A HISTORY OF CLINICAL
PSYCHOLOGY

THE SERIES IN CLINICAL AND COMMUNITY PSYCHOLOGY

CONSULTING EDITORS
Charles D. Spielberger and Irwin G. Sarason

Auerbach and Stolberg Crisis Intervention with Children and Families
Burchfield Stress: Psychological and Physiological Interactions
Burstein and Loucks Rorschach's Test: Scoring and Interpretation
Diamant Male and Female Homosexuality: Psychological Approaches
Fischer The Science of Psychotherapy
Hobfoll Stress, Social Support, and Women
Krohne and Laux Achievement, Stress, and Anxiety
London The Modes and Morals of Psychotherapy, Second Edition
Muñoz Depression Prevention: Research Directions
Olweus Aggression in the Schools: Bullies and Whipping Boys
Reisman A History of Clinical Psychology, Second Edition
Reitan and Davison Clinical Neuropsychology: Current Status and Applications
Rickel, Gerrard, and Iscoe Social and Psychological Problems of Women: Prevention and Crisis Intervention
Rofé Repression and Fear: A New Approach to the Crisis in Psychotherapy
Savin-Williams Gay and Lesbian Youth: Expressions of Identity
Spielberger and Diaz-Guerrero Cross-Cultural Anxiety, Volume 3
Spielberger, Diaz-Guerrero, and Strelau Cross-Cultural Anxiety, Volume 4
Suedfeld Psychology and Torture
Williams and Westermeyer Refugee Mental Health in Resettlement Countries

IN PREPARATION

Auerbach Clinical Psychology in Transition
Diamant Homosexual Issues in the Workplace
Spielberger and Vagg The Assessment and Treatment of Test Anxiety
Veiel The Meaning and Measurement of Social Support

A HISTORY OF CLINICAL PSYCHOLOGY

Second Edition

John M. Reisman
DePaul University

⬤HEMISPHERE PUBLISHING CORPORATION
A member of the Taylor & Francis Group
New York   Washington   Philadelphia   London

A HISTORY OF CLINICAL PSYCHOLOGY, Second Edition

1 2 3 4 5 6 7 8 9 0   B R B R   9 8 7 6 5 4 3 2 1 0

This book was set in Times Roman by Hemisphere Publishing Corporation.
The editors were Christian Milord, Lisa Warren, and Joyce Duncan; the production supervisor was Peggy M. Rote; and the typesetters were Darrell D. Larsen, Jr., Linda Andros, and Sandra Watts.
Cover design by Sharon Martin DePass.
Printing and binding by Braun-Brumfield, Inc.

A CIP catalog record for this book is available from the British Library.

Library of Congress Cataloging-in-Publication Data

Reisman, John M.
    A history of clinical psychology / John M. Reisman.—2nd ed.
       p.   cm.—(The Series in clinical and community psychology)
    Includes bibliographical references and index.
    1. Clinical psychology—History.   I. Title.   II. Series.
    [DNLM: 1. Psychology, Clinical—history.   WM 11.1 R377h]
    RC466.8.R45 1991
    616.89'009—dc20
    DNLM/DLC
    for Library of Congress   90-5381
                                                                          CIP

ISBN 1-56032-041-9 (case)
ISBN 1-56032-188-1 (paper)
ISSN 0146-0846

To my parents and to Margo and our children

Contents

Preface

It has been some 20 years since the first edition of this book was published. During that time clinical psychology has continued to grow and has made significant strides in its professional development. Today clinical psychologists are an influential, if not dominant, voice in American psychology, and clinical psychology can be found in varying stages of growth throughout the world.

Because this book describes the history of clinical psychology decade by decade, the passage of over twenty years required two new chapters to bring the account up to date. It also required changes in the earlier chapters. Some of these changes were stylistic, such as eliminating sexist language and citing references in the body of the text, and some were revisions made in the light of current information and scholarship. The changes were not always those recommended by the reviewers of this book, and I must bear the responsibility for its content; I am enough of a humanist-existentialist to accept that responsibility gladly.

I do want to thank Brendan Maher, who kindly reviewed an early draft of the manuscript, for his helpful comments and suggestions, and Charles Spielberger, who made a number of constructive recommendations and encouraged the completion of this work. I should also like to express my gratitude to the publisher for making this second edition of the history of clinical psychology possible.

John M. Reisman

Preface to the First Edition

This book begins in the late 18th century with a climate of ideas receptive to the development of clinical psychology, and proceeds to trace its growth in theoretical systems, techniques, practices, and professional organization. After the first chapter, which sets the stage for what follows, each chapter is devoted to a particular decade and is divided into these sections: a brief sketch of events, mostly outside psychology, to give a hint of the *Zeitgeist;* concepts and theories concerning "normal" personality functioning and some of the persons who advocated them; the major diagnostic techniques employed and the people who devised them; diagnostic formulations which were influential and those who conceived them; treatments proposed and used and those who practiced them; and the development of the profession and those who promoted it.

I should like to thank the Editors of The Century Psychology Series, Gardner Lindzey, Kenneth MacCorquodale, and especially Richard M. Elliott, for their many helpful comments and suggestions. Similarly, I wish to express my gratitude to those persons who make up that corporate entity "the publisher" for their assistance in making this book possible. Samuel Beck and Carl Rogers were generous in providing biographical material, and thanks are also due The University of Rochester Library, which provided most of the references used in this work.

J. M. R.

I

THE FIRST GENERATION

The early psychologists—those who identified themselves as psychologists and pursued a career in psychology—were originally physicians, physiologists, lawyers, philosophers, or ministers whose fascination with human behavior and the functioning of the mind led them to develop this new field of science. Scientific psychology began in the late 19th century, and its date of inception is usually given as 1879, when Wilhelm Wundt started a doctoral program in psychology, the study of consciousness, at the University of Leipzig. Similarly the early *clinical* psychologists were psychologists whose interests in being of help to people led them to offer their services and to do research in intellectual differences, brain damage, and psychopathology. Clinical psychology also began in the late 19th century, and its date of inception is often given as 1896, when Lightner Witmer, a psychologist who received his doctoral degree under Wundt, founded a psychological clinic at the University of Pennsylvania and began offering courses and training in the clinical method in psychology. In those early years there was no prescribed set of courses or training that identified clinical psychologists. Those psychologists who wished to become clinicians took whatever courses were available in their special fields of interest and then learned on the job in clinics, mental hospitals, schools for the retarded, and so on. Their clinical functions were mainly research and psychological evaluation, though some also engaged in training or educating people (mostly children) in age-appropriate and acceptable behaviors. Even by 1909 there were only about 200 psychologists in the United States and only a handful or so of clinicians.

MAJOR EVENTS IN THE HISTORY OF CLINICAL PSYCHOLOGY

Roots

18th century British empiricism and Rousseau's antithesis: Feelings and natural expression are superior to reason and reflection; people are harmed by their environment and class distinctions.

1

Pinel's moral treatment and the beginnings of scientific psychiatry (1793).

Itard's training of the Wild Boy of Aveyron (1800).

New Jersey responds to Dorothea Dix by building a hospital for the mentally ill (1848).

Darwin's theory of evolution (1859).

Wundt's scientific psychology and doctoral program in psychology (1879).

1890 to 1899

James's *Principles of Psychology,* containing his concept of self and practical advice on how to change habits and feelings (1890).

Hall founds the American Psychological Association (1892); Galton's and Cattell's efforts to measure intelligence; Kraepelin's descriptive psychiatry; Paris versus Nancy schools of hypnosis.

Breuer and Freud's studies in hysteria and transference phenomena (1895); Freud begins to develop psychoanalysis as a treatment and personality theory.

Witmer founds the first psychological clinic at the University of Pennsylvania and begins training psychologists in the clinical method (1896).

1900 to 1909

Freud's theory of dreams, the unconscious, and psychosexual development; McDougall's social psychology; Binet's age scale of intelligence for children; Jung's free association test; Spearman's concept of intelligence as a general ability versus Thorndike's concept.

Witmer proposes the field of clinical psychology (1907); Clifford Beers and Adolf Meyer begin the mental hygiene movement.

Founding of the National Committee for Mental Hygiene (1909); in Chicago, Healy founds the Juvenile Psychopathic Institute, regarded as the first child guidance clinic in the world; Franz's work in neuropsychology.

1

Roots

Clinical psychology is both a scientific and professional field that seeks to increase our understanding of human behavior and to promote the effective functioning of individuals. Clinical psychologists are involved in the search for and application of psychological techniques and principles that better the person. Clinicians engage in research, teaching, diagnosis or assessment, psychotherapy, and programs that enhance performance and psychological well-being.

Today, clinical psychology is the largest and certainly one of the most vigorous fields of psychology. In the United States alone there are doctoral training programs in clinical psychology in over 100 universities and 43 professional schools (McNett, 1982). Of the estimated one hundred thousand psychological personnel in the United States in mid-1983, more than half (68,148) were involved in mental health services (Stapp, Tucker, & VanderBos, 1985). It was not always this way. Although clinical psychology had its formal beginning in 1896, it entered a phase of unusually rapid growth only after World War II. This growth was not totally well received. It was opposed by other professions and by many psychologists. It has also been of concern to many clinicians (Carson, Garfield, Strupp, Adams, & Katkin, 1982).

In this book we will consider the history of clinical psychology in detail, and we will see that many of the questions that have perplexed and stimulated philosophers, psychologists, and students of the human condition down through the ages have been directly addressed by clinicians. For example, what is the basic nature of people? Are we good or bad? Aggressive or sociable? Why do we behave as we do? What influences our thinking and how we experience and understand our world? What should we do to lead a satisfying life?

This book, by presenting the history of clinical psychology, will enable the reader to see how clinical psychologists have answered these questions. The book will also provide a decade-by-decade survey of contributors to theoretical systems, diagnostic techniques, psychopathology, and treatment; information about the trends and circumstances within psychology and within the social milieu or *Zeitgeist* that affected professional development; and an appreciation of the identity of this field.

A BEGINNING

Where shall we begin? It is important to recognize that a history has no definite beginning or end. Rather than being confined by indisputable boundaries, it is a record and an interpretation carved and constructed by someone exercising deliberation and judgment from the available information. At first thought, it might seem that we should begin this history of clinical psychology with the events and leading ideas of the last decade of the 19th century.

There were many events of outstanding importance that occurred in the 1890s: the publication of William James's *Principles of Psychology,* Sigmund Freud's pioneer investigations into the causes and treatment of neuroses, the founding of the American Psychological Association, the opening of the first psychological clinic at the University of Pennsylvania, and the considerable activity that surrounded the devising of mental tests. However, to appreciate the significance of these ventures and why they met with success, we must examine the intellectual and social climate, the spirit of the times, the *Zeitgeist,* in which they took place. The fact is that favorable conditions slowly developing throughout the 17th, 18th, and 19th centuries gave increasing encouragement to the values and attitudes of a scientific psychology and its application to human problems (Maher & Maher, 1985a, 1985b).

The evolution of the sciences took place against a background of the diminishing authority of organized religion. During the gradual fall of the Roman Empire, civilization itself seemed doomed and Europeans turned to Christian religion for answers to their basic questions. They were comforted by Christianity's teaching that this world and its events were of little consequence, that this life was merely a prelude to an eternal afterlife, that human nature was weak and easily corrupted, and that there was much we could never know or hope to understand. It was through faith in God and in His goodness that people could give true meaning to their existence. The so-called Age of Faith lasted for over a thousand years (Durant, 1950).

By the 16th century, the doubts, the questionings, and the challenges to the teachings and commands of organized religion helped to foster empiricism, which is essentially a belief in the value of understanding our world and increasing our knowledge of it through sensory experiences and a conviction that all that we know is what we have learned. Empiricism can be found popping up here and there in history as far back as ancient Greece and the writings of Aristotle, but in the 16th and 17th centuries we find intellectuals such as the Frenchman René Descartes and the Englishman Francis Bacon urging the systematic study of nature and human behavior and being met with an enthusiastic response. We also find empiricism growing continuously, so that that period of history can be described as an age of reason, a time when it seemed that all the answers to the questions of this world might be settled by careful observation, unprejudiced thought, study, and reflection (Durant & Durant, 1961, 1963).

By 1749, in France, philosophy and the sciences were sufficiently established to be able to invite skepticism about their worth and criticism of their achievements. The Academy of Dijon announced a contest in which a prize would be given to the best essay on whether the advances in the sciences and arts had bettered the human condition and improved morals. The answer submitted by one contestant, Jean-Jacques Rousseau (1712–1778), was an impassioned and convincing negative.

Far from improving morals, civilization and its artificialities, according to Rousseau, corrupted our innate goodness. Rousseau went even further. In matters of importance, he argued, people should be guided by their initial impulses and feelings, not by rational thought. Our natural inclinations were preferable to any conclusion reached by reason alone (Durant & Durant, 1967).

Rousseau won the Academy of Dijon contest, which indicates his ideas struck a responsive chord. Here was an Enlightenment intellectual who argued for a return to the simple things in life, a simple faith in God, a belief in an inborn sense of what is right and wrong, a return to the joys of nature, and a shying away from the uncertainties and carping of philosophers. In his ideal world, no longer would class distinctions and intellectual elites restrict and intimidate human beings. Instead, each individual would be respected for what he or she was.

It was Rousseau who said, "Man is born free, yet everywhere he is in chains" and "I venture to declare that a state of reflection is contrary to nature; and that a thinking man is a depraved animal" (Durant, 1927, p. 284). His pronouncements, understandably enough, antagonized authorities and intellectuals. Voltaire was provoked to remark gently, "No one has ever been so witty as you are in trying to turn us into brutes; to read your book makes one long to go on all fours" (Durant, 1927, p. 270).

In what is perhaps Rousseau's most charming work, his propagandist novel *Émile,* he engagingly described the education of a boy into manhood (Rousseau, 1911). By removing Émile from civilization and rearing him in a rural environment, by permitting him to experience the natural consequences of his acts, and by accepting him and allowing him to grow freely, a happy, confident, self-reliant, guileless young man was produced. By design, any person reared in this manner would be no scholar, and for that matter Rousseau acknowledged it was impossible, if not actually undesirable, to raise a child as the fictional Émile was raised. But he sought to emphasize how certain virtues could flourish when not hampered by books and social demands. In a very real sense Rousseau was a proponent of a systems or ecological model of psychopathology. The lasting influence of his principles in the rearing and education of children is attested to by the founding of the Jean-Jacques Rousseau Institute (Jean Piaget's place of employment for many years) in Geneva in 1912.

Rousseau was a revolutionary who argued that differences between people based on social inequalities of wealth and position are wrong and should be abolished, that the individual should be allowed to develop unfettered, and that every person is naturally virtuous and sensible and capable. He saw children as innocent and honest. He saw the poor, the uneducated, and the primitive as simple, straightforward, and decent. It was largely through his teachings that a value system emphasizing the basic dignity and worth of the individual and the harmful effects of the environment, a value system at the very foundation of clinical psychology, grew. His proponents influenced the arts of the 19th century. They idealized the virtues of what is natural, venerated the poor, extolled youth and primitive societies, and argued for sweeping social reforms. Shelley and Byron made impassioned pleas for freedom and justice. Francois René de Chateaubriand saw a "holy innocence" in the poor. The very intensity of these feelings was held to be equivalent to their validity and merit (Burns, 1947).

Within literature, these sentiments were soon tempered by realism. Romantic excesses were largely abandoned in favor of a hard, unsparing examination of life and people. Middle and lower class individuals became the heroes of novels that portrayed their struggles against both an oppressive environment and their inner conflicts. Victor Hugo, in his epic *Les Miserables,* indicted the cruelty of man to man and dramatized the redemption of a criminal through trust and courage. Balzac and Flaubert, Zola and Dickens, Meredith and Twain, Melville and Turgenev, Dostoyevski and Tolstoi illustrated in their writings the following propositions:

1. Virtue and vice are not the exclusive property of any one social class.
2. People are often irrational in their actions and driven by their emotions to do what is wrong.
3. Children and the poor have feelings and conflicts; they experience and suffer from mistreatment.
4. There are characteristics of the social order that drive people to despair and that need rectification.
5. A better life is possible for all when people examine themselves honestly and look with sympathy upon their fellows.

Such convictions, presented forcefully and dramatically through speeches, plays, novels, and papers, influenced public opinion, stabbed at consciences, toppled governments, and led to reforms. Of most direct relevance to clinical psychology were the reforms in the treatment of the mentally ill.

MORAL TREATMENT

Even at the beginning of the 19th century, there was still a lingering belief among the superstitious and uneducated that the insane were "possessed" and that through their own devious actions they had brought their afflictions upon themselves, a belief that continues to find expression in popular novels and horror movies (*The Exorcist, The Omen,* and so on). Of course, this view was not shared by the medical profession. Among physicians, the mentally ill were regarded as suffering from brain lesions or an oversupply of blood, yellow bile, black bile, or phlegm (an idea dating back to Hippocrates [about 400 B.C.] and Galen [about 200 A.D.]) (Maher & Maher, 1985a). The accepted treatments for reducing humors by bleeding, vomits, and purges required little continuing medical care, so it was not uncommon for physicians to see these patients infrequently.

At "Old Bedlam" (St. Mary of Bethlehem Hospital) in England, a physician would visit once a year to prescribe treatment: bleeding of patients in April, purges and vomits in May, and bleeding again in October. At smaller institutions, where medical care was usually even more sporadic, a physician might visit once in 10 years to prescribe a regimen of treatment for the next decade. As a continuing feature of mental hospital care, patients were chained to posts, beaten, ridiculed, and fed only the coarsest of slops (Zilboorg & Henry, 1941). However, these deplorable treatments were not visited only upon the mentally ill and were no worse than the indignities suffered by many who were compelled to be in prisons or other state-supported institutions (Alleridge, 1979).

An English Quaker tea merchant, William Tuke (1732–1822), heard from some of his friends that the lunatic asylum in York was unfit. These friends had tried to visit a patient in the asylum, but they were denied admission and turned away. A few days later they were informed the patient was dead, and they suspected this death was caused by beatings. They went to Tuke, a respected leader of their community for help (Winkler & Bromberg, 1939).

Tuke visited the York lunatic asylum and similar institutions and was amazed, horrified, and angered by what he saw. He resolved to do something about it. Appealing to the Society of Friends, personal acquaintances, and physicians, Tuke enlisted support in planning "a place in which the unhappy might obtain a refuge." Years of laboriously soliciting funds followed. Finally, in 1796, the York Retreat opened its door to patients.

The retreat, built to resemble a farmhouse, was set in the countryside and surrounded by a garden and some cows. Conspicuously absent were bars and gratings on the windows and manacles on the patients. The treatment was simple: respect, good food, recreation, exercise, expressions of religious values, and friendliness in personal contacts. Tuke's principles assumed the merit of compassion and the dignity and worth of every person. He tolerated only kindness and decency in dealing with others.

Tuke devoted the remainder of his life to the York Retreat. He had the satisfaction of seeing that institution grow and serve as an example for hospitals in Europe and the United States. The humane work begun by him was continued with devotion and courage by his son Henry, his grandson, and his great grandson (Winkler & Bromberg, 1939). But the development of the retreat was not an isolated occurrence. At about the same time Philippe Pinel was promoting similar therapy for the mentally ill in France.

Pinel (1745–1826) is called the father of scientific psychiatry because he introduced the practice of taking case histories and keeping records for his patients and because he tried to formulate a nosology or systematic classification of mental illnesses. He was the son of a simple country physician in Saint-Paul. Because early in life he gave the appearance of being studious, introverted, and sensitive to suffering, it was planned that he should enter the priesthood. But Pinel abandoned plans for such a career when he came under the influence of the liberal and anticlerical writings of Voltaire and Rousseau. He decided to follow his father's profession, and at the age of 22 he enrolled at the University of Toulouse, receiving his medical degree in 1773.

For two years Pinel tutored children in Latin, Greek, and natural history. He then went to Montpellier for further studies in comparative anatomy and the classification of diseases. Still vocationally unsettled, he left in 1778 for Paris. There, his scholarliness and humility impressed his colleagues but repelled those among his prospective patients who were aristocratic and had become accustomed to expect elegance, charm, and entertaining gossip from their physicians. For fourteen years he remained obscure, impoverished, and studious: tutoring, translating books, and writing papers on medicine, physics, and philosophy.

With the second phase of the French Revolution in 1792, Pinel was appointed a municipal medical officer of low grade. His position required him to be present at beheadings, a duty which, understandably enough, he found repulsive. However, he saw in the principles of humaneness espoused by the leaders of the revolution an opportunity to alleviate the sufferings of the mentally ill—and perhaps a chance to do something that would isolate him from the violence in Paris.

Therefore, Pinel went to Thouret and Cabanis, administrators of the hospitals of Paris. He appealed to them to apply the benefits of liberty and equality to the insane. They were sufficiently impressed to appoint him, in 1793, as head of the lunatic asylum within the Bicêtre.

What Pinel found in that old, gray stone house on the outskirts of Paris has come to be questioned (Weiner, 1979; Maher & Maher, 1985b). According to traditional accounts, he saw the customary dismal combination of squalor, cruelty, neglect, and patients in chains. After overcoming official obstacles, Pinel had the chains removed from a few patients, and eventually all patients under his care were unchained, an event commemorated in a painting that has often been reproduced in texts of abnormal psychology.

Further, Pinel is alleged to have seen to it that the patients received better food and were not beaten. There is no question of Pinel's kindness and humane treatment. What is at issue is whether Pinel should be credited with *initiating* all the reforms at the Bicêtre and how much credence should be given to the romantic account of Pinel's being almost lynched by a mob that accused him of causing a cholera epidemic by poisoning wells. This story is capped by his rescue from the noose through the heroism of a former, presumably grateful, patient (Winkler & Bromberg, 1939).

According to Weiner (1979), a document by Jean-Baptiste Pussin was discovered in the French Archives, dated 1797, that claimed that Pussin had been supervisor of the ward for the insane at the Bicêtre from 1784. A former patient of the hospital, admitted for "scrofula" in 1771, Pussin stated he had immediately instituted humane measures by removing chains from some patients and placing them in straitjackets instead, by forbidding the staff to beat patients and dismissing those who continued to be abusive, and by encouraging the patients to do chores and feel useful. He also claimed to have been saved from danger by a grateful patient. There is an inconsistency in this document in that Pussin claimed to have been supervisor of the insane at the Bicêtre for almost 28 years, whereas the actual number seems to have been closer to 13.

In any case, Weiner credits Pinel with continuing Pussin's reforms and extending them by removing patients from dungeons and providing them with airy, sunny rooms; eliminating the medical procedures of bleeding, purging, and cupping; talking with patients, keeping records, and developing a case history for each patient in his care; and initiating similar practices at the Salpêtrière. That he was a pioneer of "moral treatment" is without doubt.

After being appointed director of the Salpêtrière, Pinel ordered chains removed and began a program to train personnel in his humane methods. He also requested that Pussin be permitted to join him, and they worked together from 1802 until Pussin's death in 1811. Sad to note, Pinel's career ended unhappily. Accused of harboring priests from the authorities, he was removed from his position and spent the remainder of his life in official dishonor (Winkler & Bromberg, 1939).

The ideas of Tuke and Pinel were not new. Humane treatment for the mentally ill had been urged by Hippocrates and by Juan Luis Vives and Johann Weyer during the 16th century (Zilboog & Henry, 1941). But each of these men was ahead of his time and thus had little enduring effect. In contrast, the voices of Pinel and Tuke were part of a growing chorus that sang of individual rights and social responsibility.

In the United States, that chorus was joined by Eli Todd (1762–1832). A graduate of Yale (1787), he was rich in everything but money. He had a fine family, good looks, and a brilliant intellect, but he derived little income from his work as a country physician in Connecticut. Moreover, his daily rounds were often personally distressing as he became aware of the unhappy consequences of the lack of facilities for the mentally ill. At the beginning of the 19th century, only three states—Pennsylvania, Virginia, and Maryland—had hospitals providing for their care (Deutsch, 1937). Accordingly, families were forced to improvise their own means for dealing with the mental illness of members, and since they felt ashamed about the condition, all too frequently their improvisation took the form of hiding the afflicted members from the public in one pathetic way or another. Todd saw that all those concerned suffered, and he had cause to be particularly sympathetic, since his own father and sister had experienced mental illness. Yet at that time there was little that he felt he could do to help.

In 1819, Todd moved with his family to Hartford, where medical practice was more lucrative (his fee for visits increased from 50 to 75 cents). He quickly became a leading physician in that community, and one night in 1820, at a meeting of the Connecticut Medical Society, told his colleagues of the work of Pinel. Todd pointed out that in a democracy men's hopes for success are raised high and that for many the disappointment of not attaining their goals caused insanity. It seemed, therefore, that the community had some responsibility to provide humane care for the insane; he urged that they consider the mental health needs within their state and established an institution for the treatment of the mentally ill (Winkler & Bromberg, 1939).

His colleagues gave Todd their enthusiastic support. Funds were solicited throughout Connecticut, and in 1824 an institution called the Retreat was opened in Hartford, with Eli Todd as physician in chief. The care he provided, "moral management," was based on respect for individuals and the strengths that they still possessed. Insofar as it was possible, patients were informed about their proposed treatment and were involved in their treatment planning. Every effort was made to treat the patients with dignity: "To allow them all the liberty and indulgence compatible with their own safety. . . . To cherish in them the sentiments of self-respect. . . . To occupy their attention, exercise their judgment and ingenuity, and to engage them in useful employments, alternated with amusements."

By 1826, only 2 years after the opening of the Retreat, the news of Todd's methods and of his amazing success in treating insanity spread. There were a number of important positions offered to him, but Todd refused them all and remained at the Retreat. Nevertheless, his influence was extended by his followers, who employed moral treatment in institutions arising in Massachusetts, Vermont, and New Jersey. Probably his most eminent disciple was Samuel Woodward, who became superintendent of the Worcester State Hospital and first president of an organization that was later to become the American Psychiatric Association (APA).

By 1830, five states (Virginia, Maryland, Kentucky, South Carolina, and Ohio) had publicly supported hospitals for the mentally ill, and four states (Pennsylvania, Massachusetts, New York, and Connecticut) had private institutions. Yet in the United States, the general system, or lack of system, persisted, and each community bore the responsibility for the care of its sick. Into jails and almshouses might be herded those who, for whatever reason, had to be institutionalized. It was this hodgepodge system that Dorothea Dix attacked.

Dorothea Lynde Dix (1802–1887) was born in Hampden, Maine, to a father described as a shiftless religious fanatic and to a mother portrayed as submissive (Tiffany, 1892). Around the age of 12 she went to Boston to live with her more well-to-do paternal grandparents, who maintained a proper and puritanical atmosphere. By the age of 14 young Miss Dix was gainfully employed as a teacher, and by 20 she was running a school which catered to the daughters of wealthy and prominent Bostonian families. Even at that age she evidenced concern for the less fortunate by tutoring the children of the poor in her home.

After a few years, her health failed and she became the victim of attacks of tuberculosis. During the period from 1824 to 1840, she attained some success as a writer of stories and books for children, reestablished her school for girls, fell ill once again, and finally became financially independent and able to devote herself to philanthropic activities when she inherited money from her grandmother.

The year 1841 found her teaching Sunday school in a jail in Boston. Appalled by the neglect and brutality in the prison and by the fact that the mentally ill and retarded were housed among the criminals—and starting with nothing but indignation and a fierce conviction that she was right—she proceeded to virtually terrorize the consciences of government officials throughout the world.

For over 40 years Dorothea Dix traveled throughout the United States as well as abroad. Her bearing was quiet, gentle, and dignified, but her tactics were overwhelming. She would arm herself with unshakable facts concerning the quality of the mental health facilities of a particular area, rally public support through the press, and win key legislative spokesmen to her cause by her knowledge, persistence, and dedication. Relentlessly, she preached a gospel of humane treatment and adequate facilities for the retarded, insane, and criminal.

New Jersey was the first state to respond to Dorothea Dix by erecting a hospital for the mentally ill in 1848. In the years that followed, more than 30 state institutions were built or enlarged as a direct result of her efforts. Her work also bore fruit in France, Great Britain, Italy (where she told Pope Pius IX that the insane asylum in Rome was a "scandal and disgrace"), Japan, Austria, Denmark, Holland, Russia, Greece, Sweden, Germany, Norway, Turkey, and Belgium. Seldom in history has a single person catalyzed such widespread reform. Still, it is necessary to see her work within its historical context.

I have tried to indicate that Dix, Tuke, Todd, Pinel, Rousseau were part of a movement that had been going on for over a hundred years, a movement for the amelioration of social conditions on the basis of the dignity and the rights of the individual. Their appeals were buttressed not so much by data and evidence as by feelings of guilt and compassion, and thus they represent a theme as old as the golden rule and probably as often ignored. Nevertheless, in the 19th century the popular and official support given this theme was new and historically important. From literature came a portrayal of children, the downtrodden, and men and women of all classes as sensitive, passionate, conflicted, and oppressed. From medicine came the view that the mentally ill could be cured through kindness and decent treatment. From governments came funds and reforms, not only in order to maintain themselves and to reap the eventual savings that might be derived from meeting the demands for humane treatment but also because a social responsibility was recognized and accepted and the demands were thus seen as legitimate.

By the middle of the 19th century, moral treatment was employed at a number of mental hospitals amid enthusiastic reports of high discharge and recovery rates. Twenty years later, moral treatment was largely abandoned as a therapy. Instead the view became prevalent that mental hospitals served mainly as custodial institutions for people whose conditions could not be adequately improved by current methods of treatment. What had happened to bring about this change?

It has been suggested that the improvement rates claimed for moral treatment were inflated and that the discovery of the exaggerations discredited the therapy; that the more chronic and seriously disturbed patients were referred to the hospitals and became a growing proportion of the patient population; that more dangerous, less educated patients from among the new immigrants to the United States began to flood the asylums; and that the succeeding generation of psychiatrists lacked the zeal and conviction of the moral treatment reformers (Levine, 1981). These factors, important in themselves, can best be appreciated when viewed within the broader context of advances in 19th century medicine and psychiatry, where scientific research promised new, precise, sophisticated treatments.

THE EMERGENCE OF SCIENTIFIC PSYCHIATRY

In 1799, a young boy of 11 or 12 was captured in the woods of Aveyron, France. He could not speak and appeared to be a child of nature, so there was great interest in what would happen when his fear of people was overcome and he learned to talk. Would he, as Rousseau suggested, be inherently good, decent, and aware of the existence of God? Or, as empiricists such as Locke would have predicted, would the boy know nothing of goodness, God, or manners except what he had been taught? Pinel was called upon to examine the boy and diagnosed him as an idiot, which meant that he would be able to learn nothing and treatment efforts would be wasted. However, interest in the philosophical predictions was so great that the French government appropriated funds to enable Jean Itard, a physician and tutor of the deaf, to devote himself to the education of the Wild Boy of Aveyron.

For 5 years Itard labored with great patience and ingenious training techniques to educate Victor, as the boy was named. Though Itard's efforts were not as rewarding as he had hoped, they were not as futile as was predicted. Victor was not able to talk and thus provide definitive evidence in favor of Rousseau or Locke. But he was taught some manners and learned to dress himself and to recognize a few words (Lane, 1976). Although Itard was discouraged and abandoned any additional efforts to teach Victor, suggesting that a respect for diagnosis might help avoid futility, his limited success inspired and encouraged others, such as Edward Seguin, who went on to establish the first school for retardates in Paris in 1837 and who later migrated to the United States and promoted the education of retardates on these shores. The case was therefore claimed as a minor triumph for remedial education. It gave hope where before there had been none.

During the early years of the 19th century, the rationalist tradition was attacked not only by romanticists but by scientists. In particular, the rationalist position was criticized for leading to the view that we could never hope to know our world or the causes of events within it with certainty and that thinking (or "armchair philosophy") was the best way to arrive at the truth. Some philosophers and of course many scientists argued that the best way to attain knowledge was through controlled observations or experimentation. There was an increased emphasis on doing, testing, and experiencing rather than just sitting back and pondering.

This emphasis on experience drew support from Kant's *Critique of Pure Reason*, which was published in 1781 and which contained a reasonable attack on reason. Kant (1724–1804) agreed with the British empiricists, who contended we can never know what really exists in our world since this information is limited and distorted by our sensory apparatus, but he argued that science would deal with objects only as they appear to the human mind (phenomena) and not with their ultimate reality. Moreover, he believed it is an error to suppose we can know reality through reason alone, for the mind itself is fallible and unable to grasp certain concepts or reason correctly about them.

To illustrate, our minds are so structured that we are compelled to organize events by positing cause and effect relations; to experience depth, time, and figure-ground; and to synthesize and order events to see connections that may not exist. Moreover, the limitations of our minds lead us to unresolvable puzzles. We cannot conceive of what is finite or infinite with relation to time, space, or cause and effect. Thus we suppose the universe is finite yet wonder what exists beyond it; we must think of time as having a beginning, but we also must imagine what transpired before it began; and we justify the existence of God as a first cause but are left with the question of who or what created God? The issues of God, free will, and immortality, Kant decided, can be settled neither by pure reason nor by science, though science at least could provide us with knowledge of phenomena and the processes by which they are experienced (Durant, 1927).

Progress in the science of physics, chemistry, and biology occurred rapidly in the 19th century, but let us confine our attention to the situation in medicine, particularly in psychiatry, to see how this affected moral treatment. From about 1800 to 1860, the center of psychiatric activity was the mental hospital, and the main concerns were classification and moral treatment. During this period, psychiatry became an autonomous area of specialization within the science of medicine, joining with the specialities of surgery and ophthalmology. Nevertheless, it was still possible at that time to become a physician by means of a suitable apprenticeship; one of the early leaders of American psychiatry, Samuel White (1777–1845), had been an apprentice and never graduated from college or attended medical school (Lewis, 1974).

However, the tendency in psychiatry, as in other disciplines, was to set more demanding standards for the profession and for those who would practice it. The goal was to give psychiatry a firm scientific foundation by grounding its practice in neuroanatomy and brain physiology. This thrust was abetted by the discovery in 1822 that general paresis is a specific mental disease associated with cerebral lesions. It seemed that careful observation and classification of disorders would lead to additional mental diseases and their particular organic causes and that psychiatrists must be thoroughly schooled in the sciences.

Scientific work in brain anatomy and physiology during the early 19th century produced a new and accelerated understanding of human functioning. The physician Franz Joseph Gall (1758–1828), based on his research in comparative brain anatomy, demonstrated the significance of the cortex, noted the presence of white and gray matter in the nervous system, and found commissures or neural fibers connecting the brain hemispheres. He proposed a theory of brain localizations, later called *phrenology,* which stated not only that specific cortical areas were the sites of specific personality characteristics and mental functions but also that the degree of a characteristic or function could be determined by assessing the degree of prominence of the appropriate part of the skull.

Phrenology was attacked and discredited, in large measure by the research of Pierre Flourens (1794–1867). His skill enabled him to use the method of extirpation to determine that the cerebellum largely controls coordination, the medulla is involved in life-sustaining functions such as the beating of the heart and respiration, and the cerebrum mediates learned and voluntary activities. However, he argued that within the cerebrum there did not appear to be localization; instead, functioning was dependent upon the quantity or extent of brain tissue intact or removed.

Subsequent studies supported Gall's view of cortical localization, though not the theory of phrenology: Paul Broca found the area of the cortex specifically associated with speech; G. Fritsch and E. Hitzig, in 1870, through direct stimulation of the cortex by electrodes, discovered the motor strip of the cortex; and David Ferrier found the cortical sensory strip and the function of the occipital lobe in vision (Fancher, 1979).

Meanwhile, Jacques-Joseph Moreau de Tours wrote a book about hashish that showed that this drug could produce delusions and hallucinations and thus might afford an experimental basis for the study of insanity as well as indicate a possible chemical basis for the study of its cause; Benedict-Augustin Morel described the symptoms and course of a mental disorder that he termed *demence precoce;* Jean-Pierre Falret and Jules Baillarger discovered the association of mania with melancholia and suggested one may succeed the other as parts of one disorder; Henry Maudsley's book *Physiology and Pathology of the Mind* was published in 1867; the eminent German psychiatrist Wilhelm Griesinger (1817–1868), acclaimed as the founder of German academic psychiatry, stated flatly that "mental diseases are brain diseases" (Ellenberger, 1974); the relationship of syphilitic infection to general paresis was established; and nutritional deficiencies were found to be associated with psychiatric symptoms and pathological changes in the brain and spinal cord (Brain & Walton, 1969).

One consequence of all this scientific activity was to shift the frontiers of psychiatry from asylums to university departments of psychiatry in medical schools. Formal training and professional standards had to be applied to enable the up-to-date psychiatrist to assimilate the current body of information and perhaps contribute to it. A new image of the psychiatrist was being created, that of the thoroughly schooled and knowledgeable practitioner and scientist. Within this camp, the proponents of moral treatment were regarded as old-fashioned faith healers who represented unscientific psychiatry and whose therapy, even should it be effective, would discredit the value of training in the sciences and bring into question the need for professional credentials. If moral treatment was right, some psychiatrists noted, psychiatric caregivers might just as well be ministers (Ellenberger, 1974).

These professional considerations and the advances in science undoubtedly eroded support for moral treatment, a humane but nonspecific approach to problems whose complexity and heterogeneity were just beginning to be appreciated. Accordingly, the more knowledgeable and erudite psychiatrists no longer saw moral therapy as the treatment of choice for the mentally ill. Instead the goals became to identify specific diseases, to determine their particular etiologies, and to develop methods of treatment appropriate to each. While this search for definitive treatments continued (a search that the new science of psychology was expected to contribute to), the main task of the asylum psychiatrist was often merely to ensure suitable custodial care and "management" of patients.

THE EMERGENCE OF SCIENTIFIC PSYCHOLOGY

A good many of the early psychologists were trained as physicians and physiologists and were interested in science and philosophy. They had entered professions that allowed them to pursue their interests as much as possible but were nevertheless dissatisfied by the lack of correspondence and fished about for a discipline that would be more congenial. Although Wilhelm Wundt (1832–1920) is credited with being the father of scientific psychology, since he established the first psychological laboratory at the University of Leipzig in 1875 and the curriculum leading to a doctorate, he was not alone. In that same year William James also equipped a small laboratory for psychology at Harvard (Watson, 1963). The founding of scientific psychology is usually considered to have been accomplished by Wundt at Leipzig in 1879 (Boring, 1950), and although this date is controversial, the American Psychological Association has given the date its sanction by celebrating the centenary of the founding of scientific psychology in 1979.

Among the handful of early psychologists there was no unanimity of opinion about the purpose or definition of psychology. However, one psychologist had gotten off to a running start. Wilhelm Wundt published *Principles of Physiological Psychology* in 1874 and called for the creation of a new scientific field. The content and questions of this new field, psychology, would be the same as those that perplexed philosophers, but its method of finding answers would be scientific. Adopting a positivist position, Wundt declared psychology would not embrace concepts or topics that could not be verified through observable data. It was to be an experimental science dealing with the conscious mind. Much of the experimentation would consist of varying the presentation of stimuli and determining how these variations would be experienced; hence trained introspection would be an important method for the acquisition of information—trained because those doing the introspecting were to give reports describing all the nuances of the immediate experience rather than merely naive statements of how they interpreted or made sense of it.

Psychology, according to Wundt, was to be the study of consciousness. The task of psychologists was to search for verifiable elements of experience and determine how these elements were combined into complex sensations. With Wundt and his contemporaries, psychology became the study of the mind and lost its soul. A physician by training and a professor of philosophy at Leipzig by appointment, Wundt quickly began a doctoral program in the new science. For a time, many of those who wished to become psychologists studied and trained under Wundt and his influence in those early years was very great as a result.

During the latter part of the 19th century, much was being accomplished in science and much was expected. It appeared then that scientists were noble and dedicated seekers after "pure" truth. They were not concerned about the practical applications of what they unearthed—such mundane matters were not within their province. Wundt, in particular, held to this view of science, and because the identity of psychology was new and precarious, he was understandably troubled by any attempt to expand the definition of psychology or to hasten its use. His prudence was characteristic of the first generation of psychologists, who everywhere had the task of acquainting colleges, universities, colleagues, and the public with what this new discipline was and why it should be taught and supported.

AN APPRAISAL

In this chapter the stage has been set for a more detailed consideration of clinical psychology by sketching the philosophical and scientific events of the 19th century that appear to have been pertinent to its development, including the emergence of psychology itself as a science with its own identity.

Although the movement for reform was emphasized, less attention was given to what were, by implication, the more prevalent attitudes and beliefs that seemed in need of correction: convictions about the privileges of the aristocracy; contempt for those less advantaged; and the arrogance of "superior" nationalities, races, and classes. From one vantage it can readily be seen that these attitudes about inherent differences and good breeding were attempts to maintain a semblance of stability in a world whose social order was radically changing. Civil unrest and agitation existed everywhere—in England, France, Germany, Russia, and the United States. Established governments, whether democratic or aristocratic or autocratic, were assaulted by demands for justice and were continuously reminded of their vulnerability by revolutions and assassinations.

The main thrust during the 19th century was toward the amelioration of social conditions on the basis of the rights and dignity of the individual. This thrust was pervasive. From literature came an evaluation of people of all classes as sensitive, passionate, conflicted, and deserving of respect, sympathy, and assistance when oppressed. From science came news of empirical findings and theories that challenged religious and traditional beliefs and smug attitudes about innate distinctions and differences. From governments came reforms that were largely due to the acceptance of a broadened concept of social responsibility. Such developments were part of the nourishing context of values from which clinical psychology, as a science and helping profession, was able to grow.

2

The Hopeful Psychologists
1890–1899

In this chapter and each of the ones that follow, we will direct our attention to a particular decade. In each chapter, we will first consider the events, mostly outside psychology, that set the tone or created the *Zeitgeist*. Then we will examine concepts and theories about "normal" personality functioning and the persons who advocated them; the major diagnostic techniques employed and the people who devised them; the diagnostic formulations that were influential and those who conceived them; the methods of treatment for psychological problems that were proposed and used and those who practiced them; and the development of psychology (in particular, clinical psychology) as a profession and those who promoted it.

Why did clinical psychology take hold in the United States rather than in France or Germany or Russia? What is there about a culture or society that makes it congenial or uncongenial, even downright supportive or hostile, to one sort of profession? It seems that a partial answer to the first question should involve some special compatibility between the values of U.S. society and the aims and aspirations of clinical psychology. Accordingly, it may be instructive to direct our attention to the spirit of the United States toward the end of the 19th century, the period when clinical psychology was born.

Scientific psychology began in Germany, which following its success in the Franco-Prussian War was regarded as the most powerful nation on the European continent. Ruled by a Kaiser and an aristocracy of nobles and military officers, its language requiring familiar and formal forms of the pronoun *you,* Germany was mindful of class and social distinctions. Its status throughout the world, although based on armed might, was enhanced by the achievements of its scientists (Helmholtz, Humboldt, Schwann), its philosophers (Kant, Hegel, Schopenhauer), its musicians (Bach, Brahms, Beethoven), its writers (Goethe, Schiller, Heine), and its outstanding universities. These schools had a long and proud tradition of academic freedom and were further distinguished by their programs of advanced education leading to a PhD.

In contrast, the American system of higher education was relatively new and had begun only recently to offer doctoral programs. Up to the second half of the 19th century, this system had been composed mainly of colleges and universities affiliated to some degree with churches. A liberal arts education for males was emphasized, and little provision was made for the education of females or for professional degrees and scientific research.

During the second half of the 19th century, a movement in the United States for academic freedom and reform bore fruit in the establishment of a number of secular colleges. Moreover, major efforts were made to raise the status and quality of graduate and professional education. Yale, in 1861, was the first U.S. university to give a PhD, conferring it upon three undoubtedly proud recipients. Harvard became the second, in 1872. Johns Hopkins, which opened in 1876 as a graduate school, was a leader in requiring its students to take courses in the sciences and to conduct independent research. Therefore, although it was still necessary for many Americans to study in Europe if they sought advanced knowledge in their fields, a determined and successful attempt was made by American educators to emulate the German model of graduate education and to institute research programs leading to the PhD (Watson, 1963).

This American striving for academic excellence and recognition was a manifestation of the spunky spirit and the developing maturity of the United States. By 1890, the population of the country had swelled to 63 million as a result of waves of immigration, and it was continuing to grow. The country spanned the continent, and from 1889 to 1899 Idaho, Montana, North Dakota, South Dakota, Utah, Washington, and Wyoming were admitted into the union. Moreover, like the three leading nations of Europe—France, Great Britain, and Germany—the United States was consolidating its position as an industrial and imperial power while continuing its scientific advances and social reforms (Burns, 1947).

The American people experienced feelings of accomplishment and pride, a sense of national identity and purpose. They saw an expansion in their numbers, their inventiveness, their national wealth, and the ability of their country to play a forceful role in world affairs. The Spanish-American War, in 1898, was an expression of the vigor, boldness, confidence, and self-righteousness of the American people. Ostensibly, the war was provoked by the cruelties of the Spanish in dealing with their Cuban subjects. At its conclusion, despite the altruistic nature of its intervention, the United States found itself in possession of Cuba, Puerto Rico, Guam, and the Philippine and Hawaiian islands. Suddenly the United States was a Caribbean power, a Pacific power, an Asiatic power, and a colonial power. Americans could no longer be ignored by other nations, though they could be considered brash and impudent.

Many Americans who turned to the new field of psychology shared the energy, enthusiasm, practicality, and optimism of their compatriots. They were hopeful about the prospects and attainments of psychology. They argued for psychology's recognition and championed its status as an independent new science of great interest and promise. Since at this stage psychologists were so few, each one was a trailblazer, a leader gambling on his or her ability to carve out a successful professional career in an untried field. The majority saw the establishment of the scientific credentials of psychology as the first priority.

NORMAL PERSONALITY FUNCTIONING

An appreciation of the youthfulness of the science of psychology in 1892 may be gained from a survey of its basic treatises (they were not textbooks in the current sense). In German, there was Wundt's *Grundzüge der Physiologischen Psychologie* (1873–1874); in English, there was Ladd's *Elements of Physiological Psychology* (1887) as well as the delightful *Principles of Psychology* (1890) by William James (1842–1910), the first American psychologist. If given a choice which to read, anyone would do well to select the book by James, the only one of the three to enjoy popularity in its time, to attain the stature of a classic, and to be regarded as a witty, brilliant, and highly stimulating work even today.

William James was the firstborn of an erudite and intellectually provocative family. His grandfather, "Old Billy" James, came to the United States from Ireland in 1789. Through thrift, industry, and shrewdness, he amassed a fortune as a merchant and banker and gave his children a legacy of wealth and the problem of how to justify to themselves their living on it. His father, Henry, seemed to handle that problem by embracing socialistic ideas and the passion of the day for reform (Knight, 1950). Through the James' household swirled a continuing parade of thinkers, and no thought, whether uttered by guests or family, eluded critical scrutiny. According to many of the biographers of James, an affectionate spirit pervaded these intellectual combats, rendering them innocuous. Nevertheless, it is difficult to believe that being subjected to constant challenge and criticism could fail to elicit some feelings of inadequacy. Although it is probable that many factors were involved in James's subsequent bouts of self-doubt and indecision, the intensity and chronicity of these bouts certainly suggest that he did not escape from the family arena unscarred.

During his adolescence and youth, James went through an identity crisis in which he struggled to find a suitable occupation. At first the life of an artist beckoned. James had talent, was financially comfortable, and enjoyed beer and the good comradeship of his fellow art students. However, he was displeased by his paintings and discouraged by his progress. So, at about the age of 20 he decided to become a scientist. He enrolled in the Lawrence Scientific School at Harvard, studying chemistry under Charles W. Eliot and physiology under Jeffries Wyman. After 2 years he entered Harvard Medical School and seemed well on the way to accomplishment and stability. But prior to graduation he began to experience feelings of despair, feelings from which he sought to escape by joining an expedition to Brazil.

This expedition was under the leadership of the Harvard naturalist Louis Agassiz. Its purpose was to gather zoological specimens in the jungles of the Amazon, but James's interest in collecting specimens was secondary to his interest in collecting himself. In 1865, the expedition set sail. Accompanying the intrepid scientists was Bishop Alonzo Potter, who went along to ensure that God would not be forgotten amid all the talk of evolution, which was then an intellectual sensation.

One of the early evolutionary theories was proposed by the French biologist Jean Lamarck in 1809. Lamarck stated that the use or disuse of bodily parts by animals resulted in gradual changes that were passed on to succeeding generations. The inheritance of acquired characteristics if actual, challenged the biblical conception of creation and gave importance to environmental influences in the generation of new species of life.

Lamarck's evolutionary hypothesis was called into question, or supplemented, in 1859 when Charles Darwin published *The Origin of Species,* which contained his twin hypotheses of genetic variation and natural selection. According to Darwin, environmental conditions act in such a way as to select over countless generations those variants among offspring that are best fitted to survive and reproduce. Darwin made clear in *The Descent of Man,* published in 1871, that evolutionary concepts applied to man as well as other animals. Indeed, his most enthusiastic proponent, Thomas Huxley, not only vigorously publicized Darwin's ideas but also extended them to social institutions and moral ideals.

One of the major effects of evolutionary theory was the shaking of cherished beliefs. Although it was possible for many scientists, including Darwin, to maintain a belief in God, it was no longer possible for them to maintain a literal acceptance of the Bible. An air of skepticism and intellectual humility was pervasive. The theory of evolution entailed not only that *homo sapiens* was continuous with other forms of life but also that there was an ongoing process of adaptation and change. An attitude about the transience and limits of knowledge was popularized in Huxley's doctrine of agnosticism: a frank confession that neither the nature nor the existence of God nor the ultimate character of the universe is knowable. While such ideas had been expressed before, never before had they been so widespread.

Of course Agassiz and the members of his expedition were familiar with Darwin and spent much time in debating the implications of evolution and the conflicts they experienced between their religious and scientific principles. James, noting this, asserted he was only amused, and he denied in letters to his family any personal involvement in metaphysical problems. Further, he found the rigors of the expedition and the chores of being a naturalist to confirm his inclination toward a life of thought and reflection (Knight, 1950).

Nevertheless his trip to Brazil was a personal success, and upon his return in 1866 James returned to medical school. He remained for a year before once again being overcome by depression. Tormented by doubts and thoughts of suicide, he sought relief through another change of surroundings. The next year and a half were spent in Germany, supposedly to improve his understanding of the German language and to do advanced work in physiology. Little was accomplished either intellectually or emotionally. Hoping to pull himself out of his depression, he reentered medical school and managed to obtain his degree in 1869. However, he could not bring himself to practice as a physician.

The next three years found James a chronic invalid drenched in pessimism and gloom. His own intense sufferings during this period were to make him acutely sensitive and sympathetic to those who were mentally ill. As for himself, he proceeded in the only way he knew to cope with his depression: he read and read and read in the chance that somewhere there might be something that would help him alleviate his unhappiness. Then in 1870 he came across the writings of the French philosopher Charles Renouvier (1818–1903).

People, according to Renouvier, are distinguished from other living things by the freedom they have over their lives, hardly an original idea since it is a cornerstone of the Christian religion (Robinson, 1981), but one which nevertheless was particularly impressive to James at that time. For him it meant that his depression and incapacity were choices he had made, and that if he chose to exercise his will to feel better, he could do so. We find similar treatment strategies employed today in cognitive behavior modification and rational-emotive psychotherapy (Ellis, 1973).

James regarded his encounter with the writings of Renouvier as a turning point in his life. He determined to believe in free will, and decided that henceforth he would make efforts to replace his depression with thoughts of becoming active, adventurous, and hopefully expectant. Apparently, this was no easy or sudden process for it was not until two years later, in 1872, that he was appointed an instructor in physiology at Harvard. This appointment, too, had been dictated by his indecision and confusion: Conflicted between physiology and philosophy for his academic career because he wanted the latter, he decided on the former because he felt it would be less intellectually threatening and demanding.

It is hardly surprising then, that James was attracted to psychology. By 1875 he had established a "room for demonstrational experiments" in physiological psychology, a forerunner of Wundt's laboratory. His teaching was vigorous and successful; he was wooing the future Mrs. James; he was writing; he was attracting graduate students in psychology; he was happy. In 1878 he married, and flushed with optimism he contracted to write a text that would survey and assess the entire field of psychology. It was to be done in 2 years. He underwent a common experience among authors: The 2 years stretched to 12. However, the free-flowing writing style of the *Principles of Psychology* artfully concealed James's enormous labors and difficulties.

His title was changed to professor of philosophy in 1885 and to professor of psychology in 1889. The following year the *Principles* was published. It won surprising, almost startling approval from the public, who rejoiced in its vividness, humor, clarity, and practical advice. Fellow psychologists, particularly those of a more empirical bent, were not so impressed. Essentially, James had addressed the content and questions of psychology using the methods of the philosopher. G. Stanley Hall, a former student of James who had become a leader in developmental psychology, was critical because the *Principles* neglected children and contained too much that was speculative and too little that was factual. Wundt's appraisal of the work was expressed in this backhanded compliment: "It is literature, it is beautiful, but it is not psychology."

James was hurt by these criticisms, but he had come down very hard on Wundt and those psychologists whose concept of psychology was narrow and restrictive. He felt that psychophysical "microscopic" experimentation was cold worthless and, worst of all, dull: "This method taxes patience to the utmost and could hardly have arisen in a country whose natives could be *bored*."

For Wundt, for psychology to be a science, it was essential that its results be replicable. Yet to James, who introspected and mulled over what was going on in his consciousness, replicability was impossible. Generalizing from himself, he decided consciousness did not consist of a stringing together or connecting of elements of experience but of a flowing, continuous stream of thoughts that was never the same, that never exactly repeated itself: "No state once gone can recur and be identical with what it was before" (James, 1890, p. 230). By that James meant that the experiences of the person alter even seemingly identical situations into distinctive ones. No thought, no state of consciousness, is exactly the same as a preceding one, so how can psychologists replicate results? The second time people see a rose is not the same as the first or the third or the fourth, even if it is the same rose in a very limited time span. People see it and smell it with a new freshness or a new dullness, with a new attention to detail or a new lack of interest. Fundamentally, the fact that our brains constantly undergo modifications makes it physiologically impossible for one idea ever to be exactly the same as another.

Moreover, James noted attributes of consciousness that did not seem to be functions of stimuli but implied an overriding concept that went unmentioned by Wundt and his group. People have a feeling about their consciousness, that it belongs to them and arises from within them. They recognize their thoughts to be their thoughts and do not feel that what they think has been put into their heads by someone or something else. Even when the thoughts of two people are highly similar, they experience only a recognition of their agreement, not feeling that one person has somehow exchanged thoughts with or transmitted them to the other.

People sense consciousness as a continuous, unbroken stream. The losses of consciousness, as in sleep, are not experienced as gaps or interruptions but as part of the flow, and shifts from one topic to another are not sensed as completely different: "The transition between the thought of one object and the thought of another is no more a break in the *thought* than a joint in a bamboo is a break in the wood. It is a part of the *consciousness* as much as the joint is a part of the *bamboo*" (James, 1890, p. 240).

People do not attend equally to everything in the stream but are selective and discriminating. Of the available stimulation, they ignore most of it, and from what they attend to they form their own individualized worlds. So it is of some importance to understand why they are interested in this and not that, and James supposed a major reason for attention was what seemed to be part of "me" or relevant to "me" and what did not. As James put it, "No mind can take the same interest in his neighbor's *me* as in his own."

But of what is this "me" composed? James's answer was that it was the sum total of all that a person owned. In other words, for James the personality or the self consisted of what a person felt belonged to or was part of him or her. The totality of all these possessions was the Empirical Self, which could be analyzed into three major components. First, there was Material Self, which consisted of the person's body, clothing, family, home, and property. Second, there was the Social Self, which consisted of the person's roles in different interactions: "We do not show ourselves to our children as to our club-companions, to our customers as to the laborers we employ, to our masters and employers as to our intimate friends" (James, 1890, p. 294). Third, there is the Spiritual Self, which has to do with the person's conscience and will, sense of values and morality, and psychological faculties and dispositions.

James went on to discuss conflict and rivalry between the various aspects of the Self, but such conflict was depicted as rational, polite, although somewhat troublesome. The way he described it, a person simply could not be everything to all people or fulfill every potentiality and interest. Decisions had to be made about what to be and become, and the rest of the person's inclinations had to be more or less suppressed. Those who wanted to be romantic and sexually active obviously could not be saints, and, assuming they were sensible about their decision, they need not be troubled by their lack of certain virtues. It was only when people held to aspirations and pretensions they did not achieve that they felt troubled and suffered a loss in self-esteem.

To restore self-esteem, people might simply choose to achieve greater success in the future or to abandon some of their pretensions. Since it is easier to do the latter than the former, particularly since what people want is often unrealistic or vain, James recommended giving up pretensions as the more practical and attainable course of action for the enhancement of self-esteem. After all, he might have reasoned, had he not himself lowered his aspirations and settled on a career in physiology and psychology instead of philosophy and thereby found a measure of happiness? "Our self-feeling is in our power," James (1890, p. 311) asserted, primarily because people can choose to renounce their conceits instead of belittling themselves for failing to attain them.

The *Principles* is full of practical advice. In his discussion of habits, James recommended that if a habit is to be broken or formed, it should be done immediately and without exception. That is, if people wish to stop doing something, they should stop at once and not gradually; if they wish to develop a habit, they should begin immediately the series of necessary repetitions.

Although James stressed in his psychology the importance of rational choice and volition, the freedom of a person to act and to improve, he was aware of the unconscious and devoted considerable space to its exposition.

The term *unconscious* had been introduced by Pierre Janet, but mainly in the sense of automatic—to describe behavior, such as handwriting, that is produced without awareness by the individual of its content or the fact that the act is being performed. However, long before Janet, people were familiar with the concept and had realized that much physiological functioning is not conscious. Isaac, the Abbot of Stella, pointed out toward the end of the 12th century that not all that a person knows is always directly accessible to awareness. Spinoza, in the 17th century, argued that motives and emotions are often irrational and operate without our knowledge, leading to self-deception. Johann Herbart, in the early 19th century, conceived of ideas conflicting and competing with each other for a place in consciousness; those ideas that were inhibited or passed below the threshold or *limen of consciousness* were assumed to have a tendency to strive to come back. Schopenhauer had a dynamic view of unconscious force affecting human functioning in the *will to live,* and Leibniz and von Hartmann also called attention to unconscious functioning (Zilboorg & Henry, 1941). Yet in the 1890s, the unconscious was

regarded much as it is regarded in certain quarters today: as a somewhat speculative and superfluous concept, representing a process, as in reflexes and subcortical
behavior patterns, that is of little psychological significance.

Therefore we find James presenting the following evidence to justify the recognition of the existence of the unconscious: the forgetting of dreams and thoughts,
which must be stored and exist somewhere in the mind since they often can be
recalled; lack of memory of things done while sleepwalking; the ability of people
to awaken themselves from sleep at a predetermined time; the demonstrations of
posthypnotic suggestion and of suggestions carried out automatically by persons
afflicted with hysteria.

Upon publication of the *Principles,* James became one of the leaders of psychology, and he might have led it toward practical applications and away from
Wundt. But he no longer identified with psychology and had been disappointed in
his assessment of it. One of his purposes in writing the *Principles* was to evaluate
psychology's status as a science, and he concluded that it was not yet a science but
only the hope of one. Since he had little taste for experimental research, he did not
see himself offering a valid alternative. Furthermore, he had been deeply wounded
by the criticisms of his book and his ideas. Tolerance for the ideas of others was an
attribute highly valued by James, and he strongly believed it was a quality psychologists lacked and should develop, certainly in their dealings with him (James,
1895). With not much inclination to marshal forces against the "Wundtians"—and
with some conviction that the prize was not worth the battle, with a feeling that he
was not fully appreciated and that some psychologists were not nice—James decided to pick up his marbles and go elsewhere.

Thus we find the unusual circumstance of an acknowledged leader of a field
who seeks to leave it with dispatch. In preparation for abandonment, James recommended the appointment at Harvard of Hugo Münsterberg (1836–1916), a young
German experimental psychologist and physician with a practical bent who had
attracted his sympathetic interest. Münsterberg had conducted some studies that
had been criticized—all too severely and unfeelingly in James's opinion—by
Titchener and G. E. Müller. James sought to bolster the young psychologist's
morale and, by means of some academic maneuvering, to transfer his position as
professor of psychology to Münsterberg and regain for himself a professorship in
philosophy (Boring, 1950).

In the meantime, for financial reasons, James agreed to write *Psychology:
Briefer Course,* an abridgement of the nearly 1,400-page *Principles* to a more
suitable length for use as a text. He found it a distasteful business and complained
to his publisher: "I think I have produced a tome of pedagogic classic which will
enrich both you and me, if not the student's mind" (Knight, 1950, p. 48). The
Briefer Course was published in 1892 and was an immediate success; that same
year Münsterberg arrived at Harvard.

In 1897 James's title was changed to professor of philosophy. Despite this
change in interests, his influence continued to be exerted upon all who read the
Principles and were caught up in the expansiveness, optimism, and practicality of

his trenchant and engaging style. Further, we can see his ideas still alive in current theories of the self, consciousness, and cognitive behavior modification.

DIAGNOSTIC TECHNIQUES

When we look at a population, we may summarize our impressions in terms of general characteristics, and such generalizations constituted one goal as psychologists attempted to discover the laws or principles involved in conscious functioning, the major goal according to Wundt. But this description is not complete. It is also important to know something about the dispersion of the characteristics or the variability of the population, which is referred to as *individual differences*. From the very beginning of psychology as a science, there were psychologists interested in differences, specifically those differences that exist between the mental functioning of individuals.

As we might expect, the problem was old but the scope, energy, and method of attack were new. Plato (427–347 B.C.) had recommended that tests of military aptitude be devised and administered to aid in the proper assignment of soldiers to the tasks they were best suited for. However, it was not until the beginning of the 19th century that scientists turned their attention to the serious study of the question of individual differences (Ramul, 1960).

Unexpectedly, it was in astronomy that individual differences were recognized as significant and the first systematic measures occurred. In 1816, Friedrich Bessel (1784–1846), an astronomer at Königsberg, read in the *Zeitschrift fur Astronomie* that an assistant astronomer, D. Kinnebrook, had been dismissed from his job at Greenwich observatory in England for incompetence. The reason for his dismissal was that Kinnebrook had repeatedly observed the times of stellar transits almost a second later than his superior, Nevil Maskelyne, who was the astronomer royal. Rather than simply accept the opinion that Kinnebrook was incompetent, Bessel investigated and found consistent differences between people's reaction times to stellar transits. Bessel suggested data be collected and astronomers recognize the "personal equations" that exist for each of them. This work led physiologists to study reaction times, with F. C. Donders, a Dutch physiologist, proposing that by appropriately complicating what had to be done before responding, the times needed to perform different mental functions could be determined. Many of the early psychologists were invested in this effort of *mental chronometry* (Boring, 1950).

The question of individual differences had eugenic implications for Sir Francis Galton (1822–1911). He was interested in measuring the mental and physical characteristics of the average Englishman in order to improve the British race. A man of boundless energy, curiosity, and intellectual brilliance, though not without the biases of his time, Galton's wealth and social position would have permitted him to lead a life of aristocratic ease. However, his father, alert to the social changes threatening the upper classes of England, put his faith in the future of science, while taking his money out of real estate and putting it to work in industry (Winkler & Bromberg, 1939).

Galton's youth was very similar to that of William James. His home life provided intense intellectual stimulation; his medical education was also interrupted by foreign travel to alleviate feelings of fear and "boredom"; and his resumption of college was followed by periods of restlessness and depression. Unlike James, Galton never completed his medical education but, being independently wealthy, plunged into whatever interested him. He studied geography, anthropology, and meteorology, and these interests were no mere whims; in all these pursuits he was guided by a concern for practical applications of knowledge and succeeded in making significant contributions.

It was not until he was in his forties that Galton's concerns about human evolution—he was a half-cousin of Darwin and much influenced by the theory (Fancher, 1979)—brought him into areas of research that would justify psychologists claiming him for a colleague. He had collected a mass of assorted data on all the aristocrats, professional men, and university personnel he could corner as subjects. These data were analyzed statistically using the principle of probability and the principle of the normal curve of distribution of individual differences (the former had been developed by Karl Gauss and Pierre Laplace, and the latter had been formulated by Lambert Quetelet in 1846). The results, particularly the findings derived from tracing the family trees of eminent Englishmen, led to the publication in 1869 of *Hereditary Genius*. The book's very title proclaimed Galton's major thesis that intelligence is inherited. Since, he reasoned, bright parents tend to have bright children, a better race of human beings could be developed by selecting those who are best fitted to reproduce and encouraging them to mate. Although many were favorably impressed by Galton—Charles Darwin confessed his surprise because he thought people who did not achieve had not made the proper effort or lacked persistence—there were others, such as the Swiss botanist Alphonse de Candolle, who reminded him that environmental factors might be of even greater importance in determining intelligence.

Nevertheless, Galton, in his *English Men of Science: Their Nature and Nurture,* reaffirmed his contention that heredity was decisive, and despite reasonable arguments to the contrary, he never changed his mind on this matter (Galton, 1909). It seemed to him that a pressing need was to develop objective techniques for the identification of gifted persons, and for this purpose he established an anthropometric laboratory at the Health Exhibition of the International Exhibition of 1884. Because empiricism argued all our knowledge is acquired through our senses, Galton supposed more intelligent people have better sensory acuities than less intelligent people. In support of this, Galton had observed that idiots were less able than people of normal intelligence to discriminate differences between various weights. He thought there also might be significance in individual differences in height, weight, arm span, force of blow, breathing power, reaction time, color sense, and strength. For a three-penny fee, Galton would measure these variables and provide the person with a card containing the "test" results.

After the exhibition closed in 1885, Galton moved his laboratory to the South Kensington Museum, and over the next 6 years he measured over 9,000 people.

Not much came from all this measuring (Johnson et al., 1985), for before the data were fully evaluated Galton became sidetracked by the possibilities of fingerprints.

At first Galton hoped that fingerprints might be of great anthropological significance. He examined "large numbers" of people from what were thought to be different races: Basques, East Indians, American Indians, blacks, Jews, and Chinese. Also he examined fingerprints from groups defined by different interests and personalities: students of art, students of science, Quakers, distinguished persons, and idiots at Earlswood Asylum. In no group did he find any characteristic fingerprint pattern. Although disappointed, Galton did recognize the potential importance of the whirls and loops in fingerprints as a means of individual identification, and he recommended their use in criminal investigations.

Galton's versatility bore fruit in other areas (Galton, 1909). From his endless, energetic rushing from one interest to another came composite photography; systems for describing weather; the rudimentary form of regression analysis and the correlation coefficient; the Galton whistle, which emits a pitch audible to animals but not humans; the ticker tape; the questionnaire method; the discovery of eidetic imagery; the use of free association to demonstrate the significance of childhood memories for adults; the development of percentile values; and, perhaps his greatest psychological contribution, the use of statistical methods in scientific investigation. Ironically, Galton, the father of eugenics, had a marriage that was childless.

"The greatest human being I have ever known," said James McKeen Cattell (1860–1944) about Francis Galton. Cattell graduated in 1880 from Lafayette College, where his father later became president (Watson, 1963). He was a brash, aggressive young man who fit the European conception of Americans. Armed with his BS, he studied at Göttingen and Leipzig. He then returned to the United States for a year at Johns Hopkins, where inadvertently he spent a semester as a student of G. Stanley Hall. In 1883, Cattell made a triumphant return to Leipzig and virtually hired himself as Wundt's assistant. Seemingly cowed by Cattell's chutzpah, Wundt, who generally assigned dissertation topics to his students on the basis of *his* interests and needs, allowed Cattell to do a doctoral dissertation of his own choosing on individual differences in reaction times.

After receiving his doctorate in 1886, Cattell taught for a year at the University of Pennsylvania and spent part of the following year as a lecturer at Cambridge University. While at Cambridge, he met Galton and was immediately impressed. The similarity of their interests and views, not only with respect to individual differences but also eugenics, drew Cattell to Galton and inspired him to conduct research with the same anthropometric techniques.

Cattell returned to the University of Pennsylvania in 1888 and founded the third psychological laboratory in the United States. (The first, actually less a laboratory for research than a space to be used to demonstrate techniques and principles to students, was established by James at Harvard in 1875; the second was founded by Hall at Johns Hopkins in 1883.) Within a year Cattell became the first professor of psychology at Pennsylvania.

Cattell (1890) introduced the term *mental test* in an article entitled "Mental Tests and Measurements." In that paper he insisted that psychology must rest on a foundation of measurement and experimentation. Through the use of mental tests, Cattell predicted, it would be possible to discover the constancy of mental processes, their interdependence, and their variation under different circumstances. He foresaw practical applications of the tests in the selection of people for training and as indicators of disease. However, his immediate concern was to propose a battery of 10 tests that could be adopted and administered in a standardized manner so that the results from different investigators could be compared. Already lack of standardization was becoming a problem in interpreting psychological research.

From a list of 50 tests that had been used at one time or another, Cattell nominated the following 10 for approval as a battery: Dynamometer Pressure; Rate of Movement (time used to move an arm a specified distance); Sensation-Areas (two-point discrimination); Least Noticeable Difference in Weight; Reaction-Time for Sound; Time for Naming Colors; Bi-section of a 50 cm Line; Judgment of Ten Seconds Time; Number of Letters Remembered on Once Hearing.

In a footnote to the article, Cattell expressed the hope that Galton would approve of his suggestions; in an addendum to that same article, Galton did not. He criticized Cattell for neglecting to mention the importance of comparing the tests' results with an independent measure of the same variables. (Cattell had stressed reliability; Galton was correctly, though inappropriately, reminding him of test validity.) As if to add to his reservations—and completely undermining the whole point of the article—Galton proposed several new tests of his own for inclusion in a model battery. All of this must have been most distressing to Cattell, who was eager to obtain some agreement on the issue of standardization.

The need for agreement was felt to be urgent because it was hoped these tests could be put to immediate practical use. One important task was to distinguish between the psychotic and feebleminded. That there was a distinction between these two groups was forcefully suggested by Jean Esquirol in 1838 (Zilboorg & Henry, 1941), but this distinction had significant consequences only after reformers had campaigned successfully to provide separate institutions for the mentally ill and the retarded. It then became necessary to provide some objective means for the identification of the intellectually subnormal. A similar need was experienced in educational circles, where the selection of children for newly acquired special pedagogical programs and schools could not in good conscience be satisfactorily made on the basis of subjective impressions and appraisals.

There already had been a number of attempts to devise batteries of sensorimotor tests that would discriminate between various levels of intelligence. Besides the efforts of Galton and Cattell in this direction, A. Oehrn, a student of the psychiatrist Emil Kraepelin, constructed a set of tests in 1889; Joseph Jastrow developed a set of 15 tests in 1890 and demonstrated them at the Columbian Exposition in Chicago in 1893; and Münsterberg developed a set of 14 tests for school children in 1891 (Peterson, 1925). Unfortunately, whenever the matter of validity was considered, the picture became less encouraging, because simple sensorimotor tests did not successfully discriminate among school children.

Franz Boas, at Clark University, tested approximately 1500 school children in 1891 and found little correspondence between his findings and teachers' estimates of "intellectual acuteness." J. A. Gilbert, at Yale University, tested approximately 1200 school children in New Haven. On only two tests, rate of tapping and judgment of length of distances, were the children who were evaluated as "bright" by their teachers superior to their supposedly dull classmates. Evidently the tests were far from satisfactory in differentiating among children who were not grossly different in intelligence. An understandable lack of enthusiasm for mental testing was generated, although the hope prevailed that valid and reliable measures would be devised.

In an exhaustive and exhausting review of research on mental tests, Stella Sharp (1899, p. 389) concluded that "the tests employed, considered as a whole, cannot be said to yield decisive results for Individual Psychology if applied *once* only to individuals of *the same class.*" Some worthwhile information might be obtained, she suggested, if the tests were repeatedly administered to the same person, but considering the amount of work that would be involved for what it would reveal, it wasn't worth the trouble. She was encouraged, however, by the work of Binet and Henri, who were trying to construct tests to measure complex mental processes involved in intelligence, and she felt they were on the right track.

The suggestion to test complex psychological processes had been made in the 18th century by Charles Bonnet. He proposed that minds could be ordered and measured on the basis of the number of correct conclusions they were able to draw from the same principle (Ramul, 1960), but his proposal was neglected. Hermann Ebbinghaus, who had a much greater influence on the course of psychology than Bonnet, thought that an important characteristic of intelligence is the ability to combine or organize words into a meaningful whole. In 1897, he reported promising results in differentiating between students who were grouped into good, average, or poor; the most discriminating technique he used was a sentence completion method, which he originated (Watson, 1963). This test required the child to complete sentences in a story by supplying missing words or syllables. Items similar in structure to those employed by Ebbinghaus are still found on intelligence scales and are looked upon with favor by many teachers when constructing final examinations.

In summary, psychological testing toward the end of the 19th century was still in a primitive state. There were no satisfactory psychological tests, but research into their development was beginning to occur. Already efforts had been expended on sensorimotor tests, and it was eventually determined they were of little usefulness. Nevertheless, Cattell, who had moved to Columbia University in 1891, persisted with his colleague Livingston Farrand in investigating the merits of simpler functions, trusting that they might be able to find some significant relationship between their measures and grades of college students in their freshman, sophomore, and senior years. Cattell and Farrand's tenacity was expressive of a wrong-headedness that can still be found. They dismissed the suggestion that psychologists should measure complex mental processes on the grounds of imprecision ["we find it difficult to measure definitely a definite thing" (Cattell & Farrand,

1896, p. 623)] and stuck with more objective and easily measured functions, even though these functions had no demonstrable relation to what they were trying to measure (Watson, 1953).

DIAGNOSTIC FORMULATIONS

From the middle of the 19th century, psychiatry was dominated by schools in Germany and France. As we have already noted, science and scientific values were held in the highest regard, so that where definite knowledge of etiology was absent, careful description of specific disorders and investigation into their causes were held to take priority over their treatment. Generally, French psychiatry had the lead in the study of neuroses, whereas German psychiatry led in the classification and study of psychoses.

In accord with Griesinger's dictum that mental diseases are diseases of the brain produced by physiological disturbances, the leading edge of research was in the determination of physical causes of disorders, and here the early findings were most encouraging. Morphine addiction and its psychiatric effects became known. Sergei Korsakov was studying the harmful consequences for brain functioning of chronic alcoholism. Karl Wernicke was studying the associations between lesions in different areas of the brain and different forms of language disturbances or aphasias. Richard von Krafft-Ebing's experiments were demonstrating that paresis or general paralysis was caused by syphilis, which was hailed as particularly significant support for the position that psychological symptoms have an organic cause.

At the same time, a vast amount of energy and ingenuity was expended in devising labels and classification systems of psychiatric illnesses as a necessary first step in their scientific study. Karl Kahlbaum wrote of neophrenias, enphrenias, paraphrenias, and dysphrenias. Heinrich Schüle distinguished allopathic and deuteropathic conditions, hereditary neuroses and cerebropsychoses, and cerebropsychopathies. Wernicke spoke of a kinetic, hyperkinetic, and parakinetic motility, and also of allopsychosis, somatopsychosis, and autopsychosis (Zilboorg & Henry, 1941). A major and all too easily attained goal for many psychiatrists was to invent their own new nomenclature and propose its acceptance.

Emil Kraepelin (1855–1926), known as the father of descriptive psychiatry, was probably the leading psychiatrist of this period. His research strategy was influenced by Wundt, under whom he had studied. Though capable of being pleasant and warm with colleagues, he remained professionally detached from patients, whom he viewed as clusters of symptoms. His successful and enormously influential textbook on psychiatry was first published in 1883 and came to full flower in its fifth and sixth editions (published in 1896 and 1899).

Kraepelin believed psychiatrists had to make orderly and sensible the bewildering array of disturbed behaviors by finding which symptoms clustered together into reliable syndromes of specific disorders. Once this information was gained, research could begin into causes and into the natural course of the illness, that is, whether the patients with a certain disorder seemed to improve or deteriorate or have recurrent episodes of acute disturbance. Mental diseases, Kraepelin suggested, could be divided into those caused by external conditions (exogenous), which were considered usually curable, and those caused by inherent, constitutional factors (endogenous), which were considered incurable. He assumed that the outcome and course of a mental disease was determined by the natural laws governing the particular disorder. He thought the natural laws should be the object of psychiatric investigation, not the idiosyncrasies and peculiarities of individual patients. For example, syphilis usually exhibits the following course if untreated: A sore appears at the point of infection; 2 to 4 months later a copper-colored rash appears; there is a symptom-free period of from 10 to 30 years during which the spirochetes often attack some organ of the body; and then symptoms reappear, such as blindness, heart disorder, or mental illness (paresis). This was the kind of information that Kraepelin argued should be obtained for every psychiatric disturbance.

Significantly for those patients so diagnosed, Kraepelin classified dementia praecox among the endogenous (inherent, incurable) illnesses. The term *dementia praecox* had been introduced by B. A. Morel in 1860 to describe a form of mental and emotional deterioration that had its onset around the time of puberty, a dementia that occurred early in life. For Kraepelin, *dementia praecox* had a different meaning and referred to early mental deterioration following the onset. Its major symptoms were hallucinations, delusions, incongruous emotions, and progressive intellectual impairment.

Kraepelin identified hebephrenic and catatonic forms of dementia praecox, the terms having been originated, respectively, by Evald Hecker in 1871 and Kahlbaum in 1874 (Zilboorg & Henry, 1941); these forms were thought to be caused by organic changes in the brain. Other disorders designated in the nomenclature were paranoia, an endogenous illness with an unshakable and permanent delusional system, and manic depressive psychosis and involutional melancholia, both exogenous illnesses with favorable prognoses.

Kraepelin's system was criticized, particularly since even Kraepelin admitted 13% of the patients diagnosed as dementia praecox recovered without any apparent defects. Nevertheless, his classification exerted a tremendous influence on subsequent psychiatric nosologies and on therapeutic attitudes (e.g., complacency regarding manic-depressive psychosis and other exogenous disorders, since the patients were expected to get well anyway, and resignation regarding dementia praecox and the endogenous disorders, since no recovery was anticipated).

The major neurosis at that time was hysteria, with its symptoms resembling those of many medical complaints. A prevalent attitude of physicians toward the illness was that it was peculiar to women, who more than likely employed it as a devious method by which to gain sympathetic attention, though in advanced medical circles in Europe and America its occurrence in males was recognized (Sulloway, 1974, pp. 38–41). The belief that hysteria was a female disorder, mistaken as it was, had a long and honorable history: Hippocrates (460–357 B.C.) thought the illness was due to the uterus's becoming detached and shifting its position within the body. It is a measure of the progress of medicine in this area that some 2,400 years later, in 1882, Jean Martin Charcot (1825–1893), who did believe in male hysteria (which he estimated to be 20 times less frequent than female hysteria), attributed convulsions and iliac pain in female hysterics to the compression of an ovary.

Charcot, the brilliant French neurologist, is of course better known for his teaching at the Salpêtrière than for his ovarian hypothesis. Physicians flocked from all over Europe to see "the Master" in action at that first center of postgraduate psychiatric education. They were rarely disappointed, for Charcot was in his element when using a cast of hysterics to stage a dramatic production that was both instructive and startling. His aides would bring in previously prepared hysterical patients who would obligingly fall into a deep hypnotic trance when he so suggested. Then Charcot would demonstrate in these hypnotized patients all the many symptoms of hysteria—anesthesias in various parts of the body, crying spells, paralyses, falling fits—and thus give credence to his thesis that hysteria and hypnosis were part of one and the same phenomenon (Winkler & Bromberg, 1939).

It was Charcot's contention that what the notorious and discredited Friedrich Anton Mesmer (1734–1815) called animal magnetism and what the physician James Braid (1795–1860) called hypnotism (Boring, 1950) was a condition peculiar to hysterics. Suffering from a lapse of logic, he decided (1) that because all the symptoms of hysteria could be produced in hypnotized patients, only hysterics could be hypnotized and (2) that hypnosis itself was intimately associated with the disease. Therefore, Charcot regarded hypnosis as the method of choice for investigating predispositions to hysteria (and of course since men could be hypnotized, hysteria was not confined to women). In short, Charcot's view seems to have been that no diagnosis of hysteria is possible unless the patient is hypnotized, and then it is mandatory.

Charcot's neurological reputation—in the opinions of many he had fathered neurology with his astute observations on locomotor ataxia and multiple sclerosis—ensured a respectful hearing and attentive audience to his views. Through his good offices, hypnosis acquired some scientific respectability and the condition of hysteria began to be taken more seriously. Nevertheless, his conclusions in this area were criticized from all sides. The most telling objections came from Nancy, a city in northeast France, where hypnosis and hysteria were also being studied by the physician A. A. Liebault (1823–1904) and his pupil Hippolyte Bernheim (1837–1919). They believed that hypnotism was not indicative of psychopathology and that it was a condition induced by the suggestions made by Charcot to his patients.

Moreover, Bernheim argued it is not necessary to induce a trance in order to produce a dazzling variety of hysterical symptoms. All that needed to be done was to suggest the symptoms to patients while they were in a waking state. Further, almost any person could be hypnotized and almost any person is to some extent suggestible. It was, in a way, Bernheim's misfortune to be so demonstrably correct in his assertions: They were so readily accepted that he could not found a school of thought based on them.

Pierre Janet (1859–1947), a pupil of Charcot, was his successor at the Salpêtrière. Janet also rejected Charcot's idea that hypnosis was to be found only in hysterics. He discovered through carefully reexamining the histories of his patients that a large number had suffered some emotional shock preceding the onset of their illnesses. The memories of these shocks seemed to have been forgotten by the patients and must, he decided, have been pushed into the unconscious part of their minds. At this early stage of his career, Janet concluded that the forgetting represented an abnormal and distinctive weakness in the personality of the hysteric, since the normal person was thought to have experiences much more fully integrated and accessible to consciousness.

According to Janet, then, the personality of the hysteric is split: One part of it operates automatically or unconsciously as a secondary personage that invades and takes over parts of the primary personality.

Similar ideas were published by Janet's compatriot, Alfred Binet (1890, p. 47), who also thought that in hysterics there was a "double consciousness," including a second ego able to apprehend impressions and excite ideas in the field of the main personality in such a way that "the principal Ego of the 'subject' in no wise has consciousness of it" (Binet, 1890). Even more significantly, Binet had conducted a study in which he observed hysterical phenomena, such as automatic movements, in normal subjects. But although the title of his article boldly proclaimed that normal people have a double consciousness, he was cautious in the remainder of his report and proposed only tentatively extending the concept beyond hysterics.

Meanwhile, Bernheim continued to emphasize and to expand upon his belief in the suggestibility of both normal and abnormal individuals. He believed that a broad range of behavior was due to suggestions and autosuggestions that might not be readily apparent to an observer or to the agent. On the one hand, he felt that the label *hysteria* should be restricted to cases with convulsive symptoms; on the other hand, he thought that "hysterogenous" tendencies existed in all people. Broadly speaking, this second view had more merit than the first. Bernheim's is the first known attempt to evolve a general understanding of human behavior and its motivation starting from a study of psychopathology (Zilboorg & Henry, 1941).

Bernheim went on to present a paper before the International Congress of Medicine in Moscow in 1897. There he attacked the idea of free will in mental illness and crime. He argued that through a variety of obvious and subtle suggestions all people at times engage in "automatic" acts, that is, acts that seem to arise without people being conscious of them or having any intention of performing them. Of course, the mentally ill frequently do things that seem senseless and out of control, but, Bernheim contended, criminals also behave out of an immediate yielding to a suggestion or impulse. Therefore, he proposed that society assume a more humane, less punitive attitude in dealing with those who violate its laws, since it seemed clear to him that these men and women were no more responsible for their acts than is an avalanche crashing down a mountain side. Bernheim was thus the first physician to advance the concept of the "irresistible impulse" in criminal behavior (Zilboorg & Henry, 1941). It is a concept that is still controversial. (In 1983, the American Bar Association adopted the position that it might be preferable to drop "an inability to conform one's behavior to the law" as a criterion for insanity.)

TREATMENT FORMULATIONS

It has been stated repeatedly that psychiatric treatment in this period awaited the determination of the causes of specific disorders. Although medical science progressed, the majority of patients were treated through physical procedures or the use of suggestion. Those in mental hospitals principally received custodial care, and those treated by physicians as outpatients were subjected to whatever their physicians' daring or ingenuity might lead them to prescribe. Some practitioners of a kindly bent recommended neurotics take a pleasant vacation or urged them to forget their worries. Others less kind might advise an operation.

In these circumstances, any possible method of cure might be given serious consideration for a time. Proper mastication of food until each bite was dissolved into a creamy pulp was advocated by Horace Fletcher (1849-1919), an American sociologist and nutritionist, as a means to prevent a variety of ills. Although not enthusiastically endorsed by the medical profession, "Fletcherism," during the late 19th century, was widely known and virtually a cult. "I tried it," William James remarked sadly, "but it nearly killed me."

Medically more respectable—and as popular as Fletcherism—were the ideas of S. Weir Mitchell (1829-1914). Mitchell, America's first neurologist, was the originator of the "rest cure." This treatment was not totally lacking justification. During the 18th century, John Brown had been a leading and influential exponent of the theory that irritability and exhaustion of the nervous system led to states of fatigue, weakness, and collapse (Zilboorg & Henry). The theory seemed plausible, and a century later such terms as *neurasthenia* and *psychasthenia* bore witness to its staying power.

Mitchell's treatment was intended primarily for hysterics. He had observed that "nervous fatigue" was a prominent symptom of the disorder and that anemia was frequently found in these patients. Accordingly, he charmingly advised his colleagues, "Let us bring in Dr. Diet and Dr. Quiet." Through rest, good nutrition, encouragement, and understanding, the hysteric could be helped to return to a useful life. Mitchell's book *Fat and Blood* indicated by its title what he considered to be the basic needs. Mitchell's real contributions to the treatment of hysterics— patience, respect, encouragement, optimism, hope—were apparently as little appreciated by him as they were by his fellow neurologists.

Sending patients to a spa or on a long ocean voyage was definitely a relief to the attending physician if to no one else. Charcot had even been known to send some of his hysterical patients to the shrine of Our Lady of Lourdes. At first sight this seemed rather puzzling, since it was well known that Charcot had no great love of religion. Moreover, he did not believe any miracle was likely to take place. The faith cures, he explained, were due to the latent hypnotic influence of the shrine acting on the hysterics. "What does it matter," Charcot would say when someone wondered if the Master might be thought a trifle hypocritical, "if the patient gets well?" (Winkler & Bromberg, 1939).

William James (1890) optimistically proposed that a cure of hysteria might be accomplished through hypnosis. By means of the hypnotic state he thought it possible for the physician to gain access to the secondary personage (the ordinarily unconscious part of the personality). James envisioned a kind of reasonable conversation, with perhaps some additional strong speech thrown in for the more intransigent cases, between the hypnotist and the patient that would induce the secondary personage to release control of the affected part of the body to the primary personality.

A similar proposal was made by Bernheim in 1891 in his book *Hypnotismus, Suggestion, und Psychotherapie*. Bernheim followed the lead provided by Liebeault in recommending the use of hypnosis in treating hysterics, in particular by making suggestions that would remove the harmful effects of previous suggestions. What is more, he believed that the pathological suggestions had been unconsciously accepted by the patient and led to the disorder. An interested visitor at the clinic of Liebeault and Bernheim in 1889 was the Viennese neurologist Sigmund Freud (1856–1939), who visited France to learn the latest about hysteria.

Freud had entered the University of Vienna in 1873 and received his MD degree in 1881. An outstanding, zealous student, he had been raised in a middle-class Jewish family that from his early childhood, had nurtured in him the expectation of and desire for fame: "A man who has been the indisputable favorite of his mother keeps for life the feeling of a conqueror, that confidence of success that often induces real success" (Jones, 1953, p. 5). His need for recognition and his eager anticipation of it had frequently led Freud to feel overly enthusiastic about his ideas and to present them somewhat prematurely.

Through his discovery of a gold-chloride method for staining nervous tissue, Freud had made a definite contribution to neurology, but a contribution that failed to lead to that full measure of success that he felt was destined to be his. In 1884, after finding that cocaine helped to alleviate his own periods of depression and that he could dispense with its use without ill effects, he hastily assumed the drug would be an effective antidepressant for everyone and endorsed its prescription. The unfortunate consequences that soon followed did serious damage to the reputation that he wished to have as a prudent scientist. While the sad findings of research in cocaine habituation and intoxication were being discussed in Vienna in 1886, Freud was in Paris studying under Charcot. There, too, Freud was on the track of fame, his interest in hysteria having been stimulated by the experience of his friend Josef Breuer (1841–1925).

Breuer had the unenviable distinction of being a father figure to the man who was to discover the Oedipus complex. A successful and highly regarded neurologist in Vienna, Breuer had done significant research on the functions of the vagus nerve and the semicircular canals before going into private practice. Breuer had met Freud in the late 1870s and aided him, both financially and through good counsel, in embarking on a professional career.

From 1880 to 1882 Breuer treated a young, attractive hysteric, Bertha Pappenheim (1859–1936), known in the literature as Fraulein Anna O. At one time or another this woman displayed all the symptoms associated with hysteria: anorexia (little appetite for food), paralyses, a severe cough (the symptom that first brought her to Breuer), double personality, and anesthesias. With this assortment of complaints and her engaging way with words—she was very bright—it is not too surprising that Breuer found himself becoming more and more preoccupied with her case. (Today some might say that Breuer evidenced a countertransference.) During one momentous visit, she related her memories concerning the first appearance of a symptom; to Breuer's amazement, the symptom seemed to disappear. Miss Pappenheim felt there was value in this procedure and called it "the talking cure." Breuer also thought it valuable and called it "catharsis." At this point, accounts of the story differ in detail but generally indicate the following (Gay, 1988).

As Breuer's interest in this patient grew, he began seeing her daily and then twice a day. By any standards this was an enormous amount of time to devote to one case, and Breuer's wife understandably became irritated, jealous, and suspicious. In the interests of preserving his marriage, Breuer felt compelled to refer his patient to a colleague, to terminate the treatment abruptly, and to go on a vacation with his wife. When Breuer told Miss Pappenheim that their relationship was ended, her condition took an immediate turn for the worse. Breuer succeeded in relieving her distress by hypnosis, and then left with his wife for Venice. (After several years of ups and downs, Bertha Pappenheim went to Germany and became that country's first social worker. She eventually made a significant contribution to the assistance of unwed mothers; she herself never married.)

Breuer discussed the case of Anna O. with Freud, who, after overcoming his initial amusement at his friend's discomfiture, became deeply interested. Freud journeyed to Paris in 1885 to study at the clinic of Charcot. To Freud, Charcot's productions of hysterical symptoms through hypnosis had profound meaning; they indicated that whatever the neurological or etiological basis of the disorder might be, the symptoms themselves could be treated and alleviated by verbal means alone. Moreover, Freud, like Bernheim, believed hysteria was a definite disorder and not merely an epiphenomenon produced by the hypnotist's unwitting suggestions, since hysterics everywhere presented a similar syndrome.

Freud rushed back to Vienna to share all newly gained impressions and ideas about neuroses with his medical colleagues. Having recently been embarrassed in consequence of Freud's enthusiasm for cocaine, they gave him a chilly reception. The climate of the meeting was not helped by the sight of a young, ambitious physician lecturing them on matters about which they felt informed. But Freud was not easily discouraged.

For a time he continued to treat his hysterical patients with the latest and most accepted methods, including electrotherapy (an electric shock, intended to be somewhat painful, was administered to the part of the body that the patient claimed was paralyzed or without feeling), baths, massages, rest, and direct therapeutic suggestions while the patient was hypnotized. However, his dissatisfaction with these procedures mounted daily. Relative to his earlier enthusiasm, his disappointment with hypnotism was especially keen; not all his patients could be hypnotized, and he found the whole business boring. In 1892, he began to use a "concentration" technique: The patient, while lying down, was directed and urged to recall all memories associated with a particular symptom. Gradually, Freud abandoned completely both hypnosis and directing and prodding the patient. At times he labeled this free approach "Breuer's cathartic method" and at other times "psychical analysis."

Breuer and Freud published *Studies in Hysteria* in 1895. As far as Breuer was concerned, their most important contribution was the exposition of transference, which occurs when a patient transfers to a relationship with a physician feelings and thoughts originally experienced in early years with someone else. Nevertheless, despite the importance they attached to their work, the book was not favorably received in medical circles, and Breuer became discouraged by the criticisms. Further, Breuer was reluctant to draw the same far-reaching inferences that Freud was making on the basis of his investigations of his patients' sexual life. Breuer stated with mixed feelings of fear and admiration, "Freud's intellect is soaring at its highest, I gaze after him as a hen at a hawk."

By 1896 the relationship between the two men had definitely cooled. Freud was talking about *his* new technique of "psychoanalysis" and about *his* new theory of hysteria. He announced to the Society of Psychiatry and Neurology in Vienna that the cause of hysteria was the memory of passive sexual experiences, traumatic seductions that had occurred before the patients were 8 years old. Moreover, his investigations had revealed that in obsessional neuroses there were also prepubertal seductions, but, in contrast to the seductions of hysterics, these patients had been actively aggressive in bringing them about and had found them pleasurable. These conclusions, Freud pointed out, were based on 19 "fully analyzed" cases. The reaction to these empirical findings was, to say the least, icy. Krafft-Ebing commented, "It sounds like a scientific fairy tale" (Jones, 1953, p. 263). And that was a kind evaluation.

In point of fact, Freud himself came to believe that the stories of seduction told to him by his patients were more wishful fantasies than actual incidents. Nevertheless, he used Breuer's skepticism about the validity of his conclusions and his old friend's good-natured reluctance to accept partial repayment of some debts to end their relationship. By 1900, Freud, resentful of Breuer's generous and guilt-arousing paternalism, severed all further contacts. (Some eighty years later, Freud's wisdom in coming to doubt his patients' reports of incest has been seriously questioned [Masson, 1984]).

At about the time that Freud was beginning to develop psychoanalysis on his own, Lightner Witmer (1867–1956), a psychologist at the University of Pennsylvania, initiated a training program in a new field that he soon called "clinical psychology" (Watson, 1951, 1953, 1956). It is worth emphasizing, particularly since so many people have the misconception that clinical psychology originated after World War II, that this applied field is almost as old as scientific psychology itself and that its founding occurred near the beginning of the 20th century.

Witmer, whose first name was the surname of his paternal great-grandmother (McReynolds, 1987), had graduated from the University of Pennsylvania in 1888, and in his early career he always seemed to find himself a step or two behind James McKeen Cattell. He had studied under Cattell as an assistant in psychology and followed his mentor's example by journeying to Leipzig to obtain his PhD from Wundt. But where Cattell was forceful, Witmer was pedantic, and therein lay a considerable individual difference.

Like Cattell, Witmer wanted to work on an "applied" dissertation, much against the wishes of Wundt. Unlike Cattell, Witmer accepted Wundt's suggestion and wrote a thesis in aesthetics, including research on the golden section (the most pleasing division of a line or area into two parts). Witmer received his doctorate in 1892 and returned to the University of Pennsylvania, where he took control of the psychology laboratory, since Cattell had just left to teach at Columbia. Four years later, in 1896, Witmer founded the first psychological clinic, actually the first child guidance clinic in the world, and thus gave clinical psychology its start.

There are two stories as to how Witmer became interested in clinical work, Witmer himself claimed that he became involved while teaching English at a prep school and pursuing his studies at the University of Pennsylvania (Witmer, 1907). One of his students was a boy who was impeded in articulation, and Witmer did what he could to help him. He believed that the problem was caused by a head injury suffered by the boy when he was 2 years old. What bothered Witmer most was that the boy's talent had been wasted and he had endured years of frustration, perhaps needlessly, simply because the condition had not been diagnosed and attended to earlier. Why could not psychologists, he wondered, use their knowledge to assist such individuals?

The other story is told by Witmer's friend and colleague Robert Brotemarkle (1947). Witmer was challenged by a public school teacher, Margaret Maguire, to put the new science of psychology to some practical use by helping a "chronic bad speller" overcome his difficulty. In the diagnostic process that followed, Witmer found the child had a visual anomaly, which was corrected by glasses. By then having the child tutored, Witmer was able to effect improvement, which encouraged him to initiate similar services for other children. (A more detailed and somewhat different account of this case is in McReynolds [1987]; it is also probably more accurate than Brotemarkle's recollection).

Both stories indicate Witmer's interest in being of help to people, the importance he attached to diagnosis, and his willingness to utilize whatever knowledge and skills were necessary to bring about optimum functioning. Witmer believed it was important for psychologists to work with people who were deficient in some way or other and to offer treatments that were "pedagogical" (i.e., the psychologists were to teach correct behavior). It is no exaggeration to say that the therapeutic role of psychologists as envisioned by Witmer is very similar to the role of behavior therapists today.

In 1896, during the Christmas vacation, Witmer attended the APA convention and told his colleagues about his new clinic at the University of Pennsylvania. He proposed a different role for psychologists, one in which they would continue to function as scientists but would also apply their knowledge and acquired skills. In describing his proposal, he referred to the "clinical method" in psychology. In this method, students would learn by demonstrations and contacts with those actually in need of psychological services (Watson, 1951, 1956). He explained that the psychological clinic would be an institution for social and public service, original research, and the instruction of students, and he urged other colleges and universities to follow the example of the University of Pennsylvania in supporting such a clinic. He went on to recommend the creation of a new field, "psychological orthogenics," that would include vocational, educational, correctional, hygienic, industrial, and social guidance. This was heady stuff to propose to people who believed psychologists were scientists who had no interest in the practical applications of their discipline. Witmer's talk stimulated the elevation of some of his colleagues' eyebrows but little else (Shakow, 1948).

There were at least four reasons for the unresponsiveness of Witmer's audience. First, as already mentioned, the majority of psychologists considered themselves scientists. They regarded the role described by Witmer as inappropriate to psychology as they understood it. (This factor continues to exert an influence even today, when clinical psychology is established as a profession of importance and prestige. Witness the lack of space given Witmer and clinical psychology in most histories of psychology and introductory texts.) Second, even if they had considered his suggestions admirable, few psychologists were prepared by training or experience to initiate the functions he proposed. Third, the status of psychology in those early years was too precarious to risk jeopardizing it by possibly premature applications. Fourth, Witmer had an unfortunate talent for antagonizing his colleagues.

To estrange his colleagues was the last thing Witmer wanted to do. Yet his tendencies to make overzealous criticisms and deliver his remarks in nasty-sounding tones were among Witmer's less endearing qualities. For example, at the business meeting of the APA that year (1896), he pointed out that the council was electing new members without adequately bringing them before the association for approval (Fernberger, 1931). Witmer proposed a well-defined procedure: "All names [of prospective members] nominated by the Council, shall be presented to the Association at its opening meeting in written form or visibly displayed upon a blackboard, together with a statement of the contribution or contributions to psychology, . . . and that the final action upon such names shall be taken by the Association at the final business meeting." That Witmer might be correct did not help (in 1897 definite procedures for nomination to membership were adopted, including formal nomination blanks and sponsorship by two APA members). Nor did it help when his friends argued that his aggression was directed at ideas rather than the people who espoused them; this was a subtle distinction often lost upon those whose ideas were attacked.

However, Witmer had the backing of his university (O'Donnell, 1979), and he was not the sort to bow to social disapproval or apathy. Undaunted, he proceeded the following year to expand and consolidate the services of his clinic. During the summer of 1897, he began to offer a 4-week course designed to demonstrate the clinical method in child psychology. There were case presentations and instruction in diagnostic techniques and pedagogical treatment. The large attendance provided convincing evidence that there was support for his work. Thus it might be that Witmer, unlike Pyrrhus, lost most battles but won the war.

PROFESSIONAL DEVELOPMENT

In addition to Witmer's suggestions, there were other indications during this decade of a broadening of the psychologist's role. Around 1889, Edward Cowles, a former surgeon in the Union army who had studied psychology at Johns Hopkins, encouraged the practice of conjoint medicine at McLean Hospital in Waverly, Massachusetts. A laboratory in the hospital was set aside to be used for studies and experiments in physiological psychology to determine the "exact nature and causes of departure from normal mental function" (Hall, 1894). In 1893, August Hoch was selected by Cowles to be the hospital's psychologist and pathologist. Hoch had studied psychology with Wundt and was also a physician. Later he was to become professor of psychiatry at Cornell (Meyer, 1919).

On July 8, 1892, a group of "rugged pioneers" in psychology met at Clark University at the invitation of G. Stanley Hall (1844–1924). There they founded the American Psychological Association (Dennis & Boring, 1952). Seven men formed a council, which was the governing body of the association: G. Stanley Hall; G. S. Fullerton, of the University of Pennsylvania; Joseph Jastrow, of the University of Wisconsin; William James; G. T. Ladd, of Yale; James McKeen Cattell; and J. Mark Baldwin, of the University of Toronto. The council members, together with 24 others elected to membership, constituted the entire association (Fernberger, 1932). Some of these original members were not even psychologists but were educators, philosophers, and physicians. About a third of them would be unable to meet current APA membership requirements.

The founder of the APA, G. Stanley Hall was born and raised on a farm in Ashfield, Massachusetts. His parents, hardworking, devout, and puritanical, were mindful of the importance of an education and placed great value on learning. Though they loved their son deeply, they had little time or inclination to engage in open displays of affection. (Some years after the event, Hall found out that his father had kept him from serving in the Union army by bribing a physician to certify him ineligible for conscription.). At the age of 16, Hall went away from home to teach in a country school. With the assistance of his mother and the reluctant consent of his father, he left that position for a year's study at a seminary in order to prepare himself for college. In 1863 he entered Williams College and graduated 4 years later in the bottom half of his class. Although rather skeptical of orthodox religious practices and convictions, he then went to the Union Theological Seminary, where he studied for the ministry. Hall, like many of the early psychologists, pursued his education with little zest. For 10 years he floundered, though not entirely without purpose or accomplishment.

By the age of 27, Hall had studied philosophy for 2 years in Germany, had been ordained, and had resigned from his first pastorate. Then came 4 years as Professor of Modern Language and Literature at Antioch College, followed by 2 years as an English tutor at Harvard. While at Harvard, he studied psychology with William James, found the subject to his liking, and earned his doctorate in 1878. After that he spent 2 years studying under Wundt. So by the time of his second return to the United States from Germany, Hall had a clear idea of his goals and the area in which he wished to do research.

He decided to devote himself to the study of childhood and development and began with the investigation of children's thoughts and beliefs, for which he devised interview procedures and questionnaires. One of the major findings from his study of Boston school children was that boys and girls were surprisingly ignorant about things that adults assumed were known to everyone. For example, only 10% of the children knew where their ribs were located. It seemed obvious that adults were giving credit to youngsters for much more knowledge than they possessed, and educational practices would have to take this into account so that children could understand and make meaningful use of what they were being taught.

In 1881 Hall joined the faculty of Johns Hopkins University. There he established the second psychological laboratory in the United States, served for a time as lay superintendent of Bay View Hospital, and, in 1887, founded the *American Journal of Psychology*. Two years later he left for Clark University to become its first president. He arrived with great expectations for its future as a center for graduate studies, expectations that did not correspond with the wishes of the school's benefactor, Jonas Gilman Clark (Watson, 1963). Unfortunately, a few months after Hall assumed the presidency, his wife and daughter were accidently asphyxiated. As one might expect, this tragic event affected him profoundly, and it was only through considerable self-discipline that he managed to recover. Forthwith, he plunged himself into his work.

Hall founded the *Pedagogical Seminary* (later renamed the *Journal of Genetic Psychology*) in 1891. The following year he helped to found the APA and became its first president. At that time there were only two psychological journals in the United States, and Hall was founder and editor of both. Therefore, he was in an excellent position to promote research in child psychology. Between 1891 and 1897, Hall and his coworkers published 194 articles on the thoughts and feelings of children. His book *The Contents of Children's Minds on Entering School* (1894) was the culmination of 3 years of study. It won almost instant worldwide acclaim from those who agreed that children were not "little men and women." Although later the superficiality and flaws of Hall's questionnaire method became apparent, his achievement in focusing attention on child development and establishing its significance as an area of research earned him the distinction of being referred to as the "father of child psychology."

Hall was followed in the presidency of the APA by G. T. Ladd (1842–1921), who had attained prominence through his text on physiological psychology. In his presidential address, Ladd presented a vision of the ever-increasing acceptance and prestige of psychology. He asserted that although psychology was the youngest of the sciences, it had a particularly bright future. Those within the field were aggressive, enthusiastic, and hopeful. The findings of its researchers were bound to arouse popular interest, and he was certain these findings would soon begin to enrich many areas. Moreover, he predicted that the studies of Hall and Cattell would lead to improved methods of teaching and that "in the diagnosis and treatment of the insane, the incorrigible, the idiotic, etc., scientific psychology is surely destined to exert a growing influence" (Ladd, 1894, pp. 20–21). As evidence of psychology's increasing influence, G. Stanley Hall, in addition to his other responsibilities, taught psychology to psychiatrists at Worcester State Hospital until 1895, when one of his former students, the psychiatrist Adolf Meyer, assumed this task (Meyer, 1924–1975).

Ladd was followed in the presidency by William James and James McKeen Cattell. Despite the fact that Cattell had been unsuccessful in establishing a psychological service at Columbia in 1895, his presidential address delivered to the APA later that year was bold in its claims, as though the millennium had arrived and the mantle of world leadership in psychology had passed from Germany to the United States.

Cattell's view of psychology did not correspond to the views of most of his colleagues. He argued psychology was already past the time of philosophical and speculative systems, past the time of establishing its credentials as a science, and on the threshold of advancing toward practical applications: "While our confidence in the future of psychology rests on the knowledge of its intrinsic vitality, we are able for the convincing of others to offer the brute argument of material success" (Cattell, 1896, p. 134).

With regard to mental tests, the time for action seemed at hand. At the 1895 APA convention, J. Mark Baldwin proposed the formation of a committee to consider the feasibility of enlisting the cooperation of the various psychological laboratories in standardizing the collection of data. This was a project dear to the heart of Cattell, who was appointed chairman of this committee (Committee on Physical and Mental Tests).

Shortly thereafter, the committee proposed a battery of tests to the APA membership:

1. preliminary data, social and physical
2. physical measurements
3. keenness of vision, touch, and hearing
4. sensitivity to pain
5. reaction time for sound
6. reaction time with choice
7. perception of size
8. perception of time
9. memory type
10. imagery
11. fatigue
12. color vision
13. perception of pitch
14. memory

15. apperception test of Ebbinghaus
16. perception of weight
17. dynamometer pressure of right and left hands
18. rate of movement
19. rapidity of movement
20. will power
21. voluntary attention
22. right and left movements
23. accuracy of arm
24. rate of discrimination and movement
25. quickness of distinction and movement

Cattell estimated that under ordinary circumstances it would take no more than an hour to administer all 25 tests, and he hoped this battery would be accepted and be given in a standardized manner.

The following year, 1896, James Sully organized a psychological laboratory for the study of difficult children in England (Watson, 1953), and in 1897 a psychologist, William O. Krohn (1868–1927), founded a laboratory for the study of the mentally ill at Eastern Hospital for the Insane in Kankakee, Illinois. Krohn had been a senior teaching fellow at Clark in 1892 and was a charter member of the APA. After receiving his doctorate from Yale, he founded the psychological laboratory at the University of Illinois. Krohn quickly rose to the position of head of the department of psychology and pedagogy but later entered Northwestern University Medical School, graduated in 1905, and ever after identified himself as a psychiatrist (Wallin, 1961).

We can see the dominance of a narrow conception of science in psychology. Those few psychologists attracted to individual differences and wishing to be of service either saw themselves making a contribution through research in psychopathology or gave serious thought to entering the field of psychiatry. The treatment of people with mental illnesses was not even considered as a possible function of psychologists. The treatment of such patients was regarded as the province of medical practitioners, who in the first place were not scientists and in the second place were not doing too well at it. The "treatment" used by Witmer was essentially to tutor a child to eliminate, or at least lessen, specific learning difficulties or disruptive behaviors that interfered with learning. Witmer thought of this function as teaching or training, which was natural, since Witmer had a long association with the Pennsylvania Training School for Feebleminded Children (Reisman, 1981).

Diagnostic testing was also in a very crude state of development. Few psychologists were interested in testing, and those that were tended not to cooperate. Testing was too trivial a matter to justify much attention. Shortly after being formed, the APA Committee on Physical and Mental Tests unhappily reported that the battery of tests it had proposed was not gaining any acceptance, and by 1899 no further word was heard about the committee, indicating it had decided to abandon its designated task as hopeless and inconsequential.

Although Witmer toward the end of the decade talked about the clinical psychology as a new profession that would be dedicated to the correct use of the scientific findings of psychology in the school setting, such talk did not generate much enthusiasm among psychologists. However, he did create some interest among educators in Philadelphia and among students, who would gravitate to his clinic to learn what he had to offer. It should be noted that Witmer did not question the content or methods of psychology but sought to enlarge its aim so that the findings of psychology could be applied by some psychologists for the benefit of individuals.

Clinical psychology in the 1890s was a glimmer, a baby just catching its first breath, drawing its life from the new science of psychology, itself a toddler supported more by hope and ambition than actual accomplishments. But this was in general a period of hope: hope in the future of science and the future of psychology; hope in the future and destiny of nations; hope in what the human race and the individual might achieve. Few doubts were expressed by psychologists concerning the prospects of their profession. And although psychologists were still few in number—in 8 years, the APA had grown from only 31 to almost 100 (Fernberger, 1932)—the modest increase that had occurred was, these pioneers confidently predicted, only one index of a growth in the science of consciousness they were certain would continue.

3

Early Triumphs
1900–1909

Striding across the early years of the 20th century was a man who embodied rugged individualism and direct action, President Theodore Roosevelt. During his presidency, the people of the United States absorbed an additional 8,202,388 immigrants, cheered their president's fight against monopolies and the exploitation of natural resources, and swelled with pride as a result of their country's "big stick" foreign policy and the digging of the Panama Canal.

By and large, it was still a time of peace. Of course, there had been a war between Russia and Japan and there was squabbling in South Africa, Morocco, and China. but for the most part, peace prevailed and industrialization, despite some setbacks, advanced. The push for social reforms and respect for individual rights continued. By 1909 only Russia was governed by an absolute monarch, and even there Tsar Nicholas II was obliged to make concessions to the peasants and the proletariat.

New discoveries in science seemed to conflict relentlessly not only with traditional thinking but also with established scientific theories. In 1901, the Dutch botanist Hugo DeVries published data on mutations, indicating a mechanism whereby radical and sudden innovations might take place in what was thought to have been only a slow and gradual process of biological evolution. The Japanese-American scientist Jokichi Takamine inspired research on the endocrine glands when he succeeded in isolating adrenaline and demonstrated its importance in regulating heart action. Ernest Rutherford and Frederick Soddy concluded that X-rays, light, electricity, and all other forms of energy were essentially the same, and Albert Einstein began a revolution in physics and astronomy with his theories of relativity (Burns, 1947).

Paradoxically, this very progress in understanding was once again construed by some as divesting human beings of their distinctiveness in nature and, hence, their immortality and raison d'être. New urgency was given to that old search for the meaning of life, but the metaphysical solutions proposed were rather grim.

Positivists and nihilists argued that people should believe in nothing that rested on faith, and the scientist and philosopher Ernst Haeckel (1834–1919), an avowed materialist, tended to agree. He claimed the human mind was as much a product of evolution as the body and differed only in its complexity from the minds of lower organisms. Further, he could see no fundamental difference between living and nonliving matter, except that the former was more complicated. The essayist Walter Pater believed that people, as the helpless victims of fate, deserved some compensation for living, compensation that could be gained through the judicious pursuit of aesthetic and sensuous enjoyment. However, the author Anatole France seemed to think the best one could hope to get from life was an occasional laugh; thus he advocated the cultivation of a taste for irony and placid despair.

More optimistic views were expressed in literature by George Bernard Shaw, H. G. Wells, and Frank Norris. Their writings conveyed a spirit of confidence and hope that, despite human weaknesses and errors, the world would soon prosper from the benefits of science and education. Such a hope burned with special intensity among scientists, many of whom dedicated their lives to the search for knowledge, which they believed would eventually lead to the eradication of suffering and disease and the betterment of humanity.

William James, though no longer a psychologist, still maintained an interest in the field and sought to steer it in directions that addressed human concerns. In his youth, he had saved himself from depression, mechanistic determinism, and fatalism by embracing beliefs in free will, individual initiative, and the capacity of people to change their roles and shape their future. The consequences of these beliefs, according to James, were *better* than the consequences of a belief in a deterministic universe. The latter led in many instances to mere resignation to fate, but the former led people to exercise their initiative and do something about their problems. To critics who questioned the truth of these assertions, James responded by questioning what it means for something to be true.

In a world always changing, our judgment as to the truth of a belief, James contended, should rest on the practical consequences that would result from its acceptance as true. Rather than question whether an idea is true or false, he claimed we should ask, "What sensible difference to anyone will its truth make? . . . What experiences will be different from those which would be obtained if the belief were false? What, in short, is the truth's value in experiential terms?" (James, 1907, p. 97). More specifically, to those who had come to wonder about the existence of God, James pragmatically posed two questions: "What would be the consequences after death if one believed in God and He did not exist? What would be the consequences if one had not believed in God and after death one found that He did exist?" (James, 1897).

To the energetic people of the United States, who were particularly impatient to assert their significance, James's philosophy of pragmatism made sense. It was a philosophy that urged them to test their ideas through real experiences and judge the value of the ideas by results. It counseled them to stop worrying about problems incapable of solution and to address themselves to tasks that would reward the investment of their time and effort.

However, this was not the direction that Edward Bradford Titchener (1867–1927) had in mind for psychology. An Englishman who studied under Wundt and who then exerted his influence from Cornell University for more than a generation, Titchener believed it necessary to make a distinction. *Functional* psychology (he coined the term in 1898) is interested in the purposes served by various psychological activities, in human adaptation, and in differences between individuals. In contrast, *structural* psychology (he coined the term in 1899) is interested in the basic elements or structure of the conscious mind and in how these feelings, sensations, and images are experienced and combined. It seemed to Titchener that structural analysis was what the science of psychology should be concerned with (i.e., increasing our understanding of consciousness) whereas functionalism, with its concern for adaptive uses of consciousness, more properly belonged in biology (Woodworth, 1948).

For a number of psychologists at the University of Chicago, such as John Dewey and James Angell, functionalism seemed fine. John Dewey also embraced pragmatism, and, in the spirit of Rousseau as well as James, he encouraged teachers to be flexible in their techniques and to break away from rigid pedagogical methods so that children might learn through natural experiences. In Italy, the philosopher Giovanni Papini enthusiastically supported James; that country had been particularly impressed by James and psychology since the appearance of Guilio Ferrari's Italian translation of the *Principles*. In England, H. G. Wells allied himself with the pragmatic point of view, and that probably gave Titchener some satisfaction, since Wells was identified with science fiction.

At any rate, it appeared that psychology, within 30 years of its founding by Wundt, was broadening its aims and content. James welcomed this development but was perhaps too permissive regarding what should be included. He even claimed that the supposedly supernatural and the exploits of mediums were proper topics for scientific study. Although psychologists appreciated and respected James for his tolerance of and gentle receptivity to the views of others, they were dismayed by possible damage to their reputations should they be too hasty in devising applications and extending the scope of their discipline. As Joseph Jastrow sadly noted in his APA presidential address (Jastrow, 1901), there was already confusion about what psychologists did; among large segments of the population, *spook chaser* was fast becoming a synonym for *psychologist* and the image of psychology as a science was being tarnished.

But James was not to be deterred. In 1901–1902, his Gifford Lectures were published as *The Varieties of Religious Experience*. In these lectures James tried to include some of the most vague, rare, and ill-defined of human experiences within the scope of psychology. He contended that the mystic and ascetic could not be explained merely by attributing some form of psychopathology to them. Though a neurotic temperament might well furnish the chief condition for a person's sensitivity to so-called divine inspiration, that temperament did not in and of itself yield a full understanding of that individual or of the significance of religion. It was the duty of psychologists, James suggested, to concern themselves with what there was in religion that people found valuable. Within each person, he believed, there was some need to come to grips with an urging for a relationship with a higher being; and although some intense religious feelings might be explicable as fanaticism, others were a sign of the steady growth of personality into a wider self, a maturing and flowering of the whole person, a broadening and deepening and fullness of experience that might be cultivated profitably by everyone (James, 1902).

To most psychologists, who were already having trouble enough defining their field, James's intellectual broad-mindedness and his exhortations to embrace religion as a fit matter for study were no blessing. Their immediate aim was to get psychology accepted and respected as an independent science. James's ambitious armchair speculations did not help to clarify the boundaries of the discipline, nor did they indicate an appropriate modesty and restraint or a proper regard for the scientific method. Lightner Witmer was one of James's leading critics, but then Witmer attacked not only James (for his laxity as a scientist) but virtually all the psychologists at Harvard, with Harvard's President Eliot thrown in for good measure.

Although James may have been hurt by these criticisms, he did not alter his position. He gave generously of his time and prestige to a wide range of subjects, people, and causes. It was even possible for a former mental patient Clifford Whittingham Beers (1876–1943), to gain an audience.

Clifford Beers had graduated from Yale and at the age of 24 suffered a "mental breakdown," which he believed was brought on by excessive worry about becoming an epileptic. One of his older brothers had suffered from epilepsy, and Beers became increasingly convinced that he would eventually have the same disorder. Rather than face a life of affliction he attempted suicide by throwing himself out of a fourth-story window; fortunately he landed on soft earth. For a year he languished in depression, then was committed to the Hartford Retreat.

In 1902, his depression lifted and was replaced by feelings of exaltation. Apparently in a manic phase, he decided that he would describe his experience in the mental hospital and launch a crusade for reform. His literary output, comprising an account of the abuses and cruelties he had met with together with his own feelings and those of his fellow patients, was turned out at a maximum rate of twelve feet of manila wrapping paper an hour.

An assistant physician resented Beers's journalistic interviewing of patients and retaliated by confiscating his writing materials. A vendetta followed, which culminated in Beers spending 21 nights in a strait jacket in a padded cell.

Within a few months, Beers was transferred to the Connecticut State Hospital at Middletown, and approximately a year later he was released: "I left the state hospital in September 1903, firmly determined to write a book about my experiences and to organize a movement that would help do away with existing evils in the care of the mentally ill and, whenever possible, to prevent mental illness itself" (Beers, 1908).

Beers wisely recognized that if his book was to be taken seriously, he first had to prove to himself and others that he was sane. He took a position in business, married, and, encouraged by his friends and wife, wrote an autobiography, *A Mind That Found Itself.* He avoided emotional excesses and rash accusations in the book and thus aroused great sympathy for his suffering.

Bearing a rough draft of his manuscript, he called on William James in 1906. James read the work, was favorably impressed, and sent a letter to Beers indicating his approval. That letter served as part of the book's introduction. An endorsement by James carried such significance that people of importance soon rallied to Beers's support. Among them was the leading psychiatrist in the United States, Adolf Meyer.

The relationship between Meyer and Beers began in 1906 shortly after Beers's visit with James. It was a mutually beneficial one. Meyer had long desired to bring the needs of the mentally ill to the attention of the public so that resources could be directed to those needs. He wrote of his first encounter with Beers, "I have had an unusual experience in finding in him a man not only without a chip on his shoulder, but one with a sound and worthy conviction that something must be done to meet one of the most difficult, but also lamentably neglected problems of sociological improvement. . . . It looks as if we had at last what we need: a man for a cause" (quoted in Winkler & Bromberg, 1939).

It was Meyer who suggested the movement be called "mental hygiene." In May 1908, Beers founded the first mental hygiene society, in Connecticut. There was, of course, hesitancy about financially endowing the society, but the times certainly seemed propitious. Government agencies at all levels were pushing for the prevention of diseases such as hookworm, tuberculosis, pellegra, and anemia. It seemed reasonable to expect that once people were informed about the problem of mental illness, it would get its share of community funds.

Dr. William H. Welch, an eminent pathologist at Johns Hopkins, joined the movement and notified Beers of an encouraging development: Henry Phipps, a philanthropist, had read Beers's book, which had partly induced him to endow the school's psychiatric clinic (Zilboorg & Henry, 1941). Perhaps within the near future Phipps could be counted on to make a sizable contribution to the cause. Thus, the founding in 1909 of the National Committee for Mental Hygiene, despite its empty treasury, occurred in an atmosphere of hope.

While the stage was being set for a massive effort to make mental hygiene no more shameful than any other kind of hygiene, an English physician was gaining notoriety for ripping into the "conspiracy of silence" that surrounded sex as an appropriate topic for scientific investigation. Henry Havelock Ellis (1859–1939) had published in 1898 the first of the seven volumes of his *Studies in the Psychology of Sex* (1898–1928). For the most part, Ellis took a biological and anthropological approach to his subject, describing the various manifestations and forms of sexual activity—with one exception: Little attention was given to happy conjugal love. This may not have been an oversight, since Ellis was impotent for most of his adult life (Wallace, Wallace, Wallechinsky, & Wallace, 1981).

The only son of an English merchant sea captain, Ellis, during his father's long absences from home, grew "unusually" fond of his mother and became painfully lonely and shy. For escape he turned to voluminous reading, a continuing practice that later caused him to be acclaimed "the best read man in the world."

At the age of 16, he accompanied his father on a voyage to Australia, where for reasons of health he remained. Like most adolescent males, Ellis felt keenly an amorous interest in females, but, unlike most of his peers, he seemed unable in any way to declare his feelings. Then he claimed he underwent a mystical experience that did not make it any easier for him to express love and desire but mercifully left him content not to do so (Calder-Marshall, 1962).

Ellis decided to devote his life to the study of sex and to write about it in the manner of natural history. To achieve this end, he returned to England to become a physician and obtained his MD in 1889. However, he did not practice medicine but turned quickly to literary and scientific work. Almost immediately his writings on sex created a sensation in Europe and the United States.

It was Ellis who introduced the terms *autoeroticism* and *narcissistic* to refer to self-love or self-preoccupation. These terms were later incorporated into psychoanalytic nomenclature: a fate probably pleasing to Ellis, who had been among the first to comment favorably upon the writings of Freud.

NORMAL PERSONALITY FUNCTIONING

Just before the beginning of 1900, Freud's *The Interpretation of Dreams* was published. It received mildly favorable reviews but sold only 351 copies during its first 3 years of life, which was understandably disappointing to its author. Yet Freud regarded this book as probably his best and most important work (Jones, 1953).

After the death of his father in 1896, Freud began self-analysis. Guiding him was the assumption of psychic determinism: A person's thoughts and behaviors are not accidental or freely willed but are products of natural laws. This assumption had been promoted by is teachers Brücke and Meynert, who had in turn been influenced by Herbart, a philosopher-psychologist, who protested, in 1824, against "this false doctrine of free will." For Freud the implication of psychic determinism was that any thought or act might be unconsciously determined and, through analysis, might reveal causes or motives of which the person was not aware. It followed that dreams and fantasies, so often reported by his patients (and noted by Freud himself in his own analysis), would prove a particularly rich source for the investigation of unconscious processes. Freud's ideas developed quite rapidly on the basis of this finding.

Freud's research into the meaning of dreams led him to conceive of three kinds of mental functioning that differed in the ease with which their contents could be known introspectively. Unconsciousness consists of those ideas and perceptions that are ordinarily inaccessible to awareness but that can become known if considerable effort is directed to their discovery (e.g., forgotten events during the first 5 years of life). Preconsciousness consists of those ideas that are not known at the moment but that are accessible to awareness if a reasonable effort is made to recall them (e.g., the names of an adult's grade school teachers). Consciousness consists of the feelings, sensations, and thoughts that are in immediate awareness (e.g., the sight of this page and, hopefully, the meaning of these words).

Freud thought unconscious ideas were governed by the primary process, an unlearned, illogical type of functioning in which ideas continuously press for immediate, unrestrained expression in perceptions or actions regardless of the duration of their exclusion from awareness or their current inappropriateness. Conscious ideas, in contrast, were thought to be governed normally by the secondary process, an acquired or learned type of rational, reasonable functioning in which ideas or impulses are delayed in their expression and due regard is given to the existing circumstances or situation. Functioning as a filter between consciousness and unconsciousness are preconscious processes, which repress or exclude from awareness ideas that would be too painful or distressing if known. Preconscious processes, however, allow some ideas access to awareness in a distorted, disguised, or tolerable form.

Unconscious ideas seemed to Freud to be mainly sexual wishes. More precisely, they appeared to be a person's incestuous desires regarding the parent of the opposite sex and aggressive, hostile thoughts directed toward the parent of the same sex. Such wishes reminded Freud of the legend of Oedipus, a king of Thebes who, without being aware of the consanguineous relationships, killed his father and married his mother.

At first Freud could not believe that oedipal impulses originated in preschool-age children. He decided that these wishes occurred between 8 and 12 years old but that adults misremembered them as occurring earlier in childhood. This conception of incestuous fantasies replaced Freud's previous belief that actual seductions needed to occur in the early years of his patients' lives. In either case, a Freudian childhood was far from idyllic and certainly seemed to be an exciting, important, sometimes momentous period.

During sleep, the inhibiting, perceiving, logical thought processes of an individual, which Freud called *das Ich* (translated as the *ego*), are relatively quiescent. Therefore, the relative force with which unconscious ideas press for expression in perceptions or motor acts is greater during sleep than during periods of wakefulness. In order to preserve sleep, a compromise is effected: The unconscious ideas are expressed imaginarily as a dream (though even in this form they are disguised and distorted). Among the distortions and disguises in dreams are the following: Two or more unconscious ideas might be represented by a single detail (condensation, e.g., a ring belonging to the person's father might stand for the oedipal wishes); the emphasis might shift from what is significant to what is insignificant (displacement); and an image might represent something else (symbolization, e.g., water might refer to birth). Freud called the mental processes that produced these distortions the *censor*. It seemed to him clear that dreams are essentially fulfillments of unconscious wishes and that the major purpose of dreaming is to maintain sleep (Freud, 1938).

Although most of Freud's Viennese colleagues remained unimpressed by his ideas, a small group of physicians began meeting with him to learn and discuss them. These weekly sessions began in 1902, and among the original members was Alfred Adler. Still, Freud had hoped for a more enthusiastic and widespread reception. The recognition he anticipated seemed so slow in coming that he felt that it would not be until after his death that his views would be appreciated. However, good news came in 1904. Eugen Bleuler, professor of psychiatry in Zurich, wrote that he and his staff were very much interested in psychoanalysis. Furthermore, one of his staff, Carl Jung, by using free association tests, had experimentally demonstrated one of Freud's contentions: that emotions interfere with recall. Freud, of course, was delighted.

Although Freud's books—*Psychopathology of Everyday Life* (1904), *Jokes and Their Connection with the Unconscious* (1905), and *Three Essays on the Theory of*

Sexuality (1905)—were far from best-sellers, more and more people waited for and listened to his latest ideas. Their attentiveness was taxed by his unending revisions and extensions of the theory. A vast terminology developed in which the use of old words frequently betrayed their earlier definitions. Meanwhile, new concepts were introduced rapidly. The theory leaped beyond its origins in what Freud had discovered about the neuroses, and eventually it had implications regarding virtually every facet of human life.

Freud argued quite convincingly that unconscious processes interfere with, and are a part of, the ordinary functioning of "normal" people. He illustrated his thesis by discovering unconscious reasons for a variety of commonplace occurrences that have been the grief (and apparently the pleasure) of almost everyone: the forgetting of names and numbers, slips of the tongue, mistakes in reading and writing, and "clumsy" accidents (e.g., spilling liquids and breaking glassware). But what was even more startling and significant was his extension of sexual behavior to infancy, his psychosexual theory of development.

Freud now believed he had found evidence that heterosexual behavior does not emerge suddenly at puberty but instead evolves and develops over the years from birth. Unlike other instincts (e.g., hunger and thirst), the sexual instincts do not require immediate gratification but can be postponed indefinitely and satisfied in a variety of forms: looking, masturbation, fetishism, homosexuality, heterosexual intercourse, and so on. Moreover, those forms regarded as deviant in adulthood often occur normally during the early course of an individual's life. It was the delineation of this progression from infantile sexuality to mature heterosexual behavior that was Freud's most controversial and distinctive contribution. The theory of psychosexual development became the sine qua non of psychoanalysis.

The process of human development was seen by Freud as involving changes connected with the most sensitive areas of the body, those most suitable for providing sexual gratification. These changes were conceptualized as expressions of a sexual force or energy, called the *libido,* which not only motivates the individual but also determines the vividness and intensity of the mental representations (the sensations, thoughts, and perceptions) of the sexual instincts. The distribution of libido within the body was not viewed as uniform or haphazard. On the contrary, the investment of libido, in this case the acuteness and pleasurableness with which bodily stimulations are experienced, appears to shift from the entire body surface to one specific portion of the anatomy to another in an orderly and predictable manner.

A very early phase of sexual development is the oral stage, during which the person derives erotic gratification primarily from stimulation of the lips and mouth in feeding. Then follows the anal-sadistic stage, when sexual pleasure is derived mainly from stimulation of the bowels in the act of retaining and expelling feces. If the person is overly gratified during this stage, a cluster of characteristics might occur that Freud called the *anal character*: excessive neatness or orderliness, thrift or miserliness, and obstinacy.

The phallic stage comes next, when the principal organ for sexual gratification is the penis or the clitoris. Since Freud (1959b) had recently participated in the analysis of a 5-year-old boy who evidenced fears of being castrated and wishes associated with what was now being called the Oedipus complex, he decided that the incestuous desires of children first develop during the phallic stage (i.e., when they are about 3 to 4 years old).

From about the age of 4 to 11, there is apparently a time of relative stabilization in psychosexual development, an interval that Freud called the *latency period.* After the latency period comes adolescence, which seems to be less complicated for males than for females, although troublesome for both sexes. Boys continue to experience the penis as the primary zone of erotic gratification. However, in the case of girls, the area of greatest sexual pleasure is expected to shift from the clitoris to the vagina, a shift that Freud believed was not accomplished readily. Freud supposed that because of this complication, women are in general more prone to sexual conflicts and neuroses than men.

Freud took particular pains to emphasize two points about his theory. First, although conceding that he had accumulated his evidence from neurotic patients in Vienna, he nevertheless regarded his exposition as biological, hence universally applicable and descriptive of normal psychosexual development. Second, despite the orderly changes in the principal sexual organs and zones, all areas normally provide pleasurable stimulation throughout life, just as, for example, the mouth is a lifelong source of pleasure in eating, drinking, and sucking.

The theory propounded by Freud was surely remarkable, and by 1908 there were enough people sufficiently interested in psychoanalysis to warrant convening an international meeting in Salzburg. Forty-two people attended, including A. A. Brill, Alfred Adler, Paul Federn, Otto Rank, Wilhelm Stekel, Ernest Jones, Karl Abraham, Sandor Ferenczi, Eugen Bleuler (1857–1939), Edouard Claparède, Max Eitington, and Carl Jung (1875–1961). The convention was truly unique: Freud's talk lasted 4 hours, and when he indicated they might adjourn for lunch, his eager audience prevailed upon him to continue for an hour more.

G. Stanley Hall was familiar with the news from Europe about Freud's theory and was favorably impressed. This was significant approval, coming as it did from a prominent educator and psychologist, especially since the luster of Hall's reputation had been recently enhanced by the publication of his monumental work *Adolescence* (1904). However, Hall's approval was based more on the fact that psychoanalysis seemed to demonstrate the importance of the study of childhood than on an acceptance of its specific doctrines. Still, Hall regarded the theory as of sufficient consequence to begin, in 1908, to give courses on the new Freudian psychology. That same year, Brill began his analytic practice in New York City.

Nevertheless, to Ernest Jones, there seemed to be ample cause for gnashing of teeth and lamentations over the deplorable neglect of psychoanalysis in English-speaking countries. But in fairness to the professionals of the United States and Great Britain, it should be pointed out that nothing that Freud had written had yet been translated into English.

The first article on psychoanalysis published by a U.S. psychologist appeared in 1909. Its author concluded, "The thesis here defended is that the psychoanalytic method is nothing more than an unusually skillful application of the method of suggestion and that it offers no proof for the existence of subconscious complexes of suppressed emotional ideas" (Scott, 1908, p. 373). Fortunately, Americans who could not read German could soon begin to judge for themselves. Brill's English translations of Freud's and Breuer's papers on hysteria were published in 1909, and that same year Hall invited Freud, Jung, and Ferenczi to come to Clark University to participate in the festivities celebrating the 20th anniversary of the school (Jones, 1955).

Interpreting dreams en route, Freud arrived in Worcester to deliver a series of lectures that won him several new adherents. James J. Putnam, professor of neurology at Harvard, was one of those most strongly affected by Freud's maturity and humility, by the freely given acknowledgments of the Breuer's contributions, and by Jung's enthusiasm and vigor. Although he had had some reservations about psychoanalysis, Putnam stated with deep feeling, "I have learned to believe fully in the theory and in the value of their methods of analysis and of treatment, and I am the more ready to accept their views for having made the personal acquaintance of [Freud, Jung, and Ferencz] . . . and for having found them so kindly, unassuming, tolerant, earnest, and sincere" (Putnam, 1909–1910, p. 379). He was not alone in is praise. At the conclusion of Freud's talks, William James stated, "The future of psychology belongs to your work" (Jones, 1955, p. 57).

Just the year before, in 1908, James had characteristically gone out of his way to give encouragement to a psychologist who was finding it difficult to be personally accepted but who was having better luck with his ideas: William McDougall (1887–1938). McDougall had been born in England and was fond of attributing to his Saxon and Nordic heritage "the fact that I have never fitted neatly into any social group" (McDougall, 1930, p. 192). A self-diagnosed domineering and precocious child, he matured into an adult of self-conscious arrogance, a flaw that he frequently deplored and never felt he successfully concealed. He entered the University of Manchester at 15, Cambridge at 19, and lost his faith in God at 20 when his mother died of cancer.

By the age of 28, McDougall had become a neurologist. However, he was bored by the practice of neurology because of its emphasis on diagnosis, and he turned for stimulation to anthropology. He went on an expedition to the Torres Straits in 1899 and traveled from there to Borneo. He showed tremendous promise as an anthropologist but eventually became bored by anthropology as well. Then he decided upon a career in psychology. Although he had many subsequent regrets about that choice, boredom was never one of them (McDougall, 1930).

McDougall began his career by studying briefly with G. E. Müller at Göttingen. In 1900, he accepted a faculty position at University College, London. During the following years, he helped found the British Psychological Society (12 members strong) and the *British Journal of Psychology*. In 1904, he became the Wilde Reader in Mental Philosophy at Oxford, and in 1907 (according to McDougall) or 1908 (according to everyone else), he published the book that established his professional reputation, *Introduction to Social Psychology*.

McDougall defined psychology as a positive science of conduct or behavior. Aside from his obvious intent to broaden the scope of psychology from the study of consciousness to the study of the behavior of all living organisms, McDougall wanted to get away from a rational, intellectual concept of motivation. To do this, he argued that the motivation of all human activities could be traced to innate dispositions, which he unfortunately referred to as *instincts*.

Perhaps by virtue of his predilection for heredity, McDougall held that human beings were born with a certain small number of fundamental instincts. These instincts were thought to be composed of three integrated processes. Initially there is a predisposition to perceive significant stimuli (e.g., increased receptivity to cues of food when a person is hungry). This predisposition when triggered leads to an emotional impulse, or response, which is the "core" of the instinct. The impulse then leads to a predisposition to make certain movements or overt approach responses in the direction of the goal. (This third component clearly indicates that McDougall saw purpose in behavior as an essential characteristic.)

The first and third processes of the instinct are related to environmental stimulation and thus involve learning. McDougall's compounding of hereditary and acquired characteristics was fundamental to his position and resulted in his theory's having some unique features. Beginning with 12 primary instincts, he pointed out that each of them becomes modified by learning, since (1) new and different stimuli become capable of arousing them and (2) their movements or responses to the goal become altered. For example, our tastes in food change (many people acquire a revulsion to baby food and a fondness for beer). Moreover, our eating responses are, we trust, guided by rules of etiquette, the principles of a balanced diet, and, in some cases, the prescriptions of religious ceremony. Thus McDougall was trying to emphasize that instincts are seldom, if ever, observed in forms not modified by learning and experience.

Further, two or more instincts frequently become fused or attached to a single object. When that happens, one might speak of a sentiment. In the case of the sentiment love of food, the instincts of hunger and a seeking of new tastes (curiosity) might be said to have combined to create a propensity for gluttony. McDougall thought that most behaviors of adults are motivated by sentiments, and since sentiments are largely composed of instincts, and instincts have emotions at their cores, human conduct is driven, in essence, not by reason but by feelings.

Social behavior could be viewed and evaluated in terms of its satisfaction of certain basic needs. But McDougall wanted it to be understood that he believed interpersonal activities were in the main directly motivated by sentiments, not by instincts. Although his explanations are neatly circular, it is instructive to consider some of them. People originally join others to form groups because of the instinct "to seek company," but other instincts eventually become associated with social grouping. The sentiment of patriotism is partially explained by the following instincts: The instinct of domination is aroused when people desire that their group control other groups; their acquisitive instinct is expressed in wanting to get things for their group; when their leader speaks, their instinct to submit is stimulated and they accept the suggestions of authority. However, the ideal person, in McDougall's opinion, appears capable of controlling the expression of instincts and of maintaining ideas in the face of pressures to conform; such an individual is no longer submissive to the praise or blame of the group and is sufficiently integrated to have adopted a moral code that is regarded as superior to any the group might attempt to impose.

McDougall's theoretical formulations helped to bring a new field, social psychology, into being. Although not all psychologists agreed with his conceptualizations, they heartily welcomed the new area and promptly added courses in social psychology to the curricula of their departments.

It is an interesting fact, probably due to the *Zeitgeist,* that although Freud and McDougall were not aware of each other's work, there are obvious similarities in their formulations. Both emphasized instinctual strivings, the significance of emotions in human behavior, and the minimal role played by rational considerations in much of human conduct. According to both, people are creatures often driven to do things by forces that they do not fully comprehend or control. Their view of human behavior is in opposition to the view that human beings are a unique kind of creation, can freely choose between good and evil, and are usually capable of sensibly deciding what to do. But must people be regarded one way or the other? Some psychologists believed that a reconciliation is possible between a deterministic and an elective conception of human activities. William Stern (1871–1938) was one of them.

Born and raised in Berlin, the only and lonely child of a merchant, Stern graduated from the University of Berlin in 1892. The death of his father in 1890 and of his mother in 1896 left him feeling more isolated than ever. He turned, for personal salvation, to "the philosophical discipline of psychology." Stern (1930) claimed proudly many years later, "I have never . . . become 'scientificated.'" Others agreed with his self-appraisal, although they did not consider it a matter for pride.

Stern began teaching philosophy, psychology, and pedagogy at Breslau in 1897. By 1901, he felt that the key to resolving the conflict between science and the need to find a meaning in life is somehow connected with the concept of a person. Stern's views on the subject were stated at length in the three volumes of *Person und Sache,* the first volume of which was published in 1906.

If one wishes to study human beings part by part, analyzing the workings of internal organs or examining the functioning of specific and limited physiological processes, then, Stern believed, human beings could and should be viewed mechanistically. However, if one wishes to study human beings in their entirety as functioning entities, then, since human beings have purposes, their behavior can only be understood by taking into account their goals and the degree to which they are valued. As Stern put it, a person is "a unique and self-sufficient *unitas multiplex,* whose activity as a purposive function is directed toward self-preservation and self-development."

By *unitas multiplex,* Stern meant the person's multiplicity of traits, drives, and abilities organized into a unitary developing personality. This personality is stimulated, and also inhibited, by environmental influences, and it strives to maintain equilibrium between tensions arising from internal and external circumstances. Since Stern believed a philosophical orientation is necessary to comprehend a person's system of values, he did not think that psychology alone could ever fully understand a given individual—such an understanding required the cooperation of both philosophy and psychology. What psychology could hope to accomplish within the 20th century, Stern suggested, is the determination of the psychological differences that exist between one individual and another.

DIAGNOSTIC TECHNIQUES

Of course Stern was not alone in his view that individual differences are a worthy field for investigation. Binet and Henri put the matter this way: "General psychology studies the general properties of psychical processes, those, therefore, which are common to all individuals. Individual psychology, on the contrary, studies those psychical processes which vary from one individual to another; it seeks to determine the variable qualities, and the extent and manner of their variation according to the individual" (1896).

Alfred Binet (1857–1911), whom we met in the previous chapter, had originally decided on a career in law and obtained his degree in that subject from the Lycée Saint-Louis in 1878. However, an interest in research and the influence of Charcot led him to switch to the study, but not the profession, of medicine. Beginning around 1880, Binet decided to investigate psychological problems. At first, he delved into abstruse philosophical questions and engaged in theory building, though at the same time giving some attention to thinking, hypnosis, fetishism (Sulloway, 1979, p. 285), and hysteria (Staff, 1912). Later his apparent repudiation of this phase of his professional development seemed so complete that he was criticized for a lack of theoretical perspective in his work. This criticism was not justified, for at the time of his death, Binet was attempting to make clear the place of his efforts within the framework of a theory he was trying to develop (Wolf, 1973).

One product of his early investigations was *La magnetisme animal* (1886), written with C. Féré. During their studies of hypnosis, they observed that some patients were actively participating and expending effort to overcome inhibitory suggestions, whereas other patients were passive and inclined to be resistant. They therefore recommended that a distinction be made between *active* and *passive* hypnotic states.

In 1889, Binet with Henri Beaunis, founded the first laboratory of physiological psychology in France, at the Sorbonne. The following year he obtained a degree in the natural sciences and began studying the development of behavior in his two daughters. He noted the differences between them in their learning to walk. One would hold onto a post and look for another to go to before venturing forth, whereas the other child walked boldly into an empty room undeterred by the possibility that she might fall. These personality differences were particularly fascinating to him, although he was uncertain as to how to deal with them systematically. Over the course of time, Binet also made records of his daughters' skills in recognizing objects in pictures and in giving definitions (Varnon, 1935).

Binet earned his doctorate in science in 1894 (his thesis had to do with the insect nervous system), and when his colleague Beaunis retired in 1895, he took over the direction of the laboratory. That same year the two men founded the first

French journal of psychology, *L'année psychologique,* with Beaunis as editor. It was this publication that served as the major vehicle for the dissemination of Binet's research on intelligence.

Binet was convinced that in order to study individual differences, it was necessary to sample the most intellectual and complex processes so that the spread of scores would be broad: "The more complex and the higher a process, the more it varies according to the individual: sensations vary from individual to individual but less than memory" (Varnon, 1935, p. 45). Therefore, he recommended the construction of psychological tests that sampled judgment, memory, and imagination. (Binet even proposed that imagination might be assessed through the use of ink blots.)

The basic concept for individual psychology, Binet asserted, is the norm and deviations from the norm. But he believed that ascertaining norms is only a beginning. He wanted to know additionally what the relations between the various mental processes are so that he could predict the degree of development of one process from knowledge of another. Mental tests, he thought, should also yield information about qualitative differences as well as quantitative differences, for, as he might have said, a child not only has a smaller memory than an adult but a different memory.

In 1896, Binet and Henri described a series of tests to measure attention, comprehension, memory, imagery, aesthetic appreciation, moral sentiments, sustained effort in muscular tasks, motor skill, imagination, and visual space judgment. As noted above, some American psychologists were enthusiastic about this work, but Cattell was not one of them. With the resignation of Beaunis as editor of *L'année psychologique* in 1897, Binet assumed the post and pressed on with his research into intelligence and its components.

In the years that followed, Binet continued to emphasize the importance of qualitative variables, particularly the influence of personality on intellectual functioning. His studies made it clear that psychological measurement was not absolute but ordinal: "But we cannot know, with respect to memory, if the difference between the memory of five figures and the memory of seven figures is or is not equal to the difference between the memory of seven figures and the memory of eight figures. We do not measure, we classify" (Varnon, 1935, p. 54).

Binet returned briefly to the problem of suggestibility, and found through experimentation with children that it decreased with increasing age. Nevertheless, he found enough suggestibility in adults to feel justified in cautioning his colleagues to guard against indicating to their experimental subjects what responses might be expected, no matter how subtly. Also, he thought it wise to warn lawyers about the influence they might exert on the testimonies of their witnesses by the way in which they formed their questions. Such, in brief, were Binet's ideas at the beginning of the 20th century.

Stella Sharp's unfavorable evaluation of the Cattell variety of mental test was reinforced by Clark Wissler's (1901) report of the results of this type of testing at Columbia and Bernard. Wissler's findings were as follows: (1) the scores obtained from various laboratory mental tests correlated only slightly with each other, (2) the same was true of intercorrelations between physical tests and mental tests, and (3) correlations were low between mental test scores and college grades. For example, the correlation between reaction time and class standing was − .02, whereas the correlation between grades in gym and class standing was + .53. Clearly, something was amiss. The mental tests then current in the United States had little demonstrable validity or usefulness, at least for making predictions within a relatively homogeneous college population.

Meanwhile back in France, Binet was still observing his daughters with scientific detachment. Perhaps, he thought, one might be able to determine personality types by using mental tests. He had the two girls write down a list of 20 words. By analyzing the lists, he decided that Marguerite was a practical girl whose concern was with concrete objects in the external world. Armande, on the other hand, seemed to be turned inward and had little interest in the world about her. Momentous findings to someone else, perhaps, but not to a man who was reluctant to venture far from his immediate data. Binet dismissed the whole thing as an exercise in labeling rather than explaining, as "a literary game rather than science."

Then, in 1904, the Minister of Public Instruction in Paris appointed a commission to investigate what steps were needed to ensure that defective children received the benefits of an education. Special classes were to be formed, but before a child could be removed from ordinary schooling and admitted to these classes, an examination had to be conducted to certify that the child could not profit from regular classroom instruction. Obviously, subjective examination procedures were inadequate, since authorities disagreed among themselves regarding diagnoses and the meanings of the terms used to designate the intellectually subnormal. In the hope that they might provide an objective basis for distinguishing the "degree of inferior mentality," Alfred Binet and Théodore Simon (1873–1961), medical chief of the insane asylum of Le Seine Inférieure, offered their services (Binet & Simon, 1962).

The first outcome of their efforts was the 1905 Binet-Simon scale. This scale was composed of 30 items arranged in order of increasing difficulty. Its score was simply the number of items passed. Binet claimed only that the scale provided a crude means of differentiation (e.g., an ordinary 5-year-old did not get beyond question 14). A trifle more distressing even than its crudeness was the inconsistency between the content of the scale and Binet and Simon's definition of intelligence. Although claiming that the fundamental faculty of intelligence is sound judgment, they were forced to admit that many of the 30 items did not test judgment.

However, they went on refining their work, and the result was the more sophisticated 1908 Binet-Simon scale. In it were 59 tests grouped at age levels from 3 to 13 years according to the percentages of children of a particular age who passed a given item. This determining percentage range was 67% to 75%. If a higher percentage passed the item, it was thought to be too easy for that age level; if a lower percentage passed the item, it was thought to be too difficult for that age level. Binet and Simon did not know it, nor did hardly anyone else for that matter, but a pediatrician, S. E. Chaille, had constructed a series of tests for infants up to

3 years old and had arranged them according to the percentage of various-aged children who passed them. Chaille's scale had been published in the *New Orleans Medical and Surgical Journal* in 1887 (Young, 1924).

In their 1908 revision, Binet and Simon introduced mental age as the score for their scale. Binet recognized that in so doing they might be exchanging one evil for another: The demon of subjectivity was being replaced by an illusion of objectivity. He had no such illusion, however: "It is not, in spite of appearances, an automatic method . . . an interpretation is necessary . . . all scientific procedure is but an instrument which requires the direction of an intelligent hand." The scale, he warned, did not measure intelligence alone but intelligence together with knowledge gained from school and from the environment in general. He stressed the importance of qualitative variables (e.g., the persistence and attention of the child while taking the test as a determinant of the score. In short, Binet had many reservations about the Binet-Simon scale (Varnon, 1935). Unfortunately, Binet's cautions were largely ignored.

Credit for introducing the Binet-Simon scale into the United States is usually accorded to Henry H. Goddard (1886–1957). Goddard had been one of G. Stanley Hall's students. During the early years of the 20th century, he worked as director of the research laboratory at the Institute for Backward Children in Vineland, New Jersey. While visiting Brussles in 1908, he learned of the Binet-Simon scale. Using it at Vineland, he was pleased to find that it seemed able to make discriminations, and so he began work on a revision that would make the scale suitable for general use in the United States (Watson, 1953). Even while Goddard tackled the revision, the scale was gaining acceptance. In 1909, the city of Rochester, New York, which had organized special classes for subnormal children in 1906, appointed a Binet examiner to work within the school system.

If the criteria that authorities were forced to rely upon up to that time are taken into account, the eager welcome given to the Binet-Simon scale does not appear excessive. Some physicians had struggled bravely to devise a way of differentiating between the idiot and the imbecile along the lines suggested by Pinel, who claimed that an idiot's attention was "fugitive" whereas an imbecile's attention was "fleeting" (Zilboorg & Henry, 1941). Some frankly acknowledged that their judgments were uncertain. Dr. Walter Fernald, head of the Massachusetts School for the Feebleminded, regretted that the best that he had been able to do for the classification of children was to depend on observations of their posture and motor coordination when they stepped from the vehicle that brought them to his institution. Others insisted they could tell more about a child based on feelings about the child or on the twinkle, or lack of a twinkle, in the child's eye than could ever be learned from mental testing. But these voices were drowned in the chorus of approval. In Belgium, Germany, Italy, England, and the United States, great interest in Binet's work was aroused. Here at last seemed to be an objective means of classification and a convenient device upon which could be placed the greater part of the responsibility for making decisions.

During this period, the testing of personality was not completely neglected. Some psychologists were impressed by developments in Zurich. Two psychiatrists, Eugen Bleuler and Carl Jung, who were mentioned earlier in connection with their interest in psychoanalysis, had been trying to discover a person's complexes (unconscious interrelated ideas capable of arousing strong feelings) by using free association techniques.

Jung, the younger and more inventive of the pair, had been born in Switzerland, the only son of a Protestant clergyman (Jung, 1963). His family had a rich tradition of religiousness as well as an interest in medicine, which were both incorporated by Jung in his thesis for the MD degree in 1902: "On the Psychology and Pathology of So-called Occult Phenomena." The thesis concerned Jung's observations of the trance states of a young medium. It appeared to him that during the trances a more comprehensive, promising personality was attempting to break through from unconsciousness into consciousness—a somewhat optimistic interpretation and a recurrent theme in Jung's writings. After receiving his degree, Jung studied briefly under Janet in Paris and then returned to Zurich to work under Bleuler. Very soon thereafter Jung and Bleuler began their experimentation with the free-association method.

Galton had originated free association techniques in 1879, and he quickly recognized that they were significantly misnamed: Tell a person he or she is free to say the first word that comes to mind after hearing "table," and very likely the person will say "chair." A person's associations are not really free, Galton found, but determined by past experiences and usually restricted to only a small number of words.

In 1889, Münsterberg had thought that a free association test might be useful to detect lying and criminal guilt. The only trouble was that innocent people seemed to get about as upset as guilty ones, while some guilty people did not seem to get upset at all. Nevertheless, Münsterberg had faith in the practical applications of psychology and in the potential of the technique. In a subsequent series of popular magazine articles, he predicted the eventual use of the technique to aid in the administration of justice. Jung, of course, had in mind a different purpose for the test, although he did use it on one occasion to investigate a theft at a hospital. His major interest, however, was in seeing if the technique could be developed into a sensitive instrument for the detection of complexes or conflicts and problems of which the individual was not aware.

Jung thought that hallucinations, delusions, and the other symptoms of dementia praecox were due to the activities of a complex whose dynamic force came from the strong emotions associated with it. He speculated that these emotions disturbed the individual's ideational processes and might even engender a toxin or metabolic anomaly that could irreparably injure the brain and in this manner produce a mental illness, or psychosis. This was a startling hypothesis, for it asserted that a psychic disorder could produce an organic disorder.

He prepared a list of 100 words (e.g., *sick, pride, angry, sad*) and noted carefully the behavior of people when they tried to respond freely with another word. Usually Jung used a stopwatch to measure the interval between the presentation of the word and the response, but at times he also employed a pneumograph to measure breathing rate and a psychogalvanometer to measure changes in electrical conductivity in the palm of the hand produced by sweating (the psychogalvanic reflex or response).

It seemed to Jung, in 1905, that blocking responses, unusual responses, and a delay of over 2 seconds in responding were indications that some unconscious complex had been touched upon. As a result of his experimentation, Jung became convinced that the dissociated ideas of the complex were charged with emotions and that the mechanisms that kept them isolated from awareness were the same as those described by Freud in hysterics. The symptoms of dementia praecox could thus be viewed as having, in a sense, a purpose, and the verbalizations of dementia praecox patients, far from being mad ramblings without meaning, might be analyzed, interpreted, and understood. Jung reported on his work at the Clark University anniversary celebration to an enthralled audience, many of whom hailed his free association technique as a potentially significant tool for research and diagnosis (Jung, 1936, 1963).

DIAGNOSTIC FORMULATIONS

The development of diagnostic instruments appeared to make it imperative to explain what it was that these tests were supposed to measure. In particular, the concept of intelligence seemed to have been hazy and was now in urgent need of clarification. Many people had explained intelligence in terms of so-called "faculties" or "powers" of the mind (such as perception, judgment, and moral taste), which were supposed to be relatively independent. If a person showed good judgment, his faculty of judgment was said to be well developed. Similarly, if a person seemed to remember things well, it was because his faculty of memory was well developed. Although faculty psychology had the obvious virtues of simplicity and versatility, it became quite clear that it was circular and not very enlightening (Boring, 1950).

Charles Spearman (1863–1945) was among the first to offer an explanation of intelligence based on empirical evidence. Early in his career Spearman served in the British armed forces. By 1897, he considered that his years in the military had been frittered away, and he turned to the serious study of psychology. His PhD, with a thesis on space perception, was earned under Wundt, whom he admired greatly as a scientist and as a person. Although in later years he despaired of ever reading all that should be read in psychology, he felt confident that he knew as much about the subject as most psychologists did (Spearman, 1930).

The work of Galton inspired Spearman, in 1901, to try to find out if intellectual abilities are related to each other and what their relationship might be to the capacity for making discriminations. He used the school grades of children in various subjects as measures of their intellectual abilities and tested their sensory discrimination by sounding musical chords. From an examination of his data, it seemed there were significant relationships among the different mental abilities, but Spearman realized that he had no way of numerically determining how close the relationships were. After investing a great deal of time and energy in devising the kind of statistical measure now known as the correlation coefficient, he discovered two things: The same work had already been done by Galton, and correlation coefficients had already been used by Cattell to analyze data.

Nevertheless, Spearman did notice that Cattell's results were the opposite of his own. Therefore, he concluded there must have been something wrong in Cattell's study. This led Spearman to the concept of attenuation. Attenuation occurs when correlation coefficients are spuriously decreased in value because of random errors of measurement (e.g., the measures used to compute the coefficients might not be perfectly reliable). He invented a statistical procedure to correct for attenuation, and when this was applied to Cattell's data, he was pleasantly surprised to find that the conflict between the two sets of results had been resolved in his favor.

Spearman, on the basis of his labors, devised the concept of general intelligence, or *g*. The intercorrelations between the various measures of intellectual activity, considered negligible by many psychologists, indicated to Spearman that "all branches of intellectual activity have in common one fundamental function (or group of functions), whereas the remaining or specific elements of the activity seem in every case to be wholly different from that in all the others" (1904). Thus Spearman believed that he had objectively determined the existence of a general intellectual ability that is expressed in all functioning. (Perhaps, he suggested modestly, this is the ability to discover relations.) Spearman now felt that all that remained to be done in this area was to convince other psychologists to come around to accepting the fact that he was right.

Signs arose, however, that the rush to embrace Spearman's formulation would not be too pressing. Edward Lee Thorndike (1874–1949) and Robert S. Woodworth (1869–1962) had published a paper in 1901 on the effect of training on learning aptitude that seemed to indicate the existence of specific abilities in intelligence. Essentially, they had attempted to discover whether or not there is any foundation for the belief that by learning one subject a person could more easily learn some other subject (e.g., whether by learning Latin one could learn biology more easily). Their experiments convinced them that improvements in one area rarely brought about equivalent improvements in another area. Furthermore, the improvements that did occur seemed to be attributable not to the strengthening of some broad mental or intellectual faculty but to the presence of identical elements involved in the performances of the tasks.

The interpretation offered by Spearman for his results appeared to contradict the interpretation offered by Thorndike and Woodworth for their findings. This contradiction was more apparent than real, but it persisted and was intensified by implicit demands for capitulation by one side or the other. Of all the major participants in this dispute, Thorndike seemed least comfortable, and he probably entertained the hope that such barren arguments would be put aside so that everyone could go back to pursuing profitable research.

Edward Thorndike had graduated from Wesleyan before going to Harvard for advanced studies in 1895. He was attracted there, and to psychology, by having read and enjoyed James's *Principles*. (In fact, Thorndike had enjoyed the work so much that he later voluntarily bought both volumes.) Originally, he had hoped to work with children as subjects, but he was refused permission to do so and therefore studied chickens instead. This did not end his troubles. The psychology department refused to give his chickens any space, and his landlady prudishly objected to their presence in her house. It remained for kindly William James to save the day once again by allowing Thorndike to use the cellar of his home for a chicken coop. Thorndike was able to emerge from that cellar when Cattell offered him a fellowship at Columbia and a room in an attic for his chickens.

At that time, many people believed animals thought in the same way that people did but just not as well. Thorndike's thesis, in 1898, demonstrated that animals learn by a "trial-and-success" method (trial and error) rather than by thinking their problems through to a solution the way humans supposedly do. Not only his results but his use of animals for psychological experimentation were favorably received. Although Thorndike's experiments led him to believe that learning to make or not make a response occurred when a pleasurable or unsatisfying effect followed an activity (law of effect), he felt that his own behavior was determined by a sense of duty: "I did in those early years and have done since what the occasion seemed to demand" (Thorndike, 1936, p. 266).

Such was not the case with Thorndike's colleague at Columbia, Robert Woodworth, who professed to take great delight in all his activities. He loved science and the outdoors and during his childhood wondered whether he should become an astronomer or a farmer. His parents would have preferred that he enter the ministry. Nevertheless, they did not interfere with his plans when he finally decided upon a career in teaching (Woodworth, 1932).

After graduating from Amherst in 1891, Woodworth taught mathematics for 4 years. Then he decided to enter Harvard and begin the serious study of psychology (one of his fellow graduate students was Thorndike). While at Harvard, Woodworth conducted some studies on dreams. He found that very often the content of a dream involved bringing to imagined completion an activity that had been interrupted during the day. Then he went to Columbia and received his PhD under Cattell in 1899. For a while he taught physiology in New York City hospitals. Evidently Woodworth's interest in that subject was more than passing, for he spent the academic year 1902–1903 as C. S. Sherrington's assistant in Liverpool learning more about the physiological functioning of the brain. In the autumn of 1903, he returned to Columbia with the rank of instructor. By that time Thorndike was a full professor; Woodworth became one too, in 1909.

The status of the concept of intelligence, toward the close of the decade, might be described as follows. There were disagreements among psychologists about the definition of intelligence, but no one seemed really to care too much about that. Spearman had advanced some ideas about its structure, about which he cared very much indeed. Some psychologists, including Binet, thought that the intelligence of the feebleminded was qualitatively different from that of normals. However, a study by Norsworthy (1906) favored the view that there were only quantitative differences within a continuum of intelligence. Woodworth suggested that there was no such thing as intelligence and that other psychologists, despite their claims, were actually merely concerned with evaluations of the way an organism behaved—intelligently or not so intelligently. Finally, whatever intelligence might or might not be, there was a growing demand made on psychologists to devise instruments to measure it.

In contrast to the mild state of confusion in the area of intelligence, at the beginning of the 20th century diagnostic or descriptive psychiatry was enjoying professional status and respectability. In 1903, Janet described the syndrome of psychasthenia, which had as its major symptom pathological feelings of inadequacy. Then, in 1906, August von Wassermann discovered a specific test for the presence of syphilitic antibodies. Research soon demonstrated that over 90% of the patients with general paresis tested positive. A diagnosis of paresis was thus greatly facilitated, and the theory of the syphilitic origin of the disease was supported. In 1906, A. Alzheimer reported the first case of an illness that was soon to bear his name: a precocious senile psychosis occurring as early as 30 years of age, with a rapid course culminating in severe dementia and deterioration of the brain. These diagnostic advances and the Kraepelinean classification of diseases, which helped to make the bewildering variety of disturbed behaviors seem more comprehensible and also aided reporting and hospital organization, gave a scientific air to psychiatry that was most gratifying to its practitioners (Zilboorg & Henry, 1941).

Yet, in the main, descriptive psychiatry shed little light on the problems of human personality. Nor did its professionals seem likely to shed much light, for two reasons. First, in their concern for objectivity and maintaining the appearance of being scientific, they had turned their backs on the actual thoughts and feelings of their patients. Second, they were hesitant to accept the possibility that mental illness was a continuation of the individual's psychological development. Accordingly, they were reluctant to consider that the study of the person's early life could provide information about the genesis of a disturbance shown in adulthood. Furthermore, they were unwilling to concede that the study of psychiatric disturbances could furnish information about mental health and normal psychological development. They perceived the actions of the mentally ill as distinct from those who were not ill, and they had resolved the mind-body problem by ignoring the mind.

On the fringes of descriptive psychiatry was Freud, still incurring the disapproval, and sometimes distaste, of many of his colleagues. Freud had not discarded the mind. Instead, he regarded mental processes as quasi-physical and thus obedient to natural laws.

Freud was still concerned with hysteria. He claimed that the symptoms of the illness were "conversions" of unconscious fantasies that gratified sexual wishes. Later, he emphasized that the symptoms represented compromises between the expressive sexual forces and the repressive nonsexual forces. His psychoanalytic work with hysterics showed that these patients were unaware of their complexes. In contrast, patients with obsessional neuroses were aware of their complexes but did not seem to experience the feelings associated with them.

Obsessional neurotics, Freud observed, also failed to make connections between thoughts that one would reasonably think should be related or integrated. For example, a man might say in one sentence that his parents were cruel disciplinarians and in the next sentence complain that he could not understand why he should dislike his father and mother. It appeared to Freud that the two major symptoms of obsessional neurotics were doubting and a sense of compulsion. He explained the doubting as an expression of deeply conflicted feelings of love and hate. He explained the compulsion (e.g., a strong impulse to perform a certain act) as an overcompensation for the doubting. He also considered it noteworthy that obsessional neurotics believed that if they thought something, it would have an effect or come true (Freud referred to this belief as "the omnipotence of thought"). Although the followers of Freud dined happily on his insights, interpretations, and terminology, some psychiatrists and psychologists found the opinions of Adolf Meyer (1866–1950) easier to digest.

Adolf Meyer was born in Niederwenigen, near Zurich. He believed that witnessing the sufferings of his mother during long periods of melancholia was responsible for his entry into medicine and his dedication to the alleviation of psychiatric disorders (Winkler & Bromberg, 1939). After receiving his MD, he traveled to Vienna, Paris, London, Berlin, and Edinburgh for graduate study in pathology, neurology, and psychiatry. In 1892, he came to the United States as a fellow in neurology at the University of Chicago, and he was then employed as a pathologist at the Illinois Eastern Hospital for the Insane before leaving, in 1895, for a similar position at Worcester Insane Hospital. During his 7 years at Worcester, Meyer became acquainted with G. Stanley Hall and other psychologists in eastern Massachusetts.

The division of the person into mind and body was a prime source of irritation to Meyer. On the one hand, the majority of psychologists claimed that their sole interest was in people's mental life. On the other hand, some psychiatrists asserted that their only interest was in the physical or organic condition of their patients. It seemed to Meyer that this bifurcation of the individual led to two dead ends: Many psychologists were minimizing and ignoring the individual's biological functioning, while many psychiatrists were minimizing or ignoring the individual's personal life, feelings, and beliefs.

Meyer proposed a theory of the mind and body that began to attract attention in 1897. He pointed out that a person is a mental and physical whole. Consider for a moment, he urged his colleagues, that the organism develops from a one-celled egg and throughout its life continues to grow and function as an integrated unit. Therefore, what is called mental illness should not be regarded as distinct from physical or mental pathology but as a maladjustment of the entire person. Meyer contended that frequently a psychiatric disturbance is an expression of unhealthy living, of an individual's habitual and progressive adaptations, ineffective though they might seem, to the environment. People are sensitive beings who have to be understood in all phases of their activities and in their past and current adjustments. To gain this understanding, Meyer advised psychiatrists to obtain developmental histories of their patients and to study their life situations thoroughly.

Meyer soon had the opportunity to translate his ideas into action. From 1902 to 1910, he served as pathologist and director of the New York Psychiatric Institute. While there, he developed the "psychiatric interview": a probing into the details of personality development in order to discover the reasons for a particular individual's disturbance. As a complement to psychiatric interviewing, Meyer began, in 1904, to send his wife, staff physicians, and medical students into the homes of patients so that a more complete life history could be obtained and so that relatives could be interviewed, evaluated, and become involved in whatever form of treatment was instituted. These practices marked the beginning of psychiatric social work and established closer ties between psychiatry and the social sciences. Nevertheless, the contrast between the mental and the physical aspects of functioning persisted in discussions within the sciences, and Meyer continued to hammer away that what we mean by the mind "is a sufficiently organized living being in action; and not a peculiar form of mind-stuff" (Woodworth, 1948, p. 232).

The psychiatric views then current as to the causes of criminal behavior illustrate the emphasis placed on organic etiology. Juvenile delinquency was attributed to such conditions as bad heredity, enlarged tonsils, inflamed adenoids, uncorrected refractive errors, impacted teeth, cigarette smoking, intracranial pressure, systematic absorption of toxins from focal infections, phimosis (the need for circumcision), and feeblemindedness. Regardless of what the cause of delinquency might be, there certainly seemed to be delinquents in abundance, and by 1908 a systematic attack on the problem not only was contemplated but was soon to begin.

In that year a prominent social worker, Julia Lathrop, met with William Healy (1869-1963) at Hull House in Chicago to consider what new approaches to juvenile delinquency might be of help. Lathrop and Healy were especially troubled by the tendency of judges to impose penalties on children and formulate their judgments with nothing more than a physical examination to guide them. Surely something more was needed in order to make wise decisions, especially given the great consequences for the children, their families, and ultimately society at large. As a first step, they decided to initiate a program of research to determine why children become delinquents.

Visits by Healy to the clinics of Witmer and Goddard and some suggestions from Thorndike, James, Meyers, and James R. Angell helped in formulating the organization of the program. The plan was to have interviews with each child's relatives in order to evaluate the possible influence of heredity, obtain a developmental history, and secure a picture of family interrelationships and personalities. The child's school would be asked to provide material on the child's educational and classroom adjustments, and the child would be given mental tests and interviewed. Financial support for the venture was pledged for 5 years by a philanthropist Mrs. W. F. Dummer. Judge Pinckney of the juvenile court in Chicago promised to cooperate as fully as possible with the groups, and all that remained was to select someone to direct the clinic. Influenced by the favorable recommendation of William James, Julia Lathrop invited William Healy to accept the directorship, which he did (Healy & Bronner, 1948).

William Healy had been born in England, but he received his BA in 1899 from Harvard and his MD in 1900 from Rush Medical College. He served as assistant physician at the Wisconsin State Hospital and then took the position of associate professor of nervous and mental diseases at the Chicago Polyclinic in 1903. During the academic year 1906-1907, Healy took a leave of absence for postgraduate training in neurology and psychiatry in Vienna, Berlin, and London.

Healy's work had been based upon two major assumptions: (1) he was disinclined to accept the theory that criminal behavior was inherited and (2) he assumed that serious antisocial acts indicated the presence of some psychopathology in the offender. Because of the second assumption, the clinic directed by Healy was named the Juvenile Psychopathic Institute. It opened in 1909 and was located in three rooms on the ground floor of the Detention Home. The staff consisted of Healy; a psychologist, Grace M. Fernald (1879–1950); and a secretary (Watson, 1953).

Healy's first case of delinquency was a girl who falsely accused others of committing sexual offenses. After interviewing her, it seemed to Healy that the child, far from being a born delinquent, was suffering from hysteria. Further study indicated that the girl's unconscious feelings of guilt had been aroused when she attended a revival meeting and that this incident had stimulated her to make the false accusations. Healy's studies of other delinquents did not lend much support to the concept of criminal atavism or degeneracy that had been proposed by the Italian psychiatrist Cesare Lombroso. According to Lombroso, the presence of three stigmata (unusual markings or conformations of the body) would indicate a degenerate, but very few delinquents had as many as three, although Healy did find a successful and widely respected businessman in Chicago who had five.

The Juvenile Psychopathic Institute, considered by many to have been the first child guidance clinic, was off to a promising beginning. It was blessed with a psychiatric and dynamic orientation. The psychological clinic of Witmer had been founded 13 years earlier, but Witmer was unwilling to draw the same far-reaching inferences from the concept of unconscious motivation (Shakow, 1945), and he was not a psychiatrist.

TREATMENT FORMULATIONS

The psychiatric treatment of patients had made little discernible progress. In the more "modern" mental hospitals, mechanical restraints had either been abandoned completely or been replaced by the use of drugs. However, emetics, douches, baths, static electricity, salves, and ointments were still employed, and providing a comfortable hospital environment was still regarded as about the best one could do. The disenchantment and feeling of futility experienced by many psychiatrists when they surveyed their limited therapeutic armaments caused some to give serious attention to those who spoke convincingly of the effects of ideas upon bodily functioning.

Freud was attracting both medical and nonmedical interest in his psychoanalytic theory and techniques. He had abandoned hypnosis with the assertion that its use deprived the analyst of the opportunity to come to grips with the patient's resistances. This deprivation, he believed, eventuated in an incomplete analysis and only transitory improvement. The mitigation or elimination of symptoms, which heretofore had been considered an important goal of treatment, was thus deemphasized by Freud and made secondary to the resolution of unconscious conflicts. Moreover, since it was expected that the patient would resist bringing these conflicts into awareness and dealing with them reasonably, the duration of treatment in most cases was thought to be unavoidably long. Freud did not suppose that there were any therapeutic shortcuts to the unconscious. Instead, he recommended lengthy investigations into the meaning of dreams, "accidents" and word slips, and thoughts generated through free association. By such pains-taking explorations, it would be possible, he believed, to bring unconscious ideas and impulses into awareness. But was this desirable? Some people wondered whether the patient might not become confused and even dangerous once sexual conflicts and urges were out in the open. Freud did not think so. On the contrary, he contended that making the unconscious material accessible to rational scrutiny brought it under better control than had existed before.

Another development in psychoanalytic treatment was the growing distance placed between the analyst and the patient. The analyst became more formal and less personally revealing. Freud had ended his custom of inviting patients to have dinner with him and his family, and although refreshments might still be served during the session, he attempted to keep the relationship on a professional basis (Jones, 1955).

Jung noted that Freud appeared more concerned with his status, even in their relationship. Jung reported that during their trip to the United States, Freud had dampened their game of interpreting each other's dreams by asking Jung at one point not to press him for free associations. When Jung wondered why, Freud responded, "But I cannot risk my authority" (quoted in Jung, 1963, p. 158). This remark shocked Jung, and he traced the origin of his serious doubts about psycho-analysis to this incident. Regardless of how much credence one wishes to give to Jung's anecdote, the kind of dismay he felt upon discovering that Freud had a human weakness is not uncommon in teacher-pupil relationships.

Paul Dubois (1848–1918), professor of neuropathology at the University of Bern, was another psychiatrist who argued vigorously against the materialistic bias adapted by most of his professional colleagues. In his book *The Psychic Treatment of Mental Disease,* Dubois contended that to help neurotics, psychiatrists should spend less time prescribing rest cures and bromides and more time talking with their patients. He suggested that the goal of treatment was "to make the patient master of himself," and in general he believed that the key to human happiness was self-control. The best way to achieve self-control was by a rational appeal to the intellect.

Dubois's rational approach consisted of enlightening the patient about the false premises and injurious habits out of which the patient's symptoms developed and upon which they depended. Together, he and the patient would discuss the nature of the difficulties and complaints. Then Dubois would, through reasonableness, encouragement, and moralizing, try to get the patient to exercise control over the symptoms so that they would be less debilitating. Probably of greatest significance in Dubois's success as a therapist was his respect for his patients, his boundless optimism in their ability to get well, and his infectious self-confidence: "Let one display the legend 'Master of myself!' and patients will follow it to victory" (Dubois, 1908).

William James, whose primary interest was in making life better for neurotics and everybody else, was a kindred spirit. James felt a major problem for Americans was their inability to relax. They also seemed overly disturbed by little things and overly worried about big ones. To free their minds of petty matters so that they would be able to grapple with complex problems, James advised them to acquire useful habits. It is preferable, he thought, to make one's nervous system an ally instead of an enemy. The procedure he recommended for forming habits was as follows: Resolutely start a new, beneficial habit; allow no exceptions until the habit is rooted firmly in the nervous system; put the habit into action at every opportunity; and always avoid exceptions, for, as James put it, "Every smallest stroke of virtue or of vice leaves its never so little scar" (James, 1890, p. 83).

There were other bits of good counsel. For composure in the face of adversity, James urged his fellow Americans to "unclamp" their intellectual machinery, decide on a course of action, and then stop worrying. To those who are afraid he had this to say: "To feel brave, act as if your were brave, use all your will to that end, and a courage-fit will very likely replace the fit of fear."

James himself bravely followed his own advice. At the time, James was quite sick, and the feelings of depression that had troubled him earlier in life had returned, though milder and more fleeting. He traveled to Europe in hope of finding health at various spas, and while there he lectured in Rome, at Oxford, and in Edinburgh. His welcome, particularly in Italy, was enthusiastic and warm (Knight, 1950). In person, as on paper, James was charming, witty, stimulating, and kind.

Though Witmer disagreed with James on a number of issues, he shared with him a similar concern for the prevention of psychological disturbances. Although at first it might appear Witmer addressed himself only to the problem of mental retardation among children, his conception of mental retardation was so broad that it encompassed disturbances not ordinarily considered to be in that category, including problems in conduct and self-control. Further, to the extent that any child is developing at less than full capacity, to that extent, asserted Witmer, the child is retarded (Witmer, 1908–1909b).

Within Witmer's frame of reference, a child of outstanding ability who is doing just passing work in school should be considered retarded. Witmer placed the responsibility for such a child's lack of achievement on the school. Witmer (1925) also felt that educators were unjustified in shirking their obligation to teach by claiming a child was feebleminded or ineducable. He contended the issue was not so simple. Since the diagnostic techniques were not perfectly valid and the consequences of diagnosing a child as ineducable were so great, every effort must be made to ensure that the child was not being deprived of an education unnecessarily or unjustly. He emphasized that some children, for a variety of reasons, merely appear intellectually retarded, and he insisted that only after a persistent attempt at training and mental stimulation could one hope to make a legitimate diagnosis of feeblemindedness. Witmer recognized that this would be a time-consuming and expensive process, but he judged it mandatory and emphatically worthwhile in view of what was at stake for the child.

Referring to the material, social, and intellectual deprivations experienced by children who grow up in slums, Witmer (1909–1910) asserted that "the problem calls for preventive social action. . . . We should offer the slum parent something better than a choice between race suicide and child murder" (p. 280). This awareness of a need for reform within society in order to prevent cases of "retardation" led Witmer to broaden considerably what he felt should be the concern of clinical psychology: "While orthogenics [a term coined by Witmer] concerns itself primarily with the causes and treatment of retardation and deviation, it is by definition the science of normal development, and comprehends within its scope all the conditions which facilitate, conserve, or obstruct the normal development of mind and body" (Witmer, 1908–1909a, p. ii).

A similar breadth of conception was evidenced by Morton Prince (1854–1929). After receiving his MD from Harvard in 1879, Prince engaged in private practice in Boston. From 1902 he served as a professor of neurology at Tufts Medical College, and in 1906 he founded the *Journal of Abnormal Psychology,* of which he became editor.

Prince (1906–1907) attracted the attention of psychologists as a result of his studies of dissociated or multiple personalities, a disorder which he thought was a type of hysteria. He also aroused interest by introducing the term "co-consciousness." Prince (1908–1909) felt a need to distinguish unconscious processes governed by areas in the cerebral cortex from unconscious processes governed by areas in the spinal cord and noncortical areas of the brain. He suggested that the latter processes should be properly called unconscious. However, he believed ideas dependent upon cortical functioning existed in some state of active consciousness because they could be recalled; therefore, they should be called conscious instead of unconscious. Few of his colleagues shared this need for precision, and Prince did not consider the issue important enough to raise a fuss. He was firmer in his convictions about psychotherapy.

It seemed to Prince (1909–1910) that the same principles that govern learning in general could be discerned in pathological behavior. He explained his thesis in this way: Normally, the process of learning involves integrating and relating ideas. When the association between ideas is useful, we do not become concerned about it. But when the association between ideas is harmful to the individual, we refer to it as a complex. In essence, the processes are similar, except that in the functional illnesses the processes have been perverted by trauma or inappropriate learning. Psychoneuroses, for example, can best be viewed as perversions of memory or "association neuroses," since neurotics have difficulty recalling the past.

"Theoretically," Prince claimed, "it would follow what can be done by education can be undone by the same method, and in practice we find this to be true" (Prince, 1909–1910, p. 79). He noted that psychotherapeutic techniques appear to employ ordinary learning principles to reeducate people and effect better adjustment to the environment. Old complexes "are modified by being interwoven with new ones, and new systems of ideas or complexes are artfully created and substituted for the old." In the final analysis, Prince concluded, all psychotherapies are only different forms of education.

Prince's conclusion undoubtedly startled his fellow members of the medical profession, for he implied that nonphysicians might be qualified to treat functional diseases. Equally disconcerting were public indications that the area of psychiatry did not fall neatly and exclusively within the medicosomatic domain. Auguste Forel (1907) reported success in curing alcoholics by converting them to religion, and in Boston there were signs that a Pandora's box of nonmedical practitioners of psychotherapy was being opened. Under the guidance of Rev. Elwood Worcester (1863–1940), groups of patients with nervous disorders were being given "moral" treatment.

Elwood Worcester had graduated from Columbia in 1886, studied under Wundt, and received his PhD from Leipzig in 1889. From 1890 to 1896, he taught philosophy and psychology—and served as chaplain—at Lehigh University. He assumed the rectory of Saint Stephen's Church in Philadelphia in 1896. While in Philadelphia, Worcester received his doctorate in divinity from the University of Pennsylvania and formed a friendship with S. Weir Mitchell. In 1904, he became rector of the Emmanuel Church in Boston.

Shortly after Worcester's arrival in Boston, an internist, Joseph H. Pratt (1872–1942), approached him with a request for the use of his church's facilities and for funds in order to test his idea that it would be possible to treat indigent tubercular patients without placing them in an institution. Pratt's strategy was to teach them to follow a strict routine of rest, fresh air, and proper diet. In order to save time, he proposed to gather his patients into groups so that they could learn and discuss the reasons for his hygienic methods. Pratt hoped such classes could be held in a room in the church. Worcester, going farther, wondered if the patients might not have souls as well as lungs in need of saving. The two men decided to work together.

A class began in 1905, with Worcester opening each meeting with prayers and giving spiritual counsel to the patients. This "class," conducted by Pratt and Worcester, is regarded as a precursor of group therapy. The next year Worcester and his associate, Rev. Samuel McComb, started health classes for "the nervously and morally diseased." Physicians were invited to speak on topics such as worry, anger, and suggestion, but a major purpose of the group meetings was to treat the afflicted through religion, prayer, and inculcation of faith in God. Indeed, Worcester had aims that extended beyond his classes in Boston: He hoped to achieve a revival of faith healing—and not only among the clergy but within medicine. He had a vision of mental health clinics attached to churches where psychiatrists and ministers would work hand in hand to cure the sick. He saw the luster of religion, which had been dimmed by the ascendance of science, restored by the cooperation of religion with science.

Soon the health classes attracted enough attention and enthusiasm to be christened the "Emmanuel Health Movement." Soon, too, the medical societies erupted in a storm of indignation protesting the usurpation of the physician's role in treating disease (Kiernan, 1909). And before long the effects of professional opposition and the discouragement of adherents who were unable to achieve the founder's therapeutic success led to the movement's demise.

Psychologists were hardly involved in this clash between medicine and one of their former colleagues on the issue of who was entitled to treat the mentally ill.

The issue at the time seemed to be no issue at all as far as they were concerned: Treatment of disease fell within the province of medicine, and that was that. (When Münsterberg [1909] wrote about psychotherapy, he did so as a physician.) However this attitude did not exclude the possibility of psychologists and psychiatrists working together within the same area. Psychologists could be very useful, and perhaps no psychologist better exemplified for physicians the kind of usefulness they envisioned as ideal than Shepherd Ivory Franz (1847–1933).

Following his graduation from Columbia in 1899 (he wrote a doctoral thesis under Cattell on visual afterimages), Franz spent the next 7 years teaching physiology in the medical schools of Harvard and Dartmouth. He was also psychologist at McLean Hospital and founded its psychological laboratory (Franz, 1932). His research on touch and cortical localization endeared him most to his fellow psychologists.

It was Franz who introduced, around 1900, a novel method for determining cortical functions. First, an animal was trained to perform a task, and then a certain area of the cortex was extirpated. Following the animal's recovery from the surgery, its performance of the task was reevaluated to see what role, if any, had been played by the removed portion of the brain. Almost everyone believed that when an area of the cortex was destroyed, a permanent loss of its function resulted. If the functions later recovered, they inferred that the area had not been completely destroyed. But Franz proved by his research that it was possible for other cortical areas to assume the functions of those areas that had been removed.

In 1905, Franz began applying his research findings to patients with brain damage. He initiated a training program for aphasics to help them overcome their speech handicaps. His successes with these patients immediately demonstrated to physicians that there was hope for the rehabilitation of individuals who had suffered cortical lesions.

The following year Franz left McLean to assume the positions of psychologist at the government Hospital for the Insane in Washington, D.C., and professor of physiology and professor of psychology at George Washington University. In 1907, he introduced at the hospital the practice of administering Cattell-type mental examinations routinely. His contributions were considered of such merit that in 1908 he was elected an honorary member of the American Medico-Psychological Association, later called the American Psychiatric Association (Fernberger, 1933). Franz was a tough-minded, organically oriented, brilliant, no-nonsense researcher—just the kind of psychologist any doctor would have liked to be able to order.

PROFESSIONAL DEVELOPMENT

From 1900 to 1909, the presidents of the APA were, in order, Jastrow, Royce, Sanford, Bryan, James, Calkins, Angell, Marshall, Stratton, and Judd. Jastrow, as noted above, was troubled about the public image of psychology. A facile writer and an entertaining though somewhat rambling speaker, he was particularly interested in acquainting a wide audience with the new science.

Jastrow (1930) graduated from the University of Pennsylvania in 1882 and obtained his doctorate from Johns Hopkins in 1886 with the thesis "Perception of Space by Disparate Senses." University positions in psychology were then few in number, so Jastrow was forced to remain at Hopkins as a "fellow by courtesy." He managed to supplement his income by writing popular articles for magazines until, in 1888, he received an appointment at the University of Wisconsin.

The Chicago World's Fair of 1893 found Jastrow on hand at the psychology booth explaining apparatuses and testing the sensory capacities and mental powers of adventurous spectators. In 1894, for some undetermined reason, he began to experience periods of depression. He sought out William James in the hope of getting some helpful advice, but at the time James was also depressed. If no advice was forthcoming, at least Jastrow returned to Wisconsin with the consolation that he was not suffering alone. Despite his episodes of "prostration and exhaustion," Jastrow led a very active life. Not only did he manage to fulfill his professional responsibilities, but he continued to increase the public's familiarity with psychology through lectures and books.

There was still considerable debate among psychologists as to what it was Jastrow was attempting to popularize. Much discussion centered around what the content and aims of psychology should be, and Jastrow, for one, thought he knew. In his presidential address, he urged his colleagues to become involved in the applications of their science: "Psychology and life are closely related; and we do not fulfill our whole function if we leave uninterpreted for practical and public benefit the mental nature of man" (Jastrow, 1901, p. 24).

A closely allied point of view was expressed by Stern, in 1900, in his book *Über Psychologie der individuellen Differenzen.* He attempted to outline a new discipline, differential psychology, which he believed should be given the status of an independent scientific area. Differential psychology, as he conceived it, would focus on individuals and would attempt to discover by measurement how one person differed from another. He hailed the topic of individuality as the major problem for psychology in the twentieth century.

In like manner, Mary Whiton Calkins (1863–1930), originator of the method of paired associates for the study of memory, was pushing to define psychology as the science of the self. Although Calkins (1930) had studied at Smith and at Clark, her life seemed to begin for her in 1890 when she became a student of James and Münsterberg at Harvard. She left Harvard to take charge of the psychological laboratory at Wellesley, and in 1900 she began strongly advocating a psychology of self. To illustrate how Calkins proposed to interpret all mental processes in terms of the self, we may note her distinction between perception and imagination. In perception, a person is aware of sharing a similar experience with a number of other selves; in imagination a person is aware that his or her experience is private and unique. Calkins contrasted her position (functionalism) with an atomistic point of view in psychology, the latter being concerned with the contents of consciousness and identified with Wundt and Titchener (structuralism). The self psychologists, or Calkins at any rate, were also concerned with the contents of consciousness—but as experiences of the self. She allowed that there was room in psychology for both points of view.

In her APA presidential address, Calkins (1906) argued that the self was not a metaphysical concept but a fact of experience. Although she never defined the self, she did describe its characteristics: (1) persistence or stability of identity ("The same 'I' must exist if there is to be consciousness 'in the same way' or 'of the same object'"); (2) uniqueness; (3) complexity; and (4) relations to, or awareness of, objects in the environment by observing, manipulating, and emotionally responding to them.

The self as described by Calkins, seemed to exist without a body, and her critics wondered if this were an oversight on her part. Not so, Calkins explained that to give the self a body would endanger the identity of psychologists, perhaps turn them into biologists, and so lose an important though as yet underdeveloped science. In 1909, to highlight her position, she abandoned her previously expressed tolerance for the atomistic view and came out for "a single-track self-psychology" (Woodworth, 1948, p. 242). Though most psychologists of her day were in favor of allowing her to travel her track alone, developments in the psychology of personality have since supported her stand.

During this period, there was considerable interest in functional psychology, especially at the University of Chicago, where John Dewey and James R. Angell (1869–1949) were its champions. Both of these men had been influenced by James. They defined psychology as the study of consciousness but recommended approaching the subject from a different perspective. Their position was clearly stated in Angell's APA presidential address.

According to Angell (1907), functional psychology aimed to portray the operations of consciousness as organic adaptations to a social and physical environment, in contrast with the structural approach (the atomistic approach), which attempted to analyze consciousness and describe its contents. It followed that the functionalist was interested in the evolutionary purpose, or usefulness, of mental activity, the significance of the relationship between mind and body, and the conditions under which an activity was elicited.

Moreover, Angell asserted, the functionalist did not shrink from biology but was "cheek by jowl with the general biologist" (1907, p. 69). Having placed psychologists in that intimate but rather uncomfortable position, Angell went on to describe an executive function of consciousness that both prescribed and inhibited behavior, selecting from the environment only certain aspects to which it attended: "The functionalist's most intimate persuasion leads him to regard consciousness as primarily and intrinsically a control phenomenon" (1907, p. 88). In other words, it is the function of consciousness that should be the object of study, and its major function is to control or organize stimuli.

Many psychologists found the functional position congenial, since they had been functionalists in everything but name. If psychology had been divided into a structuralist camp and a functionalist camp, then all applied psychologists would have been swept into the latter. Within functional psychology would be the approach that Witmer called clinical psychology.

Witmer (1907) used the term *clinical* to refer to a method of teaching and research and not merely as the adjectival form of the noun *clinic,* which refers to a place where people are examined. The clinical method consisted of gathering instructors, students, and those needing help for the purpose of studying, doing research into, and treating mental disabilities and defects. Although the clinical psychologist's major purpose was to examine each person with the goal of prescribing beneficial measures for development, Witmer emphasized two points: (1) as a teacher, the clinician was to conduct demonstrations in the presence of students so that they would be instructed in the science and the art of psychology, and (2) as a scientist, the clinician was to regard each case as in part a research experiment in which the effects of psychological information, procedures, and recommendations were to be discovered or tested.

Further, though Witmer recognized that clinical psychology encroached on the preserves of other professions, he dismissed the matter this way:

> While the field of clinical psychology is to some extent occupied by the physician, especially the psychiatrist, and while I expect to rely in a great measure upon the educator and social worker for the more important contributions to this branch of psychology, it is nevertheless true that none of these has quite the training necessary for this kind of work. For that matter, neither has the psychologist, unless he has acquired this training from other sources than the usual course of instruction in psychology. (Witmer, 1907, p. 7)

Witmer had, of course, been continuing his work at his clinic at the University of Pennsylvania, and by 1900 he was seeing three children a day. For some of the cases, he called S. Weir Mitchell into neurological consultation. However, the ultimate responsibility for each case, including the prescription of pedagogical treatment, rested with the precise and erudite Witmer.

Witmer succeeded in persuading the administration of the university to begin offering formal training in clinical psychology, and its catalogue for 1904–1905 announced that students could take courses for credit in psychiatry and neuropathology in the medical school. By 1907, Witmer had been able to raise sufficient funds to establish a hospital school for the training of retardates as an adjunct of his clinic and to found a professional journal, *The Psychological Clinic,* of which he became editor. Regular and continuing summer school courses were offered in child psychology, educational psychology, and the functioning of his clinic; an undergraduate course was offered in abnormal psychology. The following academic year, 1908–1909, five clinical psychology courses were offered in the graduate school: three on developmental psychology, one on abnormal psychology, and one on mental and physical defects in school children.

Not the least of Witmer's interests at this time was in promoting his coined term *orthogenics* and in encouraging psychologists to do work in the area it referred to. Issues of *The Psychological Clinic* prominently displayed the term's definition, and the journal itself was subtitled *A Journal of Orthogenics.* However, this was another of Witmer's losing battles. *Clinical psychology* was the more congenial and generally accepted of the two terms, probably because psychologists did not relish the possibility of being known as *orthogenicists*. Nevertheless, Witmer was successful in the more important aspect of his campaign: encouraging his colleagues to become involved in correcting aspects of the social system that produced harmful psychological consequences.

From its opening in 1896 to 1909, Witmer's clinic evaluated 459 children, and the University of Pennsylvania recognized its value by increasing the amount of financial support. The staff consisted of Witmer, an assistant director, five trained PhDs as examiners, one social worker, three assistant social workers, and a recorder. By then, the clinic was no longer unique (Fernberger, 1931).

In addition to Healy's clinic, mentioned earlier, there was the Iowa Psychological Clinic, founded in 1908 by Carl Seashore (1866–1949) and R. L. Sylvester. Seashore was an optimistic, self-satisfied individual: "I have been a lucky man—lucky in the place and race of my nativity, in the 'choice' of my parents, in my education, in my jobs, in my travels, in my marriage and children, in success and recognition beyond my fondest dreams" (Seashore, 1930, p. 227).

As an undergraduate, he had sung his way through Gustavus Adolphus College—in the glee club, as a member of quartets, and as a choir director. In 1895, Seashore received his doctorate from Yale, and in 1897, after two years of postdoctoral studies, he accepted the position of assistant professor of philosophy at the University of Iowa. Seashore endeared himself to the university administration by his willingness to undertake assignments even before having any idea as to how he could fulfill them, as in the following example.

Around 1900, the University of Iowa inadvertently found itself with more applicants for entrance than it could possibly handle. Seashore obligingly volunteered to accept the responsibility for solving this problem. He began giving a test devised by Thorndike as a qualifying entrance examination for incoming freshmen. As a screening device, the test owed much of its success to the fact that a sizable proportion of the applicants timidly withdrew rather than take it. Seashore had saved the day, and encouraged by his victory he began constructing his own aptitude and achievement tests.

In 1908, Seashore was appointed dean of the graduate college. The clinic he helped found that year was patterned after Witmer's. Although the major emphasis was on research, the clinic did offer remedial services for speech and reading disabilities and mental defects. Perhaps the case most fondly recalled by Seashore was that of a girl who needed help because she flatted in her singing.

The following year, 1909, Clark University established a psychological clinic. In addition, courses in clinical psychology were introduced at the University of Minnesota and the University of Washington, and both schools subsequently established clinics.

Obviously, aside from Healy's clinic, which was affiliated with a law court but which did accept some graduate students for training, psychological clinics were arising in academic settings. Their orientation, and that of their clientele, was based on the assumption that psychologists should be mainly concerned with, not people who were mentally ill, but people who had learning difficulties.

Even in nonacademic settings, psychologists, by virtue of their scientific and scholastic background, were engaged to fill positions that involved research, mental testing, and pedagogy, not treatment.

Only a few psychologists worked outside of universities. Among this hardy group were the following: R. T. Wylie, who in 1898 began research and psychological testing at the state institution for the retarded in Fairbault, Minnesota; Goddard, who became director of research at Vineland in 1906 and who began offering the first psychological internships 2 years later; Edmund Huey, who was appointed in 1909 to a position at the State Institution for the Feebleminded in Lincoln, Illinois; and F. Lyman Wells, who succeeded Franz at McLean Hospital (Watson, 1953).

Much to everyone's delight, psychology was continuing to expand in the United States and Europe. In 1901, Edouard Claparède helped found the Swiss journal *Archives de Psychologie,* and in 1903 Guilo Ferrari (1932) founded the Italian journal *Revista di Psicologia.* Cattell predicted that someday there would be a profession of applied psychology, and the Fifth International Congress of Psychology, which met in Rome, was pronounced by one and all a great success. The outstanding attractions at the congress were a paper delivered by James and a presentation of data and results attained through use of the Binet-Simon Scale.

In 1906, standards for election to membership in the APA were tightened: A prospective member had to have psychology as his profession and give evidence of research accomplishments; also, philosophers, educators, and those who merely held assistantships were no longer accepted. It was also proposed, but not agreed upon, that continued membership in the association should be contingent on continued scientific contributions. An APA committee, composed of Angell, Judd, Pillsbury, Seashore, and Woodworth, was formed to develop a series of improved group and individual tests that would have practical applications (Fernberger, 1932).

Yet, all this occurred early in the development of the profession. The APA dues had been reduced in 1904 to a dollar a year, and the membership by 1910 numbered only 222. Psychology was still largely a hope and a promise. Its devotees struggled for emancipation from departments of philosophy, yet found themselves faced with rejection by the established natural sciences. For the most part, psychologists had no secure place within academia. Unsure of their professional identity and the identity of their field, striving for recognition, and widely regarded by the academic world as troublesome upstarts whose field did not meet accepted standards for status as an independent science, psychologists still dreamed of a bright future.

"Psychology will one day, in all probability, have a dominant place among the sciences, instead of its present somewhat humble rank," said Stratton (1909, p. 83), wistfully trying to encourage his colleagues in his APA presidential address. And a similar sentiment was expressed by Judd (1910, p. 97) in his presidential address: "Psychology will boldly assert its right to exist as the science which deals in a broad way with the evolutionary processes by which consciousness arose and through which the trend of life has been changed from organic adaptation to intelligent conquest."

Some psychologists—to borrow a term from James—probably experienced a "courage-fit" as a result of Judd's words. Others no doubt mumbled and grumbled their disagreement with his definition of their science. Most psychologists, however, must have felt the exhilaration and defiant pride that comes with pioneering a new field.

II

THE SECOND
GENERATION

Clinical psychologists, in developing their profession, met resistance from psychiatrists, who saw them as encroaching on their own preserve. They did not even receive much encouragement from other psychologists, who tended to believe psychology was a pure science and its applications were not their concern. Since the majority of psychologists were teachers at colleges and universities, training in clinical psychology remained a matter of taking whatever courses might be available and then pursuing on-the-job specialization under clinical psychologists working in child guidance clinics, mental hospitals, and schools. Clinical psychologists still functioned mainly as researchers and psychometricians, though increasingly they began to consider psychotherapy or treatment as an essential part of their role. As their numbers grew, clinical psychologists began to form associations—the first in 1917. An association encompassing all applied psychologists was founded in 1937. This association sought to further the professional status of clinicians and to set standards for their training.

MAJOR EVENTS IN THE HISTORY
OF CLINICAL PSYCHOLOGY

1910 to 1919

Freud's concepts of the id, ego, and ego-ideal; intrapsychic conflict in war neuroses; recommendations for the technique of psychoanalysis.

Adler's inferiority complex and theory of compensation; Jung's collective unconscious.

Watson launches behaviorism, a new theory of psychology that attends to practical concerns and overt behaviors (1913).

Beginning of industrial psychology (1913–1915).

Terman's Stanford Revision of the Binet Scale and the IQ score.

Psychologists develop performance scales of intelligence, the Army Alpha and
    Beta, and a neurotic inventory.

Meyer's psychobiology; Bleuler's schizophrenia; Kraepelin's cyclothymic person-
    ality; Jung's introvert–extravert; Healy argues delinquents are disturbed.

Psychologists are legally recognized as expert in mental retardation.

Formation of the American Association of Clinical Psychologists (1917), which in
    1919 becomes the Clinical Section of the APA.

1920 to 1929

Freud's instincts of life and death, the superego; Rank's birth trauma, separation
    conflict, and time-limited psychotherapy; Adler's social feeling or social inter-
    est.

Gestalt psychology and Lewin's life space.

Gesell's developmental schedules and Piaget's developmental findings.

Growth in personality, aptitude, and interest tests—Rorschach's inkblot test.

Increasing awareness of testing limitations and the importance of the environment
    for intelligence and psychopathology.

Beginnings of behavior therapy, hypnoanalysis, and vocational guidance.

Founding of Psychological Corporation (1921) and American Orthopsychiatric
    Association (1924).

1930 to 1939

Association of Consulting Psychologists is founded (1930).

Anna Freud's defense mechanisms and play therapy; Adler's style of life; Rank's
    concept of will; Murray's needs and presses.

Neobehaviorism and efforts to integrate learning theory with psychoanalysis.

Cultural relativism and neo-Freudians (Horney).

Wechsler's point scale of adult intelligence; Doll's scale of social competence;
    growth in diagnostic measures and projective techniques (TAT, B-G).

Operational definitions and testable hypotheses.

Enthusiasm for psychotherapy; clinical psychologists begin to consider treatment
    as part of their professional role; American Association of Applied Psychology
    (AAAP) forms (1937); APA's Clinical Section and Association of Consulting
    Psychologists disband; AAAP begins publication of *Journal of Consulting Psy-
    chology.*

4

Psychologists Go to War 1910–1919

The beginning of this turbulent decade found intellectuals in almost all fields affirming their faith in science and confident of continued advances. This was a time of belief in human progress and ingenuity. There were breaks with tradition in art, where futurism departed from former aesthetic ideals and called for the depiction of machines and scientific achievements, and in architecture, where the beauty to be found in simplicity of design and in the imaginative use of the newest materials provided by technology was stressed. Similarly, the new realists of philosophy, while acknowledging that there was little comfort and probably some error in the truths propounded by science, nonetheless believed them to be the best available guide for ordering one's life. Accordingly, they advised people to accept them without fear and to grace their years with dignity by actively dealing with their environments and benefiting humanity.

Encouragingly, the benefits did continue to come from what some called "white magic," science. Airplanes, motion pictures, and automobiles were but three inventions that rapidly lost their novelty and became an integral part of Western life. And there were discoveries whose full implications were being pursued: the importance of the pituitary gland in the control of human growth, the necessity of vitamins for a proper diet and the prevention of illness, and the finding that electrical charges are a fundamental constituent of matter.

An important by-product of this progress was that those Americans who had directly or indirectly profited from the achievements of science made generous contributions of large sums of money to various educational causes. Henry Phipps gave $50,000 to the mental hygiene movement, thus putting it on its feet financially. Andrew Carnegie gave $10,000,000 for pensions for college teachers, $10,000,000 to advance the cause of peace, and $135,000,000 to promote human knowledge and understanding. Rockefeller gave over $165,000,000 to further the noble aims of humanity.

As might have been predicted, not everyone received these philanthropic grants gratefully. Some, Cattell for one, saw something other than hard work and thrift in the fact that one man was able to accumulate over $300,000,000 within his lifetime. Cattell was particularly indignant about the discrepancy between the incomes of those who produced ideas (e.g., college professors) and those who simply marketed and made use of those ideas (i.e., corporation executives). He made a strong argument for increasing faculty salaries and also for giving faculties greater responsibilities in the administration of their schools.

In 1910, Cattell attacked the Carnegie Foundation for the Advancement of Teaching as subversive of academic freedom. Since President Butler of Columbia University was a trustee of the foundation, a clash between the two men was virtually inevitable. Each invited the other to resign from Columbia, but neither did so. Instead, their conflict smoldered, with occasional outbursts by Cattell and others, including Jastrow, against the domination of faculties by university administrations.

Elsewhere, 2 years of minor fighting in the Balkans finally erupted, in 1914, into a worldwide conflict. By 1916, Serbia, Russia, France, Great Britain, Montenegro, Japan, Italy, and Rumania were allied against Austria, Germany, Turkey, and Bulgaria. Each side was convinced of its own virtuousness and attempted to justify its actions. However, feelings within the United States tended from the outset to be more sympathetic to the French and British cause and to grow increasingly hostile to the German cause.

In 1917, with a mingling of relief, determination, and considerable enthusiasm, the United States declared war against Germany in order to "make the world safe for democracy" and, ultimately, to end all wars among nations. Naturally, in the emotional excesses of the period, the loyalty of Americans of German descent or of those who had studied in Germany became suspect. Among those caught up by the misguided patriotism of the moment was Cattell.

Although his son McKeen was in France as part of the first group of volunteers, and although Cattell was participating in the war effort by organizing committees of scientists for the National Research Council, he found himself brought into federal court. Cattell's "crime" had been to speak out in favor of exempting conscientious objectors from combat. (Under the Espionage Act of 1917 and the Sedition Act of 1918, federal authorities arrested over 1500 people; these laws, extremely vague in sections, provided penalties for discouraging recruiting and "disloyal and abusive" language about the government.) The trustees of Columbia judged Cattell with greater speed and harshness than the judiciary, and they summarily dismissed him, minus accrued pension and salary, on the grounds of treason, sedition, and opposition to the laws of the United States. However, Cattell was not to be disposed of so easily. For 5 years he fought in the courts to regain his pension—and won. That made his war with Columbia 4 years longer, but more profitable in outcome, than the war his country had waged.

Meanwhile, sweeping changes had been taking place within the social structure of the United States. Women were assuming a new status and demanding the right to vote and to be treated as equals. They wore lipstick and rouge—a practice previously considered "immoral." And in the words of H. L. Mencken, "The veriest schoolgirl of today knows as much as the midwife of 1885, and spends a good deal more time discharging and disseminating her information."

Similar pressures for reform and just treatment were exerted by labor, which was intensifying its expressions of dissatisfaction with being dependent upon the generosity of employers (textile workers in Massachusetts were paid $10 for a 54-hour week, which even at that time was not enough to ensure survival). Demands were pressed to have management respect labor's rights to organize and bargain as equals for an equitable wage.

Disturbed by these signs of internal agitation and unrest, many people were inclined to blame influences from outside the country and to argue for a revival of isolationism. It seemed as if they hoped to restore their previous feelings of security by holding fervently to those ideals and spiritual values that, they believed, had made the United States unique and great. A red scare, a fear of Communist subversion, swept through the country in 1919. Before it ended, almost 600 aliens were deported, and a man who killed an immigrant for yelling "To hell with the U.S." was acquitted by a jury of his peers in 2 minutes.

By 1920, women had the right to vote, and an experiment was about to begin in the legislation of morals: The United States was to prohibit its people from indulging in alcoholic beverages. With the death of Demon Rum, the evangelist Billy Sunday, eloquently expressing a popular belief, predicted a beautiful future: "The slums soon will be only a memory. We will turn our prisons into factories and our jails into storehouses and corncribs. Men will walk upright now, women will smile, and the children will laugh. Hell will be forever for rent."

NORMAL PERSONALITY FUNCTIONING

The fast tempo of the times was reflected in the changes taking place within psychology. Perhaps in part because Ernest Jones became assistant editor in 1910, few issues of the *Journal of Abnormal Psychology* failed to mention the latest developments in psychoanalytic theory. Generally, even the critical articles were favorable in their conclusions, and the critics themselves were censured if their published comments indicated an uncalled-for emotional reaction against the theory. "He who cannot endure the truth should keep away from science," admonished Bleuler (Jones, 1911–1912, p. 465).

The critics seemed to agree that what irritated them most was the tendency of psychoanalysts to generalize and rush with haste into dubious applications of analytic ideas. Even Bleuler was annoyed by the "pathographies" (psychoanalyses of people long dead) that were appearing frequently in the literature. Bleuler also was unsympathetic to the view that the contents of the unconscious consisted only of wishes and not fears as well.

Woodworth (1917–1918) pointed out that any train of association, if pursued long enough, would lead to a complex. Therefore, he questioned the validity of analytic interpretations and found too many of them that seemed farfetched. He also rejected the assertion that successful therapeutic outcomes indicated the rectitude of the theory, since other forms of treatment based on different theories claimed to produce equally effective results.

Moreover, while none of the critics denied that sexual motivation is important, all wondered why Sigmund Freud insisted it was so very important. Bleuler could not see any sexual origins for a person's devotion to religion, appreciation of aesthetics, or desire to obtain knowledge. Nor did he feel that every neurosis had some sexual cause. He suggested as an alternative that it might be possible for people to have nonsexual predispositions that rendered them vulnerable to sexual disturbances later in life and that these later disorders in sexual functioning might eventually find expression in the form of a neurosis.

Yet when all was said and done, Bleuler concluded that psychoanalytic theory was essentially correct. He noted, quite reasonably,

> *That in the minor work of the whole school many details are problematical, too hastily generalized, or directly untrue, should not appear strange. It would be curious if in this freshly explored field, and in the endless complications of the mind, false conclusions were not reached as well as in every other sphere. (quoted by Jones, 1911–1912)*

Janet (1914–1915) also ended his appraisal of psychoanalysis in what was intended to be a complimentary fashion:

> *Later on we shall forget the excessive generalizations and adventurous symbolisms, which at present seem to characterize these studies and to separate them from other scientific works, and only one thing will be remembered, namely, that psychoanalysis has rendered great service to psychological analysis. (p. 187)*

Certainly psychologists were receptive to the psychoanalytic concepts of the defenses and unconscious motivation. Neither concept required allegiance to any particular theory, and both were readily inferable from overt behavior once a person had knowledge of them and was sensitive to their manifestations. Binet had been traveling in this direction and, shortly before his death in 1911, gave a hint of the framework in which his formulations would have been cast:

> *Against this theory [of rational thought] stands the new one, a theory of action, according to which mental life is not at all a rational life, but a chaos of shadow crossed by flashes, something strange, and especially discontinuous, which appeared continuous and rational only because after the event it was described in a language which brings order and clarity everywhere. (quoted by Varnon, 1935)*

Another illustration of the favor with which the concept of the unconscious was regarded may be found in an article by Ogden (1911). Ogden suggested that the reason some psychological laboratories were unable to find imageless thoughts was because the unconscious attitudes of the experimenters were being communicated without their awareness to their subjects, thus biasing these reports.

What did bother psychologists, however, was the Freudian insistence on the saturation of the unconscious with sexual content. While nonanalysts such as Borris Sidis spoke disparagingly of "Freudian twaddle," a similar discontent bloomed deep in the garden of psychoanalysis itself. In 1909, Jung wrote to Freud recommending a more discrete approach to the "unsavory topic" of sex: "Both with the students and with patients I get on further by not making the theme of sexuality prominent." But Freud would tolerate no compromise on this issue, arguing that to minimize the pervasiveness of sexual motivation would render psychoanalysis sterile. His firm stand was perceived by some of his dissident followers as personal rejection—and also a welcome signal of their maturity, because they had dared to openly challenge him.

A series of ruptures began around 1911. First, Alfred Adler left the Vienna Psychoanalytic Society to form his own group, the Society for Individual Psychology. Then Wilhelm Stekel departed for greener pastures in 1912. Neither of these losses distressed Freud personally. Adler was viewed as a morose and cantankerous fellow who never did quite fit in with the group, and the depth of Stekel's devotion to science was questioned. There were still 106 members of the International Psychoanalytic Association (with Jung serving as president), and Brill had just founded a psychoanalytic society in New York. Things were going much better than Freud had ever expected. His only worry was the use his critics might make of the defections to discredit analytic theory. To prevent recurrences, he suggested that an analyst should be "fully analyzed" so as not to "yield to the temptation of projecting as a scientific theory of general applicability some of the peculiarities of his own personality which he has dimly perceived."

Then, in 1913, Jung, the heir apparent of the psychoanalytic movement, broke with Freud. Now this was a distressing blow, one that Freud had tried to prevent. Some solace was provided by Jones's suggestion that a secret inner committee of trustworthy analysts be formed. They would be dedicated to ensuring the development of Freud's theory and therapeutic techniques. The "Committee," as it was unimaginatively called, was composed of Freud, Jones, Otto Rank, Sandor Ferenczi, Hanns Sachs, and Karl Abraham. The following year, 1914, Jung resigned his presidency of the International Psychoanalytic Association and severed his formal ties with psychoanalysis (Jones, 1955).

Freud was deeply concerned and tried to explain to the world what had happened by setting down a history of the psychoanalytic movement. Above all, he wished it to be known that it was his ideas that were in danger of being distorted and appropriated. With genuine feelings but questionable assumptions, he repudiated his former "modesty" (Freud, 1910) and rescinded much of the credit he had once accorded Breuer for helping develop psychoanalysis:

> *I have never heard that Breuer's great share in psychoanalysis has earned him a corresponding measure of criticism and abuse and as it is long ago since I recognized that to stir up contradiction and arouse bitterness is the inevitable fate of psychoanalysis I conclude that I must be the real originator of all that is particularly characteristic in it. (Freud, 1959d, p. 288)*

Because of the growing popularity of psychoanalysis—and the attendant abuses—Freud's efforts during this period were directed largely at illustrating and putting into print techniques and principles for interpretation and therapy. The outbreak of World War I and his concern for the safety of his sons, who were serving in the Austrian army, were said to have contributed to a sharp drop in the rate of his fundamental discoveries. Nevertheless, by ordinary standards Freud was still exceptionally productive, and he continued modifying, elaborating, and extending psychoanalytic theory.

It seemed to Freud that unconscious mental processes consist of wishes that have been aroused by the excitation of instincts. These wishes exist not in verbalized form but as images and sensations. This partially explains why it is so difficult to communicate the contents of the unconscious to others. Only as the wishes proceed into preconsciousness and consciousness do they become accessible to verbal concepts and labeling operations.

Within unconsciousness, all is absolute and there is no conception of time. The wish for something to happen is equivalent to its actual occurrence, and wishes of long ago that have been repressed are still experienced as current feelings and attitudes.

Repression, itself, was differentiated into two forms. *Primary repression* refers to the process by which the mental representation of an instinct is kept from awareness. *Secondary repression* refers to the process by which ideas that are connected or associated with the primary repressed material are kept from awareness. For example, a person represses not only a wish that is incestuous (primary repression) but also thoughts that might remind him or her of the wish (secondary repression). In distinguishing both of these processes, Freud devoted considerable attention to the problem of what happens to the charges of energy with which all ideas and sensations are supposedly invested. He envisioned a highly mobile, constantly fluctuating psychic system in which there are attractions and repulsions and removals of energy preconsciously.

Governing the unconscious is the pleasure principle: to seek gratification of repressed wishes and to avoid the displeasure caused by denying them expression in overt behavior. Governing conscious functioning is the reality principle: a recognition of, and adjustment to, the demands of the environment so that instinctual impulses can be gratified without bringing the individual into interpersonal conflict or causing pain.

Implementing the task of taking reality into account involves the development of perception, memory, attention, judgment, thought, and a capacity to delay gratification. Freud's view that the role of conscious functioning, or the ego, is to mediate between the demands of instinctual strivings and environmental restrictions allows psychoanalysis to encompass virtually all areas of psychology.

However, Freud did not see ego functioning as exclusively conscious. Ego processes include many that operate preconsciously or unconsciously to defend the person from awareness of instinctual impulses and, at times, to allow the impulses disguised gratification. These processes or "defenses" include repression, projection (attributing one's own feelings and thoughts to others), turning against the self (rather than expressing the impulse toward the person who aroused it), and reversal into the opposite (e.g., changing unconscious love into conscious hate for someone).

By 1914, Freud had ventured into anthropology and saw in the reported taboos and rituals of primitive peoples defenses similar to those observed in patients suffering from obsessional neuroses. He also thought he recognized another "institution," or related group of mental functions, similar to the conscience. This institution is created when, during an individual's growth, the teachings and criticisms of parents and others are internalized as a set of standards and ideals by which behavior is guided. Freud called this system of values the *ego ideal.* He suggested that with its formation not only are new demands imposed on the ego to measure up to certain standards but also feelings of self-approval or narcissistic gratifications are experienced when the person succeeds in acting in accordance with these standards. Therefore, the function of the conscience is to evaluate critically the individual's behavior in terms of the particular ego ideal and to see to it that rewards of self-satisfaction and punishments of condemnation are provided (Freud, 1959e).

In 1919, Max Eitington joined the Committee. In the meantime, Carl Jung, whose defection had been a prime reason for the Committee's formation, had been developing and expressing his own theoretical formulations. According to Jung (1963), his break with the psychoanalytic movement resulted from Freud's identification of his method of treatment with his sex theory. In keeping with this reason for dissatisfaction, Jung had redefined *libido* to mean a general psychic energy rather than an energy that was specifically sexual.

Jung envisioned libido, under normal circumstances, as rhythmically flowing back and forth. This forward and backward libidinal flow represents, respectively, progressive adaptation by the individual to the external environment and regressive adaptation to inner needs. A blockage in either direction, or a failing on the part of the person to attend to and satisfy either environmental or internal demands, is indicative of a psychological disturbance.

In order to understand the causes of these blockages, we need to recognize the importance of the present. We are dealing, Jung argued, with a person who has withdrawn libido or interest from current surroundings. For us to probe, then, into the patient's past in search of a cause in childhood will only serve to comply with the patient's desire to refrain from coming to grips with the present difficulties. The questions that should concern us, therefore, are related to the current obstacles that the person cannot overcome, the current tasks and duties that the person is seeking to avoid. Within this framework, the dreams and fantasies of the individual may be regarded as compensations for unfulfilled adaptations to reality. Jung thus questioned not only the psychoanalytic emphasis on sexuality but its focus on the past. However, his most startling innovation was the concept of the collective unconscious (Jung, 1916).

Jung called the long-recognized and much-discussed unconscious processes of the individual, those stressed by the Freudians, the *personal unconscious.* The *collective unconscious* refers to those mental processes operating within the person's awareness that are a product, not of the person's particular development, but of the development of the human race. Over countless years, Jung explained, our brains have been shaped and influenced and conditioned by the past history of the human race. The supposed result of this racial development is that each person has inherited unconscious sets or tendencies to experience and understand certain persons and events in a universal way. Jung called these preexistent forms of apprehension *archetypes.* The archetypes are illustrated by our unlearned propensity to react to birth and death, the rising and setting of the sun, and the earth and the sea with certain characteristic feelings and perceptions.

Primordial images, later also termed *archetypes* by Jung, are said to exist in the collective unconscious. These images of power, of the sun, of the hero, of the earth mother find expression in myths, folklore, dreams, religions, and mental disorders. Since the archetypes help determine our perception of the world, it is upon the inherited foundation of the collective unconscious that the entire structure of personality is erected (Fordham, 1953).

The collective unconscious and the personal unconscious were viewed by Jung as repositories of wisdom from the racial and individual past. Therefore, Jung thought that by dipping into the unconscious armed with understanding, people could gain knowledge that would help them to overcome their present frustrations. Dreams, in this context, would then become helpful guides for the solution of life's problems. This is because people, according to Jung, are constantly striving to progress to a more complete stage of development in which all their functions and processes may be acknowledged, integrated, and expressed. Pointing the way to go are symbols from the unconscious, which indicate those aspects of personality that have been repressed and ignored and that thus represent profitable lines of future growth (Jung, 1916).

Few psychologists begrudged Jung his optimistic orientation; more found it difficult to agree with his contention that human behavior is determined not only by the past but also by supposed aims and aspirations for completion and fulfillment; most, being good empiricists and Darwinians, favored natural selection and rejected his concept of a collective unconscious, with its Lamarckian-flavored inheritance of acquired characteristics, which in this case are thoughts (though there is no necessary incompatibility between the two evolutionary processes). It was this very collective unconscious that inspired Solomon (1916–1917), a reviewer of Jung's book *Psychology of the Unconscious,* to write, "Jung has presented us, in all sincerity and with the full force of his personality and the very fire of his soul, with a system of ideas than which, spite the many truths included, the undersigned can conceive of none that is a greater menace to mankind and modern civilization." Most psychologists did not share Solomon's alarm, in part because a large majority had not felt obliged to read Jung's book.

In general, it seems fair to say that the chief significance, to contemporary psychologists, of the theoretical writings of those who had broken with Freud was the fact that the psychoanalytic movement was crumbling within. Many psychologists who followed these developments with interest—and a touch of satisfaction—believed that further breaks with Freud would take place. Within a few years, they predicted, the young renegades would modify psychoanalysis to take into account the criticisms that had been made of it. There did not seem to be much point in excitedly attacking a theory already showing signs of moving toward moderation, or perhaps disintegration.

Nevertheless, nothing originating within the United States, or anywhere else for that matter, rivaled psychoanalytic theory and its derivatives in scope, depth, and comprehensiveness. Further, despite the personal disagreements, psychoanalysis was still vital. American formulations, by comparison, seemed pale, plodding, and fragmentary, restrained and cautious, and lacking dramatic fire and sweep. The emotions of American psychologists appeared to be channeled, for the most part, into heated discussions about definitions of their science and its course.

Woodworth made an effort to achieve peace among the structuralists, functionalists, behaviorists, analysts, self psychologists, and anyone else interested by proposing dynamic psychology for everyone's approval. The term *dynamic psychology* had been in circulation for a number of years. F. L. Wells and J. H. McCurdy had used it in writing on wishes, conflicts, emotions, tendencies, and inhibitions. Thorndike (1906) had used it for "the mind in action" and such processes as learning and forgetting. T. V. Moore used it in a restricted sense to imply emotion and conation. R. Dodge was mainly concerned with physiological processes and functioning, and therefore when he suggested, in 1913, that cortical operations could be measured "psychodynamically," he had in mind recording pulse and respiration rates.

It was not until Woodworth (1918) that anyone seriously advocated using *dynamic psychology* as a rubric embracing all the various schools of psychological thought. However, Woodworth did not really help his cause by stretching the term to include both the "working of the mind" and the working of the whole organism.

Few psychologists cared for his vague definition. What aroused more interest in the book than its attempt to achieve a compromise was its challenge to McDougall's view that the source energies (or motivation) for all behavior were derived from instincts. Woodworth preferred to speak in terms of "mechanisms" and "drives." A mechanism, he thought, is a course of behavior that brings about an adjustment, whereas "the drive is a mechanism already aroused and thus in a position to furnish stimulation to other mechanisms" (Woodworth, 1918).

Woodworth also held that "any mechanism might be a drive." Therefore, what had been a means to an end might also become an end in itself. For example, a person might have hunted to obtain food but later continues the activity of hunting because it becomes interesting in and of itself, even when food is no longer desired or obtained. For an activity "to be interesting," Woodworth added, "the process must present some difficulty and yet some prospect of a successful issue." It seemed reasonable to Woodworth, as it might to any person who enjoyed being with people and roaming the outdoors, that instincts did not have to be invoked to explain behaviors such as sports and social activities, since they were so intrinsically stimulating and pleasurable (Woodworth, 1932).

The immediate response to Woodworth's book, given his professed aim of unifying psychology, was not gratifying. Although Woodworth was to serve increasingly as a symbol and rallying point for a middle-of-the-road position in psychology, the next 10 years were distinguished more by contentiousness between theoretical schools and systems than by harmony. There was no noticeable rush among psychologists to leap aboard the dynamic bandwagon, and even those who might have been expected to be sympathetic seemed only to have been antagonized. Probably the most obvious case of personal injury was the reaction of the *Psychological Clinic*. Its review of *Dynamic Psychology* noted that clinical psychology had not been specifically included, nor its areas of interest adequately covered. The book was dismissed contemptuously as " 'brass instrument psychology,' with the instruments cunningly concealed from the public," in other words, as still expressive of too narrow an orientation.

DIAGNOSTIC TECHNIQUES

Clearly dominating the field of testing during this period was the Binet-Simon scale, including its revisions and derivatives. At the beginning of the decade, a prominent Italian physician, Sante de Sanctis, was using mental tests of his own making to evaluate intellectual deficiency in the feebleminded, while Goddard, who had coined the term "moron" to designate the highest grade of feeblemindedness, was pursuing investigations with the Binet-Simon scale that would shortly convince him of its great value (Watson, 1953).

In 1911, Goddard published his revision of the 1908 Binet scale. Some items were shifted about and new ones were introduced; his scale gained quick and wide acceptance. Also, a revision by O. Bobertag appeared in Germany, and Binet presented another revision of his own.

Many criticisms had been directed at the Binet-Simon scale, although almost everyone liked the idea of grouping items according to the age at which most children passed them. The comments of two critics may serve to typify the remarks of many. Ayres (1911–1912) was dissatisfied because the scale was too heavily weighted with tests involving verbalizations and the child's acquisition of knowledge. For example, the child might be asked to give the date, identify coins, write a sentence, and read a passage. Such tests did not seem to him to be a measure of judgment, which is how Binet and Simon defined intelligence, nor did they seem to be the right kind to evaluate a child's inherited intellectual ability, which is what most psychologists of that day wanted to assess and many thought they were actually measuring.

Moreover, Terman's use of the scale convinced him that it was too easy at the younger age levels and too difficult at the upper ages. He recommended a radical reclassification of items. He also thought it would be more judicious to express the score in terms of "test age" rather than "mental age." As a further safeguard against making too much of the score and misjudging native ability, Terman recommended that each child be rated as to his or her physiological age and that a comparison then be made between the two age levels, intellectual and physiological. Yet these criticisms did not diminish the enormous respect for the scale. Terman (1911–1912) expressed the confidence of a large number of his fellow psychologists when he concluded, "I believe that it is possible for the psychologist to submit, after a forty-five minute diagnostication, a more reliable and more enlightening estimate of the child's intelligence than most teachers can offer after a year of daily contact in the classroom."

After it had taken some of these recommendations into account, Binet's 1911 scale extended from 3 years of age to an adult level, but with gaps at 11, 13, and 14 years. The score was still expressed in terms of mental age and was interpreted as follows: If a child's mental age equaled his or her chronological age, the child was considered "regular" (average) in intelligence; if the mental age was higher, the child was "advanced"; if the mental age was lower, the child was "retarded."

Further, Binet continued to emphasize the importance of the qualitative aspects of performance. He suggested a possible way of differentiating among the total group of retardates by noting the means by which the children are able to maintain social relations. Idiots can do no more than communicate by gestures; imbeciles are able to maintain contact with others by speech; morons can learn to relate to people through writing (Varnon, 1936).

Following Binet's death, Henri Pieron succeeded to the position of Director of the Laboratory of Physiological Psychology at the Sorbonne. Victor Henri, Binet's earlier collaborator, had switched his interests from experimental psychology to physical chemistry and then to theoretical physics. Simon, however, continued his work in the field of mental retardation.

Nevertheless, despite the improvements that had been effected, a general feeling of annoyance with the Binet-Simon scale persisted. This irritation was that as the child grew, the intelligence score expressed as mental age also grew, assuming a normal course of development. There was thus no way of knowing from the child's mental age alone how intelligent he or she was in relation to peers. It was also thought to be confusing to have mental age increase, since few psychologists then believed it possible for intelligence to increase. A solution that would simplify things and indicate the brightness of a particular child was proposed by Stern in 1912 (an English translation of his book was published in 1914), Stern (1914) suggested dividing the child's mental age by the chronological age. He called the result of this mathematical computation a "mental quotient." If the child is of normal intelligence, the mental quotient is 1.00; quotients above or below 1.00 indicate, respectively, superior or inferior intelligence. It follows that since mental and chronological ages should increase concurrently, the mental quotient would presumably furnish a relatively stable index of intelligence throughout childhood. This seemed to be a simple solution to the problem.

At least two more revisions of the Binet scale were published in 1912; one by Kuhlmann and one by Terman and Childs. Meanwhile, back at the Psychological Clinic of the University of Pennsylvania, Witmer, never one to by swayed by a crowd, was hard at work with his colleagues on standardizing and obtaining norms for performance on certain tasks (Fernberger, 1931). R. H. Sylvester standardized the Seguin Form Board in 1913, but it proved too large and cumbersome to use comfortably with children. Witmer suggested adding another block and making the whole instrument smaller, more attractive, and easier to handle. The result, the Witmer Form Board, was standardized in 1916 by H. H. Young. Two years later, in 1918, the Witmer Cylinders were standardized by F. C. Paschal and Gladys G. Ide. This was a circular board with holes of varying diameters and heights into which appropriate cylinders could be fitted.

The Knox Cubes Test, an instrument used to assess the intelligence of illiterate immigrants at Ellis Island, appeared in 1914. The testee was required to tap cubes in a specified order. That same year, Healy (1914) published his Picture Completion Test. This test involved completing a picture that had had parts removed; the testee had to select from an assortment of pieces those that seemed most appropriate and then insert them in their proper positions. Another version of this test was introduced in 1917 and was used by psychological examiners in the army during World War I.

Robert Yerkes (1876–1956), J. W. Bridges, and R. S. Hardwick (1915) came out with their revision of the Binet scale. Yerkes received his PhD from Harvard in 1901, and from 1913 he was employed half-time as a psychologist at the Boston Psychopathic Hospital. The major innovation introduced by Yerkes's test was the use of a point scale: Items were grouped according to the processes they supposedly measured (e.g., memory and motor coordination) and were arranged in order of increasing difficulty. Each item carried a certain number of points. The testee's score was divided by the average score of other individuals of the same age, yielding a coefficient of intellectual ability (CIA), which was an index similar to Stern's mental quotient. However, despite its merits, Yerkes's scale was soon overshadowed by Terman's revision of 1916.

Lewis M. Terman (1877–1956), whose early years were spent as a farmboy in Indiana, recalled fondly that his childhood friends included a veritable collection of cases in abnormal psychology: a seriously disturbed youngster, a pathological liar, a crippled boy prone to stealing and temper tantrums, and a fellow who was a "lightening calculator." In 1892, Terman entered Central Normal College in Danville, Indiana, and by the age of 21 had earned three academic degrees from that institution, which unfortunately at that time carried little weight beyond the village limits. He became principal of a local high school, married, and became a father.

Yet Terman's ambition was to teach psychology, and for that he needed a degree from a recognized school. So in 1901 he borrowed $1200 and enrolled at Indiana University. Within two years he had a BA and an MA. Borrowing another $1200, he accepted a fellowship at Clark in 1903. What impressed him most about the psychology department at Clark was the freedom it gave students. To register, each graduate student simply told his or her name and the desired courses to Hall's secretary. Of all the courses he took, Terman thought Hall's Monday evening seminar was the best.

Each meeting began with two students reporting on their work. Following their presentations, Hall would comment generously, express some doubts, and then allow his victims to be attacked by the group. Terman's reaction was as follows:

> I always went home dazed and intoxicated, lying awake for hours rehearsing the clever things I should have said and did not. If there is any pedagogical device better adjusted to put a man on his mettle than a seminar thus conducted, I do not know what it is. To know that his contribution would be subjected to merciless criticism from every angle was enough to arouse even a naturally indolent person to Herculean effort. (Terman, 1932, p. 316)

Terman's childhood interests persisted and found expression in the study of the retarded and the gifted. He received his doctorate in 1905 with a thesis on mental tests. Because he had suffered a pulmonary hemorrhage and had been advised to live in a warm climate, Terman accepted the position of principal in a high school in San Bernardino, California. The next year he became professor of child study and pedagogy at Los Angeles State Normal School and from there went on to become professor of education at Stanford.

Around 1910, Terman was introduced to the Binet-Simon scale by a colleague, E. B. Huey, who had worked with Adolf Meyer at Johns Hopkins. Terman set himself the task of improving the scale and making it suitable for American children. Apparently, he regarded himself as a quiet individual who could make up for a lack of intellectual brilliance by careful, well-designed research. We know for certain that Terman considered himself an introvert, and that he was repelled by the self-confidence of Spearman and Thorndike and the "looseness" of Hall's studies with the questionnaire method.

Terman's revision (Stanford Revision of the Binet-Simon Scale) was standardized on 2,100 children and 180 adults. It covered a range from 3 years of age to a "superior adult" level, but there were no tests for the 11th year. The score was expressed as a mental age, and this could be converted into an intelligence quotient, or IQ; the latter score was simply Stern's mental quotient multiplied by 100 to eliminate the decimal point (Terman, 1916).

From the distribution of IQs obtained with the scale, Terman suggested a classification scheme: An IQ from 90 to 109 indicates average intelligence, an IQ below 70 indicates definite feeblemindedness; an IQ above 140 indicates genius. Much to Terman's pleasure and surprise, the Stanford revision soon became the most widely used individual scale of intelligence in the United States. In its reliability and validity it was a definite improvement over the Binet scale. Nevertheless, many of the criticisms directed at the Binet scale could be leveled at Terman's revision with equal justification.

There was still an overemphasis on verbal skills, so that the measures obtained on the foreign born and those handicapped in expressing themselves linguistically were spuriously low. Each individual task set by the test was so brief that it was difficult to evaluate an individual's persistence (this was a problem hard to avoid, since the brevity of items was deliberate and was intended to help maintain a child's interest). Without an 11th year level, the scale was really only satisfactory through the tenth year, for it was difficult to know what interpretation to give if a child passed all the items at 10 and failed all the items at 12.

Furthermore, there was still the question of what significance, if any, was to be attached to the "spread of scores" or "range of irregularity" or "scatter" (i.e., test performance where the successes of the person are distributed over several age levels). Some psychologists thought wide scatter was specific to defectives and indicated an unequal development of abilities among retardates. However, John E. W. Wallin (1917–1918) found that normals had about as much scatter as the retarded, which seemed quickly to explode that hypothesis. He did note greater scatter among epileptics and the insane but judiciously advised further investigation before accepting the validity of his observations.

Augusta Bronner (1916) described some additional variables that had to be considered in evaluating an individual's test performance. Taking her lead from

Thorndike's comment that "it is a general law of behavior that the responses to any external situation is dependent upon the condition of the man as well as upon the nature of the situation," she argued that certain test-taking attitudes could adversely affect scores. Her experiences while testing delinquents at Healy's clinic made her sensitive to factors such as deliberate deception, recalcitrancy, sportiveness, general depression, anger, resentfulness, fear, shyness, embarrassment due to onlookers, homesickness, nervous excitement, feelings of shame, and lack of confidence. Naturally, when a child adopts such "attitudes" as these, the level of performance is often lowered. Yet all too frequently such variables were not taken into account when it would have been pertinent to do so.

In 1917, Bronner pointed out that a child might have special disabilities that could lead to an invalid estimate of intelligence. Since at that time it was thought that children who could not read were probably retarded, she particularly stressed the possibility of special reading handicaps in children of average intellectual ability. The findings of Bridges and Coler (1917) of a high correlation between the intelligence of children and their fathers' occupational status raised another question. Is such a correlation due to heredity or environment? Although no conclusive answer was immediately available, the host of issues surrounding the IQ score made it apparent to clinicians that the administration and interpretation of an intelligence test could not wisely be entrusted to the inexperienced and untrained.

To aid in solving the problem of estimating the intelligence of children who were deaf, who were handicapped in their reading, or who were impaired in speaking English because they were immigrants or the children of immigrants, psychologists began combining several performance tests into what they hoped would be, with much work, a valid scale. Among the first of these performance scales was one constructed by Healy and Grace Fernald. However, the Pintner-Paterson (1917) scale was the earliest of this group to be standardized and to enjoy a measure of continued popularity. This scale was composed of 15 tests, including various form boards, Healy's Picture Completion Test, and the Knox Cubes Test. Unfortunately, as was the case with other performance tests, the scores on the Pintner-Paterson were not found to have a high correlation with the scores obtained on verbal scales, such as the Binet scale.

With the entry of the United States into World War I, Robert Yerkes (1919), who had just been elected president of the APA, became chairman of a committee of five experimental psychologists working within the medical department of the army. The committee's task was to devise methods of classifying men according to their abilities. Arthur S. Otis, who had been working on a group intelligence test, assisted the committee in developing an appropriate scale. (The members of the committee, which had its number increased from five to seven, were Yerkes, W. V. Bingham, Goddard, T. H. Haines, Terman, G. M. Whipple, and F. L. Wells.) The committee's products included a group intelligence test known as the Army Alpha, which was a verbal scale that sampled such abilities as following directions, solving problems in arithmetic, supplying synonyms and antonyms, and displaying practical judgment; another group intelligence test, known as the

Army Beta, which was nonverbal; and the Personal Data Sheet, a neurotic inventory designed by Robert Woodworth (1917) that contained such questions as, "Do you feel sad or low-spirited most of the time? Did you ever walk in your sleep?"

A school of military psychology was established at the Medical Officer's Training Camp, Fort Oglethorpe, Georgia, to provide instruction for the psychologists who were going to be testers in the army. One of the "recruits" was the experimentalist Edwin G. Boring, who later served as chief psychological examiner at Camp Upton, Long Island. Boring found the experience refreshing and broadening: "I learned about testing and about theory of probabilities, and I discovered also that the mental testers among the psychologists were, like the experimentalists, honest, sincere, intelligent, eighty-hour-a-week psychologists" (Boring, 1952, p. 35).

During the war, 1,726,000 men were tested in groups and 83,000 were examined individually. Over 500,000 were found to be illiterate, about 8,000 were recommended for discharge on the basis of low intelligence, and about 20,000 were placed in special battalions for observation and further training or put to work on intellectually nondemanding tasks. About 3% of the nation's young males were found to have a mental age below 10 years, and the average mental age of American soldiers was found to be only 13.5 years. Wide publicity was given these findings and the country was shocked. The United States seemed to be a nation of childish mentality!

Some psychologists unfortunately managed to get swept along in the stream of unwarranted inferences from the results of mental testing and found themselves out on a limb. Edgar Doll argued that since the average mental age of recruits was 13.5 years, mental growth in the average person probably stopped at 13 years. However, other psychologists took a look at the same statistics and saw little to justify coming to such a conclusion. Yoakum and Yerkes (1920) pointed out that the tests sampled a limited range of abilities, and therefore a person might score low on them yet have other skills to a superior degree. Freeman (1920) made a similar point, contending that the tests failed to adequately sample abilities ordinarily found in adults. Though the reservations of Yerkes, Yoakum, and Freeman were well taken, the pubic tended to share the gloomy appraisal of the journalist H. L. Mencken that a new breed of man was being spawned in the Western Hemisphere: Boobus Americanus.

In 1919, the APA committee on mental tests, which had been organized in 1906, peacefully passed away. Each member of the committee had succeeded in developing tests to suit his own interests: in 1911, Woodworth and Wells produced their association tests; Pillsbury worked on the determination of the auditory limen; Judd devised tests of motor processes; Angell pursued research on ideational types; and Seashore contributed to the growth of special aptitude testing by his efforts to discover musical talent through measures of rhythm, pitch discrimination, and memory for tones.

Turning now to the techniques intended to diagnose psychiatric disturbances, we find Kent and Rosanoff (1910) hoping to detect insanity by noting the number of atypical free associations produced in responding to a list of 100 words. First, they had to find out what were the typical responses. They did that by administering the list to a thousand "normal" persons and then carefully tabulating the results. Their next step was to administer the list to 250 "insane" patients. They found that patients diagnosed as having dementia praecox produced many atypical responses but those diagnosed as paranoiac and epileptic did not; they considered the free association technique promising.

In 1912, Grace Fernald came out with a set of character tests purporting to measure moral consciousness. A little later Rosanoff and Rosanoff (1913) published their research on the free associations of children. It had been noted earlier that youngsters frequently gave idiosyncratic responses to the words, and they wondered at what age children started to give associations similar to those of adults. Testing 300 children of varying ages, they found that by age 11 there was a considerable decrease in the frequency of doubtful and individual responses.

Woodworth's Psychoneurotic Inventory of 1917, labeled the Personal Data Sheet to appear innocuous to those taking it, was the first questionnaire designed to detect and measure abnormal behavior. It was intended as a rough screening device, and it served this purpose adequately.

There were few techniques designed for the evaluation of personality disturbances or functioning. This paucity may be attributed in part to the newness of the field of mental testing in general and in part to the much greater involvement of psychologists in what they considered to be pedagogical and educational rather than emotional problems. Of course, psychologists were quite successful in devising valid techniques for educational purposes, and by this time they could point with defensible pride to a variety of instruments for the measurement of intelligence. Unfortunately, in the heady warmth of public recognition, some of them lost sight of the limitations of their tests and took the scores they obtained at face value. Their error was made more poignant by Binet's forewarning against it. The movement, however, progressed—by increasing the number and diversity of tests, by making a greater effort to delineate the host of variables that might affect results, and by laying a firm foundation of healthy skepticism about the adequacy of the instruments.

DIAGNOSTIC FORMULATIONS

The ideas of Alfred Adler (1870–1937) were receiving considerable attention from psychologists and psychiatrists. What appealed to members of both groups was Adler's minimization of sexuality. Further, his emphasis on organic problems as causing feelings of inadequacy and distress made his theory especially palatable to the medical profession.

Adler, the son of a grain merchant in Vienna, was fond of recalling two events from early in his childhood. At the age of 4, when he overheard a physician telling his parents that he was in danger of dying from pneumonia, he resolved to recover from his illness and devote his life to the profession of medicine (Adler, 1962). At the age of 10, when he was failing in mathematics, he learned that his teacher had advised his father to apprentice him to a cobbler on the grounds that continuing his schooling would be a waste of time. In consequence, he resolved to apply himself to his studies and actually became the best student of mathematics in his class (Ansbacher & Ansbacher, 1956).

Adler received his MD from the University of Vienna Medical School in 1895. He began by specializing in ophthalmology, perhaps because his own vision was impaired. However, he soon turned to general medicine and became involved with Freud. Their friendly relationship formally ended in 1911, but Adler claimed he had never agreed that neuroses originated from early sexual trauma. Starting about 1907, Adler began to express his own views on the genesis of neurotic behavior.

At first Adler asserted that aggression was a more important drive than sex. Aggression seemed to be transformed or expressed in a variety of forms, including competition, altruism (when aggression was reversed in overt behavior), and anxiety (when aggression was turned upon the self). However, Adler soon abandoned the centrality of the concept of aggression, replacing it with the "will to power." He regarded the will to power as a masculine characteristic and "weakness" as typically feminine. By 1911, Adler's theory went somewhat as follows.

Neuroses have their origin in a child's feelings of weakness and inferiority. These feelings arise from the existence of a part of the body that has not developed or does not function properly. The child becomes aware of this defect and therefore feels inadequate. There are several ways to handle inferiority feelings. One is to demand support and affection from parents or other adults. This may prove to be a useful solution, since it at least helps the child's social development. Another solution is to acquire "attitudes" that compensate for the feelings of inadequacy, such as indulging in fantasy or being frequently disobedient. A third is to attempt to overcompensate for the inferior body part by striving to excel in just those functions that are adversely affected (e.g., a boy with weak legs forces himself to exercise and eventually becomes a runner in track). However, a form of overcompensation frequently found among neurotics is the "masculine protest," an attempt on the part of the individual to surpass the father in every respect, to become stronger than the father, to outdo and even dominate him.

Although Adler did not deny the importance of sex, he considered it of minor significance. The symptoms of neurotics were, for him, not compromises between impulses and repressing forces but attempts to deny feelings of inadequacy and protests against parents and others.

Following his break with Freud and the development of his own theory, which he called *individual psychology,* Adler continued to revise and extend his theory. By 1920, he no longer believed that there actually had to be a defective body part for a neurosis to occur. Instead, he emphasized the individual's subjective feelings of inferiority or incompleteness as the great driving force.

The philosopher Hans Vaihinger had claimed that all persons were guided in their behavior by fictions or beliefs that tended to grow into dogmas. Adler was impressed by Vaihinger's ideas and incorporated them into his theoretical system (Hall & Lindzey, 1957). He asserted that the neurotic person clings more intensely and rigidly than the normal person to some guiding fiction or ideal and attempts to make it into a reality: "The formula, 'I want to be a real man,' is the guiding fiction . . . in every neurosis, where it demands realization to a higher degree than in the normal psyche" (Adler, 1927, p. 35).

If we could discover the unique fiction or goal of the person, Adler believed we would be in a good position to predict behavior. Among neurotics, the general goal is to be big, to be powerful, to enhance self-esteem. It does not matter that the individual may in reality be physically big or in a position of power, since we are dealing with subjective evaluations and feelings. To safeguard self-esteem, neurotics may depreciate other people or things in their environment, blame other people for their own failures, or reproach themselves and in so doing maintain the fiction that they can achieve their goals. Regardless of the specific tactics, their general aim is to feel secure. Yet in this process the neurotic becomes farther removed from reality and less able to adjust to the demands of society. Adler was thus led to the formulation that mental disease is the result of feelings of inferiority and external demands imposed upon the individual to live sociably within the culture.

An article about Adler's theory appeared in the United States in 1915 (Tanner), and 2 years later the psychiatrist William Alanson White (1917–1918) commented favorably on his concepts. Soon psychologists and psychiatrists everywhere were talking about feelings of inferiority and compensations. Even G. Stanley Hall announced that he endorsed the Adlerian position over that of psychoanalysis. Freud, though hurt by Hall's statement, was not visibly impressed by individual psychology, which he regarded as being in essence an ego psychology and therefore too one-sided and neglectful of instinctual forces. Nonetheless, Freud's ideas were also changing (Jones, 1955).

By 1913, Freud had interpreted obsessional neuroses as fixations or regression to the anal-sadistic stage of development. He thought hysteric and obsessive-compulsive neuroses (the "classical" neuroses) generally came about when sexual impulses had to be restrained because they had grown beyond the capacity of the ego to handle them. Freud was aware of traumatic or "actual" neuroses, such as combat neuroses, and extended his theory to take them into account.

Shortly after the onset of World War I, it was observed that soldiers developed neurotic symptoms and much attention was given these disorders. At first, psychiatrists thought the explosions of shells produced minute cortical lesions and that this damage to the brain in turn produced the disorder. Hence, they called this disturbance shell shock. But soon it was noted, at least in the Canadian army, that the neurotic symptoms differed according to the rank of the soldier: Officers seemed to suffer mainly anxiety states whereas enlisted personnel usually evidenced symptoms of hysteria. This observation seemed to rule out an organic explanation, unless one could demonstrate how the same exploding shells produced discriminatory lesions among commissioned and noncommissioned officers. At any rate, a Canadian psychiatrist, S. I. Schwabb (1919–1920), claimed that the war neuroses were a personal response of the individual to trauma and that this response represented a compromise between the soldier's wish to preserve himself and his sense of obligation to his comrades and country.

Freud offered a similar explanation in terms of intrapsychic conflict within the ego. This conflict was experienced as a struggle between two ego ideals (Freud, 1959e): the soldier's desire to preserve and enhance himself versus his sense of duty, loyalty, and honor. The ego, weakened by this internal narcissistic warfare, might easily become overwhelmed by threatening external stimulation, thus causing a regression and a neurosis. Significantly, Freud explained the genesis of war neuroses, not by repressed sexuality, but by a clash between opposing value systems existing within a single hypothetical structure of the mind, the ego.

If we look at this issue more broadly, we see that shell shock produced by brain damage versus war neuroses produced by internal conflict was but one example in the repeated clash between two points of view within both psychiatry and psychology: hereditary and organic as opposed to environmental and psychological explanations of etiology. Any territory not demonstrably staked out by those favoring an organic view was quickly claimed by the other side. For example, Edith Spaulding, a psychologist working with Healy, stated in 1913 that the studies conducted at the Juvenile Psychopathic Clinic and elsewhere had failed to demonstrate any conclusive proof that criminality was hereditary; ergo, environmental factors had to be considered responsible for criminal behavior. Whatever one may think about the truth of this conclusion, the logic by which it was derived is certainly faulty. Yet it is also true that, unlike genetic variables, psychological and environmental factors are not hard to find, and so directing one's efforts toward investigating them can be more immediately rewarding and might ultimately lead to the truth of the matter.

Thus there began a deluge of information about neighborhoods, living conditions, the companions of delinquents, and school adjustments or maladjustments and their effects on crime. Yet there still seemed to be few data about the effects of emotional interrelationships within families.

In 1917, Healy hit upon the idea of asking delinquents to tell their "own story" about their feelings and attitudes toward parents and others. From these interviews, Healy concluded that delinquents are emotionally disturbed and in need of some sort of treatment. More specifically, it seemed to him that there is always some unconscious experience involved in bringing about the delinquency, though there are invariably a number of other factors, such as poor parental relationships, that have to be present to account fully for the behavior (Healy, 1915). Much interest was aroused in Healy's findings and in his novel technique of asking the children to tell him how they felt (Healy & Bronner, 1948).

In 1915, Freud held that one factor in criminality is an unconscious sense of guilt. The criminal breaks the law in order to provoke society into punishing him, thereby alleviating his guilt feelings. Thus aggression directed outward against society can at times be viewed as basically a form of aggression directed against oneself. By the same token, aggression directed against oneself can be viewed as aggression directed against someone else. Citing the extreme case of suicide, Freud commented, "Probably no one finds the mental energy required to kill himself unless, in the first place, he is in doing this at the same time killing an object (someone) with whom he had identified himself" (Freud, 1959f, p. 220).

Also in 1911, Freud interpreted the delusions of paranoia as denials of repressed homosexuality through the use of projection. Instead of experiencing the thought that he loves another man, the paranoiac denies it and claims he hates him; then, finding his own hatred intolerable, he projects it and so believes the man hates him. Therefore, delusions may be considered more or less successful attempts at resolving a conflict. Freud arrived at these views on the basis of studying the diary of a man named Daniel Schreber, who suffered from paranoid schizophrenia (Freud, 1959g).

The psychological explanations proposed by Freud, Adler, Healy, and others were novel. They were considerably at variance with the organic explanations for crime and mental illness that were predominant within psychology and widely accepted by the public. It was generally believed that the criminal, the epileptic, the defective, and the insane genetically transmitted their disturbances to their offspring. Here were new views challenging those beliefs and directing attention from inborn characteristics toward the problems and conflicts with which all individuals contend in their everyday lives.

Occupying a middle-of-the-road position was the work of Bleuler, who published his monograph *Dementia praecox, oder die Gruppe der Schizophrenien* in 1911. Bleuler argued that dementia praecox is not a disease entity, is not invariably incurable, and does not always progress to dementia. Instead, he suggested, there is a group of diseases, which he named *schizophrenia.*

The major symptom of schizophrenia is a splitting of various mental processes or a disorder in the train of associations. Thus schizophrenic patients are more or less incoherent and illogical in their thinking and speech. His description of the course of the disease was quite different from Kraepelin's description of the course of dementia praecox: "This disease [schizophrenia] may come to a standstill at any stage, and many of its symptoms may clear up very much, or altogether, but if it progresses it leads to a dementia of definite character." Furthermore, Bleuler believed a large number of cases of schizophrenia are latent. Latent schizophrenics are never hospitalized, because their behavior, although odd, is not severely symptomatic.

Among the symptoms of schizophrenia described and named by Bleuler are two that soon became widely known: ambivalence and autism. Ambivalence is the state of simultaneously having two opposite feelings toward the same person, usually both love and hate. Autism is a turning away from reality. An autistic person lives in a fantasy world in which the person's thoughts, wishes, and fears seem reasonable to him or her, though to others they appear illogical, symbolic, and not tied to reality. Bleuler not only considered autistic thinking a schizophrenic phenomenon but also claimed it appeared normally among children and even among adults when they are swayed by their emotions.

Although Bleuler thought schizophrenia was curable, and although he offered psychogenic, often Freudian, interpretations of its symptoms, he believed that the disease process itself was probably organic in origin, perhaps caused by some toxin in the body. It should be noted that there is no incompatibility between an organic cause of a disease and its alleviation. Thus in the space of a few years, the supposedly incurable illness described by Kraepelin, dementia praecox, was beginning to be analyzed as a group of reactions that could be ameliorated.

During this period, Kraepelin (1919) was far from idle, and he participated in some of the changes taking place within psychiatry. Although he continued, understandably enough, to use much of his own terminology, he joined with Bleuler in broadening the conception of psychosis. In 1913, Kraepelin described constitutional personality types that evidence to a lesser degree symptoms displayed by the mentally ill. There is the autistic personality, characterized primarily by relatively little interest in the external environment and by a preoccupation with thoughts and fantasies. Kraepelin regarded a predisposition to autistic behavior as the constitutional basis for dementia praecox. Further, he believed that there are distinguishable subtypes of the autistic personality that are similar to the subtypes of the psychosis, though of course the symptoms are not as extreme. He also described the cyclothymic personality, which exhibits in milder forms the behaviors that distinguish manic-depressive psychoses. Here, too, Kraepelin differentiated subtypes: manic, depressive, irascible, and emotionally unstable (Zilboorg & Henry, 1941).

Nineteen thirteen was a busy year for theorizing about personality types. It was in this year that Jung introduced his distinction between introversion and extraversion. Jung explained that the major difference between the two types concerns the direction of their psychic energy. Introverts direct their psychic energy centripetally (i.e., away from the environment and toward the self), and hence they seldom express their feelings overtly. Patients with dementia praecox seemed to Jung to have personalities of the introvert type. Extraverts direct their psychic energy centrifugally (i.e., toward the environment and away from the self), and hence they tend to express their feelings overtly and in an exaggerated manner. Patients with hysteria, Jung (1920) thought, have personalities of the extravert type.

Freud also spoke of the constitutional factors that were involved in the genesis of neuroses and psychoses. But having little to say on the subject other than that such factors were a part of their etiology, he pushed on with his psychoanalytic interpretations. Perhaps it was a matter of emphasis rather than a choice between mutually exclusive alternatives, although at the time many people seemed to think that if an illness had an organic cause, psychological variables were excluded, and vice versa. Yet no one could deny that certain mental diseases were organic in origin, and with the advance of science it was only reasonable to expect discoveries of bodily causes for additional psychiatric disturbances. It seemed to follow that with the finding of a definite tangible cause, all that was needed to be said was said, and it remained only to find a remedy for the illness.

The organic position thus appeared to be the position of strength. This position was buttressed in 1913 when Hideyo Noguchi and J. W. Moore conclusively demonstrated the presence of the spirochete *Treponema palidum* in paretic brains. General paresis was caused by syphilis and that was that (Zilboorg & Henry, 1941).

Among the minority of psychiatrists stressing psychological variables was Adolf Meyer. In 1910, he became professor of psychiatry at Johns Hopkins and, in 1913, also director of the Phipps Clinic. Through his training of psychiatrists, Meyer was able to impress his viewpoint upon a considerable portion of the profession. What he wished his students to realize was that mental activity should be understood as the adaptation of the individual as a whole.

Meyer called his approach *psychobiology*. The individual is a functioning whole whose organic, sociological, and psychological aspects are all to be considered. Yet often no somatic disorder can be found and the evidence for physical variables at work in the genesis of a psychiatric disturbance is equivocal. In such cases, Meyer urged his students to use such facts as are immediately available—the patient's behavioral life history and present condition. Through studying the past lives of his patients, Meyer found that they had been reacting ineffectively to their problems over long periods of time. Their faulty reactions had become habitual ways of responding to stresses, leading to (1) more severely maladaptive patterns of behavior, (2) greater inability to cope with life, and (3) further difficulties in achieving any constructive adjustments. Meyer concluded that many psychiatric disturbances should be regarded not as diseases but as psychopathological reactions, as disturbances in learning to adjust satisfactorily to the demands of living. He believed the symptoms of neuroses and dementia praecox could be interpreted as inappropriate reactions of the whole organism (Meyer, Jeliffe, & Hoch, 1911).

Meyer's position appealed to many psychiatrists and psychologists because of its simplicity and reasonableness. Moreover, Meyer was respected as an erudite man of good will. His approach stressed the longitudinal study of the individual's reactions to demands to make all kinds of adjustments. Such an approach was readily incorporated into almost every congenial psychological formulation. Thus Meyer's views aroused little opposition or conflict within the field and so lost their association with their original proponent.

Turning to the concept of intelligence, we find the persistence and amplification of the disagreements of the previous decade as well as considerable support for the one-sided view that intelligence is determined solely by heredity. In 1912, Stern defined intelligence as a general mental adaptability to new problems and conditions of life. A few years later, in 1915, Witmer similarly defined it as "the ability of the individual to solve what for him is a new problem." Witmer's views on intelligence differed greatly from the mainstream.

Witmer (1915) stressed that if intelligence *is* the ability to solve new problems, this has many implications for the measurement of intelligence. For example, he believed that retesting a person with the same scale plainly ruled out the possibility of obtaining a valid estimate of intelligence, and he recommended to psychologists that they devise scales that could grade the person's resourcefulness and creativity. It also seemed obvious to Witmer that intelligence scales were measuring, not intelligence, but a level of performance. He had no objection to psychologists doing that, so long as they were clear about what they were doing.

Witmer considered that a person's performance level is the person's average way of performing certain tasks, and he pointed out a variety of different ways in which this level could be evaluated: by age scales, such as the Binet scale; education scales that measure academic achievement; species scales, which would rank humans along with other species or organisms in the performance of a task; civilization scales; masculinity scales; femininity scales; insanity scales; and deficiency scales. Since Witmer was convinced that each type of scale measured a different kind and quality of performance, he warned,

> *The performances of the feebleminded are qualitatively and quantitatively different from the performances of normal children. Every child, normal or feebleminded, can be assigned a level on both the age scale and the deficiency scale. The deficiency scale cannot be superimposed on the age to make a single scale. (Witmer, 1915, p. 73)*

Actually what Witmer meant in that last statement is not "cannot" but "should not," and since he had neither of these scales to offer, practical considerations overruled whatever attention might have been paid to his injunction.

To a group of psychologists, devising a hodgepodge of scales to evaluate intelligence was not such a bad idea. The leading member of this group was Charles Spearman, who was still advocating his two-factor theory: "All the intellective activity of any person depends in some degree on one and the same general fund of mental energy . . . [and] his specific capacity for that particular kind of performance."

Opposing Spearman's position was a group of psychologists whose reluctant champion was Thorndike:

> *Are not our minds made up of an enormous number of highly specialized capacities to operate with particular kinds of problems? Do we have a mind with a capital M that can operate with any kind of material, and on any kind of problem, or are we a bundle of specialized capacities to do particular things? (quote in Winkler & Bromberg, 1939, p. 274)*

Obviously, Thorndike's questions were rhetorical.

Spearman could not for the life of him understand why it was so difficult for his colleagues to see that he was right. Patiently, he would reanalyze and correct their data. With great forbearance, he would answer their criticisms in the hope of resolving "a disquieting scientific discord into firm harmony" (i.e., showing that their findings agreed with his findings).

One critic of Spearman not easily dismissed was Godfrey Thomson (1881–1955). Born in England, Thomson (1952) had graduated from Armstrong College (now King's College, University of London) in 1903 and had received his doctorate in physics and mathematics at Strassburg in 1906. He had returned to Armstrong College to fulfill the obligations of a scholarship and there taught educational psychology. His interests centered on statistics, particularly factor analysis, as they related to psychological problems. In 1916, Thomson found that by throwing dice randomly he could generate a set of artificial test scores that, when analyzed according to Spearman's procedure, yielded a general factor.

After 3 more years of investigating the problem, Thomson (1919) concluded that the reason a general factor was found was that the sampling errors in coefficients of correlation were themselves correlated. The general factor was produced, he claimed, by the random interplay of small independent factors, such as test-taking attitudes and the effect of previous testings. There was thus no general intellective factor.

Spearman was stunned, though only momentarily. Soon he was as confident as ever of the rightness of his original position. Meanwhile, although psychologists disagreed about the definition and structure of intelligence, they and the tests they devised were being used more and more in measuring intellectual functioning and in diagnosing feeblemindedness.

In 1900, the British Royal Commission had defined mental deficiency as social incompetence due to mental incompetence resulting from arrested development of a constitutional, chiefly hereditary, origin. Despite the fact that almost all authorities agreed that social incompetence was an essential element in the concept of mental deficiency, after intelligence tests with some validity had been devised, the temptation became great to diagnose feeblemindedness solely on the basis of the test scores. The American Association for Study of the Feeble-Minded, in 1910, recommended that the diagnosis of feeblemindedness be established by criteria other than test scores but that after the diagnosis had been made, retardates could be classified on the basis of their Binet scale mental ages. In practice, however, the idea of social incompetence tended to be neglected and mental age became the major criterion for making the diagnosis. A mental age of 12 years in adults was generally accepted as the lower limit of normal intelligence, and in 1916 people began rigidly following Terman's suggestion: "All who test below 70 IQ by the Stanford Revision of the Binet-Simon Scale should be considered feebleminded."

At this time the preponderant view was that intelligence and scores on intelligence scales were a function almost exclusively of heredity. Therefore, when studies consistently found the average mental age of blacks to be 2 years lower than that of whites, it was generally believed the black race was of inferior intelligence (Garth, 1925).

Strong support for the hereditary position came from the work of Goddard (1912) in his study of a family he called the Kallikaks. Goddard's findings described the offspring of a man of normal intelligence who at about the time of the American Revolution first mated with an unknown defective girl and then later married a girl of normal intelligence. A defective, illegitimate son of the first union had 480 known descendants; of this lineage, 143 were judged to have had some heredity defect such as low intelligence or criminality. From the second union, 486 descendents were traced, all considered normal. These results aroused much discussion and brought Goddard some degree of fame, which eventually turned into condemnation and notoriety (Kamin, 1974; S. J. Gould, 1981) when the scientific rigor of such genetic research was questioned.

Goddard (1914) followed with another study based on the case histories of 327 families of inmates at the Vineland Training School. The records seemed to indicate to Goddard that when both parents were defective, all the children were defective; when one parent was defective, half the children were defective; and when both parents were normal but a close relative was defective, a fourth of the children were defective. Goddard concluded that feeblemindedness was inherited as a simple recessive Mendelian unit character.

Armed with these data and the means by which feeblemindedness could be diagnosed, Goddard and others vigorously urged the adoption of eugenic measures (e.g., sterilization and segregation of the defective). It was now possible, they believed, to realize Galton's hope of improving the genetic stock of mankind, by sharply reducing the incidence of mental deficiency.

Of course, the actions of legislators are not always motivated solely by idealistic considerations. Many at this time no doubt took into account the possibility that sterilization might reduce the cost of welfare programs, since not only mental deficiency but insanity, criminality, and epilepsy were thought to be genetically determined. The first state to enact a sterilization law was Indiana, in 1907; by 1919, Alabama, California, Connecticut, Kansas, Nebraska, New Hampshire, New York, North Dakota, South Dakota, and Wisconsin had similar legislation. However, perhaps because of the doubts raised about the inclusion of the criminal and the insane, there were qualms about enforcing these laws, and, with the exception of California, sterilization operations were seldom performed. Yet despite the considered reluctance to enforce sterilization laws, their enactment was to continue through the next decade and into the early thirties.

TREATMENT FORMULATIONS

For the majority of patients hospitalized with mental illnesses, the treatment was essentially the same as it had been in previous years: more or less adequate, or sometimes very inadequate, custodial care. However, a virtual revolution took place in the therapy of paresis.

Around 1910, arsphenamine (Salvarsan), an organic compound containing arsenic first used by Paul Ehrlich in antiluetic therapy, began to be employed in arresting the course of paresis. The serum was either injected into the cerebrospinal fluid or was introduced via a trephined opening in the skull. Although reports were favorable, the results still left much to be desired.

A breakthrough came in 1917 when Julius Wagner-Jauregg (1857–1940), an Austrian psychiatrist, inoculated nine paretic patients with tertian malaria. His action was based on the long-known fact that the progress of a serious illness could sometimes be favorably influenced by introducing another, less dangerous, disease. Hippocrates, for example, had commented that people with convulsions were helped when they experienced a quartan [an intermittent fever that recurs every fourth day]. In 1887, Wagner-Jauregg proposed malarial infection for paretics but decided to experiment first with tuberculin injections and typhus. Using malaria, six of the nine patients benefited, and within a short time the induction of fevers became the main treatment for arresting the course of syphilis. To many physicians, all of this demonstrated again that once the physical basis of an illness was known, the means for its amelioration would soon follow. Encouraged, they pushed on in their search for organic causes of functional or psychological diseases (Zilboorg & Henry, 1914).

Boris Sidis (1867–1923), an American psychologist and psychiatrist, thought he had uncovered the cause of mental illness. Before going into his discovery, we should note that Sidis had done some well-received work on hypnotism. In 1898, he had named and described the *hypnoidal state,* a condition in which the subject, after attending to a monotonous stimulus, appears to hover between wakefulness and sleep in a relaxed condition characterized by diminished pulse rate, deep and slow respiration, heightened suggestibility, and recall of previously inaccessible memories.

Sidis (1911–1912) noticed that all his patients either explicitly claimed to be afraid of something or else evidenced behavior indicative of fear. In one of those lapses of logical and sound judgment that even the most careful thinkers are sometimes subject to, Sidis concluded that the cause of all psychopathic diseases was the fear instinct.

Although Sidis's etiological explanation was not generally accepted, some psychiatrists regarded his techniques of treatment with favor. For example, Sidis frequently induced his patients to experience the hypnoidal state. While in that state, the patients often gained some relief from fears, tensions, and worries. The state was essentially a supervised period of relaxation, and virtually all the patients found it acceptable, including those who could not be hypnotized. Sidis thought of the hypnoidal state as an aid to therapy, but some of his colleagues regarded it as a therapy in and of itself.

Early in this decade, the foundation upon which James rested his notions about mental health was attacked by Thorndike. It may be recalled that James advised people to think themselves brave so that they might conquer their fears. This bit of advice was derived from the widely accepted concept of ideomotor action: The idea of a particular form of behavior inherently tends to produce in some degree its corresponding action or movement. Thorndike (1913) not too graciously dismissed ideomotor action as sheer rubbish. He argued that it was analogous to the beliefs of primitive peoples in the power of their thoughts to magically produce effects. Since few psychologists relished the notion that there is any similarity between their thinking processes and those of the South Sea islanders, a dark cloud passed over the concept of ideomotor action and other derivative concepts.

However, mental health is something everyone favors. Its principles are phrased in such inoffensive generalities—for example, many persons are hindered in achieving a happy life by being too sensitive, overly ambitious, and excessively self-deprecatory—that hardly anyone can disagree with them. Yet they have profound implications. "What unfavorable environment causes," F. L. Wells (1914) asserted, "correct external influences can prevent." Therefore, he urged psychologists and psychiatrists to join forces in educating the mentally ill to face their problems squarely and in a socially approved manner.

The principles of mental health, as both implicitly and explicitly applied to the prevention and cure of mental illness, were easily extended to encompass relatively mild problems of adjustment that had not previously been thought of as psychiatric in nature. Further, they seemed to endow psychiatrists and psychologists with the power of solving these problems. There was little questioning of any of these principles, although some psychologists and psychiatrists felt a trifle uneasy about finding themselves in the same strange territory.

Freud was not specifically worried about the assimilation of relatively normal behavior to the domain of psychiatry, but he was concerned about the abuse of psychoanalytic treatment by the untrained. He accordingly addressed himself to two issues: (1) what techniques should be used in psychoanalysis and (2) when should psychoanalytic treatment be advised. Freud warned against the fanatical desire to see everyone undergo analysis. Well-meaning but misguided people were recommending his treatment universally because they naively believed that analysis, if it could not help, at least would not harm. On the contrary, Freud cautioned, some patients would be harmed if deprived of the benefits obtained from their illnesses. He urged his colleagues, before prescribing psychoanalysis, to evaluate the total situation of each prospective patient, carefully consider what effects an improvement would have on the individual's way of life and on the reactions of others to the individual, and weigh the cost of treatment against any advantages that might be gained. It seemed to Freud that there was room in the world for some neuroses.

As far as psychoanalytic techniques were concerned, he advised analysts to be passive in their sessions and to avoid pushing their patients for material. An analyst is always supposed to keep in touch with a patient's current thoughts and feelings and not allow his or her interest in scientific matters to be expressed through any show of enthusiasm about the interpretation of any dream. Otherwise, Freud warned, the patient may exhibit resistance by overwhelming the analyst with dreams or by bringing up no dreams at all during the sessions.

Freud advised against taking notes or using notes because he believed those procedures would interfere with the receptive and spontaneous attitude that he felt analysts should possess. He counseled analysts to keep their personal feelings in the background while at the same time remaining alert to emotions aroused in them by their patients. Feelings experienced by the analyst toward the patient (the problem of countertransference) constitute yet another reason why all those employing Freudian procedures are encouraged to undergo a thorough self-analysis. Freud cautioned that all positive feelings are derived from sexual sources, since "originally it was only sexual objects that we knew" (Freud, 1959e). Therefore, positive feelings tend to be partially irrational and unconsciously determined. Still another problem for analysts to guard against: When unconscious impulses emerge, there may be an attempt by patients to put them into action or act them out.

As Freud recognized, all these issues make the analyst's task far from easy. Yet there is one saving piece of advice, which Freud announced in 1913: The analysis should proceed with the patient lying down and the analyst seated out of the patient's line of vision. A major reason for this tactic, Freud stated honestly, is that he himself simply could not tolerate patients looking him in the face all day (Jones, 1955).

The ink had hardly dried on Freud's writings about transference when an article appeared by Smith Elly Jelliffe (1913–1914), a neurologist in New York, giving his views on the subject. In Jelliffe's opinion the concept needed broadening and revision. He contended that transference occurs immediately after the establishment of a physician-patient relationship because of the status accorded healers within our culture: "The physician, viewed as a functional unit in society, represents for the individuals in that society, that portion of themselves given over to the protection of their bodies from the forces of disease." Therefore, transference feelings do not develop during the course of the analysis but are there at the very beginning—and from the first session they have to be understood and dealt with. Similarly, the analyst may experience countertransference feelings in the first encounter with the patient. If the analyst cannot control the contertransference, Jelliffe recommended a transference of a different sort: transference of the patient to a different analyst.

Ideas about the significance of the doctor-patient relationship were beginning to be expressed by men of differing orientations and to appear in a variety of professional areas. William McDougall touched upon its significance incidentally, since it came to his attention during service in the army. In one of those classic boners of military organization, McDougall had served for almost a year as an ambulance driver before it was recognized that he was a neurologist. He was then quickly promoted to the rank of major in the Royal Army Medical Corps and placed in charge of treating "nervous" soldiers. Although McDougall employed several techniques, including hypnosis, it was his impression that "sympathetic rapport . . . a very natural and simple human relation" was of greatest importance in benefiting his patients. At the war's end, McDougall journeyed to Switzerland for a didactic analysis by Jung, and through 1919 he continued practicing psychotherapy at the outpatient department of Oxford City Hospital (McDougall, 1930).

Guilio Ferrari (1869–1933?), an Italian psychiatrist who had studied with Binet, also commented on the therapeutic significance of his relationship with his patients. In 1910, Ferrari was in charge of running an institution for 40 children in Bologna. Half the children were mentally retarded and half were termed "normally insane," or what we might call "delinquent." He noticed that by placing the two groups together, the delinquents soon came to understand that they, as well as the retarded children, were regarded as abnormal. A great improvement in their behavior occurred, which Ferrari attributed both to their recognition of their need for change and to the manner in which he handled them. At all times he expressed confidence in their ability to better their conduct; was sincere, impartial, and honest in his dealings with them; and related to the children, not as inferiors, but as individuals who merited his respect (Ferrari, 1932).

A somewhat different perspective, one that suggests the therapist should be guided in the course of the treatment by the patient, was furnished by Edouard Claparède. A Swiss psychiatrist who included Alfred Binet among his friends, Claparède was interested in psychotherapy and the education of the retarded. Respect for the individual's uniqueness and potentialities for growth found expression in his concept of "the school made to measure" (i.e., a school whose programs were adjusted to the differences of the students). In 1912, he founded the Jean-Jacques Rousseau Institute, where he was able to translate his attitudes into action. Claparède (1930) urged teachers to learn from their pupils what should be taught. Instead of routinely and mechanically trying to instruct students, they were told to encourage children to engage in play situations where their need to be mentally active would naturally arise. By this means a child's interest in a subject could be expressed "spontaneously" and active participation in the learning process would occur. Claparède's ideas were similar to what John Dewey thought of as progressive education, and both men received international attention and support.

Claparède had been a student at the Salpêtrière under the neurologist Joseph Dejerine (1849–1917). In 1913, Dejerine's book *Psychoneurosis and Psychotherapy* appeared in the United States. Dejerine, like many others, believed that neuroses were caused by emotional trauma. In order to be cured, a neurotic has to be freed from harmful feelings through the cathartic expression of them. Yet the means by which Dejerine brought about improvements seemed to lie more in the exhortative, trusting relationship he had with his patients than in his exhaustive questions about their emotional problems. Dejerine would urge them to get well. He would untiringly point out that there was no reason why they should not get well. Above all, he would remind them that he, Dejerine, was confident that they would get well, which, if they trusted in his judgment, should dispel any doubts regarding their eventual cure (Dejerine & Garkler, 1913). Apparently many of his patients agreed with him.

Perhaps the most explicit statement made during this period about the therapist-patient relationship came from Alfred Adler (1927, pp. 46–47):

> *The actual change in the nature of the patient can only be his own doing. I have found it most profitable to sit ostentatiously with my hands in my lap, fully convinced that no matter what I might be able to say on the point, the patient can learn nothing from me that he, as the sufferer, does not understand better, once he has recognized his life-line. (Ansbacher & Ansbacher, 1956, p. 336)*

Adler saw the patient's understanding evolving in a process of free and supposedly friendly conversation with the therapist. From the very beginning of treatment, the initiative and responsibility for cure rests with the patient. The job of the therapist is to be a coworker in comprehending the patient's style of life, to communicate an understanding of it, and to point repeatedly to its manifestations in the patient's thoughts and feelings.

Adler was convinced that a neurotic patient has a strong tendency to depreciate the physician in an effort to establish superiority and that this tendency is evidenced in all significant relationships and might well be apparent from the very beginning of treatment: "I expect from the patient again and again the same attitude which he has shown in accordance with his life-plan toward the persons of his former environment and still earlier toward his family" (Ansbacher & Ansbacher, p. 336).

As Adler envisioned it, the office of the therapist becomes a battleground where two people are locked in struggle. On one side is the patient, wanting to get well yet persisting in a pattern of behavior in which mutually satisfying relationships are sacrificed for an illusion of superiority. On the other side is the therapist, wanting to be of assistance, hoping to help the patient assume responsibility, and aware that any failure to recognize and come to grips with any show of hostility will only serve to perpetuate the neurosis.

Briefly, then, some psychologists saw the doctor-patient relationship as therapeutic in itself (McDougall, Ferrari) whereas others viewed it mainly as a means of achieving (1) catharsis (Dejerine), (2) an integrated awareness of unconscious thoughts (Freud), or (3) a recognition of characteristic ways of interacting with others (Adler). All these objectives in turn were regarded as therapeutic. The relationship was promoted by social expectation (Jelliffe) and distorted by unconscious strivings and attitudes (Freud and Adler). Within this relationship, the therapist was supposed to be relatively passive (Freud and Adler), active (Dejerine), or naturally friendly (McDougall and Ferrari). The patient, not the disease or the therapist, was being held increasingly responsible for the outcome of the therapeutic venture—perhaps because it was perceived, although no one as yet seemed to acknowledge it, that regardless of the treatment employed, some patients improved and others did not.

PROFESSIONAL DEVELOPMENT

Two mutually supportive developments characterized these years: (1) A reorientation within psychology, called behaviorism, swept through the field as a powerful protest against the past, and (2) a small but growing number of psychologists, who also waged a fight against tradition, tried to involve their colleagues in applications of psychology to practical problems and to gain recognition as a distinctive profession.

The shortage of trained psychologists to administer and interpret intelligence scales was a source of dismay to the few clinical psychologists available (Porter, 1915–1916). In contrast to the swiftly rising demand for their services was the slow, dragging response of the universities, which seemed disinclined to set up graduate programs in psychology.

The APA showed little concern for the professional problems of its members. Its original purpose was to advance psychology as a science, an objective favored by its membership and to which the large majority of psychologists saw no reason to add other goals (Fernberger, 1932). As late as 1917, Cattell noted that of the 307 members of the APA, only 16 were primarily engaged in nonacademic positions involving the application of psychology. In 1918, just 15 of the approximately 375 APA members listed clinical psychology as a research interest.

Yet the demand for testing, particularly from school systems, was immediate and pressing. Teachers and principals, unable to wait, often resentful of the threat to their status posed by psychologists, but for the most part naive about testing, assumed the functions of psychological examiners. In one school system, almost half the children tested by one teacher were classified as feebleminded, an incident that, though extreme, was not unique.

J. E. W. Wallin (1876–1969) attempted in 1910 to alleviate the problem by organizing a program at the training school at Vineland in which teachers would be taught how to administer the Binet-Simon scale. Then there was, of course, the psychological clinic at the University of Pennsylvania, which offered the following: a special class, initiated in the summer of 1911, in the study of "backward" children; by 1913, a total of 14 courses related in some way to clinical psychology; a biweekly clinic, set up in 1914 and conducted by Edwin B. Twitmyer, in the diagnosis and correction of speech defects; and, in 1919, a course in remedial teaching taught by someone holding the position of clinic teacher (Fernberger, 1931).

In 1913, Münsterberg published his book *Psychology and Industrial Efficiency,* which is considered the founding work in the field of industrial psychology (Hothersall, 1990). Beginning in 1914, the School of Education at the University of Pittsburgh offered summer courses in the study of mentally retarded children, and in 1915 the first department of applied psychology was established at Carnegie Institute of Technology, with Walter Van Dyke Bingham (1880-1952) as its chairman.

Bingham (1952), who was born in Iowa, had a special interest in vocational counseling: "I have preferred to give a hand to the promising rather than to the third rate." After completing his undergraduate work—at the University of Kansas and Beloit College—he taught for 4 years. In 1905 he entered the University of Chicago and in 1908 received his PhD. From 1908 until 1910 he was an instructor at Columbia where he worked with Thorndike, and from 1910 until he went to Carnegie he was at Dartmouth.

The department of applied psychology was particularly involved in the study of aptitudes, vocational counseling, the measurement of interests, and research in salesmanship. Walter Dill Scott (1869-1955) was appointed in 1916 as professor of applied psychology, thus becoming the first of his kind in the United States, though just barely nosing out James P. Porter (1873-1956), whose position at Clark was given the same title that same year. During the war, Bingham and Scott worked on the problems involved in classifying military personnel and selecting officers.

Throughout this decade the number of psychological clinics increased. We shall list those in operation in 1914 in order to give some idea of their distribution in the United States. By then there were 19 clinics in universities, colleges, and medical schools. In addition to the clinics already mentioned, there was a psychological clinic at the Woman's Medical College in Philadelphia (established in 1910), Seashore's clinic at the University of Iowa, Gesell's clinic at Yale University (1911), Wallin's clinic at the University of Pittsburgh (1912), a Bureau of Social Hygiene to study the causes and treatment of delinquency in women at Bedford Reformatory for Women (1912), and clinics at or in the New York Post-Graduate Medical School and Hospital (1912), the Hospital of the City of New York (1912), Boston Psychopathic Hospital (1912), the State University of Iowa (1913), Albany (1913), Tulane University (1913), Rutgers University (1914), Cornell (1914), Trenton (1914), Philadelphia (1914), Los Angeles (1914), and Oakland University (1914). An important function of these clinics was training would-be clinical psychologists, since the training of clinicians was largely done through apprenticeship or on the job.

The institutions offering internships in clinical psychology included Boston Psychopathic Hospital, McLean Hospital, Western State Penitentiary in Pennsylvania, New York Institute for Child Guidance, and the Psychopathic Hospital at the University of Iowa. There may not have been many clinical psychologists but they were turning up everywhere.

In 1910, a psychologist, P. F. Lange, was appointed to the staff of the Iowa

State Institution for the Feebleminded, and the city of London engaged its first school psychologist, Cyril Burt (1952), for half-time work in 1912. Shortly before the war, Burt was joined by a social worker and a medical assistant. By that happy circumstance the first child guidance clinic in England was formed. In 1919, Alfred Adler organized the first child guidance clinic in Vienna.

Back in the United States, Healy's clinic was attracting the attention of a number of judges. They came, were impressed by what they saw and heard, and helped set up similar diagnostic services for their own courts. Among the distinguished visitors were Judges Frater of Seattle, Waite of Minneapolis, Hoffman of Cincinnati, and Baker of Boston. During the summers of 1912 and 1913, Healy taught a course at Harvard describing his work. In 1913 Augusta Bronner, who had trained at Teacher's College, Columbia University, under Thorndike, joined Healy's staff in Chicago. The following year, Cook County assumed financial responsibility for the clinic.

A book by Healy, *The Individual Delinquent: A Textbook of Diagnosis and Prognosis,* appeared in 1915. It offered descriptive case presentations and an exposition of the new field of mental testing. Its major contentions were that the current procedures for handling delinquents were ineffective and that the majority of delinquents, despite the measures taken by courts and reform schools on their behalf, did not become useful citizens and tended to continue to violate the law. Healy argued that what many of these children needed was treatment that would attempt to eliminate the emotional disturbances at the root of their delinquency, and he strongly advocated that steps be taken to ensure that such treatment was provided. Healy's book caused some alarm and provoked some action. Of most importance, it was eminently successful in influencing legal authorities and others to discard organic and hereditary concepts of etiology in favor of environmental and psychological explanations.

Healy was lured to Boston in 1917 to organize the Judge Baker Foundation, and with him went Augusta Bronner. Among the inducements that prompted their move were the treatment services available to their patients in the Boston area, the promises of cooperation by a variety of agencies, and the assurance of financial support for 10 years. The work of the foundation consisted mainly of diagnostic evaluations made for the local courts. Treatment of delinquents was provided by their probation officers (Healy & Bronner, 1948).

In spite of the paucity of clinical psychologists, by 1913 the field began to attract the attention of critics. The major criticisms were that there was an overemphasis on mental tests; the work was too exclusively diagnostic; the treatments had little practical value because they were largely confined to retardates, for whom virtually nothing could be done; the treatments were based on the wrong kind of psychology and should incorporate some psychoanalytic concepts; and the field of mental retardation would be best left to the medical profession. There was not much to say in rebuttal other than to argue that clinical psychology was still young and developing and that it wished to build upon as solid a scientific foundation as possible—which was what Rene Sylvester argued (1913–1914).

However, to some critics it appeared that the field of clinical psychology was

growing too rapidly. New terms were being constantly introduced into the literature, and, in the opinion of Shepherd Ivory Franz, they were being used vaguely
and inconsistently. Franz (1912) was particularly alarmed by all the "new psychologies," by which he meant abnormal psychology, clinical psychology, medical
psychology, psychoclinical psychology, psychopathology, and pathopsychology.
He advised his colleagues to curb their urge to go in for linguistic innovation and
suggested a division of labor:

> When an investigator is concerned chiefly with the general course of a disease and its treatment
> his interests are in psychiatry, but when his chief concern is the investigation of the development or
> interrelations of mental symptoms his interests are in psychology. (pp. 145–146)

How Franz proposed to distinguish between the "general course of a disease"
and the "development or interrelations of mental symptoms" he did not specify.

In 1915, the APA took official note of the abuses occurring in diagnostic testing
by adopting a resolution proposed by Guy M. Whipple: "That this Association
discourages the use of mental tests by those unqualified." At first not too happy
about it, the APA was being forced to become involved in the practical applications
of the science and the professional problems of its members. To avoid such an
involvement would have required unusual agility, for the status of clinical psychologists was being legally acknowledged by some states.

In 1916, Wallin, who at that time was working in St. Louis, was asked to serve
as chairman of a committee on defective children for the Missouri Children's Code
Commission. One of his recommendations, later enacted into law, was that a child
should not be assigned to a school for the mentally defective unless he or she had
been examined individually by the use of standardized tests of intelligence. Around
1917 the Illinois legislature enacted a law allowing a psychologist to serve as one
of the two members of a commission of experts certifying persons for commitment
to institutions for the retarded. The two members of the first commission were
Healy and Bronner.

Reaction from the medical profession to this threat to their authority came
swiftly. The New York Psychiatrical Society (1917), in a letter to the APA, deplored what it hoped was not a trend and officially registered its disapproval of
regarding psychologists as experts. Moreover, it objected to the activities of psychologists regarding problems of diagnosis, social management, and the institutional "disposal" of patients who evidence abnormal mental conditions. The
grounds of the objections were simple: These problems were medical in nature and
only physicians were competent to deal with them.

Franz, who was scientific director at St. Elizabeth's Hospital and had been
awarded in 1915 an honorary MD degree by George Washington University in
recognition of his outstanding medical contributions, became angry. He denounced
the contention that psychiatrists were experts whereas psychologists were not, and
he cuttingly observed, "If some states have decided to utilize psychologists as
experts regarding the normality or abnormality of the mental states of individuals,

it is conceivable that it was done because previous medical expert testimony was not satisfactory" (Franz, 1917, p. 227).

Tempers were on the rise in 1917. The APA appointed a committee to consider what qualifications were necessary to become a psychological examiner or "expert," a move that did not please anyone. At the APA convention, a group of dissatisfied clinicians got together and decided their interests would best be served by forming an organization of their own. Wallin, who claimed he had been working on just such a project since 1911, met with Leta Hollingworth, Francis Maxfield, James Miner, David Mitchell, Rudolf Pintner, and Clara Schmitt. Then and there, on December 28, 1917, at Carnegie Institute of Technology, they founded the American Association of Clinical Psychologists (AACP). Other early members of the AACP included Bronner, Fernald, Healy, Kuhlmann, Terman, Wells, Whipple, and Yerkes. Actually, early members were all there ever were, because the AACP voted to dissolve itself in 1919.

Two major factors accounted for the AACP's short life: (1) after World War I, most psychologists were opposed to the formation of splinter groups, which would have fragmented their strength; (2) the APA agreed to provide a voice for clinicians within the association and to involve itself more wholeheartedly in professional matters. An APA committee was appointed to consider methods for certifying members as consulting psychologists, and the rebels were welcomed back into the fold. Chairing the last meeting of the AACP was Arnold Gesell (Wallin could not attend the convention). On December 31, 1919, the first section or division of the APA, the Clinical Section, came into being (Wallin, 1961).

Not only clinicians but the entire field of psychology was gaining in prestige and recognition. By 1913, there were 16 psychological journals in the United States, an impressive gain of 14 journals in 22 years. Yet it seemed to a number of young psychologists that the development of psychology was being impeded by the persistence of an "Old Guard" who were bogged down in philosophical speculation. With mounting restlessness, they felt that something had to be done. That something took place in 1913, when John Broadus Watson (1878–1958) energetically repudiated the attachment of psychology to philosophy.

Watson was born and grew up in South Carolina, where he was fondly remembered by his teachers as an indolent, argumentative boy, who resisted discipline and was content to barely pass his studies. His youth was distinguished by two arrests: one for fighting and the other for shooting off firearms within the town limits. At the age of 16 he entered Furman University, and it is an understatement to remark that he was not exactly a scholar. Lonely and irritable, he resented college, seeing it as an impractical, frustrating prolongation of infancy. In 1900, after receiving his MA, Watson entered the University of Chicago. There, in a citadel of philosophers, he sulked and fumed about his inability to grasp philosophy. For the life of him, he could not understand what in blazes George Mead and John Dewey were talking about (Watson, 1936).

In the fall of 1902, Watson suffered from severe insomnia and feelings of anxiety. He managed to recover after several weeks and received his PhD in 1903. That same year he married and became a member of the University of Chicago faculty. He turned to experimentation with animals because he felt uncomfortable and awkward with people and hated to give them directions. In 1908, he went to Johns Hopkins as a professor, and in 1913, he published his manifesto, "Psychology as the Behaviorist Views It."

Watson (1913) proclaimed that psychology "is a purely objective experimental branch of natural science. Its theoretical goal is the prediction and control of *behavior*" (p. 158). He argued that since there was no dividing line between humans and other animals, by studying the behavior of animals, psychologists could understand, at least in principle, the behavior of people. He contended that all that psychology had to concern itself with were stimuli and responses: given the stimuli, to discover the responses; given the responses, to discover the stimuli.

In the new psychology proposed by Watson, the method of introspection (which he termed "verbal report") would be minimal—indeed it was to be avoided. Functional and structural psychologies were deemed unsatisfactory because they dealt with consciousness. The mind-body problem and other philosophic puzzles were best left to philosophers. Psychology, in short, was to change radically from the study of consciousness to the study of behavior. However, Watson did not mean by "behavior" only simple activities remotely related to the complexities of human life. Instead, he urged his colleagues to integrate their findings with the problems of living and to use their understanding to deal with matters of practical consequence (e.g., the psychology of advertising and of testing, areas of knowledge that he believed would make contributions to a "true," worthwhile science).

Angell thought that Watson was on the right track, although he did think Watson's program too sweeping in what it would discard. But Watson had struck at the heart of an issue, and he did not intend to compromise. Psychologists who had shared his discontent rallied vigorously to his cause. Many psychologists feared the psychological community would be split into warring factions.

A reconciliation was attempted by Warren (1867–1934) in his APA presidential address of 1913. Warren noted that "the mind-body relation is the Wandering Jew of science" (p. 79) and then proceeded to put it to rest. He advocated a double-aspect conception of the mind and body: There was only one single process observable in two ways, and the neural changes were simply the external appearance of mental changes. Having settled the issue to his satisfaction, Warren sought to resolve all differences by this new view of the mind-body problem. On the one hand, he asserted, "The hope of psychology . . . seems to lie in the study of behavior." On the other hand, he defined psychology as "the science of individual experience." Then quickly, he redefined psychology as "the science of the individual organism or consciousness, as related to its environment" (p. 99).

But Warren's attempt to combine the old and new psychologies was doomed to failure. Behaviorism was young and successful, and far from modifying its position, it became even more extreme. In 1915, Watson, now president of the APA, announced that all forms of behavior should be analyzed in terms of the conditioned reflexes espoused by the neurologist V. M. Bekhterev (Watson, 1916). His supporters cheered his stand.

There are some simple explanations for the enthusiasm for behaviorism.

First, people in general were not interested in psychology as a cerebral exercise and source of theories regarding the mind-body problem, and they seemed to have little patience for such speculations. Instead, they were interested in practical applications of knowledge: in testing, diagnosing mental deficiency, identifying talent and skills, and similar enterprises. Moreover, people were willing to give recognition, status, prestige, and financial support to those who were responsive to their needs. By attempting to serve the public, by striving to gain information that could be used, psychology, it seemed to many, could advance both as a "pure" and applied science and as a profession.

In 1916, Carl Seashore was invited to help in the organization of the National Research Council. Although at first psychology had not been formally represented on the council, at the close of the war a division of psychology and anthropology was permanently included, with the chairman and vice-chairman alternately representing one science or the other.

The development of clinical psychology was fostered by occurrences in related areas. In 1917, Smith College started its School for Social Work. That same year, a physician, Clarence M. Hincks of Toronto, after visiting Clifford Beers, founded the National Committee for Mental Hygiene of Canada. Meanwhile, the National Committee for Mental Hygiene in the United States was prospering under its medical director, Thomas W. Salmon. Following the war, Salmon helped to persuade politicians to appropriate funds for the establishment of veterans' hospitals. At the same time in order to bolster his arguments for greater financial assistance in the field of mental health, Salmon was mustering all available resources to gather data on the extent of mental illness throughout the country and the number and condition of the facilities for treatment. Under his direction, the National Committee for Mental Hygiene was preparing to embark on a massive campaign of public education concerning mental hygiene.

The significance of such developments was noted in Scott's APA presidential address in 1919. Noteworthy in itself is the simple fact that Scott, an industrial psychologist, had been elected president of the association. Although most of his remarks were restricted to the profession of personnel administration, his address had broader ramifications. Scott (1920) observed that the concept that "all men are created equal" had been replaced by a psychology of individual differences, a psychology that recognized the inequalities between human beings. From this new foundation, merit, not seniority; mental age, not chronological age; fitness for a task, not mere availability were now the crucial factors in assigning people to useful functions in society. The task and the worker were no longer seen in isolation but as a unity, as forming a kind of biological relationship, as parts of a developing, living, integrated situation in which emotions, impulses, habits, and sentiments were of extreme importance.

Society needed to fit the right person to the right job. Through vocational guidance, analyses of jobs, and measurements of talents and skills, much better results could be achieved. People and their work were to become a productive complex, with individuals profiting from their labors not only materially but intellectually and emotionally.

Thus, by 1919 psychology had attained status as a science and as a profession. In fact, its status as a science promoted its status as a profession, and vice versa. As Yerkes (1919) put it, "Largely because of the way in which it responded to the practical demands and the opportunities of the military emergency, psychology today occupies a place among the natural sciences which is newly achieved, eminently desirable, and highly gratifying to the profession" (p. 148).

5

School Rivalry
1920–1929

Within the United States, there was a continuation during the 1920s of the unsettled social conditions that seemed so distressing to so many Americans shortly after World War I. Relentlessly but very often justly, the trade union movement pressed its demands for the right to organize and bargain for higher wages and benefits from management. Women, now armed with enfranchisement, sought opportunities and prerogatives equal to those of men. A new generation of Americans struggled to free themselves from the cultures of their parents, seeking assimilation in the evolving culture of the United States. Codes of conduct were challenged and a new morality was being debated, one based on greater individual freedom, especially in regard to sex. Unquestionably the social sciences were promoted by, and played some role in promoting, this examination of traditional values and attitudes.

At the same time, of course, there was bound to be resistance and disillusionment. One great disappointment was that the prohibition of alcoholic beverages produced few of the predicted advantages. In fact, far from converting the country into a paradise of sobriety, prohibition had spawned a flagrant flouting of the law by ordinarily sober, law-abiding citizens. The feeling of turmoil and the reactions to it were epitomized in President Harding's wish to return the nation to normalcy and the recommendation of his successor to "Keep Cool with Coolidge."

On the other side of the Atlantic, there was similar unrest—and without the compensation of the material prosperity enjoyed by the United States. The League of Nations strove to maintain peace in spite of its inability to deal effectively with growing international friction and resentments. Many of those resentments had been intensified by the war. In particular, the German people, embittered by the terms of the Treaty of Versailles and periodically impoverished by inflation, brooded about vengeance and the restoration of honor. But their anger and dissatisfaction were shared by other nations in Europe. In Soviet Russia, the Bolsheviks were using their power to carve out a monolithic communist state. In Italy, the Fascists, under their leader Benito Mussolini, were urging their compatriots to accept discipline, hard work, and sacrifice for the glory of the homeland. In all areas, intellectuals were driven to the disturbing conclusion that democracy seemed to have little appeal when contrasted with political movements promising national strength and purpose.

Ironically, the twenties came to a close with the United States reeling from the impact of a serious financial crisis ushered in by the New York Stock Market crash in 1929. A period of worldwide economic depression ensued.

Yet through it all, science had progressed, and literature and art, if not unanimously regarded as having advanced or improved, had at least changed. Frederick Banting developed insulin for use in the treatment of diabetes, and Sir Alexander Fleming discovered penicillin. The medical world was excited by the discovery of filterable viruses and ascribed to them causal responsibility for yellow fever and infantile paralysis. It was not too farfetched to suppose that they, or something similar but still unknown, might be involved in the causation of mental illness. In 1927, Werner Heisenberg proposed his principle of uncertainty or indeterminacy, which states that in the subatomic world the more accurately one measures the velocity of a particle, the less accurately one can specify its position. A profound implication of Heisenberg's principle is that it assigns limits to knowledge, since it affirms that one kind of information may be purchased at the cost of another.

The most widely read writers of the day, troubled by feelings of pessimism and futility, included Erich Remarque, Sinclair Lewis, Ernest Hemingway, William Faulkner, F. Scott Fitzgerald, Andre Malraux, and Eugene O'Neill. A new literary trend, influenced in some measure by psychoanalysis, appeared. It was notably illustrated by the stream-of-consciousness writing of James Joyce, who attempted to portray the functioning of the human mind in all its symbolism and complexity. Also influenced by psychoanalysis was a new form of painting, surrealism, which tried to depict the psychic condition of people in dreamlike canvases. The public read the words and stared at the paintings and wondered why the artists seemed so troubled. Meanwhile, Sigmund Freud, godfather to them all, was having troubles of his own.

NORMAL PERSONALITY FUNCTIONING

Freud continued to encounter resistance within medical circles, particularly in Austria and Germany, but as it did not greatly trouble him, it need not trouble us. In general, recognition and honors kept coming Freud's way. Unfortunately, though, he shared the financial fate of his compatriots and saw his savings erased by inflation. As far as Freud was concerned, there was little pleasure in being a distinguished and honored pauper. Moreover, even his analytic colleagues had not greeted the ideas expressed in his latest work, *Beyond the Pleasure Principle,* with much enthusiasm (Jones, 1957).

For several years, Freud claimed, he had been pondering his new formulations. The experiences of the war had been decisive and had convinced him of their validity. Just as Schopenhauer had proclaimed, "Death is the goal of life," Freud now asserted that the basic aim of the instincts was to regress to a preceding state, which ultimately would be nonexistence.

Once again he pictured two opposing sets of instincts: the life instincts, which strive to perpetuate and preserve life, and the death instincts, which strive toward self-destruction. The life instincts, which he called Eros, are manifested in binding, integrating, and uniting activities. The death instincts, later called Thanatos, are manifested in differentiating, disintegrating, and separating activities. A new principle, the repetition compulsion, was thought to govern them both. This kind of compulsion is a tendency to repeat experiences in thought or action in order to attain a feeling of mastery over them. Of course, this tendency toward repetition may also be viewed as an effort to return to a previous state of affairs. Freud modestly explained, "It would be counter to the conservative nature of instinct if the goal of life were a state never hitherto reached." If the final goal of life is death, then aggression, even in its most violent manifestation, war, can be interpreted, paradoxically, as a defensive maneuver to preserve one's own life by displacing the destructive tendencies against oneself toward other people while at the same time courting annihilation (Freud, 1942).

Many analysts found it difficult to accept these ideas, and Jones came to suspect that perhaps they represented Freud's desire, not for death, but for reunion with his mother. However, McDougall (1925-1926) greeted them warmly even though he did not agree with them. What he welcomed, because it coincided with his own beliefs, was Freud's dethronement of the pleasure principle. It seemed to him that he and Freud agreed that instinctive urges operate independently of pleasure and pain. So McDougall hailed the latest developments from Vienna as "a great advance."

Early in 1923, cancer was detected in Freud's jaw and palate. Thus began a series of operations that succeeded in their major purpose—preserving Freud's life—but that required him to suffer serious disability. The effects of surgery made it necessary that Freud wear a prosthesis, which proved to be irritating and painful. Furthermore, his speech was made nasal and thick and his hearing was impaired. His life became one of daily torment, alleviated to some extent by the ministrations of his daughter, Anna, and by the courage he showed in continuing his work.

Possibly he was cheered by the favorable reactions of his colleagues to his book *The Ego and the Id*. Freud (1927a) described three major groups of psychological functions and named them the id, ego, and superego. The id refers to the innate undifferentiated energy and unconscious instinctual impulses that press for immediate expression. The ego, Freud supposed, originally derived its energy from the id. It was now thought to involve conscious, perceptual, cognitive, and motor processes as well as unconscious mechanisms for keeping impulses and thoughts from awareness. The concept of the superego, a newly distinguished "structure," partly included the older concept of the ego ideal. Largely unconscious in its functioning, the superego is derived from the child's identification with what is perceived to be the demands, prohibitions, and commandments of parents, especially during the time the Oedipus complex is being resolved. Conscience and the ego ideal are regarded as derivatives of the superego, and thus these functions involve punishment by feelings of guilt for "misbehavior" and rewards of self-approval for "correct" action (Jones, 1928-1929).

During this period Freud was distressed once again by the defection of one of his inner circle of analysts. The incident began with the members of the Committee being upset by the presumptuousness of their associate, Otto Rank (1884-1939) who had the temerity to publish a book without consulting them. Though Rank dedicated his work to Freud, his views, as they saw them, conflicted with the tenets of psychoanalysis.

Rank had been born in Vienna as Otto Rosenfeld. His youth was miserable. The son of a poor and alcoholic father, he suffered from rheumatism, had few friends, and fed himself mostly on a diet of books and a bountiful contempt for people in general: "If anything could drive me to suicide, it would be the stupidity and commonness of mankind" (Taft, 1958, p. 20).

After graduating from a trade school, he worked in a machine shop. At nights he tried to write poetry and fiction, but his wretchedness often led him to spend his evenings wrestling with a temptation to kill himself. Then he came across *The Interpretation of Dreams*. Inspired by his reading of Freud's work, he wrote a manuscript (published in English in 1932 with the title *Art and Artist*) using psychoanalytic principles to explain artistic productions. He showed this manuscript to Adler, and around 1906 Adler introduced him to Freud. Impressed, Freud generously helped Rosenfeld to enter the University of Vienna and obtain a formal education.

Rosenfeld legally adopted his pen name, Rank, in 1909, and in 1912 received his PhD with a psychoanalytic interpretation of the saga of Lohengrin as his thesis. During World War I, he served as the editor of an army newspaper in Poland. In 1919, he married and returned to Vienna. To those who had known him in the old days, he seemed to have become more assertive and self-confident. In 1920, he began to practice psychoanalysis.

In his book *The Trauma of Birth,* Rank proposed that the transition from the security of the womb to the painful stimulations of the postnatal environment is experienced by the infant with tremendous fear or anxiety. This primal anxiety is repressed, but throughout life the person reacts with fear to subsequent separations and strives to reinstate the bliss experienced in the womb. Despite such strivings for maternal comfort and protection, the person's feelings are conflicted. Though unconsciously desiring to return to safety within the mother's body, the person is at the same time frightened and angered by the possibility of return because of the terror that originally followed being there (i.e., the birth trauma).

Rank's formulations thus put great emphasis on the issue of separation as a universal dilemma of major significance. In line with his views, he advocated setting early in the period of analysis a termination date so that the conflict over the ultimate separation could be speedily faced and treated.

Freud did not object to Rank's experimentation with techniques and was undecided whether acceptance of the birth trauma concept necessitated ending their professional relationship. Others in the group, however, were more critical, and Rank left for New York in a huff. Anna Freud then took his place on the Committee.

Considering the fact that in those days Rank had to travel by ship and train, there followed an extraordinary and pathetic sequence of journeys. Within the year Rank was back in Vienna begging Freud's forgiveness and attributing his adherence to the disputed ideas to an unresolved neurosis, to manic-depressive psychosis, or to anything other than genuine conviction. Soon he was off again to New York, back to Vienna, off to Paris, back to New York, back to Vienna (when he broke with Freud for good), then off to Paris again, off to Philadelphia, back to Paris, and then back and forth between Paris and the School of Social Work in Philadelphia. It was certainly most fortunate for Rank's livelihood that he had hit upon the desirability of setting a time limit on a course of therapy.

Meanwhile, in 1925, Josef Breuer, the old collaborator of Sigmund Freud, died. A few years before his death, Breuer wrote an autobiography of some 20 pages in which only one paragraph dealt with his relationship with Freud and psychoanalysis. He realistically appraised his contribution to science and spoke proudly of the benefits he had received from life: "It [*Studies on Hysteria*] is the seed from which psychoanalysis was developed by Freud . . . [That I have been] completely happy in my home; that my beloved wife has given me five sturdy, fine children; and that none has ever caused me serious sorrow—then I may well consider myself a fortunate man" (Oberndorf, 1953).

Karl Abraham also died in 1925, and the position he had occupied on the Committee was allowed to go unfilled. The following year Freud was interviewed on the occasion of his 70th birthday. Despite his physical suffering and his theory of death instincts, Freud proclaimed, "Seventy years have taught me to accept life with a cheerful humility . . . I still prefer existence to extinction" (Jones, 1957, p. 126).

It was also at about this time that Freud (1936) promulgated his views on anxiety. Like Rank, he thought the first experience of anxiety occurred at birth. Unlike Rank, he did not attribute anxiety to separation but to overwhelming sensory stimulation, which at this early stage of development the child cannot handle or comprehend. Later, as the child grows older, whenever impulses or thoughts threaten to become overwhelming, anxiety is reexperienced and serves as a signal of danger. This signal anxiety operates unconsciously to set off processes, ascribed to the ego, that protect or defend the person from the excitation by keeping it from awareness or by so distorting it that it becomes tolerable.

In 1927, the Committee was dissolved and Freud published *The Future of an Illusion*. This book attempts to explain the bases for religious beliefs, and its title should be sufficient to indicate the reaction it provoked, at least in certain quarters.

Elsewhere in Vienna, Alfred Adler had done very well after his break with psychoanalysis. Regarding his own theory, he stated that "the science of Individual Psychology developed out of the effort to understand that mysterious creative power of life which expresses itself in the desire to develop, to strive, to achieve, and even to compensate for defects in one direction by striving for success in another" (Adler, 1927–1928).

As Adler saw it, people are confronted by three major problems that have to be solved in living: (1) finding a suitable vocation, (2) maintaining satisfying social relationships, and (3) experiencing satisfying sexual relationships. Actually, the resolution of all these problems requires what Adler called "social feeling" or "social interest." Social feeling is an innate potential that to be actualized, requires learning by the child as well as conscious attempts to develop it by those responsible for the child's training. Although Adler never precisely defined social interest, he described it as something very much like empathy: "To see with the eyes of another, to hear with the ears of another, to feel with the heart of another." However, this empathic effort, to qualify as social interest, has to have as its ultimate goal the creation of a harmonious, ideal community for all (Ansbacher & Ansbacher, 1956).

Not surprisingly, self-interest can be served by social interest: "The only salvation from the continuously driving inferiority feeling is the knowledge and the feeling of being valuable which originates from the contribution to the common welfare." In other words, the person can only find a path to psychic health and contentment through self-scrutiny, understanding, and, very important, being of some use to society. "A man of genius," according to Adler, "is primarily a man of supreme social usefulness" (Ansbacher & Ansbacher, 1956, p. 153).

The individual's goal in life is, therefore, of tremendous significance. All people, Adler now thought, inevitably have some feelings of inferiority. These feelings are unavoidable because children are naturally weak and dependent in relation to adults. The important thing is how the person intends to go about alleviating these feelings. Is the chosen goal to dominate others or to be of service to them? Will the child receive the training and guidance that enables the choice of a constructive rather than a destructive style of life? Adler felt it was impossible to overestimate the importance of this usually unconscious choice. The person's final goal influences current behavior, affects perceptions, and gives meaning to existence; it allows for transcending the difficulties of the moment by contemplation of future successes. Such are the ramifications of the individual's goal as Adler (1928–1929) saw them toward the close of the twenties.

Earlier in the decade there had been a fervent debate in the United States over whether behavior is fundamentally goal-directed. The leading advocate of the negative position was John B. Watson, who had come upon some hard times but was rising above them.

During World War I, Watson (1936) had antagonized his superior officers by going outside of military channels to express publicly his opinion of the use of the "rotation test" (a neurological test that seeks to detect disturbances in the vestibular apparatus) in the selection of pilots. He thought it worthless. As a result of his disregard of the chain of command, he was transferred from the United States to the front lines in Europe. Fortunately, the armistice enabled Watson's return to the temporary safety of Johns Hopkins. There he conducted research studies of infant behavior, which we shall discuss shortly. In 1920, Watson was divorced and soon thereafter married his coworker in the research just mentioned. A divorce involving a socially prominent wife, two children, and a professor at Johns Hopkins who almost immediately took another bride was a great scandal in Baltimore in 1920 and resulted in Watson's being quickly relieved of his position.

For several days after his dismissal, Watson fought against feelings of depression. All academic positions seemed closed to him, and he was at a loss as to what he might be able to do. His friends suggested that he try his hand in the field of advertising, though it would require him to be willing to start from the bottom. So start at the bottom he did. To gain familiarity with people as the salesperson sees them, Watson spent time going door to door selling coffee and asking the occupants what brand of boots they wore. In the summer of 1921, he worked as a clerk in Macy's Department Store.

Evidently he proved quite successful in this new field, for by 1924 Watson had risen to the position of vice-president of a large advertising agency. His abiding interest, however, was psychology. Through books, magazine articles, and lectures at Clark University and the New School of Social Research, he was able to continue to give expression to his opinions.

Watson believed that heredity is of negligible significance in the development of the person, whereas environment and training are practically everything. He was fond of stating this challenge: "Give me a dozen healthy infants, well-formed, and my own specified world to bring them up in and I'll guarantee to take any one at random and train him to become any type of specialist I might select" (Watson, 1928, p. 10). One of the major regrets of Watson's life was that no one ever gave him the babies to be used in the research he proposed. Perhaps, all things considered, it was just as well.

According to Watson (1924), all that people inherit are certain kinds of structure that force them from birth to respond to stimuli in certain ways. Just as a boomerang returns to its thrower because of the way it is shaped, so people respond to forces because of the way they are formed (i.e., their internal structure of bone, muscle, and nerve tissue). All behaviors are products of learning and structure. Therefore, Watson saw no need in psychology for such terms as instincts, capacities, talents, temperaments, and traits; personality is just a "sum of activities . . . the end product of our habit systems."

On the basis of his studies of infants being raised in Harriet Lane Hospital, Watson (1928) concluded that unlearned behaviors consist only of a few simple motor responses (e.g., sneezing, crying, and grasping) and three emotional reactions: (1) love, which is elicited by stroking or gentle stimulation of the skin; (2) rage, which is elicited by physical restraints; and (3) fear, which is elicited by loud noises and loss of support. More complex responses and reactions to more complex patterns of stimuli are learned through conditioning.

Watson did not hesitate to generalize from his data far beyond what was warranted. He strongly believed that child training is important and blamed most of the troubles in the world on incompetent rearing. Particularly distressing to him were manifestations of excessive parental love. He was convinced that too much affection causes children to become dependent and emotionally unstable. His advice to parents was to pay less attention to their offspring and to spend less time pampering them. He further instructed parents to give their children a rap across the fingers firmly, though gently, whenever they were caught doing something wrong. Failure to heed his advice might produce the most dire of all consequences, a child who had grown up to be a "lounge lizard."

Little tolerance was shown by Watson for anyone who disagreed with him. As far as he was concerned, only three kinds of people did not share his way of thinking: (1) those who were unable to accept the facts, (2) those who liked to think heredity was important so they could feel superior to other people, and (3) those who wished to avoid feeling responsible for the training of their children. What Watson may have lacked in sophistication, he more than made up for in zeal.

Eloquently opposing Watson was McDougall, who was appointed professor of psychology at Harvard in 1920. His description of Watson may serve to illustrate the verbal churlishness characteristic of this period:

> *Thus, by repudiating one half of the methods of psychology and resolutely shutting his eyes to three quarters of its problems, he laid down the program of Behaviorism and rallied to its standard all those who have a natural distaste for difficult problems and a preference for short, easy, and fictitious solutions. (McDougall, 1928, pp. 277–278)*

McDougall (1928) argued that behavior is basically purposive. He insisted it could not be understood only as responses to stimuli. In bolstering his argument, he left no ground unturned. He appealed to reason by showing that behaviorists were forced to assume, in order to make their findings meaningful, that their animal subjects were trying to reach some goal. He noted that at least one behaviorist, Tolman, now recognized purposiveness in the activities of organisms. He appealed to common sense by pointing out that it is impossible to know what a machine is until it is known what the machine was designed to do. Who among those hearing these words, he questioned, does not feel he or she has been working toward a desired goal? McDougall even pointed to the profit to be gained if people were seen as capable of striving "with some success to improve themselves and the conditions of their life in this strange world."

Yet McDougall was fighting a defensive war, and his appeals did not touch the hearts of many psychologists. Most psychologists mistrusted the concept of instinct or anything that smacked of innate restrictions on what a person could be taught to do. Instincts implied purposive behavior, purposiveness reminded many psychologists of teleology, and teleology was associated with the unsophisticated view that current behavior was determined by what might take place in the future rather than what had taken place in the past. Therefore, when the behaviorists threw out the concept of instinct, they also threw out purposiveness, and the behaviorists, though certainly not constituting the majority of psychologists, clearly dominated psychological thinking in the United States.

McDougall (1921–1922) recognized that instincts were taboo in psychology, and thus he tried to save his theory through revision. He said that by *instinct* all that he now meant was an innate impulse or disposition. Such an impulse was not inherently bound to any specific motor mechanism but could be expressed by means of a variety of neuromuscular connections. At the "core" of the instinct is a "capacity for desiring" the end result of the behavior or a striving to attain that particular result. To illustrate the distinction between the instinct and its associated behavior, McDougall asked that we imagine an elderly man whose "sexual fire" (sex instinct) has died out. Now this gentleman, for old times' sake, might repeat his youthful courting behavior with women. But obviously his attitudes and feelings toward women would not be the same as when he was young, and despite the same overt wooing behavior, his actions would strike others as a sad mockery of his former self (McDougall, 1925–1926).

At any rate, McDougall regretted that he had ever used the term *instinct*. He now preferred the word *horme* (a Greek word that means "animal impulse" and that had achieved scientific respectability as the root of *hormone*). Consequently, the point of view championed by McDougall came to be called *hormic psychology*.

During the early twenties, McDougall had been most interested in the sentiments. He speculated that character or personality is made up of a system of sentiments, including love, hate, contempt, respect, friendship, morality, and self-regard. Human development, he reasoned, seems to progress from strong impulses toward some vague goal to instinctive strivings that are regulated by social approval and then to the most advanced stage, the effort to realize ideals of character and conduct whether or not they meet with the approval of the group.

Although McDougall saw autonomy as the highest stage of development, he expressed his personal dilemma by making self-regard the most important of the sentiments. Self-regard, he decided, is derived from the opinions and reactions of others to the person as he or she struggles to effect a compromise between gaining their favor through acquiescence and giving expression to his or her own demands and ideas. In a formulation that anticipated Rank and Sullivan, he described the development of the self through social interactions and conflicts (McDougall, 1923).

It was McDougall's tragedy to be unable to resolve to his own satisfaction the conflict he experienced between arrogantly espousing unpopular ideas and winning the friendship of his colleagues. In the psychological community within the United States, human "instincts" had become anachronistic, yet McDougall published lists of them; environment was almost everything and heredity was being discounted in favor of learning, yet McDougall persisted in speculating that the Nordic race, of which he considered himself a member, was superior to all others; Darwin's theory of evolution reigned supreme, yet McDougall thought it possible to inherit acquired characteristics; psychologists expressed interest only in the objective and observable, yet McDougall expressed an interest in fields that many people thought of as supernatural. Each of his ideas would have been sufficient to alienate a goodly portion of psychologists; all his ideas together succeeded in alienating just about everyone.

Yet McDougall was not trying to be negativistic or cantankerous. He was for the most part sincerely trying to be a scientist by questioning and subjecting to experimental research the conclusions that he felt many others had simply assumed to be correct.

Although the majority of psychologists argued against instincts, especially human instincts, there were some, like Tolman (1922–1923), who thought a precise definition might be enough to salvage the concept. According to his own definition, an instinct is an innate connection of specific driving adjustments to specific stimulating conditions, adjustments that tend to generate particular sets of random acts until some one act occurs that provides a stimulating condition that innately relaxes the driving adjustments themselves. Other psychologists took a different tack.

Knight Dunlap rejected instincts but felt that McDougall was really talking about emotions. It didn't really matter what McDougall was talking about, because Dunlap felt the term he should have used was *desire*. In his APA presidential address, Dunlap (1923) "rashly" offered a tentative list of nine desires: alimentary, excretory, rest, activity, shelter, amatory, parental, preeminence, and conformity. He thought the last four were of major importance.

Woodworth was displeased that people were uninterested in dynamic psychology. He was also displeased that so many of them were interested in behaviorism. It seemed to Woodworth (1928) that there was more to behavior than simple stimuli and simple responses. After all, the organism is not at rest when a stimulus is presented but is engaged in some form of activity. The stimulus, therefore, is evaluated by the organism in the context of its ongoing behavior, and its response is determined not only by the stimulus but by its preexisting activity.

Furthermore, although Woodworth shared in the dissatisfaction with the concept of instinct, he thought psychology could tolerate a concept such as *need*:

> What we call 'need' is a prepotent activity, i.e., an activity not readily deflected moving forward without responding to stimuli disconnected with itself. What we see is an activity going forward in a definite direction and rendering the organism unresponsive to certain stimuli while unusually responsive to others. (Woodworth, 1928, p. 125)

Morton Prince did not care for instincts and neither did Floyd Allport. The latter talked instead about "prepotent reflexes," whereas the former (Prince, 1928) saw the human personality as the sum total of traits and neurograms. The traits of the individual could be either innate or acquired behavioral tendencies. Neurograms were traits that had become organized systems of neural dispositions. Psychologists were not noticeably enthusiastic to embrace the term *neurogram,* but Gordon Allport, for one, believed the concept of a trait had value, and many others shared his point of view.

Allport (1921) thought of a trait as a characteristic form of behavior that is more generalized than a reflex or simple habit. It can be viewed as an adjustive tendency, particularly in an individual's relationship with the social environment. Extraversion, introversion, ascendance, submission, and self-seeking are examples of traits.

Unfortunately, some psychologists described people by constructing lists of their traits. For instance, one psychologist depicted the personality of a delinquent girl as follows: "This girl is of the overactive type, intelligent, ego-centric, introspective, seclusive, excitable, and rather inclined to be depressed. She is impulsive, opinionated, sensitive, and easily offended." Allport (1924–1925) was firmly against this practice of trait cataloguing. He insisted that to picture an individual's personality adequately, the psychologist has to know and demonstrate how the person's traits combine and interact.

So we see that even though instincts had fallen into disrepute, people could rely on hormes, desires, needs, prepotent reflexes, traits, and neurograms to help them make their way in the world.

Toward the close of the decade, considerable interest and discussion centered on (1) the work of the Gestalt school and the challenges it offered to behaviorism and (2) the work of Jean Piaget (1896–1980), although to a lesser extent. Let us look at Piaget's work first.

Piaget was born and raised in Switzerland. While an undergraduate in college, he became interested in philosophy and zoology, and he earned his PhD at the University of Neuchatel in 1918 with an investigation of the distribution of molluscs in the mountains of Valais. About this time, Piaget had reached the conclusion that life could be best understood in terms of stages of development or "structures of the whole" (*structures d'ensemble,* which in his theoretical formulations are inferred and relatively stable qualities of intellectual functioning that seem to characterize behavior at a given period in the sequence of growth). His attention then turned to psychology. After studying in Zurich by reading Freud and attending lectures by Jung, he went to Paris and for 2 years worked with Simon. While there he began wondering about the wrong answers that children gave on reasoning tests and decided to investigate them. In 1921, he went to Geneva to work with Claparède at the Jean-Jacques Rousseau Institute. Five years later Piaget became professor of philosophy at the University of Geneva (Piaget, 1952).

Piaget's book *The Language and Thought of the Child* was published in 1923, with an English translation in 1926. In talking with and listening to the verbalizations of children between 2 and 11 years of age, Piaget found what seemed to be two different kinds of speech. The first, egocentric speech, had self-expression and self-stimulation as its purpose. It was characterized by a lack of concern as to whether or not people attended to the speaking or what the listener's point of view might be. It was manifested when children talked to themselves or parroted speech or when they expressed their thoughts without waiting or listening to hear what anyone else might have to say. The second kind of speech, socialized speech, had as its purpose communication with others. In socialized speech, the speakers evidenced consideration for the reactions and points of view of listeners, and Piaget thought that such speech was characteristic of adults.

Indeed, Piaget found that as children grew, their speech became less egocentric and more socialized. By citing ages and the percentages of the kinds of speech found at each age level, he stimulated psychologists to repeat his work. Many got different results, but his more abstract findings seemed to hold firm. At a time when psychology needed reminding, Piaget's work showed that careful observation of children in natural settings might shed light on human functioning.

The Gestalt school of psychology was also beginning to cause excitement. Originally it arose in reaction to Wundt and structuralism. Gestalt psychologists argued that consciousness consisted not of elements connected serially but of configurations that were perceived in their entirety, often with distinctive new properties. Movement was one example: When we go to motion pictures, the actual stimuli are photographs flashed one at a time on a screen and separated by intervals of darkness; what is experienced, however, are objects moving about.

Later the Gestalt position reacted against behaviorism, particularly Watsonian behaviorism, which posited stimuli and responses strung together in stimulus-response (S-R) chains. Gestalt psychologists pointed to the learning of relations (or transpositional learning), the learning of cognitions and expectancies, and insight (e.g., dramatic improvement in performance when a new way of viewing the situation occurred). In contrast to American psychology, which emphasized conditioning, Lockean empiricism, overt behaviors, and the environment, Gestalt psychology emphasized perception, the brain's structuring of experience, and the phenomenal field. Let us take note of the work of Kurt Lewin (1890–1947), since he was the Gestalt psychologist then most relevant to clinical psychology (Brown, 1929).

Lewin was born in Prussia and attended the universities of Freiburg, Munich, and Berlin. He received his PhD in 1914 and spent the next 4 years in the German army. Lewin then returned to the University of Berlin as an instructor and research assistant in the Psychological Institute. In 1926, he was appointed professor of philosophy and psychology. His close associates at the university were Max Wertheimer and Wolfgang Köhler, both leaders in the Gestalt school.

Like other Gestalt psychologists, Lewin disputed virtually every tenet of behaviorism. The behaviorists, he claimed, tend to ignore individual variations from the average; extreme cases are usually attributed to chance fluctuations and may even be justifiably eliminated so as not to distort the data. For Lewin, the individual case is lawful and may be sufficient to support or refute a hypothesis. Behaviorists argue that psychologists should deal only with what may be observed. Lewin argued that observable behavior or appearances (phenotypes) can be produced by a variety of underlying causes (genotypes) and that psychologists have to be concerned with the interaction of both. Behaviorists claim that each stimulus elicits a response. Lewin (1951) claimed that an external stimulus influences, directs, and regulates a response that is produced by an internal tension striving toward discharge.

According to Lewin, an individual's behavior is a function both of this tension and of the individual's immediate perceptions of self and the environment. The individual's activities tend toward the restoration of equilibrium, or the release and satisfaction of inner tensions. In seeking to obtain this restoration, the environment can be perceived as having attractions and repulsions, goals and barriers to the goals. These formulations of Lewin led to some novel experiments.

Psychologists were surprised by the reports from his laboratory of the Zeigarnik effect. Bluma Zeigarnik had found that people seem better able to recall interrupted tasks than tasks they have completed. Supposedly, the tension to attain the goal persists in the case of interrupted tasks, causing better recall of them (Osgood, 1952). Clearly, the behaviorism of Watson could not have predicted that. And does not this failing of behaviorism, it was asked, indict the entire position of the school while indicating the correctness and fruitfulness of the Gestalt approach? Well, the issue was not really so stark, though the proponents of one position or the other often made it seem that way. Each school had focused on different aspects and problems of behavior. The attention of the Gestalt school was on perception and experiencing. Both schools, and in fact all contemporary schools of psychology, shared the aim of trying to understand people, and the confirmed findings of each obviously required integration within the science as a whole.

DIAGNOSTIC TECHNIQUES

Psychologists not only continued to devise and revise tests for the measurement of intelligence, but they also turned their attention to the assessment of other facets of personality. Interests and aptitudes, as well as traits and emotions, were challenging the ingenuity of psychometricians.

The most widely used of the individually administered scales, Terman's Stanford Revision of the Binet-Simon Scale, retained its popularity. But there were revisions of previous revisions of the Binet-Simon scale by Kuhlman (in 1922) and Yerkes (in 1923) as well as a brand new revision by Herring (in 1922).

There were also many new group-administered scales of mental ability: the Otis (1923) Classification Test, Forms A and B, which measured achievement as well as "mental alertness"; the Dearborn Group Tests (1922); the Institute of Educational Research Intelligence Scale CAVD (1925), which was developed under Thorndike's direction; the Miller Analogies Test (1926); the Kuhlmann-Anderson Intelligence Tests (1927); the Terman Group Test of Mental Ability (1920); and the Northumberland Mental Test (1920), later called the Morey House Tests (1925), which enjoyed popularity in England and was developed by Godfrey Thomson.

To round out this capsule picture of mental tests, there were also the Ferguson Form Boards (1920); the Assembly Test of General Mechanical Ability, devised by J. L. Stenquist in 1923, which was the first test designed to measure the ability of children and adults to assemble the parts of mechanical devices; the Florence Goodenough Draw a Man Test (1926), in which a measure of a child's intellectual level is obtained from scoring his or her drawing of a man for completeness, accuracy, and motor coordination; and the Porteus Maze Tests, first developed by Porteus in Australia around 1913 and improved by him throughout the years, including when he took over from Goddard as director of research at Vineland in 1919 (Freeman, 1950).

Still there was a degree of dissatisfaction with most of these tests and an awareness that much more needed to be done. Three problems were immediately recognized: (1) the lack of a suitable individually administered scale of intelligence for adults; (2) the need for a suitable individually administered scale of intelligence for infants; and (3) a clarification of the concepts underlying tests in general (test theory) and such concepts as intelligence, personality, and interest. Since most clinical psychologists were involved with schools and children's agencies, virtually no work was devoted to producing an adult scale. An infant scale, however, was urgently needed, particularly for use in adoption agencies and child care institutions. Some help in filling this need was provided by Gesell's (1925) *The Mental Growth of the Pre-School Child*.

Gesell (1880–1961) had prepared himself for his area of interest with admirable dedication. He was raised in Wisconsin and there acquired a love of nature, order-liness, and serenity. In 1899, he graduated from Stevens Point Normal School. For the next 2 years he taught a variety of subjects in a high school and even served as the football coach. Then he spent 2 years at the University of Wisconsin, worked for a year as a high school principal, and went to Clark University. In 1906, Gesell received his PhD from Clark with a thesis under Hall on a genetic study of jeal-ousy (Gesell, 1952).

After receiving his doctorate, Gesell went to work with Terman at the Los Angeles State Normal School. Because he was interested in the study of child development, he visited Witmer's clinic and Vineland. Gesell felt, however, that in order to pursue his interests properly, he needed a more complete understanding of human functioning and illness. Therefore, he decided to obtain a medical educa-tion. In 1911, he became assistant professor of education at Yale University Medi-cal School. Gesell received his MD in 1915, became a full professor at Yale, and also worked as a school psychologist for the State Board of Education of Connecti-cut, helping in the identification of retarded children and the formation of special classes and programs. We may note, as he himself proudly did, that in 1918 he became a charter member of the AACP.

Gesell pioneered the use of cinematography and cinemanalysis for the study of infant behavior. From 1924, with the help of grants, he began amassing a photo-graphic research library devoted to films of child development. On the basis of his observations, Gesell presented in *The Mental Growth of the Pre-School Child* and in a subsequent publication, *Infancy and Human Growth* (1929), 195 items that could be used to evaluate the progress of children between the ages of 3 and 30 months and still other items that could be used up to an age of 60 months. These items were presented in the form of developmental schedules that described typical behaviors found at certain chronological ages. There were four broad categories of items: motor, adaptive (e.g., picking up objects and conjugate movement of eyes), language, and personal-social (e.g., ability to feed self and bowel and bladder control).

Although psychologists were happy to have Gesell's developmental schedules, they recognized there were a number of weaknesses. Obviously, not all four cate-gories were represented at each level. Furthermore, this weakness seemed un-avoidable in view of the fact that children develop rather than spring forth with demonstrable skills in every area. Criticisms were also directed at the large num-ber of personal-social items, which are largely dependent on parental training; at the items involving gross motor control, such as sitting and walking, which do not seem to be directly related to intellectual functioning; at the standardization sam-ple; and at the lack of precise directions for administering and scoring the items. All in all, the Gesell developmental schedules were not perfect, but they were unique, and psychologists and parents busied themselves seeing whether children were doing what the schedules said they should be doing.

As a little sidelight, Dorothy Hallowell (1927) published an article on her re-search in testing preschool children. Her standardization sample consisted of 657 urban boys and girls who ranged in age from 1 year to 3 years 11 months and of whom 15% were black and 85% were white. She used Wallin Peg Boards, form boards, color cubes, and digit memory span as instruments, and she obtained promising results, although little attention was given to her work.

During the twenties, then, there were all kinds of intelligence tests more or less suitable for persons of every age. By the public and by members of other professions, clinical psychologists were identified primarily as intelligence testers or psychometricians. Usually they were caricatured as stuffy scientific types because they always dressed up their reports with statistical terms—correlations, averages, standard deviations, and the like—that caused social workers and psychiatrists some uneasiness. Their obsessions were (1) precise numerical results laced with qualifiers (usually necessary, we might add) and (2) the administration of tests according to exact procedures.

Not all clinicians fitted the prevailing stereotype, and of course none was exactly flattered by it. Some of them, F. L. Wells (1927), for example, tried to stress that when they went about their job, they did so with human feelings and a certain amount of judicious flexibility:

> *The function of psychometrics is not the accomplishment of a ritual, but the understanding of the patient. The ceremony of mental tests is valuable so far as it serves to reach this end. Ability to do this [modify testing procedures] intelligently is what distinguishes the psychologist, properly so called, from the 'mental tester.' (Wells, 1927, p. 27)*

Nevertheless, clinical psychologists, psychometricians, or mental testers did not enjoy much prestige, and being alert, intelligent, sensitive people, they were aware of this fact and not very happy about it.

Although there were other tests available, they were not used as frequently as the intelligence tests, nor were they as closely associated with the function of the clinician. Interest and aptitude tests were considered to be instruments primarily used by vocational guidance counselors and industrial psychologists, who were themselves quite busy.

In 1921, Stenquist published his Mechanical Aptitude Test; in 1922, Freyd introduced his Occupational Interest Blank; and in 1927, Strong came out with his Vocational Interest Blank. Seashore's tests of musical aptitude had become well known and were of sufficient worth to move George Eastman, benefactor of the Eastman School of Music, to say to Seashore, "You have saved us vast sums of money and undoubtedly you have prevented much human suffering by the introduction of this procedure" (Seashore, 1930).

As a matter of fact, there were enough aptitude tests around that, in 1928, C. L. Hull (1884–1952) could write a book on aptitude testing. Hull is better known, however, for his work in learning theory than for his excursion into testing, and he and his students will be encountered frequently in the chapters that follow.

Hull grew up on a farm in Michigan and worked his way through Alma Academy. His plan was to become a mining engineer, but an attack of polio left him paralyzed in one leg and caused him to abandon that ambition. He spent 2 years convalescing and teaching in a junior high school. During this period he became interested in psychology. Hull went to the University of Michigan and then on to graduate work at the University of Wisconsin. He received his PhD in 1918 and became a member of the faculty at Wisconsin, where he remained for the next 10 years. In his opinion, Joseph Jastrow was a kindly, literate man who could lecture beautifully and long and yet say almost nothing of importance (Hull, 1952).

Hull wrote his book *Aptitude Testing* because he was supposed to teach a course on the subject and wanted to learn something about the field before his class began. In the process of writing about these tests, he became so discouraged about their future that, after his book was published, he would have nothing more to do with the area. (We should note that, despite Hull's guardedly pessimistic prognosis, the field of aptitude testing continued to develop and be of use.)

Hull's interest next became focused almost exclusively on hypnosis. He and his students published a number of studies on hypnotic phenomena, and in 1929 Hull described his postural sway technique for evaluating the suggestibility of a subject (how far the person swayed after being given suggestions to sway and lose balance was used as the measure). While his research into hypnosis was in progress, Hull was invited to join the faculty at Yale. He arrived in 1929, soon encountered strong opposition from the "medical authorities" to any experimentation by a psychologist involving hypnotic techniques, and thus was forced to abandon his research in this area. This setback in his career was only temporary, and it actually proved somewhat of a blessing, for it enabled Hull to devote himself to learning theory sooner than he had intended.

Psychologists were trying to construct measures of personality, character, or temperament in addition to measures of interest and aptitude. The Allport (1921–1922) brothers, Floyd and Gordon, suggested having the person's traits rated by associates and preparing a profile graph. They were willing to concede there were some flaws in rating scales. For example, Thorndike (1920) had recently demonstrated the existence of a "halo effect" in making ratings (i.e., a tendency to rate a person high or low on all scales rather than score each characteristic independently). Moreover, Hollingworth had cautioned that self-ratings are difficult to interpret because people tend to overestimate the degree to which they possess socially desirable qualities and to underestimate the degree to which they possess socially undesirable qualities. Nevertheless, Gordon Allport (1921) thought rating scales would have to be used because no other objective method for evaluating personality was in sight. Surprisingly, help of all kinds was on the way.

Voelker (1921) pointed out that it might be valuable to observe a person's behavior on a specified battery of performance tests as a method for assessing personality. This simple idea had been used in a group-administered test (the Pressey X-O) and in an individually administered test (the Downey Will-Temperament Tests).

The Pressey (1921) X-O Test consisted of lists of words. The testee was supposed to cross out certain words according to specified directions: words that the testee felt had unpleasant meanings; the word that the testee most closely associated with a given key word; words that referred to things the testee worried about; words that, in the testee's opinion, stood for moral wrongs. This test was soon put out in a new form, because school teachers objected to the sexual words it originally contained. In both forms, the Pressey X-O Test was found to be low in reliability and low in validity. Even worse, no one knew how to interpret the scores once they had been obtained.

The Downey Will-Temperament Tests made its appearance in 1919 and touched off a flurry of research. June Downey (1875–1932) was trying to measure impulsivity, forcefulness, decisiveness, persistence, attentiveness to detail, and, of course, their opposites. She attempted to do all this by timing how long it took a child to write "United States of America" at normal speed, then as fast as possible, then in a handwriting style as different as possible from usual handwriting, and finally as slowly as possible without ceasing to move the pencil. There were eight other tasks, most of them involving handwriting, their aim being to sample the child's reactions to the frustrations imposed by the psychologist.

Studies indicated that the Downey Will-Temperament Tests had some validity in differentiating between groups of delinquents and nondelinquents and between Indians and whites but that it was of little value in understanding an individual. The intercorrelations among the subtests, even those supposedly measuring the same thing, were low, and the results of some 35 pieces of research uniformly agreed that the test was, at best, of questionable validity. Regretfully, it was concluded that the test "the most carefully standardized and most highly elaborated personality test which has yet been devised," was not suitable for widespread or routine use in the school (Wells, 1927).

The free association method was still regarded as promising, although even 30 years after its introduction very little had been learned from its use. Mateer had suggested that 10 "individual" reactions to a list of 100 words should be considered indicative of "psychopathy." But the large overlap between groups of normals and psychotic patients demonstrated that the free association technique should not be used alone in diagnosing mental illness.

Woodworth's Psychoneurotic Inventory or Personal Data Sheet was the forerunner of a number of similar questionnaires. Ellen Mathews had 75 items for children 12 years old and up. There was the Woodworth-Cady revision of the Personal Data Sheet, with 85 instead of 116 questions. Laird's Personal Inventory had 75 items for college students, with a breakdown of the results into schizoid, neurasthenoid (hypochondriasis and fatigue), hysteroid (convulsions and amnesia), and psychasthenoid (obsessions and fears). Symond's Adjustment Questionnaire aimed to discover how well a person was getting along in school, at home, and with peers. There was also the Woodworth-House Mental Hygiene Inventory, and Thurstone produced a Personality Schedule of 223 items (e.g., "Are your feelings easily hurt?").

In 1924, L. R. Marston introduced some tests for introversion-extraversion, including a list of 20 items by which children as young as 2 years of age could be classified depending on the answers given by their parents. However, enthusiasm for these tests waned as their findings showed that most people occupied a middle range and rated themselves as somewhat extraverted but as more introverted than their friends rated them (Freyd, 1924).

Although not very practical for individual diagnosis, Harthshorne and May's (1928) use of real-life situations for the study of cheating, lying, suggestibility, and persistence among school children aroused interest. The testees were placed in situations where they could be dishonest without realizing that Harthshorne and May had a way of discovering just how dishonest they had been. Harthshorne and May found that a child's honesty depended on the social circumstances, just as did the honesty of psychological experimenters.

Some work was done on graphology, notably by Robert Saudek (1929). Perhaps unfortunately, psychologists, especially those in the United States, were reluctant to take handwriting analysis seriously, probably because it had been and would doubtless continue to be readily exploited by persons outside the profession.

Meanwhile Witmer was suggesting a very different approach to diagnosis. In 1924, Witmer, E. B. Twitmyer, and Henry E. Starr established a psychobiochemical laboratory clinic that was associated with and under the control of the psychological clinic. At the same time, the department of psychology at the University of Pennsylvania began offering a graduate course in "Metabolism and Behavior." Characteristically, Witmer invented a new term *psychobiochemistry*, to cover the new aspect of clinical psychology he had in mind. Psychobiochemistry is the science of the relationship between metabolism and behavior.

Feeling very enthusiastic about this latest direction in his work, Witmer (1925), in a talk before the Section on Clinical Psychology of the APA, offered the following advice: "Would you dedicate yourselves to original research in the field of science most likely to be distinguished above all others for discoveries of importance during the latter half of this century, make ready, then, in the laboratory of physiological chemistry for work in clinical psychology and diagnostic orthogenics" (p. 18).

Some psychologists had been making ready (Rich, 1928–1929). They were trying to develop a measure of emotions—and perhaps a method that would differentiate between groups of psychiatric patients—by determining the acidity and alkalinity of saliva and the creatine concentration of urine. Some were using pneumographs (to measure respiration rate), sphygmographs (to measure pulse rate), sphygmomanometers (to measure blood pressure), plethysmographs (to measure blood volume changes in a part of the body), and galvanometers (to measure the electrical resistance of an area of the body). A lot of research was conducted with galvanometers in studies of the psychogalvanic reflex, which is a drop in the electrical resistance of the skin supposedly due to emotional activity (Landis, 1930).

Such studies had a theoretical foundation in the James-Lange theory of emotions, namely, that an individual's experiencing of an emotion is actually the experiencing of the organic and physiological changes that follow the perception of some event. The James-Lange formulation was still very popular among psychologists despite known inadequacies. For example, around 1900 Sherrington had found in experiments with dogs that when the viscera were separated from the central nervous system by cutting the motor nerves leading to them, the dogs still exhibited "emotional" behavior. It had also been found that the same visceral changes occurred in different emotional states. A third difficulty was that visceral changes took place too slowly to correspond to the speed of changes in experienced emotions. A fourth difficulty was that when visceral changes were artificially produced, emotions were not experienced.

In 1919, W. B. Cannon proposed a theory of emotions that he hoped would take all the difficulties into account. He suggested that emotions were mental processes connected with activity in the thalamus that adds a feeling tone to sensations. Regardless of whether or not Cannon was correct, the evidence made it clear that physiological changes alone are not a direct index of emotions.

A further note of caution was provided by Landis (1930), who admonished psychologists to bear in mind several pertinent variables in evaluating their research on the psychogalvanic reflex. Not only emotions but changes in temperature, the pH of blood, and any variable that influences sweat secretion can affect the reflex. After reviewing the literature, Landis concluded that the psychogalvanic reflex had no more significance for indicating emotions than changes in blood pressure, the pupillary reflex, or the knee jerk.

Thus, by the close of the twenties, psychologists were finding that measurements of physiological variables were not the simple, uncomplicated, valid indicators of a person's emotions that they had hoped.

Unknown to almost all psychologists in the United States and to most psychologists elsewhere, a Swiss psychiatrist, Hermann Rorschach (1884-1922), had approached the diagnosis of personality by using inkblots. As early as 1857, inkblots had been employed for scientific studies of imagination. Among these earlier, pre-Rorschach investigators were Kerner, Binet and Henri, Dearborn, Sharp, Kirkpatrick, Whipple, Pyle, Rybakof, Bartlett, and Parsons. Not one of these investigators entered into this area of research with the complexity and breadth of conceptualization dared by Rorschach, nor were they prepared to see, as Rorschach did, that this method might reveal the intellectual and emotional functioning of a person.

Hermann Rorschach was born in Zurich, the son of an art teacher in the public schools. He was the oldest of three children. His mother died when he was 12 and his father died when he was 18. During his school years, he was an excellent but not memorable student, and he was nicknamed *Klex,* which means "inkblot" or "painter," indicating that his classmates predicted he would follow in his father's footsteps (Ellenberger, 1954).

Although Rorschach did consider becoming an artist, he decided in favor of medicine. In keeping with the Swiss custom of studying at various schools, he attended, from 1904 to 1909, the universities at Neuchatel, Zurich, Berlin, and Bern. While in Zurich, he was exposed, of course, to the ideas of Bleuler, Jung, and Freud.

From 1909 to 1913, Rorschach worked as a resident in psychiatry at an asylum in Münsterlingen. He received his MD in 1912 from the University of Zurich with a dissertation under Bleuler, "On Reflex-Hallucinations and Kindred Manifestations." During this same period he carried out some studies with inkblots but published none of them and abandoned this area of interest to concentrate on psychoanalysis.

In 1913, he went to work in Russia, his wife's native country, but returned to Switzerland after several months to take a position at a mental hospital in Waldau. In 1915, he became associate director of the asylum in Herisau. In 1917 he became the father of a daughter and, in 1919, a son. His interests focused on psychoanalysis until, in 1917, he came across the dissertation of a Polish student Szymon Hens, who had studied medicine in Zurich.

Hens had devised an inkblot test of eight cards which he administered to 1,000 children, 100 normal adults, and 100 psychotics. His intention had been to study fantasy, and, in keeping with what had been done previously, he restricted his analysis to the content of the responses. Again, as was customary, Hens concluded his dissertation with a statement that further research was needed. He also raised several questions for consideration: What does it mean when some people use all the blot for their interpretation whereas others use only parts? Would colored blots give different results from those obtained with black and white blots? Could the method be used to diagnose psychosis?

After reading Hens's dissertation, Rorschach devoted all his energy to creating an inkblot test and devising a rationale for its interpretation.

He came across the writings of the Norwegian philosopher J. Mourly Vold (1850–1907) and borrowed from him two ideas: (1) Kinesthetic imagery is stimulated by restrictions of muscular activity and is inhibited by the movements of muscles, and (2) kinesthetic perceptions form the most important part of the material of dreams. Rorschach used Vold's ideas to assert that the inhibition of impulses tends to stimulate the production of fantasy, whose content is determined by dynamic variables such as complexes and repressions.

Rorschach applied the term "introversives" to those persons who tend to inhibit their movements or impulses and who turn inward upon themselves for understanding and creativity. Such persons are expected to perceive movement in inkblots. They are characterized by a more individualized and imaginative intelligence, stable emotional responsiveness, more inner life and less adaptability to the external world, more intensive than extensive rapport, and controlled but awkward and clumsy motility.

Rorschach applied the term "extratensives" to those persons who tend to express their movements or impulses and who thus interact with the environment and direct themselves outward. Such persons are expected to use color in their responses because they tend to express their emotions and, for many people, colors are associated with feelings. They are characterized by a stereotyped or imitative and conforming intelligence, labile emotional reactions, more outward life and greater adaptability to the external world, more extensive than intensive rapport, and a restless but skilled and adroit motility.

Rorschach's conceptualization owed much to Jung's introvert-extravert typology. However, Rorschach's formulation differs from Jung's in that introversives and extratensives are not thought to represent constitutional types but two modes of psychological functioning that are not mutually exclusive. People can be more or less both introversive and extratensive, and both functions are considered necessary for optimal development and performance. Therefore, in each person both modes of functioning coexist in some proportion, ranging from individual cases where both are highly developed (the "dilatated" person) to cases where both are minimally in evidence (the "coartated" person). An individual's introversive-extratensive balance (which he called *Erlebnistypus*) was indicated, Rorschach (1921) believed, by the ratio of movement responses to color responses elicited by a standard set of inkblots.

Although he did not treat it in depth, Rorschach thought Jung's distinction between internal or semantic associations and external or verbal associations was also important. Semantic associations were inferred from delays in responding, for it was supposed that the person was producing associations but not expressing them. Such reticence was believed to be characteristic of introverts. External associations are immediate verbalizations, and they were regarded as characteristic of extraverts. When using his Association Test, Jung noted semantic associations on the left side of the page and external associations on the right. A similar framework was followed by Rorschach in recording material elicited by inkblots.

In 1918, Rorschach began experimenting with 15 inkblots, using his patients as subjects. At the same time he worked ferverishly on the preparation of his book *Psychodiagnostik*, so rapidly in fact as to impair the clarity of the text. He sent the 15 inkblots and the manuscript to seven publishers; all rejected it. Finally, in 1920 it was accepted by a publisher but only on condition that 10 cards rather than 15 would be published.

The book appeared in 1921, though with several unsolicited contributions made by the printer. The cards had been reduced in size and their colors had been altered. Furthermore, though Rorschach's original cards had uniformly black areas, the printer, in reproducing them, introduced a variety of shadings so that forms could be perceived within them. Far from being upset, Rorschach was delighted with the possibilities that the shadings of the blots might afford.

Rorschach discussed his test before the Swiss Psychiatric Society and the Swiss Psychoanalytic Society but was able to arouse little interest. His book was a complete failure and most of the copies remained undisturbed in the basement of the publishing house. Some of his colleagues were impressed by Rorschach's "blind diagnoses" (i.e., his diagnosis of a patient solely on the basis of responses to the blots), but they were not excited enough to learn how he did it.

Emil Oberholzer, who had worked with Rorschach, taught the test to an American psychiatrist studying in Switzerland, David Levy. In 1921, Levy returned to the United States and brought a set of the blots with him. That some year the test was described to the German Society of Experimental Psychology as of possible use in vocational counseling. Immediately William Stern denounced it as faulty, arbitrary, artificial, and incapable, as was any test, of illuminating the human personality. That seemed to end the matter, and on April 2, 1922, Hermann Rorschach died.

The year after Rorschach's death Ludwig Binswanger commented somewhat critically, but also somewhat favorably, on *Psychodiagnostik*. However, perhaps because Rorschach lacked the prestige associated with a university affiliation, his test was not taken seriously. In 1927 David Levy was working as chief of staff at the Institute of Child Guidance in New York City. While there, he taught the test to a psychology trainee, Samuel J. Beck, who decided to use it as the subject of his dissertation. At about the same time, Manfred Bleuler, a psychiatrist, introduced the technique at the Boston Psychopathic Hospital (Beck, 1948). Seven years after Rorschach's death, his inkblots were being used occasionally in a few psychiatric installations. Concurrently, many psychologists were still agonizing over the difficulty of devising a test for the evaluation of personality functioning. Fortunately, problem and solution were soon to meet.

DIAGNOSTIC FORMULATIONS

More or less polite debate about the concept of intelligence continued among psychologists. At issue were its definition, its structure, and the question of its origin (whether it was due primarily to inheritance or environment). Aside from these issues, intelligence was generally thought to be clearly understood.

To the definitions of intelligence were added Terman's (1921), the ability to carry on abstract thinking, and Edwards's (1928), the capacity for versatility or variability of response. T. L. Kelley (1923) believed there were three independent kinds of intelligence: verbal; quantitative, evidenced in mathematics; and spatial, evidenced in performance on such things as form boards. In view of their independence, Kelley argued against the practice of adding up the scores of all the items on a scale to come up with one final score, as in an intelligence quotient. Thorndike (1920b, 1921) also believed that there were three kinds of intelligence, but his kinds were abstract, social, and mechanical (or motor), which were evidenced by a person's ability to deal with symbols, people, and objects, respectively. It seemed to Thorndike psychologists had been mostly interested in abstract intelligence and were still neglecting the other two kinds.

Spearman (1904, 1927, 1930), of course, still held to his view of a general factor of intelligence, g. Thorndike claimed his results agreed with Thomson's in pointing to several factors in intelligence. Cyril Burt (1952) agreed with Karl Pearson that there were special factors and also agreed with Spearman that there was a general factor. In the meantime, Spearman (1922) was wondering whether he really disagreed with any of these colleagues or whether his adherence to his own view was caused by "a streak of perversity and negativism." He concluded that he was sincere and decided to issue "a friendly challenge" to Thorndike to design together a crucial study that would show that he, Spearman, was right. As far as is known, Thorndike made no published or publishable reply.

By 1927, Spearman had no less than four general factors in intelligence: g, the ability to educe relations and correlates; c, the degree of "inertia" in shifting from one task to another; w, the degree of determination or persistence evidenced in pursuing a task; and oscillation, the ease with which a person recuperates after expending effort. It also seemed clear to him, as well as to Thorndike and all other interested parties, that when there are a number of correlated variables, these variables can always be factored into either a general factor and specific factors or into a number of independent factors. Spearman's and Thorndike's systems, then, are really interchangeable, and whether evidence was found to support one system or the other depended on the method of factor analysis employed. Naturally, Spearman was delighted by this clarification, since he believed that it meant everyone had come around to his point of view.

Thorndike seemed to have grown weary of the whole dispute: "The great merit of the Binet Test is that it is a graded scale for intellectual difficulty, and it is only weakened by being interpreted loosely as a measure of some mysterious essence called intelligence which grows in man" (Thorndike et al., 1927, p. 402). His weariness was shared by Wallin (1929), who contended that clinical psychologists did not care about definitions of intelligence or whether Spearman or Thorndike was right. However, if someone did want a definition of intelligence, Wallin thought of it as a complex of cognitive activities that are interrelated and interdependent because of the similarity of processes and the integrative activity of the neural mechanism. Wallin believed that cognitive activities are initiated, modified, and directed by nonintellective factors of an affective and conative nature and that they are manifested in their highest operations as successful adjustments to novel situations and as solutions of difficult problems.

Having vented his dissatisfaction, Wallin forcefully concluded,

> There is no more important lesson for the practitioner to learn than that existing psychological and psychiatric measures . . . are far from perfect, that they are affected by the personality characteristics of the examiner and by the influences of the physical and social environment as well as by native endowment . . . and that improvement in scientific testing techniques and ability analysis waits upon the solution of fundamental theoretical questions in psychology. (Wallin, 1929, pp. 197–198)

Wallin's somewhat oblique attempt at clarifying the issues did not receive the notice accorded the frontal assaults launched by L. L. Thurstone (1887–1955).

Thurstone had at first been mainly interested in mathematics and had obtained his undergraduate degree in electrical and mechanical engineering from Cornell. From 1912 to 1914, he taught engineering at the University of Minnesota and, while there, became increasingly interested in psychology. In 1914, he began his graduate work at the University of Chicago and the following year accepted a faculty position at Carnegie Institute of Technology under Bingham. He received his PhD from Chicago in 1917. Seven years later Thurstone married and returned to the University of Chicago to teach statistics and the theory of mental tests (Thurstone, 1952).

Thurstone (1926) attacked the concept of mental age by demonstrating its illogicality when applied to adults. At the root of the difficulty was the fact that scores on a particular test did not continue to increase with increasing age. Therefore, if mental age was defined as that chronological age for which a certain test performance is average, there would be several mental ages for the same score. On the other hand, if mental age was defined as the average chronological age of people who attained a certain test score, the mental ages of older children would be grossly inflated. This problem could be easily resolved, Thurstone (1928) suggested, by using as the test score the percentile standings of individuals with reference to their age group. Thurstone's suggestion had merit, but other psychologists believed teachers understood mental ages and would be confused by percentiles, so they did little to implement his idea.

A fundamental question raised and partially answered during this period was whether or not IQ remained constant for a specific individual from year to year. This was a different problem than the statistical constancy of IQ (i.e., arranging the test items so that the average mental age equaled the average chronological age, which would thus determine an IQ of 100). It would be possible to have statistical constancy though not individual constancy if, for example, dull children grew duller and bright children grew brighter.

William Stern (1925) was pleased to report that a number of studies had indicated IQ was a relatively stable index. To be sure, he conceded, variations of five IQ points on retesting were common, but differences much greater than that were seldom found. Given this, any large discrepancy between one test performance and another would merit exploration.

Stern was less happy with his colleague Bobertag's revision of the Binet scale but was delighted with Terman's revision. However, he went on to caution his American friends against believing that IQ represented the total mental status of the person. According to Stern, it represented only the individual's level of mental alertness and not the entire personality. Therefore, an IQ score makes possible negative predictions of high probability (predicting what the person cannot do) but is less significant in making positive predictions (predicting what the person will do). Stern suggested the reason for lower positive predictability is that in such predictions personality traits (e.g., creativity and persistence) are involved.

Three years before, in 1922, another psychologist had said, "No one has ever devised an intelligence test that tests intelligence and nothing else." That psychologist was Witmer (1922, p. 65). Three years later he wrote, "The unit of observation is a performance, but the unit of consideration is personality, defined by the perfectability of behavior, which is measured or estimated in the units of progress which men make toward the perfection they prefer" (Witmer, 1925, p. 11).

Witmer's years of research in clinical psychology had led him to a discovery: People constantly strive toward perfection. He was convinced this significant discovery had been made possible only because he had studied humans to understand humans and had not tried to understand humans through the study of other animals, as some of his misguided colleagues (no names mentioned) seemed to be doing. Moreover, he urged psychologists to focus on whatever distinguishes humans from other animals—ethics, moral codes, cultures, the pursuit of what seems good and perfect—rather than the resemblances. But Witmer was plainly tired of advocating his views and bitterly disappointed by the lack of recognition: "I have received from my professional contemporaries that most sincere tribute—imitation, often enough without acknowledgment" (Witmer, 1925, p. 18).

The position that intelligence and personality are not distinct functions was held by thinkers other than Witmer. For example, Guy G. Fernald (1920–1921), a physician, argued that intelligence and character are blended. Not only that, he considered it reasonable to believe that culture can affect intellectual functioning by emphasizing or minimizing the development of certain skills. Personality, as Fernald conceived it, includes intelligence. Therefore, tests and studies of intelligence will furnish information about personality but tests and studies of personality will not necessarily furnish information about intelligence.

Thus far in this section we have discussed some ideas about intelligence current in the twenties. Next we will direct our attention to some major research findings.

Mental tests were increasingly being used not only as instruments of diagnosis but as tools for conducting experimental research. Terman (1924), in his APA presidential address, emphasized the valuable contributions that mental tests had made and could continue to make to the science of psychology. In particular, they were thought useful for measuring individual and race differences; uncovering the structure and relationship of mental traits; evaluating intellectual growth; determining the limits of educability; and understanding genius, mental deficiency, and insanity. Let us see how useful.

Catherine Cox assembled all the information that she could obtain about the childhood of 300 persons of outstanding accomplishment. On the basis of these biographical sketches, four psychologists who were expert in the field of child psychology and intelligence testing estimated what the IQs of these men would have been had they been tested in childhood. Although the estimates for some of these acknowledged geniuses varied considerably, they were, almost without exception, very high. The study demonstrated that adults of high accomplishment were usually highly accomplished children and that geniuses come from the ranks of gifted boys and girls (Hollingworth, 1926).

The accolade of genius was bestowed liberally at this time by Terman et al. (1925) on anyone with an IQ of 140 or more earned on the Stanford Revision of the Binet scale. Terman (1922, 1924) had in mind an ambitious, unprecedented, longitudinal study of "genius in the making." As the first phase of this study, approximately 1,000 school children in California with IQs above 140 were identified and evaluated. These evaluations were to be repeated over the years, but even the first results were exciting. In contrast to the stereotype of the highly intelligent child as weak, thin, short, sickly, and bespectacled, Terman found the gifted to be taller, healthier, heavier, and better adjusted socially than the average child. He planned, so far as possible, to chronicle in subsequent studies the achievements and adjustments of these gifted children as they progressed into adulthood.

Incidentally, by the middle of the twenties, Terman, in referring to highly intelligent children, was using the term *gifted* more and the term *genius* less. *Gifted* had been suggested by Leta Hollingworth based on a recommendation by Whipple. The rationale behind using *gifted* to refer to unusually bright children was that a genius is a person who has made an outstanding contribution to the enrichment of the culture. "It is only when a man's life is recognized by others as having significance for them that we call him a genius" (Alfred Adler, quoted in Ansbacher & Ansbacher, 1956, p. 153).

A possible fly in the ointment was noted by Witty and Lehman (1927). Playing the devil's advocates, they called attention to previously obtained evidence that not all gifted children become gifted adults. One plausible, even probable, reason for this lack of adult achievement is a lack of drive. Possibly this lack of drive was to be explained by the lack of a need to compensate for feelings of inadequacy. Now, if the children in Terman's study were as well adjusted as he claimed, Witty and Lehman wondered if many of these children might not progress through adulthood without becoming geniuses or achieving an outstanding record of accomplishment. Of course, only time would provide an answer to the question they raised. (To anticipate a little, their worst fears were not realized.)

Another topic of considerable interest was the extent to which human behavior is innate and the extent to which it is acquired. In the controversy about intelligence, this question of nature versus nurture (or heredity versus environment) was particularly vexing. At one extreme were those who held that intellectual ability is almost entirely inherited and that certain races and ethnic groups, because of genetically based limitations, cannot be expected to achieve the highest cultural levels. At the other extreme were those who believed that intellectual ability is almost completely acquired and that healthy children of different races raised under identical environmental conditions could be expected to function identically in school (Watsonian behaviorists were in this group).

Most psychologists were not at either extreme and simply emphasized one of the major variables over the other. For example, Goddard, Gesell, and Terman stressed the significance of heredity over environment, whereas Thorndike and Witmer stressed the significance of environment over heredity. One of the great changes of the twenties was that, within the span of a few years, a large number of psychologists shifted from a nature to a nurture emphasis and denied the existence of inherent racial and ethnic inequalities.

As late as 1925, T. R. Garth could survey the literature on racial psychology and note, "The thing most predominant is a characteristic state of mind . . . and that is a belief in racial differences in mental traits" (pp. 343–344). On the basis of his survey, Garth (1925) concluded that the white race is probably superior to all others. And most psychologists interested in the problem probably would have agreed with him. Almost every study pointed in the direction of inherent racial differences, probably because everyone believed that intelligence tests not only are supposed to measure inherited intelligence but actually do. Accordingly, Brigham (1923), after finding the Army Alpha scores of recently arrived foreign-born recruits were especially low, concluded that recent immigrants were less intelligent than earlier ones.

The position that intelligence is hereditary was shaken by several converging lines of evidence. Carmichael (1927) reported the sexual behavior of castrated animals and the inept pecking of chicks that had been deprived temporarily of visual stimulation indicated that "the development of the behavior mechanism is not alone dependent upon heredity or environment, but that it is the result of the *interdependent* action of both of these factors."

Moreover, Thorndike (1929) warned that in determining whether one race was superior to another, it was more important to consider the ranges of intellectual functioning than the averages. He pointed out that in certain studies comparing blacks with whites, the upper limit of the black scores exceeded the white average score. In view of these results and the environmental obstacles confronting blacks, he found it difficult to assert the intellectual superiority of whites.

Within the next few years, Brigham (1930) rescinded his earlier conclusion about immigrants. He warned his colleagues if they wanted to avoid similar errors in the future when comparing group performances on intelligence tests, to exercise care to ensure that the individuals in the groups have had equal educational opportunities.

In a later review of racial studies, Garth (1930, p. 348) concluded, "It would appear that it [the hypothesis of intellectual differences between races] is no nearer being established than it was five years ago. In fact many psychologists seem practically ready for another, the hypothesis of racial equality." Therefore, within a period of 5 years there was an almost complete reversal in the interpretation of the results of racial studies, and the influence of environment rather than heredity now received more emphasis.

We will note one last finding, which was provided by Mary Wentworth (1923–1924). She had administered the Stanford revision to 200 patients diagnosed as having dementia praecox. Impressed by the success of some patients on adult items and their failure on less difficult questions, Wentworth suggested the psychosis should be regarded as a volitional and affective disorder rather than one in which an intellectual defect is primary.

Wentworth's suggestion was significant in that it serves to illustrate again the tendency during this period to use emotional and interpersonal variables as explanations for illnesses previously thought to be organic or inherited. Cyril Burt (1925), after studying comparable groups of delinquents and nondelinquents, concluded that heredity is of trifling importance in the genesis of criminal behavior: "It is clear that the commonest and the most disastrous conditions are those that center about the family life." Davies (1926–1927) thought the symptoms of withdrawal and oversensitivity in dementia praecox could be attributed to the patient's wounded self-feeling. Therefore, the patient primarily needs experiences that will reinstate positive self-feelings, help to maintain contact with the environment, and exposure to confront the person with new situations that could arouse the emotions and become integrated (both in the sense that the patient has feelings that are appropriate to the situations and in the sense that the experiences are retained and recalled).

Thus we can see that the nature versus nurture controversy with respect to intelligence was paralleled by organic versus nonorganic etiologies offered in explanation of abnormalities of behavior. In this area as well, hereditary and constitutional factors were relegated to roles of minor significance in comparison with the importance assigned to interpersonal and environmental variables. Here too behaviorism made a contribution.

After the war, Watson and Raynor (1920) reported a study conducted at Johns Hopkins. They conditioned Albert, the 11-month-old son of one of the wet nurses in the Harriet Lane Hospital, to fear a white rat by pairing the presentation of the rodent with a loud noise. Not only did Albert become conditioned to fear the rat but the fear response was generalized to include rabbits, dogs, and other furry objects. Obviously, Watson had demonstrated that some fears could be acquired and had illustrated a procedure by which fear responses could be produced. Unfortunately for Albert, he was adopted and left Baltimore before it was possible to complete the extinguishing of his conditioned fear reaction. This study, despite its methodological and ethical problems, came to be regarded as a "classic" (Harris, 1979) and as having obvious implications for psychopathology.

The effects of learning and of adverse relationships within the family had also begun to occupy the attention of Adler (1928-1929). Although he still thought it possible that some feelings of inferiority are caused by a person's awareness of a certain kind of physical inferiority, he now stressed the development of such feelings as a result of the home environment. A child who is pampered or rejected or whose parents emphasize weakness and dependency and make unreasonable demands is likely to suffer from feelings of inadequacy regardless of bodily health. By decompensating (i.e., developing neurotic symptoms), children attempt to enlist the sympathy of their parents, to impose their authority over them, and to ensure that this pitiable exploitative relationship is perpetuated.

The effects of interpersonal variables on hypnosis were also becoming prominent, and study of them was radically changing the concept of hypnosis as simply a special condition. The four major symptoms of the hypnotic trance were thought to be (1) loss of initiative, (2) loss of memory, (3) increased suggestibility, and (4) rapport (or the subject's dependence on the operator). After reviewing the literature, Young (1926) dismissed the view that the subject is a helpless automation controlled by a strong-willed operator: "It is nearer the truth to regard the operator as allowing himself to play a part, and by no means an indispensable one, in a drama constructed and acted in the depths of the subject's mind." According to Young's (1927-1928) formulation of the hypnotic process, people unconsciously hypnotize themselves, but in order that this may take place, it is essential that they believe in the power of the operator and be willing to cooperate with suggestions in the unconscious act of submission involved in hypnosis.

Similarly, Gordon Allport (1929-1930) thought that interpersonal factors are of major significance in explaining the process whereby one person obtains a clear understanding or grasp of the personality of another. He suggested that this is accomplished by a process he called *empathy* (T. Lipps introduced the term in 1907). Although empathy was not precisely defined, its general meaning was made clear. Allport regarded it as a sympathetic apprehension or comprehension of the feelings and beliefs of another person, and he believed people are limited in their capacity to employ it: "The extent of our understanding of another is rigidly determined by our own attitudes and habits. . . . A thoroughly intimate appreciation of personality is a difficult accomplishment. Few people have such an appreciation for even one personality, and no one has it for an unlimited number."

Human understanding, hypnosis, psychological disturbances, and intellectual functioning were not the only areas enlightened through the use of interpersonal, emotional, environmental, often unconsciously operative variables. These variables frequently appeared as elements in credible explanations for behaviors previously dismissed as unimportant. For example, Lehman and Witty (1926) found that black children who were educationally retarded in comparison with white children played school much more than did white children. Their interpretation of this finding was that the black children used playing school to compensate for their actual lack of achievement and intellectual prestige. The point to be noted is that these concepts were no longer confined to the adherents of a particular theory but were being expressed by psychologists of varying persuasions (or of no persuasion in particular) and were thus being assimilated into psychology.

Meanwhile, Freud (1927a, 1936) who was a prime mover in fostering knowledge of these influences on behavior, continued to extend the use of psychoanalytic concepts in the understanding of pathology. He viewed psychoneuroses as conflicts between ego and id, depressions and melancholias as conflicts between ego and superego, and psychoses as conflicts between ego and the outer world or reality. As for specific kinds of neurosis, he viewed repression as the central defense mechanism in hysteria, whereas reaction formation (the opposite of a strong unconscious impulse is displayed in behavior), isolation (an impulse or wish is recognized but without knowledge of how it is related to behavior or, put differently, thoughts and feelings that might reasonably be connected or associated are not), and undoing (an activity is carried out in the hope that it will magically cancel out a previous action about which the person feels some guilt) were thought to be the characteristic defenses of obsessive-compulsive disorders.

Freud still acknowledged the importance of constitutional variables in the etiology of these disturbances but discussed them so little that the tendency of psychoanalysts was to pay them only lip service. Instead, analysts riveted the attention of psychologists on unconscious conflicts, defenses, and early childhood determinants of adult behavior. They did this so successfully that anyone who indicated the significance of current conflicts was convinced he or she was making a novel contribution to science. To illustrate, Rivers (1923) pointed out the importance of current problems: "Recent conflicts are far more influential in the production of both dreams and psychoneurosis than is now usually supposed."

It should be stressed that these widespread shifts in emphasis were not initiated by conclusive research or by positive experimental results justifying them. In other words, there was no substantial body of evidence that demonstrated environment was more significant than heredity in intelligence or psychopathology. Rather, a basic change had occurred in the interpretation of findings and observation. To a large extent, this change was brought about by a greater understanding of research methodology and diagnostic techniques and by a wish to examine new, more hopeful alternatives than those of the past. The focus on acquired, environmental explanations had the effect of infusing the field with optimism, since genetic factors were considered virtually immutable.

Arrayed against these formulations were those that emphasized constitutional differences between people. Here we find the typologies, but even here we find an exception—a typology that is acquired. However, let us first consider those systems that held to the rule.

The most popular typology was Jung's (1925), with its distinction between extraversion and introversion. Recall that this pair of concepts represented essentially innate differences in attitude: The extravert turns outward toward the external environment; the introvert turns inward toward the self. While psychologists were busy investigating this dichotomy, Jung was studying the Pueblo Indians and the natives of Africa and India to see if there were similarities between the contents of the collective unconscious of Europeans and primitive myths, cults, and rituals elsewhere. Basically, he was searching for universal symbols and archetypes.

Jung viewed extraverts and introverts as capable of relating to their world by means of four major functions that were antagonistically paired. As listed below, the first two items in each group indicate the form of the function if extraverted and the second two indicate the form of the function if introverted: thinking and understanding versus feeling and valuing; external and internal perception versus intuitive prediction (sensing what an object or person will be or has been) and unconscious perception. Accordingly, Jung envisioned an extravert relating to the environment by thinking and perceiving; an introvert, by feeling and intuiting. Furthermore, personality characteristics and functions that were not overt were considered suppressed. Within the unconscious they supposedly continued to strive for expression and, being denied accessibility to awareness, they were compensated for by the formation of symbols. Psychologists briefly focused their attention on Jung's typology, but when they found it well-nigh impossible to isolate pure types, they lost much of their enthusiasm for the typology and its elaboration (Guthrie, 1927).

Another major typology, based on body build, was first proposed by the psychiatrist Ernst Kretschmer (1888–1964) in 1921. Kretschmer distinguished four types: (1) the tall and thin *asthenic*, who has a schizophrenic temperament; (2) the muscular *athletic*, a variant of the asthenic and prone to exhibit, though to a lesser degree, schizophrenic characteristics; (3) the pudgy *pyknic*, who has large body cavities and tends to be cyclothymic; (4) the *dysplastic*, who evidences deviant physical features due largely to endocrine disturbances. The schizophrenic temperament is quiet, reserved, and unsociable; the cyclothymic is moody, emotional, genial, and cheerful. Kretschmer (1925) reported relationships between the asthenic type and schizophrenia and between the pyknic type and manic-depressive psychosis.

It was noted that in Kreschmer's sample the schizophrenics were younger than the manic-depressive patients and thus less apt to have suffered the "middle-aged spread" associated with chronological maturity. Also, other psychologists were less able than Kretschmer to locate pure types and so might be forgiven for not sharing in his excitement.

A similar fate awaited the typology of S. Naccarati and H. E. Garrett (1924). They described microsplanchnics, who are long and thin, have small trunk in comparison with their limbs and who expend their energies. At the other end of the continuum were the macrosplanchnics, who are stout or fat, have large trunks in comparison with their limbs, and conserve their energies. Midway along the continuum were normosplanchnics. Naccarati and Garrett derived, by complex maneuvers, a morphologic index as their measure. But neither they nor other investigators found much relationship between the index and scores on Woodworth Personal Data Sheets, Pressey X-O tests, or anything else.

L. Berman (1921) offered a typology based on glands, distinguishing thyroid, pituitary, and gonadocentric personalities. At about the same time, A. Rosanoff (1878–1943), a psychiatrist, presented a system based on psychiatric disorders. Rosanoff (1920) defined personality as inborn capacities, traits, and tendencies. He thought that certain abnormal constitutions were hereditarily transmitted as Mendelian recessives and that these provided the foundation for specific mental illnesses. He saw the antisocial personality as the constitutional basis for hysteria and criminality, the cyclothymic personality as the basis for manic-depressive psychosis, the autistic personality as the basis for schizophrenia, and the epileptic personality as the basis for epilepsy (the epileptic personality is characterized by fussiness, irritability, fault finding, and brief periods of elation and ecstasy). From the beginning, Rosanoff stated that there is no sharp demarcation between the "normal" personality type and its pathological manifestation and that in normality mixed types are the rule. Still, the similarities between the descriptions of cyclothymic personality and extraversion and between autistic personality and introversion caused many psychologists to believe studies based on Rosanoff's typology would yield familiar fruit. Nevertheless, some psychologists became interested in his concept of an epileptic personality and undertook considerable research on the topic.

As we pause to survey the scene, what is most noteworthy is psychologists' growing awareness of the complexity of their discipline. In every area, simple problems and concepts were the rare exception. And where new formulations or techniques were once accepted uncritically, they were now met by skepticism. There was a ceaseless questioning, and not only were all ideas challenged but the challengers were challenged in return. Further, in these disputes the weapons used were often facts garnered through controlled experiments and penetrating analyses.

The last typology we shall consider is explicitly without a constitutional reference and therefore something of an exception. The types are based on acquired value systems. This typology was introduced by Eduard Spranger (1928), who believed that behavior can be understood or experienced as meaningful only in relation to the agent's value systems. Spranger described six ideal types or value orientations, and he made no judgments as to whether one type is to be regarded as better than another. Spranger also recognized that ordinarily a person will express a preference for two or more different value systems. Briefly, in ideal or pure form, Spranger's types were the aesthetic type, valuing beauty, form, and harmony; the economic type, valuing practicality and usefulness; the political type, valuing power and leadership; the religious type, valuing mysticism and the experiencing of oneness with God and the universe; the social type, valuing the love and approval of others; and the theoretical type, valuing truth and the ordering of knowledge. Gordon Allport, for one, was favorably impressed by this formulation.

Let us now turn to the work of Shepherd Ivory Franz, which was creating a feeling of hope about a field that had been regarded as unpromising for psychologists. In his APA presidential address, Franz (1922) reported that organic problems can be circumvented and, to some extent, remedied. His studies (Franz, 1921) and those of others had indicated a general dependence of mental states on states of the brain but not, as had been believed, a specific dependence of particular functions on the integrity of definite cerebral areas. He reiterated his findings that although cerebral damage may temporarily affect psychological functioning, the disturbance need not be permanent. Franz therefore urged his colleagues to participate more in the diagnosis of central nervous system pathology: "Some neurologists have waked up to an appreciation of the necessity for finer examinations and for greater analyses along psychological lines, and it is to be hoped that psychologists will not hold themselves aloof from this field" (Franz, 1921, p. 95). However, Franz's enthusiasm was based less on his diagnostic successes than on the encouraging experiences he had in treating his patients. It is to his thoughts about treatment that we shall now direct our attention.

TREATMENT FORMULATIONS

Franz (1923) demonstrated that retraining and reeducation were useful procedures in helping patients to regain habits and functions lost through brain damage. Thus, in large part through his efforts, rehabilitation came to be seen as a feasible goal. Franz also believed rehabilitation procedures were valuable as a means of teaching social skills to motivated psychotics. But regardless of whether a patient is brain-damaged or psychotic, Franz considered the patient's motivation and relationship with the therapist to be supremely important. It is essential, he insisted, that the patient acknowledge the abnormality, evidence a desire to get well, and possess self-confidence and confidence in the therapist. The techniques alone cannot provide success.

It should be emphasized that Franz and the vast majority of psychologists thought of their approach to helping persons as a form of education. (In 1924, Franz left Washington to assume the positions of lecturer at the University of California and chief of the Psychological and Educational Clinic of the Children's Hospital in Hollywood.) They did not think of themselves as involved in treatment, a function that, as Seashore (1930) put it, was entrusted only to "duly qualified psychiatrists." Clinical psychologists, for the most part, thought of themselves as more or less working with principles of learning to ameliorate undesirable habit patterns. They attempted to correct reading and speech defects and at first viewed these problems as arising from organic causes or from some flaw in the educational process. Thus Twitmyer (1931), in discussing the etiology of speech disorders, mentioned deafness, amentia, brain injury, anatomical or functional anomalies of speech organs, and negativism. Similarly, David Mitchell (1931) described the role of the clinical psychologist in private practice as follows: "His study includes a consideration of the situation which must be set and the stimuli which must be used in order that desirable habits be strengthened and unfortunate ones modified or eliminated." In short, clinicians, perceived themselves as dealing with educational, not psychiatric, problems. But this distinction was growing increasingly difficult to maintain.

On the one hand, some psychologists saw that learning principles could be usefully applied to modify behaviors that were strikingly similar to psychiatric disturbances. Watson (1928), for example, reported investigations of the effectiveness of various conditioning techniques in the reduction of children's fears. The method of disuse was not very effective (attempting to weaken the stimulus-response association with the passage of time by avoiding its exercise), nor was verbal organization (talking about the feared object), nor was frequent and repeated presentation of the feared object, nor were social factors (observing other children playing with the noxious stimulus). What seemed to be most effective was unconditioning or reconditioning, as illustrated by the case of Peter in a study reported by Mary C. Jones (1924). Three-year-old Peter had been afraid of rabbits and other furry things. After being presented with a caged rabbit, placed closer each day, while eating lunch, Peter seemed to lose his fear of it and of other furry things as well. It appeared to Watson that many psychiatric disturbances could be explained without recourse to unconscious complexes, wishes, and the like. Instead, they could be understood in terms of conditioning and ameliorated by the application of conditioning techniques.

On the other hand, some psychiatrists saw neurotic disorders as problems in reeducation. Austen Riggs (1876–1940) reported success in treating neurotics by removing them from their stressful environments to the more insulated regimen and safety of his sanitarium. There patients were told they were in need of reeducation, which they were definitely going to obtain from their physicians and other members of the staff. Demands on them to exercise initiative and make decisions were immediately minimized. Their lives at the sanitorium were orderly and quietly regimented. It was from this very routine that they were supposed to learn to do things just because they had to be done. In the course of daily interviews with their therapists, they were given assigned readings to inspire and discipline them. They heard lectures and participated in group discussions in the psychology of adjustment. They participated in activities that emphasized the importance of cooperation in social living, and by participating they gave order to their lives. All these things, Riggs (1929) claimed, produced improvement in his patients—and without delving into the unconscious.

Thus, among both psychologists and psychiatrists, there were those who advocated that what had been thought to be mental illnesses should be considered problems in learning and adjustment. From some points of view this rapprochement of psychology and psychiatry was regarded as an exciting advance, whereas from others it was seen as having the unfortunate consequence of blurring the boundary between the two fields. What made the subject of professional identities a sensitive matter of great significance was the challenge it posed to the assertion that the practice of psychotherapy should be the exclusive province of medical professionals. Within the ranks of psychiatry, a small but influential group raised objections to this traditional claim and in so doing served to soften further the contrast between their field and clinical psychology.

Freud (1927b) did not regard a medical degree as necessary to practice psycho-analysis and could point to Hanns Sachs, his daughter Anna, and perhaps even Otto Rank as successful nonmedically trained analysts. Alfred Adler also did not believe that only physicians should undertake treatment (Ansbacher & Ansbacher, 1956). On the contrary, he made a clear distinction between juvenile and adult patients. Children, he suggested, might be helped by their parents and teachers, while adult neurotics required the services of psychotherapists.

To implement this view, Adler, in 1922, began conducting clinics where problem children and their parents were interviewed. The interviews were conducted before an audience of teachers as a way of helping to train them in understanding and dealing with psychological disturbances. Shortly after Adler began this work, he reached the conclusion that the presence of the audience in and of itself had therapeutic value. He thought this procedure made it immediately evident to the children that their problems were of concern to the community and proved to them that people in general wished to be of help. (Incidentally, Rudolf Dreikurs, a psychiatrist who was one of Adler's pupils, introduced this method of family counseling to the United States in 1928. Subsequently, he extended the method by arranging to see his alcoholic patients in groups.)

Well, is mental illness really an illness? Should physicians alone be deemed competent to treat neurotics and psychotics? Will such patients get well no matter who does what for them? Adler thought a sizable percentage of them would. He saw the therapist taking on the functions of a mother, giving patients the experience of feeling themselves close to an utterly trustworthy person and thereby strengthening and broadening their social interest. Through simple, direct, inoffensive explanations of a patient's behavior, explanations that the patient could immediately acknowledge, Adler saw the therapist building up the patient's independence and courage. Yet he believed that despite all that his theory and techniques might add, fully half his patients were already on the road to recovery simply by virtue of their wish to get well. And he did not consider this percentage to be unique to his caseload: "It is this 50 percent of 'cures' that enables all schools of psychiatry to live" (Ansbacher & Ansbacher, 1956, p. 336).

As if to demonstrate that both psychologists and psychiatrists had cause to wonder, the phenomenon of Emile Coué burst forth in the United States in 1923. Coué (1857–1926), a former French chemist, had studied hypnotism and the power of autosuggestion (Winkler & Bromberg, 1939). His theory was that imagination, when engaged in conflict with the will, is of superior strength and will triumph. Therefore, all one has to do to achieve peace of mind and mental health is to imagine vividly enough that one is well. Coué believed that mental health could be attained simply by repeating at least three times each day, "Day by day in every way I am getting better and better."

Having reputedly achieved great success in Europe, Coué was greeted in the United States as a virtual messiah. People flocked to hear him deliver his gospel and his formula in person. They jammed Coué institutes in order to make certain that they had the words right. So simple and emphatic was Coué's prescription that, inevitably, disillusionment was rapid and complete. Sadly, Coué returned to

France and Couéism became a subject for jokes ("My husband thought he was sicker and sicker until he saw Coué; now he thinks he's deader and deader"). However, Coué, in his failure, had served at least to demonstrate the enormous number of people who wished for help. Could so many persons have psychiatric problems? Were so many Americans badly conditioned?

If "curing" of roughly 50% of patients was enough to satisfy some people, it was not enough for Healy and Bronner (1926). They had studied 675 delinquent boys and girls in Chicago and Boston and found that 55% had committed crimes after supposedly having been reformed. It seemed clear to them that if only 45% were helped, the methods for treating delinquents were inefficient and ineffective. They urged judges, lawyers, and public officials everywhere to give scientists the opportunity to employ their therapeutic techniques to help delinquents become healthy, useful members of society.

The therapeutic techniques that Healy and Bronner probably had foremost in mind for meeting the problems of delinquency were psychoanalytic. Although some innovations had occurred, psychoanalytic techniques remained essentially unchanged during the twenties. Shortly after the war there had been some interest in integrating psychoanalysis and hypnosis into what was called *hypnoanalysis.* The procedure of hypnoanalysis was basically as follows: The patient, under hypnosis, would recall a traumatic incident. The hypnotist would supply interpretations that the patient would evaluate until he or she seemed to find an acceptable one. Then the hypnotist would give positive, forceful suggestions that all that had been discussed would be recalled when the patient awoke. Finally, in the waking state, the patient and hypnotist would go over the story, its interpretations, and its significance in past behavior and for future conduct (Zilboorg & Henry, 1941).

General interest in hypnoanalysis soon diminished. Not so the interest in psychoanalysis. Around 1924, William Alanson White, president of the American Psychiatric Association recommended that psychiatrists shake up their concepts and take a fresh look at mental illness with the formulations of psychoanalytic theory in mind to help them gain new insights. And by 1929, some schizophrenic and depressed patients in mental hospitals were being psychoanalyzed by analytically trained psychiatrists.

Most hospitalized patients, though, still received only custodial care. For a brief interval, many of them had found themselves subjected to teeth extractions and tonsillectomies. The rationale for these procedures came from Henry A. Cotton, a psychiatrist who believed that focal infections were responsible for mental illness and delinquency. Cotton (1921, 1922) claimed he had produced cures by removing the infected part of the body. Not many accepted his theory, but out of discouragement and in the remote hope that he might be right, a few people decided to give his procedures a trial.

Then, in 1922, a study was reported by Kopeloff and Cheney. One group of 58 mental patients had tonsils and teeth extracted, whereas 64 other mental patients, constituting the control group for the experiment, were allowed to remain intact. No difference in improvement between the two groups was discernible. Apparently there was nothing to support Cotton's theory. Another blind alley had been entered, but at least this one needed no longer to be explored.

It would appear that relatively little in the way of new developments in treatment occurred in the twenties, although more people were becoming familiar with psychoanalysis and other psychodynamic theories and were using those methods of treatment for a greater variety of disturbances. In short, the decade was a period not of innovation but of refinements and the dissemination of theories.

PROFESSIONAL DEVELOPMENT

Testing was becoming big business, and psychologists felt both delight over their success and displeasure over the extent of its commercialization. Tests were almost everywhere in use, and few school children escaped them. According to Goddard (1928), "It is in the scientific classification of pupils that the most noteworthy results, for education, of the applications of differential and clinical psychology are found."

The task of school psychologists was to detect and remedy what were thought to be "temporary" incapacities in learning. Through the use of diagnostic techniques, school psychologists tried to differentiate between those who cannot and those who will not learn. At first, this differentiation seemed easy, because it was thought that any child with an IQ below average "cannot" and all other children "will not." Unfortunately, the task became more and more difficult as the variables that affect intellectual functioning and IQ scores were recognized. Nevertheless, despite the mounting complexities in the decisions school psychologists had to make, many schools continued to rely heavily upon psychological tests to provide information to ease the demands on teachers to make judgments regarding teachability.

Testing began to be applied in the field of vocational and industrial guidance. In 1920, Morris S. Viteles set up a vocational guidance clinic at the University of Pennsylvania. The aim of vocational guidance, according to Viteles (1924), was to supply information to help in the choice of occupations by children of working age, at that time 14 to 16 years. Achieving this aim required both an analysis of the demands of various jobs and an analysis of an individual's interests, competence, temperament, health, education, physical appearance, socioeconomic condition, and experience. Obviously, testing had an important role to play in this analysis of the individual.

James McKeen Cattell, formerly of Columbia University, took the lead in founding the Psychological Corporation in 1921. He was joined in this enterprise by a group of psychologists, some 200 in number, who purchased shares of stock in the corporation. They were encouraged by reports from the British Institute of Psychology that indicated that psychological principles could be applied to increase industrial production and individual satisfaction. Far from being antithetical, high rates of production and employee satisfaction could go along very well together. The Psychological Corporation was to derive most of its income from the sale of tests, from consultations, and from the conduct of special studies and surveys for client firms. Its profits were to be devoted to the promotion of psychological research. After a touch-and-go beginning, the corporation eventually proved successful and became a giant supplier of tests as well as a moderating influence on the extravagance of claims made in behalf of diagnostic techniques.

The scope of the mental hygiene movement was also enlarged. Originally intended to promote the improvement of care for hospitalized mental patients, its aims now encompassed the prevention of mental illness and assistance of all those who suffered from any form of psychological malfunctioning. Beginning in 1919 (and in keeping with its broadened range of operations), the National Committee for Mental Hygiene (NCMH) received $10,000 annually from the Commonwealth Fund. The purpose of this grant was to support the investigation of the incidence, causes, treatment, and prevention of juvenile delinquency. In 1921, the Division on the Prevention of Delinquency was established within the NCMH, and the Bureau of Children's Guidance was established at the New York School of Social Work (Durca, 1927–1928).

From 1922 to 1926, the NCMH was engaged in conducting surveys of delinquency in New Jersey, South Carolina, Ohio, and Kentucky. During this period, demonstration child guidance clinics were arranged for communities that gave evidence of being willing to continue such psychiatric services on a permanent basis by providing the necessary funds. The first demonstration clinic was set up in St. Louis and was affiliated with the juvenile court. Its staff consisted of Thomas Heldt, psychiatrist; E. K. Wickman, clinical psychologist; and Mildred Scoville, Hester Crutcher, and Dorothy Wallace, psychiatric social workers. It was not considered successful because, although it did manage to struggle on for a number of years, it failed to obtain adequate financial support from the community. A similar fate awaited the demonstration child guidance clinics established in Norfolk and Dallas and a traveling clinic based at the University of Minnesota.

Despite these isolated instances, facilities offering psychological services were on the increase. More fiscally fortunate were clinics in Minneapolis and St. Paul (both of which were outgrowths of the demonstration clinic at the University of Minnesota) and in Los Angeles, Cleveland, and Philadelphia. In 1921, by legislative act, the Psychological and Psychopathic Clinic was established at the University of Hawaii; in 1925, James Drever organized the Psychological Clinic for Children and Juveniles at the University of Edinburgh; and in 1927, Cyril Burt helped form the Child Guidance Council of London.

Along the way, a change in the functioning of child guidance clinics began to occur. Attention was shifted from studies of delinquents and retardates to an examination of parent-child relationships. A similar enlargement of perspective can be traced in the development of the American Orthopsychiatric Association.

In December 1923, Karl Menninger sent a letter inviting 26 fellow psychiatrists who seemed interested in "medical criminology, or disciplinary psychiatry, or orthopsychics" to meet with him in Chicago (Lowrey, 1948). This meeting was held the following month at the Institute for Juvenile Research, formerly called the Juvenile Psychopathic Institute. The institute's change of name serves as another illustration of the broadened horizons in the field.

Among those present were Herman Adler, David Levy, V. V. Anderson, Lawson G. Lowrey, and George Stevenson. Together they made plans for the formation of the American Orthopsychiatric Association. (It should be noted that the term orthopsychiatry was substituted for Menninger's suggested term *orthopsychics*. This was done in order to suggest the medical nature of the group and so make it more acceptable to the medical profession. Evidently, psychologists were not the only ones concerned with status and recognition.)

The first convention of the American Orthopsychiatric Association was held later that year, in June 1924, at the Institute for Juvenile Research. William Healy was selected as its first president.

Within 6 months, the objectives of the association were sweepingly enlarged from medical criminology to "the study and treatment of problems of human behavior." Members of any interested profession were invited to participate in the organization. However, because of fears that prestige would be lost if members of the medical profession were not in control, active membership (eligibility to hold office) was restricted to psychiatrists. Quite sensibly though, and no doubt in order to promote the growth of the group, just 2 years later active membership was made available to psychologists, social workers, and other professionals involved in the diagnosis and treatment of behavior disorders.

The membership of the American Orthopsychiatric Association increased from 23 in 1924 to 83 by 1929. Within its roster of early members these familiar names may be found: Augusta Bronner; Edgar Doll, who had taken over from Porteus as director of research at Vineland in 1925; Shepherd Franz; Henry Goddard; Adolf Meyer; and Lightner Witmer.

Another example of psychology's widening scope occurred in 1921, when the *Journal of Abnormal Psychology* became the *Journal of Abnormal and Social Psychology*. Although practical considerations having to do with publishing costs may have entered into the reasons for this change of title, the reason given to the public was that social psychology, perhaps more than any other branch of the science, is interested in the forces underlying human behavior and is enriched by the findings of psychopathology.

As a final example of developments in psychology, in 1926 Morton Prince appeared at Harvard with a check for $75,000 from an anonymous donor. It was proposed that this gift be used to establish a "department of abnormal psychology" within the university as a means of bringing normal and abnormal psychology into a closer relationship. At Boring's suggestion, it was decided to protect the university in the event that abnormal psychology should cease to exist as a separate field by stating in the deed of gift that the new Harvard Psychological Clinic was to give instruction and conduct research in abnormal *and dynamic* psychology. In 1927, the Harvard Psychological Clinic was founded by Morton Prince.

The APA was not insensitive to these signs of change but vacillated in responding to them. At issue was the concern of many members that in enlarging the scope of the association, psychology's recently acquired, and still fragile, identity as a science might be threatened. To appreciate the legitimacy of this concern, it may be helpful to consider the following.

To begin with, mediums and spooks still tended to be associated with psychology in the mind of the general public. In a desperate effort to dissociate psychology from what were claimed to be supernatural phenomena, the *Journal of Abnormal and Social Psychology,* in 1925, made a public offer of $5,000 to anyone who could produce supernatural events under rigid laboratory and scientific conditions (Prince, 1925–1926). Forty-four persons responded to this offer in the hope of picking up some easy money. According to the opinion of the panel of psychologists acting as judges, only three of the respondents were genuinely interested, the remainder being cranks and phonies. Moreover, no one made further inquiry when informed of the conditions under which they would have to make contact with the otherworld. Somewhat hastily and presumptuously the offer was withdrawn, leaving many mediums, no doubt, grumbling to their ethereal associates about the unfairness of earthly psychologists.

A second consideration was that opposition from psychiatrists to the diagnostic function of clinical psychologists continued. Particular irritation centered on the issue of mental retardation diagnosis, which the medical profession contended was solely a medical responsibility.

Once again Shepherd Franz (1922) attempted to win peace with honor. He tried to achieve this desideratum by making a distinction between the abnormal and the pathological. For example, an IQ of 180 was abnormal but not pathological. He suggested that clinical psychologists were concerned only with deviations from the norm, the abnormal, and were content to leave to the medical profession the determination of whether the deviations should be considered symptomatic of disease. Franz also expressed the hope that interdisciplinary ill feelings were due only to semantic misunderstandings and that there would be harmony between the two professions once each understood the language of the other. He recommended that "psychological psychiatrists" and "psychiatric psychologists" play the role of mediators between the disciplines. Unfortunately, the conflict went deeper than difficulties in communication.

For psychiatrists opposed psychologists engaging in treatment as well as diagnosis. In 1925, A. A. Brill published, in a New York newspaper, an article against the practice of psychoanalysis by anyone who was not a physician. About a year later in Vienna, one of Theodor Reik's patients sued him on the grounds of harmful treatment and also accused him of quackery. Reik, who had his PhD from the University of Vienna, was acquitted, but Freud, troubled by rumblings within the analytic ranks, published *The Problem of Lay Analyses* in an effort to settle this issue. In 1926, the New York legislature passed a bill declaring lay analysis illegal, and the American Medical Association warned its members against any cooperation with lay analysts.

Freud emphatically stated his position. Not only did he favor lay analysis, but he strongly urged the separation of psychoanalysis from medicine. Psychoanalysis, he contended, was a part of psychology and not psychiatry.

Analysts within the United States, almost equally emphatically, took the opposite position. They insisted that analysts should attain and maintain an identity within the medical profession. One compromise was proposed based on the supposition that the analyses of children were easier and less professionally demanding than analyses of adults: In 1929 the New York Psychoanalytic Society, reluctantly agreed to permit lay analysis of children.

The actions of the APA seem to have been determined by a desire to preserve its inoffensive, respectable appearance while decorously stifling demands that it become involved in the professional problems of some of its members.

In 1921, the APA reaffirmed that its sole objective was the advancement of psychology as a science. Scrupulously avoided were any overt signs of enthusiasm for psychology as a profession. In keeping with this single-mindedness, the requirements for membership in the association became a PhD in psychology and published postdoctoral research of an acceptable nature. At the same time, an APA committee recommended the formation of a section of consulting psychology, the initiation of a program for the certification of consulting psychologists, and the elimination of the Section of Clinical Psychology. A group of dissatisfied clinicians banded together and formed the New York State Association for Consulting Psychology.

Events at the Carnegie Institute of Technology were probably not completely unrelated to the concern for scientific legitimacy that pervaded the upper echelons of psychology. In 1924, the Division of Applied Psychology was discontinued by the institute and its staff were scattered. According to Bingham (1952), first and only chairman of the division, this was done to avoid competition with the graduate program in psychology at the University of Pittsburgh. Whatever the reason, Bingham packed his bags for New York City and the private practice of industrial psychology.

Meanwhile, the APA's certification program for consulting psychologists was not very successful. During its first 2 years, only 24 psychologists applied for certificates. Even the APA's membership was increasing at a slower than expected rate. Some psychologists, Wells (1924) for one, felt the standards for certification and membership were too high. They also believed the APA should assume the responsibility for setting ethical and professional standards for applied psychologists. However, the APA, by its inaction, made known that it felt things were going along just fine.

In 1924, the Section of Clinical Psychology, which had survived despite its poor prognosis, attempted to set standards. It recommended that a clinical psychologist should have a PhD from an approved graduate school and 4 years of professional training, with at least 1 year of supervised work in practical psychological diagnosis. These were high standards, everyone agreed, but it was felt that high standards were necessary. Furthermore, clinicians believed that some action had to be taken to prevent unqualified persons from engaging in testing, and there was incessant pleading with the APA to set up standards for the training programs that were needed. The pleas of L. Crane will serve as an example.

Crane (1925–1926) argued that if psychologists were to achieve the status and receive the financial rewards they desired, a legal definition of the profession and a specific program of education in clinical psychology were necessary. He advocated a minimum of 3 undergraduate years followed by a 4-year graduate course. The first 2 years of graduate training would focus on medicine; the next 2 years would focus on testing, psychoanalysis, and topics of lasting interest (whatever they happened to be at the time). Upon successful completion of the program, the student would be awarded a PsD (doctor of psychology), with all the rights and privileges attached thereto. The response to Crane's plea was imperceptible.

The Section of Consulting Psychology was changed to a division in 1924, and in 1925 the APA became a corporation and purchased the journals of the Psychological Review Company. The purpose of incorporation was to relieve individual members of financial responsibility for the journals and to have that responsibility vested in a corporate body. It was also recommended that associate membership be established. The requirements for associate membership were a PhD in psychology and full-time work in the field or sufficient distinction to be recommended for such membership by the council.

In 1926, associate membership was established, and Morton Prince generously gave the *Journal of Abnormal and Social Psychology* to the APA. The dues, which had been 2 dollars a year in 1919, were raised to 10 dollars for members and 6 dollars for associates, with a subscription to *Psychological Abstracts* included. The following year the APA certification program was abandoned on the grounds of lack of interest. Besides, or so went the argument, the standards for certification were so high that those who could meet them did not need certification to attest to their competence.

Some psychologists feared that the requirement of published research for election to the membership was having an unhealthy effect on the composition of the association. In 1928, 16 members and 206 associates were elected; in 1929, 6 members and 222 associates were elected. Within 3 years, the APA had more associates than members and the imbalance was growing. Obviously psychologists felt that it was desirable to belong to the APA but perhaps not at the price of doing postdoctoral research.

Fernberger's (1928) analysis of the composition of the APA in 1928 showed that 616 members had PhD degrees. Of that number, 324 (53%) had received their doctorates from just four universities: Columbia (135 PhDs), Chicago (80), Harvard (56), and Clark (50). Nineteen members were practicing industrial psychology and 104 were engaged in clinical work. Moreover, although approximately 77% of the membership of the APA held academic positions, 48% indicated research interests in some area of applied psychology.

By the close of the twenties, there was obviously a shift in the balance of forces within the APA. A steadily increasing minority of clinicians were attempting to gain recognition within the organization and striving to shake it from its policy of complacent inaction in the face of increasingly urgent professional problems. There were disagreements among psychologists about their science and what direction it should go. Simultaneously the field was expanding and external pressures were mounting. Society was demanding that psychologists apply their knowledge, skills, and techniques through many forms of service. Yet these demands also brought psychology into conflict with other professions in areas where the status and value of psychology had still to be demonstrated.

The field had changed enormously in the past 20 years. As Dunlap (1932) wistfully asked, "The questions concerning introspection as present observation or memory; interaction vs. parallelism; two-level or multi-level attention; bidimensional or polydimensional feeling; and a host of other 'problems': who is willing to discuss these now?" (p. 57).

Joseph Jastrow (1930) could survey the field and say without fear of much contradiction, "Psychology as we know it, along with many another discipline, is a twentieth-century achievement." He undoubtedly stirred up more controversy with this opinion: "Yet of all the applications, that of clinical psychology appears to me the most momentous."

To a large extent, the changes within psychology had been directly or, more often, indirectly brought about by psychoanalysis. Thurstone, Leuba, Lashley, and Jastrow (1924) regarded the following contributions of Freudianism as having been the most influential: its study of the basic and permanent tendencies in human nature; its emphasis on the demands of the organism and the behaviors by which these demands were satisfied; and its determinism, particularly the significance of childhood experiences as these affect adult behavior. G. Stanley Hall phrased his evaluation more personally: "I have the deepest appreciation of the service Freud has rendered our specialty by doing more to popularize and give zest to it among all sorts and conditions of intellectuals than any other man in the history of the science" (Hall, 1923, p. 411).

Then there were the schools of psychology, some growing and some dying: behaviorism, Gestalt psychology, self psychology, structuralism, hormic psychology, associationism, functionalism. A representative of the expiring structuralist school, Madison Bentley (1926), reflecting upon his feelings of isolation within his science, voiced a moving plea for tolerance:

> Our underlying notions are then useful . . . but we must remember that they represent less an ultimate truth than our own individual preferences. More is to be gained than men commonly acknowledge by a sympathetic insight into alien points of view and into the possible utility of concepts which one has not learned how to use. The history of the sciences is eloquent upon the enormous wastefulness of prejudice. (Bentley, 1926, p. 105)

Mary Calkins (1930) held fast to her beliefs: "For with each year I live, with each book I read, with each observation I initiate or confirm, I am more deeply convinced that psychology should be conceived as the science of the self, or person, as related to its environment, physical and social" (pp. 41–42). Yet here too the emphasis had changed—from a "self" that was introspective to a "person" in interaction with the world.

However, McDougall (1930) could not hide his disappointments under the strength of his convictions. Looking back on a career that to most would appear outstanding in its accomplishments, he felt a keen sense of failure. From a detached, intellectual point of view, he claimed psychology was "the most difficult of the sciences, and the most unsatisfying of all fields of research" (p. 221). He was also aware of the irony that psychologists, seemingly unable to agree on an answer to any major question, were surrounded by an admiring public, eagerly seeking only immediate and dogmatic solutions to their problems. But what seemed to trouble him most was his corrosive belief that it was only his inability to contain his arrogance that had alienated people and prevented them from embracing his views. For reasons that he could never fathom, he had not been able to win the friendship of his readers, unlike his model William James. Somehow, he was convinced, he had failed to convey his humility and warmth and so was forced into the awkward position of a leader pathetically devoid of followers.

To many psychologists, Bentley, Calkins, and McDougall were voices from a far distant past. Dominating psychology were behaviorism and psychoanalysis, with Gestalt formulations challenging them both. Representatives of each school seldom neglected an opportunity to criticize their rivals. Yet Boring (1929) thought that probably every school had its serious errors: "The more you fight for the truth the less you see it" (p. 99).

Although Boring conceded that the leaders of the opposing factions were brilliant, he felt the distinction of being right belonged to those who were less dazzling and extreme. The eclectics and the middle-of-the-roaders, really the majority of psychologists, would gather the most worthwhile fruits of the controversies between schools. There is a paradox in all this—that those who argue most vigorously for what they believe are driven to some extent from the truth by the need to emphasize their positions. But Boring (1929) concluded; "Psychology needs both judiciousness and effective prejudices, and I cannot resist the impression that we shall do well to cultivate and welcome both" (p. 121).

Disagreements, unsolved problems, and dissatisfactions were certainly to be found in abundance. But we must remember that these were only by-products; as a whole the profession continued to make revolutionary advances. In 1929, James McKeen Cattell was elected president of the Ninth International Congress of Psychology. His remarks, although a trifle chauvinistic, may serve to throw a positive light on the situation and help to explain the vitality of psychology within the United States:

> *Our people had curiosity, acquisitiveness, and energy with ever-increasing wealth. We were able to take over what we wanted from abroad; we were not bound by procedure and tradition. The psychologist has some reason to thank God when he is born a happy and irresponsible American child. (quote in Winkler & Bromberg, 1939, p. 236)*

6

Shared Values
1930–1939

Throughout the world during the thirties there was ample reason for feelings of bewilderment and despair. Within the United States, millions of people were unemployed or attempting to adjust themselves to greatly reduced incomes, and the prospects for the country's recovery from the Great Depression were bleak. The financial situation elsewhere was little or no better. In such dire circumstances, economic competition between nations was intensified, and governments felt extraordinary initiative was required to surmount their internal problems.

The United States set about righting its domestic affairs in a peaceful manner through such steps as ending Prohibition, establishing a system of social security, adopting minimum-wage and maximum-hour laws, and spending unprecedented sums for the construction of public works. However, other countries sought to stimulate their economies and rouse the spirit of their people by appeals to nationalistic pride, by stepping up the production of armaments, and by military conquests. Starting in 1931, when Japan invaded Manchuria, the decade was marked by wars and a succession of triumphs for dictatorial forms of government: Adolf Hitler became chancellor of Germany in 1933; Spain's civil war began in 1936 and ended with the consolidation of Franco's power; Japan invaded China in 1937; and in 1939 Italy invaded Ethiopia, Germany seized Czechoslovakia, Russia attacked Finland, Germany invaded and conquered Poland, and in response, Great Britain and France declared war on Germany.

In particular, the Hitler regime, with its cold disregard for human life and a ruthlessness unmatched in history, had repercussions for eugenics and psychology. Shortly after assuming power, Hitler enacted sterilization laws that applied to people suffering from mental deficiency, epilepsy, schizophrenia, manic-depressive psychoses, Huntington's chorea, severe alcoholism, and hereditary blindness, deafness, and deformity. Some idea of the zeal with which these laws were enforced can be gained by noting that in a period spanning close to 30 years and involving some 30 states in the United States, approximately 20,000 sterilizations had been performed, whereas in a period of about four years, approximately 225,000 sterilizations were performed in Germany, in many instances in utter violation of the rights of the individual and the intent of the laws. Accordingly, in much of the Western world outside Germany, even reasonable and humane eugenic measures lost virtually all support.

Even more directly related to psychology were the effects produced by Hitler's policies of anti-Semitism and his intolerance of any opposition, which resulted in the closing of many of the centers for psychological research in Germany and Austria. Though psychologists suffered greatly in the upheaval, fortunately a sizable number managed to emigrate to the United States, where, assisted by their American colleagues, they secured positions in their profession and unquestionably contributed to the preeminence which psychology in the United States now enjoys.

Among the sciences, it was physics, however, that achieved the greatest prestige. Its discoveries were also the most ominous: In 1939, physicists succeeded in splitting atoms of uranium, thus releasing gigantic quantities of energy. Compared with what was happening outside the laboratories, this momentous event attracted little public notice. For the attention of the world was on the progress of a war unparalleled in its degree of mechanization and its destructiveness.

NORMAL PERSONALITY FUNCTIONING

The deaths of a number of prominent psychologists—Freud, Adler, Rank, McDougall, and Stern—contributed to the decade's atmosphere of gloom. Yet of more enduring importance were the many exciting innovations and the auspicious intermarriages between various points of view within psychology as well as between psychology and other sciences.

In 1930, Freud's mother died, and the following year his relationship with Ferenczi, which for many years had been strained, was seriously tested. One major point of contention was Ferenczi's belief that the analyst's relationship with the patient should be less passive and more affectionate and giving. Freud was particularly distressed that Ferenczi sometimes kissed his patients and in other ways indicated his fondness. In 1933, before the matter could be satisfactorily resolved, Ferenczi became ill and died (Jones, 1957; Gay, 1988).

That same year, the International General Medical Society of Psychotherapy, a largely German organization, came under the influence of the Nazis. Kretschmer resigned the presidency of the society, and Jung assumed the position, ostensibly with the hope of protecting psychotherapy and his Jewish colleagues. However, his belief in the collective unconscious led Jung to express his sympathy for the task of discriminating between German and Jewish psychology. Such a statement during those years led to much resentment, and though Jung tried to explain he intended no anti-Semitism, the episode did not enhance his reputation (Hannah, 1976).

Germany "abolished" psychoanalysis in 1934, and Eitingon managed to escape and settle in Palestine. It was a time of much physical suffering and many bitter disappointments for Freud. However, he undoubtedly derived some comfort from seeing his daughter, Anna, attain a position of eminence in psychoanalytic circles.

In 1937, Anna Freud published *The Ego and the Mechanisms of Defense*. Her book focused on the use of defenses in normal growth and as a means of dealing with external as well as internal threats to the organism. Among the defenses noted were fantasy in thought and action (e.g., daydreaming and playing), identification with the aggressor (e.g., a boy's display of the mannerisms and personality characteristics of his father as a device for seeming to be less afraid of him), and asceticism (a defense prominent during puberty and adolescence in which a person seeks to control impulses by repudiating them and avoiding situations that might arouse them, such as dances, movies, or dates).

When Austria joined with Germany in 1938, the lives of Freud and all other Jews in the country were in danger. Yet circumstances were still such that the Nazis were at times willing to appear to be reasonable men of good will. Therefore, after Mussolini and President Roosevelt made requests for the safe treatment of Freud, the Nazis consented to allow him and his family to leave Vienna. First, however, Freud had to undergo the formality of intimidation and the confiscation of his property. Further, as a final galling indignity it was demanded that he sign a document stating he had been treated with fairness and courtesy. Being a realist, Freud did not hesitate to put his signature to the release, but he cleverly added this ironic endorsement: "I can heartily recommend the Gestapo to anyone" (Jones, 1947, p. 226).

Accompanied by Ernest Jones, Freud left for England, where he died the following year, 1939. A study by Park (1931) assessed the influence of Freud on psychology. Park reported that of 50 popular texts in general psychology published between 1910 and 1930, only 4 failed to mention Freud, and no text after 1917, with the exception of Dunlap's, ignored psychoanalysis. She concluded that "the status of Freudianism in academic psychology seems to be rather firmly established."

Within psychoanalysis, the ideas of Melanie Klein (1882–1960), although given little serious notice in the United States, were attracting favorable attention in England. Klein was the youngest child in a Viennese family. Her father was a dental surgeon, so it is not too surprising that she hoped to pursue a career in medicine. But she became engaged at 17, was married at 21, and began to have children; as a result, she abandoned her plan. She attended the University of Vienna and went into analysis with Ferenczi and then Karl Abaraham. Her marriage was unhappy, her older son died in early manhood, and she became estranged from her daughter. Around 1921, she began formulating her own ideas about analysis. She went to England in 1926, and her first book, *The Psycho-Analysis of Children*, was published in 1932 (Isaacs, 1961).

Klein believed that children exhibit details of their unconscious fantasy life when engaged in free, undirected play, and she thought that since play may be considered equivalent to the verbal free associations produced by adults, children as young as two or three can be analyzed and their unconscious conflicts interpreted to them.

From her psychoanalyses of children, Klein began to evolve theoretical formulations of her own. It seemed to her that the child in early infancy feels in serious danger. This fear is experienced as a persecutory anxiety. Later in development, between 4 to 9 months, this fear changes from an anxiety about being harmed to an apprehension about harming loved ones by swallowing or incorporating them. This fear is experienced as depressive anxiety. Actually, according to Klein, the persecutory anxiety is produced by a projection of the infant's own intense aggression and sadism, and the depressive anxiety is a form of guilt brought about by recognition of hostile feelings. Some analysts, when they contemplated the innocent faces of babies sleeping in their cribs, found it difficult to agree with Melanie Klein—but then one never knew. They did find it much easier to accept her suggestion that it was possible to psychoanalyze youngsters through play, and they recognized this as a definite contribution to the study and treatment of children.

Meanwhile, Alfred Adler (1930) was still busy broadening his theory and casting it in a more positive mold. Instead of a striving for superiority, Adler now posited a longing for perfection and fulfillment that is evidenced in all behavior, a longing that is expressed throughout all psychological functioning. As can be seen, Adler's views had mellowed with the years. He had moved from the assumption that an actual organ inferiority underlies neurotic behavior and instead emphasized the importance of people's perceptions of themselves and their external environments.

More specifically, Adler now believed that early in life each person sets a personal goal that imposes a unity upon his or her actions. This goal setting is compelled by an innate striving for perfection. But the particular goal selected by each person is unique and is determined uniquely by the person's inherited equipment and his or her perceptions and interpretations of events and experiences. By the age of 5, the person has developed a *style of life*, which has been considerably influenced by the person's appraisals and conceptions of his or her bodily functioning, strength, and vitality. This style of life is the pattern—the means or method—through which the person seeks to achieve perfection or superiority. It supplies consistency and stability to the person's behavior. These characteristics, we might add, are to be regarded, in part, as advantageous, since they contribute to the person's sense of identity. However, the maintenance of this stability and consistency may be purchased at the cost of excluding or distorting whatever threatens the style of life—in other words, at the cost of resistance to personal change and distorted perceptions of reality. (The Spanish philosopher Miguel de Unamuno [1864–1936] beautifully phrased ideas very similar to Adler's: "To propose to a man that he should be someone else, . . . is to propose to him that he should cease to be himself. . . . A man can change greatly, almost completely even, but the change must take place within his continuity" [Unamuno, 1954].)

Further, Adler thought the unique goal of the individual could be either normal or pathological. Normal goals are dominated by social feeling and based on an interest in reality, an interest in others, and cooperative action. In contrast, pathological goals are private and self-centered, and the individuals are preoccupied, not with benefiting others, but with obtaining something from them. Of course, it is through normal goals that people best serve their own interests as well as those of their societies.

Finally, toward the close of his life, Adler came to regard feelings of inferiority, not as abnormal in and of themselves, but instead as an inescapable condition of being human. Indeed, he thought such feelings provide the impetus for much that is desirable, as well as undesirable, in humans (Ansbacher & Ansbacher, 1956).

In 1935, Alfred Adler and his family moved to the United States. His children Kurt and Alexandra became, like their father, psychiatrists. While on a lecture tour in Scotland in 1937, Adler died suddenly from a heart attack.

At the same time that Adler was modifying his formulations, Otto Rank (1950) was placing a similar emphasis on the more constructive aspects of human functioning. He was now discussing and making central to his theory his concept of will which he defined as "a positive guiding organization and integration of a self which utilizes creatively as well as inhibits and controls the instinctual drives . . . [something] that acts, not merely reacts." Resistance in analysis, as well as a child's refusal to obey his or her parents, though often frustrating to those who encounter or provoke the opposition, may be viewed positively as a conflict between wills in which the patient (or child) attempts to assert individuality in the face of what is perceived as demands for submission.

Conversely, Rank saw that acquiescence has both positive and negative aspects. Through submission to the ideas of another, a person gains a measure of safety and security, because alienating the other individual is not risked, but the person also sacrifices some uniqueness. Unlike Adler, who focused on the benefits of cooperation, Rank stressed the need for self-assertion and made basic the striving to assert one's will. From birth onwards, the person struggles to separate from others and to express his or her own wishes, feelings, and ideas. This growth in autonomy is far from easy. Each step away from the influence of others eventuates in feelings of guilt for having estranged them, feelings of loss, and a fear of being totally abandoned, yet each act of compliance results in a sense of guilt and self-reproach for having betrayed or compromised oneself and often elicits a fear of losing one's own individuality.

Admittedly a difficult process, and yet, Rank insisted, within each person this conflict and the striving for independence are to be found. Its ideal resolution he conceived of as an artistic, creative integration in which the person accepts his or her own will as right without feeling guilt for self-expression and still maintains relationships with others in which their wills are accepted, when it is reasonable to do so, without feeling a loss of self.

Coincident with the development of his theory, a resolution seemed to occur in Rank's personal life. Although he continued to experience periods of depression and still found it necessary to undertake frequent transoceanic voyages between Paris and New York, in 1934 he decided to "settle" in New York City. He taught at the Graduate School for Jewish Social Work and lectured at the New York School of Social Work, at Stanford, and in Philadelphia, Cleveland, Rochester, and Buffalo. Unfortunately, his marriage had not been happy, and with the arrival of his wife in the United States he appeared again to suffer intensely from feelings of depression. Three years later, in 1939, there was a divorce; Rank remarried, seemed briefly happy, but died that same year (Taft, 1958).

Among the other psychologists who made their way to the United States was Kurt Lewin. His description of personality functioning aroused much excitement and interest. Lewin, who was successively at Stanford, Cornell, and the University of Iowa, saw each individual existing in a world of perception that he called the *life space*. A person's life space is everything that is experienced. It includes needs, persons, objects, memories of the past and thoughts of the future as they are perceived in the present. Lewin (1935) believed that as a person develops, his or her life space tends to become differentiated into various regions of phenomena that are either connected to some degree or kept firmly apart.

Heightening the fascination of Lewin's ideas were his ingenious diagrams representing life spaces. These diagrams tended to be elliptically shaped and to contain the person (P), arrows ("vectors" representing forces in a given direction), plus and minus signs ("valences" indicating whether the object is attractive or repulsive), and lines (boundaries) demarcating certain areas (regions and barriers within the life space). Human functioning was understood in terms of needs arising from within the person. Such needs arouse tensions that confer positive valences on regions perceived to be instrumental in satisfying the needs and negative valences on regions perceived as threatening to increase tensions. Movement or locomotion was supposed to be toward positive and away from negative valences. Lewin pointed out that his diagrams represented a topological space (i.e., representations of magnitudes were completely arbitrary and only ordinal relations were fixed). Therefore, his "vectors" were not the same as the mathematician's vectors and could not be used quantitatively. Nevertheless, a semblance of scientific precision appeared to be introduced into the phenomenal world.

McDougall, who in 1927 had gone to chair the psychology department at Duke, could not understand why so many psychologists were excited about Lewin's work. He was not impressed and saw only one merit in the theory: Its recognition of the existence within the person of "springs" of motivating energy (McDougall, 1936-1937). The theory as a whole he regarded as hopelessly inadequate: "All the multitude of personal peculiarities . . . Lewin's theory requires us to interpret in terms of his basket of potatoes, one differing from another merely in respect of size, position in the group, and thickness of its skin" (p. 81). All in all, McDougall failed to appreciate the significance of Lewin's work as a stimulus to the growth of an experimental social psychology, and it appears that he was still finding it difficult to effect the creative integration that Rank cherished.

For his own theory of hormic psychology, McDougall (1930) had words of praise and the hope of success. It seemed to him that almost everyone now agreed behavior was purposive, and so he saw a possibility for the eventual acceptance of many of the other ideas he had championed. Although he now minimized instincts, they were still used in his theory to explain the energy source or motivating impulse for behavior. His concept of behavior, though, was quite different from the common view: "Hormic activity is essentially mental activity, involving always cognition or awareness, striving initiated and governed by such cognition, and accruing satisfaction or dissatisfaction" (p. 15).

The terms *horme* and *hormic* had been introduced by P. T. Nunn (1920) to refer to both conscious and unconscious drives in animals. By adopting these terms, McDougall acknowledged that hormic processes could be unconscious, but he held that even unconscious processes involve, no matter how dimly, some foresight or knowledge of goals. Each human activity, McDougall insisted, is done in pursuit of some goal that is foreseen and that the agent, instinctively or by the person's very nature, desires to achieve. McDougall recognized that his emphasis on instincts rather than on external stimuli as the source for the arousal of behavior antagonized his colleagues and made it more difficult to predict what behavior would occur. However, when they questioned him as to why he allowed this room for uncertainty to exist, he justified his point of view by citing the principle of indeterminacy in physics as evidence that even in the most esteemed of sciences exact predictability was being abandoned as an attainable goal.

Until his death, McDougall continued to espouse unpopular views, often simply because they were unpopular and he felt they deserved an opportunity to be heard: He began experimentation on Lamarckian evolution to see if learning could be passed from one generation of rats to those following; he welcomed J. B. Rhine (1936-1937) to Duke for research on clairvoyance and mental telepathy; and he provided a faculty position for William Stern at a time when Stern was no longer in favor.

Stern had fallen from grace because of his attacks on the Rorschach test and because he engaged in armchair philosophizing and was proud of it. He also still talked about the "person," which he defined as "an individual, unique whole whose activity is goal directed, who is related to the self, is open to the world, and who lives and experiences." Stern (1935-1936) agreed with other psychologists that the person has certain potentialities, such as character and intelligence, that require appropriate interaction with the outer world to become actualized. But since Stern held firmly to his opinion that psychology is the science of the experiencing person and so does not in itself include the environment, he insisted that psychology is only a *partial* science of the person—a conviction not likely to win him many followers among psychologists.

During this period there was much talk in psychology about traits of character, and Stern maintained that they could be described intrinsically (a person's attitude toward something), comparatively (how one person's attitude compared with the attitudes of others), and personally (how a person's attitude related to the person's total character). Stern defined character as the person's disposition to act or to will changes and exert influence in the world, a definition that coincides with popular usage but that makes character virtually identical with personality.

For Gordon Allport (1897-1967) of Harvard University, character was a quite different concept, namely, the evaluation of behavior in ethical terms. According to Allport, personality was "the dynamic organization within the individual of those psychophysical systems that determine his unique adjustments to his environment" (Allport, 1937, p. 48). His conception contrasted markedly with the behavioristic and social formulation of personality advanced by Vernon (1933) and others. They asserted that personality is simply behavior that is socially evaluated, and therefore it ceases to exist when there is no one available to judge a person's actions—all that remains is a person exhibiting behavior. (However, it is reasonable to argue that people themselves evaluate their own behavior according to standards they have developed as a result of contact with others.)

In Allport's (1937) schema, the concept of a trait is introduced to provide for the consistency and uniqueness that is to be found in every personality. A trait is "a generalized and focalized neuropsychic system (peculiar to the individual)" that initiates and guides adaptive and expressive behavior. What gives maturity to the personality is, for Allport, the operation of the principle of functional autonomy.

By functional autonomy, Allport meant that an individual may be motivated to continue engaging in an activity for entirely different reasons or purposes than the original ones. For example, an activity may have originally been motivated by the gratification of instincts or early needs or tensions but may then become largely independent of them. The activity may now be pursued because it has become interesting, rewarding, or stimulating in its own right. What makes it so is the continuous challenge it presents to the individual to perfect its performance while engaging in it. This is, of course, very similar to Woodworth's (1930) idea that mechanisms may become drives.

Woodworth, by the way, was still trying to promote a reconciliatory and unifying definition of psychology. It troubled him to see schools of thought acting belligerently, since he felt strongly that all psychologists were sincere in their beliefs, were competent investigators, and were searching as best they could for the truth. Woodworth (1930) suggested that psychology be defined as the study of the individual organism's activities, especially in relation to the environment. Woodworth hoped psychologists would rally round his definition, but many insisted on taking more specialized positions. Yet, at least in terms of general principles, some unification was being achieved.

Many personality theorists could agree that what is most important to know is not the objective situation in which a person exists but how the person perceives that situation. This phenomenological approach to understanding human behavior was becoming more and more popular. For example, Paul Schilder (1886–1940), a psychiatrist, developed the concept of the body image, which is the individual's conceptualization of his or her body and its boundaries. Schilder (1934–1935) conceived of the body image as an evolving, changing picture affected by emotional disturbances and everyday events; in turn, the individual's body image strongly affects the experiencing of self and the environment. To illustrate these interactions, Schilder urged his audience to imagine an injured person. For such a person, he predicted, everything would be perceived as closer to the body and about to touch the injury. Others with phenomenological leanings included Stern, Rank, Lewin, Adler, and McDougall.

Of more significance, it was possible for two major unifying developments to begin because of the very fact that definite and "opposing" schools in psychology had become established and had gained recognition. We will first examine the early steps toward making the two major schools, psychoanalysis and behaviorism, more compatible. We will then consider attempts by psychologists to reach out to embrace formulations from other disciplines, particularly cultural anthropology.

It had been argued by some behaviorists that the concept of emotion should be eliminated from psychology as superfluous. After all, their argument went, emotions are only behavior; therefore, when behavior is understood, emotions will ipso facto be understood. Buttressing their contention were the disappointments experienced in evolving a satisfactory theory of emotions. Cannon's theory, Lashley (1938) pointed out, had run into some difficulties. To be sure, experimentation had demonstrated the localization of motor centers for emotional expression in the hypothalamus, but no evidence had been found to indicate the existence of special centers for "feeling tone." Nor, for that matter, were there any other areas of the brain where existence of a neurological basis for affect could be demonstrated.

But unfortunately for those who advocated parsimony, it no longer appeared feasible to throw out emotions, for they seemed more important than ever in understanding behavior. The results of at least nine studies agreed that recall of the pleasant occurred more frequently than recall of the unpleasant, regardless of whether the items were school grades, nonsense syllables paired with odors, or previous experiences. Of more significance, even the behaviorists were starting to become involved with the investigation of feelings. These *neobehaviorists* were willing to consider more than observable stimuli and responses in understanding behavior, and they spoke of "intervening variables" and "hypothetical constructs" that were related to observables.

Clark Hull had not been frustrated for long by the ban on the continuation of his hypnosis research at Yale. After publishing *Hypnosis and Suggestibility* (1933), he turned his full attention to "pure" research and learning theory. Around the same time, the Institute of Human Relations was established at Yale to bring together ideas from psychology, anthropology, psychiatry, and sociology. The learning theory being developed by Hull provided a framework for integrating the formulations and concepts of the various disciplines at the institute.

Among Hull's colleagues at the institute were Neal Miller (b. 1909), who had a PhD from Yale and underwent a training analysis at the Vienna Institute of Psychoanalysis in 1935–1936; O. H. Mowrer (1907–1982), who received his doctorate from Johns Hopkins in 1932 and arrived at Yale as a Sterling fellow in 1934; Robert Sears (1908–1989) who had spent the interval between earning his PhD from Yale in 1932 and his return there in 1936 as an instructor at the University of Illinois; and John Dollard (1900–1980), who obtained his doctorate in sociology from the University of Chicago in 1931. Together these men tried to combine Hull's learning principles and psychoanalysis.

One of Hull's (1937) major principles is that the tendency for a reaction to occur ("habit strength") is strengthened whenever the response is closely associated with the reduction of a need (i.e., whenever the response is reinforced). The concept of anxiety, of great importance in psychoanalysis, can be considered a learned response whose reduction is reinforcing to the organism (a negative reinforcement). Mowrer (1939) thought that since anxiety generally occurs in advance of an actual danger, it can be viewed as an anticipatory reaction that motivates the organism to cope with a potential threat and thereby diminishes the likelihood of any harm. According to his formulation, those actions that reduce anxiety are reinforced or tend to be learned.

The crowning achievement of this Yale group during the thirties was the publication of *Frustration and Aggression* (Dollard, Doob, Miller, Mowrer, & Sears, 1939). The major hypothesis of the work is that aggression is always a consequence of frustration.

Very briefly, the theory ran somewhat as follows: When people are being frustrated, their tendency to make aggressive responses varies directly with the amount of frustration. However, even with much frustration, the potential display of aggression in overt behavior might not occur. In such a case, the display has been inhibited, and the likelihood of this inhibition taking place depends on the amount of punishment that person expects to receive if hostility is openly expressed. These inhibited aggressive responses tend to be displaced or expressed in some modified form. But no matter how the person expresses aggression, whether displaced or directed at the frustrating object, any expression will lessen the probability of other aggressive responses being aroused. By these few principles, the Yale group attempted to explain a variety of behaviors, such as delinquency and adolescent turmoil, in terms of differing manifestations of aggression generated by frustration.

Frustration itself was analyzed in an article by Saul Rosenzweig et al. (1938–1939). They regarded the frustrating situation as being brought about by external and internal deprivations, privations, and other conflicts. In this context, people are seen as differing in two respects: First, they differ in their capacities to tolerate frustration, and second, they differ in their reactions to frustration. Now it is also possible to evaluate a reaction to frustration along four dimensions: (1) its adequacy or inadequacy in coping with the situation, (2) its specificity or nonspecificity (one nonspecific reaction to frustration, for example, is falling asleep), (3) its directness or indirectness in relation to the frustrating object, and (4) its perseverativeness or defensiveness. Defensive reactions can be further broken down into cases of aggression directed at some external object (extrapunitive reaction); cases of aggression directed at the self, such as self-condemnation or guilt (intrapunitive reaction); and cases in which the aggression might be repressed or the frustration denied (impunitive reaction). With the help of this analysis, a way now seemed open for launching an experimental attack on the problem.

A very different analysis of frustration was being made at Harvard by Henry A. Murray (1893–1988). Murray received a BA in history from Harvard in 1915, an MD from Columbia in 1919, an MA in biology from Columbia in 1920, and a PhD in biochemistry from Cambridge in 1927. He also received training in psychoanalysis and, in 1928, became director of the Harvard Psychological Clinic.

Murray (1938) made use of two basic concepts: need and press. A need was defined by him as a construct (hypothetical concept) representing a force in the brain region that organizes perception and action so as to modify an unsatisfactory situation. Needs may be aroused by internal processes, but generally they tend to be elicited by circumstances in the environment (press) that affect in some way, favorably or unfavorably, the well-being of the person. Murray tentatively listed 20 needs, including achievement, affiliation, aggression, autonomy, and deference; he took note of 16 forms of press, including danger, loss, family insupport, sex, and inferiority. When the individual perceives a press, a need is aroused that eventuates in some pattern of behavior for reducing the tension (need) thus generated; this interactive process between needs and press is called a *thema*. We can see that, in contrast to the hypothesis of the Yale group, Murray saw aggression as only one of the possible needs that might be aroused by a frustrating press (although, of course, it can be argued that the other needs that appear in response to some frustration, such as abasement, are variants of, or defenses against, aggression). In any case, the important point is that psychoanalytic concepts were being assimilated into the mainstream of psychology. Let us now consider the press exerted on psychologists by the work of the cultural anthropologists.

During the early thirties, Edward Sapir (1884–1939) seemed to express the self-confidence of most cultural anthropologists when he claimed their discipline was of great value in specifying which forms of behavior might be universal and which forms seem to be inherited and which acquired. On the basis of anthropological investigations already completed, Sapir (1932–1933) described a different way of looking at personality:

> *A personality is carved out by the subtle interaction of those systems of ideas which are characteristic of the culture as a whole, as well as of those systems of ideas which get established for the individual through more special types of participation, with the physical and psychological needs of the individual organism, which cannot take over any of the cultural material that is offered in its original form but works it over more or less completely so that it integrates with those needs. (p. 239)*

By "culture" Sapir meant what Ralph Linton (1893–1953), a fellow anthropologist, defined as the "sum total of the behavior patterns, attitudes, and values shared by members of a given society" (p. 425). Linton (1938) pointed out that no individual can be fully aware of the entire culture of which he or she is a member or participate in all its ramifications. Nevertheless, the members of a culture are differentiated into families and into age and sex categories, and demands are imposed upon those in each category for performing certain tasks according to certain procedures. Therefore, Linton claimed that with knowledge of the culture and the categories to which an individual belonged, a foundation would be provided for predicting the behavior of the person in a given situation.

The idea that a culture requires its members to act in certain prescribed ways was carried a step further by Ruth Benedict (1887–1938), who stressed that a specific culture tolerates the expression of only certain personality characteristics and behaviors and that the appearance of deviations from these are considered abnormalities. Therefore, what is normal or abnormal is relative to a particular cultural setting (Benedict, 1934). In the same vein, Abram Kardiner (1939) offered the concept of a basic personality type. Supposedly, the primary institutions (the prescribed patterns for obtaining food, dealing with aggression, and forming families) result in a modal kind of personality structure for that culture. This basic personality, Kardiner suggested, attains uniqueness by the individual's idiosyncratic ways of coping with the primary institutions in order to ameliorate their tyranny.

However, not everyone thought that culture is only tyrannical. Some cited instances where a culture allows its members opportunities for expressing in one medium what it prohibits in another. Drawing upon Adler, Beaglehole (1938) thought that when a culture represses a segment of behavior, it is forced to offer a socially approved compensation for what is repressed through media such as the dance, art, and religious ceremony.

The studies of cultures were also clarifying the extent to which human behavior is learned. Among others, Margaret Mead (1935) reported how sex behaviors, which many had considered to be innate patterns of response, appear to be products of social learning. On the island of New Guinea, Mead studied three cultures. She noted that among the Arapesh both males and females were gentle and cooperative, among the Mundugumor both sexes were violent and aggressive, and among the Tchambuli there seemed to be a reversal of the behaviors found in Western cultures, since the males were artists and dancers and the females provided the food and dominated the household. (Some psychologists were uncertain that this really differed from a pattern observed in the United States.) Evidence such as Mead's was most compelling. It was generally agreed that the anthropologists had established the point that behaviors that some had thought to be instinctive or inherited are actually capable of modification by the culture and might even be completely a product of learning.

Anthropologists also vigorously criticized those psychologists who had postulated qualitative differences between the mentalities of primitive and civilized human beings. They argued that what distinguishes primitive societies from those called civilized is the lack of a written tradition, which thus makes cultural transmission dependent on the memories of some members of the group. But they did not consider this illiteracy sufficient cause to justify hypothesizing a dichotomy in intellectual functioning between primitive and "modern" peoples. For one thing, it is obvious that the various primitive cultures differ considerably from each other. Furthermore, in some respects (e.g., the kinship system among the Australian aborigines) their customs and practices are more complex than those found in Western societies. Accordingly, it would no longer do, anthropologists warned, to make a distinction between cultures on the basis of primitiveness. Nor would it be possible to claim knowledge of a culture by superficial observations of the living habits of its people and the mechanical conveniences they enjoyed. Anthropologists had discovered with cultures, just as psychologists had discovered with individuals, that they have to be studied as wholes, against their ecological backgrounds, and with knowledge of their training methods, norms, and deviations (Mead, 1934–1935).

Most psychologists responded to admonitions from anthropologists with good grace, feeling, no doubt, that the criticisms were surely directed at members of the profession other than themselves. There is, after all, ample room for the concept of a culture, and it fitted nicely into justifications for the significance of acquired, as against innate, behaviors. Perhaps as a humorous paradox, T. L. Kelley (1930) suggested that cultural changes passed on from one generation to the next could be viewed as an instance of the inheritance of acquired characteristics. Unfortunately, heredity and Lamarckian evolution were serious matters among psychologists in the thirties, so it is unlikely that many relaxed sufficiently to laugh at Kelley's little joke.

The contributions of cultural anthropology created much excitement in the social sciences and psychiatry, and we shall consider them further in the sections and chapters that follow. A related development was experimentation concerning the effects of social variables on psychological processes, such as remembering and perception. Bartlett (1932) showed that a person's recollection of the events of an incident is distorted in the direction of agreement with cultural values and expectations, and Sherif (1935) published one of the first studies that aimed to show the influence of a group in shaping an individual's perception.

Sherif hypothesized that perceptual patterns are molded in different ways in different cultures. Therefore, what people perceive individually might be altered when they engage in the "same" act of perceiving within a group. Sherif tried to demonstrate this by an experiment involving autokinetic movement. (Autokinetic movement is a phenomenon in which a person observing a stationary pinpoint of light in a totally darkened room will report after a few moments that the light appears to be moving.) Sherif obtained estimates of autokinetic movement from individuals sitting alone in a darkened room and from groups of people sitting together. In the case of groups, the estimates tended to converge toward a common standard (i.e., a social norm of the extent of movement seemed to become established). Whether this represents an alteration in perception or merely in the reports of perception is not clear. Nevertheless, Sherif was successful in demonstrating experimentally the effects of social variables on psychological processes. The hope for a simple stimulus-response formulation of behavior, which had seemed feasible only 20 years before, had now, under the impact of various psychoanalytic and interpersonal considerations, become virtually untenable, and what was going on within the individual seemed to be more and more important for understanding why humans act as they do.

DIAGNOSTIC TECHNIQUES

During the thirties, a deluge of new tests rained down upon psychologists and the public. Most of them were developed in the United States. On the European continent, the growth of psychological testing was being obstructed by the repressive measures of dictatorial regimes.

For example, in 1936 the Central Committee of the Communist Party of the Union of Soviet Socialist Republics formally abolished the construction and use of psychological tests. The committee based its proclamation on the work in genetics done by I. V. Mitchurin and T. D. Lysenko, who believed inheritable characteristics could be induced by an individual's experiences or by environmental manipulations. This meant that Mitchurin and Lysenko supported Lamarck's doctrine that acquired changes could be passed on to succeeding generations. It therefore seemed unnecessary to study or test for innate abilities, since by placing individuals in suitable environments it would be possible to change them so that they could perform any designated task. Mitchurin and Lysenko's theory predicted a considerable dividend, because after an individual had learned the task, his or her descendants could learn it even more easily.

Within a democracy, the freedom to manipulate fellow citizens has definite limits. Since environments cannot be strictly controlled and people cannot simply be moved higher and thither, it still made sense to do testing whether one believed in partly or wholly acquired intellectual functioning. During 1936, the most frequently used tests in the United States were the Stanford-Binet, Porteus Mazes, Arthur Point Scale of Performance Tests, Healy Picture Completion, Pintner-Paterson, Stanford Achievement, Merrill-Palmer, Gesell Developmental Schedules, and Kuhlmann-Anderson. Up through 1936, the six tests that had the largest number of studies published about them were the following: Stanford-Binet, with about 141 studies, ranked first; Rorschach, with 68 studies, had come up rapidly to capture second place; Bernreuter Personality Inventory; Seashore Measures of Musical Talent; Strong Vocational Interest Blank; and American Council on Education Psychological Examination for College Freshmen. Other tests were emerging in profusion, so let us note the essentials of what was happening.

Most psychologists engaged in the field of test construction considered themselves, and were considered by others, to be psychometricians. Their efforts were directed at devising techniques that would arrange or order persons according to the degree of possession of whatever trait, ability, or attribute they hoped to measure. In the general classification of intellectual functioning, their testing methods seemed to be satisfactory. But in the evaluation of most other characteristics, psychometricians were encountering difficulties. Simultaneously, clinical psychologists, frequently referred to as *psychometrists* (and not too happy about this label), were impatiently casting about for techniques that would assess "latent" personality functioning. Troubled by what they felt was a lack of professional status, clinicians hoped that through the use of more global and less statistical personality measures they would earn the understanding and respect of their psychiatric colleagues (Crane, 1931–1932).

Two well-received performance scales appeared early in the decade. In 1930, Grace Arthur published the Arthur Point Scale of Performance Tests. Intended primarily for use with children between the ages of 6 and 16, Form I of the scale was composed of eight restandardized tests from the Pintner-Paterson, plus the Kohs Block Designs and the Porteus Mazes. Arthur planned her scale to correlate highly with the Stanford-Binet, and it seemed to do so satisfactorily with children up to age 12. The Cornell-Coxe Performance Ability Scale was published. It covered the same age range from various sources. Ethel Cornell and W. W. Coxe constructed their scale so that it would have little correlation with the Stanford-Binet, and in this they seemed to be successful. The two scales were thus designed to serve different purposes: the first to be a nonverbal substitute for Binet revisions; the second to supplement them (Freeman, 1950).

The most popular Binet revision, the Stanford-Binet, was published in revised form in 1937. Tests were provided at age levels from 2 years to a Superior Adult III category, including items for those levels that had been absent from the 1916 revision, 11 and 13 years. There were two equivalent forms of the scale, L and M, the letters presumably referring to the first-name initials of its authors, Lewis Terman and Maud Merrill (1937). The revision was standardized on a sample of about 3,000 American-born white children ranging in age from one and a half to eighteen years, with efforts to control the influence of geographic location and socioeconomic status.

Criticisms of the 1937 revision were similar to the criticisms of the 1916 scale: There were too many verbal items; the test was of questionable value for assessing adults; the use of "mental ages" at the upper end of the scale was misleading; the test items were a hodgepodge.

Nevertheless, it was agreed that the 1937 revision was a marked improvement over its predecessor, and the scale was widely and quickly accepted by clinical psychologists. Early studies encouragingly reported "constancy" with children of school age (i.e., ordinarily IQs did not vary more than 5.5 points from one administration to the next).

Efforts to evaluate the significance of scatter on the Stanford-Binet continued to prove fruitless. There was no consensus with regard to any quantitative measure of scatter, nor had any numerical computation of spread of scores revealed any significant differences between groups of children thought to be normal, feebleminded, delinquent, or neurotic. It had been found, however, that in cases of mental illness, the scores on the vocabulary subtest seemed less affected than the scores on the other items. Harriet Babcock (1877–1952) thought it might be advantageous to make use of this finding as a means for determining the extent of intellectual deterioration in psychiatric disturbances.

In the early thirties, Babcock's Deterioration Test attracted the attention of psychologists working in state hospitals (Wittman, 1933–1934). The test involved administering the vocabulary items of the Stanford-Binet to obtain an estimate of the patient's preillness level of overall intellectual ability and then administering 24 tests sampling speed of response and capacity for learning to obtain a measure of current mental functioning. The discrepancy between the two estimates was supposed to indicate the extent, if any, of mental deterioration.

J. M. Hunt (1936) warned of two difficulties in evaluating test results and experimental findings when the test was used with psychiatric patients: (1) there was an alarming tendency for psychologists to naively accept psychiatric diagnoses and nosology as factual when, in reality, both the classification scheme and the diagnosis were relative to the predilections, training, skills and biases of a particular psychiatrist, and (2) most psychologists ignored the problem of the patient's motivation. Therefore, samples of the same diagnostic grouping might not be comparable and the nomenclature might be largely unreliable and invalid. Further, in most studies it was virtually impossible to determine whether the patient could not or would not perform the task in question or was simply uninterested in what was being asked. The relevance of Hunt's remarks for tests such as the Babcock was obvious.

Mental deterioration was given some consideration by Wechsler (1939) when he published his intelligence scale, the Wechsler-Bellevue. Deterioration was evaluated by comparing the scores on subtests that supposedly did not decrease with the passage of time with the scores on those that did. But this diagnostic feature was tentative and, as it were, so much frosting on the cake. For the Wechsler-Bellevue was an instrument designed specifically to measure the intellectual functioning of adults as precisely as was then possible.

David Wechsler (1896–1981) had received his PhD from Columbia in 1925. At first his published interests centered on evaluating the significance of the psychogalvanic reflex, but later he turned to the problems of measuring intelligence. In 1932, Wechsler accepted the position of chief psychologist at Bellevue Psychiatric Hospital in New York, and while there he developed his test (Matarazzo, 1981). It was composed of a verbal and a performance scale, with five subtests in each. The verbal subtests included information, comprehension, arithmetic, similarities, and memory span for digits; the performance subtests included object assembly, picture arrangement, block design, digit symbol, and picture completion. A vocabulary test was included as an alternate.

The Wechsler-Bellevue was standardized on 670 white children from 7 to 16 years and 1,081 white adults aged from 17 to 70 years, all of whom resided in New York City and surrounding areas. Efforts were made to control for education and occupation, and the scale was intended for use with persons from 10 to 60 years.

Wechsler (1939, p. 3) defined intelligence as an "aggregate or global capacity of the individual to act purposefully, to think rationally and to deal effectively with his environment," a definition that indicated his support of Spearman's two-factor theory. He rejected the mental age concept in favor of point scales: an IQ value of 100 was assigned to the mean score of an age group; an IQ value of 90 was assigned to a score that is minus one probable error from the mean. This done, it became possible to calculate IQ tables for conversion of scores for a particular age group on the verbal, performance, and full scale into IQ estimates. Therefore, in the case of adults the score obtained by an individual is compared with the scores of others of approximately the same age. In contrast, on the Stanford-Binet, the adult's score is evaluated only in relation to the successes obtained by children and adolescents.

By virtue of the way the IQ tables were constructed, the classification of intelligence on the Wechsler-Bellevue is symmetrical. Approximately 2% of the population—the group considered "defective"—were assigned IQs of 65 and below. Approximately 2% of the population—the group considered "very superior"—were assigned IQs of 128 and above.

In his development of the scale, Wechsler found that scores on some of the subtests began to decrease gradually between the ages of 15 and 22 and fell more rapidly after age 35. Wechsler's findings indicated to some psychologists that intellectual abilities continue to grow until early adulthood and then they decline. But to other psychologists, Wechsler's results only illustrated again that intellectual growth varies with the specific ability and the means by which it is assessed.

Kuhlmann introduced another revision of the Binet in 1939, but it was far overshadowed in popularity by the Stanford Revision and the Wechsler-Bellevue. The California Tests of Mental Maturity, group scales of intelligence, were introduced around 1937. They reflected the view of Thorndike and Thurstone that intelligence is composed of independent abilities or factors. Intended primarily for school children, the California Tests of Mental Maturity sample factors of visual acuity, motor coordination, auditory acuity, memory, spatial relationships, reasoning, and vocabulary.

Around 1938, Thurstone came out with his Primary Mental Abilities Test. Based on the results of his factor analytic research, his group scale was supposed to measure reasoning, word fluency, verbal comprehension, number facility, spatial perception, and rote memory.

Also in 1938, Gesell and Helen Thompson provided developmental schedules for the evaluation of infants between 4 and 56 weeks of age. Meanwhile, research studies were indicating that it was not possible to predict later intelligence scores accurately from scores made on tests administered in infancy.

Edgar Doll (1935) introduced a novel developmental schedule, the Vineland Social Maturity Scale, intended to measure social competence. Designed for use with persons from infancy to 30 years of age, the Vineland was unique in that its scoring was based on an interview with someone well acquainted with the person rather than the person him- or herself. There were 117 items, grouped in age levels, ranging from "balances head" to "directs or manages work of others." The scores on the scale were expressed in terms of social age, which, when divided by the chronological age, produced a social quotient (SQ). Doll's rationale for this new use of division was that some individuals, such as delinquents, may be high in intellectual level but low in social maturity, and vice versa. However, with preschool children the items were so similar to those found on the Gesell Developmental Schedules that the Vineland provided a means for estimating the children's developmental levels when it was not possible to test them.

The Strong Vocational Interest Blank made its appearance in 1938. Earlier in the decade, a somewhat similar test, the Allport-Vernon (1931) Study of Values, was first published. The Allport-Vernon test was based on Spranger's typology and was therefore a device for discovering an individual's value systems, including the order of preference regarding aesthetic, theoretical, economic, social, political, and religious values (Vernon & Allport, 1931–1932).

Among the many personality inventories introduced in this period were the following: Thurstone Personality Schedule; Bernreuter Personality Inventory; Bell Adjustment Inventory; Rogers Adjustment Inventory; Humm-Wadsworth Temperament Scale; California Test of Personality; Aspects of Personality; Maller Personality Sketches; and Guilford Inventory of Factors STDCR (social introversion, thinking introversion, depression, cycloid tendency, and rhathymia, i.e., carefreeness). In most of the inventories, the interviewee was confronted with straightforward questions, such as "Are you troubled with shyness?" The task was simply to answer each item as truthfully as possible by checking Yes, No, or Don't Know (Freeman, 1950).

One of the difficulties with some of the inventories was that they seemed to measure more than they were supposed to measure. A "simple" test of extraversion-introversion was found by the Guilfords (1933–1934) to contain a minimum of 18 group factors, such as impulsiveness and interest in self. Another difficulty with the inventories was that they did not seem to measure the same thing, even when it was reasonable to expect that they would do so; it then became a problem to know what it was they did measure. Moore and Steele (1934–1935) reported a study in which they used the Thurstone Personality Schedule, Allport's Ascendence-Submission Test, Laird's Personality Inventory, the Neymann-Kohlstedt Submission Test, the June Downey Test, and the Pressey X-O Test; they found little correlation between the results on any two tests.

A third difficulty with the inventories was that the scores could easily be faked. Kelly, Miles, and Terman (1935–1936), using the Stanford Test of Masculinity-Feminity, observed that their subjects, both male and female, would obligingly shift their scores considerably in either direction when asked to respond to the items as they thought a member of the other sex would. The transparency, or obviousness, of the inventories was an issue that troubled many clinicians greatly, not only because people may choose to misrepresent themselves, but also because certain items may be alarming to those who are oversensitive to being asked questions concerning abnormal behavior.

Rosenzweig (1938) suggested that an experimental rather than a statistical approach to test construction would greatly improve matters. Instead of asking people Yes-No questions that it is hoped will prove related to personality, he urged the development of techniques based on well-defined hypotheses that yield performances or actual behaviors that can be evaluated. If, however, his test-constructing colleagues should persevere in asking obvious questions, he strongly recommended that they at least regard the responses as raw data in need of interpretation and not as necessarily valid answers.

Yet even if success in measuring traits had been more clearly demonstrated, a number of psychologists would still have regarded the psychometric approach to personality as bankrupt. "Too atomistic," would have been the contention of some. "There is a need for qualitative as well as quantitative knowledge," would have been the argument of others. The demand was fast growing for global, qualitative test procedures that were both simple and disarming.

Graphology certainly provided a sample of behavior for interpretation, and Robert Saudek, a leading graphologist, enjoyed considerable favor among psychologists. Saudek had founded the journal *Character and Personality*, which was later called the *Journal of Personality*. One of his interesting studies showed that identical handwriting could be produced by different persons. Such an occurrence is rare—Saudek (1933–1934) guessed that the chances were one in ten thousand—but happen it did in some cases of identical twins and even in cases of people not related or known to one another.

Saudek's death in 1935 was undoubtedly a setback to graphology and probably made it more difficult for the field to gain acceptance in the United States. However, it is doubtful that Saudek's efforts could have altered the outcome much. Graphology's easy corruptibility and consequent notoriety dampened what little appeal it might have had as a diagnostic technique.

A few psychiatrists suggested diagnostic procedures. Appel (1930–1931) thought it would be a good idea to ask children to draw a house or people, including family members, and then obtain their comments about their drawings. He found this procedure helped him to understand a child's unconscious problems. The same was true when he had children make ink blots and noted their comments about them. Schwartz (1932) reported on his use of pictures showing children in different kinds of social situations. He would ask the youngsters to describe the pictures and answer questions about them. Along the same lines, David Levy (1939) claimed he found it profitable to present children with dolls representing family members and then observe how they played with them. Not only was this technique diagnostic, but Levy thought some of the children derived therapeutic benefits from just expressing their feelings in play. Although Levy seemed to have lessened his interest in the Rorschach test, his former student Samuel J. Beck (1896–1980) was enthusiastically engaged in studies using the inkblots.

Beck had concentrated on the classics during his first 3 undergraduate years at Harvard. He was prevented from continuing college by a lack of money and so took a job as a newspaper reporter in Cleveland. That job lasted 10 years, the last 3 of which Beck spent covering the criminal and juvenile courts. His career in journalism was regarded by Beck (1963) as a profitable interlude in which his skills in analyzing information objectively and precisely were sharpened. He returned to Harvard in 1926 and obtained his BA. He earned an MA and a PhD from Columbia in 1927 and 1932. During his graduate school days, he spent a year as a Commonwealth Fund Fellow at the Institute for Child Guidance in New York, where he met Levy and became acquainted with the Rorschach. He then spent a year as psychologist at the Jewish Board of Guardians in New York, followed by 3 years as senior resident psychologist at Boston Psychopathic Hospital. In 1933, Beck became a research associate at Harvard Medical School, and the next year he was awarded a fellowship that enabled him to study the Rorschach with Oberholzer in Zurich. Beginning in 1936, Beck headed the clinical psychology laboratory at Michael Reese Hospital in Chicago.

A study conducted by Beck (1930) involving the diagnosis of feeblemindedness using Rorschach's inkblots was the first research based on the Rorschach test published in the United States. Other studies (Beck, 1933, 1935, 1936–1937, 1937) using the instrument quickly followed, and Beck's research efforts were soon joined by those of Marguerite Hertz and Bruno Klopfer. In Beck's view, there were two initial problems in developing the test: (1) obtaining statistical norms so that good form responses could be specified and "rare" detail areas of the blot delineated, and (2) testing patients representing a variety of diagnostic categories so that their differential personality patterns could be ascertained.

By 1935, there was still no standardized way to administer the test or score its responses, and the studies reporting positive findings about its reliability and validity were few. Yet Hertz (1935) concluded her survey of the Rorschach literature with the prediction that the test would grow in popularity, because it "is another form of the free association technique which has been found useful in the past for describing personality" (p. 58).

It seemed reasonable to expect little encouragement from studies or experimentation with the Rorschach until some agreement could be reached on how to administer, score, and interpret it. Tending to make such an agreement more and more difficult to achieve was the fact that, as familiarity with the test increased, so did the complexities of scoring and interpreting it.

Some psychologists remembered that Rorschach had made distinctions within the categories of introversion and extraversion. He distinguished active or voluntary introversion from passive or pathologic introversion. The former is exemplified by a poet and the latter by a catatonic patient. Similarly, the active extravert (e.g., a socialite) is to be distinguished from the passive extravert (e.g., a manic individual). Implicit in Rorschach's distinction is the issue of how much control the person has over his or her behavior. Perhaps, it was thought by some of Rorschach's followers, this control could be evaluated by the appropriateness of form in color and movement responses.

On a somewhat broader scale, Beck took note of some general principles. All Rorschach determinants (color, form, movement) are dependent on the person's ability to organize stimuli into a meaningful relationship. Moreover, all responses having the same determinant involve the same psychological process. However, the same determinant does not always have the same interpretative significance and can represent behaviors of differing social value. For example, movement always indicates the "inner ability to create fantasy" but might be overtly expressed in artistic productions, daydreams, or delusions. The psychologist skilled in the use of the Rorschach, Beck concluded, should be able to uncover such meaningful differences.

In 1937, Beck published a manual of the Rorschach and introduced several innovations: an organization score (Z); substitution of the term *experience balance* for *Erlebnistypus*; a classification scheme for content categories; and some normative tables for determining good form responses and rare details. Klopfer and Kelley (1937) also provided instructions for administering the Rorschach.

During the early thirties, shading determinants had not been formally recognized by American psychologists. Back in Switzerland, though, H. Binder had stressed their significance. Binder (1937) believed an emphasis on the dark shadings indicated a dysphoric mood whereas a touch of euphoria is evidenced by percepts determined by light shadings. On the other hand, Klopfer (1938) thought shading responses indicated sensitivity or a cautious desire for contact with the environment. Whatever their meaning, all Rorschach experts agreed shading responses now had to be scored.

Meanwhile, the Rorschach was encountering criticism from psychologists on three counts: (1) It was too subjective in administration, scoring, and interpretation; (2) it was of questionable reliability; and (3) it was of dubious validity.

Yet much to the consternation of its critics, the test grew in popularity. There simply was no other technique that allowed clinicians to make statements about global personality functioning, and it was hoped that the legitimate objections to its use would eventually be proven groundless. Encouraging its users were occasional positive reports, such as the one by Hertz and Rubenstein (1939). They reported a Rorschach record had been presented to three experts, Hertz, Beck, and Klopfer, who made their interpretations "blind" (i.e., they had seen neither the patient nor his case history). Happily, their interpretations were very much in agreement and were substantiated by the case history material. It surely seemed that with increasing experience, equal successes could be had by all serious students of the Rorschach.

So enthusiastic had been the response of clinicians to the Rorschach that one of its early and most severe critics made an ambivalent attempt to "jump on the bandwagon." If psychologists wanted ambiguous stimuli, well then William Stern was willing to supply them. Stern (1937–1938) asked his colleague Karl Struve to make three pictures of clouds of unsurpassable nebulosity. These cloud pictures had neither symmetry, not contours, nor backgrounds. They were just broad expanses with internal variations in shading. Probably Stern intended his cloud pictures to be a bitter joke. If so, he was successful, for few clinicians took his test seriously.

In 1935, Christiana D. Morgan and Henry Murray presented the Thematic Apperception Test (TAT). The TAT consists of 30 pictures, mostly of people in a variety of situations, and a blank card. The testee is supposed to make up, for each picture, a story that describes what has happened, what is happening, what will happen, and what are the feelings of the characters. Only 20 cards (10 at a sitting) were to be administered to any one person, with the selection of cards determined by the person's sex and age. Each story was recorded verbatim and analyzed for its thema (i.e., the interaction of needs, press, and outcome). Obviously, the TAT is a time-consuming procedure and has the additional disadvantage of taxing the clinician's stenographic powers to the limit. Nevertheless, when its cards became available in 1936, it was received with enthusiasm as a promising technique for determining an individual's conflicts and attitudes.

Some interest was shown in two tests developed by Margaret Lowenfeld. The Mosaic Test (1931) required the testee to make a design from tiles of differing geometric shapes and colors. She hoped the designs produced by the testee would yield information about personality functioning and aid in establishing a psychiatric diagnosis. At the time, however, she regarded the test as still being in an early stage of development and therefore best restricted to experimental uses and continued investigation. In the World Test (1939), the testee is asked to construct an environment using settings and models of people, animals, houses, and other objets d'art. Naturally, once the scene is constructed, a story can be elicited. Like the Mosaic Test, the World Test was in need of considerable study in order to ascertain its usefulness.

Another device that had diagnostic possibilities, in particular, as an instrument to evaluate the blind, was the tautophone (Shakow & Rosenzweig, 1939–1940). The tautophone was based on Skinner's verbal summator, which had been used to study latent speech. An individual heard a voice speaking conversationally but unintelligibly and had to guess what the voice was saying. It was hoped that the guesses would reveal something about the individual's personality.

The Bender-Gestalt Test made its appearance in 1938. Lauretta Bender, a psychiatrist who received her MD in 1926 from the State University of Iowa, in 1930 became a member of the faculty at New York University, and in 1936 married Paul Schilder. Her test is composed of nine geometric designs based on figures devised by the Gestalt psychologist Max Wertheimer in his work on perception. The testee is told simply to copy them to the best of his or her ability. It was thought that disturbances in the process of perception and reproduction would indicate pathology and, more specifically, organic brain disease and schizophrenia. Furthermore, in using her test with children, Bender found a chronological progression in the accuracy with which the figures could be reproduced. Therefore the test, in addition to its possibilities for helping in psychiatric diagnosis, had potential value in assessing the level of maturation of visual motor coordination; it was thus quickly accepted for use.

L. K. Frank (1939) proposed the term *projective methods* for those techniques, such as the Rorschach, the TAT, and the tautophone, where the correctness of the response is not determined by the tester but by "the personality who gives it, or imposes upon it, his private idiosyncratic meaning and organization" (p. 403). Therefore, according to Frank, what made a test projective was not the test itself but the method by which its responses were evaluated. Any test can be considered projective if the individual's performance is analyzed and interpreted in terms of its processes and configurations; the projective method can be applied to behavior elicited by any scale and by any situation.

The tests thus far presented, although impressive, were not the only methods put forth during the thirties for diagnosing human behavior. Some advocated the evaluation of personality by an investigation of the functioning of the endocrine glands. Charles Dickens (Fantham, 1933–1934) was one of many notables treated to a postmortem glandular analysis: He suffered from insufficient parathyroids, an overstrained thyroid, overtaxed adrenals, and an enlarged pituitary. Few psychologists were receptive to this approach.

Research papers of more lasting interest to clinicians were those about individual differences in electroencephalographs (EEGs). Hans Berger, a German neuropsychiatrist, after 15 years of trying, was the first to successfully record electrical activity from the intact human head. This event took place in 1929. In 1934, at the Harvard Medical School, the first record of human brain waves in the United States was made on an ink writer.

A large number of EEG studies followed, and by 1939 certain findings about the technique were generally accepted. Among them were the following: Whether or not the person is psychotic, an unstable EEG pattern indicates emotional instability; conversely, a stable pattern indicates emotional stability. Predominantly alpha type patterns are associated with passive, dependent individuals; nonalpha type patterns are associated with active, driving individuals. A feebleminded person without brain damage can have a normal EEG. Epileptics tend to have abnormal EEGs. Patients treated at a psychoanalytic institute have the same EEGs during and after their analyses that they had before their treatment began. It is not possible to separate a normal from an abnormal EEG solely on the basis of specific factors—the pattern of the record as a whole has to be evaluated (Davis, 1940).

In summary, it appears that though the thirties may have been a time of desperation in the world at large, never before had clinical psychologists been so productive in developing diagnostic techniques. From the seeds of ideas, satisfactions, dissatisfactions, and needs sown in previous decades, a rich crop of new instruments had grown and ripened. The immediate task was to harvest, process, and digest them.

DIAGNOSTIC FORMULATIONS

The controversy about the structure of intelligence dwindled. Thorndike had never been a willing combatant and had sufficient integrity to follow his own advice that "the time spent in replying to an attack could better be employed in doing a relevant experiment." Spearman and Thurstone, however, carried on gamely.

Some psychologists advocated that the concept of intelligence be eliminated from psychology. They noted matter-of-factly that IQ could be viewed as merely an index of certain types of adaptation whenever definite relationships between IQ and those adaptations could be demonstrated. Since intelligence scales sample heavily what people have learned, they can be regarded as a form of achievement test. Therefore, it was concluded, the concept of intelligence should be abandoned, because testing "intelligence" was simply a matter of sampling what a person had achieved as a basis for predicting what he or she would achieve.

Most psychologists were willing to part with instincts but were not so eager to lose intelligence. Thurstone (1931) had devised a new statistical technique, multiple-factor analysis, which he believed was a scientific method capable of resolving the issue of the structure of intelligence, among other problems.

According to Thurstone, Spearman's two-factor methods of factor analysis encounter difficulties in dealing with group factors (factors common to only some of the variables) and more than one general factor. In contrast, he claimed, multiple-factor analysis asks how many factors have to be postulated to account for the experimentally given table of correlations and imposes no restrictions on the number of group and general factors.

In his APA presidential address, Thurstone (1934) discussed some of the early results of using his multiple-factor analytic method. He had analyzed 60 adjective traits and had found five factors. Perhaps, he suggested, this meant that it is possible to describe and study the complexity and variety of personality along only five dimensions. Similarly, he had factor-analyzed psychotic symptoms and found five clusterings, which he named *catatonic, manic, depressive, cognitive,* and *hallucinatory*. Perhaps, he thought, this meant that psychiatric disturbances could be reduced to five syndromes. But more work would be needed before a definite answer could be reached. The important point, in Thurstone's opinion, was that these results gave an inkling of the contributions that might be expected through use of the method of multiple-factor analysis.

The following year, Thurstone (1938) launched another experimental attack on the structure of intelligence. Fifty-seven tests sampling intellectual functioning were administered to 240 students in eighth grade, high school, and college. During factor analysis of the results, a correlation of less than .40 was used as a critical value to eliminate a test from participation in a factor.

Six "primary" factors or mental abilities emerged from the data: (1) number, or the ability to perform numerical calculations; (2) verbal comprehension; (3) space, or the ability to manipulate an object in space by using one's imagination; (4) word fluency, or the ability to think of isolated words rapidly; (5) reasoning; and (6) rote memory. There were possibly two other factors—a perceptual factor and a deductive factor—but they were "not yet sufficiently clear." In addition, Thurstone discovered that the tests were intercorrelated and concluded there was a general factor, but only of a "second order."

Spearman (1939) insisted that the alleged second-order general factor found by Thurstone was not a second-order factor at all but was really the primary general factor he had been talking about over the many years. It was becoming increasingly evident to all concerned, especially to the bystanders, that factor analysis was an arbitrary method.

Thomson, an internationally recognized expert on factor analysis, publicly expressed his doubts that the procedure was worth much. Stephenson (1935–1936) suggested that instead of factor analyzing tests, psychologists should factor analyze people by giving a large number of tests to a small number of people and then obtain the factor saturations; it might be that this method would help uncover personality types. Thurstone acknowledged that there is no unique result of a factor analytic study and attempted to evaluate three criteria that had been proposed for deciding whether the results of an analysis are valid.

The first criterion was the invariance of results (i.e., the factorial structure has to remain constant under differing methods of factor analysis). Thurstone felt this criterion was inadequate because the factor loadings change with the addition and removal of tests supposedly measuring the same thing. Also, the correlations seem to fluctuate depending on the particular sample of subjects.

The second criterion was the psychological meaningfulness of the results. In practice this meant that it should be possible to discern some common factor among those correlated items that clustered on tests. This seemed to place a large burden on the ability of the experimenter to perceive similarities among diversities, and it also appeared to be a fairly arbitrary procedure in its own right.

The third criterion was the practical value of the results (i.e., the usefulness of a factor in describing an individual and its superior meaningfulness in comparison with the unanalyzed test score). The results should be sufficient to repay the efforts made to obtain them. To put it differently, do the results of a factor analysis have any application or make any real difference to anyone? In the final analysis, a pragmatic standard seemed to count most.

Other things being equal, most clinicians valued a scale that yielded a profile of mental abilities over one that furnished a single estimate of intelligence. It would have been of significance to them if one theory of the structure of intelligence produced a scale that differed from other scales. Yet not too surprisingly, one scale based on Spearman's theory, the Wechsler-Bellevue, was just as capable of yielding a profile as Thurstone's Primary Mental Abilities Tests. Therefore, it did not seem to make much difference, as far as the appearance of scales, whether one subscribed to Spearman's or Thurstone's theory of intelligence. When the smoke of battle cleared, the fine distinction between a general factor and specific factors versus specific factors and a second-order general factor had an evanescent subtlety that was unimpressive to those not personally involved in the dispute.

A similar truce, born of futility, seemed to have been reached in another quarter of psychology. Pacific overtures were drifting across the no-man's-land separating the camp of the nature-heredity-organicists from that of the nurture-stressing environmentalists. The environmentalists had entered the thirties in a position of strength. But just when the hereditarians seemed to be on the run, a sensible reconciliation was effected (Dashiell, 1939). Let us see what happened.

The nurture position with respect to intelligence gained tremendous support when Beth L. Wellman (1895–1952) reported that children of average intelligence and above who attended nursery school had a mean increase of about five IQ points as compared with those who did not attend a preschool (Wellman, 1932–1933). Other studies indicated that feebleminded mothers could have children of normal intelligence, retarded children who were properly trained could become socially useful adults, and children who at one time seemed of average ability could later score in the feebleminded range if reared in an educationally impoverished environment. Far from being constant, IQs could vary 5 to 20 points and more. Wellman (1938) reported the case of a child who at 3 years scored 89, at 10 years scored 149, and at 13 years scored 132. It seemed clear to Wellman, as well as to other psychologists, that IQs should be dated; that the particular tests by which they were obtained should be noted; and that marked losses in IQ could come from impoverished environments and gains could come from enriched environments.

In further support of the nurture position, it had been found that blacks living in the North scored higher on intelligence tests than those remaining in the South. However, the nature camp attempted to vitiate this finding by the hypothesis of selective migration (i.e., those blacks who left the South tended to be more intelligent than those who remained). Otto Klineberg (1935) evaluated the evidence for selective migration and found it lacking. It appeared that blacks who came North were not on the average superior to those in the South but instead obtained higher scores after living in the North's more favorable environment.

At first each bit of evidence in support of environmental effects on intellectual functioning was marshaled in favor of the view that intelligence was acquired and not innate. The nature camp was on the defensive, but it counterattacked at every opportunity. Terman (1932) expressed his conviction that "the major differences between children of high and low IQ, and the major differences in the intelligence test scores of certain races, as Negroes and whites, will never be fully accounted for on the environmental hypothesis" (p. 329).

Even in the case of "mongolism," which generally was believed to be genetically determined, advocates of nurture argued that the disorder might be produced by some environmental deficiency in utero. Then in 1935, the British psychiatrist Lionel Penrose reported two cases of mental retardation produced by a genetically determined deficiency of phenylalanine hydroxylase. This deficiency resulted in an incomplete oxidation of the amino acid phenylalanine, which could be detected by the presence of phenylpyruvic acid in the urine. If the disorder was detected shortly after birth, preventive measures could be taken to avoid irreparable intellectual damage.

Thus toward the close of the thirties, victories could be claimed by both sides of the nature-nurture controversy. The studies on impoverished and enriched environments cast serious doubt on the validity of the 1930 White House conference committee's definition of feeblemindedness: social incompetence due to arrested mental development from organic causes. Still it was clear, if for no other reason than the existence of retardation due to by phenylpyruvic oligophrenia, that the environmental position was not able to explain all cases of mental subnormality. A synthesis between the nature and nurture positions was in order.

Steps toward effecting such a synthesis were taken throughout the decade. Witty and Lehman (1933) tried persuasion to bring the two groups together. They noted that although most psychologists rejected the term *instinct*, the term *maturation*, as applied to the development of behavior due to normal processes of growth entirely uninfluenced by learning, was being given a definition that sounded distinctly familiar. There were few studies, they pointed out, that provided unequivocal support of the nature position. Even the fact that IQ scores of near relatives are more highly correlated than those of distant relatives might be explained by the fact that environments are more likely to be similar in cases of close consanguinity. They concluded that it is futile to attempt to dichotomize behavior into learned or innate categories. Most behaviors are due to interactions between heredity and environment, and both are essential to a full understanding of growth.

The integration of the nature and nurture positions was exemplified by an American Orthopsychiatric Association meeting on aging held in 1939. George Lawson (1940), a member of a panel which discussed this topic, emphasized that senescence has a double aspect. Biologically, there are declines in the functioning and performance of some abilities but usually not in all of them; nor are abilities impaired at the same rate. Psychologically, there is a transition from autonomy and self-sufficiency to increasing dependence on others, but this transition is often affected by enforced occupational retirement as well as by impaired functioning. It thus appears that chronological age, in and of itself, has little predictive value for assessing the ability of a person to perform a useful function in society and that senility is the product of an interaction between biological and environmental effects. Therefore, the feelings of helplessness, despair, and worthlessness so frequently experienced by the aged might well be prevented. Such dreadful and unnecessary psychological consequences of aging would probably not take place if the elderly were helped to find some task in keeping with their abilities and if employers were flexible about retirement ages.

A similar integrative process was at work in areas of personality functioning other than the intellectual. Many of these areas had been dominated, by default, by psychiatry, and thus organic, hereditary explanations tended to be favored. A strong reaction against the traditional position was displayed, during the thirties, in newly developed theoretical formulations.

Adler's (1930; Ansbacher & Ansbacher, 1956) revised personality theory buttressed the modern functional architecture. He had traveled some distance from the notion that neurosis is caused by the inferiority of some organ. Now he saw the neurotic as someone lacking in social interest, as someone whose symptoms are unconsciously motivated, artful creations intended to exploit others and to protect self-esteem. Through the use of safeguarding mechanisms, the neurotic strives to avoid coming to grips with the problems of life and confronting basic feelings of worthlessness. Yet, to the trained observer, the neurotic constantly reveals true feelings and the subtle means of dealing with them. These attitudes and mechanisms are apparent in verbalizations, expressions, mannerisms, movements, and posturings. When a neurotic patient is being seen by a therapist, one important task is to get the patient to correct these methods of distorting the world and to accept a mature view of it. For only if this happens is the patient able to derive a feeling of true worth through benefiting others instead of abusing them.

But Adler was not the only psychiatrist who stressed the significance of the social environment in the genesis of neurosis. The very title of Karen Horney's (1937) popular book *The Neurotic Personality of Our Time* reflected the current emphasis on culture. Horney (1885–1952) had received her MD from the University of Berlin in 1911 and began her psychoanalytic training in 1914. This included a personal analysis with Karl Abraham and Hanns Sachs. In 1920, she became an instructor at the Psycho-Analytic Institute in Berlin. Coming to the United States in 1932, she assumed the position of associate director of the Chicago Psychoanalytic Institute. However, she became increasingly dissatisfied with the theory that psychosexual development was genetically determined and universal in nature, and she broke with the Chicago group. From 1934, she practiced privately in New York and taught at the New School for Social Research and the New York Psychoanalytic Institute (Hall & Lindzey, 1970; Oberndorf, 1953).

Horney held that "neuroses are generated by disturbances in the interhuman relationships." She insisted that many of Freud's theoretical formulations were culture-bound, true only with reference to his particular time and place of practice. Not only might much of his theory be invalid in the United States of the thirties, but what psychiatrists today would consider neurotic is probably quite different from what would have been considered neurotic in Freud's day.

Horney accepted the contention of cultural anthropologists that what determines whether a behavior is neurotic depends on the standards and values of the culture in which it occurs. The culture of the United States, she asserted, was based on individual competition, which caused people to feel isolated and hostile. What made adjusting to this culture more difficult even than its competitiveness were its many inconsistencies. On the one hand, people were urged to achieve and get ahead; on the other hand, meekness, humility, and brotherly love were held up as virtues. On the one hand, advertising, movies, books, and magazines stimulated sexual and material needs; on the other hand, the country's economy and its moral and legal codes frustrated these needs and restricted their expression. On the one hand, individual freedom was cited as an important value; on the other hand, there was an endless stream of written and unwritten social prohibitions. It was Horney's opinion that within this uniquely confusing culture a new sort of neurotic had emerged.

Horney took pains to make it clear that her discussion did not relate to all kinds of neuroses. She excluded hysteria, obsessions, and compulsions, and she also differentiated between situational and character neuroses. Situational neuroses occur in relatively intact personalities as a reaction to some conflict or stress in reality; character neuroses, which had already been discussed to some extent by Franz Alexander, Wilhelm Reich, and Erich Fromm, among others, are attributable, in Horney's phrase, to an "insidious chronic process" of personality deformation. Her theory was directed toward explaining character neuroses, which, she thought, were especially prevalent in the United States at the time.

Horney noted that children are at first helpless and utterly dependent on their parents. If parental love is not genuine, children sense this and react to this rejection and to the demands of their parents with feelings of basic hostility. This hostility is repressed for a variety of reasons: in order to maintain parental protection; to minimize fears of punishment, abandonment, and complete loss of love; and to avoid feelings of guilt. However, when children continue to experience a lack of affection from people with whom they come in contact, or if the rejection by their parents is severe, a feeling of being isolated develops and their hostility is projected onto the world about them. Horney called this feeling of being alone in a hostile, frightening, and dangerous environment "basic anxiety."

Once children acquire basic anxiety, they begin a process of adopting defenses or maneuvers to alleviate it. They may withdraw from people, become submissive, strive to gain affection, or attempt to gain power and prestige. Usually two or more of these forms of incompatible striving are adopted by neurotics in their chronic efforts to gain reassurance. Therefore, no matter how successfully they have fulfilled the dictates of one striving, they will have betrayed the dictates of at least one other and will thus feel constantly conflicted and torn. Moreover, these strivings, by their persistence and intensity, actually serve to alienate people. The rejections that ensue only make matters worse for a neurotic person. Being highly sensitive to any rebuff, perceiving the requests of others as demands, and perceiving these demands and those of the culture as burdensome impositions, the neurotic's basic anxiety becomes intensified, which in turn produces an intensification of the ineffective patterns of relating and causes more people to become alienated, and so on and so on. The entire process is a vicious circle in which the individual's very struggle to achieve acceptance and security brings about the frustration of those ends and the continuance of maladaptive behavior.

In Horney's formulation, symptoms no longer define a neurotic disorder. Instead of traditional symptoms she saw certain forms of repetitive and inept behavior that are perceived by individuals, for better or worse, as part of themselves. What seems to make a person neurotic is the belief, or the belief of responsible people, that the person's characteristics are unsatisfying, distressing, inefficient, or maladaptive. According to Horney (1937), the absence or presence of symptoms is often irrelevant for the nature of a neurosis. This broadening of the concept of neurosis made virtually everyone open to the charge of being neurotic. In fact, it was claimed that all Americans are probably neurotic and that they suffer from this disorder because of the neurotic culture in which they live. It is at this point that a potshot was fired by the nature camp. Of course all human beings are neurotic, agreed hereditarians, since "it's just the way our phylum is."

The concept of culture relativism was applied not only to neurosis, but also to schizophrenia. According to Devereux (1939), it is not true, as was formerly maintained, that schizophrenics have reverted to a primitive or immature level of thinking. Instead, it appears that they are unable or unwilling to think in the manner or patterns demanded by their society. They are aware of their environment, not withdrawn from it, but rather than using the values and purposes shared by the members of their culture to make sense of their world, they interpret events according to their own private, limited, and idiosyncratic code. Therefore, what is considered schizophrenic behavior in one community might not be considered unusual or abnormal in another, and, conversely, the normal behavior of one culture may be the psychotic behavior of another. Inevitably, cultural relativism led to the seriocomic proposal that a country should benefit its schizophrenics by distributing them among the peoples that would find their behavior perfectly acceptable.

During the thirties, emotional disturbances thus seemed to be everywhere and nowhere, depending on the cultural frame of reference of the moment. Even speech and reading disorders, if one believed what the experts were now saying, were no longer caused by physical defects, unfavorable attitudes toward learning, and inappropriate habits. Instead, they were thought to be produced by unconscious conflicts, and when these conflicts were resolved by psychotherapy, these children were supposed to be able to learn to read and to speak correctly without the need for special tutoring (Blanchard, 1935; Bryngelson, 1935–1936; West, 1936–1937). Thus clinicians who had been laboring in the hard field of remedial teaching found the value of their work questioned and themselves facing a Hobson's choice: Either they would have to begin abandoning their efforts in this area or they would have to give up their role as tutors and assume psychotherapeutic responsibilities.

As might be expected, the concept of psychosomatic illness attracted considerable attention (Dunbar, 1938). Ulcers, asthma, skin rashes, and so on, which formerly had been classified as physical ailments, were now thought to be partially determined and exacerbated by tensions and unconscious conflicts and desires. H. A. Murray (1937) reported that the following unconscious wishes were especially important in the etiology of psychogenic or psychosomatic disorders: (1) to avoid something, (2) to atone for something, (3) to injure someone, (4) to elicit sympathy or support, (5) to die, and (6) to gratify one's sexual desires. Although many people understood that psychosomatic disturbances were psychological problems which produce certain physical illnesses, the view of a few psychologists was that all disturbances are psychosomatic, that any sickness or injury or trauma has psychological consequences which have an important bearing upon the course of treatment. This way of looking at afflicted persons is well expressed in Goldstein's statement: "The aphasic is not a man with altered speech but an altered man."

Kurt Goldstein (1878–1965), whose theoretical position came to be called holistic and organismic, obtained his MD from the University of Breslau in 1903. During World War I, while serving as director of the Military Hospital for Brain-Injured soldiers, he observed that the behavior of the brain damaged is more concrete than normal in that they seemed bound more tightly to the immediate stimulus situation and found it more difficult to consider future possibilities or to see relationships between different stimuli. Goldstein used observations such as these to help in the formulation of his general theory. In 1930, he accepted the position of professor of neurology and psychiatry at the University of Berlin, but with the rise of Nazism he left Germany in 1933 and went to Amsterdam. While there, Goldstein wrote *The Organism*, which appeared in an English translation in 1939. He arrived in the United States in 1935 and became clinical professor of neurology at Columbia University (Goldstein, 1967; Hall & Lindzey, 1970).

For Goldstein (1939), the only motive of the organism is the inborn, somewhat abstract striving for self-actualization (in other words, the striving to realize potentialities and to be expressive). All other motives, such as thirst, hunger, sex, and affiliation, are simply ramifications of this one basic master motive. Put simply, Goldstein viewed the organism (person) as born into the world with certain innate potentialities. These potentialities are sometimes frustrated and sometimes promoted by the environment. If the organism is to survive and flourish, it must come to terms with the environment and achieve some sort of stability and balance. But this coming to terms is a continuing process, both because the organism's striving for self-actualization persists and because the external stimuli are always changing (Purdy, 1936–1937).

Goldstein saw self-actualization as essentially good and the environment as, to a large extent, limiting and frustrating. Thus, like Rousseau, Goldstein thought that the basic and worthwhile potentialities of people are distorted and thwarted by a world that is largely oppressive.

The emphasis on nurture in the etiology of neuroses received additional support from experimental studies within psychology (Hall, 1933–1934). Working with animals, some psychologists had been able to produce neuroticlike behavior by frustrating the animals or forcing them to attempt to make impossible discriminations (Stogdill, 1934). Rats could be made to exhibit such "learned disorganized behavior" when the experimenter blocked the paths they had taken to get to food. They could be "cured," or made to attempt once again to traverse these paths, by increasing the strength of their drive or by depriving them of food. Although these findings were not crucial, the deliberate creation of disturbed behavior in cats, rats, dogs, sheep, and other domestic animals was certainly very interesting, and the studies demonstrated that neuroses might indeed be brought about by situations in which the person could do no right.

A prime target of both those who argued for the tremendous formative significance of the culture and those who contended that neuroses are learned was Freud. He was criticized by the first group for his neglect of interpersonal variables, by the second group for his emphasis on unconscious functioning, and by both groups for the tenacity with which he and his followers held to a view of psychosexual development as naturally evolving. Yet Freud's influence was established and pervasive.

Early in the decade, affixing proper names borrowed from mythology to complexes, which was a habit of Freud's, became a full-blown fad. In addition to the Oedipus complex and the Electra complex, there were proposals to name complexes after Medea, Clytemnestra, Phaedra, Heracles, Amphitryon, Jehovah, Belshazzar, and Manfred. In line with the *Zeitgeist*, Henry Starr (1933) offered up *the Prometheus complex* as the name for an urge toward an ideal too far above the level of the individual's social group, an urge that therefore has to be repressed because of cultural taboos. Such supplements to the contemporary nomenclature were fashionable and entertaining for a few years, but they were not lasting and did seem needlessly confusing.

In the meantime, Freud, despite advanced age and poor health, had been far from idle, unproductive, and subdued. Though he still paid homage to constitutional predispositions to certain kinds of personality functioning, his attention continued to be directed to their psychological characteristics, as was illustrated in 1931 in his discussion of three libidinal types whose physical bases went unmentioned. The *erotic* type is mainly interested in being loved. The *narcissistic* type is preoccupied with self-preservation and self-assertion and tends to be confident and aggressive. The *obsessional* type is dominated by his or her superego and fear of not being loved. Freud recognized, however, that only the rare person embodies the characteristics of just one type and that people usually evidence the characteristics of two or all three, with perhaps one type being the most prominent (Jones, 1957).

Though Freud's typology aroused interest within psychoanalytic circles, the *Zeitgeist* was not propitious for more widespread acceptance. The trend was to attack or belittle suggestions of inborn differences and to concentrate on observable, measurable behavior. Thus, although Jung's introversion-extraversion dichotomy was popularly accepted as descriptive of important individual differences, the supposed constitutional foundation for these traits was minimized or rejected outright.

Even less interest was displayed in other typologies that made their appearance during this period. Among them were Jaensch's integrated and disintegrated perceptual types, Kroh's extensive and intensive attentional types, and Kretschmer's cycloids and schizoids. Each of these typologies has differentiations basically similar to those of Jung's typology. Kretschmer's typology, since it is related to physique, is the most easily tested. Katherine Campbell (1932–1933) reported that height and weight curves for populations of patients suffering from dementia praecox and manic depressive psychosis were highly similar. Her study was one of several that failed to support Kretschmer's observations (Farber, 1938).

In fact, so reluctant were psychologists to accept organic etiologies for "functional" disturbances that some research by Kallmann (1938) in support of a genetic basis for schizophrenia was criticized for the "Teutonic thoroughness" with which Kallmann had conducted the study. Franz Kallmann (1897–1966), the recipient of that irrelevant reproach, was a German psychiatrist who in 1936 accepted a position at the New York Psychiatric Institute. His study carefully noted the occurrence of schizophrenia among near and distant relatives of a sample of 1,087 schizophrenic patients, and he concluded that the psychosis is in part conditioned by general tissue defects having germ-plasm determiners. In other words, schizophrenia is to some extent genetically determined.

Kallmann's conclusion was disputed on the familiar grounds that people who are closely related are brought up in similar environments, an argument of some merit. Unfortunately, in attempting to vitiate organic explanations, the implication was fostered that parents were to be held solely accountable for the psychological disturbances of their offspring. This "accusation" had become more grave, since more severe disorders were now thought likely to occur in childhood. We should note that although psychoses in children had been recorded in the 19th century, it was not until the late twenties and early thirties of the 20th century that psychiatrists considered certain patterns of symptoms to be indicative of schizophrenia as modified by childhood (Potter, 1933; Bradley, 1941). Therefore, although the presence of schizophrenia among the very young is capable of being interpreted as the result of an organic defect or a nurturing defect, the tendency at the time was to attend more closely to whatever evidence supported an environmental explanation, particularly evidence of the existence of pathological family relationships.

Although the symptoms of schizophrenia in childhood generally appeared to be fewer and more simple than those manifested by adults afflicted with this psychosis, they are fully as dramatic and heartrending. In making such a diagnosis, psychiatrists agreed that no single symptom is definitive and that the total behavioral pattern of the child has to be considered (Lutz, 1937). The forms of behavior indicative of this most severe disorder were seclusiveness, bizarre speech, anomalies of thinking, greatly reduced interest in the environment, regressive activities, and disturbances in the expression of emotions (Potter, 1933). By the end of the thirties, and even earlier, as we shall soon see, it was widely believed that the most helpful course to adopt in treating childhood schizophrenia was to remove the child from the family environment and place him or her in an institutional setting that would be therapeutic.

As the decade came to a close, there existed a considerable consensus supporting the position that heredity, with few exceptions, should not be considered the sole cause of mental abnormalities. The most reasonable view seemed to be that the individual's genetic endowment provided certain potentialities or capacities whose realization or fulfillment were dependent on appropriate environmental conditions. It was generally agreed that the individual is best understood as a unitary functioning organism. Accordingly, emotional stresses and strains could have a damaging effect on bodily functioning, and physical ailments and disabilities could have a damaging effect on the person's self-image and on psychological functioning. It appeared that in any disorder the person's symptoms are best understood in relation to the cultural setting, their effects on the person, and the meanings they have for the person.

TREATMENT FORMULATIONS

While the nurture position was growing in popularity, a minor revolution in the psychiatric treatment of hospitalized mental patients by physical means was taking place. During the thirties, vigorous and bold techniques were inaugurated to benefit psychotics. Although the ultimate effectiveness of the assault was debatable, the sincerity and good intentions of those leading it were unquestioned. And, at the very least, sustained efforts were made on behalf of patients who might otherwise have merely languished.

In the early thirties, Ladislas Meduna (1896–1964), a Hungarian psychiatrist, began to experiment with the induction of seizures in schizophrenic patients. He had come across a report describing an antagonism between epilepsy and schizophrenia; this had led the researchers to inject the blood of schizophrenics into epileptics in an effort to reduce the frequency of seizures. This did not prove very successful, but it led Meduna to speculate that perhaps inducing epileptic seizures in schizophrenics would reduce the severity of the psychosis.

Beginning in 1933, Meduna searched for an effective convulsive agent among strychnine, thebaine, nikethamide, caffeine, absinthe, and camphor. The last was tried on an adult catatonic, who after seven camphor injections was able to return home. Later, Meduna switched from camphor to pentylenetetrazol (Cardiazol, Metrazol) as a safer, more reliable seizure-inducing agent. Despite its advantages, there was still a 15-second delay between the injection of the solution and the appearance of the convulsion. Nevertheless, the treatment did seem to be effective in helping about half the patients who had been ill for less than 4 years (Fink, 1984), and its use was shortly thereafter extended to melancholic and manic-depressive disorders as well as schizophrenia (Zilboorg & Henry, 1941).

Metrazol therapy was soon supplanted by electroshock therapy. In 1938, two Italian psychiatrists, V. Cerletti and L. Bini, found that they could induce convulsions by passing a current through the temporal regions of the patient's head. Loss of consciousness was immediate, the seizure was usually not very severe, and ordinarily the cost of treatment was low. Both Meduna and Cerletti emphasized that the essence of the treatment was the production of an epilepticlike seizure, not the specific manner by which the attack was produced. In 1939, Lothar Kalinowski and Renato Almansi introduced the method to the United States.

Another form of shock treatment was discovered by the Viennese psychiatrist Manfred Sakel. While working in Berlin, Sakel treated the withdrawal symptoms of morphine addiction by injecting doses of insulin sufficient to produce coma, or hypoglycemic shock. Pleased with his success in making the withdrawal more bearable, he thought it might also be helpful to give hypoglycemic shocks to schizophrenics. He began his work with psychotic patients in 1933, and in 1938 he demonstrated his insulin shock method in the United States. The therapy did seem to be effective in certain cases.

Generally, either insulin or Metrazol shock was used in the treatment of psychoses. But sometimes, and especially with patients who were particularly disturbed or unresponsive to one or the other, the two types of shock treatment were combined, the Metrazol following the insulin.

Narcosis therapy was used with agitated or excited patients as a means of inducing prolonged sleep and making them more receptive to what was said to them by members of the staff. The principal drug for this purpose was sodium amobarbital. In some cases, the conflicts of the patients could be discussed with them during the period of awakening, a time when they seemed most amenable to suggestion.

The most drastic of these new procedures, psychosurgery, was first performed by the Portuguese neurologist Egaz Moniz. Originally, Moniz had hoped to abolish chronic delusions by injecting alcohol into the prefrontal lobes, the area of the brain thought to be the locus of intellectual activity. But his technique underwent an evolution, and by 1936 it consisted of severing the fiber tracts connecting the prefrontal lobes with the thalamus. Refinements of and variations on this basic strategy soon followed. The outcome of Moniz's early operations demonstrated that though the content of delusions might be little changed, the patient's feelings about these delusions, along with feelings about almost everything else, became bland and apathetic. Psychosurgery was introduced to the United States in 1937 by W. Freeman and J. W. Watts (1942).

Each of these shock and surgical methods at first lacked an acceptable explanation for its efficacy. Nevertheless, all of them were apparently able to effect improvements in some psychotic patients. The theories that originally led to their development were quickly found to be groundless. There was little support for Meduna's hypothesis that epilepsy and schizophrenia are antagonistic, and Moniz's early work soon demonstrated that the prefrontal lobes are not the sole locus of cognition. In order to provide some basis for their continued use, aside from the simple fact that they were of some help, a variety of psychological explanations were offered. Perhaps the shock treatments punish the patient and afford relief. Or perhaps the superego functions are located in the prefrontal lobes and it is they that are surgically isolated in a lobotomy. Unfortunately, the abundance and equal plausibility of such explanations pointed to the absence of any definitive explanation.

More importantly, the results of studies evaluating the therapeutic outcomes when these techniques were employed were equivocal. Yet, for two major reasons, their use continued and expanded: (1) there was little else to choose from in treating psychotics, and (2) the introduction of the techniques raised morale among the staffs of mental hospitals, since it seemed they were providing treatments that actually helped their patients (this was a benefit not to be lightly dismissed).

Despite the fact that psychoanalysts were attempting to adapt their method to the treatment of psychotics, Freud believed such efforts were doomed to failure. He contended that these patients did not have enough remnants of a normal ego intact to be able to cooperate in the manner needed for an effective psychoanalysis. His belief in the futility of these efforts was shared by Paul Schilder (1938), but for a different reason. Schilder thought that since schizophrenia was an organic illness, no form of psychotherapy would be of much value in ameliorating the condition. Freud's and Schilder's pessimism was not shared by many workers in the field. On the contrary, the popular attitude was that psychotherapy could be quite helpful if it were only made available.

The belief in the beneficial effects to be derived from psychotherapy can be partly explained by the widespread appreciation of the importance of social variables and the enthusiasm for psychological etiologies in general, among other things. In short, the situation in psychology was conducive to the development of psychotherapeutic approaches and produced a generation of clinicians who were most attentive to the latest thinking of the leading therapists: Freud, Jung, Adler, and Rank.

Drawing on his vast experience as an analyst, Freud expressed his opinions on a variety of issues. He felt that neuroses, since they did not involve a repudiation of reality as severe as that found in psychoses, were most amenable to psychoanalysis, especially in those cases where their onset seemed to be brought about by some recent trauma. He acknowledged the possibility that the constitutional strength of an instinct might be of less significance than its strength at a given moment (i.e., the present might be of more significance in a given case than the past). He conceded that the fixing of a termination date for analysis could be effective if it were done at just the proper time. His feelings about his practice, however, were essentially negative, and he referred to it as a "blackmailing device."

Freud (1959c) thought that determining when an analysis should be judged completed required taking into account practical considerations. The analysis should not be pursued until the patient is a psychologically perfect human being. That would be expecting too much. It is reasonable to terminate analysis if the patient's condition is improved, even though there may still be a chance for the recurrence of symptoms. However, speaking ideally, possibly only when the basic theme that is unconscious is brought into awareness and fully explored (the wish for a penis in the case of women and the struggle against passivity or the fear of castration in the case of men) should the analysis be judged truly complete. Yet sometimes Freud seemed to feel that no analysis ever really comes to an end. Once begun, analysis is an interminable task in which both patient and analyst continue throughout life to examine their own feelings, conflicts, and problems.

Such concepts as ego functioning, defense mechanisms, and resistances, including the fear of recovery itself, appeared to be assuming an ever-larger place in Freud's thinking:

> *Our therapeutic work swings to and fro during the treatment like a pendulum analyzing now a fragment of the id and now a fragment of the ego . . . Our object will be not . . . to demand that the person who has been 'thoroughly analyzed' shall never again feel the stirrings of passions in himself or become involved in any internal conflict. The business of analysis is to secure the best possible psychological conditions for the functioning of the ego; when this has been done, analysis has accomplished its task. (Freud, 1959c, pp. 341, 354)*

In the meantime, Freud's former colleague Jung had been concentrating much of his therapeutic work on middle-aged patients. Many of these patients complained chiefly that they felt their lives were empty and meaningless. It seemed clear to Jung that this neurosis, like all others, is an attempt to compensate for and draw attention to neglected or repressed aspects of the personality. Perhaps, he thought, in the second half of life sexuality and self-assertion are of less importance than earlier and are not as significant as the drive to express a spiritual or "natural religious function." What the middle-aged have repressed that is now causing them so much anguish, assuming their development has proceeded satisfactorily thus far, are their spiritual yearnings and their need to relate to a being superior to themselves. As this need and these wishes obtrude into consciousness, they are regarded as bad, and the patient feels guilty and worthless as a result of experiencing them. But fortunately relief can be obtained and this conflict resolved if the person confesses or acknowledges these repressed yearnings and frankly discusses them with an honest, warm human being, such as his or her Jungian analyst.

As Jung saw it, the early stage of this type of analysis would deal with the contents of the personal unconscious, examining those problems and conflicts that are specific to this individual. As the analysis progressed, and especially in its later stages, material from the collective unconscious (the problems and conflicts shared by all people) would come into prominence and be discussed. Working together, patient and analyst would form a relationship in which both might become changed as they consider spiritual problems and search for new meanings to give to the patient's life:

> [Psychotherapy then becomes] freed from its clinical origins and ceases to be a mere method for treating the sick. It is now of service to the healthy as well, or at least to those who have a right to psychic health and whose illness is at most the suffering that tortures us all. (Jung, 1933, p. 54)

In contrast, Adlerian therapy seemed to reach its end about where Jung regarded his kind of therapy as just beginning: "Individual psychology considers the essence of therapy to lie in making the patient aware of his lack of cooperative power, and to convince him of the origin of this lack in early childhood maladjustments" (Adler, 1930, p. 404). According to Adler, the prime task of the therapist is to enlist the patient's cooperation in the psychotherapeutic process, to provide the experience of contact with an understanding and accepting fellow human being, and to help the patient transfer the favorable attitudes of the therapeutic relationship to dealings with other persons.

Not cooperation but self-expression is what came first with Rank (1950). The individual should take joy in the expression of self and yet be so at ease and certain of his or her identity that attention to and acceptance of the will of another can be given without self-reproach. Rank did not claim that as a therapist he could "make" the patient become aware of personal problems, principally because he did not believe that the therapist is the best judge as to what those problems are. "Psychology does not deal with facts as science does," he said, "but deals only with the individual's attitude toward facts" (Taft, 1958, p. 149). Therefore, Rank asserted that in therapy the person is not so much taught or convinced as helped to experience self-understanding and knowledge of self. Since Rank saw people striving to assert their own thoughts and feelings, their resistance to analysis was not regarded as something to be broken by the therapist but as a positive force that could facilitate self-development. The task of the therapist was to provide a relationship in which the patient could learn to use that force constructively and assert his or her will without feeling excessively guilty or fearful about being independent.

Freud, Jung, Adler, and Rank all shared a belief in the far-reaching importance of the relationship that develops between the therapist and patient. Although differing in the details of what they considered to be the ideal form of this alliance, all agreed that it is a vehicle for achieving the goals of analysis and that at least a minimum of cooperation must exist if the patient is to be helped. But such an awareness was not confined to these leaders. Talk of "the relationship" blossomed in profusion everywhere in the literature of this period.

For many, such as the psychiatrist John Levy (1897–1938), the relationship was of importance mainly because the patient will probably use the same tactics and defenses in relating to the therapist as he or she uses with others. However, there is a big difference in the reaction that will occur. The therapist will not respond in the same way as other people have done to these maneuvers. Rather than becoming emotionally upset or involved, the therapist will only understand, clarify, and interpret the patient's feelings and needs, which produces a different kind of relationship from any the patient has ever experienced. Then, gradually (and in some manner not quite clear) the patient's maladaptive attitudes will "drop off" and in their place effective functioning will be restored. Levy (1938) called this approach "relationship therapy," but we should note that by this term he meant that it is essentially the relationship that is treated. A quite different stance was taken by others who saw the treatment relationship as so significant and meaningful that they regarded it as a kind of therapy in and of itself.

This was the position taken, to some extent out of necessity, in the social work profession, where depth analysis was thought to be seldom feasible or desirable. Although explorations of unconscious motivation and conflict were ruled out, the attachment of the client to the case worker could still be employed in what was called "supportive therapy," which involved conscious attempts to alleviate the client's hunger for protection, help, and solicitude. In supportive therapy, the social worker expressed interest and deliberately gave advice, encouragement, and affection. The assumption was that the client would eventually be able to move beyond the close, dependent attachment that was to be engendered toward greater self-reliance and personal freedom (Axelrode, 1940).

Although the idea of supportive therapy appealed to many members of the mental health professions, some psychologists, psychiatrists, and social workers expressed doubt that this kind of therapy was the best way, or even a satisfactory way, of helping people. In their view, supportive therapy was based on an underlying theory that people were weak and dependent and had needs that were essentially infantile. In contrast, Rank, for one, depicted individuals as striving for independence and needing to be self-assertive. In was Rank's view that struck

Fredrick Allen (1890-1964) as more meaningful and that most influenced his thinking as to what the most favorable therapeutic relationship would be like.

Frederick Allen had earned a bachelor's and a master's degree in psychology from the University of California. For about 3 years, he worked as a school psychologist and then entered Johns Hopkins to study medicine. He received his MD in 1921, became a psychiatrist, and in 1925 assumed the position of director of the Philadelphia Child Guidance Clinic.

Allen (1934) felt that as a child therapist his main task was to accept and respect children as they were at the moment, without feeling any need to change them or assume the responsibility for directing their decisions. He did not see himself, nor did he wish others to see him, as omnipotent. Allen's cardinal assumption, emphasized again and again, was that respect for individuals as they exist, respect for their ability to help themselves and to take responsibility for their own lives, would be of most benefit to them and enable them to use the healthier modes of self-expression fostered by the therapeutic relationship in interactions with others.

The relationship between the therapist and the patient is valuable, in Allen's opinion, not because it is a reexperiencing of past events, but because it is a meaningful reality satisfying in the present. Since Allen, in line with his assumptions, minimized the giving of interpretations and advice and stressed the activity of the patient and the receptivity of the therapist, his colleagues called his approach "passive therapy." However, Allen disliked this term and felt that it embodied a misunderstanding of his concept of the therapist's proper role. In 1933, he attempted to clarify his position:

> I am interested in creating a natural relation in which the patient can acquire a more adequate acceptance of himself, a clearer conception of what he can do and feel in relation to the world in which he continues to live . . . I am not afraid to let the patient feel that I am interested in him as a person. (Allen, 1934, p. 201)

Though Allen's work was mostly with children, he felt there was nothing to prevent his formulations from applying equally to adults. His ideas interested some psychologists, and Carl Rogers, whom we will encounter later, was one of those favorably impressed. But on the whole Allen's concepts, deceptively simple in appearance, could not compare with Freud's in popularity or in the enthusiasm they generated.

Throughout the thirties there was considerable development in those psychotherapeutic techniques and methods that reflected the significance attached to interpersonal variables. The growing importance of the therapeutic relationship was but one manifestation. There were two others: an increasing interest in the treatment of children and in the use of group therapy. (At the same time, whatever interest there had been in hypnosis as an aid to treatment declined. Some experimentation did continue; for example, Freidlander and Sarbin [1938] suggested a standard method for trance induction and a scale for measuring depth of hypnosis in order to allow comparison between the results of different studies in this area. However, little attention was given to the therapeutic uses of hypnosis, possibly because there was less concern about the rapid alleviation of symptoms and more concern about effecting changes in basic personality functioning, the latter presumably requiring a long and deliberate involvement by the patient.)

In 1931, the first residential treatment center for children in the United States, the Emma Pendleton Bradley Home, was established. It was designed to serve severely emotionally disturbed and psychotic children ranging from 5 to 12 years of age. What made the Bradley Home unique was its attempt to make an entire environment therapeutic, not only by judicious selection and indoctrination of all its personnel but also by having rules, procedures, furnishings, and rooms constructed to meet the needs of the children rather than of the institution.

By and large, play therapy (Newell, 1941) was the form of treatment children received when they were seen individually. Its usefulness had been amply demonstrated by the pioneering efforts of Hermine von Hug-Hellmuth (1921), Anna Freud (1928), and Melanie Klein (1932). In their formulations, play served two major functions: (1) It is an appropriate or natural medium through which a child can express fantasies and conflicts, and (2) the therapist can use it to favorably impress the child and win his or her confidence and admiration. The first function is, or course, by far the more important of the two. It is through a relatively free and expressive form of play that children seem best able to communicate.

David Levy (1939) offered some additional observations about play therapy. He saw no reason why play could not be deliberately made to serve as a diagnostic technique. The therapist could choose toys and materials that would be likely to draw the child out or be pertinent to the case, employ them in creating or describing a situation (usually interpersonal), and then encourage the child to react to it. Further, Levy was convinced that play alone could provide the child with therapeutic benefits simply because it allowed the expression of feelings and impulses (he called this "release therapy").

Another important addition during the thirties to the repertory of psychotherapeutic methods was group therapy. We may recall some of the group approaches of the early 1900s, such as the Emmanuel Movement, which were tentative forerunners of this "new" kind of treatment. One of the pioneers of that earlier period, Joseph Pratt, was still active in the field, although in a somewhat different way. In 1930 he established a clinic at the Boston Dispensary using his class method to help, not tubercular patients this time, but people who complained of physical ills when nothing organically wrong could be detected. Although Pratt seems to have become more psychiatrically oriented over the years, his influence on work with groups was confined to only a very few colleagues (Corsini, 1957).

In 1931, L. C. Marsh, a psychiatrist, began to publish accounts of the use of group treatment with schizophrenics. Marsh had the idea of establishing a therapeutic community and, in his treatment, relied heavily on his ability to generate a healthy enthusiasm among the members of his groups, something we might perhaps have surmised from his credo: "By the group have they been broken; by the crowd shall they be healed." He claimed that he had been involved in working with groups since 1900 and that another psychiatrist, by the name of E. W. Lazell, had antedated him. But it cannot be said that the work of either of these men had much effect.

Someone who did have a significant effect was Jacob Levy Moreno (1892–1974). It is he who introduced, in 1932, the term *group therapy*. Moreno was born in Rumania. During his childhood he had a love for the theater and would act out elaborate, improvised dramas. He received his MD from the University of Vienna in 1917, and while there he acquired a distaste for psychoanalysis. At the beginning of his career, Moreno used group discussions in an attempt to rehabilitate prostitutes. Later, in 1922, he founded a spontaneity theater, in which individuals were encouraged to throw themselves freely into specified roles in a given situation and to improvise both their lines and their actions as they went along. Subsequently, this method, called *psychodrama*, was developed as a technique for the diagnosis and treatment of psychological problems.

Moreno left Austria for the United States during the late twenties and began practicing psychiatry in New York. He defined group therapy as follows: "a method of psychotherapy which combines the technique of assignments with the technique of spontaneous treatments." This somewhat unusual definition originated in Moreno's (1932) attempt to work out a therapeutic approach to the classification or grouping of criminals in prison. His idea was to evaluate prisoners individually and then to group them so that social and personal improvements would be produced by the interactions of appropriately arranged personalities. To implement his theories, Moreno developed sociometric techniques. A sociometric technique attempts to measure preferences of the members of a group for one another, usually by asking each member to name those in the group with whom he or she would like, or not like, to be involved under a specified set of circumstances. It was this work that led Moreno, in 1937, to establish the journal *Sociometry*.

In 1934, the psychiatrist S. R. Slavson began what he called "activity group therapy," a form of treatment intended specifically for use with emotionally disturbed children. His idea was to help youngsters about 8 to 11 years old by placing them in a group and allowing them to freely engage in constructive, destructive, and other expressive activities, at all times with a highly permissive therapist in attendance. The atmosphere of an activity group is like that of a social club. Refreshments are served and outings may be held. However, Slavson believed that the group functions as a secondary family and that the therapist comes to be seen as a substitute parent. The group members become increasingly important to each other, and insight is gained, not by interpretations from the therapist, but mainly through the reactions of the children to the behavior that takes place in the group (Slavson, 1940).

Paul Schilder was also enthusiastic about group therapy, and his enthusiasm seemed to infect others. By the end of the thirties, almost everyone in the mental health field had heard of the method and quite a few had tried their hand at it. As generally understood, group therapy involved seeing conjointly a small number of persons with problems and encouraging them to express their feelings to everyone present. The therapist undertook to clarify the expressions and interactions of the members, including, of course, any comments or actions that related to him- or herself.

Few clinical psychologists spoke out on the subject of therapy during this period, but those that did seem to have been swimming against the mainstream of interest and experimentation in interpersonal and group psychotherapy. Their approaches to treatment were still geared to the conviction that they were dealing with problems in learning, and thus they emphasized the value of making use of principles of conditioning. Tendler (1933), for example, urged his fellow clinicians to pursue work in psychotherapy, and he offered his method of treatment by "detensors" as a possible technique. In this method, the clinician was to reduce the patient's tensions by presenting relaxing ideas (e.g., reassurances and comforting explanations), by advocating new and delightful situations (e.g., telling the patient to go on a vacation or trip), and by helping the patient make use of those who might be of assistance (e.g., advising the patient to confide in friends, members of the clergy, or the clinical psychologist). Knight Dunlap (1932) recommended the breaking of habits such as stuttering, thumb sucking, and masturbation by "negative practice." This procedure required the person deliberately to repeat the habit so that it eventually could be brought under conscious control and thus be eliminated. Mowrer and Mowrer (1938) advised using an apparatus for treating enuretics similar to one devised by the German pediatrician M. Pfaundler in 1904. Whenever the child urinates in bed, the urine serves to complete an electrical circuit which rings a bell that awakens the child. According to Mowrer's information, 30 enuretic children had been treated by the bell-ringing technique and all abandoned the habit without substituting any other behavior that was maladaptive! (First results with a treatment are almost always the best.)

These conditioning approaches did not greatly appeal to American psychiatrists and social workers. Nor were psychiatrists especially inspired by the offer of psychologists to subject psychotherapy to scientific investigation. Contributions from psychology were interesting, to be sure, but, as Carl Rogers (1931) pointed out, they implied that psychotherapy was a process which could be examined and refined by scientific methods. At that time, probably a majority of psychotherapists felt strongly that their treatments were more art than science and that they would lose something essential in the very process of being experimentally dissected and studied. They believed deeply in the worth of what they were doing, were personally convinced of its value, and on occasion even argued that such deep conviction is necessary for psychotherapy to be most effective. Far from questioning the effectiveness of psychotherapy, the major concern of this period was to try to extend its use to the mentally retarded, to the psychotic, and to anyone who might be benefited or feel benefited by its use (August, 1935).

Despite such enthusiasm, there were few who claimed that psychotherapy was always successful. Healy, who had been among the first to advocate therapy for juvenile delinquents, was also among the first to report that the outcomes had been most discouraging (Healy & Bronner, 1948). However, he held the disorder and not the treatment responsible for these disappointing results, and he concluded that the prognosis for children with "abnormal personalities" was in general not good.

Healy and Franz Alexander had conducted another investigation (Alexander & Healy, 1935). Although their research had to be curtailed during the Depression due to a lack of funds, they had been able to devote about 9 months to the psychoanalysis of five criminals. According to Healy, "The material obtained bearing upon unconscious motivation is extremely illuminating; the curative results in the face of long-standing internal conditions and external vicissitudes were meagre."

Healy's verdict was sobering to many members of the mental health professions, but it elicited from others contentions that the treatments described in these studies had not been long enough or else were not of the proper kind to produce the desired changes. In fact, the variety of different therapeutic methods and techniques, the growing emphasis on the significance of the personality and experience of the therapist in the course and outcome of treatment, and the complexities due to the variables in the therapeutic relationship enabled anyone who believed strongly in a particular form of therapy to attribute, quite sensibly, instances of failure to some problem arising from the large constellation of method and other interacting variables. Often enthusiasts conveyed the impression that some measure of success could be obtained with any patient, regardless of his or her condition, if he or she was matched with the appropriate practitioner and seen for a sufficient length of time. They held to this belief with such tenacity and seemed so impervious to contradictory evidence that some members of the mental health professions began to wonder if these enthusiasts did not suffer from an unshakable resistance to the idea that psychotherapy might sometimes be ineffective. Gregory Zilboorg (1890–1959) was one of several who gave some thought to this intraprofessional matter.

Zilboorg was a psychoanalyst who obtained his MD from Columbia in 1926. By 1938, he could safely proclaim, "Ours is an age of psychology" (Zilboorg, 1939, p. 86) and yet at the same time he entertained some misgivings about psychology's popularity. He asked himself why so many people had come to attach so high a value to psychoanalysis and psychotherapy. His answer was not a very flattering one. Zilboorg believed that a large number of people, including members of the mental health professions, had a repressed demand for individual perfection. By virtue of their own narcissism, psychotherapists felt they could help others to change for the better simply by the use of words. These words were, perhaps not entirely unconsciously, endowed with magical properties and powers (as may be recalled, Freud referred to this as a belief in the "omnipotence of words"). Zilboorg argued that in order to satisfy their own emotional needs, psychotherapists had made psychotherapy into a form of dogmatism maintained by rationalizations and intellectual insights and dedicated to the perpetuation of the delusion that its practitioners were capable of improving anyone.

Accordingly, Zilboorg urged his colleagues to evaluate themselves unsparingly and to recognize and accept their limitations. In particular, he advocated caution and restraint in acquainting the public with what they had to offer. It is all to easy, he noted, to oversell psychology, not only to people in general but to those who seek to apply it professionally as well.

Thus we see that by the close of the thirties serious doubts about the unqualified effectiveness of psychotherapeutic approaches had arisen. These doubts were quickly dismissed, however. More prevalent were feelings of hopefulness and excitement as new and evolving techniques were applied to an ever-increasing variety of groups. The "modern" conception of mental illness encompassed any degree of maladjustment from childhood through old age. Although there was some question about the universality of these disorders, there was a general feeling of confidence that everyone could be treated satisfactorily by some form of psychotherapy.

What, then, could disturbed persons expect in the way of professional assistance? Disturbed children might be treated through the use of play (either individually or in a group), negative practice, or conditioning. Almost certainly any disturbed child would encounter a practitioner who would treat him or her with respect, with acceptance, and, to the best of the therapist's professional knowledge and skill, with understanding. Disturbed adults would not, of course, engage in play therapy in our sense of the term, but they would have an impressive number of other psychotherapies to choose from. An adult hospitalized psychotic would be more likely to encounter treatment with insulin and electroshock therapy than an understanding relationship alone. But, even for adult patients, there was a growing conviction as to the intrinsic effectiveness of psychotherapy and its superiority to other forms of treatment.

PROFESSIONAL DEVELOPMENT

Hunter (1932), in his presidential address before the APA, expressed a view shared by most of his colleagues: "Psychology seeks to describe and explain, to predict and control, the extrinsic behavior of the organism to an external environment which is predominantly social." The disputes between various schools of psychology no longer seemed to arouse the emotion or even the interest that they had done only a few years before. It was as though most psychologists had tacitly reached an agreement that speculations and polemics were not the means by which their profession could be advanced and so had decided to unite in developing experimental methods to study human behavior objectively. Guthrie (1933) had observed that "the extent to which psychologists are divided into schools measures the extent to which psychology is not a science, but a field for speculation." It seemed reasonable that investigation should take precedence over argumentation, since when facts and natural laws are established they will be binding on all psychologists and all schools of thought.

Of course, this agreement about certain principles did not mean that by the end of the thirties all controversies had vanished from psychology. Obviously they had not, and even in the midst of this relative accord Yerkes (1933), for example, claimed that psychology should be restricted to the systematic study of the self and its relations to other selves, whereas the study of various organisms should be a different discipline called *psychobiology*. Nonetheless, psychologists who thought of themselves as scientists shared the goal of understanding human behavior through research that was as objective (reproducible) as possible. Therefore, they turned away from arguing about what they should or should not study and began to seek to establish certain basic rules by which all scientific investigations and theoretical constructions, regardless of particular opinions and persuasions, could be conducted.

Naturally there were misgivings and recognized limitations. Skraggs (1934) noted that the more specific and manipulable problems became, the more they became simplified and restricted in scope. Conversely, the more problems were treated globally, the more difficult it became to delineate and appraise the relevant variables objectively. Furthermore, awareness of the probably unavoidable restrictions on the acquisition of truth was not confined to psychology. Within the physical sciences a similar trend was dramatically apparent: Determinism gave way to indeterminism; certainty gave way to probability; an insistence on a rigorous and pure objectivity was replaced by a skeptical recognition of the possible ubiquitousness of subjectivity; relative rather than absolute statements became the rule; and experimental hypotheses instead of axioms were held up as the most worthwhile fruit of science. As a result, psychologists began turning once again to philosophy, but this time to the philosophy of science, for help in erecting firm methodological foundations for their discipline.

An essential need, it was agreed, was for clear definitions of terms. Bridgman and Stevens suggested that terms and constructs should be defined operationally (i.e., according to specifiable, "public," and repeatable operations). "To experience," Stevens (1935) asserted, can be operationally defined as "to react discriminatively." Since operations are always changing, all concepts require continual revision, and any term not capable of being specified in terms of shareable and repeatable observations would, in Steven's opinion, best be ejected from the body of science.

Hull (1937), in his APA presidential address, described what most psychologists could subscribe to as an ideal model for building theories: a set of explicit postulates with operationally defined terms and deduced series of interlocking theorems. If the statements or hypotheses derived from the theorems failed to be supported by the facts, the theoretical system was to that extent false and in need of revision or abandonment. If it was not possible to derive testable hypotheses from a theory or to relate observations to it, that theory, according to Hull, was scientifically meaningless.

Although no theory in psychology at that time satisfied the rigorous standards advocated by Hull, the majority of his audience agreed that his criteria were worthwhile goals and should be strived for. There was thus a ground swell of harmony within psychology as well as an attempt to integrate the findings of this science with those of related disciplines. Psychologists, as they looked about themselves and examined the signs of development, had ample cause for satisfaction.

The science of psychology had continued to grow, and the United States had become the leader in terms of sheer volume of research and professional expansion. During the 40 years between 1894 and 1933, there had been 138,820 studies listed in the *Psychological Index*; of these, 41% were in English, 29% were in German, 13% were in French, with the remainder in various other languages. If numbers of publications and increase in the number of members of the American Psychological Association are reasonable criteria of professional vitality, the facts are striking: 1,312 papers were published in 1894, whereas in 1933 there were 6,286; in 1930 there were approximately 1,100 members of the APA, whereas in 1939 the membership was approximately 2,200.

Nevertheless, Fernberger's conclusions about the APA in 1931 applied just as forcefully to the organization in 1939. He felt the association had succeeded very well in giving psychologists a group consciousness, an identity, and prestige in the academic world. Due to its high standards for membership, it had made APA affiliation both an honor and an economic necessity, since employers favored applicants who had attained this distinction. Further, the association performed an important scientific service through its ownership and publication of a balanced group of journals. Certainly here were reasons enough for self-congratulation, although Fernberger (1940) did see a persistently vexing debit side: "The Association has completely and signally failed at every direct attempt to control psychology or psychologists, whether . . . in matters of terminology, technique, or personnel." These were urgent matters, and equally as pressing, in Fernberger's opinion, was the need for the APA to assume responsibility for formulating some sort of legal definition of a psychologist.

Other psychologists, particularly clinicians, were even more dissatisfied with the situation. It is somewhat of a paradox that this distress was especially acute among clinical psychologists, for their self-confidence and success were greater than ever. Although the role of clinical psychologists as constructors, administrators, and interpreters of tests was increasingly accepted by other kinds of professionals (in 1931 Augusta Bronner and in 1936 Edgar Doll were elected to the presidency of the American Orthopsychiatric Association), many clinicians felt this role was restrictive and even distasteful. Tulchin (1930) declared, "The clinical psychologist is just beginning to get recognition and help in his attempt to emerge from the IQ-indicator stage and to develop a technique in treatment of behavior and personality problems. . . . The psychologist is no longer satisfied with the mere giving of tests."

Tulchin gave the following reasons why clinical psychologists felt discontent. First, they wished to break free of the rigid adherence to standardized testing procedures, an adherence apparently invoked to set limits on the pursuit of the major objective, which was to understand people. Second, they recognized that individual patients cannot be expected to confine the expression of emotional reactions to meetings with psychiatrists and that therefore psychologists also should have the right to deal with these reactions when they were expressed. Third, they believed they should be involved in the actual conduct of treatment, since they were already participating in the planning of treatment for specific patients and were doing research on psychotherapy. Fourth, due to the fact that clinicians were engaged in remedial teaching, they were in a strategic position to deal with school maladjustments "while ostensibly tutoring." (That Tulchin should feel it necessary to point out a subterfuge that would enable clinicians to broaden their role without attracting undue attention indicates the likelihood of considerable resistance to such a change, especially resistance on the part of the medical profession.) Finally, there was a growing demand for clinicians to undertake vocational counseling as well as testing, a demand that they did not feel they could satisfy (as Tulchin put it, "The sooner we recognize the fact that there are few vocational tests of real worth the better").

Wallin (1929–1930) offered some additional reasons for discontent. He noted with justifiable concern that there was a growing tendency for psychologists to be relegated to "second-string" jobs while physicians took over the positions of heads of clinics and bureaus. As might be expected, along with inferior positions of responsibility went lower salaries, lower by as much as $1,200 to $3,000 a year. Yet there was nothing diabolical in all this. According to Wallin, the heart of the problem was the absence of standards, regulations, and a prescribed training program for clinical psychologists. Anyone who wished to become a clinical psychologist still was forced to take whatever courses were available and to receive additional training on the job (Machover, 1980). Phony psychologists were able to advertise their services in the daily press so that, as far as the public was concerned, being called a psychologist was not always a guarantee of competence. Moreover, those who presumed to function as "mental testers" often had limited abilities and little, if any, training.

In these deplorable circumstances, students were best advised to leave whatever clinical programs they were in and to pursue a career in some other profession. But Wallin saw a more sensible and desirable alternative. He urged psychologists to meet their responsibility to develop the profession. Satisfactory training standards would have to be set up and enforced, and better jobs would have to be created by arousing the public to the pressing need for them and by lobbying for favorable state legislation. Wallin preferred that the universities should assume these profession-development responsibilities, but other clinicians felt they should be assumed by the APA.

The APA still wavered, seemingly ambivalent about venturing into nonacademic professional problems, and in consequence, in 1930, the Association of Consulting Psychologists was formed. This organization was in effect an extension and expansion of the New York State Association of Consulting Psychology, which had been in existence since 1921. The new name indicated its intention to reach out for membership beyond the boundaries of the state of New York.

In 1931, the Section of Clinical Psychology of the APA made an effort to establish a prescribed training program in clinical psychology that would be accepted by the universities. The Committee on Standards of Training for Clinical Psychologists was created to develop the program.

At that time there were approximately 800 psychologists in the United States engaged in clinical work. The need for them to offer their professional services in the area of treatment was formally recognized the following year, 1932, when the Executive Committee of the Association of Consulting Psychologists established a subcommittee on psychotherapy.

The APA Committee on Standards of Training (Report of Committee, 1935) defined clinical psychology as "that art and technology which deals with the adjustment problems of human beings." The committee recommended that any person, before being called a clinical psychologist, should be required to have a PhD and a year of supervised experience (fifteen hours of clinical work a week for forty weeks). An MA and a year's experience would entitle someone to be called an assistant psychologist. Following publication of the report, the committee, considering its task finished, disbanded.

In the same year, Poffenberger (1936), president of the APA, exhorted the association to accept the responsibility of setting up a "hallmark" for the qualified psychologist and establish conditions or standards for defining competence. Poffenberger pointed out that the composition of the APA was changing: 530 members had jobs with no academic affiliation, and too many were unemployed and finding it difficult to obtain positions, particularly in universities. Therefore, if psychologists were going to get work during the economic depression, an even larger number would have to consider expanding their services to include applications of their science, and they would have to look for employment in clinics, schools, courts, and mental hospitals, Psychology, Poffenberger claimed, was compelled to revise its image and become an applied as well as a pure science. At the same time, psychologists had to ensure that both the public and their own reputations were protected from damage by incompetents.

Poffenberger's concern about unemployment and the Depression should not obscure the fact that, despite the state of the economy, the number of clinics and clinical positions was increasing. In 1930, there were about 500 clinics in the United States offering psychiatric services, of which about 125 were child guidance centers staffed by psychiatrists, psychologists, and social workers (American Psychological Association Clinical Section, 1935). By 1936, there were approximately 676 psychiatric clinics and 87 psychoeducational clinics (compared with 20 in 1914). The psychoeducational clinics were mostly affiliated with universities and colleges and directed by psychologists.

Within psychiatric clinics, the major activities of the clinical psychologists were diagnostic testing and interviewing. Nevertheless, a sizable percentage (approximately 44%) were engaged in remedial teaching, and about 35% reported that they conducted therapeutic interviews with people suffering from mild personality disorders. Within the psychoeducational clinics and state hospitals, there was a similar distribution. Obviously, the majority of clinical psychologists were not active in psychotherapy, and some, contented that this was so, even felt the name of their profession should be changed to "consulting psychology" to avoid any implication that they were involved in treatment.

In 1936, the department of psychology at Columbia University established a tentative curriculum for clinical psychologists, which consisted of 2 years of graduate work and 1 year of internship. Just such a 3-year training program was endorsed as a satisfactory model by the Boston Society of Clinical Psychologists in 1937.

Also in 1937, Witmer retired from the University of Pennsylvania. Earlier in the decade he had proposed another goal for the field he had named and helped create: "psychonomic personeering . . . clinical psychology oriented toward the creation of a personal character of surpassing superiority" (Witmer, 1930). This objective, like many proposed by Witmer, had merit but seemed inopportune and attracted little interest.

Out of a sense of futility, the Clinical Section of the APA disbanded in 1937, and the American Association of Applied Psychology (AAAP) was formed. The AAAP swallowed up the Association of Consulting Psychology and organized itself into four sections: consulting psychology, clinical psychology, educational psychology, and business and industrial psychology. In 1938 the AAAP also started publishing the *Journal of Consulting Psychology* (which had been originated, in 1937, by the Association of Consulting Psychology).

Toward the close of the decade, the situation in clinical psychology was as follows. Some clinical psychologists still made up a small but distinct minority group within the APA. Some 888 members and associates of the APA (approximately 40%) did not hold academic positions, and of this number about 270 were clinical psychologists. An increasing number of psychologists were going into the clinical field, and an increasing number of clinical positions were available to them. This was especially true in the United States and in England, where the number of child guidance clinics had increased from 4 in 1929 to 20 by 1939.

Nevertheless, more psychologists were looking for jobs than there were positions to be filled. The situation was particularly acute in universities and in large metropolitan areas, especially New York City. Although some skeptics suggested the problem was confined to the more desirable positions in the more desirable locations, the matter seemed of genuine concern to those out of work, and several factors could be adduced to explain why unemployment existed. To some extent, the Depression had probably slowed expansion in psychiatric and psychological facilities and academic positions. Moreover, psychologists fleeing from Europe undoubtedly took some jobs that might otherwise have been held by Americans. But what was most distressing was that some employers reported that they were unable to offer positions to self-proclaimed clinical psychologists because the applicants were poorly trained and seemed unlikely to contribute much professionally.

Clinical psychologists were still thought of primarily as diagnosticians or mental testers, but there was talk of enlarging their role to include psychotherapy. Any such proposal encountered major opposition from psychiatrists and from the entire medical profession. There was also considerable discussion about getting state legislatures to enact certification laws for psychologists, and this also aroused strong opposition from physicians. Little could be accomplished in broadening the profession until clinicians defined their role to their own satisfaction, saw high standards of training adopted by the profession, and gave evidence of their professional maturity by formulating and following an explicit code of ethics.

Once again the APA took the lead by setting up the Committee on Scientific and Professional Ethics in 1938. However, the APA still seemed unwilling to come to grips with the issue and took an ineffectual stance. The committee reported in 1940 that it would be premature to devise a code of ethics, yet it recommended that a standing committee be formed to handle ethical infractions.

Clinicians were still determined to include psychotherapy within their role definition. This was certain to introduce a number of serious problems. Measures were called for to meet the all-too-predictable opposition from the medical profession. Criteria for the selection of clinical psychology trainees would have to be set. Graduate students were going to have to be more carefully screened by the universities in order to filter out those who seemed unsuited to function as psychotherapists. The universities would have to establish graduate-level courses in methods of treatment (Report of Committee on Clinical Training of Psychologists, 1940).

Referring to the selection of trainees, Carl Rogers (1939) recommended that students in clinical psychology should have the ability to enter into warm human relationships, give evidence of an interest in people as individuals, and have a sincere desire to be of help to others. Further, their training should assist them to gain insight into their own motives and needs while developing their integrity and maturity. Rogers' recommendations were eminently reasonable, and psychologists could generally agree that everything should be done to see that they were put into practice.

The war in Europe had thrust the responsibility for scientific progress in psychology on the United States. Mixed with pride went the sobering recognition that American psychologists had an obligation to the discipline, not to particular points of view. Gordon Allport (1940), in addressing the APA as its president in 1939, advised his colleagues to be tolerant of their differences and to avoid authoritarian attitudes. The test of a theory, he observed, rested not on persuasive discourse and forceful argumentation but on its success in predicting, understanding, and guiding human action.

At the end of the thirties, when so many people had taken up arms to settle their grievances, psychologists did well to remind themselves that they belonged to an international group that shared the purposes and values of a scientific discipline.

III

THE THIRD GENERATION

In 1944, the APA attracted back clinical and other applied psychologists by agreeing to broaden its objectives and address professional concerns. The first certification law for psychologists was enacted by Connecticut in 1945, marking a significant step in the long process of gaining legal recognition, protection, and status for the profession. As World War II came to an end, people recognized there would be an enormous need for clinical psychologists to meet the psychological problems of returning veterans. University graduate programs in clinical psychology were encouraged through the use of federal funds, and the APA assumed the responsibility of determining which programs satisfied standards and merited support. Doctoral programs in psychology were expected to train their clinical students to be scientists and practitioners of psychotherapy and psychological assessment. The goal of training all clinical psychologists in research methodology at the expense of assessment and treatment skills became increasingly untenable. Programs were instituted to train practitioner-scientist clinicians and clinicians devoted to professional practice. The PsyD degree and the emergence of professional schools in psychology indicated that clinical psychologists were of sufficient number and strength to claim a measure of autonomy and independence for their profession.

MAJOR EVENTS IN THE HISTORY OF CLINICAL PSYCHOLOGY

1940 to 1949

Neo-Freudians (Fromm, Sullivan); growth of interest in the ego and the self-concept; Maslow's hierarchy of needs; psychodynamics in experimental psychology.

Boom in psychological testing: WISC, MMPI, college entrance examinations, achievement tests, interest inventories, figure drawings.

Growing interest in individual, group, and brief psychotherapies; founding of the

American Group Psychotherapy Association (1942); Rogers' client-centered therapy.

APA broadens its objectives to include professional concerns (1944); the AAAP disbands and merges with the APA (1944).

The VA, NIMH, and USPHS provide funds for clinical training; the APA assumes responsibility for accrediting training programs in clinical psychology; there is a rapid increase in the number of universities offering clinical training.

Connecticut enacts first certification law for psychologists (1945).

Graduate programs in clinical psychology required to provide training in psychotherapy, assessment, and research (1947).

1950 to 1959

Erikson's theory of psychosocial development opens psychoanalysis to the life span and to the concepts of Adler, Rank, Horney, and Sullivan.

Existential-humanistic ideas; Selye's studies on stress and the general adaptation syndrome; behavior modification, verbal conditioning, Ellis's rational-emotive therapy, Wolpe's systematic desensitization.

Mounting criticisms of test utility and validity, effectiveness of psychotherapy, clinical judgment; introduction of tranquilizers, antipsychotic drugs, psychoactive drugs; systems and communication explanations of psychopathology.

APA publishes a code of ethics for clinical and consulting psychologists (1951).

Clinical psychologists gain legal recognition as experts in determining mental illness.

1960 to 1969

Beginnings of affirmative action in recruiting women and minorities as graduate students and faculty in psychology; Association of Black Psychologists forms (1968).

Importance of infancy; early childhood education; Piaget; learning disabilities; cultural deprivation; deemphasis on testing.

Community mental health centers and community psychology (1963); deinstitutionalization and prevention of disorders (1963).

Humanistic growth movement; encounter groups; sensitivity groups.

Behavioral movement; token economies; Skinner; behavior therapy.

Information explosion; over 30,000 psychologists in U.S., about 12,000 clinicians; about 20,000 scientific articles and books published a year.

PsyD program begins at University of Illinois (1968).

Founding of California School of Professional Psychology (1969).

7

To the Victors
1940–1949

The war in Europe, which began in 1939, was markedly different in nature from the kind of trench warfare anticipated. The German army launched a blitz-krieg consisting of fast-moving attacks. In 1940 the British army was driven from the continent, and Germany conquered Denmark, Norway, the Netherlands, Belgium, and France. Meanwhile, Germany's main ally, Italy, launched an invasion of Greece. In 1941, Germany conquered Bulgaria, Yugoslavia, and Greece. During the summer, the German army surged into the Soviet Union, and in December 1941, Japan threw its might against the United States, transforming what had been a European war into World War II.

After a series of additional victories, the tide turned against Germany, Italy, and Japan. In 1943 Italy surrendered, and in 1945 so too did Germany and Japan. The war had been an extremely savage and costly one. Approximately 16 million men in the armed forces had been killed and many millions more wounded. Millions of civilians, including women and children, had died in bombings and the vicious persecutions conducted by the Nazis.

The United States emerged from the war the most wealthy and powerful nation on earth and deeply resolved not to repeat its mistakes of the post–World War I period. Accordingly, it eagerly joined and hopefully supported the United Nations, an organization dedicated to seeking rational, peaceful solutions to world problems. For a moment, but only a moment, there seemed to be peace.

The illusion was quickly dispelled when civil war was renewed in China and the Soviet Union embarked on a policy of promoting communist governments wherever possible—a policy opposed by the United States with resentment and growing determination. All too swiftly it appeared that one enemy had been replaced by another. By 1949, two great coalitions of nations confronted each other: the nations of the West led by the United States and including Great Britain and France versus the nations of the East led by the USSR and including the recently established communist regime in China. Each of the leaders of the two blocs possessed atomic weapons and thus the capacity to exterminate each other and, it was widely feared, everyone else besides.

Yet World War II and its aftermath were not without some positive results. For one thing, the war had had an enormous vitalizing effect on the American economy. Billions of dollars in aid were extended by the United States to countries all over the world and vast sums were spent on rejuvenating nations. One highly desirable consequence in the United States was the GI Bill, which provided veterans with an opportunity to acquire a college education without cost. Not too surprisingly, the enrollment in schools of higher learning for the academic year 1949 was nearly double what it had been 10 years before. Many of these students, 2,659,021 in number, chose to specialize in psychology, perhaps encouraged to do so by the favorable publicity that psychology had earned through its contributions to the military effort and its applications in other fields, notably mental health, and by the films that dramatized these accomplishments, such as *Spellbound* and *The Dark Mirror.*

Moreover, the fruits of the research stimulated by the war were many and diverse: electronic devices of all sorts, jet aircraft, miracle drugs, antibiotics, insecticides, rockets, detergents, and atomic energy. Taken all in all there had been 10 years of rapid change—for individuals, for nations, and for the profession of clinical psychology.

NORMAL PERSONALITY FUNCTIONING

The field of investigation when Freud began his epoch-making discoveries bore little resemblance to the field at the time of his death. Few psychologists could expect to attain Freud's stature, yet reactions to his contributions, including sharp dissent, continued; and even among those who considered themselves Freudian in orientation, there were shifts in emphasis and movement into areas that were thought to have previously been neglected (McLean, 1946; Wolff, 1948).

Many psychoanalysts focused on the functioning of the ego. In so doing, they were drawn into the task of integrating their findings with those of psychology as a whole. They were supported by Anna Freud's observations that ego processes defend against external as well as internal stimuli and by the formulations of Hartmann, Kris, and Loewenstein (1946) concerning the autonomy of ego functions. These ideas were leading to a different psychoanalytic conception of human development in which instinctual forces were held to be less powerful and considerably less dominant than had been thought.

The organism was now conceived of as having been endowed from birth with both instinctual impulses (id) and "apparatuses" or structures for motility, perception, and memory (ego). Even without conflict or a need to control these impulses, the ego processes function to adapt the individual to the environment, including interpersonal relationships. The autonomy of the ego was proclaimed in theory by departing from the previous belief that it derived its energy gradually from the id. Instead, both the ego and id were thought to be differentiated from a common matrix and the processes of each to have their own supplies of energy. Furthermore, in analytic circles a concept was developed similar to functional autonomy but called *neutralization of drives.*

Neutralization of drives is a progressive process whereby energy associated with instinctual gratification becomes divorced from this aim and serves the function of environmental adaptation. For example, though painting might have originally provided pleasurable gratification through giving expression to smearing impulses, it could later come to serve as a vehicle for the communication of feelings and a source of livelihood. Through neutralization, energy associated with the functioning of the id would become associated with ego functioning.

The concept of neutralization served to bring the present more sharply into focus and to stress its importance in understanding the individual. The past, however, was still emphasized, and it was still agreed that the essential structure of personality is formed by the time a child is 5 or 6 years old. Another idea that brought out the significance of the present was the suggestion that a stimulus of little relevance in one stage of development might become decisive at a later stage. For example, a boy might see a nude woman early in his life when this would have little meaning for him, but later this memory might be reactivated and contribute to the development of fear of castration.

A similar change of view occurred with regard to the importance attached to the gratification of drives. Not only instinctual gratification but also its frustration, as well as the maturation of perceptual equipment, was now seen as necessary for psychological growth and the development of interpersonal relationships. An optimal balance between satisfactions and deprivations is needed if the child is to become mature in all respects.

Despite these modifications, psychoanalytic theory continued to encounter much criticism from cultural anthropologists. Cross-cultural studies had shown that infants could be subjected to widely varying child-rearing practices and still seem to develop into "normal" adults. Two major conclusions emerged: (1) though children's early experiences might predispose them to acquire certain personality characteristics, their later experiences could actualize, modify, or nullify them, and (2) child-rearing practices are of much less significance for personality development than the attitudes, feelings, and motives communicated to children by their parents (Orlansky, 1949). Both these empirically supported conclusions were swiftly recognized and incorporated into psychoanalytic teaching.

"There is no psychology of man in a vacuum . . . only a psychology of man in a certain concrete society and in a certain social setting within this concrete society." These are the words of Otto Fenichel (1897–1946) in his book *The Psychoanalytic Theory of Neurosis* (1945). Fenichel felt a great love for psychoanalytic theory and a great fear that in trying to meet the enormous demand for therapeutic services psychoanalysis would be modified and compromised until its uniqueness as a form of treatment was lost. He had taught at the Berlin Psycho-Analytic Institute before leaving Germany in 1933. After teaching analysis in Oslo and Prague, Fenichel arrived in the United States in 1938 and spent his few remaining years in California. Fenichel concluded from his studies that the Oedipus complex is not universal and inevitable but that it is a product of family structure and influences. Therefore, he hypothesized that when the composition of the family departs from the Western model—a nuclear family structure with an authoritarian father and a passive mother—the pattern of the Oedipus complex changes. Fenichel thus took another step toward making psychoanalytic theory consistent with findings from cultural anthropology (Simmel, 1946).

Freud's death instinct (or aggression instinct) was also revised to make it compatible with results of experiments and more current points of view. Karl Menninger (1942) asserted that the aggression instinct is fostered and intensified by frustrations of the love instinct. Such frustrations are produced by parents who unconsciously reject their children. A vicious circular process is set in motion, for these children, when they grow up and become parents themselves, unconsciously rejecting their children in turn. If this vicious circle is to be broken, Menninger recommended that people should become aware of their aggressive impulses and cultivate expressing their love. Karen Horney, it would seem, might easily have returned to the psychoanalytic fold. But she did not, and she was joined by others, including Fromm and Sullivan, who shared with her the conviction that personality is largely determined by culture.

Erich Fromm (1900–1980) grew up in Germany, received his PhD from the University of Heidelberg in 1922, and trained as an analyst in Munich and at the Berlin Psychoanalytic Institute. In 1933, he came to the United States and lectured at the Chicago Psychoanalytic Institute before entering private practice in New York.

According to Fromm (1950) humans, by their very nature, need to experience a sense of belonging and relatedness. Yet with each step in their growth as unique persons, with each step forward in their awareness of separation from the natural environment, they come to feel more lonely, isolated, and uncertain of the desirability of their supposed progress. Their lives may easily come to seem empty and meaningless, and the temptation is to fill this void by conformity and submission to others. But at the same time they are reluctant to part with their individuality. A choice has to be made: to unite with the world in the spontaneity of love and productive work or else to seek a kind of security by such ties with the world as destroy freedom and the integrity of the individual self.

Naturally Fromm favored the alternative of personal growth and social usefulness. But coming from Germany, Fromm was acutely aware that a whole people could sacrifice their freedom in order to gain a feeling of security and a sense of identity through submission to a totalitarian regime. Obviously, the more healthy choice is not always made—with consequences that may be calamitous and catastrophic. Therefore, Fromm believed, in view of the dangers confronting democratic forms of government, an immediate human need was to have "faith in life and in truth, and in freedom as the active and spontaneous realization of the individual self" (Fromm, 1950).

Although Harry Stack Sullivan (1892–1949) shared Fromm's appreciation of the importance of interpersonal relations, he approached the subject from a different direction. Although it may be denied that people inherently need to relate to others, it cannot be denied that from birth we are involved in interpersonal situations. For Sullivan, "the relatively enduring pattern of recurrent interpersonal situations which characterize a human life" is personality (Sullivan, 1953, p. 111).

Sullivan obtained his MD from the Chicago College of Medicine and Surgery in 1917. He studied under the psychiatrist William Alanson White, and from 1923 until 1930 was connected with the Medical School of the University of Maryland. During that period Sullivan conducted studies of schizophrenia and was a pioneer in its psychotherapeutic treatment and in interpreting its etiology primarily in terms of disturbed relationships in early childhood. In 1933 Sullivan became president of the William Alanson White Foundation, and in 1936 he became director of the Washington School of Psychiatry. The journal *Psychiatry*, which began publication in 1938, served as the chief vehicle for the communication of his ideas.

Sullivan (1953, pp. 19–20) defined psychiatry as "the study of processes that involve or go on between people." This rather ambitious and certainly overinclusive definition contains an implication that Sullivan recognized and explicitly discussed: The individuality of the person is not itself the object of scientific scrutiny. Instead, it is the interactions between a person and other people, including interactions with the scientist or therapist, that are to be observed, studied, and interpreted. Thus, what the person says or does has meaning only insofar as it is related to someone else. Therapists, scientists, and other "participant observers" (Sullivan, 1954) can no longer consider themselves passive or neutral and let it go at that. They have to understand what effects they might have—including what effects their attempts to have no effect at all might have—on the individual's personality.

It was thought that, from birth, interpersonal interactions are of paramount importance in shaping the self. According to Sullivan (1947), the self-system, the sanctioned potentials that the person seeks to develop and integrate, originate in the infant's empathic sensing of the mothering one's feelings. (For example, the infant is supposed to be able to sense the mother's feelings of anxiety, hostility, and affection. To a large extent, these feelings are thought to be communicated by the way the mother feeds, holds, and otherwise interacts with her child.) Further, the self-system is built up over the course of years from the child's appraisals of the attitudes of significant people. When the child experiences rejection, frustration, or insecurity, tension or anxiety is felt. This anxiety sets up disruptions in the process of communication and disturbs integrative actions and growth. Ordinarily, efforts are made to alleviate tension and anxiety through the satisfaction of needs and through regaining a feeling of security. But when these efforts fail, the individual tends to resort to feeling apathetic or sleepy. Thus indifference, drowsiness, selective inattention, withdrawal, and distortions of reality are seen more as a means for preventing an overwhelming feeling of tension or anxiety from coming into awareness and less as defenses against instinctual impulses.

The various stages of development described by Freud were perceived by Sullivan as representative of modes of interaction between the child and others. For example, the anal stage centers around the activities of toilet training, and the child's retention and elimination of feces can produce melodramatic interpersonal reactions. The anal stage is not simply a time when the anus serves as a zone of special sensitivity and gratification.

Although the self-system has its foundation in infancy, it continues to grow in scope, complexity, and integration throughout childhood and adolescence. Among other things, sex roles, cultural values, and occupational goals are supposed to become included. Clearly, Sullivan regarded personality as capable of changes and modifications throughout the normal course of development, and during this growth interpersonal variables are of major importance, particularly the relationships between the mother and infant, the parent and child, and the child and peers and authority figures.

Since the self-system functions to safeguard a feeling of security and to protect the person from feeling anxious, Sullivan claimed it tends to exclude information incompatible with its state of organization. A similar view was advanced by Prescott Lecky (1945). Lecky regarded personality as an organization of consistent values—consistent because the individual is motivated to resist accepting information inconsistent with personal values and to assimilate experiences that correspond with these beliefs. In the same vein, Angyal (1941) conceived a symbolic self that tends to falsify and distort reality, with the result that the person's behavior is often based on or guided by unreliable and inappropriate information. In theories such as these, the concept of the self found its way back into psychology.

Hilgard (1949), in his APA presidential address, pointed out that feelings of guilt have to be understood in relation to a self-concept since they indicate that people conceive of themselves as capable of either good or bad choices. A person's defense mechanisms also imply a self-reference, in the sense that they protect the person against a loss of self-esteem. Therefore, Hilgard believed it necessary to obtain a picture of the individual's self-concept ("his image of himself") in order to understand the individual fully.

But to ask people simply what they think of themselves does not constitute a satisfactory way of obtaining information about their self-concepts. Even if they want to be honest and cooperative, unconscious factors will distort the reported self-concept, because not all that we believe about ourselves is in awareness. It seemed to Hilgard that the best way to avoid both conscious and unconscious bias is to infer the self-concept from observations of a person's behavior, either by noting a sample of performance in interviews or by using projective techniques.

Many psychologists agreed with Hilgard that self-concepts are important but disagreed with his contention that the self has to be inferred. All that is necessary, they claimed, is to define the self-concept as consciously held and readily acknowledged thoughts, feelings, and strivings. Other psychologists felt that such a public concept of the self is not very sophisticated. It became apparent, however, that regardless of which self psychologists wanted to talk about, they at least were discussing once more a self. William James and Mary Calkins would have been pleased.

At least four factors contributed to this renewed interest in the self. Two of them we have already noted and discussed: the growing attention paid both to ego functioning and to interpersonal relationships. A third was the experimental demonstration of support for the hypothesis that people exist in a world of their own perceptions. A fourth was the increasingly popular belief in the dignity and uniqueness of the human being. Let us now briefly consider the last two factors.

Everyone agreed that perception is a function of maturation, and Heinz Werner (1940) specifically described what that might mean. In general, Werner saw mental development as a progression from products of perception and conceptualization that are diffuse, labile, and indefinite to those that are more differentiated, integrated, stable, and definite. To the child, objects have a personal meaning. They appear alive and expressive, and their fine details do not seem to be perceived. As children grow, their perceptions become more discrete and less influenced by personal feelings and needs. However, these maturational changes seem to be more a matter of degree rather than of distinct types of perception, one occurring only in childhood, the other occurring only among adults. A number of studies investigating the effects of needs and feelings on perception supported the view that these effects are normally found in adulthood. We shall mention only two of them.

Schafer and Murphy (1943) had subjects learn names for each of four outlined faces presented tachistoscopically. Whenever two of the faces were presented, the subjects were regularly rewarded with money, whereas presentation of the other two was regularly accompanied by "punishment," taking money from the subjects. A rewarded face and a punished face were then combined along their common profile to form a single ambiguous figure. When the composite face was presented, the subjects more frequently called out the name of the rewarded face than the name of the punished face.

McClelland and Atkinson (1948), after establishing a set by projecting faint pictures onto a screen, projected blanks and asked three groups of hungry naval trainees what they thought these "faint pictures" might be. The more hungry the naval trainee, the less he tended to see food but the more he tended to see objects related to food (e.g., plate, spoon, fork). This finding was interpreted as showing there is an inhibition against thinking about food itself when hungry.

Because of the insights gained from such experiments, psychologists began to talk enthusiastically about "a new look in perception," referring to the demonstrations of the influence of values and needs upon perceptual processes and hence the artificiality of demarcating content areas within psychology. As Bruner and Cecile Goodman (1947) put it, "For too long now, perception has been virtually the exclusive domain of the Experimental psychologist with a capital E." It seemed clear to them that a full understanding of perception would require the cooperative efforts of psychologists specializing in different fields of research.

A similar conclusion might have been reached in every area of psychology. There was no longer much question that the individual is an organism, an integrated whole, who cannot be broken up into separate functions or processes that are fully understandable in isolation. The new look in perception had given support to the position of psychologists who had argued for more emphasis on the self. Some of these psychologists defined the self as a conceptual system organized from perceptions of the environment, especially perceptions of the attitudes and feelings of others that affect subsequent perceptions of self. But regardless of the particular definition employed, the experimental findings compelled most psychologists to entertain a much broader conception of stimulus and response than before.

During the preceding 40 years of psychology, a picture of humans as a higher form of animal had emerged (some psychologists would stop there), a form of animal whose behavior is determined in large part by thoughts and feelings and impulses of which it is not aware, who unknowingly distorts the world on the basis of needs and fears, and whose lifelong patterns of responding have been laid down during the first 5 years of development. Now a reaction to this conception of humans was mounting. Adding impetus to this reaction were the very real prospects for human annihilation—prospects made vivid by the recent spectacle of destruction in which millions of egos and selves perished. It was thought that part of the solution was for human beings to develop a sense of responsibility for their own actions and then strive to live by an ethics based on an appreciation of the worth of every person. Perhaps at the crux of the matter was the need for each individual to refute the apparent meaninglessness and insignificance of his or her own life.

Human significance, dignity, worth, and responsibility for behavior had certainly always been emphasized by religion, but such ideas had seldom found a place within textbooks of psychology. The time seemed ripe for them to make a forceful appearance.

Sullivan (1953) pointed out that even the lowest level of human integration is far superior to that of the most highly developed nonhuman organism. Even the genius and the idiot, Sullivan asserted, are more similar to each other because of their shared humanness than either is to any nonhuman member of the animal kingdom, and the human species is so distinctive that it can only be understood by studying it, not by merely drawing conclusions from the study of other organisms.

Of course, James, Freud, Adler, Jung, Rank, Horney, and so on, had each in his or her own way discussed human uniqueness. But where before this uniqueness had been taken mostly for granted and the continuity with other forms of animal life had to be made explicit and stressed, now the continuity of humans with other forms of animal life was taken for granted and there was a felt need to make human uniqueness vivid and of great consequence. Not every psychologist, however, experienced this need.

According to some psychologists, what makes us unique are our needs, especially our higher needs, and our ability to deal creatively with our environment. Abraham Maslow (1908–1970) described the person as possessing a hierarchical structure of needs, which in ascending order are physiological needs; safety; belongingness and love; esteem; and self-actualization (Maslow, 1943). (*Self-actualization* was the same term used by Goldstein to indicate a continual striving for completion and the fulfillment of potentialities.) Physiological needs are basic, shared with other organisms, and demanding of relatively immediate gratification if the individual is to survive. But with their satisfaction, the next higher group of needs in the hierarchy emerges to dominate conscious functioning and to serve for a time as the immediate motivation of behavior. With satisfaction of this group, the next higher group of needs emerges, and so on. In short, as the lower needs are satisfied, the person becomes free to manifest the higher ones (Maslow, 1948). Conversely, when the lower needs remain chronically unsatisfied, the person may never have the opportunity to satisfy the more altruistic, lofty, and human needs. In a land where people starve and fear for their lives, the need for self-actualization may rarely manifest itself.

John Anderson (1948) presented an overall picture of the nature of children that was shared by many of his colleagues in developmental psychology and that can also be taken as descriptive of human nature. He depicted children as active energy systems coping with and creating personal worlds, not passive organisms victimized by stimuli from the environment. Children respond selectively, ignoring as well as attending to stimuli. The past is largely forgotten, and children live mostly in the present. They have a tendency to retain whatever has repeatedly been encountered, including cultural values, persistent family attitudes and problems, and more or less successful patterns of adjustment. Children, as thus conceived, evidence resiliency and a substantial capacity for tolerating and recovering from stresses and frustrations.

Anderson's description of children may easily be substituted for a description of the self, and it is further evidence that psychologists were again interested in theories of the self, though less abstract and less extreme theories than those of the late 19th century and early 20th. Psychoanalysis had discarded the completely rational adult self capable of free will. Behaviorism also represented a reaction against free will, self psychology, and the indulgence in a whole class of mentalistic concepts. But here was the self again—a self less rational than its predecessor, more aware of its environment, less capable of pulling itself up by its own bootstraps, and with a history of continuous development. Its reappearance represented a formidable reaction against determinism by the unconscious (as in psychoanalysis) and against bundles of habits or empty organisms (as in behaviorism).

DIAGNOSTIC TECHNIQUES

Like personality theories, diagnostic techniques were increasing in quantity, complexity, and comprehensiveness. Some idea of the number of psychological tests in 1940 was provided by Buros (1941), who published reviews of about 325 and who listed approximately 200 others. Only a small proportion of these techniques was employed to any great extent by clinicians. The remainder were either instruments devised for use in other areas of applied psychology or tests that did not enjoy much popularity.

With war raging in Europe and Asia, psychologists were again asked to develop group tests for the evaluation of military personnel. In 1940, a committee consisting of Walter Bingham (chairperson), C. C. Brigham, H. E. Garrett, L. J. O'Rourke, M. W. Richardson, C. L. Shartle, and L. I. Thrustone was formed to advise the adjutant general. These psychologists assisted in the development of the Army General Classification Test, a group test administered to approximately 10 million servicemen during the course of the war (Bingham, 1952). A number of other tests were devised for use in the selection of naval officers, pilots, instructors, and candidates for assignment to particular kinds of training (Freeman, 1950; Staff, 1946).

To meet the special demands of wartime, a variety of screening devices and modifications of existing procedures were produced, including a personal inventory of 145 items for detecting psychiatric disturbances, the Kent (1942) EGY tests for the rapid evaluation of intelligence, a group administered Rorschach

(Harrower-Erickson & Steiner, 1943), and shorter forms of the TAT. At the other extreme were highly elaborate situational tests that involved lengthy stress interviews and subjecting testees to diabolical frustrations. These were used to select the candidates best fitted for the dangerous, precarious, highly important work of the Office of Strategic Services (OSS Staff, 1948), the U.S. intelligence and espionage service of World War II.

Hardly a male adult with military potential escaped psychological testing (Hunter, 1946). It was estimated that during 1944, 60 million standardized tests were administered to 20 million persons. In particular, the College Entrance Examination Board and American Council on Education administered 26,781,759 tests to 11,493,407 people; the Adjutant General's Office administered 4,993,142 tests to 2,302,919 people; the Bureau of Naval Personnel administered 9,000,000 tests to 1,250,000 people; the Army Air Force administered 10,000,000 tests to 400,000 people; the Civil Services Commission administered 1,800,000 tests to 30,000 people; and the Bureau of Medicine and Surgery administered 240,000 tests to 80,000 people (Wolfle, 1947).

Within Great Britain, the principal test for purposes of military classification was the Raven Progressive Matrices. This was a nonverbal test of homogeneous items in which the testee was required to select the missing section that would complete a sequence of designs. In each item there is some logical principle of progression, and this principle becomes increasingly more difficult to detect. The test was devised by L. S. Penrose and J. C. Raven and was first published in 1938 as a technique for measuring general intelligence that would minimize the effect of culture and education. Although based on Spearman's theory of intelligence and thus designed to measure g or the ability to perceive relationships (more specifically, "insight through visual survey"), the Raven Progressive Matrices did not prove very effective in predicting success in most training courses. However, it did seem useful as a predictor of performance in visual signaling and the operation of radar sets (Freeman, 1950).

Surprisingly, in view of official declarations against their use, diagnostic techniques even managed to survive and find a place in Nazi Germany. Testing had ostensibly been abandoned in 1942, probably for two reasons: (1) Because psychological testing is essentially a democratic procedure, since selection for positions is based on an individual's psychological functioning and skills rather than on membership in a favored political party or social group, and (2) because there was a wish to deny the presence of psychological problems within the German armed forces. Nevertheless, clandestine psychological testing went on within the German slave-labor program. Individual industrialists sanctioned testing as a method of placing laborers in proper jobs and ensuring worker satisfaction (Ansbacher, 1950). Approximately 425,000 slave laborers were given group placement tests patterned after those used in the American army in World War I. It is satisfying from a scientific point of view, but chilling from another perspective, to note reports that the slave laborers who had been assigned to their jobs on the basis of testing were more productive than slave laborers who were assigned arbitrarily (Fitts, 1946).

Publication of the Wechsler-Bellevue was well timed, since the war created a great demand for the evaluation of adult intellectual functioning. It rapidly became the leading individually administered adult intelligence scale. Its appeal to clinicians was increased when Wechsler hypothesized that certain patterns of scatter among subtest scores might be useful in the diagnosis of organic brain disease, schizophrenia, mental deficiency, juvenile delinquency, and psychoneurosis. Almost immediately there was a flurry of studies aimed at assessing the instrument's validity as a diagnostic tool in psychiatry. An early evaluation of these studies by Rabin (1945) indicated that the various measurements of Wechsler-Bellevue scatter and patternings might differentiate between groups of individuals who manifested certain psychiatric disturbances but that they were not sensitive enough to warrant a diagnosis in a specific case on their evidence alone.

Nevertheless the Wechsler-Bellevue fulfilled its major objective of providing a measure of adult intellectual functioning. In 1949, the similarly constructed Wechsler Intelligence Scale for Children (WISC) was published. The WISC had been standardized on 2,200 children: 100 boys and 100 girls at each age level from 5 through 15 years. This standardization sample consisted of white youngsters only and was controlled so as to represent proportionately geographic areas in the United States, urban and rural populations, and occupational classifications of the fathers (Wechsler, 1949). Clinicians liked its division into subtests and into verbal and performance scales, and before long the WISC challenged the Stanford-Binet as the most popular individually administered intelligence scale for children, particularly in children over 8.

For testing infants, the developmental-intelligence scale constructed by Psyche Cattell (b. 1893), daughter of James McKeen Cattell, became the most widely used. This scale included items at each age level from 2 to 30 months. It was designed to overlap with the Stanford-Binet so that testing could be extended upward and downward between the two instruments. Standardization was based on 1,346 examinations of 274 white children of North European parentage living in the Boston area. Since Cattell's scale provided standardized administration and scoring procedures, it was a decided improvement over Gesell's Developmental Schedules, which lacked both. Yet even at the time of its introduction, Cattell (1940) acknowledged its dubious reliability and validity. Research seemed to make it clear that until children reach school age, their IQs as measured by tests are not very reliable or predictive of scores that they may obtain later.

There were three rather disparate occurrences that we will take notice of before proceeding to a consideration of some techniques for determining personality in general. Among other devices introduced during this period for the evaluation of intellectual functioning were the group administered Stanford Achievement Tests (1940) and Forms R, S, and T of the Otis Classification Test (Otis, 1941). The Kuder Preference Record appeared in 1942; it consisted of 168 items selected to provide a measure of the person's interest in nine areas: artistic, clerical, computational, literary, mechanical, musical, persuasive, scientific, and social service. In

1947, the Education Testing Service was established at Princeton, New Jersey, taking over and coordinating the functions formerly performed by the Graduate Record Office, the College Entrance Board, and the Cooperative Test Service.

The Minnesota Multiphasic Personality Inventory (MMPI), constructed by the psychologist Starke Hathaway and the psychiatrist J. C. McKinley (1940, 1943), began to receive attention. It eventually consisted of 550 statements that a testee has to categorize as True, False, or Cannot Say (e.g., "I very seldom have spells of the blues"). The responses to such statements were initially standardized on 1,500 normals, 220 psychopaths, and 50 hypochondriacs, but standardization was soon extended to nine diagnostic groupings: depression, hypochondriasis, hypomania, hysteria, masculinity-femininity, paranoia, psychasthenia, psychopathic personality, and schizophrenia. Although the MMPI was intended primarily to assist in differential psychiatric diagnoses, its 550 items and its scales, which could be regarded as descriptive of personality characteristics, provided a large field for exploration and tempted the ingenuity of clinicians to devise other uses for the inventory.

A great deal of activity centered around projective techniques, particularly the Rorschach inkblot test (Monroe, 1941). From 1930 to 1938, approximately 142 articles had been published on clinical applications of the Rorschach; from 1939 to 1947, there were 436 publications on this one projective technique alone. A significant step in the development of this test occurred when Klopfer and Kelley (1942) published their scoring system, which included a major innovation, the scoring of animal and inanimate movement responses.

Bruno Klopfer (1900–1971) was born in Germany, the son of an authoritarian banker. He expressed the belief that his poor vision made it necessary for him to develop his abilities to concentrate on and think carefully about a problem. He received his PhD from the University of Munich in 1922. Then for about a year Klopfer underwent analysis with Jung, and while in Zurich he spent the time between analytic sessions studying the Rorschach. When later asked how he could study and master so complex a test in so short a time, he replied, "Well you see, it wasn't so complex, till I made it complex" (Vorhaus, 1960).

Klopfer came to the United States in 1934 and worked with Franz Boas as a research associate in anthropology at Columbia University. He began teaching the Rorschach and two years later founded the Rorschach Institute and the *Rorschach Research Exchange*, a publication that changed its name in 1949 to the *Journal of Projective Techniques*. In 1946, he was appointed associate clinical professor at UCLA. The scoring system proposed by Klopfer and Kelley was widely adopted and rivaled S. J. Beck's (1944, 1945) in popularity. The major difference between the two systems was that Beck scored only human movement responses.

The Rorschach, consisting as it does of ambiguously structured inkblots, seemed at first to be an ideal culture-free instrument and as such suitable for evaluating the personality functioning of diverse peoples. However, it soon became clear that it is not as culture-free as had been thought, and even if it had been, the psychologist who administers and interprets it is not. Although the anthropologist Jules Henry (1941) discussed the Rorschach with reference to its use in cross-cultural studies, his comments have the same relevance whether the subjects are natives of the United States or Pilaga Indians of Argentina.

Henry thought that in testing people who are not testwise, a reason has to be given for their being tested, one that does not clash with their particular culture. If the psychologist, through ignorance of a person's value system, unwittingly justifies the test administration for reasons that conflict with what the person feels is right, then the results, supposing that testing is still allowed to take place, will probably be invalid. Furthermore, to make meaningful interpretations, the psychologist has to have some frame of reference for evaluating responses in a particular culture, including knowledge of the language and its nuances and of the emotions associated with particular flora and fauna (e.g., among some inhabitants of the United States a donkey is a good omen and an elephant a bad one). Henry concluded that valid Rorschach interpretations can only be obtained if the psychologist has been thoroughly informed about the culture in which the testing is to be done.

Following the war, a number of projective techniques made their debut. There was still interest in graphology, though relatively little. Somewhat more attention was given for a time to Dollard and Mowrer's (1947) Discomfort-Relief Quotient. This was a method a measuring "tension" in a document by dividing the number of words it contained indicating discomfort by the total number of discomfort and relief words. However, there was less enthusiasm for this method than for certain drawings and other projective devices.

The Rosenzweig Picture-Association Study for Assessing Reactions to Frustration consisted of 24 cartoons. Each cartoon depicts two people in frustrating circumstances, and the character at the left makes a statement that is frustrating in itself or expresses frustration (Freeman, 1950). The person taking the test is asked to write in what the other character will say about the unhappy turn of events. These responses are thought to reveal something about the tolerance for frustration; the direction aggression might take (hostility toward the environment or the self or an attempt to appear nonchalant and avoid any expression of hostility); and the reaction type (defensiveness, being overwhelmed by frustration to the point of helplessness, or persisting in attempts to overcome the obstacle and achieve gratification of need).

David Rapaport (1911–1960) brought the Szondi Test to the United States when he emigrated from Hungary, but it did not attract much interest until after the war. Constructed by Lipot Szondi (1947), a psychiatrist, the test is composed of 48 facial photographs of (European) psychiatric patients. There are 6 photos in each of 8 psychiatric categories: passive male homosexuals, male sadistic murderers, hysterics, epileptics in the paroxysmal phase, catatonic schizophrenics, paranoid schizophrenics, manic-depressive depressed, and manic-depressive manic (Deri, 1949). A person taking the test is asked to pick the two photos liked most and the two disliked most in each of 8 sets. It was supposed that these selections indicated the strength of latent tendencies to the pictured conditions. Those pictures liked were thought to indicate tendencies available for expression in overt behavior; those disliked were thought to indicate tendencies that are repressed or sublimated;

those not selected were thought to indicate tendencies that were already overt. Szondi's rationale was that the eight syndromes represent genetically determined basic drives and that people respond to the photos according to the relationships between their drives and those of the patients pictured. A *Szondi Newsletter*, established in 1949, made it possible for those interested in the test to communicate with one another.

E. S. Schneidman's (1947) Make-A-Picture-Story Test requires people to construct a picture and then tell a story about it. The sentence completion test provides the testee with the stem of a sentence that he or she is asked to finish (Symonds, 1947). Karen Machover's (1948) Draw a Person Test requires the testee to draw pictures of one person and then a person of the opposite sex. These drawings are analyzed for evidence of anxiety about certain body parts, for suspiciousness, for inadequacy, for insecurity, and so on. In J. N. Buck's (1948) House-Tree-Person Test the person has to draw a house, a tree, and a person on a sheet of paper. G. S. Blum's (1949) Blacky Test asks the testee to tell a story and answer questions about pictures of a cartooned dog family, each picture depicting one or more dogs in a situation related to—and supposed to arouse the idea of—some aspect of personality functioning derived from psychoanalytic theory (e.g., the Oedipus complex, anal and oral impulses, etc.).

Of inventiveness and activity there was obviously plenty. But of validity there was all too little evidence (Ellis, 1946). Guilford (1948), evaluating the role of psychology in aviation during the war, concluded that its major contributions had been rather undramatic. Psychologists did improve training procedures by suggesting techniques that made it possible for the trainees to get immediate knowledge of how well they were performing. But a variety of personality tests were found to have little value in predicting success in pilot training. Objectively scored personality inventories such as the Bernreuter, MMPI, and Guilford-Martin had validity coefficients around .20. Projective techniques fared no better. Neither the Rorschach nor the TAT were of much use in making predictions about pilots. In fact, intuitive clinical judgments were found inferior in validity to objective scores. What did seem to be of help in predicting who would make a good aviator was biographical information—not exactly clinically demanding data.

However, in rebutting the negative verdict of their critics, clinicians quite legitimately pointed out that they had not been given the chance to do their job properly. They had been expected to predict success in pilot training without first being given an opportunity to find out what are the personality characteristics of the successful military pilot (Staff, Psychological Research Project, 1946). Under the unrelenting pressures of war, there had not been the time to gain this knowledge (Britt & Morgan, 1946; Hunter, 1946).

The new studies of perception were introducing other variables for the clinician to ponder while evaluating tests results. Some experiments indicated that transitory deprivations and frustrations could distort an individual's perceptions. For this reason, it seemed important to know a person's experiences just prior to administering a projective test. Could it be that recently frustrated drives would turn up in responses to projective techniques? Of course, things would be much simpler if the tests proved insensitive to situational variables. Everyone hoped they were not. But, unfortunately, the evidence indicted that they were (Benton, 1950). For example, when a man had become angry with the examiner or had recently seen nude photos, his responses to the Rorschach differed from his responses when he approached the test situation with more poise and less provocation. Accordingly, the testee's performance came to be seen as a function of both current and relatively enduring response patterns, and the task of the clinician was now to discover approximately how much weight should be given to each.

There was even some question as to whether the techniques actually furnished any unique pieces of information about testees. In the opinion of Rosenzweig (1948) and others, they did not:

> *The view is indeed current that the projective techniques serve in large measure not to elicit new facts regarding the personality, but to underscore certain knowledge already available from history and interview and thus to indicate the degree and type of relevance these aspects may have in the patient's actual present approach to his environment.*

"The literature abounds with signs proposed as indicators of this or that trend or characteristic," said H. F. Hunt (1950) after reviewing publications in psychodiagnostics. The Rorschach was the favored projective technique for generating diagnostic signs, such as the presence or absence of movement responses or the number and type of color responses that would help in making differential diagnoses. There were signs for schizophrenia, signs for suicide, signs for homosexuality, signs for brain damage, signs for mental deficiency, signs for hysteria, signs for depression, signs for obsessions, signs for paranoia, but very few signs for normality. Moreover, there was growing irritation over the swelling mass of studies of dubious value for making predictions.

Despite criticisms and discouraging reports, many clinical psychologists retained their enthusiasm for projective techniques and the projective method (Frank, 1948). Admittedly, there were occasionally tongue-in-cheek questions as to whether the person or the clinician had been doing the projecting, but such sarcasm did not diminish the ardor of some clinicians for their inkblots, pictures, and drawings. It was generally felt by the group favoring these devices that the psychometric tradition had, to be sure, yielded standardized personality tests but that these were capable only of telling the extent of an individual's deviation from a norm—rather dry stuff. In contrast, projective techniques were regarded as an avenue into the fascinating world of the unconscious, where people were continuously engaged in creating, maintaining, and defending their private perceptions and beliefs.

Thus, to some psychologists it seemed that psychological testing had attained maturity. In their view, the ultimate tests for the evaluation of personality had been developed, and although much remained to be done to understand them fully, these instruments were, so to speak, inviolable. Their conviction was not shared by many other psychologists, who, though they admired these creations, were still poking about seeking to discover if this plot of turf was in need of weeding.

DIAGNOSTIC FORMULATIONS

Despite the growing number of disputed points, such as those concerning projective tests, in some areas general agreement was being established. The formerly heated nature-nurture controversy was one such area, with each side now recognizing that the position of the other had some validity. Exaggerated claims that mentally deficient children can be brought up to an average level of intellectual functioning by being reared in suitable environments were generally discounted, as were adamant assertions that the IQ is a completely stable index of native ability (Katz, 1941). Some 50 studies agreed that attendance at nursery school could raise the mean IQ of children by about five or six points (McNemar, 1940; Wellman, 1954). Environmental effects, it was concluded, can mildly to markedly impair or improve the level of intellectual functioning. Presumably, though, the functioning of the basic neurophysiological processes involved in intelligence cannot be radically improved by experiences later in life (e.g., as far as we know, a Down syndrome child, even if raised in the best environment, will remain intellectually subnormal).

Another controversy that had persisted over the years was also drawing to a close. Cyril Burt (1940) demonstrated that the results of any factor analysis can easily be transformed into the results of another. Hence, the disagreement between Spearman and Thurstone about the structure of intelligence was shown to be largely a product of two different statistical methods as well as the restricted range of scores in Thurstone's University of Chicago sample. At any rate, Spearman acknowledged the existence of certain group factors, and Thurstone wound up with a general factor, although he considered it a second-order factor.

Nevertheless, the search for factors or abilities went on. Guilford (1940) found g, verbal, numerical, spatial, memory, speed of perception, fluency, and alertness factors in intelligence, and he also uncovered some leads for other factors. Meanwhile, Thurstone, after second thoughts about the matter, decided to eliminate the induction factor. He also had his doubts about the perceptual and deductive factors but dealt with these less drastically.

Thurstone (1948) explained that first-order factors represent primary abilities, which function as media for the expression of intellect and are probably connected with separate organs of the body. The second-order factors are supposed to represent more central and universal parameters, which influence the activities of the primary factors. By this time, Guilford had discovered 27 factors in human abilities. Among them were space (awareness of spatial arrangement in which reference to the body is important), visual memory, rote memory, reproductive memory, and mechanical knowledge.

Oddly enough, Thurstone's earlier conclusions were used to justify a course of social action, not in the United States, but in Great Britain, Spearman's own country. Using, or perhaps it is more accurate to say "misusing," Thurstone's initial finding that there is no general ability factor, the British Education Act of 1944 set up a tripartite classification of secondary schools for three types of children: grammar schools for the literary or abstract type, technical schools for the technical or mechanical type, and "modern schools" for the practical or concrete type. Cyril Burt (1958) in describing this system a few years later, reported that in his judgment it had not really worked well, although there was disagreement with his assessment.

How to define intelligence was still a lively issue. Stoddard (1943) offered the following definition:

> *Intelligence is the ability to undertake activities that are characterized by (1) difficulty, (2) complexity, (3) abstractness, (4) economy, (5) adaptiveness to a goal, (6) social value, (7) the emergence of originals, and to maintain such activities under conditions that demand a concentration of energy and a resistance to emotional forces.*

Garrett (1947) disapproved of Stoddard's definition. He suggested that intelligence should be considered an attribute of behavior, not an ability: "An intelligent person does not possess 'intelligence' but rather exhibits the capacity to act intelligently (make a high score) when faced by tasks demanding the use of symbols (words, diagrams, numbers, mazes) in their solution."

In keeping with Werner's theory of perceptual development, Garrett hypothesized that as a person grows older, intelligent behavior gradually becomes differentiated and changes from being fairly unified and general into a loosely organized group of abilities or factors. Garrett's hypothesis was supported by evidence that correlations between various tests of ability decrease as age increases. Probably the basis for this developmental trend, Garrett suggested, is to be found in the differential effects of maturation, in divurging interests, and in concentration on the cultivation of certain skills or talents to the neglect of others. From such a hypothesis, it could be predicted that tests that yield a single score, such as the Stanford-Binet, are most useful with children, whereas tests providing part scores, such as the Wechsler-Bellevue, are most useful with adolescents and adults.

If intelligence is an attribute of behavior, it follows that intelligence depends on the frame of reference of those who propose to evaluate the behavior. Some psychologists were not comfortable with a relativistic concept of intelligence, but there seemed to be no alternative. Doll (1940), in his definition of mental deficiency, asserted that the primary criterion of mental subnormality is social inadequacy, which certainly would seem to vary depending on the criteria of adequacy prevailing in a particular society. Incidentally, Doll's complete definition of mental deficiency runs as follows: social incompetence due to mental subnormality of constitutional origin, that is evidenced over the course of development and at maturity, and that is essentially incurable.

In the majority of mental defectives, the "constitutional origin" of their retardation was not specifically identified and their subnormality was assumed to be genetically determined. They were called familial or "garden variety" defectives or, according to Strauss and Lehtinen (1947), endogenous defectives. However, Strauss and Lehtinen (1947) distinguished another group of mental defectives, exogenous defectives, who are brain injured and who might compose perhaps 15–20% of all retardates. When examined as children by neurologists, signs of defective neuromotor systems sometimes showed up. Generally, though, the neurological reports were negative, supposedly because the symptoms were relatively minor and subtle. Instead of being evident in pathological reflex functioning, these abnormalities were observed in the psychological examinations of perceptual processes, thinking, and other complex forms of behavior. Since the diagnosis of exogenous mental deficiency usually rested on evidence solely from psychological tests, the supposed etiology of the syndrome seemed based on circular reasoning and was of questionable validity, at least until some external criterion of brain injury could be found to substantiate and rescue it. But this did not diminish the accomplishments of Strauss and Lehtinen in the identification of children with cognitive disturbances.

At the other extreme of the continuum of intellectual functioning, Terman and Oden (1947) reported on the results of their follow-up of a group of gifted children. Most of these children retained their superior standing into adulthood, possessed better than average physiques and health records, and did well in college and in their chosen professions. Rates of divorce, sickness, and mental illness were about the same as in the general population.

On the basis of her study of approximately 30 children who earned IQs of 180 and above on the Stanford-Binet, Leta Hollingworth (1942) concluded that these children tend to feel, and actually are, isolated by their unusually high level of intellectual functioning. They are likely to be social misfits, in part because they do not appreciate fully their own superior abilities, and for this reason they experience much unhappiness. Apparently, an extremely high IQ may be, in its own way, as much a social liability in the United States as a low IQ. In any case, it appeared that those children who have the best prospects for developing well-rounded personalities and achieving "good" adjustments in our society possessed IQs between 125 and 155. In intelligence as in many other things, it seemed possible to have too much of a good thing.

Let us now turn from intelligence to personality. The issue of whether personality is constitutionally determined was being examined with new vigor. A fresh empirical attack on this issue was inaugurated by William Sheldon (1899–1979), even though typologies based on relationships between physical characteristics and personality were no longer fashionable. Sheldon was raised in Rhode Island on a farm owned by his father, a naturalist and breeder of animals. He received his PhD in psychology from the University of Chicago in 1926 and his MD in 1933. For about 2 years he studied psychiatry abroad, mostly with Carl Jung. In 1938, he went to Harvard, and, after a period of service in the army during the war, in 1947 accepted the position of Director of the Constitution Laboratory, College of Physicians and Surgeons, at Columbia University (Hall & Lindzey, 1957).

During the early stages of Sheldon's research project, he sought to determine the principal variables that account for variation in physique by using the nude photographs of 4,000 male college students and the considered opinions of several judges. The task of the judges was to detect primary components of physique, that is, characteristics that could be used to rank each and every subject, that are reliable, and that could not be accounted for by combining two or more other variables. Three major body types were defined: *ectomorphy* refers to a thin, lightly muscled body with a flat chest, fragile appearance, and a large central nervous system in proportion to size; *mesomorphy* refers to a muscular physique with well-developed bones; and *endomorphy* refers to a body characterized by softness, relatively large body cavities containing the viscera, and underdeveloped bones and muscles. Sheldon (1940) noted that individuals generally exhibit all three of the body types to some degree and that it is possible to classify individuals by rating them on a seven-point scale with respect to each type. Thus, there are theoretically 343 patterns of physique, or somatotypes, and in his early studies Sheldon identified 76 of these.

In another phase of his research, Sheldon (1942) attempted to isolate the major components of temperament. After concluding that 50 personality traits seemed to adequately describe an individual, an intensive study of 33 young men was conducted in which each subject was rated on each trait. These rating scores were intercorrelated and three primary clusterings of personality traits emerged: *cerebrotonia*, which describes the inhibited, introverted, controlled, secretive, self-conscious, and perhaps thoughtful person; *somatotonia*, which describes a person who is energetic, extraverted, aggressive, inclined to be noisy, and brave; and *viscerotonia*, which describes a person who is sociable, relaxed, and preoccupied with seeking companionship, comfort, and food.

A study of 200 male college students, which took about 5 years, sought to discover relationships between physique and temperament. Sheldon (1944) claimed that his results indicated high correlations between ectomorphy and cerebrotonia, mesomorphy and somatotonia, and endomorphy and viscerotonia. These findings are similar to those reported by Kretschmer during the twenties, and, just as Kretschmer had done, Sheldon investigated the relationship between physique and psychiatric disturbances and also found significant positive correlations between endomorphy and affective psychiatric disturbances (e.g., manic-depressive psychosis) and between ectomorphy and heboid disorders (e.g., schizophrenia of the hebephrenic type).

However, unlike Kretschmer, Sheldon offered explanations for his correlations that recognized the importance of environmental interactions and mediators as well as constitutional predispositions. Thus, he thought it likely that cultural stereotypes about the personality characteristics of people with certain physiques might play some part in shaping the behavior of individuals to fit the stereotypes (the "tall, silent type") or that certain body builds restrict persons to certain patterns of action, as in the case of the frail individual who would not be encouraged to participate in sports and so might turn to books and ideas as compensation.

Sheldon's reasonable explanations made his work more acceptable than it might have been had he insisted on genetic determiners alone for physique and personality characteristics. Although few psychologists were convinced that the correlations between the variables are as large as he claimed, they appreciated the worth of his classification of physiques as a research tool and admitted that, at the very least, Sheldon's studies served as a reminder that people's bodies might have some bearing on how they function as personalities (Sheldon, 1949).

Of course, organic disorders are often clear-cut illustrations that physical changes can have dramatic consequences for behavior. One of the significant findings of this decade was the discovery, around 1940, that alcoholic psychoses are not mainly due to the direct effects produced by the consumption of alcohol but are largely traceable to vitamin B deficiencies. Jolliffe (1940) described four possible factors in evaluating the indirect effects of alcoholic intake on nutrition: (1) the irritating action of alcohol on the gastric mucosae; (2) alcohol's interference with the absorption and utilization of vitamins; (3) the substitution of vitamin-free alcohol for vitamin-containing food; and (4) an increased requirement for vitamins because of the large number of calories provided by alcohol. This advance in understanding the etiology of alcoholic psychoses made high vitamin intake and adequate nutrition essential components of treatment.

On the other hand, support (if support was needed) for the alleged significance of interpersonal relationships came from two unexpected sources. A number of studies agreed that relatively few neuroses occurred among children or adults who had been subjected to frequent bombing (Vernon, 1941). It was thought that their experiences had been made less traumatic by the fact that they had been shared with others and by the mutual support and encouragement they received and gave. Here were persons able to endure considerable stress when in the company of fellow human beings. Moreover, several studies of institutionalized children substantiated the clinical impression that being mothered is essential for satisfactory personality development. Particularly in the case of infants, deprivation of warm, human contacts seemed to have damaging effects on physical and intellectual growth (Spitz, 1946; Ribble, 1941). Although the experimental procedures used in some of these studies left something to be desired, it was generally conceded, even by the most severe critics, that being mothered, whether by the actual mother or not, is very important.

The importance of parent-child relationships was also emphasized by findings in studies of prejudice. Much of this research was spurred by the war's demand for a unified America (Myrdal et al., 1944), and one of its noteworthy products was an impressive amount of information on the nature of the authoritarian personality. An authoritarian person, it was shown, while submitting to those in positions of power and glorifying the values and virtues of his or her particular in-group, deprecates and even vilifies the characteristics and beliefs of members of outgroups, perceives the world as dangerous and unpredictable, and finds it difficult to tolerate ambiguous situations. Unconsciously, such persons appear to have hated their parents and felt worthless, though they vehemently deny these feelings and at the same time displace their hostility and direct it toward people belonging to minority groups. Complicating their problems even further is their need to justify their attitudes and actions within a culture that values democratic ideals. Often their justifications rest on rationalizations and projections of their own conflicts, which makes their aggressive attacks seem strikingly unrealistic and irrational (Adorno et al., 1950; Frenkel-Brunswik & Sanford, 1945).

Although the plight of an authoritarian personality is deplorable, the sympathies of most social scientists leaned toward the defense of the persecuted minorities, who suffer not only obvious abuses and assaults but who also, it was thought, may fall prey to psychosomatic diseases induced by the tensions engendered by their being discriminated against. Yet it is also true, as Bruno Bettelheim (1947) observed, that the victims of bigotry may likewise stereotype their persecutors.

Let us now briefly examine a severe disorder of childhood identified during this decade. In 1943, the psychiatrist Leo Kanner described the syndrome of early infantile autism, a psychotic disturbance of childhood characterized by a lack of relationships with people and a fascinated preoccupation with inanimate objects. The primary criteria for the diagnosis of this condition were "from the start an extreme autistic aloneness," failure to use language for communication, and an obsessive insistence on sameness. Secondary criteria were the onset of these symptoms before 3 years of age and evidence of average or better intellectual functioning in certain areas. After Kanner's delineation of the syndrome, others began reporting the diagnosis of early infantile autism among children they had observed, but some varied from the standards previously specified, thereby creating needless confusion.

Meanwhile, there was still considerable controversy about the etiology and the nature of schizophrenia. One question had to do with the fact that usually whenever a group of schizophrenics are compared with a group of normals on the performance of a task, they do less well. Does this mean that this psychosis necessarily eventuates in a deterioration of the abilities under study? If so, schizophrenia could be viewed as a disease affecting the functions of the cortex. This appeared to be the conclusion of Lauretta Bender (1947), who, impressed by the impaired functioning of schizophrenic children, suggested that the disturbance might consist of a "developmental lag of the biological processes from which subsequent behavior evolves by maturation at an embryological level." However, Hunt and Cofer (1944) questioned whether there are actual impairments in the abilities of schizophrenics and suggested that the deficits in performance are more probably attributable to impaired motivation.

Sullivan (1947) proposed that the term *schizophrenia* should be reserved for those psychotic disorders of living that have an acute, traumatic onset and that the term *dementia praecox* could be used to refer to an organic, degenerative psychosis that has an insidious onset and poor prognosis. Similarly, Darrah (1940) believed that *dementia praecox* implies a schizoid prepsychotic personality which progresses toward deterioration and that *schizophrenia* is the correct term to use when the prepsychotic personality seems to have been adequate and there has been an abrupt onset followed by a milder, nondeteriorating course.

Bellak (1948) thought one could detect a continuum of etiological factors in cases of schizophrenia ranging from the completely organic to the completely psychogenic. Duval and Hoffman (1941) noted that soldiers evidencing symptoms of dementia praecox had, typically, an abrupt onset, a stormy course, and a better prognosis than patients who manifest the illness in civilian life; they suggested that the best diagnosis for the military disorder might be somewhere between hysteria and acute schizophrenia.

At any rate, a new distinction was being drawn between types of schizophrenic patients. On the one hand were those who evidenced a long history of poor psychological adjustment that eventually culminated in hospitalization; in the etiology of such cases, organic factors were thought to predominate and the prognosis was poor. On the other hand were those who seemed to make an overtly satisfactory psychological adjustment prior to hospitalization and in whom the psychotic onset was sudden and usually contemporaneous with some trauma. Psychogenic factors were thought to predominate in the etiology of this form and the prognosis was good.

It was hoped that clarification of these subtypes of schizophrenia would help explain and prevent conflicting experimental results and also assist in the evaluation of the validity of psychological tests. Of course, the fact that practically every large medical teaching center had its own unique nomenclature made for additional difficulties in appraising research results and in obtaining consistent information about diagnostic techniques used with psychiatric patients. The American Psychiatric Association had previously attempted to remedy this problem in 1933 by publishing the *Standard Classified Nomenclature of Disease*. Unfortunately, this manual was intended to meet the needs of mental hospitals treating civilian patients, so that when World War II broke out, only about 10% of the military psychiatric cases could be satisfactorily diagnosed. The nomenclature had no category for combat neuroses, and patients with relatively minor personality disorders had to be classified either as psychopathic personalities or as psychoneurotics because there were no appropriate labels.

An army revision of the manual was adopted in 1945 by all branches of the armed forces and, in 1946, by the Veterans Administration. In 1948, the revised *International Statistical Classification* was published. Thus during the forties at least three major nomenclatures enjoyed some degree of popularity. In addition, almost all the psychiatric teaching centers had their own varying emphases and diagnostic groupings. Some order had to be brought into this chaos, and as the decade drew to a close, the Committee on Nomenclature of the American Psychiatric Association (1952) was hard at work on this problem.

It was against this background of diagnostic inconsistency that clinical psychologists attempted to validate their instruments, assess the functioning of patients manifesting various psychiatrically diagnosed disturbances, and evaluate the effects of different treatment procedures.

TREATMENT FORMULATIONS

Insulin and electroshock, both singly and in combination, continued to be used in the treatment of schizophrenia, manic-depressive psychoses, and melancholia (Shipley & Kent, 1940). For chronic psychoses, psychosurgery was becoming popular, and enthusiastic accounts of it were not uncommon in the daily press and in magazines.

It appeared to psychologists that the prefrontal lobes were involved in planning, persisting at a task, thinking about the future, and functions related to conscience. What contributed to this impression was the fact that patients who had lobotomies became less inhibited, found it difficult to contemplate prospective courses of action, and were less able to sustain attention (Freeman & Watts, 1941, 1942). There was some question whether such functional impairments outweighed the improvements in behavior produced by the surgery. Even more serious was the question whether any benefits at all were derived from the operation or whether all observed favorable changes were traceable to the care the patient received before and after the lobotomy (Robinson, 1946).

Toward the end of the forties, a study was conducted by the staff at Greystone State Hospital in New Jersey and a research team from Columbia University. A group of chronic schizophrenic patients had topectomies performed (a topectomy is a refinement of lobotomy in which only a few selected areas of the prefrontal lobes are severed). A control group of similar chronic schizophrenic patients were prepared for surgery, wheeled into the operating room, did not have topectomies, but did have their heads bandaged and did receive postoperative surgical care. Neither the patients nor those ministering to them knew which patients had had the operation and which were controls. It was found that favorable changes occurred just as frequently among the nonoperated controls as among the patients who had received topectomies (Columbia-Greystone Associates, 1949).

Although the decade closed on a disappointing note as far as psychosurgery was concerned, psychotherapy was benignly thought of by almost everyone. Clinical psychologists, social workers, teachers, clergy, and other professionals were being attracted to psychotherapy in ever greater numbers. Kraskin (1940), an optometrist, recommended that his colleagues engage in the practice of psychotherapy, since ocular problems are exacerbated by emotional problems and sometimes even engendered by them ("There is more in this than meets the eye," one might say). Schwing (1940), a nurse and lay analyst, urged members of the nursing profession to treat psychotic patients. Her own work was primarily with schizophrenic women, for whom she aimed to function as a giving mother-substitute.

Psychiatrists were far from delighted by this trend toward psychotherapeutic intervention by nonmedical professionals (Menninger, 1950). Some were sufficiently alarmed to attempt to induce general practitioners to accept the role of psychotherapists. Their hope seemed to be that by enlisting the help of the kindly family doctor, proprietary rights to psychotherapy could be fixed exclusively within the province of medicine. However, this was not easy to accomplish, if for no other reason than that psychotherapy had little appeal to physicians, who were already burdened by the pressures of their ordinary practice.

Yet the public, in its demand for psychotherapy, was unmindful of the distinctions between professions and was concerned only that relatively fewer therapists were available to meet its need. Karen Horney (1942) suggested that in certain cases an individual might be able to conduct analysis alone. After all, self-analysis was good enough for Sigmund Freud, William James, Alfred Adler, and John B. Watson, among countless others. Through a planned system of self-treatment involving introspection, meditation, reading, prayer, work, and so on, Horney believed that the person might be able to gain greater self-understanding, become better socially adjusted, and in general become more relaxed and satisfied. She called this consciously directed self-analysis "autonomous therapy."

Group therapy was a method particularly suited to meet the increased need for psychotherapy that was caused in part by the war and its aftermath. In consequence, this form of therapy experienced an acceleration in growth.

In 1942, Moreno established the Psychodramatic Institute in New York, and Slavson helped found the American Group Psychotherapy Association. Like everything else, group therapy became more complex, and various forms were developed. Slavson (1940, 1943) described four types: play or release group therapy; activity group therapy; interpretive group therapy, in which the personality functioning of the individual members of the group was discussed; and group work, which Slavson thought may lack therapeutic value but help members socially and educationally. In 1947, Moreno founded the journal *Sociatry*, later named *Group Psychotherapy*. Moreno was notable as a vigorous and untiring proponent of and proselytizer for this form of treatment.

As group therapy became more widely used, its unique advantages and disadvantages became clearer. Among the advantages claimed for the method were the following: It helped resistant or reserved patients who found it difficult to participate in and obtain benefit from individual sessions, and it quickly helped people who took comfort in knowing that they were not alone in their unhappiness and their struggle toward self-improvement. Group therapy also provided opportunities for the members of a group to reassure and support one another and to offer alternative solutions to problems; moreover, it allowed the leader of the group to observe and explore the interactions of the patients.

Among the reported disadvantages were the following: The therapist could not devote as much time as might be wished to particular patients; the therapeutic experience was often more intense and more superficial than in individual therapy; hostility tended to be acted out in the group and sometimes members were injured; a resistant member might interfere with the efforts of others to gain self-understanding as well as thwart his or her own treatment; and one member might copy the symptoms of another. Despite such disadvantages, the economic and other benefits of group therapy made it the treatment of choice in many circumstances, especially in situational settings (Pratt, 1945).

Another line of attack for meeting the demand for services was to develop methods for abbreviating the duration of individual psychotherapy. Berliner (1941) discussed the possibilities of brief psychoanalysis. The psychoanalyst, instead of dealing extensively with repressed content or id material, might deliberately choose to focus on the ego and those aspects of superego functioning readily accessible to awareness. By this means the course of treatment would be shortened and more patients could be served.

A method of treatment called *semantic therapy*, which is a special branch of general semantics, began to receive attention. General semantics is the study of human responses to signs (anything that is perceived to have significance) and symbols (anything that is intended to communicate significance). One of the exponents and leading popularizers of semantic therapy, Alfred Korzybski (1880–

1950), claimed that maladjustments were often the result of emotionally charged, inaccurate interpretations of experiences. The person then came to use symbols irrationally and had to be helped to evaluate them intelligently and precisely. Korzybski (1941) mentioned four general rules that, if accepted, would help correct mistaken beliefs:

1. The symbols have to be dated (i.e., the time of events and actions have to be specified). For example, a father is not always cruel. The patient has to note the times and circumstances when the father acted harshly. By this means, the patient may be led to accept partial responsibility for the punishments received and acknowledge that the father possessed positive characteristics and experienced positive feelings toward the patient. In short, an equation such as *father = cruelty* is false; the correct equation is *father = cruelty when*. . . .

2. The symbols are not all-inclusive (i.e., a partial resemblance to an object does not necessarily signify that object, and the patient has to make this differentiation). This rule has relevance to the concept of transference. The person has to recognize when reactions to an individual are being determined by some aspect of the individual or their relationship and when they are based on feelings toward someone else.

3. The symbols have to be indexed (i.e., individuals have to be specified and distinguished from other members of their group). This rule bears on the subjects of prejudice and stereotypic thinking. A patient has to recognize that, for example, unpleasant experiences with his or her mother does not justify feeling antipathy toward all older women.

4. The symbols are not the objects symbolized and therefore should not by themselves elicit emotional responses. This means that a person should learn to control feelings when reacting to words, pictures, and thoughts. Excessive affective reaction is not only inappropriate but may do great harm. Korzybski believed that by a thoroughly rational evaluation of symbols, a person could be helped to face problems objectively, clearly, expeditiously, and successfully.

As might be expected, there was at this time an awakened interest in narcoanalysis and hypnosis. Narcoanalysis or narcosynthesis seemed to be particularly useful in treating combat or traumatic neuroses. Sodium amobarbital or thiopental sodium was administered to produce a light narcosis during which the patient reenacted the trauma. This was followed by interviews that aimed at synthesizing the material in awareness. The method was particularly effective in alleviating feelings of guilt and thus helped many soldiers to return to their duties in a relatively short time (Grinker & Spiegel, 1945).

By the early part of the decade, some agreement had been reached about the nature of hypnosis. A number of experts in the field felt that hypnotic behavior should be regarded as a form of meaningful, goal-directed striving. The general goal being strived for was to behave like a hypnotized person as this role was continuously defined by the hypnotist (through suggestions and commands) and understood by the subject (White, 1941).

Hypnosis as a form of treatment (hypnotherapy) seemed to have six major uses: (1) to allow relaxation and rest by employing prolonged hypnosis; (2) to remove symptoms by direct suggestions that they disappear; (3) to bring about by direct suggestions the disappearance of the attitudes underlying the symptoms; (4) the abreaction of traumatic experience or the reduction of emotional tension by recalling the incident; (5) specialized techniques (e.g., anesthesia during what would otherwise be the extremely painful exercise of muscles to prevent their atrophy while in bed; and (6) hypnoanalysis (Brennan & Gill, 1944).

Two of the better-known proponents of hypnoanalysis were the psychiatrist Lewis Wolberg (1945) and the clinical psychologist Robert Lindner (1946). As expounded by them, hypnoanalysis was a method that integrated hypnosis and psychoanalysis. First, the patient was taught how to be hypnotized and to experience a deep trance state. Free associations in the "normal" state were elicited, and whenever resistances were encountered, hypnosis was resorted to in order to clarify or circumvent them. With the patient once again in the "normal" state, there were syntheses of material and attempts at reeducating, which were reinforced by posthypnotic suggestion. The goals of this treatment were the same as those generally attributed to psychoanalysis: to uncover the unconscious motives for behavior, to enable the patient to experience an abreaction, and to strengthen the healthy aspects of ego functioning. Lindner (1946) believed that hypnoanalysis was most successful with cases of alcoholism, anxiety neurosis, homosexuality, and somnambulism but was contraindicated for psychoses.

As the forties came to a close, there occurred a perceptible waning in enthusiasm for the use of both hypnosis and procedures involving drugs. The feeling was that these were largely techniques adopted as expedients during wartime and were best confined to the battlefield and its victims. Few civilian patients seemed to give evidence of the same dramatic improvement that had been shown by soldiers, and in peacetime there was less urgency and more concern for thoroughness and making the effects of treatment last as long as possible.

Here, too, exceptions could be found. Some analysts contended the treatment could be shortened and still be effective. Franz Alexander and Thomas French (1946) advocated variations in psychoanalytic technique to abbreviate the therapy, and they reported good results when this was done. They recommended (1) enlisting the cooperation of people in a strategic position to ameliorate environmental pressures on the patient, (2) setting a time limit for the end of analysis, (3) manipulating the frequency of analytic sessions, and (4) accepting the validity of apparent improvements produced after even one meeting.

Within this context, we may note two forces at work: (1) the greater weight given to expediency as a reason for briefer forms of therapy in view of the many people in need of treatment and the relatively few available therapists; and (2) a growing conviction, based on a belief in the resiliency of human beings that patients might be changed through corrective emotional experiences within a short time. These forces and the need for a form of psychotherapy closely identified with, and offered under the aegis of, clinical psychology provided a set of circumstances that predisposed many clinicians to accept the eloquently expressed and thoughtfully developed ideas of Carl Rogers (1902–1987).

In 1940, Carl Rogers described the process of psychotherapy as follows: The therapist and client establish rapport; the client freely expresses feelings; the client experiences a recognition and acceptance of the spontaneous self; and the client, aided by the therapist, makes responsible choices, gains insight through assimilated interpretations, and becomes increasingly independent. In 1942, Rogers stated, "Effective counseling consists of a definitely structured, permissive relationship which allows the client to gain an understanding of himself to a degree with enables him to take positive steps in the light of his new orientation."

Roger's (1942) approach, at first called "nondirective therapy" due to its prohibition of counselor interpretations, probing, and giving of advice, emphasized the significance of the therapeutic relationship as in itself a growth experience. Its stress on the importance of feelings over intellectual insights, on the present rather than the past, and on the role of the counselor in assisting the client to become more expressive and independent demonstrated its indebtedness to the formulations of Otto Rank and Frederick Allen.

Rogers was a middle child in a large, close-knit, conservative family. His parents prohibited dancing, cards, sodas, movies, and all other frivolous, enticing activities. According to Rogers, "I was a pretty solitary boy, who read incessantly, and went all through high school with only two dates" (1961).

Rogers entered the University of Wisconsin majoring in agriculture. During his junior year he went to China for 6 months to attend an international World Student Christian Federation Conference. On this trip he began to admit to himself more frankly his doubts about organized religion and about his dependence on his parents. Following his graduation from Wisconsin, he married and entered Union Theological Seminary. After 2 years he left the seminary for Teacher's College at Columbia, where he studied psychology.

At Columbia, Rogers was influenced by the ideas of John Dewey, enjoyed the atmosphere of free thought, interned at the Institute for Child Guidance, and learned to work with children under Leta Hollingworth. He accepted a position as psychologist at the Society for the Prevention of Cruelty to Children in Rochester, New York, in 1928, became director of the society in 1930, and received his PhD in 1931. That year a test developed by him, *A Test of Personality Adjustment* (Rogers, 1931), was published. It is a paper and pencil test that samples children's wishes, aspirations, affection for family members, and the areas in which they feel a discrepancy between what they are and what they would like to be. In 1939, Rogers helped establish and served as director of the Rochester Child Guidance Center. His book *The Clinical Treatment of the Problem Child* (Rogers, 1939) was published and received favorable reviews. A major theme of this book—that treatment may become a science if we are willing to subject it to careful examination—recurs throughout his work. From 1940 to 1945 he was professor of psychology at Ohio State University, and in 1945 he accepted the positions of professor and executive secretary of the Counseling Center at the University of Chicago.

Rogers (1959) listed four major principles that his many years of clinical experience had taught him: (1) authorities are not always right; (2) coercion in therapy or counseling is never more than superficially effective; (3) the client, not the therapist, is most aware of the best direction of movement in psychotherapy; and (4) there is a discoverable orderliness in the process of counseling and therapy.

At first Rogers (1942) believed that the nondirective approach was appropriate for only a select group of clients, clients that were experiencing some degree of tension and wanted to be helped. They had to have some capacity to cope with life and to express feelings. Further, they needed to be of at least dull normal intelligence, between 10 and 60 years of age, free of excessive instability and severe organic impairment, reasonably independent of close family control, and able to plan meetings with the counselor and keep them as scheduled.

Later, Rogers (1946) spoke of his approach as "client-centered therapy," which unfortunately sounded presumptuous, since all psychotherapists feel that the well-being of their clients is central to their efforts. The cardinal assumption of Rogerian therapy is the existence within the individual of forces that potentially make for growth. These forces are supposed to be spontaneous in their working and in their capacity to integrate and creatively reorient the organism (person). Thus, an individual's behavior is determined not by past influences but by current perceptions of self. The role of the therapist is to provide a setting in which these constructive forces can operate and to create a relationship in which the client feels understood and free to understand and alter the self. In keeping with this new assumption, all admonitions as to the suitability of particular kinds of clients for nondirective therapy were abandoned. Instead, Rogers was in favor of trying this new method with anyone and everyone.

In his APA presidential address, Rogers (1947) emphasized the importance of perceptions in the behavior of the person. Like Lewin, he argued that behavior is not immediately determined by organic or environmental factors but rather by the individual's perceptions of these factors. He contended that when changes occur in the individual's perceptions of self and the world, there will be related changes in feelings, behavior, and social interactions.

From Roger's point of view, psychological maladjustment represented a more and more extensive denial to awareness of significant experiences. Such denial prevented self-perceptions from being integrated into the structure of the self. Failure to integrate what should have been integrated produced a state of psychological tension. When someone was able to integrate all self-perceptions into a conscious concept of self, a feeling of relief and comfort would result, which may be thought of as psychological adjustment. Rogerian therapy, he proposed, was one means—for him the best one—by which this comfort or adjustment could be attained.

The Rogerian approach was criticized for being superficial and placing inordinate demands on the client to assume responsibility. Frederick Thorne (1944) contended that some patients were better served by directive techniques and that the therapist has a responsibility to evaluate continuously how much potential the person has for effective self-regulation. It seemed to Thorne that the crucial factor in therapy is not the method adopted but the skill with which a particular method is used. Directive and nondirective approaches both have a place, depending on the needs of the person at the time. Accordingly, Thorne (1948) advocated an eclectic method of psychotherapy that had as its goal the replacement of emotional-compulsive behavior by rational-adaptive behavior. Emotional reactions are handled in the initial phases of therapy, and later the patient is to be in certain respects reeducated or trained. Throughout the course of treatment, any available technique or method may be used if it is appropriate.

A similar view as to how the therapist can best meet treatment responsibilities is expressed by Sullivan in the following statement: "From beginning to end, to the best of his ability, the psychiatrist tries to avoid being involved as a person—even as a dear and wonderful person—and keeps to the business of being an expert" (1954, p. 34). Sullivan regarded the therapist as a participant observer, an expert in the field of interpersonal relationships whose tasks are to respect the patient and to demonstrate expertness by understanding the patient in the interview. The interview is serious business. There is to be no joking or fooling around, and if patients disgress from their task, they are to be brought back to it. Through listening and skillfully asking questions, the therapist gains an understanding of the patient and of the nature of the interaction between the two of them. Sullivan deemphasized free associations except when they might prove useful in overcoming silences or resistances. However, Sullivan did urge the therapist, when an interview seemed to lag, to ask what had occurred to make the patient experience anxiety and find it difficult to continue the discussion. At the conclusion of an evaluative or therapeutic interview, the therapist should tell the patient what had been learned, prescribe a plan of action, and later assess the possible effects of this plan on the patient's life.

From experiences gained in his work with schizophrenics, Sullivan advocated a therapeutic relationship grounded on mutual respect and urged the therapist to refrain from arousing the patient's anxiety by making "deep" interpretations.

From experiences gained in *his* work with schizophrenics, the psychiatrist John Rosen (1947) advocated a therapeutic relationship in which the therapist played an active, nurturant, "maternal" role and offered deep, direct interpretations of the patient's behavior.

Despite these islands of dissent, there were pacific atolls of psychotherapeutic agreement. Almost everyone concurred that the environment is important, and so there was general interest in "milieu therapy," which was popularized by Bruno Bettelheim and Emmy Sylvester (1948), both at the Sonia Shankman Orthogenic School of the University of Chicago. Milieu therapy makes use of thoughtfully selected and arranged physical surroundings, personnel, and general procedures as a means of contributing to the patient's mental health. For example, in an institutional setting, there should be a pleasant and stimulating physical plant, friendly interpersonal relationships, flexibility in schedules and routines, and opportunities for each patient to experience a meaningful involvement with at least one member of the staff. Although milieu therapy was first used in residential treatment centers for children, it was speedily adopted as the treatment of choice in many mental hospitals, although often without any noticeable difference in conditions.

Estes (1947) observed, "There now appears to be almost complete agreement among therapists of all schools that the social relationship between therapist and client is critical with respect to whether there will occur the thinking and doing on the part of the client which are essential for his improvement." It remained true, however, that the significance attributed to the relationship varied from one approach to another.

According to Estes (1947), transference phenomena resulted from a fusion of four variables: (1) repetition compulsion (in general, *repetition compulsion* refers to a need to repeat a behavior pattern or to think about an incident again and again in order to allay anxiety; with specific reference to transference, it refers to a need to perceive and to relate to people in the present as they were perceived and related to in the past); (2) infantile neurosis (the unresolved conflicts of childhood, particularly those related to one's parents); (3) early experiences with significant persons that have an influence on later reactions to others; and (4) current social relationships that affect what and how rapidly the person learns. It seemed to Estes that Rogers, Alexander, French, and a number of other therapists were stressing the last variable and neglecting all the rest. But, he conceded, it was still a matter for conjecture whether dealing with the other three variables was really essential in order that the person should be helped.

Among clinical psychologists (Krugman, 1945), there was general agreement that psychotherapy should be recognized as a proper function of their profession and that it should be offered to all who might benefit from it regardless of socioeconomic status, race, religion, creed, level of intelligence (Sarason, 1949), and severity of disturbance. Not all psychologists were enthusiastic about this program. Brotemarkle (1947) noted dryly that clinical psychology had originated in a case of bad spells and was now encountering a spell of bad cases. Hathaway (1951) questioned the effectiveness of psychotherapy and wondered how often improvement is a matter of a "hello–goodbye" social situation in operation ("hello" refers to the client's need to begin by giving reasons for seeking help and "goodbye" to the need to tell the counselor at the end of their meetings that help was gained). Walter Bingham (1952), wanting to avoid contention with psychiatrists over the right of clinicians to practice psychotherapy, declared, "We should thank them [the psychiatrists and social workers] for their willingness to relieve us of all responsibility for therapy, thereby freeing the psychological profession for the more congenial and, I sincerely believe, more socially useful task of augmenting the productivity and the happiness of the mentally well" (pp. 25–26).

But the opposition was too meager to stay the onrushing tide. Far from heeding those who advocated erecting a stout wall between counseling and psychotherapy, the majority avidly sought to remove any obstacle that would bar psychologists from attempting to help individuals deal with their psychological problems. And there was some merit to their point of view (Bordin, 1950; Snyder, 1947).

To those who accepted the basic principle of integration and appreciated the implications of organismic theories, the separation of a person into problem areas seemed artificial and arbitrary. A woman who faces a vocational problem ipso facto has a personal problem. A boy doing poorly in school has an emotional response to his education difficulties. A man with a broken leg has feelings about his injury and the effects it may have on his ambitions.

Furthermore, it did not seem possible any longer to conceive of psychotherapeutic influences magically confined within the four walls of the therapist's office (Raimy, 1948). They were seen everywhere—in diagnostic evaluations, in talking with friends and enemies, in eating and drinking, in dancing, in sports, in arts and crafts, in listening to music, in scrubbing floors, in any activity that might be pleasurable or the least bit instructive. As the implications of such a point of view became accepted, the number and complexity of the variables that had to be considered in helping people and in evaluating the effectiveness of psychotherapy swelled to the point of encompassing every facet of life, and restrictions as to who may do therapy seemed almost impossible to impose.

The professional literature burgeoned with case histories, descriptions of new therapeutic approaches and techniques, and research that tested the concepts of therapy, both old and new. Between January 1948 and August 1949 there were over 400 publications on psychotherapy. Much of this research was flawed. All too frequently it took the form of a therapist announcing that something was going to be done, then demonstrating that it had been done, yet failing to show whether the techniques employed were related to variables outside of therapy or had any usefulness. But still the volume of research and publication mounted. More and more links were forged between the therapeutic process on the one hand and learning theory (Salter, 1949), perception, and social interactions on the other. Psychology was aggressively extending itself into psychiatry, while psychiatry was hardly less aggressively extending itself into psychology.

PROFESSIONAL DEVELOPMENT

Psychology's robust growth is illustrated by the changes in the profession during the forties. To begin with, the situation in the APA in 1939 was critical (Fernberger, 1940). There were 618 members and 1,909 associates. Everyone knew what the roadblock to status as a member was—the postdoctoral research requirement. If this requirement had been eliminated, there would have been 1,759 members and 768 associates. In 1940, a committee was appointed to review the matter.

In 1941, the AAAP had 615 members. Despite occasional criticisms of the APA, AAAP members looked to the APA for leadership and support in dealing with professional problems. Their expectations were soon to be fulfilled. That very year William Malamud and Walter S. Hunter, who had been working as members of the Committee on Problems of Neurotic Behavior of the National Research Council, issued a report urging cooperation between psychiatrists and psychologists in the interest of national defense. Their report was sent to the

Surgeon General, and it probably helped pave the way for the recognition of military clinical psychology (Hunter, 1946).

In 1942, following spadework by a subcommittee of the National Research Council on planning in psychology (with Robert M. Yerkes as chairperson), the APA and AAAP began plans for a constitution that would be acceptable to both groups and that would lead to the incorporation of the latter within the former. The following year a joint convention was held and an APA-AAAP constitution committee was appointed. Under the leadership of Yerkes, a new constitution was drafted.

The new association was to be "federal." Eighteen divisions of the new APA were to be established, each representing a special-interest group, and provision was made for the addition and dissolution of divisions as needs changed.

Henceforth, the objective of the APA was "to advance psychology as a science and as a means of promoting human welfare." It was intended that the association devote more attention to the professional problems of its members. As a tangible expression of its professional interest, the APA was to publish a new journal, *American Psychologist*, devoted largely to professional issues.

The new constitution established two classes of membership in the APA: fellow, which required a PhD plus acceptable research or professional experience in psychology, and associate, which required either 2 years of graduate work in psychology or a year of graduate work and a year of professional experience. Both fellows and associates could vote in the organization and hold office, but associates were restricted to holding relatively minor positions. Provisions were also made for student and division affiliates, who would not be eligible to vote or hold office and would not be considered members of the APA. The association's governing body was to be the Council of Representatives, with a board of directors as its administrative agent. The board consisted of six members of the council and the elected executive officers of the APA (Wolfle, 1946).

In 1944, the APA voted to accept the constitution. At the same time, the AAAP voted to go out of existence and to transfer its membership to the APA. Dues were raised from $10 to $15 for fellows and from $8 to $10 for associates. The *American Psychologist* began publication in 1946, and in 1948 the dues were raised to $17.50 for fellows and $12.50 for associates.

Approximately 1,710 psychologists had served in the armed forces of the United States during World War II, their average age being about 32 (Britt & Morgan, 1946). Many of them had been involved in devising methods for the selection and training of personnel. Others had helped in designing extremely complicated instrument panels to ensure that they conformed to human sensory capacities and could be operated efficiently and effectively. Not only had clinical psychologists evaluated the fitness of men or their suitability for particular assignments, but over half had also engaged to some extent in counseling and psychotherapy (Hutt & Milton, 1947). The contributions made by psychologists obviously covered a broad range (Hunter, 1946). We shall point to just two. The adjustment of a recruit was likely to be facilitated by the book *Psychology for the Fighting Man*, by Boring and his associates, and upon leaving the service and reentering civilian life he could find help in the companion book, *Psychology for the Returning Serviceman*, also by Boring and his associates (Committee of the National Research Council, 1945). An outstanding contribution by a psychologist to the war effort was the suggestion by Walter Miles (1943) that people could secure and maintain the adaptation of their vision to darkness by wearing red goggles. It would be difficult to overestimate the significance of Miles' simple prescription for men and women who had to be able to perform their duties under ordinary illumination and then emerge abruptly ready to function efficiently at night.

As we have already seen, even before the conclusion of the war in 1945 psychologists were making ready to deal with their postwar problems. The keynote was sounded in Gardner Murphy's presidential address before the APA in 1944, in which he declared that psychology was on the threshold of becoming an integrated, dynamic science. This was a time, he suggested, not only for integrating the various areas of psychology but also for exercising the freedom to become immersed in all its ramifications and to apply its findings to the great problems confronting nations. If we look for a moment beyond the obvious content of Murphy's speech, we can appreciate better its significance as an indication of the confidence now felt by psychologists.

In the period after the war, Murphy devoted much of his energy to the Society for the Psychological Study of Social Issues, which was founded in 1936 and which he was president of in 1937–1938, and to UNESCO. Many of his colleagues shared a similar concern to meet their responsibility as psychologists to assist in the alleviation of international tensions and the preservation of peace (Cantril, 1949). Essentially, they worked to create an atmosphere in which people would be willing to strive toward a goal of maximum social justice. Therefore, they emphasized that aggression cannot be dismissed as an unfortunate and unavoidable consequence of human nature and that the irritants which provoke it must be faced. (It is interesting to note that William James, in 1904, identified himself as a philosopher to his audience and then proceeded from the premise that there is a "rooted bellicosity" in man to argue that the hope for a lasting peace rests in directing this militancy into a warfare against injustice and nature.)

As one might expect, public interest in psychology had never been higher. The constant increase in the number of college students majoring in psychology attested to that interest and to the growing prestige of the profession (Fischer & Hinshaw, 1946). Approximately 53% of those affiliated with the APA in 1945 expressed an interest in the clinical field (Hilgard, 1945), thus confirming the vision of Cattell, who predicted years earlier that there would come a day when the majority of APA members were engaged in nonacademic work. Yet, as we pointed out, there were not enough clinical psychologists to meet the demand.

A few facts will show the extent of the problem confronting psychology at that time. There were 16 million veterans of World War II and 4 million veterans of previous wars. Forty-four thousand neuropsychiatric patients were in the hospitals of the Veterans Administration (VA). The VA claimed that it alone needed 4,700 clinical psychologists and vocational counselors. The states asserted that they required 2,100 vocational advisers. There were 1,500 positions in vocational guidance waiting to be filled, yet there were only 1,000 vocational counselors in the entire United States. It was clear that something had to be done (and done quickly) to train clinical psychologists and counselors and devise acceptable professional standards. Further, this had to be accomplished without resorting to shortcuts that might do injury to the public or the hard-won reputation of psychology.

A joint APA and AAAP committee (1945), with David Shakow serving as its chairperson, had foreseen the emergency and decided in 1944 that rather than attempt to develop new schools or departments, the training of clinicians should be entrusted to the existing graduate programs in psychology. Through the cooperation of the VA, whose chief of the Division of Clinical Psychology and Neuropsychiatry was James Miller, a physician and psychologist, and the U.S. Public Health Service (USPHS), funds became available to assist in clinical training. A 4-year graduate program was proposed: The first year or so would be needed to provide the student with a foundation in the science, research methodology, and theory; in the second or third year practicums and internship training would be introduced; and the fourth year would include completion of the doctoral dissertation.

In its essentials, that was the graduate program endorsed by the APA for clinical psychologists. Standards were set for graduate departments, and the APA assumed responsibility for evaluating training facilities and informing the VA and the USPHS which universities and other schools were meeting its criteria. In 1946, the National Institute of Mental Health (NIMH) began its program of training grants. During 1948, the NIMH awarded $212,000 for graduate training in clinical psychology.

By requiring the doctorate for clinicians seeking employment in its installations, the VA was helping to raise professional standards. Moreover, by providing training facilities, personnel to assist in the training, financial support for trainees, and job opportunities for graduates of clinical programs, it fostered the development of graduate programs and exerted a strong influence on the type of clinician produced. Clinicians now were likely to be experienced in working with hospitalized male adults but relatively inexperienced in working with outpatients, especially with women and children (Miller, 1946), a strange turn for a field that began largely devoted to the problems of youngsters.

The APA Committee on Training in Clinical Psychology (1947) reported that a graduate program for clinicians should include courses in general psychology, statistics, psychotherapy, psychodynamics, and diagnostic methods; an internship or externship and training in research methods; and courses in related disciplines (e.g., anthropology, clinical medicine, physiology, and sociology).

This emphasis on a well-rounded background in psychology, coupled with a decision not to add to the length of graduate education, ensured that students would acquire knowledge of psychological principles at the cost of some proficiency in clinical techniques—an outcome not altogether pleasing to everyone. In 1949, a conference sponsored by the APA was held in Boulder, Colorado, to consider training policies. Although the conferees recommended continuing the solid grounding in principles and techniques, they urged graduate schools to experiment in their training approaches.

The upshot of all this activity and interest was that within an incredibly brief period of time there was a great increase in graduate education in clinical psychology. During 1947, twenty-two universities had a total of 210 trainees in the VA training program for clinical psychologists. By 1949, there were forty-two schools in the United States offering the doctorate in clinical psychology, and each had far more applicants than it could accommodate (Heiser, 1950). Thus psychologists were faced with the difficult though not unpleasant task of selecting students with outstanding intellectual abilities and with personalities fitted to clinical work. No one questioned any longer the drawing power of psychology or of clinical psychology in particular.

The prospects for clinical psychology were brightened further by developments in the attempt to obtain legal recognition for psychologists. Legislators were being asked to enact licensing and certification laws. A licensing law restricts the performance of certain functions or practices to members of a specified profession. A certification law restricts the use of a title, for example, *psychologist*, to people who meet certain standards specified by statute and whose qualifications satisfy an official board of examiners. Since psychologists would engage in activities that are also performed by members of equally reputable professions, licensing laws did not seem feasible, nor on the whole did they seem advisable in view of possible complications caused by prematurely defining the psychologist's role (Safir, 1950).

The first general certification law for psychologists was enacted by the state of Connecticut in 1945; it required possession of a PhD and 1 year of professional experience. Certification for clinical psychologists went into effect in Virginia in 1946, and required the PhD and 5 years of professional experience.

By 1949 *school* psychologists were certified in 11 states: Arizona, California, Connecticut, Delaware, Florida, New Jersey, New York, Ohio, Pennsylvania, Wisconsin, and Wyoming. Registries for school psychologists were maintained by 7 other states: Illinois, Indiana, Maryland, Minnesota, North Dakota, Oregon, and Utah (Hall, 1949).

The APA favored certification over licensing, but bills for both forms of legislation ran into stiff opposition from the medical profession. William Menninger (1950) expressed the position of many of his fellow psychiatrists when he stated his belief that "clinical psychology is essential to the best practice of psychiatry." However, he added that he felt the major contributions of clinical psychologists would be made in the areas of diagnostic testing and research. Although most psychiatrists could accept the idea of psychologists' performing psychotherapy in medical settings, they tended to agree that psychologists should be barred from private practice. Menninger concurred with this point of view and justified his position by saying that physicians are trained to feel a life-and-death responsibility for their patients. He doubted that psychologists felt as deep and genuine a concern.

Since laws for the certification of psychologists were not likely to be enacted soon in all states, it was decided in 1946 to establish certification within the profession by setting up as a certifying authority the American Board of Examiners in Professional Psychology (ABEPP). This board was to consist of nine APA fellows who would serve 3-year terms and administer the agreed standards for professional competence. In order to protect the APA from possible damage suits arising from allegedly improper actions by a certifying body, the ABEPP was organized as a separate corporation in 1947.

The requirements for an ABEPP diploma or certificate in clinical, counseling, or industrial psychology were satisfactory professional, moral, and ethical standing; membership in the APA; a doctorate in psychology; 5 years of professional experience; and passing scores on written and oral examinations. (A grandfather clause, which expired at the end of 1949, waived examinations for those who had sufficient experience and were able to satisfy the other requirements.) In 1949, the first ABEPP written examinations were held.

Toward the close of the forties, there could be no doubt that the United States held the position of professional leadership. In other countries of the world there was comparatively little professional activity, and what little there was centered on teaching, research, and diagnostic testing.

Psychologists were regrouping and attempting to reestablish their field in Germany and Scandinavia. In Zurich, the C. G. Jung Institute was founded in 1948. In England, clinical psychology was moving forward, and there was research and experimentation related to chemotherapy, nutrition, and personality characteristics (Bartlett, 1947). However, it was still commonly maintained that psychotherapy was alien to the role of the clinician. Hans Eysenck (1949), one of England's leading clinical psychologists, gave his American colleagues the following reasons for viewing psychotherapy as inappropriate for their professions: (1) treatment is a medical problem; (2) therapy dilutes the clinician's specialty, which is diagnosis and research; and (3) psychotherapy spoils objectivity and forces the psychologist involved in its practice to become biased in its favor.

For the most part, then, the enthusiasm among clinical psychologists in the United States for psychotherapy was of relatively recent origin and was not necessarily shared by clinicians elsewhere. But, of course, psychology in the United States had become to a large extent an applied field and so was quite different from psychology as practiced in other countries. Some 54% of the positions open to psychologists in the United States were nonacademic. Clinical psychology and counseling alone accounted for 43% of all psychological positions, both filled and available (Black, 1949). Salaries for a psychologist with a PhD had risen from approximately $3,400 in 1940 to $6,400 in 1949, and in that year 250 PhDs and 1,350 MAs in psychology were awarded. There were now approximately 149 graduate departments that offered clinical training, with a total registration of approximately 5,600 students, half of whom were majoring in clinical psychology. Practically all these budding clinicians had been attracted to the field by the prospects of doing psychotherapy. The membership of the APA had increased from 4,500 members in 1946 to 6,735 at the close of the decade, and there were 1,047 members in the clinical division alone.

The APA, by adopting the position that psychotherapy is a legitimate function of the clinical psychologist, showed that it recognized the possibility of interprofessional conflicts. The association adopted this position from a feeling of respect for the integrity and quality of its membership and with confidence in the ability and competence of psychologists to meet their obligations and responsibilities fully.

8

Questions, Doubts, and Responsibility
1950-1959

This was a perplexing decade, distinguished by both prosperity and recession, by duplicity and a sinister form of patriotism, and by a great deal of general bewilderment. Consider what occurred in 1950 when the army of North Korea invaded South Korea, and the United Nations intervened with force to halt the aggression. Technically, the Korean War was not a war—for want of a better term President Truman referred to it as a "police action." Yet in this police action the United States armed forces alone incurred 157,530 casualities, including 54,246 deaths. The use of euphemisms was prevalent during the fifties.

Another of the less commendable characteristics of the decade was anti-intellectualism. Distrust of people who were learned as well as moderate and conscientious was fanned when many intellectuals adopted the position that the manufacture and testing of atomic weapons ought to be stopped, a position that struck some Americans as distinctly subversive of the best interests of the United States. A few instances of treason by educated individuals contributed to a hysterical feeling that the nation had been betrayed by its liberals and that communists had infiltrated the government. In some places, oaths of loyalty to the United States were required, and mere insinuations that someone had socialistic leanings were often sufficient to wreck a career.

Naturally, psychologists were troubled by the spreading of suspiciousness, especially when some universities required their faculty members to sign a loyalty oath. Aside from objecting to the foolishness of expecting communist agents to reveal themselves by refusing to sign such an oath, there was resentment at the imputation of lack of patriotism and at the threat to academic freedom presented by the pressure to conform. The furor was greatest at the University of California, with Edward Tolman as the leading and most eminent dissenter.

During this time, psychologists were also becoming more actively involved as shapers of social legislation and legal briefs (McCary, 1956). Their counsel was being sought by the judiciary in considering the social consequences of laws, a matter which, as the noted jurist Louis Brandeis emphasized, is of great importance. For example, in 1943 Hawaii passed a statute prohibiting the teaching of languages other than English to children below the age of 10 years in public schools. This law was based on the alleged fact that bilingualism in children could produce academic retardation and emotional disturbances. In a brief that successfully contested the law, psychological findings were introduced to show that bilingualism in and of itself did not result either in emotional disturbances or in intellectual retardation and that while some retardation in academic achievement might occasionally be attributable to bilingualism, this effect could be avoided by improved and already available methods of teaching.

The Supreme Court, at one time, had ruled that racially separated but equal public school facilities were constitutional. In legal briefs contesting the constitutionality of separate but equal facilities, psychological studies were used to point out that separate facilities, even if equal, were discriminatory and eventuated in undesirable social and psychological consequences. Further, when a poll of 849 anthropologists, sociologists, and psychologists was taken, 90% of the 517 who responded claimed that in their (expert) opinion enforced segregation would have detrimental effects even if equal facilities were provided. Such studies and expressions of opinion led the Supreme Court, in 1954, to reverse its earlier ruling and to decide that the doctrine of separate but equal facilities was unconstitutional and that the public school system within the United States should be racially integrated (Kendler, 1950). It would be difficult to point to a more significant legal case in which psychologists participated. However, as might have been expected, this did not increase the esteem with which psychologists were regarded in certain quarters.

Fortunately, the wave of anti-intellectualism was not long lasting. It suffered a marked reverse when Russia placed a satellite in orbit around the earth in the autumn of 1957. Intellectuals were suddenly regarded as a valuable national asset. Talk turned to programs for utilizing the gifted, to the need for concentrating extra effort and funds in promotion of the sciences, to missile lags, to the restoration of American prestige in the eyes of the world, and to the care that had to be taken to create and preserve a favorable image. Newspapers and magazines frequently referred to this period as an age of anxiety, and they published cartoons depicting the analyst's couch and vending machines dispensing tranquilizers. There is little doubt that this was a time of fear and reactions to fear (e.g., the "beat" generation and the popularity of adult westerns and rock and roll) as well as a time of accelerated advance in science and technology (e.g., the Salk and Sabine antipolio vaccines, electronic computers, automated machinery, transistors, and new advances in the theory of relativity).

Within psychology, the integrating and synthesizing tendencies of the previous years continued (Shaffer, 1953). A method-oriented conception of the nature of science had to a large extent replaced the content-oriented conception. Although a few psychologists were still uneasy about the study of, for example, extrasensory perception, there was general agreement that what defines a science is not the subject being investigated but the method by which those working in an area obtain and order their data. Any topic may become part of science if the "scientific method" is used in its exploration.

Contemporary views on matters having special relevance for clinical psychology included the following: Both heredity and environment are essential, interactive, and ubiquitous, and the question is not which is more important than the other but how hereditary and environmental variables affect human behavior and growth. Frustrations and gratifications are each necessary to some degree for optimum psychological development. Mental health does not imply freedom from worry and anxiety but an ability to tolerate and deal effectively with problems and fears. And finally, the results of any psychological evaluation constitute only a sample of the individual's functioning.

Of course, there were still different emphases and points of view. Probably there will always be a place in psychology for precision and the kind of "tough-minded" experimental focus so highly esteemed by the "pure scientist." Likewise, there will probably always be a place for the "tender-minded" humanism characteristic of the "caring professional." But particularly in this decade, when so many Americans seemed tormented with problems of conformity, identity, self-expression, and despair, there was a heightened interest in those who stressed that people were beings unique in nature and who focused on the scientific study of our distinctive needs, feelings, beliefs, and potentialities. (As an aside, psychoanalysis perhaps occupied the middle ground, with an attitude of tough-minded humanism.)

NORMAL PERSONALITY FUNCTIONING

As psychoanalysts directed more of their attention to ego processes, some of the results and conclusions of experimental psychology were woven into the fabric of psychoanalytic theory (Gill, 1959). The writings of many psychoanalysts during this period were, to a large extent, either embroideries or restatements of both empirical findings and behavioristic theories concerning early childhood development. Perhaps the most widely discussed analytic author of this period was Erik H. Erikson, who had graduated from the Vienna Psychoanalytic Institute in 1933 and later settled in the United States.

In essence, Erikson (1950) integrated a psychosocial theory of development with Freud's psychosexual theory. In this amalgamation, each psychosexual stage is supposed to confront the individual with social demands or tasks that are considered universal—for example, the acquisition of a sense of trust in one's world, in the functioning of one's own body, and in others. However, the typical solutions for each interpersonal conflict vary from one culture to another. Furthermore, although the traditional psychoanalytic model ended with the attainment of genital sexuality, Erikson postulated later crises of adjustment that extended into adulthood and old age. The successful resolution of one developmental crisis or problem increased the likelihood, but did not guarantee, a successful resolution of the next, whereas an unsuccessful resolution appreciably reduced an individual's chances of dealing appropriately with subsequent stages of development. Moreover, later experiences could change a resolution for the better or worse.

Erikson characterized each phase of the life cycle as a more or less successful attempt to deal with a specific central conflict that had come into prominence. He believed, however, that the resolution of the conflict was not an either-or matter, although in healthy growth it is weighted toward the positive or desirable alternative. Since this general perspective was extended through adulthood, it was assumed that the normal developmental crises of parents will interact with the normal developmental crises of their children.

The specific alternative outcomes at each stage in growth were identified as follows: in the oral-sensory stage, a basic sense of trust versus mistrust; in the muscular-anal stage, a sense of autonomy or independence versus shame and doubt; in the locomotor-phallic stage, a sense of initiative versus guilt; in latency, a sense of industry or accomplishment versus inferiority; in puberty and adolescence, a sense of identity versus role or identity diffusion; in young adulthood, a sense of intimacy or friendship and love versus isolation; in adulthood, a sense of generativity or productivity versus stagnation; in old age, a sense of integrity versus despair and disgust. Of particular interest, and requiring special mention, is Erikson's concept of identity.

When he spoke of identity, Erikson (1959) referred to the awareness of continuity in one's development, self-knowledge, and a sense of consistency between what one has been and what one wishes to become. This concept seemed especially meaningful to many persons of middle and high social status in the United States, where discontinuity appeared rife. Discontinuity took diverse forms, such as geographic and social mobility, the decreasing importance of the extended family, the role of unconscious motivation, the alienation evident in modern art and architecture, divorce, and concern about the preservation of individuality. The college educated, especially intellectuals, were troubled about conformity and how a person could maintain uniqueness in the face of pressures to conform and about the meaning of life and how to carry on even when life seemed to have no meaning. The old answers were no longer satisfactory. There were new answers, although some perhaps were not so much new as newly discovered and bandied about in popular discourse and in the media. Thinking to obtain answers that would satisfy, many persons were turning to psychoanalysis, psychotherapy, Zen Buddhism, and existentialism (Pervin, 1960).

Existentialism can be traced back to the writings of the Danish philosopher and theologian Sören Aabye Kierkegaard (1813–1855). Kierkegaard, as well as other existentialists, was concerned with how people are to understand their situation in the world. Although existentialists did not tend to see the human situation as an easy or enviable one (since people are alienated from nature and aware of their limited existence), they strongly emphasized the worth and significance of each person as a unique and irreplaceable being. The major, if not the only, problem facing each person is to exist as an individual, to be oneself, to fulfill one's potentialities. Unlike other organisms, humans are regarded as free to determine their actions, to become aware of themselves as apart from other beings, to be reflective, to question their behavior, and to ponder the reasons for their existence. This very freedom places on a person the responsibility to be genuine and authentic. To refuse this freedom, to attempt to escape this responsibility, produces, perhaps, temporary relief, but it will eventuate in a state of boredom mingled with dread and despair. To accept this freedom and responsibility and genuinely to strive to bring one's potentials to fruition is the only legitimate means that existentialists see for living with dignity and meaning (May, Angel, & Ellenberger, 1958).

Existential thought appears in the writings of psychologists such as Erich Fromm, Gordon Allport, Rollo May, and Carl Rogers. Very much as Goldstein had stated earlier, Rogers (1951) declared, "The organism has one basic tendency and striving—to actualize, maintain, and enhance the experiencing organism" (p. 487). This striving is in the direction of increasing differentiation and integration, self-government, autonomy, and, in a broad sense, socialization and away from control by external forces. For Rogers (1951), as for Lewin, "Behavior is basically the goal-directed attempt of the organism to satisfy its needs as experienced, in the field as perceived" (p. 491).

Karen Horney (1950) also viewed the individual as striving for growth and self-realization, and, in a sense, so did Erich Fromm. To fully understand humans, Fromm contended, it is necessary to understand the needs that arise from the conditions of their existence. These needs are for relatedness or productive love, transcendence or creativeness, security or rootedness, identity, and a stable frame of reference or a consistent perception of the world. These are human needs not found in other organisms, and the forms in which they are expressed are determined by the mores of the social order in which people live. Fromm (1955) believed that all known societies have failed in some degree to meet the basic needs of our existence, and he sketched as his ideal a psychologically perfect social system: humanistic communitarian socialism. In this social system, every person would have an equal opportunity to become fully human and to gain "a sense of self by experiencing himself as the subject of his powers rather than by conformity" (Fromm, 1955, p. 362).

Gordon Allport (1955) introduced the term *proprium*, which seemed a mouthful for a concept suspiciously like the self: "the regions of our life that we regard as peculiarly ours . . . and which make for inward unity." Once our basic needs are satisfied, we are free to grow, to become. Therefore, people strive not only to reduce tensions but to maintain some kinds of tension. The maintenance of tensions falls within the province of propriate strivings and includes endeavors to attain goals, realize values, perfect behavior, and pursue interests.

Existentialism as a development within psychology emphasized the responsibilities of the individual to self rather than social responsibilities. Obviously, when there was so much concern about conformity (Crutchfield, 1955), such a point of view was of interest to a sizeable portion of the public. But just as psychoanalysis was unfortunately distorted by some people into a rationalization for sexual license, so existentialism was often distorted into a rationalization for narcissism, perverse negativism, and groping after egocentric experiences. All too frequently overlooked was what existential writers demonstrated by the simple fact of their writings—that self-actualization takes place within a social context. As they illustrated, a valuable way to give meaning to one's life is to be of help in giving meaning to the lives of others.

Closely allied with existentialism was a view of people as actively dealing with their environments and capable of initiating constructive changes in their functioning. However, this view was expressed by some psychologists who are not ordinarily associated with existentialism. George A. Kelly (1905–1966) asserted that the ordinary person performs in much the same way as does the scientist, in that both have theories and personal constructs or beliefs, both test hypotheses, and both weigh whatever evidence they acquire for the purpose of predicting and controlling their world. Kelly (1955) envisioned the growth of a person as the development of a unique system of constructs, capable of change and of varying degrees of integratedness, fragmentation, or incompatibility. To understand people, we have to understand their constructs, and to understand a construct, we have to understand the two construct poles that form it. For example, a man may believe that women are gentle and males are not; thus he has certain expectations about the ways individuals of each sex should behave when an act to which he would apply the construct "gentleness" is involved. Moreover, people not only make predictions but direct their behavior so that it will be appropriate to the events they anticipate.

Under nonthreatening, experimental conditions in which people have an opportunity to validate their constructs, they may undergo modification. Kelly believed that humans have the conceptual freedom to alter their construct systems and realize their potential, that they can invent their own ideas. Unlike psychologists who viewed people as dismayed by their finite existence or striving to fulfill themselves within their environment, Kelly focused on human beings attempting to deal with the environment actively and creatively by making representations of it through which they come to understand it better. His model of human nature is related to an ideal held up by ancient philosophers as the best means to happiness: spending one's life searching for knowledge, truth, and understanding.

Another Kelly, Everett Lowell Kelly (1955), reported that after years of research on the consistency of adult personality he had been most impressed by its flexibility. Whereas values and vocational interests professed by adults seem stable, self-ratings and certain attitudes do not. Further, when the results are seen in broader perspective, there is evidence of much change in all measured variables. Kelly (1955) concluded,

> Our findings indicate that significant changes in the human personality may continue to occur during the years of adulthood. Such changes, while neither so large nor sudden as to threaten the continuity of the self-percept or impair one's day-to-day interpersonal relations, are potentially of sufficient magnitude to offer a basis of fact for those who dare to hope for continued psychological growth during the adult years.

As we can see, people were coming to be regarded by some psychologists and psychoanalysts as less driven and irrational in their behavior and as more capable of reason, modification, and the exercise of responsibility (Hartmann, 1958). Before we go on to consider the views of human nature that were emerging from "tough-minded" experimental studies, it is important to note that within both modern existentialism and science the universe is postulated not to have a purpose, although, of course, these systems differ considerably in their attitude to this. Nevertheless, many persons, influenced by science and existentialism, felt their religious beliefs shaken (although it is difficult to determine whether the influence came before the feeling). So widespread did this skepticism become that even members of the clergy questioned the existence of God in public. One of the few psychiatrists who spoke out strongly for religion as essential to the well-being of humans was Carl Jung.

It seemed to Jung that the public and psychology were neglecting a "natural religious function" that exists within the collective unconscious, ignoring at their peril a powerful need to relate one's inner being to one's conscious world. Through religion, we are provided with a means to give expression to our inherited and unconscious spiritual experiences, our archetypes related to a superior being: the God-image or archetype of the self, the archetype of the great mother, the archetype of the old wise man. Each person, Jung believed, needs to experience these archetypes within and to feel their correspondence with the particular forms his or her own religious upbringing gave to them: "Too few people have experienced the divine image as the innermost possession of their own souls. Christ only meets them from without, never within the soul; that is why dark paganism still reigns there." In order to express the strength of his conviction that a deep belief in a supreme being satisfies an unconscious human need, above the entrance to his house Jung had these words carved: "Called or not called, God is present" (Fordham, 1953).

Let us now consider some of the studies of this decade that influenced how people conceived of human nature. The physiologist Hans Selye (1956) of the University of Montreal concluded that any living organism adjusts to stresses of all kinds by a general adaptation syndrome. Any stress, whether due to infection, extremes of temperature, injury, fatigue, or psychological conflict, produces physiological changes that elicit a definite reaction pattern. The goal of this reaction is to restore inner equilibrium. It is composed of a general response, common to all forms of stress, and a specific response peculiar to the particular form of stress afflicting the organism at that time. There are three stages in this reaction.

Selye called the relatively brief first stage "the alarm reaction." The organism reacts to the stress with increased activity of the autonomic nervous mechanisms and an outpouring of glandular secretions. If the organism successfully maintains the production of these secretions and still survives, the next stage, adaptation, occurs. In adaptation a homeostatic balance to the stress is sustained, and the organism is relatively insensitive to further stresses of the same kind. But this represents a successful adjustment to what is still an abnormal situation. If the stress persists, the organism becomes less able to tolerate other stresses and enters the third and final stage, physiological exhaustion. In this terminal stage, homeostatic mechanisms no longer function effectively and symptoms of illness appear.

One test of Selye's theory consisted in housing rats in refrigerators. At first there was a short period of disruption manifested in disturbed mating and feeding habits. But the rats survived and thereafter appeared to carry on "normally." Finally, as they were forced to maintain their adjustment to the polar environment, the rats suffered physiological exhaustion, became ill, and died. This study clearly demonstrated the general adaptation syndrome.

Selye's work has a number of implications, of which we shall mention but two.

The first is that an organism may be better able to tolerate a continued stress if supplied with substances that compensate for the physiological strain that it endures. Some support for this deduction was provided by the fact that using glandular extracts in the treatment of human rheumatoid arthritis and other complaints was found helpful. The second implication is that an appearance of health and vitality in a stressful environment may be deceptive, that an apparently successful adjustment to psychological pressures may mask progressive physiological debilitation culminating in illness and premature death. This, or course, is of major psychological significance.

While Selye was reminding psychologists of the frailty, as well as the sturdiness, of human beings, another way of looking at humans was gaining in popularity. This was to depict people as a glorified electronic computer, a system into which information is fed through statements (Mowrer, 1954). In order to understand a person, one has to understand the information that is being introduced and to analyze how much it reduces the number of alternatives (Miller, 1953). At times, statements may be meaningless or equivocal. Bateson et al. (1956) spoke of double-bind communication, a statement that places a person in a situation where no matter what is done, there is dissatisfaction (e.g., "I don't want you to feel that I'm forcing you to do this"). Such messages may foul the system. At any rate, people were seen as exceedingly complex, elegant mechanisms that have their inputs, outputs, communication channels, programmings, servomechanisms, and feedbacks and that sometimes get their wires crossed.

A huge number of empirical studies supporting, challenging, and extending these and other theories were being published (Jensen, 1958), including studies of empathy, rigidity, perceptual defense, creativity, and subliminal stimulation (to give just a sample). The last of these topics, subliminal stimulation, is, as we will soon see, particularly pertinent to our discussion.

Experiments were done in which ideas or commands (e.g., "Eat Popcorn") were flashed at speeds so fast that viewers claimed to be unaware of their meanings yet gave evidence of having believed them or acted in some way to carry them out (McConnell et al., 1958). If the existence of so-called subliminal stimulation was confirmed, it would have implications for advertising and other forms of persuasion. Yet it is obvious that the technique might be seriously abused and that in any case its use raises ethical issues. It can be contended that ordinarily a person recognizes an idea or suggestion as coming from an external source and is free to evaluate it critically. But supposedly in subliminal stimulation (if this does really occur), the person is not cognizant of the external source, and the idea is regarded as self-originated. Thus by trying to affect people without their knowledge, their right to evaluate information is violated. This was a particularly sensitive matter at that time, not only because of the dangers posed to civil liberties in the United States—dangers arising from the public's extreme reaction to the threat of communist infiltration—but also because so much was heard about "brainwashing" during and especially after the Korean War.

A small but damaging percentage of U.S. soldiers taken prisoner in Korea were known to have cooperated with the enemy. This was disheartening news to the

American public, and a strong demand for an explanation was voiced. Inquiries into the experiences of the men after they had been captured disclosed a certain similarity in the way some soldiers had been handled. They had not been beaten or tortured physically but had been placed in isolation with little to see or hear or do. Shortly after their solitary confinement began, they started to experience hallucinations, difficulties in thinking, a decrease in the ability to concentrate, and feelings of helplessness, futility, and abandonment. Eventually they experienced a childlike dependence on the generosity and sympathy of their captors and became receptive to thoughts and suggestions given to them.

Before the Korean War, brainwashing had been inferred when political prisoners in various communist nations abjectly confessed to the crimes with which they were charged. So complete were these confessions that it was thought the prisoners had been drugged or that their "minds had been broken" by compelling them to examine their darkest fears. To help evaluate the veracity of the more recent reports from Korea, controlled laboratory investigations into the effects of sensory deprivation were carefully planned. Beginning around 1952, dogs were reared in isolation, college student volunteers were bundled and bandaged on couches in soundproof rooms, and some subjects were suspended in tanks of water kept at body temperature. On the basis of the results from the research conducted with dogs, Hebb (1958a) concluded that "the normal development of behavior depends on a normal perceptual environment. The animal, reared in isolation is a permanent screwball at maturity: motivationally, socially, intellectually abnormal."

The studies of human beings cut off from virtually any external stimulation confirmed the fact that within a short period a person becomes highly suggestible and experiences hallucinations and delusions. Moreover, suggestions and propaganda were far more lasting in their effects than were any of the other changes produced during the period of deprivation. In other words, although the subjects were no longer in isolation and although they did not seem to be abnormal in their behavior, they continued to profess beliefs that had been suggested to them. It seemed clear that the human organism requires a certain amount of stimulation from the environment in order to function normally, realistically, and critically.

From a different line of research came additional demonstrations of the significance of central stimulation in motivating organisms and further alarming intimations that people might one day be controlled with relative ease and economy. W. R. Hess (1954) succeeded in permanently implanting electrodes in the brains of living cats. This made it possible to stimulate the brain electrically while the organism was in a "normal" unanesthetized state. Evidence soon accumulated from studies with rats and cats about the effects of such stimulation. It appeared that the electrical stimulation of certain areas of the brain that induce eating responses could also motivate the organism to perform learned instrumental acts that had been reinforced by food. According to the findings of James Olds, rats would learn to press a bar and would continue to do so with electrical stimulation of portions of their brains serving as a powerful reward (apparently, the only one).

Neal Miller (1958) reported the discovery of other areas where stimulation served as punishment. At the very least, such findings demonstrated that the organism could be motivated by direct central stimulation as well as by drive or tension reduction.

The response of the press to photographs of rats performing tasks while wearing implanted electrodes was to envision a day when people would labor for electrical stimulation rather than money. This dream (or nightmare) of authoritarian control and dehumanization was reinforced by the success of B. F. Skinner and his followers in shaping behavior.

Skinner (1958) had abundantly demonstrated that a response pattern can be "shaped" or built up by quickly reinforcing any initial crude approximation of the final behavior desired and by following this up with a careful scheduling of reinforcements of each closer and closer approximation to the final behavior. In this way animals could learn to perform acts not at all normally characteristic of their species. Chickens could play a minor league variety of baseball. Pigeons could play a game of ping-pong before climbing into the cockpit of a missile to give their all for psychology and country. Children sitting in front of teaching machines that almost immediately informed them of the correctness of their responses to questions seemed to learn certain academic subjects with an efficiency ordinarily considered beyond their reach. Human behavior, Skinner asserted, could be analyzed in terms of its schedules of reinforcement, and many activities could be modified and manipulated by altering these schedules.

Experiments on verbal conditioning supported Skinner's contentions (Daily, 1953). A casual "uh-huh" or "good" uttered by the psychologist as the person speaks serves to increase the frequency of any verbal response temporally associated with it. Hostile verbalizations (Buss & Durkee, 1958), references to the past, and the use of plural pronouns could all be reinforced and increased in frequency during the span of a single interview, with the person reporting no awareness of what was taking place and the reinforcement usually consisting simply of "uh-huh" or "yes" or "good," (Buss & Gerjuoy, 1958).

Whereas these experiments implied that people were less free, or human, than had been supposed, other studies implied that monkeys, at the very least, were more human than previously thought. Many psychologists believed a child's love for its mother is a learned or secondary drive acquired by associating the mothering figure to the drive reductions produced by feeding. Fromm, however, as spokesman for a dissident group, argued that among the unique human needs are productive love or relatedness and rootedness or security. Both of these views were challenged by Harry Harlow's experiments with macaque monkeys.

Groups of infant monkeys had been nursed on constructed models of monkey "mothers." Some of these surrogate mothers were made of bare wire; others were covered with foam rubber and terry cloth. Regardless of whether the infant monkey had been nursed on the wire mother, it preferred to spend much of its time clutching to and resting on a terry cloth mother. When strange and presumably frightening objects were introduced into the room, the infant monkey would run to the model and press itself against the foam rubber. Only after a time would it begin to explore the situation, and always the mother remained the base to which it retreated or returned whenever it appeared disturbed.

Harlow (1958) believed that his experiments supported Watson's suggestion that love is an innate emotion elicited by cutaneous stimulation of the erogenous zones of the skin. He also thought that his work made it clear that love is not unique to humans and that it is more dependent on tactile than oral stimulation.

As the decade closed, the crush of research caused one reviewer (Atkinson, 1960) to cry out, "Gad, what a mess!" Many of the studies contradicted each other or were fragmentary. So many investigations were being done that the content of one experiment or theory was hardly assimilated before another experiment or theory appeared to refute or extend it. Relatively new statistical techniques, such as nonparametric methods, were often unfamiliar and evoked skepticism when their use led to statistically significant results. There were theories in abundance, journals in profusion, and, like an awesome iceberg, the published research represented but a small fraction of all the research in progress.

Some terms had become so popular that they had lost their distinctive meaning. For example, most psychologists in using the term *dynamic psychology* wished to imply that they were speaking of the causes of behavior, especially motivation. But as English and English (1958) pointed out, "'dynamic' is often a mere cliché to imply that something is happening of which the speaker approves." Other long-honored concepts seemed to have become so refined, so exclusively specified in terms of their operations, and so intertwined that they were threatened with extinction. Cofer (1959) concluded his review of the literature on motivation with this statement: "Motivation, as a distinctive concept, coordinate to other psychological concepts, may well disappear." Blake and Mouton (1959) decided on the basis of their survey that "as an independent, isolated compartment, personality is on its way to oblivion."

Nevertheless, there were terms that served as rallying cries for many psychologists: The organism! The self! Psychodynamics! Identity! Interpersonal relations! Reinforcements! Feedback! However, this should not obscure the fact that the majority of psychologists, regardless of their particular area of interest, valued precision in measurements, in formulations, and in technology as the best means for understanding people. A minority disagreed, often eloquently arguing that the essence of what they were seeking to study and understand in humans was lost in the very act of scientific scrutiny. Perhaps unwisely, this disagreement regarding orientation was sometimes phrased in the form of alternatives, with psychologists exhorted to choose one position or the other. William McDougall had succinctly put it this way: "Men or robots?"

Obviously this issue—whether human dignity and the essential characteristics of human beings become lost in the process of reducing behavior to relatively small units—had troubled some psychologists for many years, even before the fifties. William James, as we know, grappled with this problem, and it may be that he had it in mind when he offered this apologia for all the questions that after a lifetime of inquiry still remained unanswered: "What has concluded that we might conclude in regard to it?" Yet it is clear that at least one conclusion can be offered. We are certain that it is possible to put together from the results of normative and clinical studies a portrait of human beings that is more complete and accurate than any that can be assembled from the findings of one orientation alone. Accordingly, the important thing is not to choose between orientations but rather to be open to any information that advances our understanding of human behavior.

DIAGNOSTIC TECHNIQUES

Although the number of available tests increased markedly during the fifties, clinical psychologists remained loyal to the techniques and their modifications that had been developed during the thirties and forties. Buros (1953) listed 793 mental tests, an increase of approximately 250 instruments in a span of about 10 years. With so many tests appearing so rapidly, it is small wonder that the clinician preferred to rely on those that, if not altogether tried and true, at least were familiar and of some demonstrated value.

And these tests certainly seemed to have been tested, if number of publications is any criterion. Through 1951, there had been 1,219 publications dealing with the Rorschach, 493 with the Stanford-Binet, 371 with the Wechsler-Bellevue, and a respectable demonstration of interest in the TAT and MMPI. Amid all this research, interest in some tests seemed to die (e.g., the Szondi) as a result of negative evaluations, although interest in others held up stubbornly despite many criticisms (Sundberg, 1954, 1961).

Relatively speaking, the intelligence scales appeared to be solid rock, a place of refuge and security for clinicians in an otherwise ambiguous world of tests. Only one individually administered scale in this field made its debut in the fifties and attained wide popularity, the Wechsler Adult Intelligence Scale (WAIS).

The WAIS had the same structure as its forebear, the Wechsler-Bellevue. It was standardized on a population of 1,700 subjects of both sexes ranging in age from 16 to 64, with an additional 475 subjects 60 or more years old. This sample was stratified, with a proportionate selection of cases representing different occupational groups, levels of education, geographic locations, and urban versus rural populations within the United States. A noteworthy feature of the standardization sample was that 10% of the subjects were nonwhite (Wechsler, 1955).

Wechsler (1958) did not alter his definition of intelligence and remained firm in his adherence to Spearman's theory of its structure. The Wechsler-Bellevue and the WAIS seemed to resemble each other factorially, both having g, verbal comprehension, performance organization, and memory. However, the age range of subjects who scored highest on the WAIS was 25–29, whereas on the Wechsler-Bellevue it had been 20–25. What did this mean? Well, it did not mean that people were still getting smarter at a later age than formerly, and in order to understand what Wechsler thought it might mean, we have to consider two of his concepts.

The concept of ability, according to Wechsler (1950), refers to the manner in which certain mental operations are performed; the concept of intelligence refers to the relevance or relation of those operations to certain goals and ends. It would seem to follow from this distinction that, for example, a person may show great ability in performing arithmetical computations but, if nothing of any value is gained from the computations, his or her dedication of long hours to this work would not be considered intelligent. Since Wechsler believed that intellectual ability did not increase beyond the age of 15 or 16 years, he thought the gains in scores on his tests found after those ages should be attributed to an increased familiarity with the culture and a rise in educational level, both of which contribute to make a person's behavior more intelligent. Presumably, the population used in the standardization of the WAIS was more attuned to the culture and better educated than the population used in the standardization of the Wechsler-Bellevue.

Despite discouraging reports (Guertin et al., 1956, 1962; Rabin & Guertin, 1951) concerning the validity of patterns of scatter when the Wechsler-Bellevue was used to make psychiatric diagnoses, Wechsler (1958) in his new test still offered patterns of subtest scores for differentiating anxiety states, organic brain disease, delinquency, schizophrenia, and mental deficiency. He suggested that a difference of 15 IQ points between the verbal and performance scales was probably significant clinically, and advised his colleagues to take two or more scaled score units from the mean as a measure of scatter. Furthermore, he recommended that clinicians employ the method of successive sieves in arriving at a diagnosis: One test pattern would be used to identify a percentage of a diagnostic group, then another test pattern would be employed to filter out a percentage from the previous percentage, and so on. For example, the first sieve might be a difference of 20 or more IQ points between verbal and performance scale scores; the second sieve might be lower scores on picture completion and object assembly than on picture arrangement and digit symbol; the third sieve might be higher scores on vocabulary and comprehension than on similarities and digit symbol. The hope was that after such a series of siftings the clinical psychologist would be better able to bake a diagnostic cake composed of clearly identified ingredients.

The following techniques, which received a great deal of attention during the fifties, will serve to demonstrate the diversity within the clinical area and the tenacity of old truths, even though for a time they may have been ignored.

Price and Deabler (1955) reported that the perception of a visual aftereffect is useful in discriminating between those who have suffered brain damage and those who have not. This test requires the subject to stare at a spinning Archimedes spiral. When the spinning is stopped, the "normal" person seems to see the spiral expanding or contracting, but the person with central nervous system pathology does not seem to experience this aftereffect. A later study claimed that children perform in the same manner as those who are brain damaged. Subsequent research, however, challenged these findings and led psychologists to question the validity of earlier reports. This skepticism was partly due to a study in which children were presented with balloons with Archimedes spirals painted on them. They were asked to describe what seemed to happen to the spirals when the balloons were inflated and deflated. Once a child's way of describing what he or she saw was ascertained, the child was tested for the aftereffect. In most cases, the child seemed able to see it, although the report was in the child's own words. It was thought probable that the children in the earlier study had also perceived the aftereffect but, owing to idiosyncrasies of expression, had not been able to communicate what their experience had been in such a way that the psychologist could understand (Gollin & Bradford, 1958).

Q-sorts enjoyed some popularity, particularly as a research technique for Rogers and his followers (Rogers & Dymond, 1955). A Q-sort consists of a number of descriptive statements (usually having to do with feelings and personal beliefs) that the subject has to arrange according to their appropriateness as self-descriptions. In most cases, the subject is asked to sort the statements at least twice, first according to how well they describe the kind of person the subject thinks he or she is (self-concept sort) and second according to how well they describe the kind of person the subject would like to be (ideal self sort). The extent of the discrepancy between the self-concept sort and ideal self sort serves as a measure of the person's self-satisfaction. The closer the correspondence between the two sorts, the greater, supposedly, is the individual's self-satisfaction and the better the psychological adjustment. Unfortunately, it was soon found that psychotics and others who are obviously maladjusted often show high correlations between the two sorts. This prompted the ready explanation that these individuals are very defensive, but, of course, it also raised the question how one is to know whether a sorter has been honest or defensive.

An attempt was made to solve this problem in the case of the MMPI by having items that were designed to detect, on the one hand, either carelessness or poor comprehension and, on the other hand, intentional falsification. As mentioned earlier, the amount and quality of the research on this instrument was impressive, and high hopes were held for it as an objective means for making psychiatric diagnoses. This goal was, for the most part, abandoned during the fifties, and the scales were regarded as descriptive of personality patterns rather than immediately diagnostic of the specific disorders for which they were named. Therefore, like practically everything else, the interpretation of the MMPI had become more complex, while at the same time more uses were proposed than those for which it had originally been intended. Hathaway and Meehl (1951) published an atlas to help in its interpretation. This consisted of a collection of 968 short case histories, with one or more associated MMPI profiles for each. Items from the inventory were used by Janet Taylor (1953) to construct a scale of manifest anxiety, which was employed in a number of studies (testing Hullian learning theory) to identify groups of individuals supposedly differing in drive level. Barron (1953) took 69 items from the MMPI and made an ego-strength scale that appeared to differentiate between groups of patients who would and would not benefit from psychotherapy. And by 1959, there were almost 200 different MMPI scoring keys for the purpose of assessing characteristics ranging from dependency to baseball talent.

Despite these indications of acceptance, the MMPI was not without its critics. A major criticism, directed not only at this technique but also at others of its kind, was offered by Edwards, who pointed out that people's responses on questionnaires are frequently influenced by what they think is socially acceptable.

Edwards noted quite sensibly that some of the items on personality inventories require an individual to admit to or deny characteristics or forms of behavior that differ greatly from what is culturally approved. Thus Edwards thought it probable that many individuals yield to the tendency to select the alternative that is more desirable as descriptive of themselves. As a way of dealing with this problem, which he hoped would prove successful, Edwards (1954) designed the Edwards Personal Preference Schedule. The schedule was intended to measure 15 personal needs on the basis of choices between 225 paired comparison statements. Each pair of alternatives had been matched so that they were approximately equal in social desirability, and Edwards recommended to his fellow psychologists that in the future they consider this variable in constructing tests.

In 1953 Aserinsky and Kleitman reported that rapid conjugate eye movement (REM) is associated with dreaming. While the individual is in a light sleep, as defined by EEG criteria, the usual slow drift of the eyes is sometimes replaced by REM. REM, which is measured by electro-oculograms, is apparently a valid indication that dreaming is taking place. Subsequent research indicated that dreams last from 3 to 50 minutes (much longer than had been thought) and occur at intervals of 70 to 104 minutes throughout the night (more frequently than had been thought). The technique thus proved to be a valuable tool in investigations of dream activity, dream deprivation, and dreamers (Dement & Kleitman, 1957).

As we have seen, questions about the validity of diagnostic instruments were prominent during the fifties. For example, Margaret Lowenfeld (1954), even after her test had been in use for 25 years, still regarded it as being in the beginning stages of development. Studies of the test in the United States indicated that cultural factors probably would have to be considered in interpreting the designs constructed by the people who take it. The intervening years of research, instead of simplifying matters, had only added more variables that needed to be taken into account in the complex task of interpretation, and Lowenfeld could no longer suppress doubts that her test would provide a reasonably simple technique for evaluating personality. Somewhat more encouraging were the results from investigations of the Bender-Gestalt. They indicated that reasonably valid mental ages from 5 to 10 years could be estimated from the drawings of the designs. (Below the mental age of 5, the drawings were too crude to allow discriminations; above the mental age of 10, the task was not difficult enough.) Moreover, the test appeared to have some value in distinguishing between psychotic and nonpsychotic adults and supplying clues for the detection of central nervous system pathology when used in a battery of tests (Billingslea, 1963).

As for the general concept of validity, it was itself being analyzed and its ramifications were becoming more fully appreciated. The APA Committee on Test Standards (1952) attempted to clarify some of the problems involved in validating diagnostic techniques. They distinguished between four kinds of validity. *Criterion* or *predictive validity* refers to the correlation between test results and subsequently obtained criterion measures, such as success in training or therapy or school. *Concurrent* or *status validity* refers to the correlation between test scores and some external criterion available at about the time the test is taken, such as a psychiatric diagnosis or ratings by teachers or therapists. *Content validity* refers to the extent to which test items sample the universe of content specified by the instrument's purpose (e.g., an intelligence scale samples intellectual behavior but not feelings about oneself or other persons). *Congruent* or *construct validity* refers to the degree to which the test measures the psychological variable it is supposed to measure, which is indicated when the test correlates with other tests of accepted validity or when scores on the test correctly predict differences in behavior deducible from the same theory that led to the test's construction.

To illustrate construct validity, the following example may be cited: In theory, people who are authoritarian are supposed to be rigid in their psychological functioning. Therefore, those who score high on a test of authoritarianism should be more rigid in their behavior than those who score low. If an experiment is conducted that substantiates that prediction, its results would demonstrate construct validity of the test as well as the validity of the theory itself. However, failure to support the prediction would indicate the test, the theory, or both lacked validity.

Further, it should be noted that the congruent or construct validity of a test is no guarantee that it also has predictive validity. A test may measure a certain characteristic very well, but that characteristic may have no demonstrable relationship to anything else of interest. Thus knowledge of scores on our test of authoritarianism may not help us to predict grades in school or success in a course of training because whether the person is authoritarian may not be related to academic or vocational accomplishments (Cronbach & Meehl, 1955).

The distinction between predictive validity and construct validity is pertinent to understanding psychologists' assessment of the Rorschach, which had been severely censured for the failure of its scores to relate to certain predictive criteria, such as improvement in psychotherapy and successful performance as an airplane pilot. Some clinicians, in spite of these statistical failures, felt the Rorschach was a valuable instrument and of great help to them in their work. Far from being persuaded to abandon the test, clinical psychologists in greater numbers than ever became convinced that their interpretation of the Rorschach must depend less on the significance of specific test scores than on their acumen, sensitivity, and understanding of subtle aspects of the entire testing situation (Sarason, 1954).

This shift from an emphasis on scores to an emphasis on the total set of circumstances in evaluating the Rorschach was exemplified in Schafer's *Psychoanalytic Interpretation in Rorschach Testing.* Schafer (1954) argued that content, test scores, expressive movements, the testee's verbal comments or asides, the qualitative aspects of verbalizations, and the relationship between one response and another are all to be analyzed and integrated in an attempt to comprehend the individual's defenses, conflicts, and interpersonal reactions. In general, he viewed the situation in which the testee is placed as a challenge to his or her ability to relax defenses, to "regress in the service of the ego" and meet the demands imposed by the examiner for imaginative productions.

The number and complexity of variables that had to be taken into account increased not only with respect to the interpretation of tests but their construction as well. When selecting a standardization sample, the psychologist had to consider the relevance of the population's age, sex, geographic distribution, education level, personality characteristics, socioeconomic status, racial and ethnic composition, and mental health—and perhaps other variables as well. Items on tests had to compensate for response biases, such as the general tendency of people to agree with statements (especially clichés), to mark extreme positions on degree-of-agreement scales, to describe themselves in socially desirable terms, to deny symptoms, and to develop sets (i.e., to respond based on the kind of answers they have previously given). Furthermore, the hypothesis of "levels" suggests that the ambiguity or definiteness of a test might be related to the extent to which unconscious processes would normally be expected to affect responses to its items. This means that the less ambiguous psychological tests, such as intelligence tests, would be expected to tap higher levels of conscious functioning than the more ambiguous projective techniques (Stone & Dellis, 1960).

By the close of the fifties, clinical psychologists as a group seemed to be trying to catch their breath while attempting to assimilate the vast amount of new information that had accumulated. Being an extremely self-critical group, they berated their research. "One cannot read in detail the contemporary literature in diagnostics without being overwhelmed by the tremendous expenditure of time, money, and labor involved in bringing forth inconclusive or trivial results," said Ann Magaret (1952). "A large number of publications mostly making little or no contribution to theory or practice," was the judgment of E. L. Kelly (1954). Yet much had been learned.

The consensus regarding factor analysis was basically this: "Factor analysis remains a powerful tool for simplifying correlational data, but it now seems clearly not to be a means of discovery, and it is not reasonable to expect that it can transcend the limitations of the original test data or be a substitute for new experimental analyses" (Hebb, 1958b).

Evaluations of personality functioning in real-life situations, especially those where examiners stood around taking notes, had negligible predictive validity (Mackinnon, 1953). Interviews by clinical psychologists and by psychiatrists of candidates for professional training had little value in identifying the students who later proved successful (Kelly & Fiske, 1950). Even more remarkable, the more confident clinicians were in their judgments, the less accurate their predictions turned out to be. What seemed to be at least temporarily reassuring was that the studies of predictive validity had neglected to ascertain which characteristics are necessary for later success and which will ensure failure before demanding clinical predictions.

Results with the Rorschach, TAT, MMPI, and other personality techniques were not particularly helpful in indicating those who would benefit from psychotherapy (Zax & Klein, 1960). One weak ray of sunshine was the fact that global tests of personality were less predictive of specific characteristics than tests specially devised for predicting them. After reviewing over 100 studies having to do with the prognostic usefulness of psychological tests with neurotic and psychotic patients, Fulkerson and Barry (1961) concluded, "The variables which appear to have the strongest relationship to outcome [of psychotherapy and other forms of treatment] have been nontest variables, severity and duration of illness, acuteness of onset, degree of precipitating stress, etc." The consensus finally reached was that the analysis and understanding of an individual's total behavior in the testing situation integrated with past data (case history information) seemed to be of more value in making predictions than isolated test scores.

It appeared that the clinician's race, sex, and body size produced only minor interactive effects on projective test results under ordinary circumstances. What seemed to be crucial in altering responses was the testee's attitude toward the total test situation, and this attitude seemed to be affected in turn by the personality characteristics of the psychologist, particularly his or her friendliness or hostility. "Thus," concluded Masling (1960), "the procedure [the Rorschach] that many clinicians hoped would serve as an X-ray proves, on close examination, to function also as a mirror, reflecting impartially the S[ubject], the E[xperimenter], the situation, and their interactions."

Test results, unless gross screening was intended, were also not found to be very useful for predicting psychiatric categories. However, recognition of the arbitrariness of psychiatric diagnoses and groupings vitiated, for the time being, the importance to be attached to failures to demonstrate concurrent validity. Clinicians tended to draw away from psychiatric labeling as the goal of a psychological evaluation and moved toward descriptions of personality functioning. Whether a diagnosis of brain damage or schizophrenia was substantiated was now thought to be less important than understanding and accurately representing the person's behavior.

Clinicians saw their main diagnostic task as grasping the uniqueness of each individual. For this purpose they employed a variety of diagnostic techniques, including the Rorschach, Draw a Person, TAT, Bender-Gestalt, Stanford-Binet, WAIS, MMPI, Draw-A-Man, and WISC, all high in popularity. But they and other psychologists wondered if this testing, even assuming that it yielded a valid understanding of the person, was of any practical value.

There seemed little doubt that psychological testing had an established and significant place in education, but whether or not it had any real merit for psychiatry was still questioned. The deemphasizing of psychiatric nosology was welcomed by proponents of testing who had been disappointed by studies failing to demonstrate the concurrent validity of their instruments as well as by those who had also recognized the unreasonableness of the task they had set for themselves. But becoming aware of the futility of a goal is never a completely satisfactory substitute for reaching it, and some psychologists were compelled, in good conscience, to continue wondering just how seriously results of personality tests should be taken in arriving at meaningful decisions about a patient (Challman, 1951; Rotter, 1953; Windle, 1952).

That they may play a minor role in influencing the course of psychotherapy was indicated in a thought-provoking report by Meehl (1960), who noted that only 17% of the therapists polled in one study claimed that a diagnostic evaluation based on tests was helpful in accelerating treatment. Likewise, using tests to gain an understanding of patients did not seem cost-efficient, since therapists usually reached a fairly accurate and stable impression of their patients after four interviews or so. Moreover, Rogers (1951) argued that a psychological evaluation as a prelude to treatment is unnecessary and may even hinder progress in psychotherapy, because it implies that the responsibility for the client's self-knowledge and growth belongs, not to the client, but to the psychologist.

As if these criticisms were not enough, psychological testing was also under fire from antagonists outside psychology who flayed it, as an invasion of privacy, a devious method for imposing conformity in thought and behavior, and an obstacle that stood between decent people and the attainment of worthwhile positions (Cronbach, 1956). Psychologists in general rallied to the defense of tests when under attack, but they were also aware that the true value of clinical psychology is to be found elsewhere than in the particular instruments employed: "If there is anything that justifies our existence . . . it is that we think scientifically about human behavior and that we come from a long tradition . . . of being critical of ourselves as cognizing organisms and of applying quantitative methods to the outcomes of our cognitive activity" (Meehl, 1960).

Actually, most clinicians did not feel that the situation had to be viewed so starkly. Quite a few, even those working in psychiatric settings, asserted that their diagnostic appraisals were useful and had practical value and that this estimate was shared by colleagues in other disciplines who were in a position to know what clinical psychologists were doing. They were also prepared to admit that psychological testing had little importance in situations where, regardless of test findings, patients were handled in about the same way.

Yet the fact remained that for reasons of urgency and necessity, the use of certain tests had spread before their usefulness had been rigorously demonstrated. This kind of acceptance did not relieve clinicians of their obligation to evaluate the worth of their instruments but, if anything, made careful evaluation even more imperative. Clinical psychologists in the fifties agreed that they had this responsibility, and some discharged it, in part, through research, through the development of new techniques, and by acting as their own most severe critics.

DIAGNOSTIC FORMULATIONS

Although progress had unquestionably been made toward improved diagnostic formulations, the advances were usually new insights into the complexities of problems rather than solutions to problems (Yarrow, 1961). The structure of intelligence and the relative weightings of hereditary and environmental variables in psychological functioning and malfunctioning were still matters for debate and investigation. Moreover, definitions that had formerly been taken for granted were now called into question. Here, too, advances were to be measured not so much by the attainment of final answers as by difficulties more fully appreciated (Liverant, 1960).

Since clinical psychologists had come to agree that nonintellective personality characteristics affect intellectual functioning, much of their interest at this time centered on evaluating the effects of psychiatric disturbances, levels of anxiety, and the need for achievement on intelligent behavior. In general, the results indicated that there are optimum levels of anxiety and a felt need for achievement. Above these optimum levels there are disruptions of functioning, whereas below them individuals seem unmotivated to put forth their best efforts.

There was also general agreement that intellectual functioning is a complex process that depends on satisfactory interpersonal relationships for normal development. Although some question was raised as to whether the studies of maternal deprivation should be considered studies of sensory deprivation, there was overwhelming evidence to justify the conclusion that disturbances in family interactions could adversely affect a child's learning.

Nancy Bayley (1955) reported that intelligence test scores influenced by the testees' ability to use verbal concepts and abstractions continued to increase in adulthood in the case of superior adults. Thus, determining the age when highest intellectual capacity is reached appeared to be a complex issue dependent on what functions were being assessed, on the procedures used to evaluate those functions, and on the intellectual level of the population being studied.

The structure of intelligence was regarded by most clinicians, at least implicitly, in accordance with Spearman's two-factor formulation. As elaborated by A. W. Stern (1956) an up-to-date follower of Spearman, the primary mental abilities possess characteristics analogous to those of nuclear particles (i.e., they exhibit collective as well as independent behaviors and possess group as well as individual properties). Their duality of function, both discrete and interactional, was attributed to the fact that the brain is an interactive system. Stern called their collective characteristic *connectivity*, referring to a coupling among separate factors. He defined intelligence as "the resultant collective behavior among the intellective factors," and g as "the measure of the strength of the resonance evoked by the coupling process."

On the basis of the formulations of Stern and others, Wechsler (1958) was led to the following conclusion about the construction of intelligence scales: "In order completely to measure intelligence, it is insufficient to extend the range of abilities measured, . . . we must also find tests which manifest both greater coupling potential and greater resonance characteristics" (p. 23). In other words, Wechsler advocated the construction of intelligence scales in which there are relatively high correlations between an extensive variety of subtests, or a relatively high saturation of g.

To some extent Wechsler's conclusion was echoed by J. P. Guilford (1959). Following his factor analytic investigations into the structure of intelligence, Guilford erected a model of intellect in the shape of a $5 \times 4 \times 6$ cube. He listed five major factors (cognition, memory, convergent thinking, divergent thinking [Guilford, 1950], and evaluation), four content factors (figural, symbolic, semantic, and behavioral), and six products factors (units, classes, relations, systems, transformations, and implications). Thus there were 120 predicted unique abilities (e.g., cognitive figural units, cognitive figural classes, etc.). However, Guilford's cube model and his factor analysis were soon called into question when later studies revealed that some cells contained more than one factor. Therefore, Guilford concluded somewhat tautologically, to know an individual's intellectual resources thoroughly, psychologists would have to obtain many scores on many tests—or perhaps not so many, since a number of the factors seemed to be intercorrelated.

As a result of what he found in his studies on the structure of intelligence, Cyril Burt (1958) came to favor the views of Spearman. One of his findings was that intellectual structure changes with age. Although g appears to account for 50% of the variance in childhood, as the person matures specific group factors contribute more to the variance. Burt's finding was in keeping with a generally accepted principle in developmental psychology, namely, that growth tends to progress from a general or relatively undifferentiated matrix toward greater differentiation and specialization in functioning and behavior. This is also in keeping with Garrett's hypothesis referred to in the previous chapter of intelligence becoming more differentiated into abilities or factors with increasing age.

The crude question of whether heredity or environment is more important had become virtually a dead issue. The more interesting question of how heredity and environment influence the individual's functioning became the focus of investigation (Anastasi, 1958). It was agreed that every observable characteristic is the product of heredity and environment, that what the individual inherits are only tendencies to develop in certain directions, and that these tendencies require appropriate environmental conditions in order to be realized. Given a society in which adequate nutrition, good health, and opportunities for advanced education are the rule, it might be reasonable to conclude, as Burt (1958) did, that most of the variance in intelligence was due to heredity and that "improved environmental amenities can of themselves ensure no lasting results; but the changes in a nation's genetic constitution are likely to prove irreversible." However, in a society that is undernourished, impoverished, or unable to provide adequate education, it seems quite likely that favorable modifications of the environment could bring about lasting improvements in the intellectual functioning of its people.

It had long been held that there are 48 chromosomes in the human cell. Joe Hin Tjio and Albert Levan, however, reported that the correct number is 46. Later, Jérome Lejeune found that people afflicted with Down syndrome (mongolism) have 47 chromosomes, and subsequent research indicated the presence of a metabolic disorder in this form of subnormality. Lejeune believed that partly because of the extra chromosome, people with Down syndrome produce an excess of an enzyme that breaks down tryptophan, an essential component of the proteins involved in brain functioning.

Other metabolic anomalies, probably genetic in origin, found to impair effective brain function include a deficiency of ceruloplasmin or copper protein, apparent in Wilson's disease; a deficiency of galactose in the disorder galactosemia; and the previously mentioned deficiency of phenylalanine hydroxylase in phenylpyruvic oligophrenia. Naturally, it is not unreasonable to expect any metabolic anomaly to have some effect on brain functioning in an intricately interrelated system such as the human organism (Brackbill, 1956).

Psychologists were still hoping to clarify the issue of whether differences in mean scores on mental tests between blacks and whites were primarily a function of hereditary or environmental variables, though it is no secret that they thought it was probably the latter. Dreger and Miller (1960) reviewed approximately 200 studies concerning this topic conducted during the period from 1943 to 1958. In general, whites had higher intelligence and achievement mean scores and blacks had a higher prevalence of psychosis. Still, no unequivocal conclusion about racial differences could be reached in view of the inferior social status of blacks. Unfavorable environmental and educational conditions seemed to confront blacks regardless of where in the United States they lived. Until equality existed in fact as well as in words, it was unlikely that any definitive answer to the question could be obtained. At any rate, it was clear from the high accomplishments of many blacks, both in the United States and in Africa, that a broad range of intellectual functioning exists within that race as well as within the white race.

Although Franz Kallman (1959) did not overlook the influence of environmental variables, his research strongly suggested to him the presence of some gene-specific metabolic deficiency at the heart of schizophrenia. His primary evidence was an observed trend toward an increase in the frequency of schizophrenia among the relatives of a schizophrenic in proportion to the degree of consanguinity with the known case. Given a schizophrenic patient, the probability that a relative suffers from the same disorder is higher if that relative is an identical twin than if a full sibling, higher if a full sibling than a half-sibling, and higher if a half-sibling than a step-sibling. Nevertheless, it was still argued that the environment also tends to be more similar in proportion to the degree of consanguinity to the schizophrenic relative. Although most clinicians were willing to assume, as did Freud, that constitutional predispositions to various psychiatric disturbances probably existed, they were unwilling to assume that such predispositions were transmitted in the germ plasm (it is possible that the psychological changes which accompany a mother's disturbance affect the developing organism within her before birth) or that they were ordinarily of much practical significance.

Clinical psychologists gave a considerable amount of attention to a large number of psychological explanations for schizophrenia, especially explanations involving childhood and family interactions. Arieti (1955) attributed the disorder to some severe trauma in childhood that, by being repeatedly experienced, causes the person to retreat into archaic forms of thinking, emotional detachment, and desocialization. He regarded the metabolic and endocrine changes associated with schizophrenia as psychosomatic aspects of the psychologically initiated disease process. Lidz (1958; Lidz et al., 1958) thought a person who became schizophrenic was probably raised in a severely disturbed family whose members distort the shared meanings, particularly the linguistic meanings, of the culture. Faced by conflict between the demands of society and the demands of the family, such a child withdraws from the culture's imposed semantics and logic. This withdrawal eventuates in further isolation and immersion in the distortions of the family.

Margaret Mahler (1958) thought the two major symptoms of childhood psychosis or schizophrenia were a severe disturbance of self-identity and an alienation or withdrawal from reality. The first symptom is obvious in a symbiotic psychosis, where the child and mothering person have been virtually inseparable and may be seen as extensions of one another. The second symptom is prominent in early infantile autism, where the child has apparently not progressed to the stage of development in which people are differentiated from other objects in the environment. Kanner, who at first had been impressed by autistic children's compulsive desire for sameness and their tendency to relate to others as though they were inanimate objects, thought the disturbance might be produced by a lack of emotional responsiveness on the part of the mothers. Later, impressed by the early onset of the illness, its resistance to significant amelioration, and the genuine concern of some of the parents for their children, he thought it probable that organic factors were involved in its etiology and that it should be classed as one of the schizophrenias (Kanner, 1951; Kanner & Eisenberg, 1955).

Cameron and Magaret (1957) suggested that virtually all behavior disorders are the end products of cumulative learning resulting from patterns of reaction that have become overlearned, overgeneralized, and self-perpetuating. These reactions or symptoms are therefore not abandoned when they are no longer appropriate. It follows that the withdrawal pattern of a schizophrenic, for example, might have been initiated and perpetuated by traumatic experiences but that with the passage of time the symptom becomes intrinsically satisfying to the person and thus persists even in the safety of the mental hospital.

It was suggested that, among adults, two kinds of schizophrenics could be distinguished. Reactive schizophrenics evidence a satisfactory prepsychotic adjustment, extraverted behavior, a sudden onset of the disturbance in association with some trauma, and a favorable response to treatment. Reactive schizophrenia is supposedly psychogenic. Process schizophrenics evidence a lifelong history of maladjustment, introverted behavior, a gradual onset of psychosis, and a poor response to treatment. Process schizophrenia is supposedly organic. An obvious distinction between the two kinds is the duration of schizoid symptoms prior to hospitalization. Reactive schizophrenics supposedly show psychotic symptoms only just prior to psychiatric intervention, whereas process schizophrenics supposedly have manifested symptoms of maladjustment over a long period of time, symptoms that eventually become so severe that hospitalization is required (Kantor, Wallner, & Winder, 1953). After reviewing some 50 studies in this area, W. G. Herron (1962) concluded that the process-reactive formulation clarified many heterogeneous reactions found in investigations of schizophrenia. Yet, despite the merit of the distinction, he considered that the dichotomy was to some extent artificial and that it would be an error to believe all schizophrenics can be easily classified as having one kind of schizophrenia or the other. Usually a schizophrenic is found to have both process and reactive signs, which suggests that there is a continuum of personality organization or that the method of classification is imprecise.

A diagnostic category called *pseudoneurotic schizophrenia* was proposed by Hoch and Polatin (1949). Pseudoneurotic schizophrenia is a disorder that appears like, and may be mistaken for, a neurosis. The symptoms of the disturbance were pan-anxiety, pan-neurosis, and pan-sexuality. Along similar lines, Dunaif and

Hoch (1955) suggested a diagnostic category that they termed *pseudopsychopathic schizophrenia*, which refers to an apparent psychopathic personality with an underlying schizophrenic process. The symptoms of this disturbance were pan-neurosis, pan-sexuality, an acting out of antisocial behavior, and indications in the case history that, after imprisonment, full-blown psychotic episodes had occurred. At about the same time, clinicians seemed to become apprehensive lest the proliferation of pseudoschizophrenias became a full-blown diagnostic trend that had post-hoc-ergo-propter-hoc reasoning as its major symptom.

The failure of experiments to support Goldstein's contention that schizophrenic functioning is concrete led him to offer some clarification by way of defending his view. Goldstein (1959b) suggested that the motivation in schizophrenia can only be explained if one carefully considers the patient's situation and determines whether it is likely or not to arouse anxiety. Given an anxiety-arousing situation, the schizophrenic performs concretely. Otherwise, the schizophrenic's behavior may be either concrete or abstract. By abstract behavior, Goldstein meant symbolic behavior (i.e., behavior that transcends immediate sense impressions and is appropriate). For example, a person entering a dark room but not immediately turning on the light because there might be someone asleep is behaving in an abstract manner (abstract because the person has contemplated the consequences of his or her actions).

Impairment of abstract behavior (or the abstract attitude) seems to occur not only in schizophrenia but in patients with known brain damage. Goldstein (1959a) believed this impairment among the brain damaged could not be obviated, although each patient was not equally handicapped, the severity depending upon the location of the lesions and the extent of the cortical damage. But regardless of whether the disturbance was organic or psychogenic, Goldstein emphasized that the symptoms should be considered as performances of the total personality. Symptoms are not caused directly but are products of the affected organism's attempts to cope with inner and outer demands while struggling to realize capacities to the highest degree possible.

In the same way, Agostino Gemelli (1952), an Italian priest and psychologist, pointed out that psychoses are both organic and mental diseases, since "what we call 'personality' . . . is the whole man considered in the light of his organic factors and activities" (p. 117). Therefore, a mental disease is not psychogenic or organic but rather is to be thought of as "organic alterations, regressions or modification which are necessarily accompanied by psychopathological disintegrations" (p. 119). Given this frame of reference, Gemelli believed it reasonable to consider psychology as a biological science concerned with people in their entirety.

According to these formulations, schizophrenia appeared to be a disturbance toward which some children might be constitutionally predisposed. However, the probability of developing schizophrenia was a function of both the degree of the constitutional predisposition and the degree to which the person is compelled to adjust to deviant circumstances. In any case, the symptoms of the disorder were to be regarded as not only expressions of a defect, but as reactions to it, including attempts to somehow overcome it. Similar conclusions could be drawn for neuroses.

During this decade, practically every explanation of neurosis previously entertained remained viable, though in some cases in a modified but still recognizable form. Dollard and Miller (1950) published their integration of psychoanalysis and Hullian learning principles. They saw transference as a special case of stimulus generalization. Repressed conflicts were thought to be conflicts that the individual simply cannot "label," whereas maladjustments were attributed to conflicts between two strong drives producing incompatible responses. Unfortunately, both learning theorists and psychoanalysts had reservations about the Dollard-Miller integration. On the learning theory side, there were those who believed that Hullian principles were outmoded; on the psychoanalytic side, David Rapaport (1953) criticized their proposals as "clinically unsophisticated" and modeled after Freudian theory prior to 1923.

Mowrer (1950) claimed that maladjustments arise from a learning deficit that results from a failure to incorporate parental and social values into the structure of the ego. Thus neurotics, because they are lacking in superego or conscience, feel they have committed some transgression or actually have "sinned." In Mowrer's (1960) view, the neurotic is not a sick person but a "sinful" person. Mowrer interpreted the great interest in existentialism as a reflection, on a broad scale, of this loss of moral values, one that led many individuals to question their identity and the meaning of their lives. Although psychologists were critical of Mowrer's introduction of the concept of sin, they noted that in practice the therapeutic approach that he advocated was not markedly different from most. Since the sinner (or neurotic) has a rejecting attitude toward self, the task of Mowrer's therapist was to be accepting and to help the person face his or her sins rather than refuse to acknowledge them.

Hans Eysenck (b. 1916), who received his PhD from the University of London in 1940 and continued on there, was using factor analysis to gain an understanding of personality. He suggested that "psychoticism" and "neuroticism" were two independent dimensions of personality, each a continuous variable in normals and abnormals. Introversion-extraversion appeared to be a third dimension, with its basis, he hypothesized, in constitutional differences in the capacity for developing and dissipating cortical inhibition. Eysenck (1952b) thought that extraverts generate stronger cortical inhibitions more quickly, but dissipate them more slowly, than introverts. It followed from Pavlovian learning theory and Eysenck's assumptions that extraverted neurotics, who he believed to be hysterics and psychopathic personalities, should evidence quick, strong, lasting inhibitory processes but weak, slow excitatory processes. He predicted that just the reverse would be the case with introverted neurotics, who he believed to be subject to reactive depressions, anxieties, and obsessive disorders.

Since social training was thought to consist largely of conditioned anxiety reactions, Eysenck supposed that extraverts are undertrained and so exhibit a tendency to act out their impulses, whereas introverts are overtrained and overcontrolled. But when attempts were made to test these predictions, they yielded unimpressive and conflicting results. Diligence is often rewarded in this fashion, as the next two topics will also demonstrate.

A consistent finding in extraversion-introversion research was a positive relationship between extraversion and various measures of satisfactory adjustment and a positive relationship between introversion and various measures of unsatisfactory adjustment. (We may recall at this point that evidence of extraverted behavior is a criterion for placing patients in the good-prognosis reactive schizophrenic group and that evidence of introverted behavior indicates membership in the poor-prognosis process schizophrenic group.) The usual explanation given for these relationships was that within the culture of the United States the extraverted pattern is more highly valued by the public than the introverted. But then it was fair to ask whether these relationships also occur in cultures where introversion is more highly valued. In these cultures is extraversion associated instead with unsatisfactory adjustment? Furthermore, is it possible to state whether these two personality patterns are wholly learned or based in large part on constitutional differences? After surveying many years of research on extraversion-introversion, Carrigan (1960) concluded that many fundamental questions still remain unanswered and as challenging as ever.

The nature of hypnosis continued to be a topic of interest and controversy. Many effects associated with the trance state were now thought to be epiphenomena. People who are not hypnotized can, if given appropriate suggestions, tolerate pain, "regress" in their behavior, produce alternations in gastric and pancreatic secretions, recall memories, and even produce localized blisters and alter their blood glucose levels. There seemed to be no physiological way to differentiate "the hypnotic state" from "the waking state."

Studies indicated that what individuals know about hypnosis has a significant bearing on their behavior when hypnotized. It also appeared clear that what the person thinks is being demanded and the nature of the demand characteristics of the experimental procedure are important determiners of performance while in the trance. The question seemed to be this: Does hypnosis actually consist of a unique kind of functioning or is the person playing a role based on a conception of what a hypnotized subject is supposed to do?

On one side of the question, Orne (1959) suggested four characteristics of hypnosis that distinguish it from an individual's normal state. First, the person who has experienced a deep trance feels that the trance is not continuous with normal waking behavior. Second, the person reports being unable to resist the hypnotist's suggestions. Third, the person claims to actually experience the alterations, distortions, or denials of reality that are suggested, such as "not seeing" an individual who is clearly visible in the room. Fourth, the person appears able to tolerate logical inconsistencies in the trance that would normally be disturbing or unacceptable. Obviously, whether we accept these as distinguishing characteristics depends on how much confidence we have in the validity of self-reports regarding hypnotic trances.

On the other side of the issue, Barber (1956), following his review of over 100 studies of hypnosis, asserted that its nature is still elusive. Rather than continue to focus directly on hypnosis, psychologists, he suggested, might find it more profitable to direct research efforts toward uncovering those biographical and situational variables that may possibly explain why some people exhibit hypnotic behavior whereas others do not.

Before proceeding, we would do well to pause and consider the significance of the fact that questions were being asked that would stimulate investigation and experimental research. In and of itself, the raising of questions represents progress—though no doubt not as much as arriving at conclusive answers. Charles Darwin commented on a similar situation in this way: "False facts are highly injurious to the progress of science, for they often endure long; but false views, if supported by some evidence, do little harm, for every one takes a salutary pleasure in proving their falseness."

The Committee on Nomenclature and Statistics of the American Psychiatric Association (1952) published a revised nomenclature in 1952. In it neurasthenia, hypochondriasis, and hysteria were dropped as separate diagnostic categories, and hysteria was broken down into phobic, conversion, and dissociated reactions. Personality disorders, transient reactions to special stress, and the adjustment reactions of childhood, adolescence, and later life were added to the general class of psychiatric disturbances. The number of schizophrenic reactions was increased to allow more detailed diagnoses. Manic-depressive reactions were reduced in number and grouped as "affective reactions." The use of IQ limits to distinguish mild, moderate, and severe mental deficiency was abandoned. Psychosomatic disorders became a separate category under a different name, *psychophysiologic autonomic and visceral disorders*. *Psychopathic personality* was replaced by *sociopathic personality*, but the use of either label was discouraged.

Quite sensibly, in view of the fact that the information furnished by psychiatric diagnoses was both limited and likely to be only transitorily applicable, the goal of the clinical psychologist changed from putting diagnostic labels on patients to understanding each patient as a unique personality and predicting behavior. Additional support for this change came from the observation that some psychiatric disorders, the "classical" neuroses (hysteria and obsessive-compulsive neuroses), formerly quite common, were now almost rare, whereas personality trait disturbances (passive-aggressive personality, compulsive personality, emotionally unstable personality, etc.) were now frequently reported "illnesses." Most clinicians were inclined to think the changing picture of the neurotic could be attributed to the relatively more permissive methods of rearing children and to a relaxation of moral standards. Both developments may have been, in part, produced by the influence, direct and indirect, of psychoanalytic formulations on the public. Whatever the reasons, the "new" neurotic, unhappy and dissatisfied with life or self, seemed even more difficult to help than those hysterically paralyzed and perplexingly ritualistic predecessors (Garner, 1958; Wright, 1957).

Along with a recognition of the blurring between the normal and abnormal came an attempt to conceptualize what constitutes positive mental health. Marie Jahoda (1958) suggested the following criteria are involved in the concept: growth and self-actualization, accepting attitudes toward the self, integration, perception of reality, autonomy, and mastery of the environment.

But the question may be raised as to whether positive mental health is such an eminently desirable condition. After all, it cannot be denied that out of psychological suffering has emerged creative productions whose unique worth can be traced to their creators' pathologies. Is it wise to encourage creative individuals to undergo psychotherapy? Moreover, is it possible that some day in the future people will no longer consider the grotesquely beautiful, the tragic, and the pathetic as viable forms of human expression? The conclusion of M. Brewster Smith (1959) was that mental health "is a cluster of values that compete with other values in the arena of personal and social choice. We will not always want to give it priority." However, other psychologists were not so certain that the matter was closed to debate.

TREATMENT FORMULATIONS

The comments with which the preceding section opened will serve equally well here. What progress was being made in psychotherapy came not so much from the resolution of differences and from answers to questions as it did from recognition of additional variables that have to be taken into account. Unlike forms of physical therapy, where some may fall into disuse and become completely abandoned, the basic methods of psychotherapy all seemed to thrive and to generate apparently limitless varieties.

At the beginning of the decade, electric and insulin shock therapies were the primary forms of psychiatric treatment employed with psychotic patients. Electroshock seemed most effective with those depressed patients who were agitated and anxious but did not seem to work well with depressed patients who reported somatic complaints and who were openly guilt-ridden. Attempts had been made to use electroshock with neurotics and children, but the improvements in behavior tended to be temporary and so the practice was not encouraged. However, this is not a sufficient explanation, since temporary improvements were also not uncommon with psychotic patients. It seemed likely that psychiatrists regarded the procedure as too drastic to be employed routinely with nonpsychotics in view of its hazards, the availability of other kinds of treatment, and the outcome.

A 14-year follow-up study of 781 schizophrenic patients who had been given courses of insulin coma therapy showed that approximately 68% had responded favorably to the initial course, but of these, 63% suffered a relapse. A second course of insulin treatment produced improvements in 52% of the relapsed patients. Thus, of an original group of patients, about 47% benefited from either one or two cources of insulin shock. Favorable response seemed to be associated with the following factors: a psychosis of less than 6 months duration, comas totaling 30 to 60 hours, and a gain of approximately 30 pounds in the patient's weight during the course of the therapy.

Some psychiatrists were trying ether and carbon dioxide inhalations as a method of treatment and reporting encouraging results. Studies on the outcomes of lobotomies, topectomies, and transorbital leucotomies, however, were discouraging. Few or no significant differences were found between patients who had undergone these forms of surgery and their controls. In consequence, the use of these surgical procedures sharply declined.

Doses of glutamic acid were administered to mental defectives in the hope of raising the level of intellectual functioning. There was some early enthusiasm for this form of medication, but later it was sadly concluded that what mental stimulation it provided was not sufficient to alter in any marked degree the prospects of the intellectually subnormal (Zimmerman & Burgemeister, 1951).

Around 1952 a major change in the treatment of psychiatric disturbances occurred. A pharmacological agent, reserpine, extracted from the roots of the rauwolfia plant, seemed to have a beneficial effect on psychotic patients, calming them and helping them to maintain better contact with their environment and to become more cooperative. Two years later, another drug, chlorpromazine, which had been used earlier in Europe, was introduced in the United States. It seemed to alleviate anxiety and to make psychotic symptoms less intense and disturbing. A related development was the discovery that lysergic acid diethylamide (LSD) could produce transient psychotic symptoms. This touched off a search for drugs that would counteract the effects of LSD and thus might prove useful in the treatment of psychoses.

Within a relatively short time, a large variety of ataractic or tranquilizing drugs were produced, and their effects in treating psychotics and neurotics of all ages were extensively studied. Of particular interest was the question as to just how these drugs worked to bring about the benefits associated with their use. Reserpine was connected with the release of serotonin in the brain, but the significance of this association, if any, was conjectural. Some psychologists and psychiatrists wondered if the modifications in symptoms might be due less to the drugs themselves and more to the warm interest shown by those who administered them. Or perhaps, on a more analytic level, what was involved was the gratification of the patients' dependency needs when they received and took their pills from the giving therapist. In any case, and regardless of how the drugs worked, beneficial effects were being produced.

In just a few years, 4,500 studies were reported in the world's medical literature on just one of these drugs, chlorpromazine. There seemed to be general agreement that it accelerated the termination of acute psychotic episodes, that it could rapidly produce a reduction in motor activity and aggressiveness, and that it contributed to more logical thinking and to a feeling, in some paranoid and catatonic patients, of "distance" from their hallucinations.

It was also generally agreed that these pharmacologic agents made patients more accessible to individual psychotherapy (although in the first wave of enthusiasm there was expressed the almost exultant hope that the drugs might do away with any need to resort to such expensive and time-consuming "traditional" methods). Yet another benefit, and one by no means to be ignored, was the virtual disappearance from mental hospitals of disturbed wards with screaming, babbling patients milling about. The hospitals were more quiet than they had ever been and the patients more easily managed. Whatever might be said of the drugs from the patients' point of view, they raised the morale among nurses, physicians, and attendants by making their working conditions less clamorous.

Since the drugs were relatively cheap and easily administered, it became feasible to discharge patients whose psychoses were, so to speak, controlled and have them continue their medication outside the hospital, in the same way, for example, that people who suffer from convulsive disorders (e.g., epilepsy) can control their illnesses by barbiturates or other drugs. The tendency in state hospitals, therefore, was to step up the turnover of patients by returning them to their families as quickly as possible, even though some might continue to show disturbed behavior.

As far as the public was concerned, tranquilizers seemed to be one of the "miracle drugs" invented by humans to make life a little more palatable. Magazines and newspapers described their wonder-working effectiveness in glamorous, overdrawn reports and endorsed their use as though there were no side effects or cases of therapeutic failure. People feeling "nervous" and "tense" were encouraged to take them to gain a feeling of relief and relaxation in the face of onrushing stress. From media accounts, it appeared that the mental hospitals would soon be emptied, that immediate and lasting comfort for all neurotics was at hand, and that the Brave New World described by Aldous Huxley, the contentedly drugged society with its blithe motto "Half a gram is worth ten damns," was soon to be realized.

Understandably, there were at this time signs of concern and even anxiety over the future of psychotherapy. This uneasiness was largely confined to the professional men and women engaged in this form of treatment. As far as the public could see, the only problem with psychoanalysis and psychotherapy was cost and limited availability. There was little question that going to an analyst had become virtually a status symbol in American society, but psychologists were less easily impressed.

Although the books that described any method of psychotherapy usually recorded only morale-inspiring instances of success, soberly conducted empirical studies of outcomes reported, on the average, that one-third of the patients had not improved. Nor did it seem likely that any therapist had avoided, or would be able to avoid, experiencing moments of ineptitude and failure. On a purely intellectual level, furthermore, all psychotherapists could agree that it was unreasonable to expect any one form of treatment to be completely effective in treating even just one form of illness, not to mention the varied assortment of maladies ranging from vague feelings of dissatisfaction to pronounced psychoses, from transitory adjustment problems to entrenched patterns of lifelong maladaptive behavior, from disturbances in which people eagerly seek help to those in which they fight help with every resource they can command, from a child's difficulties in accepting toilet training to an elderly man's difficulties in accepting death. It could be agreed that psychotherapy is of limited effectiveness and that psychotherapists are limited both in their skills and what they can reasonably hope to achieve. Yet when failures and limitations were pointed out, some psychotherapists responded not intellectually but self-critically, perhaps even with a sharply defensive attitude that rejected out of hand any criticism of this method of treatment.

With the stage thus set, we will now consider some of the variants in method espoused in this period. We will see that a major distinction among variants concerns what might be called the "depth of interpretation."

At the shallow end of the continuum, Frieda Fromm-Reichmann (1889–1957), who had been influenced greatly by the ideas of Sullivan, joined with others in recommending modifications in psychoanalytic technique, such as the use of a chair instead of the traditional couch and seeing a patient less often than once a day. She strongly urged her colleagues to consider each patient as a person of his or her actual age and not to insist that the patient must have somehow regressed and become fixated at some infantile stage of development. And along with other analytically oriented therapists, Fromm-Reichmann (1950) desexualized the Oedipus complex into a wish for "closeness" and "tenderness" with one parent while feeling "envious resentment" toward the other.

Near the deep end of the continuum, Marie Sechehaye (1951) believed it is helpful when the therapist participates directly in the psychotic reality of the schizophrenic patient. Instead of necessarily endeavoring to interpret her patients' symbols to them, Sechehaye often used them directly as a means of communicating with them and demonstrating her understanding of their needs. For example, she might present a patient with food to symbolize that she was prepared to gratify the oral needs that had been frustrated early in life. Or perhaps she might offer a patient a book to signify that she realized the patient yearned for definite limits and self-control. In these concrete and symbolic ways, Sechehaye attempted to establish a therapeutically meaningful relationship, although she hoped that eventually she would be able to provide interpretations of this material that her patient would accept.

Although Sechehaye regarded interpretations as necessary during the course of treatment, a view shared by most analysts, Carl Rogers believed that they should be avoided. In his book *Client-Centered Therapy*, Rogers (1951) explained that the aim of the counselor should be to perceive a client's perceptual field and to communicate understanding of it to the client. He believed that his aim is best accomplished through attending to the client's feelings and then clarifying them, which, if done faithfully, precludes a probing, interpretative approach. Rogers further assumed that since the client (supposedly) introduces whatever material comes up in the session, the client will be capable of dealing with it, for otherwise he or she would not have been free to bring it up in the first place. This belief in the capability and strength of the client was the cornerstone of Roger's method: "The counselor chooses to act consistently upon the hypothesis that the individual has a sufficient capacity to deal constructively with all those aspects of his life which can potentially come into awareness" (Rogers, 1951, p. 24).

It is to Rogers' credit that he consistently endeavored to subject his ideas to empirical investigation. A study done by him and his colleagues at the Counseling Center of the University of Chicago (Rogers & Dymond, 1955) indicated some of the changes that occur during a course of psychotherapy. Clients seemed to become more satisfied with themselves, not only in meeting their own standards but also in how they "stack up" against others. Indications of such changes were found in higher correlations between Q sorts for self and ideal self and between self and the "ordinary person." The general trend was for people in therapy to move toward less rigid conceptualizing and more inner comfort, optimism, self-confidence, spontaneity of feelings, and comfortable relations both with others and self.

Rogers (1958) felt that the counselor, as well as the client, gained from the therapeutic relationship. What he had learned from his many clients was that the individual has a propensity for positive growth, the counselor should be genuine in the relationship, the counselor should feel free to try to understand the client, and the facts of scientific inquiry, whatever they might be, are friendly.

In 1957, Rogers accepted a professorship in the departments of psychology and psychiatry at the University of Wisconsin. Part of his purpose in leaving Chicago for Madison was to be able to conduct a research program evaluating the effectiveness of his therapeutic approach with schizophrenic patients. Regardless of the outcome of such a program, Rogerian therapy had now become an internationally recognized and widely adopted form of treatment.

Markedly different from Rogerian therapy was Albert Ellis's (1958) rational-emotive therapy. According to Ellis, neurotic behavior is a product of illogical or irrational assumptions. The job of the very active, rational psychotherapist, then, was to examine the patient's assumptions, to demonstrate that these beliefs are both at the root of disturbed behavior and without any sensible foundation, to persuade the patient to work against neurotic attitudes, and to help substitute new attitudes that will be more serviceable. Ellis reported that his approach was the most effective of any that he had tried.

Let us now look at two additional methods of treatment that made little attempt to deal specifically with unconscious conflicts. George Kelly (1955) described a combination of diagnosis and psychotherapy that he called "fixed-role therapy." The procedure he recommended called for a diagnosis of the person's psychological constructs in significant interpersonal relations by means of responses on the Role Construct Repertory Test (REP). Using the diagnostic information gained from the REP, the counselor prepares a personality sketch of the kind of person the client might reasonably be expected to become if favorable changes occurred. This personality sketch, in particular its development as a possible role to be played for the next several weeks, is discussed with the client. Perhaps after the role has been tailored, the client playacts it with the therapist and then is encouraged to playact it in significant situations outside the counseling sessions. Finally, the client reports to the counselor and discusses the progress made in playing the role, including the feelings aroused while playing it and the responses it seems to elicit from other people. Kelly believed that the client was helped to bring about personality changes that were personally desired through the practice of such a role, and he reported encouraging results from the use of his method.

John Wolpe (1958) advocated a learning-theory-based therapy for neurotics called variously "reciprocal inhibition," "desensitization," and "deconditioning." In essence, it consisted of efforts to elicit responses that would be incompatible with and would thus inhibit the neurotic symptoms. The techniques used by Wolpe and his followers were similar to those used by Watson when he attempted to eliminate fears of furry objects and by Dunlap when he tried to remove habits through negative practice. However, Wolpe's theoretical framework was Hullian.

In desensitization, the therapist listed the patient's anxiety-arousing stimuli from the most to the least feared. After the patient was helped to relax somewhat, either by means of hypnosis or verbal suggestions, the least frightening stimulus on the list was presented. Following this, the next higher up on the list was presented, and so on, until the patient signaled a feeling of distress. Wolpe reported that after a number of similar sessions, the vast majority of his patients, about 90%, became able to tolerate what had previously been the most anxiety-arousing of all the stimuli without any alarm. By treating symptoms alone, and without attempting to ascertain any particular causes for the neurotic behavior, improvements appeared to be obtained (Rachman, 1959).

Before we examine some of the variables and problems that make the evaluation of treatment difficult, we will complete this survey of methods by taking a look at group therapy, which was now more popular than ever. Few professionals still regarded it solely as an expedient, and many preferred it as the treatment of choice for certain kinds of disturbance under certain conditions. One of its leading advocates, Slavson (1951), defined it as "a special application of the principles of individual therapy to two or more persons simultaneously which also brings into the situation the phenomena and problems of interpersonal relations." But this definition did not please everyone, because it made group therapy seem more an extension of individual psychotherapy than a unique method requiring its own distinctive principles and techniques.

Corsini (1957) expressed his belief that the growth in the practice of group therapy might be a reflection of a cultural demand for a treatment procedure that immediately alleviated feelings of being alone and socially isolated. Whatever the reason, there could be no doubt about the growth. During the years from 1931 to 1940, 89 publications concerning group therapy appeared. By 1950, the total was 739, and by 1955, the number rose to 879.

One of the interesting developments in group therapy was the attempt to extend residential treatment to delinquent children (Glueck & Glueck, 1950). This attempt was inspired by the success reported by the psychoanalyst August Aichhorn (1878–1949), who shortly after World War I arranged to have 12 adolescent delinquent boys live together in a house in Vienna. He reasoned that the antisocial behavior of the boys was due, putting it in psychoanalytic terms, to a failure on the part of their egos to integrate the reality principle (i.e., to postpone gratification and to evaluate their environments realistically). These ego weaknesses had led, Aichhorn (1935) believed, to deficiencies in the growth of superego functions—or to put it another way, the boys did not feel guilty after they did something wrong. Consequently, he decided it would be of therapeutic value to allow these boys to gratify their impulses with virtually no restrictions and thus let them experience in full the consequences of their own behavior. At first, the boys responded to their freedom with almost wild destructiveness. But then, receiving no punishment from external sources, they became seemingly depressed and self-reproachful. Following this period of open expressions of sadness, grief, and a sense of worthlessness, they accepted appropriate modes of social behavior and became receptive to reeducation.

Redl and Wineman (1951) tried to use an approach similar to Aichhorn's with severely disturbed, hyperaggressive, preadolescent children in Detroit. Just as in the case of the Viennese boys, there was at first a period of destructiveness. Unfortunately it went on and on. There appeared to be no end to the hatred and the aggression shown by the children, and the professional staff experienced considerable difficulty in dealing with the impulsiveness and lack of emotional control displayed by their charges. Redl and Wineman (1951) concluded that their boys not only had deficient egos but also "solidification of their hatred into an organized department of shrewdly developed defenses" and thus were protected from realizing the moral implications of their behavior. What these boys seemed to need were environmental supports and "a counter-balanced design" to help them perceive their world realistically and maintain self-control in their dealings with it. Moreover, such growth had to take place before the usual therapeutic approaches could even be attempted. How exactly this was to be accomplished was a subject for further investigation and research, for as Redl and Wineman observed, "Our trouble is that we don't know enough about Hate."

Despite admitted gaps in their knowledge, Redl and Wineman and practically all others engaged in residential treatment for children agreed on several basic principles for the construction of a therapeutic milieu. First, the children should be completely protected from any traumatic handling by personnel. Second, they should be provided with gratifications regardless of whether they earned or "deserved" them. Third, there should be tolerance of symptomatic and regressed behavior, although the staff should have techniques for dealing with such behavior in order to prevent the children from harming themselves or others. Fourth, the physical design of the milieu should allow the boys as much freedom as possible; for example, fragile, expensive furnishings should be avoided (Bettelheim, 1950). These principles seemed to make sense, and so whenever possible they were incorporated in the construction of treatment centers, clinics, and mental hospitals and in the policies of these institutions.

Morita therapy, named for Shoma Morita (1874–1952), a Japanese psychiatrist, was widely used in Japan. It was based on the principles of Zen Buddhism (Maupir, 1962). Patients were prompted to stop thinking about themselves and their problems and instead to take an interest in the activities going on in the world about them while maintaining a realistic attitude toward life. Included in this "realism" was an acceptance of the belief that problems and unhappiness are a part of life shared by everyone. Patients were encouraged to recognize that all people must at times live with suffering and that it is best to bear one's troubles with equanimity (Kora & Sato, 1958).

Within the Soviet Union (London, 1953), psychiatric treatment was guided by traditional Pavlovian formulations about conditioning and brain functioning and consisted chiefly of occupational therapy or plain work, physiotherapy, and "active therapy." This last kind of therapy included insulin shock and electroshock, sulphotherapy, and the induction of sleep and relaxation by means of sodium amo-barbital and other drugs. Psychosurgery or leucotomy had been introduced as a procedure in 1947 but was banned 3 years later on grounds that it was un-Soviet, cruel, and ineffective. Psychotherapy, either in a psychoanalytic or a Rogerian form, was not practiced to any considerable extent (Chauncey, 1959).

A vast amount of thoughtful attention and research was devoted to counseling and psychotherapy during the fifties (Shoben, 1956). These efforts succeeded in shedding light on a number of complex variables but, if anything, made the task of evaluating the outcomes of treatment methods appear even more stygian. Individu-als came to be seen as parts of interpersonal systems in which efforts to ameliorate their condition may become disruptive to and elicit resistances from the other members of the network who are dependent on their pathology for the gratification of their own needs. For example, an alcoholic's wife may interfere with rehabilita-tion because her husband's recovery would deprive her of the satisfaction of being a compassionate, long-suffering "mother." If we grant that this can occur, then the following question is raised: In some cases, is the lack of improvement following psychotherapy due, not to defects in the method, but to a failure to take into account (and deal adequately with) the actions of persons of significance to the patient?

The personality of the therapist came to loom ever greater in importance. The therapist's friendliness and genuine interest and concern for the patient were seen to be variables of major significance in helping the patient feel positively toward the treatment relationship. Yet it was found that the therapist's values, usually middle-class values, appeared to prevent full understanding and acceptance of patients with different values. It was recognized that therapists preferred treating people who shared their frame of reference and that they also tended to feel that the well-to-do were most likely to benefit from their help. It now became essential to discover whether a therapist's middle-class cultural biases precluded being able to help to a significant degree those whose status was low but whose need for assistance was undeniable.

At the same time, there was much discussion about the "arousal" value of each person involved in the therapeutic interaction (i.e., the nature and intensity of the feelings the therapist tends to arouse in the patient and of those the patient tends to arouse in the therapist). All therapists could agree that if either party almost imme-diately aroused negative feelings in the other, psychotherapy became more difficult than when the feelings were positive.

Edward Bordin (1950) emphasized the variable of ambiguity-structuredness in the counseling situation. He suggested that counseling can be distinguished from psychotherapy by reference to this factor. At the beginning and during the course of the relationship, the counselor (or therapist) structures the topics appropriate for discussion, the closeness and character of the interactions, and the goals to be attained by means of the sessions. In counseling, as compared with psychotherapy, the relationships tend to be more structured and less ambiguous, the topics dis-cussed more specific and circumscribed, and the goals more limited.

Further, Bordin thought it likely that as the situation becomes more ambiguous, the client is more apt to experience anxiety and to react in a more personal and affective manner. Therefore, if desired, anxiety and the intensity of the transference may be increased by increasing ambiguity. On the other hand, if the client shows evidences of benefiting from the counseling or treatment, the tension and investment can be diminished even more by reducing the ambiguity of the situation.

A cynical view of psychotherapy was offered by the psychiatrist Jules Masserman (1955), who believed that it might actually establish or strengthen what he called "ur-defenses." Ur-defenses were regarded as certain delusions necessary to all humans in order to help them adjust to the harsh realities of life. One such delusion helps people deny the constant threat to their existence and the inevitability of death. Patients, by being seen in therapy, are encouraged to believe that they possess a self that is of value and significance, a self whose momentous effect on the selves of others can reverberate and persist through countless generations. A second ur-defense is the delusion of the omnipotent servant. Patients are led to feel that they must indeed be very worthy and important, since they have at their command the powerful, deeply involved, all-wise, and all-understanding therapist. A third ur-defense is the fiction that people are kind to their fellows. In the unreal world of the therapist's office, an attempt is made to build up the delusion that the patient can hope to find help, warmth, and concern outside the therapeutic milieu similar to what was experienced inside it.

It was one of Masserman's contentions that these false beliefs are fostered by denials on the part of the patient and therapist that their relationship is an economic transaction in which a fee is paid for services rendered. Patients wish to deny the fee so that they can believe more easily that they are persons of worth who would be listened to by the therapist regardless of whether or not they paid money. Therapists deny the fee so that they can see their work as noble, pure, and altruistically motivated, even though they would probably be quite distressed if their clients did not pay their bills.

Not many psychotherapists were aware of Masserman's sardonic analysis of their profession, but nonetheless most gave signs of discomfort when confronted with studies of therapeutic outcomes. The results of a number of investigations indicated that the degree of improvement depended more on the acuteness of onset and the subtype of the illness than on the method of treatment, whether insulin or electroshock or psychotherapy. On the other hand, Lauretta Bender (1956) believed she had found evidence that with brain-damaged children the prognosis and behavior manifestations are far more dependent on the way in which the children are accepted and helped than on the degree, or even the presence, of organic factors.

Kanner and Eisenberg (1955) reported a follow-up study of 63 children with a diagnosis of early infantile autism. Approximately 9 years had elapsed between the time of their original diagnoses and the follow-up evaluations. Thirty-four of the children were then in residential treatment, whereas 29 were still living at home. Of 31 children who had been mute at the age of 5 years, only one showed any improvement. Of 32 children who could speak at least some words at 5 years, 16 showed later improvement. Most discouraging to Kanner and Eisenberg were the signs of disturbance and the need for close supervision even among those children who had made some progress. They noted that none of the various treatments was superior to any other, which in this case meant that all were equally ineffective.

Hans Eysenck (1952a) published the results of his survey of the literature of the effects of psychotherapy. Different investigators had adopted different standards for what they would consider "improvement," with psychoanalysts being more demanding of themselves in this regard than others. Estimates of the percentage of patients who had improved from psychotherapy ranged from 39% to 77%, with 66% a fair average estimate. But it also appeared that anywhere from 66% to 72% of neurotic patients who had had custodial care but no psychotherapy also improved. Therefore, Eysenck concluded, the research failed to justify rejecting the hypothesis that the results of psychotherapy were due to chance or random effects. In other words, whatever supposed "effects" were observed after psychotherapy were probably not uniquely related to the therapy itself.

Eysenck's conclusion touched off an outburst of dismay and indignation. Despite the soundness of many of the objections raised to his survey (e.g., he had unjustifiably combined studies with widely differing frames of reference and patient populations as if they were of equal merit and relevance), the fact remained that the responsibility for demonstrating the effectiveness of psychotherapy rested on those who asserted that it was effective and to date that responsibility had not been fully met. Symptomatic of this was the proposal brought forward to use multiple therapy; two or more therapists would see a single patient, and the patient might play the role of a participant-observer while his or her therapists analyzed one another.

A meeting of some of the leading figures engaged in research in psychotherapy was held in Washington, and a report of that meeting was published by the APA. Rubenstein and Parloff (1959), who summarized the proceedings of the conference, were impressed by the ingenuity of the research designs and methods for investigating the process of psychotherapy. They were puzzled, however, by the glaring absence of any attempt to deal with the issue of its outcome, and they concluded that, despite monumental efforts, "there has been relatively little progress in establishing a firm and substantial body of evidence to support very many research hypotheses."

Zax and Klein (1960), following their review of studies of the measurement of personality and behavior changes during and after psychotherapy, concluded that no relationship had been demonstrated between measures of process or reported concepts of self and the everyday behavior of patients.

In a study based on a survey of the literature up to 1958, Eysenck (1961) was led to an even more forceful conclusion that the one he had reached in 1952: "With the single exception of the psychotherapeutic methods based on learning theory, results of published research with military and civilian neurotics, and with both adults and children, suggest that the therapeutic effects of psychotherapy are small or non-existant."

Thus, by the close of the fifties psychotherapy was being severely criticized and yet simultaneously advocated for a variety of disturbances from infancy through senility. Its proponents were convinced of the worth of their methods despite the lack of any quantitative evidence obtained by adequately controlled research that would support their convictions. Although the burden of demonstrating the effectiveness of psychotherapy rested on them, and although it would have testified to their confidence and their prudence had they tried to provide a thoroughgoing and valid demonstration, those who investigated psychotherapy seemed satisfied with concentrating their efforts on examining antecedent variables and the process itself.

Raimy's (1952) appraisal of psychotherapy was as valid in 1959 as it had been when he earlier observed that "the field of psychotherapy appears to have an enormous but somewhat leaderless vitality." Yet perhaps it would have been more accurate to charge that the field was so heterogeneous and vital that no one person could make a statement that a majority of his or her colleagues would endorse. There were many leaders, yes, but no leader.

Turning to the problem of evaluating the effectiveness of physical methods of treatment, we find a similar situation. After the first wave of enthusiasm for the ataractic drugs had ebbed, it appeared that 65% to 75% of schizophrenic patients remained severely handicapped, a percentage approximately the same as had been reported years earlier during the time of Bleuler. Robert White (1959), in concluding his review, made a statement in reference to a psychotic population that might have been said of the entire spectrum of mental illness:

> Thus we are left with a curious uncertainty concerning what it is that improves chronic hospital patients. One is almost tempted to think of a single scale of improvement on which a patient's position can be bettered by a given unit of chlorpromazine, or L-glutavite, or respect, or structured tasks.

PROFESSIONAL DEVELOPMENT

Each year of this period was marked by growth in numbers, influence, status, and prestige. In 1950, the APA had 7,250 members; in 1959, 16,644. After 1958, there were only two kinds of voting members (fellows and members), and both required a doctoral degree based on a psychological dissertation and continued professional work that was psychological in nature.

During the fiscal year 1952–1953, the U.S. government appropriated $11,000,000 for contracts and grants for psychological research (Young & Odbert, 1960). During the fiscal year 1958–1959, $31,300,000 was appropriated for research in psychology and closely related areas. In 1950, *Psychological Abstracts* took note of 6,563 publications; in 1959, 11,242. The APA journals alone published approximately 870 original articles. The National Institute of Mental Health in 1956 awarded $1,674,664 in graduate training grants for clinical psychology, a sum approximately eight times what was allocated in 1948 (Sanford, 1958).

Further evidence of growth is provided by the increase in legal recognition and status. In 1950 Kentucky passed a certification bill, and in 1951 the Georgia legislature passed a licensure law for psychologists. Also in 1951 Minnesota passed a certification law and the New York legislature passed a licensing bill, subsequently vetoed by Governor Dewey of New York because of strong opposition from the medical profession. Despite the temporary setback in the Empire State, legislation elsewhere marched on: Maine passed a certification law and Tennessee passed a licensure law in 1953; Washington passed a certification law and Arkansas passed a licensure law in 1955; at last New Yorkers had their certification law in 1956; certification followed in California, Florida, New Hampshire, and Maryland in 1957; and Utah passed a certification law in 1959.

The competence of the profession was given legal recognition by the Supreme Court of the State of Michigan when it ruled, as did various other courts, that the testimony of a clinical psychologist on questions of mental illness could be admitted as expert witness testimony.

Judging by their actions, psychiatrists seemed torn by disagreements within their profession over the stance that they should take with regard to the certification of psychologists. Although it had consistently resisted such measures over the years, in 1952 the Council of the American Psychiatric Association passed a resolution favoring the certification of clinical psychologists. But when, in 1957, the American Psychiatric Association rescinded this resolution, understandably enough, relations between the two professions, at least on the formal level, could fairly be said to have become "strained" (Joint Report on Relations Between Psychology & Psychiatry, 1960).

However, psychiatrists were not alone in feeling ambivalent about licensure and certification (Deutsch, 1958). There were psychologists who feared that legislation designed primarily to be applicable to clinicians in private practice might have the effect of restricting or hampering the activities of other psychologists (Tryon, 1963). In order to circumvent such possible discrimination, they urged their colleagues to institute a policy of voluntary certification (i.e., certification by the psychologists themselves rather than by the states), and this policy was adopted in Illinois, Louisiana, Massachusetts, Nebraska, New Jersey, Ohio, Oregon, and West Virginia.

Finally, to close this survey of certification, we should note that the number of states certifying school psychologists had risen from 11 in 1949 to 23 by 1959. Newcomers to the list, in addition to the District of Columbia, were Colorado, Hawaii, Illinois, Indiana, Iowa, Kansas, Massachusetts, Michigan, Missouri, Oklahoma, Oregon, and Rhode Island (Hodges, 1960).

Our review thus far has focused on the increased support and recognition given to psychology by the public. However, one sign of the growth and greater maturity of the profession was the preparation of a code of ethics. As a beginning, in 1951 the APA published a tentatively formulated ethical code for clinical and consulting psychologists (APA Committee on Ethical Standards for Psychology, 1951). In the following years a formulation of the ethical standards that should apply to all forms of practice by psychologists was adopted. This code, of course, was considered subject to continuing revisions and amplifications as demanded by new and changing circumstances (Ethical Standards, 1959).

In 1955 the APA initiated the practice of conferring Gold Medal Awards on those psychologists who had made an outstanding contribution to the science. The first recipient of a Gold Medal Award was Robert Woodworth. A similar honor, the APA's Distinguished Scientific Contribution Award, was bestowed on two clinical psychologists, Carl Rogers (in 1956) and Paul Meehl (in 1958).

The United States had attained incontestable leadership in the profession. In 1952, it was estimated that there were 18,000 psychologists in the United States, 2,500 in England (Summerfield, 1958), 700 in Japan (McGinnies, 1960), and 24 in all South America. In Austria and West Germany in 1953, there were 209 graduate students working for doctorates in psychology at 15 universities (Lehner, 1955). However, neither of these countries had any formulated clinical psychology training program, although some psychologists were functioning as clinicians. In Turkey and the Arab countries, psychology was still almost exclusively an academic discipline (McKinney, 1960). Egypt did have about 40 psychologists, a handful of whom worked as clinicians at an outpatient child and student clinic affiliated with the Institute of Higher Education for Men in Cairo. They used an adaptation of the Binet, and the Egyptian army employed intelligence and aptitude tests. There was some teaching of clinical psychology at the Syrian State University in Damascus. Aside from Egypt and Syria, there was little to report about the profession in the Arab states (Protho & Melikan, 1955).

By 1959, there were approximately 2,000 psychologists in the Japanese Psychological Association. Six centers in Japan were devoted to teaching the Rorschach, a modified version of the TAT was in use, and the method of psychotherapy identified with Carl Rogers was very popular. Great Britain had about 400 clinical psychologists, many of whom expressed interest in the practice of psychotherapy. Clinical psychology appeared to be growing in France, Germany, and elsewhere in Western Europe (David, 1959).

In the United States, there were 56 APA-approved doctoral training programs in clinical psychology and 27 in counseling. During the 4-year period from 1957 to 1960, 3,074 PhDs were awarded in psychology, of which 1,047 were in clinical psychology (Harmon, 1961). ABEPP (1959) diplomas had been awarded to 1,403 psychologists, of whom 965 were clinicians. The Clinical Division of the APA, largest in the association, had 2,736 members.

It was now generally agreed that an internship had to be an integral part of doctoral training for clinical psychologists. Such an internship had to include at least 1 year of supervised experience in a clinical setting treating people demonstrably in need of diagnosis and psychotherapy. Interns were to be given the opportunity to maintain intensive, intimate, long-term contacts with clinical problems. They were to be encouraged and aided in developing professional independence, self-confidence, and facility in communication with the members of allied professions. Their immersion in the vital problems of human begins, in addition to sharpening their clinical skills, was intended to acquaint them with the raw data of a field in which they must be prepared later to undertake relevant, sophisticated research (Raimy, 1950; Foster, Benton, & Rabin, 1952).

At the same time there was a need not only for proficiency but for flexibility.

Clinical psychologists were extending their services in new directions. Some worked closely with neurosurgeons to evaluate the fitness of patients to undergo operations intended to alleviate the symptoms of Parkinson's disease. Some assessed the effects, direct and indirect, of surgical and other medical procedures. Some participated in the training of physicians in comprehensive or humanistic medicine. Some worked in the areas of executive appraisal, leadership counseling, and the analysis of man-machine systems.

But this expansion in vigor and recognition, rather than marking a final stage in the development of clinical psychology, is better seen as marking a phase of its beginning. There was confidence of still much to come, and there was certainty that as clinical psychologists continued to further the growth of their profession, they should be aware of but not constrained by their history. For although a great number of words speak to us from the past, there are other voices that must await our advances before they can be heard.

Lightner Witmer died in 1956. Even his name sounded a bit anachronistic, and so, not surprisingly, his death was for the most part overlooked, as he himself had been, in the forward rush of the profession he had named and amid the celebrations commemorating the centennial of Freud's birth. Yet 50 years before, in the article that introduced the field of clinical psychology, Witmer concluded with words that retained their importance: "But in the final analysis the progress of clinical psychology, as of every other science, will be determined by the value and amount of its contributions to the advancement of the human race" (Witmer, 1907, p. 4).

9

The Oppressive Environment
1960–1969

What can one say about a period in American history in which a young idealistic President is assassinated, a winner of the Nobel Peace Prize and preacher of nonviolence is murdered, a U.S. senator is slain, the United States announces that it is in a war of attrition with North Vietnam, riots and protests sweep the cities and schools, crime increases, communication between the generations appears to break down, withdrawal is recommended as a way of life, and everywhere there seems to be disruption and change?

Some have characterized this period as a time of excessive hope and disappointment, as a time when such tremendous strides were made in so many areas of human rights and human needs that some falling short of expectations was bound to occur. Others have characterized it as a sewer in the stream of history.

The sixties were colored by an air of urgency, by confrontation, by nonnegotiable demands, by hate, by fear, by a feeling of discontinuity with the past and a desperate faith in the future. "War" was used to describe the government's programs to alleviate poverty, its foreign policy vis-à-vis most communist nations, its attempts to reduce crime and drug use. This was the time of A New Frontier, The Great Society, and humankind's giant step forward on the moon. The population was a "bomb," and so was the air and the water. Revolutions were supposed to be occurring in sexual practices, among racial and ethnic minority groups, among women, in psychiatry, in religion, and throughout the culture—from hair styles to music to language to art to dancing to attitudes. "Make Love, Not War," said one popular bumper sticker. "Due to Lack of Interest, Tomorrow Has Been Canceled," said another. "Turn On, Tune In, and Drop Out," said a third.

The author of that last slogan was Timothy Leary, once a respected clinical psychologist and scholar at Harvard University's Center for Research in Personality. Leary was dismissed from that position after his enthusiasm for and encouragement of the use of LSD made his judgment suspect, and he soon developed into a kind of Pied Piper of drugs, touting their mind-expanding, mind-blowing, quasi-religious properties. By 1966 he had attained such notoriety that he was summoned to testify before the Senate Subcommittee on Juvenile Delinquency, and shortly thereafter he was arrested on charges of illegally possessing marijuana (Sann, 1967).

Leary was not the only clinician to become a public figure. Two books by Haim Ginott, *Between Parent and Child* and *Between Parent and Teenager*, made the best-seller list and sold in the hundreds of thousands of copies. Both books engagingly revealed to parents how to talk with their children. And a book by Rollo May, *Love and Will*, was highly popular. Clinicians were also gaining publicity through the success of *Psychology Today*, a magazine that featured entertaining and informative articles about psychology.

Yet these popular successes may also be viewed as indicative of the widespread discontent that afflicted this country. People hungered for meaningful, honest communication. They wanted their loneliness reduced. They wanted answers, and not from their parents or elders but from the experts—and many were not even sure about them. Suspicion and mistrust of the establishment, old values, authority, the administration, the police, the armed forces, the FBI, the CIA, the haves, the ins, and those in power was rampant.

Fired by the civil rights movement, a host of minorities (Puerto Ricans, Chicanos, Indians, feminists, the physically handicapped, and homosexuals) organized to protest their grievances. Some American psychologists were party to these grievances, many more were sympathetic to them, and efforts were made by the APA to see that they were redressed. Policies of "equal opportunity" or "reverse discrimination" were encouraged, and graduate schools and faculties were exhorted to make special efforts to recruit women and members of minority groups as graduate students and faculty so as to increase their representation within psychology.

The Association of Black Psychologists was formed in 1968 to exert pressure on the APA to become more involved in remedying the problems of racism. That year was one of the first in which the convention meetings of the APA were disrupted by protesters of one kind or another who objected to what scheduled speakers might say. The APA canceled its 1969 convention in Chicago, holding it in Washington instead, because many of the members were outraged by reports of police brutality in Chicago at the 1968 Democratic National Convention. Further, the APA announced that its 1969 convention would have a theme: "Psychology and the Problems of Society."

In this atmosphere, it is not surprising that psychological tests were attacked for their invasion of privacy, condemned for their discriminatory impartiality, and ridiculed for their irrelevance. In the *New York Times*, psychoanalysis was said to be dying, the death of God was announced on the cover of *Time* magazine, and there appeared to be renewed interest in astrology, fortune-telling, mediums, and mysticism.

A third revolution was announced in psychiatry. The first had been the humanitarian reforms of Pinel. Psychoanalysis was the second. The third seemed harder to pin down, because so much was going on at once. Some said it was humanism. Others said it was behaviorism. A few thought it was primal therapy. Many considered it to be community psychiatry or psychology (Bellak, 1964).

On October 31, 1963, The Community Mental Health Centers Act was passed. This piece of legislation provided federal support for the establishment of community mental health centers, which were to offer primarily outpatient mental health services to communities of 200,000 or less. Within 4 years, there were almost 300 centers located in 45 states. There was the expectation and the hope that by 1980 there would be 2,000.

These centers were required, if they were to receive federal funding, to provide a certain mix of services: inpatient facilities for brief periods of hospitalization; outpatient services for children and adults; crisis intervention, preferably on a round-the-clock basis; outreach programs, so as to make the center accessible to clients who otherwise might not avail themselves of it; day-care programs, so that patients who might have been excluded from the community could be maintained within it; drug and alcoholism clinics, intended to deal with drug and alcohol abuse; consultation services, whose purpose was to change policies and practices in agencies, schools, and the community and thus reduce the prevalence of psychological disorders; after-care, so that those discharged from a mental hospital could remain within the community; and research or a continuing assessment of effectiveness.

Implicit in the establishment of community mental health centers were criticisms of previous programs and practices. For example, previous programs were claimed to be restricted to the middle and upper classes, officebound and aloof from the community, insensitive to the fact that people could be harmed by long periods of hospitalization and prolonged psychotherapy, preoccupied with the individual client, neglectful of social issues, and fragmented and disorganized in approach. The community mental health centers were supposed to change all that. They were to offer continuity of care (from childhood through adulthood, assuming the person did not leave the community), vigorous involvement in and responsiveness to the issues and needs of the day, and services based on confidence in the resilience of human beings. But what if people varied in their resilience? What if the anguish of the hard-to-reach was promoted by such mundane matters as poor food and inadequate housing? What if the establishment that was supposed to be favorably influenced by consultative services did not appear to be touched by them? What then?

NORMAL PERSONALITY FUNCTIONING

Psychoanalysis occupied an established position among the personality theories. Despite the fact that it was constantly changing and assimilating the research findings and the views of many innovators and critics, it represented tradition and a bedrock of theory concerning psychosexual, instinctual, and intrapsychic phenomena. It was attacked by behaviorists for being mentalistic, stodgy, unresponsive to the problems posed by psychotics and retardates, and pessimistic about the changes that people might undergo after brief periods of intervention. Its belief in the importance of unconscious motivation, the irrational, and infantile experiences was challenged not only by behaviorists but by humanists and by psychoanalysts themselves.

Humanists such as Abraham Maslow, Rollo May, Carl Rogers, and Fritz Perls criticized psychoanalysis for emphasizing negative aspects of personality. They insisted a strong case could be made that constructive, reparative, self-actualizing forces existed in the individual. People have a need to grow, to realize potential, to become all that they are capable of becoming. This was supposed to be true of everyone, and hence every person might be assisted in the process of growth. Psychiatric and psychological services were to be thought of as open to all who might wish to move forward in their development and to become more and more aware of their experiences and themselves.

Unfortunately, people, ordinary normal people, were cut off from one another and themselves. They were not fully aware of their bodies, their sensitivities, their feelings, and the joys they might experience by being touched, both literally and figuratively, by those around them. They could heighten their awareness and become more whole, more alive, by making themselves accessible to any and every experience. A slogan of the movement—and the humanists referred to themselves as a movement in the same way that many behaviorists regarded themselves as a movement and many analysts had felt they were involved in a crusade years before—was attributed to Perls: "Lose your mind and come to your senses." (Compare this slogan with Rousseau's emphasis on feelings over reason.)

Unlike psychoanalysis, which extolled secondary process thinking and which regarded instincts as forces to be inhibited and brought under rational control, the tenor of humanism and behaviorism at this time was decidedly emotional and anti-intellectual. The former glorified spontaneity, natural expression, the beneficial effects of catharsis ("Let it all hang out!") and acting on impulse and intuition. The latter movement tried to proceed without giving undue attention to mental functioning and emphasized environmental manipulations instead (Reisman, 1974).

Both behaviorism and humanism stressed the importance of trusting a person's conscious motivation and striving. Their faith in intention, in people doing what they set out to do, was reminiscent of William James's confidence in the will and the simplicity and straightforwardness of his belief in conscious motivation. They made little mention of resistance, of people failing to do as they were asked, of missed appointments and the persistence of undesirable behaviors. Instead they had a deep trust in the modifiability and responsiveness of people, the pleasure to be derived from small gains and triumphs, and the deliberate creation of services that required limited goals and brief, intense involvements, a trust that meshed beautifully with the needs of an alienated, rootless society intent on exploring inner space.

This would have been a perfect time for the rediscovery of Otto Rank and his ideas, but there appeared to be little interest among psychologists and their students in history, including the "dark ages" of 30 years ago. This was a relatively ahistorical period that emphasized the present and the future. "Autonomy and individuation," "doing your own thing," "I am I, and you are you" were frequent themes in the literature and discussions of the sixties, but it was rare to find them associated with Rank.

The developments in psychoanalysis seemed relatively minor and measured in comparison to the information explosion and frenetic activities going on around it. A year's worth of *Psychological Abstracts* contained about 1,000 pages at the beginning of the decade and about 3,000 pages toward its end. Yet psychoanalytic theory was still largely Freudian, although slightly modified and extended by Erikson and others. Freud had written so much that it was rumored half-seriously he had jotted down both sides of every issue he had ever considered. In truth, he could be quoted in support of a variety of views, and when read he remained brilliantly timely, insightful, and cogent. The major criticism concerned what he had failed to write.

Erikson's ideas were given wide currency. The concept of identity and the need of the individual to acquire a sense of who he or she uniquely is was much discussed. It seemed to Kenneth Keniston (1968) that this was such a problem in American society that a new, prolonged stage in human development had emerged, a stage between adolescence and adulthood in which young people who ambivalently questioned the values and beliefs of previous generations groped for years toward their own convictions. He called this stage "youth."

The very concept of stages of development increased in importance. The failure of children raised in orphanages and institutional settings to display feelings of trust and affection for others, reports by Harlow (1962) that his monkeys deprived of mothering grew to be socially and sexually inept, the difficulties encountered in overcoming early handicaps in language acquisition, and research on imprinting all suggested that there are critical stages or periods in growth when certain kinds of learning are most propitious. Moreover, the concept of stages of development had two major implications for psychoanalysis that made it more compatible with the *Zeitgeist*: (1) stages implied temporary disruptions and crises in development that were to be regarded as relatively normal and readily alleviated, and (2) stages implied conflicts of the moment that might be situationally influenced and relieved by environmental manipulations.

Jean Piaget's theory of children's intellectual development was a stage theory. Although burdened (or blessed) with an extensive nomenclature, Piaget's theory attracted great interest because it was richly illustrated with observations of children's mental activities, because it emphasized their explorations and constructions of knowledge, and because at the same time the federal government of the United States was spending considerable sums of money to back research and programs in early childhood education. Federal involvement in this area was prompted by arguments that early childhood deprivations were responsible for the subsequent lower performances of black children in intelligence and achievement tests and their lack of success in academic careers. If compensatory educational experiences could be provided, it was argued, then perhaps these children would do better in school, get better jobs, live in better neighborhoods, and thus help break the cycle of poverty and racism.

All of this was probably of secondary interest to Piaget, who lived in Switzerland and had little sympathy for attempts to accelerate the development of children. He and his colleagues described in great detail a sequence of stages in the child's perception of volume, space, number, and so on. The sensorimotor stage corresponded to infancy and consisted of the child's learning that certain actions are associated with certain effects and that things continue to exist even when they are not seen. This is followed by the preoperational stage, which roughly covers the period from 2 to 7 years. During this time the child tends to assume causality and relationship among closely associated events and becomes more aware of other people and of the need to take their feelings and wishes into account. Of course, by the end of the preoperational stage the child has begun to learn to manipulate symbols, as evidenced by the acquisition of reading and arithmetic skills.

From 7 to 11 years, or thereabouts, is the concrete operational stage. Concepts of time, constancy, and reversibility are grasped but often only through demonstrations and actual examples. The formal operations stage extends from about 11 years through adulthood. Here the person becomes capable of mentally shuffling abstract symbols, deriving hypotheses and implications, predicting future events, and considering extenuating circumstances. These stages give only a hint of the complexity of Piaget's observations, descriptions, and terminology, and it is difficult to convey how much hope and excitement were generated by them (Maier, 1965).

Surely, it was thought, Piaget's theory could be put to work in improving preschool education, preventing failures in school by teaching concepts such as conservation of mass, and eliminating the biases of traditional intelligence scales by having scales that assessed the stage of the child's mental development. Much hope was indeed raised, but it was little encouraged by Piaget. He continued his prodigious research and writing, with their implication that personality characteristics are a function of the person's intellectual ability to organize experiences.

Although stage theories are essentially descriptions, they can provide an illusion of greater understanding than may be justified, in the same way that naming something gives a feeling of being able to control it. Certainly there were many in the United States who sought to increase their understanding of infants and children by struggling gallantly with the books by Piaget and the books about him.

In stark contrast to Piaget's theory were the views of Jerome Bruner. Bruner asserted that "any idea or problem or body of knowledge can be presented in a form simple enough so that any particular learner can understand it in a recognizable form" (quote from Sprinthall & Sprinthall, 1974, p. 219). All children, according to Bruner, have curiosity, a wish to be competent, and a need to work cooperatively with others. These are intrinsic motivations, but they can be "turned off" if the level of work is not appropriate. When the learning task is too difficult, the child becomes discouraged and confused; when too simple, the child becomes bored and is not involved. This means that the teacher must present the work at a level that is challenging and rewarding for the child. With young children, actions and physical demonstrations are frequently the best way to present material. This would include what Bandura (1971) called "modeling" the behavior that you wish the child to acquire. As children become older, material might better be presented through images and diagrams and eventually through verbal explanations.

If Bruner was correct, a great burden lay on the inventiveness and skill of the teacher. Nonetheless, many educators were inspired by his position. It was cer-

tainly compatible with the aims of federally funded compensatory educational programs and with what teachers presumably should have been doing anyway. The
"catch" lay in determining the appropriate means of presentation and whether
people would agree that the simplified form was still recognizable as the original
concept (Sprinthall & Sprinthall, 1974).

When looked at from a broad perspective, it is possible to conceive of Bruner's
suggestions within the context of *expectations*. People approach tasks with certain
expectations, including expectations regarding the level of difficulty. If the work
proves to be more complex and burdensome than they expected, they may feel the
impossible is being demanded of them and may thus avoid the situation. Yet if the
work is easier than expected, they may find it tiresome and demeaning. An additional complication is that, according to theorists such as David McClelland (1961)
and Leon Festinger (1957), people strive to reduce discrepancies between what
they expect and what actually occurs, though minor discrepancies were thought by
McClelland to add spice to life. This would suggest that if people expect a difficult
(easy) task that is actually easy (difficult), they may achieve consistency or reduce
cognitive dissonance by thinking of themselves as more clever (dumb) than they
did before.

Expectations and the striving of people to make their perceptions consistent
with their expectations was a dominant theme in the literature. Robert Rosenthal
(1967; Rosenthal & Jacobson, 1968) emphasized the significance of expectancy
effects when expectations were held by teachers and scientific investigators. Much
attention was given to a study of his in which teachers were told at the beginning of
the school year that certain of their pupils (randomly identified by the researchers)
would soon experience a growth spurt. Not only were these pupils favorably regarded by their teachers, but they did evidence greater gains in academic performance and IQ than their peers. Moreover, children who did show gains but had not
been identified by the researchers were denigrated by their teachers. Presumably
the self-concepts of children would be affected by how they were handled by their
teachers, and they would continue to show the effects, expecting more or less of
themselves and thus encouraging teachers to expect more or less of them, and so
on, in a vicious or benign circle, depending on whether the halo was positive or
negative.

Although Rosenthal's work was criticized because the effects he found were not
readily duplicated, the attitude seemed to be that the implications of his work were
so great that it would be better to try to prevent such effects than worry about
whether they could ever be reproduced. Even if they weren't reproducible, they
seemed reasonable.

This line of research fit into the concern about the many children, especially
black, lower-class children, who did not do well in school. Carried into adulthood,
the negative concepts that these children were thought to have of themselves,
reinforced by failure in school and low appraisals and expectations of teachers,
would constitute a handicap in becoming gainfully employed.

However, another line of research into expectations was more closely tied to
adult experiences. This had to do with the locus of control, and it was aided by

Rotter's (1966) development of a measure of this dimension (the I-E Scale). Some people, it was thought, expected rewards and punishments to come as a direct result of their own efforts (internal control), whereas others believed that what they did made little difference and that their gains and losses were determined by external forces, whims, fate, and chance (external control). A number of studies were done to show that the poor tended to feel externally controlled and that raising them from poverty would be complicated by their sense of futility and their general expectation that hard work was not always rewarded.

As one surveyed the scene in the United States of the sixties, it was not difficult to see why many people might reasonably feel externally controlled. Violence that fell on the innocent filled each day's newspaper, international crises that promised a nuclear holocaust would occur because of a wall built in Berlin or missile launching sites constructed in Cuba, government programs and promises would dangle precariously and then be withdrawn or gush forth funds, automation and the formation of conglomerates threatened jobs, the draft seemed capricious and unfair, and disruptions and heated challenges to established ways of doing things sprang up everywhere.

So many Americans felt alone and struggled desperately to find themselves and a meaning for their lives—the beat generation, the hippies, the yippies, the flower children, the drug freaks, the Jesus freaks—that some psychologists and psychiatrists, notably Viktor Frankl (1960), saw a basic motivational force in human beings driving them to find their own meaning in life (Hall, 1968). But others wondered if the nuclear family structure and the environment, with its rapid changes, were not playing major roles in fostering this concern.

Erikson had spoken about identity, and many were familiar with the concept. However, it was less often mentioned that Erikson believed a sense of continuity, a feeling of being united with one's past and having come to grips with its values, was essential for establishing one's identity.

Rank had made the drive to achieve a sense of autonomy or individuality central to his theory. Yet he believed the ideal person was not only capable of standing alone but was capable of accepting the ideas and wishes of others without feeling threatened. The existentialists emphasized self-awareness and responsibility. However, they also thought of people existing within a context. When this context, this network of significant social relationships, was lost, then a person's identity would be gravely threatened and much anxiety would be experienced.

Adler had seen people striving for mastery and feelings of adequacy to compensate for their feelings of inferiority. But he thought that seeking superiority was a meaningless pursuit and that people were best advised to enrich themselves by giving of themselves to others. And Freud, when asked to give his criteria of normality, implied a social context in casually remarking that the normal person is one who loves and works well.

What psychologists and psychiatrists had been trying to say for 30 or 40 years was that a person could not find a place in the sun by moving away from everyone else or climbing over their bodies to get there. Rather the individual had to be at peace with the past, had to join responsibly, intimately, and considerately with others in the present, and had to possess a sense of purpose or direction in the future. Somehow, in all the din, part of this message was being lost.

DIAGNOSTIC TECHNIQUES

A variety of external forces in the United States greatly influenced the development of diagnostic techniques. Concerns about civil rights and the rights of the individual to privacy made suspect intelligence and personality assessments. The MMPI was severely criticized as a screening device because some of its items inquired about religious beliefs and sexual practices. Although assurances were given to congressional committees that responses to specific MMPI questions were not deemed significant, the possibility remained that they could be misused, and it was true that some clinicians regarded responses to certain of the questions as of special diagnostic importance (Anastasi, 1967).

The entire November 1965 issue of the *American Psychologist* was devoted to attacks on psychological testing and statements in its defense. According to John W. Macy, Jr., chairperson of the U.S. Civil Service Commission, "present personality tests and inventories to not justify use as selection methods" and therefore would no longer be used in determining civil service positions.

Many psychologists, for a number of different reasons, joined in these attacks. Some had never seen the value of certain assessment devices, and now their opinions were being given a respectful hearing and much publicity. A concerted body of criticism by behaviorists was directed at projective techniques in particular. The Rorschach, the TAT, and figure drawings had no obvious relationship to what they were supposed to measure. In the thirties and forties that had been considered one of their major strengths. By the sixties it was viewed as one of their major weaknesses (Rabin & Hurley, 1964).

As might have been expected, behaviorists had little patience with instruments intended to measure, by subtle and indirect means, unconscious conflicts, defense mechanisms, and responsiveness to stress (Goldberg, 1965). They suggested that if psychologists desired to assess a specific personality characteristic, this could be done best by developing measures for just that characteristic. For example, if psychologists desired to measure anxiety, then specific scales could be employed for that purpose or physiological indices (e.g., galvanic skin response, pulse rate, and respiration) could be recorded under appropriate conditions (Greenspoon & Gersten, 1967).

Further, behaviorists urged that, insofar as possible, people's behavior should be observed and assessed in natural settings. Of special interest, according to them, would be the identification of those behaviors that were to be increased or decreased in frequency (controlled) and the determination of the stimuli or conditions that would be effective in modifying those behaviors (a "functional analysis" of behavior).

Behaviorists were taking potshots at "traditional" and "establishment" procedures, (after all, the validity of projective techniques had been debated for over 20 years), and many of their targets retreated under the fire. In relatively short order, their views became influential among students and in the design of graduate school curricula. In many departments offering clinical psychology, the teaching of projective techniques was deemphasized or entirely eliminated, a situation that would have seemed inconceivable in the forties but that a psychologist who had lived through the twenties might have found oddly familiar.

Whether out of an expression of broadened interests or out of self-defense (no doubt, its action was overdetermined) the *Journal of Projective Techniques* changed its name to the *Journal of Personality Assessment* in 1963. There was still a feeling of optimism while Kennedy was president, but that soon changed. No cow was sacred, and soon abuse was piled on the relatively inviolate intelligence scale with its magic scores, the IQs.

Intelligence scales were denounced because they had often failed to include minority groups in their standardization samples. Since it would not have made much difference if there had been proportionate representation of racial and ethnic groups in such samples, they were also criticized because the ghetto child or adult was being compared with an advantaged group. When such comparisons were made, it was alleged the disadvantaged were discriminated against in schooling and hiring. Children who scored low on these tests were thrown into ungraded or special classes, where education was inferior. Adults who scored low were refused employment.

No comparison need be unfair so long as people are clear about what it is they are comparing. What can be unfair are the conclusions and actions based on the comparisons. To conclude that racial inferiority existed on the basis of mean IQ differences between races in the United States was not justified, nor was it justified to use these scores as a reason to further deprive low-scoring children and adults. However, it also makes no sense to pretend a problem no longer exists by ridding oneself of the means by which the problem can be identified. In the sixties that also was done.

New York City discontinued the use of group intelligence tests within its school system, and this approach to reducing racial biases was adopted by several other cities. Civil rights groups, parent groups, and liberal organizations were against psychological testing because they perceived it as an assault on individual privacy and as a violation of the right to due process and the right not to incriminate oneself. What made this so ironic was that intelligence testing began as a way to counter the biases of teachers. The early reports of its use contained case after case of children who had been thought to be retarded but were found instead to be gifted. As a result, it was regarded as a democratic procedure. It identified abilities and achievements regardless of race, religion, class membership, or what have you. In many quarters, its lack of discrimination was judged to be its major liability.

One might think from all this that testers were mainly engaged in seeking safe places to hide. To the contrary, although embattled, they continued to be productive, and strangely enough some of the reasons for their productivity were related to the reasons for their harassment.

A primary concern of the civil rights movement was breaking the cycle of poverty, and one means for accomplishing this was by early childhood education. With special attention directed to preschool-age children, there was a renewed effort to develop measures of intellectual functioning to assist in the assessment of enrichment programs. An individually administered scale, the Wechsler Preschool and Primary Scale of Intelligence (WPPSI), was introduced in 1967.

In the manual for the WPPSI, Wechsler (1967) took a stand against Piaget's theory by presuming that "mental abilities are continuous and not disparate, and that consequently one can use the same or similar tasks in appraising them." By that Wechsler meant to indicate the WPPSI had the same structure as the WISC and WAIS. Of equal interest to test users was that his sample consisted of children between the ages of 4 and 6½ who were both white and nonwhite.

Two years later the Bayley Scales of Infant Development (BSID) were introduced. These scales had been standardized on 1,262 children 2 to 30 months old who were supposed to be representative of the U.S. population within this age range. The test contained a mental scale, which gave a mental development index as its score; a motor scale, which yielded a psychomotor development index; and an infant behavior record, which had rating scales of the child's attitudes, interests, emotions, and energy (Bayley, 1969). Much was expected from the BSID, since previous infant scales, the Gesell and Cattell, had been standardized 30 to 40 years before and had been found to be of low reliability.

The question of why children do not do well in school had long been asked but seldom with such urgency. Witmer and the psychologists of his day had considered mental retardation and learning disabilities of many kinds. It may be recalled that in one of Witmer's early cases, the child had been helped by being fitted with glasses. Later, unconscious conflicts and emotional disturbances were thought to be responsible for many school problems. The pendulum was now swinging back to physical or organic etiologies.

Within a short time, children having difficulties with reading and arithmetic—children who might earlier have been judged emotionally disturbed underachievers—were diagnosed as having minimal brain damage or minimal brain dysfunction or perceptual handicaps or learning disabilities or learning handicaps or dyslexia. Often this was diagnosis by exclusion. The child had a learning problem. That seemed certain. But the etiology of the problem was less certain, and some etiologies were not as easily accepted as others. That also seemed certain. Learning disabilities were not offensive and helped put the problem and the child in a sympathetic light. Therefore, they were sometimes diagnosed because no other diagnosis was indicated.

Theoretically, a disorder in the central nervous system could be manifested in almost any conceivable deficiency on any psychological test. Accordingly, scatter on the WISC or poor performance on the Bender-Gestalt was not necessarily due to a learning disability. Yet these tests might not adequately pick out the particular area of the handicap. Therefore, additional tests were developed whose major purpose was to assess skills essential to reading. Three of these tests were the Minnesota Percepto-Diagnostic Test, the Frostig Test of Visual Development, and the Illinois Test of Psycholinguistic Abilities (ITPA).

The Minnesota Percepto-Diagnostic Test was introduced in 1963 and restandardized in 1967 with children ranging in age from 5 to 18. It required that the person draw a few of the Bender-Gestalt designs. Each design had the same series of different figure-ground relationships brought about by varying the shape of the card on which the design was reproduced (e.g., a rectangular and diamond-shaped card). Based on how much the child rotated drawings of the designs, the test was supposed to distinguish among normal children, emotionally disturbed children, and children with reading problems having a physical or an organic component (Fuller & Laird, 1963).

Both the Frostig and the ITPA were not intended to be of use in diagnosing brain damage but instead were purported to sample important abilities and determine the degree to which children had these abilities. Further, their results were tied to remedial programs and specific education recommendations. Whether any deficiencies they uncovered were due to brain damage was a moot point. However, it was believed that such deficiencies were probably related to difficulties in school, especially reading difficulties, and that their alleviation might very well contribute to academic success.

Both tests were standardized on local samples of preschool and early school-age children. The Frostig (Frostig & Horne, 1964) could be individually or group administered and had subtests of motor coordination, figure-ground discrimination, and perception of reversals. The ITPA (Kirk, McCarthy, & Kirk, 1968) was an elaborate, individually administered procedure based on Osgood's theory of communication. Accordingly, the linguistic process was divided into (1) making sense of incoming information (decoding), (2) organizing and integrating the information (organizing), and (3) expressing ideas in some form of communication (encoding). Several subtests were developed as measures of these processes: auditory and visual reception (decoding); auditory-vocal and visual-motor association (organizing); and verbal and manual expression (encoding). This was perhaps the most sophisticated psychological test of learning disabilities, certainly one of the most demanding and time-consuming to administer, and it created a great stir of excitement in the fields of clinical child psychology and special education.

Ralph Reitan had assembled a battery of tests, including the WISC or WAIS, as a means to identify the location of brain injury in children and adults. The Reitan battery attracted much interest, but little notice seemed given to a simple instrument developed by Tien (1960), the Organic Integrity Test. This consisted of 10 sets of three colored pictures each. The testee was shown the first picture and then had to select which of the other two matched it. In each set, one of the pictures shared the same color and one shared the same shape or form with the standard (e.g., a yellow hat, a yellow dog, and a red cap). Presumably matching on the basis of color is more primitive than on the basis of form, and organics were reported to differ significantly from normals on that basis.

Another test that appeared to receive a somewhat disappointing response from clinicians was the Holtzman Inkblot Technique (Holtzman, Thorpe, Swartz, & Herron, 1961). The Holtzman was designed to answer many of the criticisms that had been directed at the Rorschach. It had two equivalent forms so that, in retesting, familiarity was less of a problem. There were 45 cards in each form, and the testee was required to give one response to each card. This controlled the number of responses in a record and should have enhanced the appeal of the test as a research instrument. Further, the scoring was clearly defined and norms were provided. The problem seemed to be that clinicians who were fond of the Rorschach remained loyal to that instrument, whereas those who were not fond of the Rorschach were not especially drawn to the Holtzman.

Although subjected to an enormous amount of criticism, the Rorschach remained an exceptionally popular test. Buros (1970), in a review of personality tests, estimated there were 379 in print in the United States during the latter part of the sixties. Of this number, 296 were nonprojective and 83 were projective. Yet projective tests were extensively used and continued to be heavily researched. The Rorschach was far and away the instrument about which most had been written, but the MMPI was rapidly narrowing that lead. Other personality tests that had stimulated considerable research were the TAT, the Edwards Personal Preference Schedule, the Allport-Vernon-Lindzey Study of Values, the Bender-Gestalt, Raymond Cattell's 16 Personality Factors, and Gough's California Psychological Inventory (Lanyon & Goodstein, 1971).

In the field of psychological testing in general, public and professional criticisms did not appear to slacken the pace of growth. Each edition of Buros's *Mental Measurements Yearbook* was a thick, ponderous volume that did not supplant but supplemented the editions which preceded it. The seventh edition in fact was composed of two volumes. There were 957 tests listed in the fifth edition, 1,219 tests in the sixth, and 1,157 tests in the seventh. About 50% of the tests in the seventh edition were new, about 39% were revisions, and only about 6% were "old." Psychological testing, although under fire, seemed to be wearing a thick, protective coating.

DIAGNOSTIC FORMULATIONS

The continued use of "old" tests and "old" ideas may have been a comfort to some clinicians, but it was an extreme irritant to others. Seldom in the history of clinical psychology had criticism been so incessant, and rarely had it sought to bring about nothing less than capitulation. In previous generations there seemed to have been room for mutual respect. During the sixties, lines were sharply drawn and each side portrayed the other as not only in error but as malicious and destructive. In those circumstances, compromise and tolerance were unthinkable. These were wars of annihilation in which many traditional beliefs had to go.

In 1960 Thomas Szasz, a psychiatrist, published an article entitled "The Myth of Mental Illness" in the *American Psychologist*. Szasz argued that most psychiatric disorders are expressive of "problems in living" and are not due to diseases or chemical imbalances in the brain. To treat many of these disorders by physical, surgical, or drug therapies was to perpetrate a fraud that concealed the real problem from both the practitioner and the public. It had been a long time, perhaps 20 years, since any psychiatrist had argued so forcefully on this issue, and clinical psychologists were most eager to join in.

Variations of this theme, that the medical model (disease or illness model) of abnormal behaviors found in psychiatric and abnormal psychology texts was wrong or out of date, appeared repeatedly throughout the decade. Putting people into mental hospitals in and of itself can be a matter of grave consequences, for it places them in a situation where they are expected to act like patients. Any assertiveness and independence will be discouraged by staff members, who prefer to deal with helpless, dependent patients. People in the mental hospitals soon learn what behaviors are expected, and many of them try to act accordingly, that is, admit being ill and in need of help, comply with the hospital rules and regulations, confess weaknesses, and behave in a crazy or sick fashion.

Schizophrenia was derided as a "put-on," because many of its symptoms could be acquired and extinguished in accordance with the principles of learning. This was true not only for schizophrenia but also for mental retardation and a host of other disorders. Behaviors that seemed to be intrinsic to a disorder could be modified. As a result, it was suggested that the concept of almost every psychiatric disturbance be held in abeyance until its essential nature could be determined. In the meantime it would be best to think of mental disturbances as simply collections of behaviors and do away with diagnostic labels.

Diagnoses were denounced by humanists as a screen that interfered with relating to the person as a human being. They were denounced by behaviorists as arbitrary, inconsistent, meaningless abstractions that gave no real understanding of the treatment to be used. And they were condemned by almost everyone because there were indications they might be misused in assigning lower-class patients to somatic forms of therapy.

In books and movies (e.g., *One Flew Over the Cuckoo's Nest* and *A Fine Madness*), the suggestion was made that mental health professionals would stop at nothing, including psychosurgery, to squelch individuality and ensure conformity within their domains. The patient was portrayed as the victim of a system, a lunatic society that drove its more sensitive members to rebellion and then cast them into mental hospitals, where vindictive psychiatrists and nurses lay in wait.

A psychological (behavioral, social learning theory) model was advocated as a replacement for the medical. Of course it was acknowledged that there were brain disorders and physical disorders that resulted in anomalies in behavior. However, it was argued, as Albee (1968) put it, "that most disturbed behavior consists of learned operant anxiety-avoiding responses."

Incredibly, during this time some psychologists were working assiduously to have psychological services covered by health insurance. Moreover, evidence was accumulating in favor of constitutional components in a number of psychiatric disorders. Although the genetic determination of schizophrenia was not as strong as Kallmann had suggested, study after study in this area gave support to the conclusion reached by the psychiatrist Kringlen (1966): "The more accurate and careful the sampling, the lower the concordance figures. . . . These concordance rates support a genetic factor in the etiology of schizophrenia; however, the genetic factor does not play as great a role as had been assumed."

Buss and Lang (1965) reviewed the research on schizophrenia and believed it pointed to a defect in attention. Schizophrenics seemed to have great difficulty in inhibiting irrelevant or interfering stimuli and maintaining concentration on a task or on what they were trying to communicate. The results of these disruptions were impaired performance and peculiar speech, particularly for chronic (process) schizophrenics, paranoids, and recent first admissions. They thought the psychological deficit pointed to some problem in the reticular activating system.

A similar disorder was suggested for children who were diagnosed as early infantile autistics. Many studies indicated these children and those diagnosed as schizophrenic during childhood had a poor prognosis, especially the more severe their condition seemed to be. The refractoriness of these children to treatment and the severity of their problems made a growing number of professionals think some organic or physical factor was involved in the etiology and that psychodynamic explanations that implicated the parents were unfounded.

For those who favored organic explanations, new breakthroughs always seemed to be in the offing. Biochemists were constantly making discoveries that appeared to have significance for human behavior. Refinements in genetic techniques led to such startling findings as the presence of an extra male chromosome in a greater number of male criminals than would have been expected. The anthropologist Ashley Montagu (1968) supposed that the Y (or male) chromosome might somehow possess an aggressiveness potential, although he undoubtedly would have been among the first to acknowledge the validity of Hirsch's (1967) statement: "The expression of any gene depends upon both the prevailing genetic background and the prevailing environmental conditions."

But this did not seem to be a decade for sober statements and qualifications. The emphasis was on the exciting, the sensational, the innovative. Enthusiasm and personal endorsements carried much weight, and a failure to share the enthusiasm marked one as old-fashioned. Conservativism, traditionalism, and differing attitudes toward youths, minority groups, the poor, and the disadvantaged, although often unspoken, frequently smoldered and flared and made disagreements bitter and ugly.

Anna Freud (1965) had offered a psychoanalytic scheme for diagnosing a child according to the child's development along various "lines," such as psychosexual and psychosocial development and relationship forming, play, and impulse control. This scheme had virtually no impact outside analytic circles. The American Psychiatric Association introduced a new nomenclature (Committee on Nomenclature and Statistics, 1968) that had some peculiar features. Runaway reaction (it was estimated there were about 1,000,000 runaways in the United States in 1972) was a disorder but early infantile autism was not. There was a "maladjustments" category that should have ensured that no one would be overlooked: "This category is for recording the conditions of individuals who are psychiatrically normal but who nevertheless have severe enough problems to

warrant examination by a psychiatrist." Hysteria, neurasthenia, and hypochondriasis were back. Regardless of how one felt about the nomenclature, it could
not be totally ignored.

There were little hotbeds of controversy and research interest. These will be
mentioned briefly to convey the breadth of activity.

Everyone sleeps, and the study of REM indicated that everyone also dreams.
About 20% to 25% of the time spent in sleep is composed of four or five dream
periods lasting roughly 20 minutes each. People seemed to have a need to dream
that was independent of their need for sleep. It was found that people who were
allowed ample sleep but were awakened when they started to exhibit REM became
irritable and, in some cases, even hallucinated and reported delusions. Infants,
cats, rabbits, and rats were found to exhibit REM (Dement, 1960). However, it
was not necessary to conclude that all God's creatures have dreams as well as
rhythm. Instead, it was thought that REM may serve as a stimulus for dreaming in
some organisms and play another role in others.

The eye was also revealingly associated with how much interest the person had
in what was visually presented. When heterosexual males looked at pictures of
women, their pupils became larger than when they looked at photographs of men.
Just the opposite happened when homosexual men looked at photographs of
women and men. This seemed to provide a subtle way of detecting homosexuality,
but in the sexually permissive atmosphere of the sixties the importance of such a
diagnosis appeared to diminish. Nevertheless, the technique was thought to have
promise in attitude and opinion research (Hess, Seltzer, & Shlien, 1965).

Psychologists continued to put people into extreme groups along various dimensions and then see what differences could be associated with those placements. The
REM research indicated that everyone dreams but not everyone remembers
dreams, so studies were conducted to determine how people who recall their
dreams differ from those who do not (Lerner, 1967). There were investigations of
repressors and sensitizers, high and low dogmatics, field dependence and field
independence (Witkin, 1965), levelers and sharpeners, sensation seekers and sensation avoiders, dominance and submissiveness, overinclusion and concreteness,
hysterics and nonhysterics, neuroticism, psychoticism, achievers and nona-
chievers, good and poor premorbids, process and reactive schizophrenics, introverts and extraverts, social desirability, and isolators—and even a study or two in
support of Sheldon's theory of somatotypes and temperament (Cortes & Gatti,
1965; Luborsky et al., 1965).

The question of whether hypnosis is a special state was being answered increasingly in the negative. Barber (1965) continued to accumulate evidence in support
of his position that hypnosis was not a unique phenomenon. Simply telling or
encouraging people to push on and "bite the bullet" could help them exceed their
usual limits of strength and endurance. Further, performances on some intellectual
tasks, such as the digit symbol task on the WAIS, could be improved, and people
would more readily exhibit certain physiological effects, such as salivating, when
suitably urged. If people were told they were in an experimental study involving
hypnosis, they were more responsive to a variety of suggestions, including sugges-

tions to hallucinate and tolerate pain, than if they were told the study was a test of imagination. What seemed to be important was that the person believe hypnosis would increase suggestibility, that the situation be defined as a "hypnosis" situation, that the person be motivated or encouraged to be cooperative and to experience the intended effects, and that suggestions be given which would make a lessened criticalness seem reasonable. The last could be accomplished by using suggestions associated with "trance" induction: "Your eyes are getting heavy, heavy, heavy, and you are beginning to fall asleep."

An ingenious study to check on the validity of hypnotic phenomena was conducted by Leonard (1965). He asked his subjects to learn a list of nonsense syllables paired with digits (A). Two weeks later they were required to learn another list (B). Then some of the subjects were hypnotized, asked to "regress' to the date of the first session, and given trials on list A. Theoretically, if the subjects had truly regressed, there should have been no interference from list B. However, both hypnotized and nonhypnotized subjects had about the same number of interlist intrusions. Of course, this may only indicate that hypnotic phenomena are not readily obtained in the laboratory despite the valiant efforts of subjects to do what they think is wanted of them by their experimenters. At any rate, a growing number of psychologists came to believe that hypnosis might best be conceived of as an exercise in exerting influence rather than bringing about or creating a special condition or state.

Clinicians were dealt a share of the lumps, and many felt they got more than their fair share. Their testing instruments had been criticized, but such criticism was acceptable and clinicians themselves had engaged in it. They could live with the possibility that scatter on the Stanford-Binet might have no diagnostic significance, that projective techniques might have little predictive validity, or that the conscious verbalizations of clients might be of greater importance for understanding them than subtle signs on the Rorschach or figure drawings. But now came a drumbeat of suggestions that clinicians might be replaced as diagnosticians.

Although the substance of what was said was generally reasonable and fair, the issue was usually framed in terms of antagonistic alternatives. On one side was the clinician, the expert, the seer, the clinical. On the other side was the computer, the novice, the sign, the actuarial. Implied was the threat of automation and extinction.

Four lines of research appeared to menace the diagnostic function of the clinician. First, studies employing the MMPI, and sometimes the Rorschach and TAT as well, generally found an actuarial or sign approach to be as accurate, or more accurate, than clinicians interpreting the data. Kleinmuntz (1967), for example, found that a computer could be programmed to do as well as the best interpreter of MMPI profiles and better than the average performance of eight clinical judges. It seemed reasonable to conclude that "it may be well to assign this chore to machines rather than to trained clinicians."

Second, biographical or case history information seemed to be of great importance in formulating clinical judgments, and these judgments did not seem to gain in accuracy from the variety of test results generated by the usual test battery.

Quite the reverse appeared to happen. When clinicians were given a wealth of information and test data, their accuracy decreased. The results suggested that the clinician could neither handle the amount of data nor work with the consistency of a computer.

Third, experienced clinicians did no better than novices or clerical help in making predictions and judgments from the MMPI, the Bender-Gestalt, and figure drawings. The problem appeared to be that the experienced clinicians did not know, any more than the novices, which signs were valid for making certain judgments and which signs were not.

Fourth, impressions that clinicians' test reports were valid and their interpretations determined by careful observation of relationships between performances and personality characteristics were thrown into doubt. It could easily be demonstrated that statements from psychological reports were often of universal applicability and that such statements, when presented to a wide array of people, drew from them enthusiastic endorsements that the descriptions uniquely applied to them. Thus, the fact that a client asserted a report was accurate was no assurance of skill. The client may simply have been agreeing with comments true of almost anyone. Moreover, clinical signs were often determined by verbal links or cultural associations rather than by psychodiagnostic evidence. The beady eyes, narrow mouth, and large head in a drawing may be more indicative of what we have come to associate with these characteristics through folklore and literature than what we have learned through matching them with personality attributes (Chapman & Chapman, 1967, 1969).

The most disheartening aspect of these studies was their suggestion of the intransigence of clinicians. Errors would persist despite encouragement to make more careful observations. Training to improve accuracy had little effect. A not very pretty picture was painted of professionals who performed ineptly on techniques which had little value and to which they clung stubbornly and irrationally.

Many clinicians regarded this picture as grossly distorted and unfair. Their work did not consist of handling masses of data about people they had not seen while being subjected to the artificialities of a research study. Instead, they examined individuals intensively, and their appraisals were integrated with the appraisals of other professionals in arriving at plans of treatment. They thought of themselves as competent and judicious, as performing a valuable and valued service, and as quite willing to use all the help they could get, regardless of its source. Was nothing sacred? they wondered. Would motherhood be attacked next? Well, in point of fact, motherhood, along with fatherhood, *was* under attack.

Being a parent had never been an especially enviable position, but until the advent of psychoanalysis the consequences of being a bad parent had not seemed so enduring and destructive. Like Oliver Twist and Huck Finn, actual children could suffer cruelties and indignities, deprivations and neglect, and still emerge sweet and lovable. After Freud, all that was changed.

The concept of the bad parent had also changed to include the overprotective and seductive mother and father. Tenors could no longer sing of their filial devotion and of their wish to have "a girl just like the girl that married dear old dad" without seeming a little ridiculous and immature. Yet in spite of the criticisms leveled against parents for mishandling their children, there had been no suggestion that the family be eliminated as an institution. In the sixties, that suggestion was made.

Virtually every established way of doing something was under attack in the United States and other countries. With reference to the family, there were questions about the concept of marriage and the legal and religious bonds that might require two people to live together who no longer loved one another, there were questions about abortion and the right of women rather than the state to determine whether life should be allowed to grow within their bodies, and there were questions about whether a family was actually the best means for raising children.

Lidz (1963) noted that the nuclear family is structurally discontinuous. The discontinuities allowed the mobility and the emphasis on individuality that are so highly prized within our culture. But they also gave rise to anxiety and doubts about being a parent, since appropriate models were not readily available. For advice, the nuclear mother and father, woefully unsure of how to function as parents, were usually compelled to turn to supposed experts.

It would be pleasant to record that the experts agreed how to raise children, but that was not the case. Some argued that parents were not doing such a bad job. They saw the confidence of parents undermined by authoritative pronouncements, and although they recommended that some assistance be given, they thought parents bear the major responsibility for raising their offspring. Others were less sanguine.

These experts tended to see the family as a system of communication. Many of their observations were based on the study of schizophrenics and their families, although the observations were often extended to families in general. According to Bettelheim (1967), the autistic or schizophrenic child felt at the mercy of an insensitive, irrational home environment that threatened destruction. A similar observation was made by Laing and Esterson (1964) in working with adult schizophrenics. The parents of these patients sent out messages that tied their children in emotional knots, bewildered them, and threatened their identities. Much the same thing could be observed in the families of neurotics: People said one thing and meant another; they gave orders that could not be followed; they did not feel what they said and did not say what they felt. Families did not seem to be the best or the sanest place in which to live.

At the same time there were indications that the attitudes of parents were an important link in compensatory education programs (Jablonsky, 1971). Results were supposed to be less impressive or long-lasting when the parents did not value education and when their cooperation was not enlisted. That attitudes of apathy and powerlessness were not easily changed and that such cooperation was not always obtained led some soldiers in the fight against poverty to wonder if there was not a better way to raise youngsters than in families.

Rabin (1958) reported that children raised in kibbutzim, the collective farms of Israel, seemed to get along better with their peers and with their parents than children raised in nuclear families. In kibbutzim, the children lived together and were cared for by "professional" mothers while the parents worked. In the evenings, a mother and father and their children would spend some time together as a family, but for the most part each child's world consisted of age-mates. Bettelheim, who had achieved a measure of popularity and who had long been impressed by the harmful influences of the family, saw in the kibbutz an alternative model of child rearing, and he stimulated audiences by provocatively questioning the right of people to raise children simply because they succeeded in producing them.

Studies of schools, including nursery schools, in other countries led some professionals to argue that the sooner the baleful effects of the family could be counteracted, the better. Kindergartens and day-care programs were funded in states that had never before had them on the understanding that the resulting educational experiences would benefit the learning skills and improve the self-concepts of children. Although frequent attempts were made to involve parents in these programs, the feeling was widespread that, whether because of their own disturbances or their own chronic histories of deprivation, a large number of American mothers and fathers were ill-equipped to effectively carry out their roles.

In writing of his term in office, President Johnson (1971) stated,

> Experts tell us that most of a child's full potential is achieved before he reaches school age. Half his eventual capacity has been established by the age of four. By the time he is six, two-thirds of his adult intelligence has been formed. . . . The Head Start program led the way in the application of these discoveries to the classroom. Focused on culturally deprived children, Head Start was responsible for calling attention to several incredible facts. Almost half the children we reached with this program came from homes that had no toys, books, magazines, crayons, paints, or even paper. Some of those children, particularly those from city slums, could not recognize pictures of animals from the zoo. . . . The progress of these children under our Head Start program astounded and gratified us all. I urged that Head Start and its companion programs be made available to all 8 million poverty-level youngsters in this country below the age of ten, and not just to the million who currently are benefiting (pp. 220–221).

Johnson's rhetoric was typical of the era of the New Frontier and the Great Society. A problem would be identified, its seriousness and urgency would be stressed, the force and funds of the government would be pledged to solve it, and the results of the efforts would be declared pleasing and promising. It is probably impossible to calculate how much money and skilled effort were expended in this "war." During the mid-sixties, there were roughly 244 compensatory education programs in 31 states. By the end of the sixties, there were only about 50 left. At approximately the same time that Johnson was writing his assessment of the success of Head Start, a more sombre evaluation was being expressed by Jablonsky (1971):

> The frustration and anger of the lay critics of "education for minority-poverty children" because of the failure of schools to meet the demands for palpable evidence of success on any or all criteria is matched by the concern and despair of those professionals responsible for producing results. Rationalizations used in past years that the programs were too new, the funding too weak, the staffs too few and unprepared, the social problems too pervasive, are no longer acceptable to the community supporting the schools.

Jablonsky went on to try to determine what characteristics distinguished the programs that had been effective from those that had not. A major distinction seemed to be the persistence, dedication, "competence, enthusiasm, and belief that these children can learn, can turn the tide of deprivation."

In short, the government of the United States had been involved as never before in trying to modify intellectual development. There were some reports of improvements, many reports of no significant change, and a general finding of immediate gains that were lost as the children continued to attend school. There was little disagreement that these were the findings, but the implications of these findings for concepts of intelligence and educational planning touched off one of the most acrimonious debates in the history of psychology.

About 10 years before, it had been possible for Cyril Burt to be honored for his work in psychology, including his view that intelligence is largely determined by genetic factors. Arthur Jensen (1969) surveyed the evidence of the sixties and reached a similar conclusion. He felt the failures of many compensatory education programs and the trend for blacks to score lower than whites were based on genetic differences between the races. Possibly there were two kinds of performances or learning involved in intelligence. One type, Level 1 learning, consists of acquisitions or relatively simple associations, such as would be found in serial learning, digit span memory, and paired associate learning. The second type, Level 2 learning, is relatively more complex and consists of cognitively integrating material and forming abstract concepts, the kinds of intellectual activity found in reasoning, seeing similarities, and logical thinking. Jensen supposed that children of all races might be similarly endowed with Level 1 abilities but that Level 2 abilities might be differentially distributed among races and social classes and hence account for the differences in mean IQs when these groups are compared. He acknowledged, of course, that in dealing with the individual child, predictions based on group studies are invalid because of the variability in the distributions. For several years after making his views known, Jensen spent a considerable portion of his time vigorously defending his reasonableness, his fairness, and his wish to be helpful, not harmful.

In a sense, it almost makes no difference what Jensen actually said and meant. The plain fact is that many people interpreted his remarks as racist half-truths based on inadequate and selected evidence with dangerous implications. It was feared that his beliefs would be used to justify cutbacks in federal spending and the abandonment of special efforts to improve the education of children (Kagan, 1967). That may not have been what Jensen intended—he insisted it was exactly what he did not intend—but it was what people feared would happen.

The atmosphere of the sixties was sensitive, troubled, and hostile. It could absorb, and be little affected by, Raymond Cattell's (1968) statement that there were two kinds of intelligence (a fluid g consisting of abilities to perceive relationships and a crystallized g consisting of abilities heavily influenced by educational and cultural experiences), but it could not tolerate beliefs that aggravated wounds still sore and festering. What was particularly disturbing about this atmosphere was its pervasiveness. No place seemed entirely safe for the expression of ideas, and an honest exchange of convictions was frequently prevented by intimidation, derision, and vituperation. That these circumstances should exist within psychology, as well as outside it, augured ill.

TREATMENT FORMULATIONS

There were four major developments in treatment methods in this period, each of which was called a "revolution" or a "movement" by its advocates. Few advances were referred to as "modest contributions" in the sixties. Yet, although almost any seeming improvement might be described by someone as "revolutionary," "exciting," and "a breakthrough in our understanding," these four treatment approaches did attract much attention. They were (1) community psychology or psychiatry (depending on whether the practitioner was a psychologist or psychiatrist), (2) behavior therapy, (3) humanistic psychology or psychiatry, and (4) chemotherapy or drug therapy. Since the use of drugs was somewhat insidious, let us consider it first.

Within psychiatry, the use of drugs had become highly important in the treatment of anxiety, depression, convulsive disorders, psychoses, and neuroses. It was generally conceded that medication was effective in reducing the frequency and severity of symptoms, and in many cases this was all that one could hope to accomplish. The patient's disorder became less obvious and more manageable, periods of hospitalization became more frequent but less lengthy in duration, and the use of maintenance dosages became an accepted procedure in psychiatry and presumably an acceptable way of life for the patient. Chemotherapy involved periodic visits to a drug clinic, where the patient's response to medication and progress could be monitored and medicines prescribed or dispensed (Rome et al., 1966).

It is no exaggeration to say that the treatment of schizophrenia was remarkably altered by the use of drugs. Return of the patient to the community and maintaining the patient within the community were feasible goals. The day of the large mental hospital was declared at an end, and although some wags spoke of "a revolving door policy," the emphasis was on avoiding chronic hospitalizations.

Drugs were also used more extensively than before in the treatment of children. For virtually every disorder, from bed-wetting to learning problems, there existed a practitioner willing to attempt to treat it with a drug. However, for the most part medication was not used widely in reducing minor behavior problems. It did see much use, to the point where some proclaimed it a national scandal, in the alleviation of hyperactivity. Stimulants, such as amphetamines and Ritalin, were found to have a paradoxical effect in reducing the hyperactivity associated with brain damage. Accordingly, these drugs were prescribed for many children whose parents or teachers complained of their activity level. And if a youngster responded favorably to the medication, that response was taken as evidence of "minimal brain damage" or "minimal brain dysfunction." Although there was little disagreement about the beneficial effects of these drugs, there was much controversy about their possible abuse, their employment as a means of ensuring conformity, and the harmful psychological consequences their use might have for the child.

Outside of psychiatry, there was an obvious "drug culture." Drug addiction had been a problem for many years, at least from the time nations made it a criminal offense to traffic in drugs, but the sixties differed from other periods in the extent of usage and in the patina of respectability that professionals bestowed on users.

Drugs were hailed as mind expanders, as a means to achieve mystical experiences, attain new levels of consciousness, and become more self-aware. Aside from those possible benefits, the sensuous pleasures and the speed and immediacy of the experiences were praised. Further, whereas it would have seemed prudent to caution against the use of drugs until their long-range effects could be determined, it was sometimes argued by professionals that unless there was conclusive evidence to the contrary, it could be assumed they were safe. Suggestions were made that the older, established generation had the money for expensive drugs like alcohol and were jealously keeping the younger generation from "turning on" with a cheap drug like marijuana.

LSD, marijuana, and heroin were illegally used by so many people during the sixties that estimates of usages varied widely and alarmingly depending on whether the figures included casual users. At any rate, few American communities believed they had no drug problem, and every large city had an area where illegal drug use was reputed to occur. Heroin usage seemed of most concern to federal authorities, and to reduce its incidence the government sponsored a substitute narcotic, methadone, which it was willing to have prescribed for addicts who would agree to remain off heroin.

Drug and methadone clinics were frequently found in community mental health centers, as were clinics offering other services now regarded as traditional, such as individual psychotherapy, play therapy, and group therapy. The professionals who provided these traditional services were sometimes criticized because they seemed to be making little effort to offer them to the poor; they were also criticized for offering them at all, since psychotherapy did not appear to be an especially effective form of treatment; and finally they were criticized for not using their time more efficiently by engaging in primary prevention.

As was mentioned earlier, *primary prevention* refers to "the communication of psychological principles and insights to the public so that the incidence of conflict, unhappiness, and maladaptive behavior may be reduced and so that the best functioning of each person is encouraged." One analogy is public health (e.g., by ensuring a safe water supply and sanitary conditions public health officials help prevent the occurrence of disease). If psychologically damaging institutional policies could be modified, then, it was reasoned, great numbers of people might be helped at relatively little cost in professional time.

A combination of factors argued for the urgency of greater professional involvement in primary prevention: (1) The population was increasing and the number of people requiring psychological services could be expected to grow rapidly; (2) there was a shortage of personnel in the mental health professions and there seemed little likelihood that this shortage would be alleviated in the near future; (3)

prevalence studies indicated that more people were in need of mental health services than had been suspected; (4) the pressures, tensions, and crises within American society and the world were generating much anxiety and concern and could best be dealt with at their source; and (5) it seemed impossible for traditional approaches ever to meet the demand for psychological services.

This demand was supposedly coming from people of every social class. Of course, it was conceded that the lower classes did not appear particularly receptive to psychotherapy, nor were therapists enthusiastic about involving themselves in individual treatment with lower-class clients. To be sure, there were exceptions. For example, some therapists reported excellent results working with lower-class children and adults who were eager to be seen in individual psychotherapy. Nevertheless, the generalizations were accepted, and the issue was how to deliver services to all who needed them.

Two major strategies were adopted for the delivery of services. One was to expand the number of service providers through the use of training programs and consultation. The other was to increase the visibility and accessibility of the services (Page, 1967).

The ingenuity and zeal with which these two strategies were implemented was breathtaking. A select group of housewives were trained within a few months to function effectively as psychotherapists (Pines, 1962). Mothers were recruited to function in schools as warm and sympathetic sources of comfort to children who seemed to be experiencing distress in the classroom. Attendants were transformed into leaders of group therapy programs for psychotic patients. Teachers were encouraged to deal constructively with emotionally disturbed children (Hobbs, 1966). Community aides and mental health aides were created from the ranks of the poor as the best means for reaching the poor. Parents were helped to treat the problems of their children. Former patients, friends, college students, classmates, and neighbors were reported to perform surprisingly well in therapeutic roles. Consultation was used to make police, clergy, day-care workers, teachers, and government officials more sensitive and responsive to mental health problems (Cowen, Gardner, & Zax, 1967).

Crisis intervention centers were established to provide round-the-clock services to people who felt they needed help. The staff members of these centers conceived of people in emergency situations as being particularly vulnerable to psychological reorganization and thus capable of responding positively to timely aid. Satellite clinics were established to spread professional personnel throughout the community. Neighborhood or stonefront clinics were established to make mental health services available to target populations and less threatening or burdensome than they presumably would have been at a formal clinic.

Traditional concepts of treatment were being shaken to their very roots (Ford & Urban, 1963). Psychotherapy had been regarded as a kind of Holy Grail, and if people were not sufficiently motivated to endure hardships to gain it, that was their tough luck. Now psychotherapists were enjoined to get off their rumps and out of their offices and to do whatever was necessary to make their skills of use to those who needed them. This push was part of the antiprofessionalism, antiestablishment, "get with it," "hang loose" spirit that characterized community psychology, American society, humanism, and behaviorism.

Group therapies and group-based self-development techniques swept the United States and many other countries. These therapies and techniques were incredibly diverse, but they shared these points in common: (1) Present, ongoing events and feelings were emphasized and discussions of the past were discouraged; (2) they were relatively brief, but during their limited time they sought to stimulate intense affect; (3) the leaders of the groups, if professionals, tried to appear casual and informal, and often the leaders were not psychologists or psychiatrists; and (4) the aim was to develop human potential to the fullest, so that the group members were not always patients or clients in the traditional sense (Blank, Gottsegen, & Gottsegen, 1971). Undoubtedly the success of these therapies and techniques was spurred by the intense loneliness experienced by so many people, yet the discontinuities inherent in their very structure raised questions about their ultimate benefits.

T-groups (or training groups) developed out of the seminal work of Kurt Lewin. They became popular as a means of dealing with personnel problems in business and industry. Essentially, a group of executives or businessmen would meet and strive to better understand themselves and group processes through their own interactions. The meetings took place in a different setting from the usual workplace, a setting where the sole task was to concentrate on acquiring new perspectives for dealing with problems while coping with the lack of structure in the group (Shaffer & Galinsky, 1974).

Encounter (basic encounter, sensitivity, intensive, open encounter) groups were promoted by Carl Rogers, Frederick Stoller, William Schutz, and a host of others. The names given to these groups and their myriad variations kept a legion of followers in a dither. Affectionately known as "touchy-feelies," their purpose was to break down social barriers quickly and to have the individual "come alive." Rogers' approach to encounter groups was probably the most conservative and stressed the honest expression of positive and negative feelings among the members.

Stoller and George Bach introduced an element of dramatic intensity to the encounter by requiring group members to meet nonstop for 24 hours or more—with or without a break for sleep, depending, one supposes, on the convictions and stamina of the group leader. The sheer duration was supposed to induce fatigue and pressures for disclosure that would cause defenses to weaken and provide opportunities for extended discussion not possible in the conventional group. This kind of encounter was called a "marathon group encounter," and a much discussed variation was the nude marathon.

Schutz's approach was called "open encounter," and it emphasized the body and physical expression. Rather than talk about feelings, each person, with the assistance of the group, was encouraged to pantomime or act feelings and problems. Dreams and fantasies might also be portrayed and their resolutions dramatically achieved. The aim was to reduce blocks against expression, and in pursuit of this aim, breathing exercises, screaming, and pillow beating might be introduced.

With the introduction of body procedures and physical contact among group members, there appeared to be groups which engaged in these exercises and techniques for the sheer pleasure and joy that they afforded. Massage, fondling and caressing one another, yoga exercises, dance, meditation—there seemed to be no limit to what might be done in a group. Serious consideration was given to the issue of when, if ever, a therapist would be justified in having sexual relations with a client, and great interest was expressed in the occult and parapsychological. The leaders of some groups took on the dress and bearing of a guru, and no one did this better than the psychiatrist Frederick Perls (1893–1970).

Fondly known as Fritz, Perls had a full gray beard, a corpulent physique, and a look of inexhaustible patience and kindliness wreathed in cigarette smoke. He had been trained as an analyst but had been critical of Freud and psychoanalysis for many years. The Gestalt therapy that he formulated and helped popularize was at first a kind of Fletcherism. In order to express aggression (the suppression of hostility being regarded as a prime source of difficulty), Perls had advocated thoroughly chewing one's food (Perls, 1969a).

During the last few years of his life, Peals devoted himself tirelessly to workshops and the preparation of training materials. His therapy could be conducted individually or in groups, but it was the group form that Perls eventually focused on almost exclusively. The essence of Gestalt therapy was to bring everything in the person's awareness into full relief and to highlight messages that the individual was communicating nonverbally. Dreams were not so much interpreted as experienced, and while they were being brought to life and experienced (often by having the person pretend to be inanimate objects in the dream), unexpected insights would be gained. However, Perls was not interested in the person's verbalizing these insights. Instead, he wanted to see the effects of the insights in relaxation, relief, comfort, warmth, courage, and self-confidence (Perls, 1969b).

Perls' charisma and the engaging, colorful terms he used no doubt helped Gestalt therapy become popular. A person who was asked to come before the group and become its focus was invited to the "hot seat." Conscience and its imperatives were the "top dog," and the poor person who struggled under the yoke of these internal demands was the "underdog." Anxiety had its anticipatory quality made prominent by being referred to as "rehearsal." And a complex terminology awaited those who wished to plumb Gestalt therapy deeply.

Something of the same appeal, a gamelike quality and a set of "with-it" terms, characterized transactional analysis (TA). This form of analysis swept the country as the result of two enormously successful books, *Games People Play* by Eric Berne and *I'm OK—You're OK* by Thomas Harris (1967). The idea was that people engage in repeated patterns of behavior in order to compel other people to interact with them in certain reassuring but ultimately self-defeating ways. These patterns are games, and the trick is to get the person to see that he or she no longer needs to practice them. Instead of interacting with others in such a way as to say, "I'm not OK, but you're OK," or "I'm OK, but you're not OK," or whatever, the person had to come to act in such a way as to say "I'm OK, you're OK."

Further, people's communication with each other could be analyzed to determine when they were not communicating appropriately. Injunctions, moral judgments, and criticisms came from the Parent; wishes, fears, and expressions of helplessness came from the Child; and reasonable statements about the reality of the situation came from the Adult within each of us. Supposedly, adult communication was the most desirable, and by TA the individual could be helped to communicate in that fashion. If the person failed to respond as expected to TA, there was the dark suspicion that he or she had been participating in the whole thing as a game.

One of the concepts of TA that virtually everyone liked was that people needed to be "stroked," or given messages affirming their value and worth. Strokes, whether verbal or nonverbal and whether called "rewards," "reinforcements," or whatever, were certainly much discussed, perhaps especially much because criticism, attack, and feedback were rampant. Behavior therapists, of course, were highly mindful of the significance of rewards and of their positive and negative consequences.

Behavior therapy had grown so rapidly in this decade that its proponents found themselves no longer a beleaguered minority but a powerful group that could soon expect to have their promises called due for an accounting. They had reaped a harvest of dissatisfaction with psychotherapy and had sown seeds of hope where there had been precious few. With guarantees of effectiveness, with unbounded confidence in their abilities to produce change, with youthful determination and energy, they tackled every conceivable problem of behavior in every conceivable place (Ullmann & Krasner, 1965; Wolpe & Lazarus, 1966).

Loosely called *phobias*, sexual deviations from fetishes to troubling fantasies, hoarding, mutism, head banging, marital problems, hallucinations, delusions, and rituals were treated by conditioning therapies such as desensitization, aversive conditioning, and implosion (Stampfl & Levis, 1967). Entire wards and institutions were turned into token economies, where the performance of certain activities earned specified points or tokens that could be exchanged for rewards, privileges, food, and so on (Ayllon & Azrin, 1968). The success of these activities encouraged behaviorists to think of how much better it would be if prisons, schools, clinics, businesses, and society in general were run along the same lines (Hall, 1967).

Children who were psychotic, autistic, and retarded and who had not been appreciably helped by any previous treatment were taught to talk, to behave more sociably, and to cease their self-punitive behaviors. Much attention was given to these efforts, particularly to the dedicated work of Ivar Lovaas, and it appeared that with patience and sufficient time these children could be trained to a semblance of normality.

On the periphery of the four major treatment movements described above were related developments, some of which represented continued growth in earlier movements and some of which were the first stirrings of movements to come. Family therapy, with its insistence that the patient was the scapegoat of disturbances in communication and relationships within the family system that hence the entire family had to be seen in treatment as a group, rallied many to its banner.

Bruno Bettelheim (1967) and Margaret Mahler (1968), by their reports of success in treating autistic and schizophrenic children, encouraged those with psychoanalytic leanings, and Bettelheim was to find himself a public figure as a result of his warm and sympathetic account of the residential treatment of autism, *The Empty Fortress*. Viktor Frankl's (1962) logotherapy, which "focuses on the meaning of human existence as well as man's search for such a meaning" and whose technique of *paradoxical intention* was reminiscent of negative practice, became popular, as did William Glasser's (1965) reality therapy, with its emphasis on getting the person to be practical and take responsibility for dealing with the problems of the present and the immediate future.

Yet, overall, progress in some areas had been slow. Near the beginning of the decade, Saslow (1962) had evaluated a meeting of the leaders in psychotherapy with these words: "I had the impression that dissatisfaction was general, even with such a central concept as 'anxiety,' although many people felt it had some usefulness." Toward the close of the decade Dahlstrom (1972) surveyed the research in personality and wrote, "Some large part of the sprawl and diversity in our field . . . can be attributed to the fundamental differences in the definition of personality. Rather than methodological ineptitude or negligence, the central problem for personologists at this stage in the development of our field seems to be lack of any consensus in conceptualization."

A decade of research in psychotherapy, much of it generously funded by the U.S. government, had yielded a mixed crop of fruit. The treatment of schizophrenics with Rogerian therapy (Rogers, 1967) suggested some clients benefit more and some get worse than those who are simply left alone. It now appeared that psychotherapy could damage as well as help, and so it became necessary to give thought to which patients would respond best to the various forms of treatment (Bergin, 1966). Studies by Rogerian therapists pointed to empathy and warmth as important characteristics for the therapist to possess, and other studies indicated experience and satisfactory psychological adjustment were attributes not to be neglected. Yet these findings were at variance with others in the literature, and perhaps the only conclusion to be drawn was that investigations of appropriate matchings of therapists and clients needed to be done (Luborsky & Strupp, 1962; Lorr, 1965).

Some 50 years before, Freud (1959a) had peered into the future and had seen a day when the governments of nations would establish clinics for the psychological treatment of the poor. No doubt, he mused, psychoanalysis would be called upon to make its contribution, and some modification of its treatment method would be necessary:

> We shall probably discover that the poor are even less ready to part with their neuroses than the rich, because the hard life that awaits them when they recover has no attraction, and illness in them gives them more claim to the help of others. Possibly we may often only be able to achieve something if we combine aid for the mind with some material support. . . . It is very probable, too, that the application of our therapy to numbers will compel us to alloy the pure gold of analysis plentifully with the copper of direct suggestion; and even hypnotic influence might find a place in it again. . . . But whatever form this psychotherapy for the people may

take, whatever the elements out of which it is compounded, its most effective and important
ingredients will assuredly remain those borrowed from strict psychoanalysis which serves no
ulterior purpose. (Freud, 1959a, p. 402)

As a prophet, Freud seemed to be at least partially right.

PROFESSIONAL DEVELOPMENT

When Freud talked about anxiety, he noted its association with a flooding of
information or a feeling on the part of the person of being overwhelmed with
stimulation. This was a common feeling during the sixties. There was fear of an
information explosion, a worry that so much was happening so fast that people
were stunned and in a state of shock. The sheer numbers of psychologists and
publications created a nostalgic feeling for the "good old days" of only 30 years
before, when Thorndike was able to boast of being able to keep up with the
literature and the APA still seemed a proper organization of scientists and friends.
But, then, as the bumper sticker proclaimed, "Even Nostalgia Isn't What It Used
to Be."

The APA had begun in 1892 with 31 members. By 1968 it was impossible to
achieve an exact count because of the rapid turnover, but it was figured there were
27,250 members, a large percentage of the estimated 35,529 psychologists in the
United States. The National Register of Scientific and Technical Personnel calcu-
lated that 29% (about 12,000) of the psychologists were clinicians (Cates, 1970).

In 1927 *Psychological Abstracts* began publication, and there were 2,730 cita-
tions. There were 6,063 in 1937; 4,688 in 1947; 9,074 in 1957; 17,202 in 1967;
19,586 in 1968; 18,068 in 1969; and a whopping 21,722 in 1970. No one could
keep up with the literature, and there was even a question whether *Psychological
Abstracts* could cope with it.

Clinical psychology was still largely an American phenomenon. In comparison
with the thousands of clinicians in the United States, it was estimated there were
39 in Belgium (Buckle & David, 1967), 90 in Czechoslovakia (Moss, 1967), 134
in Denmark, 2 in Bulgaria, 76 in Finland, 14 in Ireland, 183 in Norway (Bard,
1966), 280 in Poland (Kaczkowski, 1967), 94 in Rumania, 253 in Sweden, 345 in
the United Kingdom, 60 in Yugoslavia, maybe 30 in Greece (Vassiliou & Vassiliou, 1966), several in Egypt and Lebanon, 1 in Syria, 6 in Iraq, 1 in Jordan
(Melikan, 1964), 1 in Kuwait, perhaps 300 in France (Sanua, 1966), a few hundred in Japan (DeVos, Murakami, & Murase, 1964), and several hundred in Canada and Latin America (Abt, 1964).

These clinicians varied widely in training and responsibility. In Poland they
enjoyed a status comparable to that of physicians. In France they were subservient
to physicians and had little professional standing. In Scandinavia the doctoral
student was required to take a 6-hour oral examination, produce a dissertation that
could be published as a book, and deliver two public lectures. In Mexico most
psychologists performing clinical functions were "psychotechnicians" who had no
graduate degree.

The profession was growing. Of that there could be no doubt. There were 56 graduate programs in clinical psychology approved by the APA in 1960; by 1969 there were 71. However, there was an uneasy feeling about this growth. Three prestigious universities, Harvard, Northwestern, and Stanford, had dropped their clinical training programs. There were rumors that this might be the beginning of a trend and that clinicians had best look for ways to safeguard their profession. What would they do if universities suddenly stopped training clinical psychologists?

Not that they were entirely happy with the training provided by universities. The scientist-practitioner model seemed to produce clinical psychologists with very little enthusiasm for science and limited skills as practitioners. Moreover, it was supposed to take 4 or 5 years to get through a university program and earn a PhD. Unfortunately, about one-half of those who began that arduous journey did not complete it, and many who did finish required 7 to 9 years (Lockman & Thorne, 1966).

A substantial proportion of graduate students claimed they were unhappy with the scientist-practitioner model. Practicing clinicians claimed they were unhappy with the performances of interns and new doctorates. "Tough-minded" psychologists said they were dissatisfied by the fact that about 30% of the clinical group did not publish at all and that publications by clinicians averaged out to approximately one per person. That was hardly an impressive output, and it called into question the value of training clinicians in research skills they would not utilize.

Whereas it could be agreed there was extensive dissatisfaction and unhappiness, it could not be agreed what to do to solve the problem. David Shakow (1965), an elder statesman of the profession, argued that in view of the undeveloped state of both psychology and clinical psychology, the most important responsibility of the clinician was research. He thought clinicians needed to be involved in less private practice and to get better training, to be less defensive and to acquire more self-respect, and to receive less criticism and more understanding and acceptance from psychologists in other areas.

However, the mainstream of thought on training in clinical psychology was responsive to the *Zeitgeist* and the concerns about manpower shortages, the delivery of services, getting away from the medical model, and subdoctoral careers. The discussions about these matters generated a frantic atmosphere in which there seemed to be little capacity for delay in translating ideas into action. Questions were posed within the context of pressing social issues, as though resolving doubts about the identity of clinical psychology would somehow help to settle the contributions clinicians could make to mental health and community psychology (Albee, 1966, 1968).

A training conference held in Chicago in 1965 concluded there should be some degree of professional preparation throughout the years of college. At an undergraduate level, the student could be trained in interviewing and basic testing. At a subdoctoral level, the student could be trained in counseling or statistics and find employment as a mental health worker and statistical technician. The doctoral student would require "adequate role models distributed over all of the scientist-professional continuum. This implies and requires inclusion on the faculty of skilled, mature, and dedicated practitioners." Then, of course, there would also be postdoctoral education in clinical specialities, such as neuropsychology, clinical child psychology, and so on (Hoch, Ross, & Winder, 1966, p. 45; Bergin, Garfield, & Thompson, 1967).

One problem in implementing such a career ladder was that it was based on the assumption that there was a close correspondence between the rudimentary appearance of a task and the level of sophistication needed to perform it. Some clinicians, however, did not think of interviewing as a simple skill, although this seemed to be a presupposition of the career ladder. Another problem was that some graduate schools, in trying to meet the needs of their communities, were giving extensive training in clinical practice to students at the master's degree level, and even if they were not giving that training, the jobs for which their graduates were hired frequently demanded diagnostic and treatment functions. In other words, there was no uniformity in the level of training signified by the various degrees. Nor was there any assurance that such uniformity could be imposed, since (1) the public often expected to get the same services from someone with an MA as they expected to get from someone with a PhD, and (2) some graduate schools, in order to be competitive, tried to offer attractive, innovative programs. A third problem was that some clinicians wanted the doctorate to signify a lofty level of policy planning, conceptualization, consultation, teaching, and formulation of research. "The model we will develop will be a social-learning model, and the professional users of this model will be Bachelors-level people working in tax-supported institutions more like schools than like hospitals," was the way George Albee (1968) put it. On the other hand, some clinicians liked doing diagnostic testing and providing psychotherapy.

The majority of clinical psychologists who worked in APA-approved graduate school programs followed and endorsed the scientist-practitioner model, supported the concept of subdoctoral training, but were not enthusiastic about a simple practitioner model. Yet students, the public, and practicing clinicians seemed very much in favor of developments that would enhance professional skills. Concern was expressed that psychotherapy and diagnostic assessment could not be taught properly in a patronizing and skeptical atmosphere. Presumably this atmosphere existed in graduate schools (Thelen & Ewing, 1970).

Complaints were voiced about the small value placed by some faculties on the expert work of clinicians as compared with the high value placed on research skills. Repeatedly throughout the sixties, APA committees addressed themselves to this problem by exhorting schools to recognize and reward clinical proficiency. The need for these exhortations suggested the problem continued to exist (Goodstein & Ross, 1966).

One recommendation was to form a new profession that would draw its recruits from the fields of psychiatry, clinical psychology, and psychiatric social work. A psychiatrist, A. S. Mariner (1967), confessed that little of his work involved the use of medicine and that psychotherapists, regardless of their discipline, performed similarly and with about the same effectiveness. He proposed the formation of a field of mental health, with its own schools, outside the dominion of medicine: "The mental health profession, then, is really working in the field of applied psychology. . . . That jurisdiction over this field should be claimed by a profession [psychiatry] whose basic education usually includes not a single course in psychology is, when viewed dispassionately, little short of fantastic" (Mariner, 1967). Psychologists liked that kind of talk, particularly when it came from a psychiatrist, but it did little to compensate for the inferior status and income awarded them by the public. They also did not think it likely that Mariner's opinions were shared by many of his colleagues.

A second recommendation was to recognize the practitioner model as a viable alternative to the scientist-practitioner model in graduate education, as had been done at the University of Illinois. This university began a program in 1968 that allowed its clinical students to pursue either a PhD or a PsyD. The course of instruction for the PsyD was distinguished by less emphasis on research and by a series of "laboratories in clinical psychology," which were year-long practical courses in specific treatment and assessment methods. A PsyD student had to take five of these "laboratories," whereas a PhD student had to take but two. Donald Peterson (1971), who was directing the new program, regarded it as quite promising.

A third recommendation was to start independent professional schools of psychology. The California School of Professional Psychology (1972–1973) was founded in 1969 and offered a 6-year PhD program designed to produce competent journeyman psychologists. The duration of the program was supposed to be significantly less than the 9 to 11 years that might be required to complete a comparable course of study in "traditional academic settings." Of interest are the "four crucial needs" that prompted the school's founding:

> *(1) The requirements of our society for drastically more professional psychologists than are being trained by our universities; (2) The unmet interest of students which has culminated in as many as forty qualified applicants for each opening in a doctoral program; (3) The long overdue need for a complete overhaul of the current APA approved clinical training model to render it relevant to the later activities of a practicing professional psychologist; (4) The importance of providing a realistic career and educational ladder within psychology, beginning with the AA degree as the basis for a paraprofessional cadre and through the PhD degree itself.*

The tenor of the sixties is manifest in the above quotation: "crucial needs . . . drastically more professional psychologists . . . unmet interest of students . . . long overdue need for a complete overhaul . . . relevant . . . paraprofessional." On the other hand, although many people were interested in becoming professional psychologists, few were willing to be "hassled" about it. For example, few of the eligible clinical psychologists took the trouble to obtain an ABEPP diploma.

Perhaps a major reason for this lack of enthusiasm was that the consequences for failing to get an ABEPP diploma were not especially grave. Although some employers rewarded diplomates, many gave the diploma no particular notice. Moreover, an important purpose of the ABEPP at its inception was to serve as a means of signifying to the public which psychologists met certain standards of professional competence. This purpose was certainly needed in 1946, when less than a handful of states had certification or licensure laws (APA Committee on Legislation, 1967). But by 1969 the situation was reversed, and only three states, Hawaii, Indiana, and North Carolina, had no provision, either statutory or nonstatutory, for certification or licensure. Further, there were now laws regulating psychologists in six Canadian provinces: Alberta, Manitoba, Ontario, New Brunswick, Saskatchewan, and Quebec. A clinical psychologist in most states was thus obligated to be certified or licensed. Did the public require a dual system of protection?

In 1968, the ABEPP, faced with little demand for its services and with annual budget deficits, did what many organizations have done in similar straits. It changed its name to the American Board of Professional Psychology (ABPP), dropping the Examiners and so perhaps softening its image but making pronunciation of its acronym a problem. "To strengthen its services to the public and the profession," it began to award its diplomas at the APA convention, issue ABPP awards for distinguished professional achievement (the first recipients were Ralph Berdie, Florence Halpern, Rensis Likert, and Carl Rogers), and award diplomas in school psychology. It also announced that it would issue a directory of diplomates (Morrow, 1969).

The ABPP was not the only psychological organization confronted with a crisis of sorts. The APA was dealing with the problem of how to be all things to all psychologists. Its situation was very similar to that described by Heinz Werner in the development of organisms. According to Werner, development proceeds from a stage of little differentiation to a stage of greater growth and differentiation. However, the organism must be able to integrate what has been differentiated; otherwise there is a fragmentation of parts. For the integration to occur, there must be a central organizing core.

Obviously there had been growth and differentiation in psychology. The sheer number of psychologists had grown, and there were 22,726 graduate students in psychology in the United States in 1969, as compared with 10,677 in 1960. Specialization within psychology had increased, with specialties within subareas of specialization. At the beginning of the decade, there were 21 APA divisions; by its close, there were 29, despite an effort by the APA to reduce the number. The new divisions included Community Psychology, The Experimental Analysis of Behavior, Psychological Hypnosis, Psychopharmacology, and Psychotherapy. Within clinical psychology there were clinicians who regarded themselves as specialists in clinical child psychology, neuropsychology, community psychology, behavior modification, behavior therapy, psychotherapy, family therapy, group therapy, consultation, hypnosis, and so on.

The danger of differentiation leading to fragmentation had been of concern in American psychology for at least 40 years, ever since its first division had been created as a way of keeping a group of clinicians in the APA. Now the APA was being pulled in at least three directions by its membership. First, it was being implored to hold to its original purpose—the advancement of psychology as a science. Second, it was being exhorted to become more active in professional affairs and to do more to promote psychology as a profession. No doubt with this aim somewhat in mind the APA had constructed an impressive eight-story head-quarters in Washington, D.C., to which its central office moved in 1964 and from which it could conveniently monitor and hopefully influence federal bills and legislation. Third, it was being challenged to address itself to the great social problems of the United States and the world: racism, war, overpopulation, and poverty. (One of the APA's responses was to invite Martin Luther King to speak before the APA convention held in Washington in 1967.)

As might easily have been predicted, not all psychologists were enthusiastic about each of the above three aims, and in striving to meet all three, the APA antagonized those of its members who believed its resources should have been directed toward meeting just one. Psychologists whose major interest was in a scientific organization formed, at the initiative of Clifford T. Morgan, the Psychonomic Society in 1959 and began holding their own meetings and publishing their own journal. Most of these psychologists retained their APA membership, but about 8% did not (Hilgard, 1987). Other newly formed organizations included the American Association for Humanistic Psychology, the Association for Advancement of Behavior Therapy, and the American Academy of Psychotherapists. Of course, this by no means exhausts the list of organizations and special interest groups. Each year new calls would go forth to bring together psychologists of like minds on some matter.

The APA was sufficiently worried about fragmentation to create the Committee on Scientific and Professional Aims of Psychology (1967). The committee's report made clear that dissension existed among the leadership of the APA about the objectives of the association. Moreover, not only was doubt expressed about the continued existence of the APA as a single body, but its fragmentation was seen as possibly desirable.

Frankly, psychologists who saw themselves as scientists and academicians resented the use of a portion of their dues to support such professional matters as negotiations with the American Medical Association and American Psychiatric Association, lobbying for psychological services to be covered in health insurance plans, and assisting in the passage of certification and licensure legislation. They disliked mingling with practitioners at APA conventions and competing with them for meeting time and journal space. They did not like the APA, an organization with which they were identified, going before congressional committees to argue in favor of psychological tests, and they wanted it to deal only with issues directly related to psychology as a science.

Professional psychologists, on the other hand, now constituted the majority of APA members. Therefore, it seemed reasonable to them that they should be represented proportionately in the association's governing bodies. They complained about the control over professional training exercised by academic psychologists, and they wanted a greater voice in that training. Naturally they wanted the APA to play a greater role in promoting professional interests.

Three different kinds of recommendations were offered to help bridge these two apparently divergent aims. Milton Wexler proposed a reorganization of the APA that would allegedly increase its efficiency by eliminating unnecessary divisions and committees. In part this streamlining of the APA might help it to channel its energies so it could respond to the needs of its members better than it had in the past.

Stanford Ericksen thought that what unified psychologists was their humanitarian concern. All psychologists wished to be of help to their fellow human beings. Therefore, the APA might well direct its energies to the social utilization of psychological knowledge.

Lloyd Humphreys thought the best strategy might be to consider the differences among psychologists to be irreconcilable. Recognize there are scientists and practitioners, have separate training programs for each, award them different degrees (Humphreys was a professor at the University of Illinois and thus had first-hand knowledge that such a two-degree program could be successful), and when they are fully trained, let them hold their own meetings and publish in their own journals. It might be possible to contain these different groups under the sagging umbrella of the APA, but the legal and tax complications might make separation more reasonable. In any case, the existence of separate groups might foster an atmosphere of mutual respect that would be preferable to the hostility and recrimination currently pervasive.

Confronted with these recommendations, the APA membership seemed to favor letting things ride and making do. There was no strong push in favor of fragmenting the organization, but neither was there much agreement about what it was that unified psychologists. A moment's thought was enough to demonstrate that the humanitarian ideals of psychologists were not distinctive. Most rational, sensitive, intelligent people claimed to favor peace, civil rights, and a decent life for all. Although it was comforting to think psychologists shared those aims, they appeared to be a flimsy basis for a scientific or professional association—not to mention that a number of psychologists professed to doubt if such ideals were really held in common.

But undergraduate enrollment in psychology courses was booming, competition was stiff for admission into graduate school, and jobs seemed plentiful. The U.S. Department of Labor predicted the number of psychologists employed by state and local governments would increase from 3,300 in 1965 to 6,000 in 1975, that the number of bachelor's degrees in psychology would jump from 14,700 in 1965 to 32,700 by 1975, and that the number of PhDs awarded in psychology would go from 800 in 1965 to 2,000 in 1975. Federal support for training, research, and the construction and renovation of graduate facilities (46 grants totalling over 11½ million dollars had been awarded for this last purpose alone during 1960-1966) had been generous. And humanitarian and employment prospects were brightened by such decisions as were handed down in 1966 in the U.S. Court of Appeals for the District of Columbia in the case of *Rouse v. Cameron*. Chief Judge David Bazelon asserted that persons who were involuntarily committed had a right to receive satisfactory treatment as speedily as possible and that "continuing failure to provide suitable and adequate treatment cannot be justified by lack of staff or facilities."

In 1969 Ken Little, a clinical psychologist, became the executive officer of the APA. So heady were these times that a Cassandra of the profession predicted clinical psychology would cease to be a form of practice because all the clinicians produced would be needed for teaching and administration and none would be left to do diagnosis and treatment (Albee, 1970). President Nixon had just begun his first term of office, and the times they were a-changing.

Yet within clinical psychology some things remained the same (Wildman & Wildman, 1974). Clinicians were still wondering about their identity, as they had been wondering for over 40 years. Some felt they were scientists, others that they were practitioners, and still others that they were just warm human beings. The profession was growing. Of that there was no doubt. The Clinical Division of APA had over 3,500 members, and the future of the profession, though tinged with uncertainty, seemed destined to be long and fruitful.

IV

THE FOURTH GENERATION

Clinical psychology became the largest single field within psychology, with roughly as many members as all the other fields of psychology combined. As a result, clinicians were assured a position of dominance within the APA, and that organization, although still very much involved in furthering the science of psychology, became increasingly concerned with professional issues. At this time, there were 155 doctoral training programs in clinical psychology approved by the APA, most of which were in colleges or universities. There were also 45 professional schools offering doctorates, usually PsyDs, in clinical psychology (most of these schools were free-standing or not part of a college or university). Clinical psychologists were legally recognized throughout the United States and in many other countries of the world. The applications of the field in addressing human problems enabled the profession to remain attractive even during a constrictive economic period and indicated the likelihood of its continued growth.

MAJOR EVENTS IN THE HISTORY
OF CLINICAL PSYCHOLOGY

1970 to 1979

Cognitive behaviorism and social learning theory; modeling, vicarious learning, and self-efficacy of Bandura; Rotter's I-E.

Depression viewed as learned helplessness and incorrect beliefs.

Cognitive behavior modification, social skills training, relaxation training, and stress reduction techniques.

Growth in PhD and PsyD programs and professional schools and emphasis on clinicians as practitioners.

Clinical psychology differentiates into areas of specialization and independent fields.

Clinical psychologists are legally entitled to receive third-party payments for their services.

The APA affirms the doctoral degree is required for professional practice in psychology, defines a basic curriculum for psychologists, and endorses continuing education; about 20,000 of the 50,000 psychologists in APA are clinicians.

1980 to 1989

Life span psychology, with emphasis on infancy and old age; renewed interest in the self and the unconscious as explanatory constructs and in temperamental or biological variables.

Health psychology or holistic medicine; the significance of stress and Type A and Type B personalities.

Involvement in testing continues to decline; computer scoring and interpretation grows; revisions of WPPSI, MMPI, and Stanford-Binet; IQ is abandoned as score by Stanford-Binet.

Meta-analyses demonstrate effectiveness of psychotherapy; hypnosis widely regarded as attention, without need of trance for treatment.

Clinicians receive hospital admitting privileges, admission to psychoanalytic institutes, and payments for their services under Medicare; about half the psychologists in the APA are clinicians.

10

A Professional Establishment 1970–1979

This was a decade that again demonstrated psychology's vulnerability to economic conditions and the ingenuity and adaptability of psychologists. During the administrations of Presidents Nixon, Ford, and Carter, the United States and the world seemed in the draining grip of ever-worsening inflation, with countries once considered underdeveloped merging to form a powerful cartel, the Organization of Petroleum-Exporting Countries (OPEC). For a time this cartel held much of the planet hostage to high prices for oil. An energy crisis was widely publicized, and as the costs of fuels rose, so did almost everything else.

Caught in the crunch of rising prices, rising taxes, and the lower purchasing power of the dollar were those whose incomes were relatively fixed, including teachers and tax-funded programs and institutions. The War on Poverty, with its wide range of social welfare programs, was reduced to an inconclusive series of skirmishes, and the federal commitment to community mental health centers was left in tatters. Within a short few years the prediction there would be far more jobs in psychology than psychologists to fill them, whether in clinical settings or colleges, proved wrong. Just the reverse happened. The need for psychological services grew, but financial sources lowered expenditures and there were relatively few jobs, particularly in academic settings. As a result, some psychologists could not find employment in the field for which they had been trained and needed to seek retraining in professional psychology or a less congenial vocation.

As one commentator put it,

> The '70s were a disconcerting decade. For the first time in the memory of most Americans, people felt they had lost control over events that shaped their lives. The mood was mainly one of bewilderment. Individuals were simply unprepared for so many shocks and disappointments that came in quick succession. (Hacker, 1980, p. 129)

What were these shocks and disappointments? There were in fact so many that it is impossible to detail them all here, but let us note a few of the more significant ones.

The American dream of job security and a growing standard of living was shaken, if not destroyed, as was the very concept of progress itself. People no longer thought things would inevitably get better and better. Nuclear energy, far from becoming a technological marvel and an inexpensive source of power, was transformed into a dearly bought nightmare of cost overruns, safety hazards, and threats of ill-defined proportions. Confidence in the country's leadership, weakened by the growing involvement in the war in Vietnam under President Johnson, was not appreciably strengthened by that war's continuance under President Nixon, nor by the unprecedented resignations of Vice President Agnew and President Nixon and the ineptitude of President Carter's government in dealing with the Iranian seizure of the U.Ş. Embassy and its occupants in Teheran. Along the way were the dispiriting bombings in Cambodia, revelations of "dirty tricks," the killings of college students on campuses by police and National Guardsmen, airplane hijackings, the abandonment of Vietnam, the suicide of 900 followers of the Jim Jones religious cult, the Watergate scandal, disclosures of questionable activities by the FBI and CIA, the Symbionese Liberation Army, riots, protests, the reestablishment of diplomatic relations between the United States and China, genetic engineering, and test-tube pregnancies.

American society no longer appeared to be a melting pot, and that very image was repudiated as an ideal amid all the talk of ethnic pride, bilingual education, and the rights of one group at the expense of another. Women's rights, gay rights, the acceptance of extramarital sexual relationships, the right to have an abortion, and birth control devices were credited with defusing the "population bomb" and leading to a new concern about the "graying of America." Contentious factions emerged within psychology itself. There was disagreement among psychologists about the merits of the arguments and the actions advocated for many of these issues; there was consequent distress when the leadership of the APA committed the organization to one side in these disputes, such as when it decided APA conventions would no longer be held in states that failed to ratify the Equal Rights Amendment to the Constitution or when it endorsed the right of gay parents to be awarded custody of their children.

The Moral Majority, consisting of Americans who claimed devotion to traditional values and beliefs, arose as a loosely organized political movement whose purpose was to counter the growing number of abortions, over a million a year, and to reassert the influence of conservative religions. According to its members, society was falling apart because each person was "looking out for Number One." Individualism and self-interest were thought to be at the foundation of a number of social evils: divorce rates at an all-time high; crime at record levels; growing numbers of single-parent families; children coming to be regarded as burdens and dispensable career impediments instead of blessings; and the breakdown of the traditional family, with Dad the breadwinner and Mom the chief cook and bottle washer going the way of romantic ballads and the schmoo.

Some said this was the "me decade," and some said it was the "culture of narcissism." Whatever it was called, the bicentennial of the founding of the United States came and went without any notable surge in patriotism. Many argued national boundaries were of less importance than the interests and profits of international corporations, and others argued the rights of citizens took precedence over any so-called obligations to the country: "The United States was entering its third century less a nation than an aggregate of individuals. People may have had higher estimates of themselves than in any previous generation" (Hacker, 1980, p. 137).

To what extent were these currents and culture changes determined by clinical psychologists and to what extent did they affect clinical psychology? Obviously, clinical psychology had long championed the worth of the individual, and for over 30 years humanistic psychologists had discussed self-actualization as a major human motive, if not the only one. These views had been given wide currency in psychology and education texts and were presented to the public by the mass media and any number of popular self-help books. It would certainly be incorrect to minimize the significance of these teachings and to contend psychologists were reclusive scientists and practitioners who had nothing to do with what was going on in their society. Similarly, it would be wrong to regard psychology as unaffected by national and world events. Both involvement in social issues and an exclusive focus on intimate relationships characterized this period. As we look at this decade in more detail, we will be able to better appreciate the pervasiveness of the interactions between these two extremes.

NORMAL PERSONALITY FUNCTIONING

Although the influence of psychoanalysis within psychology waned, its predicted demise did not occur. In fact, psychoanalysis did not even deign to respond to the attacks on it and went about its business of becoming a comprehensive personality theory. Its jargon was as esoteric and intimidating as ever, but its most noteworthy ideas, refurbished and rarely mentioned in connection with those who originated them, were there to be uncovered.

Erikson's psychosocial stages of ego development opened the way for Horney (trust versus mistrust), Rank (autonomy versus shame and doubt; identity versus confusion), Adler (industry versus inferiority), and perhaps a bit of existentialism and Jung (intimacy versus isolation; generativity versus stagnation; integrity versus despair). Theoreticians such as Kohut (1971, 1977) emphasized the development of the self (Sullivan, Rogers) in the infant's interactions with the mothering person and the significance of these early experiences in personality growth. Infancy came to be seen as far more important than the Oedipal stage, since it preceded it and thus in large measure determined it. At any rate, more and more attention was given this period (Mahler, Pine, & Bergmann, 1975) and analysts were most receptive to the empirical findings of infant psychologists and the theory of Piaget (who was sufficiently removed from analysis to be acknowledged by name).

At times the analytic terminology would fade from view, and discussions of "self-actualization," "growth," and the concept of resistance as a positive sign of individuality might lead one to believe one was reading Rogers or Rank. Certainly the ego had never before been given so much attention, and although the psychosexual theory and its drives were not forgotten, their status was decidedly reduced. Human growth and mothering and its effects in nurturing and encouraging the child's sense of self and independence were much discussed:

Organization can only take place in a manner consistent with the level of development. Organizational formations and malformations, then, represent given levels and qualities of development. Normalcy, therefore, is the result of organization and development, while pathology is the result of malformation in the organizing process. (Blanck & Blanck, 1979, pp. 18–19)

Many analysts were willing to think of the ego as having its own instinctual energy and drives, perhaps drives to explore, to learn, to be competent, and to establish mastery, which when frustrated lead to distress and conflict and efforts to deal with the obstacle. These theoretical suggestions seemed daring and controversial within analytic circles, but they would hardly have excited most psychologists, who had long entertained similar notions. In contrast to the frenetic pace in psychology, psychoanalysis moved with glacial speed, slowly assimilating what seemed appropriate, yet retaining its core Freudian identity.

The Freudian core was continuously criticized for its emphasis on the past, the unconscious, and aggressive and sexual instincts. But it was also misrepresented as being the sum total of psychoanalysis. Even Erikson, who stoutly maintained his psychosocial stages were meant to complement, not supplant, Freud, saw his ideas displayed as an alternative to psychoanalysis. And poor Freud, who had been dead for over 30 years, was taken to task for what he said, for what he didn't say, for not changing the theory, and for constantly changing the theory. The feminist movement was indignant about his concept of penis envy, and the comedian Woody Allen, playing an analyst in his movie *Zelig*, admitted, "I broke with Freud over the concept of penis envy because he wanted to restrict it to women." Moreover, although few personality theories stimulated more research than psychoanalysis, and although Silverman (1976) reported on two research programs whose findings supported the significance of unconscious wishes for behavior, the unjust criticism that the theory was untestable continued to be voiced.

Behavioral psychologists, among the foremost critics of psychoanalysis, were distinguished by their rejection of unconscious conflict and Freud's theory of instincts. They occupied a dominant position within American psychology and had ascended to a similar lofty perch in clinical psychology. B. F. Skinner (1904–1990), who was acclaimed by many as the greatest American psychologist and who even attained a degree of popularity during the seventies, was behaviorism's eloquent spokesperson.

B. Frederic Skinner was born in Pennsylvania and graduated from Hamilton College in 1926 with a major in English literature. He aimed to be a creative writer, and for 2 years struggled to make a name in this field while living in Greenwich Village in New York. Little rewarded for his efforts, he began graduate studies in psychology at Harvard, earning his PhD in 1931. After teaching at the University of Minnesota and the University of Indiana, he returned to Harvard in 1948, where he remained for the rest of his career (Skinner, 1967). Though a leading behaviorist by the mid-forties, Skinner's aversion to theory put him into eclipse through most of the fifties, when psychologists were enamored of elegant theory building and were thus more attentive to the constructions of Hull and Tolman.

His novel *Walden Two*, published in 1948, dealt with the creation of a utopian community, the product of a benevolent social engineer who controlled behavior by a clear, consistent use of reinforcement principles and a steadfast refusal to worry overmuch about inner states. It and Skinner did not really attract widespread attention until the sixties, when a generation of clinical psychologists, disenchanted with psychodynamic formulations and the seemingly ineffective results of psychotherapy, turned to behaviorism in order to put their discipline on a firm empirical footing and to increase the effectiveness of treatment.

To the astonishment of many—probably to the surprise and delight of Skinner himself—clinical psychologists embraced and honored him, perhaps more so than if he had been one of their own. The Association for Behavior Analysis, an organization dedicated to Skinnerian work, was launched in the seventies, and Skinner, an articulate and stimulating advocate of radical behaviorism, became a celebrated figure, featured on the cover of *Time* magazine because of the controversy aroused by his book *Beyond Freedom and Dignity* (Skinner, 1971).

In this work Skinner simply said what he had been saying for years: that societies would be better off if they acknowledged that human behavior is determined and concentrated on seeing to it that their citizens were consistently rewarded for desirable behaviors and were not rewarded for doing what is wrong. He repeated this theme and made explicit his assumptions in *About Behaviorism* (Skinner, 1974). He did not deny that people have inner workings and that the world is complex. The point was to get on with it, to ignore complexity and what could not be changed, to focus on what could be changed, and to see how much might thereby be accomplished: "It is the environment which must be changed. . . . In the behavioristic view, man can now control his own destiny because he knows what must be done and how to do it" (Skinner, 1974, p. 251).

Terms such as *personality, neurosis, anxiety, instinct*, and *habit* had no place in Skinner's system; all of them merely referred to certain forms of behavior. The task of the psychologist, according to Skinner's radical behaviorism, was to do a *functional analysis* of the individual's behavior, that is, to determine what was rewarding or maintaining or controlling the behavior in question or to determine what would be rewarding and controlling and then to institute an appropriate system of rewards for desirable behavior.

By these simple means and with astonishing displays of ingenuity and patience, behavioral psychologists reported all sorts of accomplishments—from teaching a chimp how to use words or signs (Premack, 1972) to discovering that attraction to a stranger is a function of number of rewards (Byrne, 1971). What was notable was the intoxicating degree of self-confidence and power conveyed by behaviorists. For example: "Our studies suggest that Sarah [a chimp], who knows more than 120 words, has mastered four important functions of language. This does not mean that she can produce all the functions of language, or that she can do everything a human can: but then, we have only been working with her a relatively short while" (Premack, 1972, p. 135). Such optimism was shared by behavioral clinicians, who saw in learning principles and techniques a guarantee of some measure of success in dealing with every behavioral problem.

However, just as there were neobehaviorists (Hull, Tolman) after Watson, so too were there cognitive behaviorists and social learning behaviorists who differed with Skinner and his followers. Chief among the social learning behaviorists was Albert Bandura, who was president of the APA in 1973.

Bandura (b. 1925) received his BA from the University of British Columbia in 1949 and his PhD from the University of Iowa in 1952. After a clinical internship at the Wichita Guidance Center, he went to Stanford University, where he remained throughout his career. A major theme in his work is that much of human learning occurs without obvious rewards provided. In many instances, learning takes place when we observe the consequences of behavior for others; we see someone rewarded or punished for doing something and thus learn what to expect for engaging in that behavior (vicarious learning). Another major form of learning consists of emulating or modeling the behavior of someone we like, admire, or respect. A third major form of human learning consists of acquiring information of behaviors in order to meet our own standards; here we administer approval (rewards) or disapproval (punishments) to ourselves when we live up to or fail to live up to our values and ideals.

Thus Bandura (1977), within the framework of behaviorism, introduced the concept of the self. This self was very similar to the self posited by James and Rogers, a set of cognitive structures or beliefs, including expectations as to whether one is competent to deal with a situation (self-efficacy). Moreover, this self system was capable not only of self-regulating but also of regulating the environment so that rewards would be forthcoming for valued behaviors. A process of reciprocal determinism was described, in which the environment acts on the person and the person acts on the environment, and these actions affect their targets and their agents as they see the effects produced. Since Bandura had little sympathy for unconscious processes, the self he posited was very rational and reasonable and in that sense similar to the self described by James.

A great deal of research was stimulated by Bandura's ideas, and the significance of modeling, particularly the effects of watching violence on television, generated discussion and concern. Rotter's notion of internal-external (I-E) control also served to spur research. By 1976, Phares's book dealing with the locus of control reviewed the findings of about 200 studies, and that number increased yearly. Also by this time the consistency of the findings attained through use of the I-E scale seemed less than formerly. Some found it difficult to replicate the research or obtain similar results. This led Rotter (1975) to explain that expectations as to whether one's behavior was internally controlled were most likely to have an effect in somewhat ambiguous situations. For example, in certain circumstances almost everyone would agree that personal control was or was not possible, such as picking what to eat for breakfast versus influencing the toss of a coin. Rotter's argument was that only in settings where there was uncertainty about control could I-E expectations come into play and affect behavior. A similar rationale might be appropriate for any number of expectations, including Bandura's efficacy expectation.

Self-regulations figured prominently not only in social learning theory but also in Piaget's theory: "We must think in terms neither of the exclusive action of the environment nor of an innate preformation, but of self-regulations functioning in circuits and having an intrinsic tendency towards equilibrium" (Piaget, 1972, p. 60). Equilibrium was presented not as a static state but as a progressive process leading to new assimilation, accommodations, structures, schemas, and equilibriums. Significantly, Piaget noted that because early learning (the sensorimotor period) occurs when the infant is without language, the basis of intelligence is essentially unconscious.

The dominant trend in the seventies was the increasing importance of behavioral positions, with social learning theory representing a conscientious effort to address the complexity and subtlety of human behavior in a rigorous, experimental manner.

Skinner was criticized, somewhat unfairly, for ignoring complexity, for stripping people of their freedom and dignity, and for encouraging a tide of manipulativeness and depersonalization (Smith, 1973). More justifiably, the Skinnerian position was taken to task for emphasizing the consequences of behavior and not the information given by those consequences: "Contrary to the mechanistic metaphors, outcomes change behavior in humans through the intervening influence of thought" (Bandura, 1974).

The research, of which there was more than anyone could possibly know and in more journals than most psychologists could afford, was evaluated negatively. On the one hand, Epstein (1979) was disappointed that so much of the experimental research was not replicable and so often dealt with variables that were easily manipulated instead of being highly relevant. Similarly, Rorer and Widiger (1983) concluded from their review of personality research that "the obsession with pseudo-rigor has resulted in well-controlled studies that are virtually irrelevant to the questions they are supposed to answer. . . . [They] focus instead on the minutiae of . . . previous studies."

On the other hand, many of the constructs in personality theory were taken to task for having more factors than would have been supposed. Locus of control, for instance, appeared to be composed of four or five factors rather than two (Jackson & Paunonen, 1980). Many of the critics thought the solution might be to try a different approach, the idiographic or idiothetic approach, rather than the nomothetic approach so long employed. The individual would be studied and personality would be described—yet not in terms of how the person compared with others but in terms of the person's actual behavior in a given situation compared with what the person could have done in that situation (Lamiell, 1981). The individual would be his or her own frame of reference and would be judged in relation to fulfilling his or her potential.

DIAGNOSTIC TECHNIQUES

Throughout the seventies, psychological testing came under attack from critics inside and outside the field. The major criticisms were the same ones as have previously been mentioned: that tests were used to segregate children and deprive people of educational and vocational opportunities; that they sampled a narrow range of skills and behaviors; and that for many reasons they were often, if not usually, invalid.

Suggestions were made to do away with psychological tests entirely and to (1) devise entirely new ones that would sample more appropriate abilities and accomplishments and that would be better standardized than the old; (2) develop highly specific measures for highly specific attributes, such as a specific scale for depression or a specific scale for emotionality; or (3) make a judgment about the behaviors in question by observing the person's performance in those natural settings where the behaviors would be elicited (Bersoff, 1973). This last suggestion, it may be recalled, had also been made by Witmer (1909–1910).

An APA committee studied the matter and issued a report to the membership in 1975. The report presented certain differences between populations of blacks and whites when standardized tests of intelligence and achievement were administered: The means for white children tended to be about one standard deviation higher than the means of black youngsters. These differences were found consistently and throughout the school years. However, these differences did not provide any justification for the segregation of children by race, nor were they evidence of genetic differences between the races. The committee offered a state-of-the-art definition of intelligence that differed 180 degrees from the most widespread previous definition: "Intelligence is defined as *the entire repertoire of acquired* [italics added] skills, knowledge, learning sets, and generalization tendencies considered intellectual in nature that are available at any one period of time. An intelligence test contains items that sample such *acquisitions* [italics added]" (Cleary, Humphreys, Kendrick, & Wesman, 1975, p. 19). The committee concluded by urging the "better and fairer use of tests."

The committee's report drew an immediate response from a spokesperson for minority psychologists: "Psychological testing historically has been a quasi-scientific tool in the perpetuation of racism . . . it has provided a cesspool of . . . fallacious data which inflates the egos of whites by demeaning Black people and threatens to potentiate Black genocide" (Jackson, 1975). He urged immediate sanctions against the further use of tests.

Despite the strong condemnations of psychological tests and their improper usage, the numbers of psychological tests continued to grow. Efforts were made to develop new measures of intelligence that would be non-culture-bound or reflect Piaget's stages of intellectual development or sample creativity. The results attained with these instruments, however, did not suggest they were much of an improvement (Anastasi, 1982). Most new tools for personality measurement were self-report questionnaires, many of which could be computer scored and interpreted, though here, as might be expected, criticisms were voiced similar to those expressed some 50 years before: People may not report information or may distort it, they may be unaware of their behaviors, the questions may not sample significant aspects of personality, and unconscious conflicts and functioning are not available for self-report.

Significantly, training in psychological testing was becoming less essential in graduate programs in clinical psychology. Behavioral psychologists favored assessments of behavior, community psychologists favored analyses of the system or measurement of the social milieu, and existential-humanistic psychologists preferred to help clients gain in self-understanding.

All things considered, what was amazing was the continued popularity among clinicians of certain tests and projective techniques whose use had been discouraged and whose validity had been suspect for over 20 years. This failure of clinicians to modify their behavior no matter how much aversive stimulation they received from their colleagues was not taken as a refutation of Skinner's theory but as evidence of a tendency to distort information. A spate of studies showed that clinicians persisted in seeing relationships when evidence to the contrary was presented, were less accurate than statistical predictions, and were reinforced by vague interpretations that could apply to anyone. Nevertheless, some clinicians, such as Holt (1970), maintained that astute, sensitive professionals could be aware of cues in making informed judgments that were simply not accessible to machines. Disciplined, refined diagnostic evaluations by such professionals were argued to be superior and more attuned to the clients than any computer printout, regardless of empirical findings. Much sadness was felt in some quarters about the dwindling investment of clinical psychologists in their tests and their assessment functions.

Yet another Rorschach scoring system was proposed (Exner, 1974) to increase reliability in scoring and interpretation. This seemed to complement Rorschach's and Beck's theme of scientific rigor and precision by emphasizing the structural analysis of responses to the inkblots, although in the crunch of actual practice many clinicians still relied heavily on the analysis of content and their intuitions.

Scientific breakthroughs in diagnostic techniques did occur, but they were not in clinical psychology. Computerized axial tomography (CAT scan) provided cross-sectional, pictorial representations of the brain. In the first rush of enthusiasm for this technological marvel, it was thought the CAT scanner would be able to locate lesions and tumors of all kinds; although not that successful, it certainly did appear to be a valuable diagnostic tool. However, neuropsychological evaluations were still in order, since even when the location of damage could be specified, the consequences for psychological functioning needed to be determined. Meanwhile the field of biochemistry continued to identify neurotransmitters, metabolic products, and other types of biological "markers" that seemed to be associated with one or another form of psychopathology. For example, a low level of norepinephrine seemed to be associated with depressive behavior and a low level of serotonin with fearful or anxious behaviors (Ellison, 1977).

DIAGNOSTIC FORMULATIONS

The problems in relating biological markers to particular forms of psychopathology were made worse by the low reliability of psychiatric diagnoses, the number of unofficial psychiatric disorders with ambiguous criteria (e.g., early infantile autism, hyperactivity, minimal brain damage, borderline disorder, borderline retardation), and the vague standards for many disorders in DSM-II. "The current state of the biological approaches to psychopathology is chaotic; no markers have been accepted despite the fact that dozens have resulted in promising, if not dramatic, results" (Buchsbaum & Haier, 1983).

A new nomenclature, DSM-III, was produced by an American Psychiatric Association committee in 1980, but even before its official publication it received unprecedented attention and criticism. In part this was due to the committee's sincere desire to consider a broad range of opinions, which antagonized those whose views were rejected or ignored, and to present whenever possible the diagnostic criteria in a reliable form, which troubled those who felt the specifications were invalid or still imprecise. Another problem was that, with very noble intentions, the committee had wanted to provide an appropriate diagnostic label for any person who might come to a psychiatrist. Accordingly, a number of behaviors formerly regarded outside the purview of psychiatry were made part of the nomenclature. Thus, shyness (avoidant disorder), stubbornness (oppositional disorder), tobacco smoking (substance use disorder), and significant deficiency in reading or arithmetic (specific development disorder) became official psychiatric problems, and there was no telling what effects this might have on those so diagnosed and on the prevalence of "mental illness," except that the figures would unquestionably be much higher than they had been (Garmezy, 1978).

DSM-III included many terminological changes and refinements in diagnostic criteria that reflected genuine advances in understanding: psychological tests were made essential in the diagnosis of mental retardation and school achievement problems; homosexuality was a disorder only if the individual was dissatisfied with this sexual preference (ego-dystonic homosexuality); psychophysiologic or psychosomatic disorders were replaced by the more comprehensive designation *psychological factors affecting a physical condition*; the criteria for functional enuresis, functional encopresis, and schizophrenia were made explicit, which gave promise for advances in research (Spitzer, Williams, & Skodol, 1980). Most impressive of all was the modesty with which the nomenclature was offered. The need for a DSM-IV and later revisions and the work toward filling that need were anticipated, and frank ignorance about the etiology of most disorders were confessed.

The etiological confusion about schizophrenia was particularly distressing, since so much research had been directed to determining its causes. All seemed to agree genetic factors were involved. It was argued that there was not necessarily a progressive course, but there was a vulnerability to the disorder brought about by experiences and stresses; the person might recover or improve but the vulnerability remained, as did the probability of improvements and relapses (Zubin & Spring, 1977). Others pointed to everything from an unhappy home to something in white bread to problems in the level of dopamine to a delayed response to a virus infection as the cause of schizophrenia. Yet by the end of the decade, the cause was still unknown: "Fundamental understanding of the roots of mental illness and advances in treatment continued to be discouragingly slow, and 1980 provided only scant cause for expectation that the pattern would soon change" (Buchsbaum & Haier, 1983).

Although exaggeration and distortion were to be expected in popular accounts of scientific findings and efforts, the professional literature was not immune to strident claims. New techniques, and even old techniques given new names, were "breakthroughs" and "revolutions." Various problems were portrayed as "diseases" of "epidemic proportions" and "of mounting concern." These were obvious signs of rashness. Further, the volume of mental health literature made some wonder if the importance of the topics was not being inflated. Gould (1981) suspected the prevalence of mental illness in the United States was being blown out of proportion. He noted that while U.S. mental health professionals contributed 75% of the world's articles in their field, the contribution of U.S. scientists to the total literature in other areas of medicine and science was only 40% to 50%. "It could be suggested," and Gould (1981) did so suggest, "that the incidence . . . of reported disorders of the mind bears a direct relationship to the magnitude of the professional effort devoted to their study and treatment."

Racial differences in intelligence continued throughout the decade to be a volatile issue. The debate about heredity and environment raged on as if a single argument could be decisive. Scholarly reviews attempted to put the evidence in reasonable perspective (Robinson, 1970; Loehlin, Lindzey, & Spuhler, 1975; Block & Dworkin, 1976); however, they did not settle matters.

Attacks on those who had argued for the greater importance of heredity in determining intelligence increased. Terman, Goddard, and Yerkes were denounced as biased (Kamin, 1974), and the research of Burt, Jensen, and Goddard was called "shoddy." Indeed, Goddard's and Burt's data were said to have been manufactured so as to confirm their suppositions (Dorfman, 1978; Jensen, 1978; Gould, 1981; Lewontin, Rose, & Kamin, 1984). It was suggested psychologists recognize that IQ tests do not measure intelligence but achievement, that the assignment of any numerical value to the amount of intelligence inherited is meaningless and objectionable, and that researchers in the area of racial differences bear a special social responsibility to assess carefully the possible harm of their interpretations of findings (Block & Dworkin, 1976).

Appropriately, there was more than ordinary interest in the topic of depression, and the February 1978 issue of the *Journal of Abnormal Psychology* was devoted to just one of its aspects: learned helplessness. Learned helplessness occurred when dogs, for example, were subjected to inescapable electric shocks. When the dogs were later placed in a situation where they could escape the shocks, they did little or nothing to avoid them—they had learned to be helpless. Seligman (1975) related such canine behavior to the behavior of depressed humans, and he suggested depressives could be helped by being encouraged or trained to deal more actively with their circumstances and to see they had some control over them.

A different view of depression emphasized the avoidance by depressives of situations where they might be rewarded and the low probability of their doing things that might result in positive reinforcement (Ferster, 1973). This analysis stressed the lack of rewards from the environment and the tendency not to do what might be socially rewarding.

A third widely discussed view was associated with A. T. Beck (1972). The depressive's self-critical cognitions and incorrect beliefs about being a "loser" and failing to measure up to unreal standards of perfection were thought by Beck to be of greatest importance. Although changing such beliefs was the major focus of Beck's (1976) cognitive therapy, all the above theories could accommodate improvements in behavior brought about by training.

From the perspective of psychiatrists, biochemical findings generated much excitement. An excess of the hormone cortisol was associated with those who had endogenous depressions (DePue, 1979). Moreover, norepinephrine, serotonin, and thyroid levels seemed involved in affective disorders. Such findings were said to signify yet another revolution in psychiatric understanding and treatment, although, as usual, the more these findings were investigated, the less reliable they seemed to be. For example, the hypersecretion of cortisol was found in only half the cases of endogenous depression in adults and appeared even less often among younger patients similarly depressed (Puig-Antich & Gittelman, 1980).

A dismal fate had befallen the extra Y chromosome as a significant biological marker for aggression in men. Research found that the prevalence of XYY in normal males is 0.13% and that among criminals it does occur at a statistically greater frequency of 1.9%. Nevertheless, for practical purposes it was of little use, since many males with an extra Y chromosome are not violent and the great majority of aggressive male criminals, not to mention all the aggressive females, are not XYY (Jarvik, Klodin, & Matsuyama, 1973).

What progress did seem to occur was of a peculiar sort—the exciting and the mysterious were reduced to the banal. Biofeedback training to increase the frequency of alpha rhythms and relaxation was found comparable in its effects to meditation, which was found to be not significantly better in reducing stresses and strains than simply sitting down, closing one's eyes, and trying to relax (Holmes, 1984). Hypnosis was no longer regarded as an avenue to accurate recall of information (Turkington, 1982) and could be thought of as a narrowing or focusing of attention. The more the person attended to the voice of the "operator" or hypnotist, the more suggestible the person became and the more the behavior exhibited trancelike characteristics. This explanation of hypnosis, which was developed by the hypnotist Milton Erickson, suggested that everyone who could attend or listen could be to some extent hypnotized and that hypnotic phenomena, far from being rare, occurred whenever people gave their attention to someone else (Erickson, Rossi, & Rossi, 1976). Since attention is given in the classroom, in watching television, in reading a book, people's exposure to suggestive influences (hypnosis) occurs daily and almost continuously.

The behavioral movement had started with heady claims about controlling behavior and using appropriate reinforcers to make people do whatever was desired. Nothing seemed beyond reach, and it appeared that the individuals who were the targets of these efforts need not be consulted about them. All one had to do was cleverly manipulate rewards and punishments and observe the behavior change. As the decade progressed, there was talk of how to generalize effects (early studies frequently noted generalization of desired behaviors to many situations as a pleasant by-product), of how to bring about self-control and intrinsic rewards, or negotiating behavioral contracts, and of enlisting cooperation. These topics came into prominence as the limitations of behavioral methods came to be recognized and cognitive concepts were invoked:

> More recently, biofeedback, despite its dependence upon electrophysiological equipment, actually emphasizes the attainment of voluntary control through feedback in line with the intentions of the persons being treated. . . . The behavior therapists themselves are paying more attention to the person's expectations and plans as influential in producing the changes that are desired. (Hilgard, 1980)

Social learning theorists were usually disarming as a result of the straightforwardness and simplicity of their views. Their main argument might be put as follows. In working with nonhumans, it is often necessary to train without taking the subject into our confidence. However, we do have an advantage with human beings. Very often we can tell them what we would like them to do and they will do it. Or we can discuss the matter with them and work out some mutually agreeable compromise. At the very least, we can in most instances explain what we are about and hope they will see it is to their benefit to be cooperative. Given these obvious facts, what is to be gained by pretending people are empty organisms or black boxes?

Behavior modifiers followed a different line of reasoning but to the same end. Notice was taken of growing concerns within the society about the rights of the individual. Skinnerian approaches were criticized for violating rights in institutional settings by making various "privileges" and "rewards" contingent on the performance of certain behaviors. Accordingly, legal judgments forbade the use of token economies and the employment of aversive techniques, and careful attention was paid to determine when behavior modification constituted an invasion of privacy and a threat to personal dignity. To allay these concerns, it was recommended that behavior modifiers affirm their intent to protect the rights and welfare of those who might receive their services and that they solicit cooperation on the basis of informed consent (Stolz, Wienckowski, & Brown, 1975).

TREATMENT FORMULATIONS

Claims about psychotherapeutic techniques reached a height and frenzy from which, thankfully, there was nowhere to go but down. For a short time serious discussion was given to the circumstances (if any) in which it might be appropriate for a therapist to have sexual relations with a client. The textbook and exhibit area at the APA convention in New Orleans in 1974 assaulted the senses and the sensibilities of anyone who might be sexually innocent or feel some restraint was proper: Booths offering electronic instrumentation mingled with masturbatory devices and films showing intercourse. Further, there was an unseemly interest in the merchandising and franchising of psychotherapeutic services. Amid the hubbub it was difficult to remember that only a few years before some psychologists talked of donating their services, primary prevention, and career ladders.

Clinicians were reminded again of how few of their treatment methods dropped into oblivion. Instead, the popularity of a theory or technique waxed and waned, and many, like a diva in a tragic opera, died long, interminable deaths. Beutler (1979) surveyed the field of psychological treatment and estimated there were over 130 different kinds. Among the new treatments was primal therapy (Janov, 1972), although its *primals*, or early memories of painful events, did not differ much from the *engrams* of dianetics (a form of treatment introduced about 30 years before that found it advantageous for tax purposes to transform itself into a religion, scientology). Among the old treatments were methods based on the teachings of Freud, Adler, Jung, Horney, Rank, and Sullivan.

Five major categories of psychological treatment were identified: (1) *cognitive modification*, or behavioral approaches that emphasize the use of verbal mediation; (2) *behavior therapies*, where imagery is employed to bring about change, as in systematic desensitization and, conceivably, modeling; (3) *behavior modification*, or contingency management without worries; (4) *cognitive insight*, or psychodynamic approaches; and (5) *affective insight*, or existential therapies that stress current problems and the assumption of responsibility. Within each of these categories were individual, family, and group variations.

At the beginning of the decade, it seemed behavioral methods were more effective than others, at least in attaining relatively modest and specific goals, but by the end of the decade there was less certainty about their efficacy. Professionals were at least agreed that it was not easy to demonstrate the superiority of one form of psychotherapy. Therefore, there was much interest in seeing what the various methods had in common.

Frank (1973) noted all therapies probably succeed in arousing the client's expectations of being helped, and this giving of hope may provide the thrust toward growth and improvement. After surveying the field for uniformities, Reisman (1971) concluded what all psychotherapies have in common is the communication of understanding, respect, and the wish to be of help. However, the spur for a considerable research effort was Rogers' (1957) contention that essential to effective therapy was the therapist's genuineness, unconditional positive regard for the client, and accurate empathy.

By the end of the sixties, the relevant research had appeared so highly supportive of Rogers' contention that training programs were encouraged to select therapist candidates on the basis of their ratings on these variables (Truax & Carkhuff, 1967). By the end of the seventies, the situation was muddled.

Mitchell (1974) drew on the findings of a 4-year study of 75 therapists, most of them psychoanalytic and eclectic. Unconditional positive regard and accurate empathy were not significantly related to client change, and the correlation with genuineness was only "modest." The results of 20 years of research on Rogers' conditions led to the inconclusive conclusion that "it makes no sense to talk in terms of effective and ineffective training programs." Also, Parloff, Waskow, and Wolfe (1978) concluded on the basis of their review of the literature that "the evidence for the hypothesis that the conditions of accurate empathy, warmth and genuineness represent the necessary and sufficient conditions for positive change in patients independent of the school of therapy is similarly in doubt" (p. 248).

What was not in doubt? Well, there was no uncertainty that stress was an important and ubiquitous variable worth taking into account no matter what the psychological problem. Hence the reduction and management of excessive stress were highly desirable goals in almost any treatment program. Physicians could see psychologists working with them to reduce the stress arising from any number of medical conditions, and new fields came into being (e.g., health psychology and behavioral medicine) in which psychologists used their skills to alleviate symptoms and aid adjustments to disorders not previously regarded within their domain.

There was also no uncertainty that the deinstitutionalization of mental patients had been seized as a policy by the states, although there was a question whether the motive was to benefit patients or to cut costs. In 1964 the state hospital population in Illinois was 38,137; in 1974 it was 7,590 (Rosenwald & Gould, 1975). In the United States the mental hospital population had gone from about 600,000 in the forties to about 150,000 in 1978, despite the growth in U.S. population. So deinstitutionalization was a fact. Whether it was a success was a different matter. There were disquieting reports of patients dumped unceremoniously in communities where they were neglected or ostracized, and the large number of relapses and readmissions to mental hospitals led this policy to be dubbed "the revolving door."

Finally, there was no uncertainty that the use of drugs was a mixed blessing. The biochemistry of the brain was better understood, and new chemical substances, such as more neurotransmitters and endorphins, were discovered, substances that all hoped would lead to more effective treatments. It was also acknowledged that drugs seldom "cured" a disorder, although they did alleviate symptoms. That they helped patients become more receptive to psychotherapy was readily conceded, as was the fact that psychotherapy was usually not provided. More often, drugs were used to "manage" or "control" patients. Unfortunately, medications were not without their risks. For example, the prolonged use of phenothiazine evidently could result in a disorder of its own, tardive dyskinesia, a muscular problem of repetitive grimacing and lip smacking that often persisted after the medication stopped.

Behavioral approaches increased rapidly in acceptance and stature. It was not until 1955 that the first course in behavior modification was offered by Arthur Staats (Benassi & Lanson, 1972), and it was not until 1965 that these courses accelerated in number. By the early seventies, about two-thirds of the psychology departments in the United States offered courses in behavioral methods, and by decade's end it would have been a rare school that did not provide such instruction. Of course, this growth was accompanied by corresponding increases in texts, training materials, journals, and research (Garfield & Bergin, 1978). Equally significant was the use of behavior therapy and behavior modification in medical, psychiatric, and psychodynamic settings (Masterson, 1972; Davids, 1975; Spence, Carson, & Thibaut, 1976).

There were three major reasons for this widespread acceptance: (1) For almost any purpose, whether overcoming shyness or being more assertive or applying for a job, training procedures might be helpful; (2) for certain purposes, such as teaching retarded or autistic children how to talk, behavioral techniques were among the few means available to provide assistance; and (3) for other purposes, such as pain management and stress reduction, behavioral procedures offered a highly desirable alternative. Coupled with these reasons were the zeal, optimism, patience, and ingenuity of behavior therapists, who were perfectly willing to try their methods on anyone for anything. The result was that behaviorists soon received the kinds of cases for which other treatment methods were unsuccessful.

It was now fairly evident that any method of psychological treatment followed a predictable cycle of stages. In the introductory stage, the method is introduced as distinctive and superior in every way to one or more other methods, and its success in treating many disorders is reported to be significantly greater than any previous therapy. In the endorsement stage, many studies showing the success of the method in treating many problems and disorders are published. In the acceptance stage, the similarity of the method to other methods is noted, and the treatment success rates decline to the point where it appears hardly different in effectiveness from competing approaches. In the assimilation stage, the method adopts some of the attributes of approaches previously condemned, the claims for effectiveness are modest and the limitations of the method are recognized, and what makes the method most distinctive are its label and the professional organizations and journals that bear its name.

In the seventies, behavioral methods moved from the endorsement to the acceptance stage, whereas encounter groups, sensitivity groups, and so on, were on their way from the acceptance to the assimilation stage.

At the beginning of the decade, the number and variety of group approaches boggled the imagination. It seemed that whatever might be done to induce an "experience" was done—from nude marathons to massage to death-in-life to holding one's urine (Blank, Gottsegen, & Gottsegen, 1971; Bry, 1975). The techniques and gimmicks that were used created an atmosphere of excitement and confusion. Here the humanistic movement held sway.

People were encouraged to enter groups to expand their consciousness, to increase their sensitivity, to grow. Target populations included not only patients and clients but students and executives and many other kinds of people, whether they wanted to join groups or not. Carl Rogers found himself associated with these efforts and swept along by them. He suggested his therapy be known as "person-centered," and he and his colleagues founded the Center for Studies of the Person in La Jolla, California, "the zaniest, most improbable, and most influential nonorganization imaginable" (Rogers, 1980, p. 72).

However, amid this giddiness began to appear reports of "deterioration effects" and "casualties" in encounter groups. Horn (1973), in a survey of noteworthy developments in the field, reported a study that found almost 10% of the participants in encounter groups suffered adverse effects from the experience. Hartley, Roback, and Abramowitz (1976) reviewed the growing literature and found that estimates of the percentage of "casualities" ranged from 1% to 47%, with the best guess being about 8%. Breakdowns were caused by forced participation and by leaders who were charismatic and authoritarian and so might compel participation.

As the seventies drew to a close, a more professional and sober tone began to prevail. Economic conditions—unemployment and underemployment of psychologists, job retraining because experimental areas of psychology had no openings, competition for jobs and private practices, and applications for licenses to become legally recognized as psychologists by members of other disciplines—created demands for higher standards and more cautious assessments. Phillips and Bierman (1981) detected a sense of urgency regarding demonstrations of the effectiveness of psychotherapy—perhaps for the less-than-noble reason that a national health insurance plan was in the wind and psychologists wanted their services to be included.

Demonstrating the effectiveness of psychotherapy was usually understood to be a matter of showing that its results were significantly superior to the results found without formal treatment. As we have seen, this modest demonstration was not easily achieved. However, Smith and Glass (1977), by a relatively new statistical treatment (meta-analysis) of the data from 375 controlled studies of psychotherapy and counseling, found that, although there was a considerable overlap in outcome between treated and untreated groups, nevertheless the typical patients receiving therapy were higher rated than 75% of those untreated. They concluded that they had supplied convincing evidence for the effectiveness of therapy but that "unconditional judgments of superiority of one type or another of psychotherapy, and all that these claims imply about treatment and training policy, are unjustified."

Another issue that began to be discussed was the cost-effectiveness of psychotherapy. That is, were the financial gains from treatment sufficient to offset its cost? It was argued, for example, that the provision of psychotherapy reduced the person's use of more costly medical services and procedures. Such a consideration was helpful in arguing the case for the coverage of psychotherapy by insurance plans. Nevertheless, it should be remembered that this dollars-and-cents justification was somewhat irrelevant, since (1) it is very difficult to place a monetary value on even a minor improvement in health or how people feel, and (2) the insurer's possible debits and profits ought not be the issue in determining the provision of treatment.

PROFESSIONAL DEVELOPMENT

The U.S. economy and its effects on the employment of psychologists were an overriding concern throughout the decade. Such a concern had existed during the thirties but certainly not to the same extent. At that time there were approximately 2,000 APA members. In the 70s, there were about 40,000 members of the APA, about 95,000 psychologists in the United States, and almost 24,000 students in psychology graduate programs (National Science Foundation, 1974). Particularly scarce were jobs in colleges and universities, and particularly affected were those who had recently obtained their doctorates, of whom almost one in five did not find immediate employment (Stein & Sauta, 1975).

Only a few years before, Albee (1968) had written, "Elsewhere I have argued that the future available supply of clinical psychologists and social workers is at least as inadequate as the prospective supply in psychiatry. The demands for academicians in psychology, for example, can absorb most of the PhDs we produce over the next decade or two." And only 2 years after Albee's 1970 APA presidential address, in which he predicted so dire a shortage of clinical psychologists that few would be available to practice, Perloff (1972) was writing of a PhD glut and a dismal employment picture. A sobering lesson for those who hazard predictions.

So what was to be done? A number of suggestions were made and actions taken, some of which were in direct response to unemployment but many of which were seemingly unrelated, though probably influenced by, the scarcity of positions. It was suggested that fewer graduate students be accepted and fewer psychologists be produced. It was suggested that psychologists be more broad-minded in assessing their skills and the range of positions for which they would be suitable (Stein & Sauta, 1975). It was suggested that the government increase its spending for research, training, and psychological services. It was suggested that psychologists develop new applications and expand into new markets (Zimet, 1981).

There was little evidence of any support for the suggestion to reduce the number of graduate students. The number of APA-approved programs in clinical psychology rose from 70 in 1969 to over 100 by 1979. Among the additions were five PsyD programs. In fact, despite employment troubles, the number of professional programs grew significantly—from 2 in 1978 to 21 by 1980. Some of these professional programs were affiliated with universities (Adelphi, Rutgers, and Denver) and some were free-standing institutions (California School, Chicago School), that is, schools whose sole purpose was to train psychologists for professional roles. About half awarded PsyD degrees and half PhDs. These professional schools were producing psychologists: The University of Denver and Rutgers University were each awarding about 30 PsyDs a year, and it was estimated that in the near future the number of graduates from professional programs would exceed the output of all other programs combined (McNett, 1982).

The implications of this growth in professionalism were momentous for clinical psychology. First, it meant clinical psychology had arrived as a profession and discipline and was likely to endure. Its existence was not dependent on whims and vagaries outside the field and instead rested on the ingenuity of clinicians in meeting challenges. Now that they had their own schools, faculties, and administrations, their own bureaucracies and organizations, there would be a strong tendency toward protectionism and self-perpetuation. Admittedly this was not without its dangers and disadvantages. Nevertheless, it was a significant development in the history of clinical psychology.

Second, this growth signalled a major change in the role of the clinical psychologist. Originally the clinical psychologist had been a teacher and researcher; then a teacher, researcher, and psychometrician; a diagnostician, researcher, and teacher; a diagnostician, therapist, and researcher; and finally a therapist, consultant, diagnostician, and researcher. Clinical psychologists were increasingly being trained in service functions at the expense of scientific training, rather than the reverse, which had been the case.

Thus, a definite trend toward a professional-practitioner emphasis in clinical psychology—comparable to the emphasis that exists in medicine and the biological sciences—was institutionalized. And this trend, far from reducing the numbers of graduate students during this period of national economic uncertainty, acted to increase them. Yet the new clinicians, in spite of the difficulties, did find employment.

Many entered the field of private practice. One factor that made this possible was the bringing of legal suits against those who tried to obstruct the payment of psychologists by medical insurers. In *Blueshield of Virginia v. McCready* and *Wyatt v. Stickney*, the courts held mental health professionals (psychologists, psychiatric nurses, and social workers) were entitled to treat patients without the supervision of psychiatrists and to receive third-party payments, which was a way of saying patients should have freedom of choice in deciding which kind of professionals should treat them. The result, according to one psychiatrist, was the "dethronement of the psychiatrist as head of the mental health team" (Stone, 1981).

Litigation was also used to compel governments to provide treatment to persons who were in institutions (ostensibly for the purpose of receiving treatment). Judgments were handed down declaring people could not be deprived of their rights and liberties until such time as states allocated adequate funds for their assistance. The courts ruled that any community incurred a responsibility to expeditiously treat those it removed and to see that they were returned to the community as soon as possible. In many states, positions were created in mental hospitals and prisons to satisfy these rulings and meet these responsibilities.

Legislation was used to gain admitting privileges in hospitals and to enable psychologists to be on the medical staffs of hospitals. In 1979 a law of this kind went into effect in California. At the same time, clinical psychology was being divided into various health-related fields: clinical neurophysiology, health psychology, pediatric psychology, clinical psychophysiology (Feuerstein & Schwartz, 1977), and behavioral medicine. Accordingly, the average number of psychologists affiliated with a medical school increased from 4.4 in 1955 to 20.7 in 1976 (Nathan, Lubin, Matarazzo, & Persely, 1979). Moreover, some psychologists offered health-related services to the public in ways not previously imagined—smoking cessation clinics, weight reduction clinics, tension reduction clinics, pain management clinics, and sexual dysfunction clinics—and thus created additional job opportunities.

Therefore, the employment picture in clinical psychology was brighter than in many other areas of psychology. This resulted in pressure to retrain psychologists, that is, to allow psychologists to return to graduate school and take the additional courses and practicums that would enable them to meet standards for licensure and practice as clinicians.

Pressures came from other directions. Graduates of guidance or counseling or various nonpsychology programs sought certification or licensure as psychologists. When their applications were questioned or denied, they challenged the laws on the grounds that there was no specific definition of what constituted psychology or a psychological training program. In addition, state laws were challenged on the grounds that they were detrimental to consumers because they restricted those who could provide services. In 1979 Florida and South Dakota allowed their psychology laws to end, and although they shortly reenacted them, it soon became evident that psychologists could ill-afford to continue to be liberal and indecisive on the issue of licensure (Nemir, 1980).

The APA was compelled to take a stand by defining what constituted a psychology training program. Significantly, the APA required knowledge of the history and systems of psychology as well as courses in the individual, social, biological, and learned bases of behavior. The APA's definition went into effect for APA-approved training programs in 1980 and was also adopted by many states in determining qualifications for certification or licensure as a psychologist.

Despite the undoubted benefits of the APA's action in defining a core psychology curriculum, attention needed to be paid to its hazards: Academic freedom was restricted by requiring certain courses to be offered and taken, and a rigidity was introduced that might well interfere with the introduction of new material. This loss of freedom, however, seemed at the time a fair price to pay for the setting of standards, and it was a commitment to standards that appeared necessary.

The sixties had been characterized by jobs aplenty and by the discontinuities and anti-intellectual stances of both the humanistic and behavioral movements (Reisman, 1975; Strupp, 1976). As a result, a national conference on the professional training of psychologists held in Vail, Colorado, endorsed career ladders and various levels of education and training within the profession (Korman, 1974). But to no apparent effect. The APA adopted the position that the doctorate was the only professional degree in psychology, and it discouraged schools from offering terminal master's degree programs. Even beyond that, the APA encouraged continuing education courses for professionals, and a few states took the step of mandating the psychologists they licensed to take such courses (Jones, 1975). So the seventies brought a tightening rather than a relaxing of professional standards.

Clinical psychology assumed a strong position within American psychology and the APA. Membership in APA rose from 30,830 in 1970 to 50,933 in 1980; about 44% of the membership toward the close of the decade consisted of clinical psychologists, and four of the APA presidents during the 70s were trained as clinicians. Yet a critical mass seemed to have been reached, and clinical psychology began fragmenting into different professions.

Twenty years before it had been possible to suggest that a school psychologist was a clinical psychologist who worked in a school. No longer. School psychology had become an independent profession (Graff & Clair, 1973). A similar process was occurring in clinical community psychology (Sarason, 1976), and in 1978 the first four students graduated from the University of California at Berkeley with a Doctor of Mental Health (DMH) degree. The 5-year program had an emphasis on psychoanalysis and offered courses in biology, psychology, and the social sciences. Of what significance was it that the series of annual volumes entitled *Progress in Clinical Psychology* ceased publication in 1971?

However, in other countries of the world the numbers of clinical psychologists had nowhere to go but up. Norway was training about 100 psychologists a year at a PsyD level. Certification or licensure of psychologists existed in Austria, East Germany, the Netherlands, Norway, Portugal, Sweden, and Canada. Switzerland

and Great Britain recognized psychologists as competent to practice psychotherapy (Dörken, 1980). South Korea had about 33 clinical psychologists and a training program with 12 doctoral candidates (Barcus, 1982). Clinical specialization was also available in Australia, Belgium, Denmark, France, West Germany, Ireland, Italy, New Zealand, Poland, Portugal, and the Soviet Union (Fichter & Wittchen, 1980; Lomov, 1982).

It was particularly encouraging to note the acceleration in the numbers of clinical psychologists in Canada, where there were seven PhD programs and a PsyD program (Coleman, 1971), and in the German Democratic Republic, where training was available at Humboldt University in Berlin and at Karl Marx University in Leipzig (Kossakowski, 1980). Clinical psychology was also emerging in Turkey (LeCompte, 1980), Cuba (Averasturi, 1980), Greece (Borehoutsos & Roe, 1984), the People's Republic of China (Ching, 1980), and Mexico (Nunez, 1976).

Of course, there was always concern about the future. "The Golden Era of clinical psychology is over," stated Cummings (1984), one of the four clinical psychologists to have held the APA presidency during the seventies. Sharing this feeling of troubled waters ahead was Sigmund Koch, one of a number of psychologists (Wetheimer et al., 1978) who peered into the future and saw irreconcilable differences among psychologists and fractionalization of the field.

But there were those who saw psychology being created anew—being loosened from its physiological origins and connected more with the attributes of the human condition. "Modern scientific psychology is rooted in hope," said Leone E. Tyler (1973) in her APA presidential address. She called for less emphasis on determinism and more on the feeling of having choice so that people will believe their decisions can make a difference. Similarly, W. J. McKeachie (1976), in his APA presidential address, saw a return to the view that people are "active, curious, social, human learners" capable of rational choice, responsibility, and participation in determining their world and its future.

The seventies, then, was no different than any other decade in presenting overwhelming forces, complex issues, and hard decisions. But in dealing with the difficult issues in these difficult times, clinical psychologists had demonstrated a confidence in their profession and a resourcefulness and an adaptability that bode well for their continued survival and evolution. They had met the exigencies of the day and they emerged from the decade in a position of undeniable and growing influence and strength.

11

Openness
1980–1989

These were the years of Ronald Reagan, referred to as the teflon president because his popularity did not seem to be affected by the corruption and ineptitude within his administration. An overwhelming victor over President Carter in the election of 1980, Reagan campaigned on a platform of lower taxes, higher defense spending, and a return to "conservative" values, such as patriotism, religion, and individual initiative. He also favored a restricted role for the federal government, which meant less government support for social welfare and education, including the training of graduate students in clinical psychology (West & Lips, 1986).

Surprisingly, since many experts predicted his economic programs would be disastrous, under Reagan the ruinous inflation of preceding years was checked and reduced. Also surprisingly, since many experts predicted Reagan's arms buildup would intensify the Cold War and bring the United States into conflict with the Soviet Union, the reverse happened. Relations between the United States and the Soviet Union improved, an arms reduction agreement for nuclear weapons was reached, and by 1989 the media proclaimed that the Cold War was over and the Western democracies had won. During 1989, democratic reforms were instituted in the Soviet Union, China, and Poland; communist governments were toppled in Hungary, East Germany, Czechoslovakia, and Rumania; and the Berlin Wall, a symbol for over 20 years of the division of people and the repression of freedom, was breached, danced upon, and broken into chunks to be sold as mementos by enterprising capitalists. The teflon that protected Reagan from blame also appeared to shield him from credit: *Time* magazine, in its last issue of 1989, not only refrained from naming Reagan Man of the Year, it proclaimed Gorbachev, leader of the Soviet Union from 1985, Man of the Decade. Gorbachev had advocated a policy of *glasnost*, or openness to ideas, dissent, and reform.

But the happy events of 1989 were a dramatic culmination of forces and values at work from at least the time of Rousseau. Accordingly, these changes held promise not only for peace, but also, more parochially, for the growth of psychology and clinical psychology within Eastern Europe. At times it was difficult to discern whether these forces and values were still operating amid all the violence and confusion of the eighties.

Some historians believed this decade was a period of global anarchy (Geyer, 1985). There were conflicts in Lebanon, El Salvador, Nicaragua, Iran, Iraq, Haiti, Ethiopia, India, Cambodia, Israel, and South Africa. Leaders who supported peace were assassinated (Anwar Sadat in Egypt and Indira Gandhi in India), and

President Reagan and Pope John Paul II were both wounded during attempts to kill them. Airplanes and passenger liners were hijacked, bombs were exploded, and the random terrorism of desperate people seemed to be matched by the planned or unintended terrorism of desperate governments, as when the United States bombed Tripoli or mistakenly shot down an Iranian passenger plane. Fraser (1988) was disturbed that the violence of this century had by now come to be accepted as routine and that the incompetence of governments in preventing and perpetuating violence was little noticed.

What did seem to attract attention was the incessant striving for more and more money to buy more and more things. The Reagan years were thought to epitomize vulgar materialism (Landi, 1989). On television were prime-time soap operas such as *Dallas* and *Dynasty*, which showed the trials and tribulations of millionaires, and the real-life though perhaps more fantastic program *Lifestyles of the Rich and Famous*. Nevertheless, some questioned the propriety of the former president and Mrs. Reagan accepting over 2 million dollars for their personal appearance in Japan in 1989, indicating there might be a limit to how far flagrant materialism would be allowed to go.

There were also spirited discussions and genuine concerns about ethics, human rights, and the effects of human actions on the environment. Depletion of the ozone layer, acid rain, and the destruction of rain forests worried and aroused many people. These potential and growing hazards were exacerbated by immediate threats from oil spills, radioactive contamination by nuclear power plants, and chemical and radioactive waste. The concept of the interrelationship of all things (the ecological balance) had long been familiar within the social sciences; it gained public currency during the eighties.

Within that ecosystem known as the family there was also violence. The first National Conference for Family Violence Researchers convened in 1981 and reported some shocking estimates of the extent of the problem: 1.7 million children seriously abused each year; 50,000 children missing; 100,000 children kidnapped by parents in disputes over custody; one in four adolescent girls sexually molested. Psychologists and teachers were legally required to notify the appropriate authorities of suspected instances of abuse. Over 700,000 such cases were reported each year, of which 40% to 45% were substantiated. Many clinicians were involved in working with abused children and abusive adults and in doing research to determine effective programs and interventions.

Psychologists also tried to play a significant role in alleviating other national problems. AIDS (acquired immune deficiency syndrome) was identified as a serious public health problem in 1981. A fatal disease that still has no cure, AIDS was originally thought to be confined to the homosexual population, which did have a disproportionate share of its victims. As more information was gained about AIDS and its transmission through bodily fluids, chiefly blood and semen, alarm within the general population grew (Batchelor, 1984) and radical changes in behaviors were recommended to prevent the spread of the disease. The danger of AIDS was credited with or blamed for, depending on how one viewed the change, an increase in fidelity and commitment in personal relationships, a drop in divorce, a decrease in sexual freedom and impulsiveness, and a jump in the sale of rubber gloves and condoms.

From time to time, the plight of the homeless seized attention and raised questions about the allocation of national resources. How could billions of dollars be spent on weapons when so many social and psychological needs were not adequately met, from the day care of preschool children to the day care of the elderly? Deinstitutionalization, an aim of community psychiatry and psychology, had been a great success—if a reduction in the number of patients in mental hospitals and individuals in institutions for the mentally retarded was the sole objective. But the programs needed to support these individuals within their communities were often lacking or poorly funded. It was estimated that anywhere from 25% to 50% of the 250,000 to 3,000,000 street people in the United States were mentally ill.

Whatever was to be done about whatever problem had to be mindful of the rights of individuals. People could not be compelled to accept what other people thought was for their own good if they did not want it. Litigation, the possibility of being sued even when one had the best of intentions, was an ever-present consideration. Courts held that patients had the right to refuse antipsychotic drugs and electroconvulsive therapy and that the homeless had the right to refuse shelter if they wanted to remain on the street.

Two major developments in medicine were of special significance to clinicians. First, there was increasing acceptance of holistic medicine and the notion that in treating any condition the patient's attitudes, expectations, and feelings were of great importance. This was certainly not a novel notion, and it can be traced to the teachings of Adolf Meyer and Kurt Goldstein, among others. However, it was now being implemented in the general practice of medicine and the procedures of institutions. As one example, patients with chronic conditions, such as cancer, might be helped to cope with their illness through participation in a support group. As another example, the delivery and care of infants became homelike and open to the entire family. More and more psychologists were becoming involved in health psychology.

Second, there were new techniques for creating images of the brain: computerized axial tomography (CAT), single photon emission computed tomography (SPECT), positron emission tomography (PET), regional cerebral blood flow (RCBF), and brain electrical activity mapping (BEAM) (Andreasen, 1988). It was difficult to predict what might be learned from these techniques, but they held great promise for research and for understanding how the brain functions.

Technological advances in medicine were a reflection of general technological advances. For many, this was the age of technology, particularly electronic and computer technology. Advances in circuitry and miniaturization were taking place at such speed that computers were out of date within a year or two after their introduction. Personal computers were available to help, befuddle, and frustrate their users. The power that they gave to organize and reorganize, to store and to imagine, to calculate and entertain had become commonplace.

These technological changes were said to be changing the economies of the world and the relations between countries. Technologies, not raw materials, were the basis of wealth. The cities and the industrial centers of the United States had to accommodate to the change from the production of goods to the production of services. To keep pace in this world, countries, businesses, and individuals needed to be flexible, to be adaptable, to be open and ready for change.

Gone were the days when people could train for jobs and then work at them for the rest of their lives. Instead, people were told to expect to make two or more career changes. The functional psychologists at the turn of the century had been impressed by human intelligence as a means of adaptation and survival, and in 1989 intelligence was also being emphasized as an economic asset. Clinical psychologists could be expected to be open to that message. Being members of a service-oriented profession, clinicians were somewhat protected from the vicissitudes endemic to manufacturing and business. Moreover, if they were mindful of their history, they recognized they had a tradition of resourcefulness and coping with change while helping others to cope. For change, as William James and many others before him had noted, is a constant, and people are best advised to be open to its opportunities and invigorated by its challenges.

NORMAL PERSONALITY FUNCTIONING

Bits and pieces of new information about human functioning were gradually being integrated and assimilated into comprehensive conceptions of development. From infancy, and some might even argue before birth, people were active organizers of experience, striving to make sense of their world and to cope effectively with it. Advances in experimental techniques, such as videocassette recording, were making possible the more intensive study of infant behavior and documenting skills that had previously been unsuspected.

At the other end of the life span, advances in understanding the variables that affected health, such as proper diet and habits, were helping more people to live fuller, longer lives. Questions were also being raised about whether, or to what extent, the progressive deteriorations in health and intellectual functioning seen among adults were unavoidable consequences of old age. Alzheimer's disease, which had previously been conceived of as a premature disability in memory, was increasingly diagnosed among the elderly, since it was argued that a significant deterioration in intellectual functioning was abnormal regardless of the person's years. In any case, the APA began publication of the journal *Psychology and Aging*, and clinical psychologists were being encouraged to specialize in research and work with the elderly (Santos & VandenBos, 1982).

Erikson's theory, despite his protests that it was part of psychoanalysis, was usually presented as a separate doctrine, one that provided a good perspective on psychological growth throughout the life span. The problems and changes in the ego that he described fit well with the conception of the person as always having to struggle to come to grips with one thing after another. Moreover, the feelings and beliefs about oneself and one's world that were consequences and shapers of these experiences could readily be seen as aspects of the self—and the self seemed to be a fairly robust concept in psychology (Singer & Kolligian, 1987).

Of course, the self was important in humanistic psychology, for example, when Rogers and Maslow talked about self-actualization. It was also important in social learning theory, when Bandura talked about self-efficacy and when Rotter talked about the locus of control. The self was also prominent in psychoanalysis, where the ideas of Kohut were being given attention. According to one interpretation of Kohut, the significance of sex and aggression was not so much that they were innate drives to which people had to adjust but that people whose selves were easily wounded would respond to slights by being aggressive and would seek to stimulate themselves and feel vital by being sexually active (Kahn, 1985). Both Kohut and the analyst Otto Kernberg had conceptions of how the self develops that stressed the importance of child-rearing experiences during infancy and the pre-school years. Though developmental research did not support some of the details of their speculations (Weston, 1989), the self remained a concept of endless fasci-nation. (For example, Kohut thought that by school age, children were capable of having and being aware of conflicting feelings toward the same person at the same time; however, research with children of 6 to 10 years old indicated they could not understand how they could love a person with whom they were angry.)

In social psychology Aron and Aron (1986) suggested interpersonal interactions of love and attraction were motivated by a desire to expand the self. People who could stimulate, educate, and enrich the self would be sought; conversely, relation-ships would not be maintained with those who could no longer seem to expand the self or who were boring. Although explaining all personal relationships on the basis of self-expansion seemed no more satisfactory than explaining them on the basis of rewards (of which self-expansion could be considered one), the use of the self in explications of social behavior did increase during the decade (Schlenker, 1985).

An entire issue of the *Journal of Social and Clinical Psychology* consisted of articles about the self and illusions that it might hold which were adaptive and constructive (Snyder, 1989). It was argued that because certain illusions about self-efficacy and having an internal locus of control are correlated with mental health, the conception of the healthy person as being entirely realistic needed to be modi-fied. False beliefs are not so bad if they give hope and enable the person to keep up the good fight.

Freud, who had been sympathetic to people's need for illusions but unsparing in ridding himself of them, would probably have been concerned that the focus on the self or the ego was distracting people from the significance of his psychosexual theory of development. The psychosexual theory of oral, anal, oedipal, latency, and genital stages was often discussed in a paragraph or two and dismissed as hopelessly culture-bound and dated. In other words, Freud's psychosexual theory was not regarded as his major and distinctive contribution; in fact some thought it was a major and distinctive embarrassment, since, on the one hand, it led him to make comments about females that many found offensive and, on the other hand, it was alleged to have made him dismiss the reports of his patients about being sexually abused as wishful fantasies (Masson, 1984).

What was regarded by many as Freud's great contribution was his pioneering emphasis on the pervasiveness and importance of unconscious functioning. Back in the fifties and sixties there had been a concerted effort to test this aspect of Freud's theory through research on subliminal stimulation (i.e., studies of how wishes, fears, and needs might distort perceptions without the person's awareness). The research on subliminal stimulation had not supported the theory that people could be affected in their behaviors by messages below the threshold of consciousness, whether the messages were delivered forwards or backwards (Vokey & Read, 1985). However, during the eighties there were positive reports of a series of studies based on predictions from psychosexual theory and involving subliminal stimulation.

According to this research, everyone has unconscious wishes to be reunited with the good feeding mother of infancy. When the message "Mommy and I are one" was presented subliminally to various groups of people, mostly males, it gratified their unconscious wish and was found to have the following effects: improved self-concept, better ability to refrain from smoking, improved scores in mathematics, and reduced pathology among schizophrenics (Silverman & Weinberger, 1985). Another subliminal message, "Beating Daddy is okay," supposedly improved the performance of males in competitive situations, such as throwing darts. Unfortunately, the latter findings did not appear to be easily replicated (Vitiello, Carlin, Becker, Barris, & Dutton, 1989). What did seem to be more readily demonstrated was that when people really stopped to think about it, much of their psychological functioning and behavior occurred beyond their awareness.

This somewhat surprising fruit of introspection particularly impressed cognitive psychologists. Whereas it had been thought that cognitive psychology dealt with conscious ideas and thinking, it was now argued that people are aware of the products or outcomes of decision making but are curiously unaware of how they actually make the decisions (Mandler, 1984). There is an unconscious leap from the weighing of options and alternatives to settling upon a choice, and during that lapse in awareness no one is quite certain of what variables come into play.

Further, more behaviors than are usually recognized are automatized and thus performed to some extent unconsciously. People talk unconsciously, being aware of what they *intend* to say but not deliberately selecting each and every word that occurs in the flow of their speech. The schemas in Piaget's theory—the conceptions that people have about things that help them to order and organize and make intelligible their experiences, of which the self-concept is one—are not entirely in awareness and are often out of awareness. Some psychologists were bold enough to declare there is a *cognitive unconscious*, or an aspect of unconscious functioning involved in the process of cognition. People are aware of "declarative knowledge" (facts and information), but they are not aware of "procedural knowledge" (how they store and retrieve facts and memories) (Kihlstrom, 1987). This is unconscious—or as Freud might have put it, unconscious ego functioning.

Even brain research was providing support for Freud's view of the unconscious. The amygdala can elicit emotions without the involvement of the hippocampus, which is a focus for cognitions and not mature at birth. This suggests that fears and emotions can be learned and retained without cortical involvement and that they can be elicited without thought or conscious awareness (Goleman, 1989). Also, the important learning that occurs in infancy, when the child lacks the language to label experiences, seems to take place somewhat unconsciously.

Rosenzweig (1985) suggested that if psychology is to advance as a science, research during the next few decades must focus on how the unconscious operates in experimental situations. There must be a determination of how the unconscious beliefs and attitudes of the experimenter, the unconscious beliefs and attitudes of the experimentee, and their interaction in the experimental situation influence results. Especially significant would be the identification of unconscious or preconscious self-deceptions ("I've got to do what's necessary to show this guy he can't order me around").

This acceptance of the unconscious would not have entirely pleased Freud. It is said that when told that his ideas had met with an enthusiastic reception by some group, Freud wondered what had been left out. In the eighties what seemed often to be missing from the unconscious was the id (sexual and aggressive impulses and wishes) and what was accepted was the ego.

Although Freud had recognized the importance of the mother-infant relationship, he had stressed the later years of childhood in his writings. This relative neglect was being redressed by the attention being paid to infancy, just as the growing status of the ego might be said to have corrected his emphasis on the id.

More was being learned about prenatal and infant development. Before birth, the balance of sex hormones within the fetus appears to masculinize, feminize, demasculinize, or defeminize the person's sexual orientation. Although this prenatal hormonalization, primarily of the brain, disposes the child to a heterosexual, bisexual, or homosexual orientation, sexual preference is strongly dependent on postnatal or subsequent socialization as well as other experiences (Money, 1987). The information about socialization and experiences had been known for some time, and in fact it had once served to balance explanations that were largely based on genetics and temperament or innate dispositions. There appeared to be a shift away from environmental explanations of personality to genetic or biological explanations. Perhaps it would be more accurate to say there were frequent reminders of the importance of both kinds of variables. As the old formula put it, the person is a product of heredity interacting with environment.

An analysis of identical-twin research indicated both genetic and environmental variables were significant in determining intellectual development and achievement. However, emotional stability seemed little affected by differences in environment, suggesting that temperament or genetic endowment under ordinary circumstances is of crucial significance in determining how well people deal with stress and anxiety (Loehlin, 1989).

Similarly Kagan, Reznik, and Snidman (1988) found what they believed to be a biological basis for shyness and sociability. In their longitudinal study of a group of children (starting at age two and ending at age seven), a small percentage, about 10% to 15%, reacted to strange situations by consistently becoming quiet, subdued, alert, and inhibited in their behavior; an equal percentage of the youngsters consistently responded to novel circumstances by enthusiastic, spontaneous involvement in the setting. To Kagan, these differences in characteristic response suggested temperamental predispositions to shyness or sociability, which he recognized gave support to Jung's distinction between introverted and extraverted personalities. Moreover, physiological measures including a relatively simple test of saliva for cortisol, led to the speculation that the biological basis for shyness was a low threshold for limbic-hypothalamic arousal and consequently higher sympathetic nervous system activity (Kagan, Reznick, & Snidman, 1988).

That there is a biological basis for the infant's attachment to the mother was emphasized by Bowlby. Even before the child had any feeding experiences, there were inborn reflexes and dispositions for the infant to grasp, gaze, and respond to the mother, which rewarded the mother for her care and stimulation. Bowlby (1988) was certainly mindful of the significance of the mother's sensitive responsiveness to her child's signals and cues and of the importance of subsequent interactions, but he laid special emphasis upon inherent predispositions for response.

The topic of attachment stimulated much research. A series of studies of how 1-year-old infants responded to being in a strange situation, to separation and reunion with their mothers, and to the presence of a stranger indicated the children's attachments were of three kinds. The majority, those who were securely attached (about 70%), showed distress or cried when left by their mothers and sought to be comforted by them when they returned; these children used their mothers as a safe base for exploration and as a haven when strangers approached. The remainder of the children were thought to be insecurely attached to their mothers, and they exhibited two different patterns of reactions. About 20% were *avoidant* and showed little distress when separated from their mothers, nor much in the way of relief when reunited. The other 10% were *anxious/ambivalent*, and although they were upset when their mothers were gone, they both sought to be and angrily resisted being comforted by their mothers when they returned (Ainsworth, Blehar, Waters, & Wall, 1978).

Research stimulated by these investigations sought to determine what accounted for the differences in attachment and to assess what the implications of these differences would be in the development of these children. Because of its longitudinal nature, the required research could not provide many answers by the end of the decade, but it did indicate, as would be expected, better social adjustment for those children who were securely attached. Further, some investigators tried to infer what kind of attachment adults might have experienced as children by their endorsement of statements indicative of different ways of relating to others. The majority of adults seemed to be securely attached and had trusting, close relationships that they generally found satisfying and positive; they also tended to see their mothers as having been caring and accepting of them. Avoidant and anxious/ambivalent patterns of attachment were also inferred in the case of adults with social relationships and attitudes that corresponded to these patterns (Shaver & Hazan, 1988). Thus attachment in infancy seemed to have long-range consequences for adjustment, as Erikson predicted when he described early infancy as the stage in which a fundamental sense of trust in others and one's world usually develops.

L. A. Pervin (1985) looked at the personality research of the 1980s and concluded "On the whole, I continue to feel than I am more in touch with and learn more about people in my office than I do reading the personality literature." Nonetheless, the decade did generate its fair share of knowledge and advances in understanding human behavior.

DIAGNOSTIC TECHNIQUES

At the beginning of the eighties, the future of testing did not appear bright. Criticisms of diagnostic techniques as devices biased in such a way as to perpetuate the prejudices of their developers and users continued, while the appeal of psychological assessment as a clinical role appeared to be in decline. Yet another issue of *American Psychologist* (October 1981) was devoted entirely to testing and its endangered status, but that very attention implied there was still some interest in preserving the species. Korchin and Schuldberg (1981), in their assessment of the field, saw signs of improving health.

To be sure, clinicians were spending a smaller proportion of their time testing. In 1959 it was estimated that about 44% of the clinical psychologist's time was spent in diagnosis, and this had dropped to about 24% by 1976. However, this decline could be attributed in part to the growing role of clinicians in psychotherapy, university teaching, and mental health administration. Korchin and Schuldberg (1981) recognized that what had been so ardently desired by clinical psychologists in the twenties and thirties had come to pass: They were no longer just psychometricians or psychological testers. Thus, despite indications that the body was still alive and twitching, such as renewed interest in the Rorschach, the creation of 14 computer programs to score and interpret the MMPI, and growth in the fields of neuropsychological and behavioral assessment, it was highly unlikely that clinical psychologists as a group would be as closely identified with testing as they had been before World War II.

The number of tests continued to grow, nourished by an outpouring of behavioral assessment devices, mainly of the checklist and paper-and-pencil type (Sweetland & Keyser, 1983, 1986). Checklists were often constructed of statements descriptive of a variety of disorders. The patient or, more often, someone who knew the patient, such as a parent or teacher, would indicate which of the statements applied; the ratings then gave an indication of the nature and perhaps severity of the problem.

Rating scales were developed for problems that might be difficult to detect in overt behaviors and that were consequently dependent on self-reporting: depression, loneliness, shyness, fears, suicidal thoughts, and anxiety, to mention a few. Scales were also developed for behaviors that were overt but that might more easily be assessed through informants than by direct observation (e.g., hyperactivity). These latter scales were somewhat troubling to behaviorists, who believed in the importance of analyzing behavior by directly observing its occurrence in natural settings. Their concern was that the rating instruments would be substituted for more valid observations. There was also concern that the reliance on self-report measures would repeat an error made some 50 years before: accepting reports at face value and not allowing for the possibility that people might not have access to all the information requested nor any special desire to share it.

Speaking of 50 or more years before, that was a time when physiological measures were attracting much interest. The polygraph, a carryover from that period, was an instrument intended to measure several aspects of physiological functioning (respiration rate and heart rate) indicative of anxiety and presumably related to lying. Known to the public as the lie detector, there had long been doubt about its validity for determining honesty. The research indicated that much depended on the skill of the examiner in conducting the interrogation and in framing the questions; a great deal also hinged on the belief of the person being tested that the polygraph could detect lying. Given the fact that some people could lie without being anxious and some people could be quite upset while telling the truth, the procedure yielded too many false negatives, false positives, and inconclusives, although it did appear to have some merit if judiciously used (Saxe, Dougherty, & Cross, 1985).

Questions about validity bedeviled almost every diagnostic technique, especially the projective techniques. But despite years of criticism and their relative neglect in clinical training programs, projective techniques were still widely used (Piotrowski & Keller, 1989). A survey of five different professional settings disclosed that among clinical psychologists the top 10 tests were almost the same as in decades past: the MMPI, WAIS, Bender-Gestalt, Rorschach, WISC, Sentence Completion, TAT, Draw A Person, Rotter Sentence Completion, and the drawing of a House-Tree-Person (Lubin, Larsen, Matarazzo, & Seever, 1985).

Those who persisted in the use of favored instruments of dubious validity could take heart. A century after Galton had collected his anthropometric data, they were analyzed and found to be both reliable and of some validity. People from different social classes did tend to differ in ways that would have been expected; for example, the poor tended to be smaller, weaker, and less acute in their sensory functioning than the well-to-do (Johnson et al., 1985).

Of major interest was the most recent revision of the Stanford-Binet (Thorndike, Hagen, & Sattler, 1986). Gone was the age scale format that had been the hallmark of the Binet scale, and in its place were 15 tests with items of increasing difficulty. The examinee would take anywhere from 8 to 13 of these tests, depending on age and entry level. Despite appearances to the contrary, the tests did not represent specific factors or abilities, any more than the subtests of the Wechsler scales did. The revisers of the Stanford-Binet, like Wechsler, continued to believe that there was a general factor in intellectual functioning, g, which they conceived of as a broad reasoning ability.

Although presumably all the tests had some g in them, they could also be categorized into one of three second-order factors: crystallized abilities, which are those most influenced by learning, such as comprehension and verbal and quantitative abilities; fluid-analytic abilities, which are thought to be much less influenced by learning, such as the ability to copy geometric designs and analyze patterns; and short-term memory, such as memory for digits, bead patterns, and sentences.

Therefore, the revision (1) addressed the criticism that the test consisted of a hodgepodge of items, and (2) afforded clinicians the opportunity to make reasonable statements about strengths and weaknesses in a number of areas of cognitive functioning.

Of greater significance than the change in structure was the change in attitude about what the test measured. Gone were the terms *mental age, intelligence*, and *IQ*. They were replaced by *cognitive development* and the *standard age score*. A person's raw score on the test was converted to a standard age score (SAS) by using an appropriate table for that person's age. This was a momentous revision for the scale that, about 70 years before, had introduced the IQ.

What had brought these changes about? According to some critics, they were an attempt to reverse the 20-year-long decline in the use of the test (Spruill, 1987). Obviously, they were also an attempt to break with the past and to correct mistakes. Granting in large measure the success of the revision in answering criticisms, it was somewhat disappointing to find the standard deviation of the SAS still set at 16 when most other scales had standard deviations of 15. This meant that the SAS would have a slightly different meaning than an equivalent IQ, just as the Stanford-Binet IQ was a bit different from the same numerical IQ on most other scales. It seems some traditions are less easy to give up than others.

The fourth revision of the Stanford-Binet sought to avoid the controversy that previous revisions had largely helped to bring about by purging itself of the emotionally charged IQ. Whether this purification would help matters and whether other scales would follow were questions for the future. At any rate, *standard age score* better indicated the nature of the test than *intelligence quotient*.

A revision of the Wechsler Preschool and Primary Scale of Intelligence appeared in 1989. The scale was restandardized on children 3 to 7 years, had nicer drawings, had other changes, but was fundamentally the same scale. Similarly, a revision of the MMPI, the MMPI-2, became available in 1989. It was restandardized using a sample with equal numbers of men and women and proportionate representations of minorities. Most of the sample had been picked randomly from telephone directories in Minneapolis, Cleveland, San Diego, Seattle, Norfolk, Philadelphia, and Chapel Hill.

There were still over 500 true-false items in the MMPI-2, but an effort had been made to eliminate statements that had been confusing or offensive in the original (e.g., "I think Lincoln was greater than Washington," "I have never had any black, tarry-looking bowel movements"). Also, the implications of some statements had to be changed in light of the differences in endorsements between the original Minnesota sample and the restandardization group: In the thirties, only 9% of the Minnesota normal adults had agreed with "I am an important person," where 49% of the men and 69% of the women in the modern group did, indicating agreement with it no longer pointed to self-importance and grandiosity. Thus, in spite of its similarity to the MMPI, the MMPI-2 would be significantly different in interpretation, and new items had been added to assess such topical concerns as Type A behavior and eating disorders (Adler, 1989).

Scoring and interpretation of the MMPI had long been accomplished by computer, and it was reasonable to suppose that not only would this be done with the MMPI-2 but also that computer-based psychological test interpretations (CBTIs) would be employed by an increasing number of tests by an increasing number of psychologists. Estimates were that thousands of psychologists owned microcomputers and that about 500 clinical psychologists had computer links that enabled them to do CBTIs. During 1983–1984, there were 300,000 test administrations interpreted by computer, and with the VA prepared to have 62 psychological tests computer interpreted, some were predicting that by the year 2000 virtually all psychological tests would be automated.

Possible precautions regarding this development were noted by Groth-Marnat and Shumaker (1989). They pointed to the need for continued research to determine the validity of many of these automated tests and the interpretations that were generated. Research was also needed to determine whether there were differences between a test administered by a clinician and that same test administered by computer. There were also ethical concerns about the qualifications of those who used CBTIs, the timeliness of the interpretations and their need for periodic revision, the qualifications of those who developed the software, and the extent to which programs might be loaded with statements of vague generality that applied to almost everyone.

As the decade closed, so did almost a century of psychological test development. Great progress had occurred in the number of techniques and the variety of functioning they sampled and in the sophistication of interpretations. One danger was that that sophistication might be confined to a smaller and smaller proportion of clinicians, with a growing number being content to be critical of diagnostic techniques or to make use of them without being sufficiently informed about their administration and interpretation.

DIAGNOSTIC FORMULATIONS

Health psychology, holistic medicine, and the theory that mental functioning and attitudes affect physical conditions and vice versa had been championed by Adolf Meyer and Kurt Goldstein. Thus, these ideas were not exactly new, but in this decade they achieved popular acceptance and were implemented in medical practice. A central concept was stress, and being able to control stress was generally held to increase psychological well-being (Spielberger, Sarason, & Milgram, 1982).

In general, stress seemed to be experienced when almost any kind of change was brought about, whether desirable or undesirable, if the person felt somewhat pressured in dealing with it. It could also be experienced when the person was frustrated or annoyed by minor and major irritations or hassles. Therefore, potentially stressful situations were apt to be encountered daily by everyone, and the question was how to deal with them effectively and to come to a better understanding of their effects.

Friedman and Rosenman (1974) suggested that men who suffered heart attacks seemed to exhibit a constellation of behaviors, which they called *Type A behav-*

iors. These men responded to stress by becoming angry and aggressive. Further, they placed themselves under stress by being perfectionistic and impatient, by feeling a great sense of urgency about not wasting their time or having it wasted, and by driving themselves to higher and higher levels of achievement. In contrast, men with Type B behaviors appeared to be less at risk for cardiovascular problems. These men were relaxed, patient, and less concerned about achieving goals in competition with others. This research had obvious implications for health and the kind of personality one should have to prevent coronary heart disease (Wright, 1988).

People were urged to respond to stressors with greater equanimity, to lighten up, and to be mellow. Relaxation and imaging techniques helped people to feel more in control not only of stressful feelings and situations but also of illnesses and medical conditions. Indeed, it was increasingly recognized that the patient's hope, optimism, and confidence were important in promoting health. Whether such techniques could also reverse the course of cancer and other serious diseases, as some claimed, was more debatable. The wisdom of advancing such claims was questioned by those who argued it placed too much responsibility on the patient to counter illnesses that were usually chronic or fatal, but it did appear that feelings of anger, hostility, anxiety, depression, helplessness, and hopelessness were linked to ill health and debility (Friedman & Booth-Kewley, 1987).

Moreover, there was evidence of a physiological process that might account for how stresses could eventually lead to medical problems that had been thought to be unrelated to stressors. Research pointed to significant decreases in the immune system when the person was undergoing stressful life events. This suggested a general vulnerability of the person under stress to viruses, illnesses, and disorders. Although the evidence was scant that decrements in immune status brought about by stressors led to particular illnesses, it was foolish to ignore the preventive implications until more evidence was accumulated (Geiser, 1989).

Although in the eighties physicians and the public were more ready to accept psychological variables as determining medical conditions, they were also more willing to accept biological variables as bringing about psychological disorders. Many psychiatrists believed that schizophrenia was to some extent genetically determined, perhaps as some sort of inherited vulnerability to the disorder, which would then be brought about by stressors—the diathesis-stress hypothesis (Mirsky & Duncan, 1986).

The history of biological explanations for schizophrenia could be traced back 100 years to Kraepelin, and there was still no definitive answer, although no shortage of possibilities. Biochemical explanations had been thoroughly investigated over the past 4 decades, including theories that it was due to problems with one or more neurotransmitters, accumulations of formaldehyde in the brain, or a viral infection, more specifically, a cytomegalovirus (Gould, 1982). Surprisingly, an article flatly asserting schizophrenia was a brain disease was published in the *American Psychologist*, with the recommendation that psychologists so regard it (Johnson, 1989).

Johnson's article presented no conclusive evidence but instead offered the following argument: Schizophrenia produced such profound changes in the person's behavior that it must be caused by correspondingly profound changes in the person's brain. Other siblings were usually not schizophrenic, or even seriously disturbed, so it could not be caused mainly by environmental factors. The patient and the family would feel less stigmatized and at fault if schizophrenia were not attributed to family factors, and there would be more hope for the cure and prevention of schizophrenia if it was a brain disease and not a product of interpersonal problems. (Why there should be more hope for improving a brain disease than a family problem was never made clear.)

A similar line of reasoning was often used to explain why autism was regarded as an organic disorder. By the eighties, few professionals working with autistic children agreed with Bettelheim's (1967) psychodynamic explanation, and in DSM-III autism was listed as a pervasive developmental disorder, implying some early problem interfered with the infant's growth. What this problem was could not be stated with certainty. However, research had explored genetic factors, brain damage resulting in various cognitive and sensory deficits, and biochemical abnormalities. The tantalizing inconclusiveness of this research did not discourage the belief that the causes were organic, but it led to the reasonable hypothesis that autism was a heterogeneous disorder and thus might have a number of different causes (Rutter & Schopler, 1987). In addition, Kanner's diagnostic criteria for early infantile autism had been ignored and altered over the years and significantly changed in DSM-III. Kanner, it may be recalled, insisted that the social isolation of the child had to be described by the parents as existing virtually from birth. In DSM-III the corresponding criterion was that the onset of the disorder had to occur before 30 months.

"The current state of nomenclature and diagnostic criteria in the field of adult psychopathology is barely more than one of organized confusion, but compared to the chaos that reigns in the realm of child psychopathology it is one of rigorous exactitude," began Ross and Pelham (1981) in their review of child diagnosis at the beginning of the decade. At that time there was hope that diagnosis would be made more reliable and valid by the new psychiatric nomenclature, DSM-III. A major problem with DSM-III was its inclusiveness. In order to ensure that no visitor to a psychiatrist's office would escape a diagnosis, many conditions were included in the nomenclature that had not been thought of as psychiatric disorders: smoking too much, drinking too much coffee, having a learning disability, being shy, being stubborn and oppositional to authorities, and so on. Some psychologists were so concerned about the consequences DSM-III would have for research and the diagnosis of disorders that they hastened to see if they could develop a better nomenclature. By the end of the decade no such nomenclature had appeared, but the psychiatric nomenclature had meanwhile undergone some unexpected changes.

DSM-I had been published in 1952 and listed 60 disorders; DSM-II had been published in 1968 and listed 145; DSM-III had been published in 1980 and listed about 230 disorders. A pattern of long intervals, at least 12 years, between revisions of the nomenclature had been established, and it was expected that the next version would appear in the nineties. Reinforcing that expectation was (1) the widespread discussion of DSM-III that had taken place for years before its official adoption in 1980, (2) the publication of DSM-III in hardcover and softcover and in an abbreviated version, and (3) a series of workshops to acquaint professionals with the system. Imagine then the surprise when DSM-III-R[evised] was published in 1987 (American Psychiatric Association, 1987).

Although only a revision, DSM-III-R had significant changes in so many disorders that DSM-III became outdated: ego-dystonic homosexuality was a disorder in DSM-III but not in DSM-III-R; the criteria for autism were altered; self-defeating personality was a new, suggested diagnosis. Of more concern than the changes was the absence of any compelling justification for them. Quite the reverse! The research that compared diagnosis using DSM-III with diagnosis using DSM-III-R indicated greater validity for the former. The use of DSM-III-R led to a significant overdiagnosis of autistic disorder among children with learning disabilities (Volkmar, Bregman, Cohen, & Cicchetti, 1988) and blurred distinctions among a number of personality disorders (Spitzer, Williams, Kass, & Davids, 1989). Further, it did not seem that matters would be set right by DSM-IV, which was supposed to be published in 1992 and was expected to contain disorders of relationships, such as spousal abuse, marital problems, and incest (Group for the Advancement of Psychiatry Committee on the Family, 1989). The relatively rapid appearance of new nomenclatures did not permit the research into etiologies promised by the appearance of DSM-III, and it was hoped that forthcoming changes would reflect more informed consideration than seemed to have been the case with DSM-III-R.

Improvements in diagnostic techniques and understanding (Cacioppo & Tassinary, 1990) were markedly changing psychologists' views of the significance of prenatal development. It now appeared conclusive that a host of substances could have adverse consequences for the fetus. These harmful agents were termed *teratogens*, and they included a number of common drugs, such as nicotine and alcohol. Pregnant women who consumed too much alcohol over the course of pregnancy placed their offspring at risk for fetal alcohol syndrome: low birth weight and possibly retarded intellectual functioning (Jones, Smith, Ulleland, & Streissguth, 1973; Abel, 1984). Evidence of the consequences of maternal behaviors for the fetus suggested many infant and childhood problems might be prevented if mothers took relatively simple measures, although it was acknowledged that changing habits is not easy for many people to do.

The concern of the U.S. government about drug abuse focused attention on the taking of cocaine, heroin, and other illegal substances by pregnant women and the consequent damage to their infants. Although there was no denying drug abuse was cause for concern, there was also ample documentation in the scientific literature that sufficient food and good nutrition for pregnant women was extremely important for healthy development. At times, this bit of information seemed to be overlooked, which complicated the evaluation of research on teratogens, since people taking drugs often neglect to eat adequately.

Another genetic disorder associated with mental retardation, called the *fragile X syndrome*, was identified (DeLaCruz, 1985). On chromosomal analysis, a specific region of the distal end of a long arm of the X chromosome appeared to be constricted or pinched or in the process of breaking off and gave the impression of being fragile. The defect is expressed in males, who have an X and a Y chromosome, as a form of moderate mental retardation. Affected females (females have two X chromosomes) did not appear to be mentally retarded, although they did seem more apt to have learning disabilities. Early studies of the disorder indicated that it was second only to Down syndrome in frequency among genetic aberrations and thus served as a partial explanation for why males outnumbered females among the intellectually retarded.

As the decade came to a close, the oft heard recommendation to diagnose people based on their competencies and skills rather than their weaknesses or symptoms was made once again (Masterpasqua, 1989). Most clinicians could fondly recall from their training the frequent injunction of their teachers and supervisors to make careful note of their patients' strengths and assets in their reports. Anna Freud (1965) made a similar argument for diagnosis using *developmental lines*, a delineation of the progress to be expected in the acquisition of various social or psychological skills, with the patient's achievement noted for each. Sigmund Freud's psychosexual theory was one possible developmental line, Erikson's psychosocial theory was another, and the developmental psychology literature could quickly yield many more. But it was unlikely that such a nomenclature would gain wide acceptance in the foreseeable future.

TREATMENT METHODS

Although psychosurgery and insulin coma therapy were rarely used for the treatment of psychoses during the eighties, electroconvulsive therapy still had its proponents. In modern practice the patient was often put to sleep through administration of a general anaesthesia, given a muscle relaxant to reduce the likelihood of damage, and then induced to have a seizure by the placement of a unilateral electrode to the temple. A single electrode seemed to be just as effective as two and resulted in fewer cognitive deficits. Electroconvulsive therapy was particularly indicated for the treatment of major depression, especially when it was essential to have rapid improvement in order to minimize the risk of suicide (Fink, 1984; Burrows & Deunerstein, 1981).

Drugs continued to be developed and used for the treatment of an ever-growing number of disorders. Lithium was regarded as the treatment of choice for mania or cyclothymic disorders, whereas MAO inhibitors were widely prescribed for depression. There was the suggestion that Anafranil, the trade name for the antidepressant clomipramine, was useful in reducing obsessive-compulsive behaviors in children and adults (Rapoport, 1988; King, 1989); the majority of these patients were said to respond favorably to this medication. Another drug, Wellbutrin, was said to enhance sexual responsiveness among its users; with the drug, 19 out of 30 patients became able to engage in sexual intercourse, whereas this was true for only 1 out of 30 in the placebo group (Carey, 1989).

Exactly how drugs worked was not clear, although it was speculated they might increase levels of brain serotonin or dopamine. Despite the lack of understanding, it was nevertheless asserted that the effectiveness of a drug in treating a condition indicated that a biochemical problem had brought the disorder about. There was no logical justification for that conclusion, which was further weakened by reports of the effectiveness of cognitive therapies and behavior therapies in alleviating depression and obsessive-compulsive disorders (King, 1989).

Moreover, the use of drugs over long periods of time led to problems. It was reported that taking benzodiazepines such as Librium and Valium could lead to reduced tolerances for stress and impaired motor performance (Gould, 1982) and that the probability of incurring tardive dyskinesia was quite high when major tranquilizers or antipsychotic drugs were taken for 10 years or more. Among psychiatrists, there were concerns about the prescriptions of these medications by physicians who were untrained in their use, just as there were concerns about junior psychiatrists being delegated to administer electroconvulsive therapy (a study indicated that in far too many instances relatively inexperienced psychiatrists were not aware that they should vary the strength and duration of the electrical pulse for the individual patient [Gould, 1983]).

Some psychologists raised the possibility of clinicians being suitably trained so that prescription privileges for psychotropic medications could be granted to them. The issue was debated and studied, and it says something positive about the robust health of the profession that predicted opposition from psychiatry was not among the major considerations. Many clinical psychologists believed their appeal as therapists was based on the fact that their treatments did not include the use of drugs. In any case, surveys of the field indicated the majority of clinical psychologists had no interest in gaining prescription privileges (Piotrowski & Lubin, 1989).

The view that hypnosis was a state of narrowed attention and heightened suggestibility dominated thinking in the area of hypotherapy. Gone was the "trance" as an important or necessary condition for achieving improvement. With the trance gone, hypnosis did not differ much in its essentials from the prescription by Coué in the twenties to repeat each day, "Day by day in every way I am getting better and better."

Of course, if a trance could be obtained, so much the better. However, the induction of a trance was no longer considered essential in hypnotherapy, so both the patient and hypnotherapist need not be hung up on that as an issue. Research had indicated a trance was not essential to alleviate pain (Hilgard, 1978; Barber, 1982); instead, pain reduction and greater tolerance of discomfort were attributed to the patient's receptivity of the therapist's suggestions of increased comfort and well-being. Further, just feeling more relaxed was beneficial to the patient. Although some authorities in the field continued to argue that there was something special about hypnosis, that it was not just mere relaxation and heightened suggestibility (Hilgard & LeBaron, 1984; Hilgard, 1987), the dominant "modern" tendency was to be pragmatic and do what one could to help patients. What seemed almost universally helpful was to relax as best one could and to be given—and to give oneself—suggestions to feel or do whatever was desired in attainable steps (Golden, Dowd, & Friedberg, 1987). Thus, hypnosis had come to be a much less esoteric, mysterious, and dramatic procedure than it had been in the days of Charcot.

Studies of the effectiveness of psychoanalysis had been conducted for quite some time, and perhaps the most lengthy and rigorous of the evaluative research programs was at the Menninger Hospital in Kansas. Over a period of more than 20 years, there had been various reports that the gains were modest. These reports were consistent with Freud's appraisal of psychoanalysis as a treatment method of limited usefulness, but they were nevertheless somewhat disappointing. An article by Wallerstein (1989) described one of the research projects.

Forty-two patients were seen in treatment, half in what started out to be "classic" psychoanalysis and half in other forms of psychoanalytic psychotherapy. All patients were white, upper-middle-class or upper-class neurotics of better than average intellectual functioning, and they ranged in age from 17 to 50 years. In short, demographically they were ideal candidates for psychotherapy. Each patient was given the form of therapy thought to be most appropriate, and neither the patients nor the therapists were aware that they were part of any research.

It was found that none of the patients received a classic form of psychoanalysis throughout the course of treatment and that changes in method also occurred in the psychoanalytic psychotherapy group. About half the patients required hospitalization during the course of their treatment, which again made it difficult to specify what might have been effective. Still, it was concluded that classic psychoanalysis led to less favorable outcomes and psychotherapy, including support from groups and removal from a stressful environment to a relatively benign one, led to more favorable changes than had been expected. Put another way, the degree of insight achieved by the patients was not very predictive of changes to more effective behaviors; many patients achieved changes that surpassed what was expected from what little insight they had gained, whereas many of those who had achieved much self-knowledge from their long-term analyses fell short of the improvements expected.

These results were perhaps sobering to therapists who believed insight was curative, although they were congenial to those who emphasized the treatment relationship. A piece of information that should have sobered all therapists was that there were diminishing returns as the number of sessions of psychotherapy increased (Howard, Kopta, Krause, & Orlinsky, 1986). From 10% to 18% of patients improved even before they had their 1st therapy session, 50% improved the 8th to 13th session, 75% by the 26th session, and 85% by the 52nd session. Since no therapy has been found to be 100% effective for any disorder, the data seemed to demonstrate the merit of considering 52 sessions as an upper limit in long-term psychotherapy.

Limits on expectations have never set too well and have always inspired people to challenge them. This is almost a tradition in psychotherapy, and social learning theory emphasizes the importance of positive expectations. However, it may put matters in some perspective when it is recalled that serious questions had once been raised about whether psychotherapy is effective at all. In the seventies, meta-analyses of outcome studies with adult patients demonstrated psychotherapy was effective. In the eighties meta-analyses of outcome studies with children and adolescents also demonstrated the effectiveness of psychotherapy (Casey & Berman, 1985; Weisz, Weiss, Alicke, & Klotz, 1987). Thus, there was a general conviction among psychotherapists that science had finally arrived at the point of justifying their impression that the services they rendered were of significant help.

Some misgivings were experienced about the statistics involved in the meta-analyses. Individual studies with nonsignificant differences between treatment and control groups became significant, another illustration of the whole being greater than the sum of its parts. But skepticism was overcome, and it was concluded that the "evidence suggests that deliberate psychotherapeutic interventions are more useful than their absence, and that the magnitude of their effects . . . is substantial" (Parloff, London, & Wolfe, 1986).

Years of research on psychotherapy and comparisons of one form with another indicated specific techniques for the treatment of a specific disorder are usually more effective in a limited period of time than a nonspecific treatment; no form of psychotherapy is always more effective than others; a positive outcome is related to a cooperative relationship, a client who is intelligent, open, eager for change, and not too disturbed and a therapist who is seen by the client as skillful, involved, understanding, and caring; and there is not much agreement among therapists, clients, and observers in describing what occurs in psychotherapeutic process. "Psychotherapy is a complex intersubjective phenomenon, and naively 'objective' approaches to its study are likely to prove inconsistent," said Orlinsky (1989) in proposing a generic model that he believed would facilitate researching the process.

Kazdin (1988) appraised the field and decided research could turn from the broad issue of effectiveness to the determination of which components of a treatment package were effective and which were not. In addition, the variables involved in treatment could be systematically varied to answer questions such as these: How much time should a session be? How often should a session be held?

Bednar, Burlingame, and Masters (1988) surveyed the research in family therapy but made observations pertinent to all of psychotherapy. In far too many instances, certain fundamental issues were ignored. Researchers were presumably investigating the same topic but defining it differently. This often resulted in substantial differences in what was observed, inconsistent sets of data, and confusion. Professionals had to arrive at substantial agreement about the definitions of their terms, including *psychotherapy*. A second important consideration was the method used in research or the means by which the variables were measured. Over 50 years before, Stevens (1935) urged psychologists to consider defining their terms operationally. Keeping in mind operational definitions was still important when looking at data from different studies. For example, improvements in one study might mean an increase or decrease in a specific behavior, in another study it might mean a feeling of general well-being, in another it might mean closer correspondance between how one saw oneself and how one wished to be, and in another it might mean a gain in insight. Moreover, in whose judgment was there improvement? Such issues would continue to bedevil research until more clinicians realized that definitions were not to be ignored or treated casually but were central to communication and an understanding of their activities.

Movements were afoot to integrate the different systems of psychotherapy. Dollard and Miller (1950) presented psychoanalysis as a kind of Hullian learning theory, and every so often there would be attempts to amalgamate two or more systems. Over many years many clinicians had speculated that common to all psychotherapists, especially the more experienced ones, was their establishment of a friendly relationship with their clients. Also, a large proportion of clinicians thought of themselves as eclectic and willing to use, for a given client, whatever was appropriate from whatever treatment system (Norcross, Prochaska, & Gallagher, 1989). However, research seemed to indicate substantial differences between therapists of different orientations (Reisman, 1986), and Patterson (1989) suggested that an integrated system might not be possible because therapists held incompatible views about human nature and their roles. Some saw people as needing training to cope more effectively with internal and external pressures, whereas others saw people as stymied in the process of growth and in need of acceptance and understanding in order to move on. Nevertheless, it did seem these integrative efforts were steps in the right direction.

The range of problems for which psychotherapy or therapeutic techniques were used continued to grow larger and larger: stress and pain management, physical and sexual abuse (Walker, Bonner, & Kaufman, 1988), prevention of substance abuse, crisis management, and coping with transitions. When disasters struck or when some terrible event occurred within a community, it was not unusual to see psychologists meeting with those affected and helping them deal with the situation. Psychotherapy had changed from a treatment used by those who felt they had exhausted their own resources to a way of interacting that strengthened and invigorated people during a time of need. Clinical psychology had changed from a profession that worked with a small segment of the population to a profession eager to provide services of value to everyone.

PROFESSIONAL DEVELOPMENT

Clinical psychology achieved a position of dominance within American psychology and the APA during the eighties. Five of the 10 APA presidents were clinical psychologists, and 4 of these 5 were elected consecutively (from 1986 to 1989): Logan Wright, Bonnie Strickland, Raymond Fowler, and Joseph Matarazzo. Further, the next two presidents, Stanley Graham for 1990 and Charles Spielberger for 1991, were also clinical psychologists, while Raymond Fowler became executive vice president and chief executive officer of the APA in 1989. (Fowler assumed that office following the resignation of its previous occupant, Leonard Goodstein, who had the temerity to state openly that the APA had become more of a professional than a scientific organization. Clinical psychologists preferred to walk softly.)

The facts attesting to clinical dominance were many. Before 1940, 70% of PhDs awarded in psychology were in experimental psychology, and almost all doctors of psychology worked in academic settings. By the eighties, the majority of doctorates were awarded in clinical psychology, counseling, and school psychology. More PhDs were awarded in clinical psychology than in any other field, and most of these degreed psychologists were working in health care settings (55% in clinics; 22% in schools, government, business, and other; 14% in academics; and 9% in private practice). Half the members of the APA, which listed over 68,000 members in its 1989 directory, were clinical psychologists, and about two-thirds worked as health service providers (Howard et al., 1986; Stapp, Fulcher, & Wicherski, 1984). There were 155 doctoral training programs in clinical psychology accredited by the APA, 51 in counseling, and 37 in school psychology (Nelson, 1989). There were 45 professional schools in psychology, 22 of which had APA accreditation.

Clinical psychologists were legally recognized as a profession and were certified or licensed in all 50 states, the District of Columbia, Puerto Rico, and several Canadian provinces. Clinical psychology was a popular and growing field in Australia (Day & Taft, 1988); Hungary (Reisman, 1988); Mexico, Brazil, Colombia, and Venezuela (Ardilia, 1982); the United Kingdom, Austria, Poland, Switzerland, Sweden, Norway, Iceland, the Netherlands, Portugal, East and West Germany, Spain, Italy, Finland, and France. In 1981 the European Federation of Professional Psychologists Associations (EFPPA) was founded with the aim of promoting cooperation in the practice of professional psychology and interaction between national psychological associations. Nineteen national organizations, including the APA, affiliated themselves with the EFPPA (McPherson, 1986).

An office of professional practice was established within the APA in 1986. Its purpose was to support practitioners, assist in legislative efforts, and foster the right of psychologists to practice their profession. Clinicians had hospital privileges in several states, which meant they could admit a patient to a hospital and continue to provide treatment without needing to have a "supervising" physician, and there was a push to extend these privileges to clinical psychologists throughout the country (Tanney, 1983).

Litigation and threats of litigation had enabled clinical psychologists to receive reimbursement for their services under all major federal insurance plans, including Medicare (Buie, 1990). In 1989 it was reported that, after 5 years of legal action, the suit of *Welch et al. v. American Psychoanalytic Association et al.* had been resolved by giving psychologists and other mental health professionals access to psychoanalytic training and membership in the International Psychoanalytic Association. Further, for a minimum of 10 years, at least 28% of the new students accepted by the American Psychoanalytic Association had to be nonphysicians (DeAngelis, 1989). What reasoned argument, even from the founder of psychoanalysis (Freud, 1927), had not been able to accomplish was finally achieved by legal means. Although it was doubtful that many clinical psychologists would avail themselves of this opportunity, the transfusion of psychologists into psychoanalysis could be expected to increase the receptivity of psychoanalysis to empirical findings and other theoretical positions.

Clinical psychology, Strickland (1988) announced in her APA presidential address, had come of age. As elsewhere in American society, psychology responded to the thrust for civil rights for minority groups and women. Minorities constituted about 5% of new clinical psychologists in the seventies and about 10% in the eighties; women constituted about a third of new clinicians in the seventies and a little more than half in the eighties (Howard et al., 1986). The profession was less elitist and more open to diversity that it had been.

Although the majority of doctorates in psychology were still PhDs, the PsyD was growing in acceptance and numbers. It was proposed once again, as Crane had proposed in 1925–1926, that the PsyD should be the degree for all professional psychologists (Fox, Kovacs, & Graham, 1985). A National Conference on Graduate Education was held at the University of Utah (Brickman, 1987), and although it endorsed professional schools in psychology and acknowledged the legitimacy of the PsyD, it concluded that research was still essential to every psychologist's training and recommended that after 1995, professional programs, in order to be APA accredited, should be formally affiliated with a regionally accredited university.

By this time APA-accredited professional schools of psychology had banded together into an organization of their own, the National Council of Schools of Professional Psychology, and they too were able to hold conferences. After meeting at Mission Bay, they reported they continued to endorse the APA requirement that training programs in psychology provide a core curriculum in experimental areas of the field. However, they challenged the recommendation of the University of Utah conference that the APA deny accreditation after 1995 to professional programs without university affiliations. They noted there was no evidence that university affiliation led to better education and training, and they argued that each program be judged on its individual program and situation (Bourg, Bent, McHolland, & Stricker, 1989). At the very least, their resistance suggested that schools of professional psychology had increased in strength and that dissension within the ranks of psychology was probable should this issue be pushed.

Dissension had seldom been out of place in psychology, and this decade had more than its share of disagreements. As the APA got bigger and bigger, it changed from a small chummy group into an organization with many members who did not even know the people elected to be their leaders. Clinical psychologists had been among the first to believe their interests might better be served by forming a group of their own, which they did in 1917—the American Association of Clinical Psychologists. This group disbanded in 1919 and became the first section or division of the APA. By 1989, despite efforts to reduce their number, there were 45 APA divisions. These groups addressed the special interests of psychologists and elected representatives to the APA council. The council and the APA board of directors considered recommendations for action by the organization.

On several occasions during the eighties the APA took actions that members believed were presumptuous. The most immediately ruinous of these actions was the 1983 purchase of *Psychology Today*, a magazine that disseminated the findings of psychology to the public in a relatively readable and engaging fashion. This magazine, modestly priced on the newsstand but inordinately expensive when purchased lock, stock, and barrel, changed the APA from a fiscally sound organization to a deficit- and debt-plagued one within 2 years (Fowler, 1985).

To meet its debts, the APA was forced to sell its major asset, its headquarters in Washington, DC, and two office buildings in Virginia. It was also forced to sell its major liability, *Psychology Today*, which, for the 6 years that the APA owned it, served as a continuous stressor for the membership (Spielberger, 1989). With the sale of *Psychology Today*, the APA's finances took an immediate turn for the better, and in December 1989 ground was broken for a new headquarters building in the capital, to be completed in 1992. Other problems, however, were not so easily solved.

A revision in the APA Code of Ethics appeared in 1981 (APA, 1981). Some of the principles set restrictions on advertising, client referrals, and the sale of practices, restrictions that some members believed interfered with their right to practice and make available their services. They threatened to sue the APA, and the offending passages were finally deleted in 1989. Other psychologists objected to laws and ethical principles that required them to break confidentiality with their clients in certain circumstances. They argued confidentiality should never be broken, even in instances of child abuse. Although a study of the matter indicated therapists who reported clients who abused their children did not necessarily experience a deterioration in the treatment relationship, many psychologists continued to refuse to break confidentiality when required (Watson & Levine, 1989).

The January 1986 issue of the *APA Monitor* featured notable achievements in psychology during the previous 15 years, predictions for the coming decade, and bones of contention. One article dealt with the continued controversy regarding psychological testing and with efforts to redefine intelligence (Cordes, 1986). Another article dealt with the growing numbers of psychologists working in applied fields and the increasing involvement of the APA in professional matters (Turkington, 1986). By the eighties, the balance had so firmly shifted from the view that psychology was a "pure" science to the view that it was both a science and a profession that those psychologists who held the former view felt alienated and resentful. They were unhappy that the APA used its resources, which they contributed to by their membership dues, to deal with professional matters, and they felt the organization was not representing, as it should, psychology as a science. Unless something was done to correct this situation, they threatened to withdraw from the APA and form their own association. To prevent such a split, a plan for the reorganization of the APA was proposed.

Briefly, the proposal was to divide the APA into separate assemblies of academic and nonacademic members. The two assemblies would be somewhat autonomous and were to have two different dues. Of course, those psychologists who wished to support the APA's promotion of the profession were expected to pay higher dues than those whose interests related only to the science. This proposal had the support of a number of former presidents of the APA, who hoped that by its adoption the APA would continue to represent all psychologists. "Despite internal tensions APA, with its historical ties to other scientific societies, continues to represent the common heritage of American psychology" (Hilgard, 1987, p. 771).

However, the growing number of psychologists with special interests had led to the formation of many organizations (Fagan, 1986), with no appreciable effect on the power of the APA. Therefore, there was not much concern about this threatened split being implemented (Sechrest, 1985b), at least in some quarters. This almost blasé attitude about a possible split among psychologists was relatively new. There was even some evidence to suggest a split might be inevitable and for the best (Kimble, 1984; Krasner & Houts, 1984).

For example, Kimble (1984) asserted there were two cultures within psychology: One valued a scientific, nomothetic, deterministic, reductionistic, experimental approach to understanding human behavior; the other valued a humanistic, indeterministic, intuitive, naturalistic, ideographic, holistic view. In Kimble's opinion, the differences were not reconcilable and the field would be fragmented, with psychologists of similar value systems going their separate ways.

In 1988, the reorganization plan for the APA was submitted to the membership for their approval, and they voted to reject it. Immediately thereafter a group of dissident psychologists formed an organization dedicated exclusively to scientific psychology, the American Psychological Society. Its first president was Janet Spence, who had been president of the APA in 1984. The first convention of the society was held in Alexandria, Virginia, in 1989, and it was announced that its membership had reached about 5,000 and that it would soon publish a journal, *Psychological Science*. It was highly unlikely that the APA would reorganize itself and alter its aims to accommodate these psychologists, as it had done in the forties to accommodate clinical psychologists. The difference was that clinical psychology represented a growing trend and the society did not. Moreover, both the APA and the American Psychological Society were open to members wishing affiliation with both groups. This openness reduced the probability of APA concessions.

Nevertheless, many psychologists were troubled by the division and wished for a reconciliation. To some extent the division and the resulting distress were expressive of broader trends of differentiation and fragmentation on the one hand and strivings for synthesis and union on the other. Thus in the same year and in the same journal it was possible to have one article heralding the arrival of school psychology as a profession in its own right (Fagan, 1986) and another article calling for the combination of clinical psychology, counseling, and school psychology to form a new profession: human services psychology (Fitzgerald & Osipow, 1986).

Similarly, the multiplicity of personality theories and their attendant therapeutic systems bothered some psychologists. The enduring theoretical and technical diversity was alleged to be a symptom of weakness in psychology as a science and of the ineffectiveness of its current treatment methods. The situation in other sciences was claimed to be in stark contrast to the sorry and dismal state that exists in psychology, especially in clinical psychology, where contradictory theories and techniques seem never to be abandoned.

But which of the other sciences had really attained an idyllic state of agreement?

Physicists, biologists, and astronomers would willingly admit they have many unsettled issues within their fields, and they could mention the nature of magnetism, life, antimatter, and black holes to show there are still a few questions they have not definitively answered. Moreover, even if it was argued that psychology and its problems are distinctive and that its solutions need not correspond to those in other disciplines, psychology does in fact have a knowledge base that is integrative and cumulative, and social or cognitive behaviorism and psychoanalysis are two relatively comprehensive and open theoretical systems.

This history began by discussing the period when values conducive to the development of clinical psychology first gained currency. It is fitting to end by making those values explicit.

Truth. Truth is not always easily determined, particularly in psychology, when what may be true for a group or population is not usually true for many of its individual members. Nevertheless, psychologists are supposed to value truth and be willing to modify their theories and beliefs should they conflict with what is true.

Surprisingly, what is at the basis of much truth is agreement or consensus. Therefore, if psychologists wish to increase what is true in their discipline, one sure but neglected means is to arrive at standard definitions of their terms. Through the years psychologists have been amused and distressed by their lack of consensus about the meanings of *intelligence, psychotherapy,* and *clinical psychology,* to give just three examples (Sechrest, 1985a).

It is compatible with the goals of the APA in advancing psychology as a science to have a scientific committee deal with matters of definition and to publish a glossary of terms.

Honesty. A commitment to honesty requires psychologists to report their findings and convictions accurately. It also requires them not to traffic in exaggerated claims and distortions of the positions of others.

Throughout psychology's history this value has not always been honored, most glaringly in the use of deception in research and reactance techniques in psychotherapy (Hoffman, 1981). It is never violated without cost and is best scrupulously observed.

Fairness. To be fair means to be just and equitable, to be free of favoritism or bias. What is fair in a given situation, however, depends a great deal on the judgments of the people involved. It may be fair that every psychologist should have his or her say in an APA journal. It may also be fair to restrict publication to those whose statements have merit, to those most in need of being published, or to those who have worked hardest to write something. Fairness is not a simple matter.

During the eighties there was some concern that criticisms of some historical figures whose honesty had been called into question might be unfair. Henry Goddard, for example, was charged with deliberately retouching photos of the Kallikak family so their "retardation" would be more evident and his position (that intelligence was inherited) would be supported. However, it was also possible the photos were retouched by the publisher because they were of poor quality (Fancher, 1987). In any case, fairness seems to require that there be a presumption of innocence and that historical figures be judged within the contexts of their times.

People. Psychologists value people, and clinical psychologists value every person, without regard to race, creed, religion, or belief system. What drew them to the field of psychology is the value they place on people and the understanding of human behavior. The high value placed by psychologists on truth, honesty, fairness, and people to some extent unifies them.

One of the things psychologists can gain from the study of the past is humility. They will discover that long ago there were men and women who puzzled over many of the same behaviors that are still enigmatic. Although some of these predecessors' thoughts about people were incorrect, many of their speculations, studies, and insights have merit.

Psychologists are also people, and, like other human beings, they hope for recognition and approval and lasting reknown. Many of them are deeply sensitive to criticism of their efforts. Perhaps the teachings of humanistic psychology and all the research on stress will foster a more compassionate and less critical stance in their interactions with each other.

In 1989 Fowler, chief executive officer of the APA, rushed events a bit by anticipating the celebration that would occur in 1992 to mark the hundredth anniversary of the founding of the organization. His comments had an optimism that echoed the attitude of early APA presidents such as Hall, Ladd, and Cattell: "We're just now at the end of our first 100 years and we're having the kind of impact our fathers dreamed about. For the second 100 years, the sky's the limit" (quoted in Denton, 1989). We shall see.

References

Abel, A. (1984). *Fetal alcohol syndrome and fetal alcohol effects.* New York: Plenum.

Abt, L. E. (1964). Clinical psychology in Latin America. In L. E. Abt & B. F. Riess (Eds.), *Progress in clinical psychology* (Vol. 4). New York: Grune & Stratton.

Adams, D. K. (1939). William McDougall. *Psychological Review, 46,* 1–8.

Adler, Alexandra. (1962). Adler, Alfred. *Collier's Encyclopedia* (Vol. 1). New York: Crowell-Collier.

Adler, A. (1927). Individual-psychological treatment of neuroses. In *The practice and theory of individual psychology.* New York: Harcourt, Brace.

Adler, A. (1927–1928). Individual psychology. *Journal of Abnormal and Social Psychology, 22,* 116–122.

Adler, A. (1928–1929). The cause and prevention of neuroses. *Journal of Abnormal and Social Psychology, 23,* 4–11.

Adler, A. (1930). Individual psychology. In C. Murchison (Ed.), *Psychologies of 1930.* Worcester, MA: Clark University Press.

Adler, T. (1989). MMPI-2: Revision brings test "to the 21st century." *The APA Monitor, 20*(11), 1, 6.

Adorno, T. W., Frenkel-Brunswik, E., Levinson, D. J., & Sanford, R. N. (1950). *The authoritarian personality.* New York: Harper.

Aichhorn, A. (1935). *Wayward youth.* New York: Viking.

Ainsworth, M., Blehar, M. C., Waters, E., & Wall, S. (1978). *Patterns of attachment: A psychological study of the strange situation.* Hillsdale, NJ: Erlbaum.

Albee, G. W. (1966). The dark at the top of the agenda. *The Clinical Psychologist, 20*(1), 7–9.

Albee, G. W. (1968). Conceptual models and manpower requirements in psychology. *American Psychologist, 23,* 317–320.

Albee, G. W. (1970). The uncertain future of clinical psychology. *American Psychologist, 25,* 1071–1080.

Alexander, F., French, T. M., et al. (1946). *Psychoanalytic therapy.* New York: Ronald.

Alexander, F., & Healy, W. (1935). *Roots of crime.* New York: Alfred A. Knopf.

Allen, F. H. (1934). Therapeutic work with children. *Amerian Journal of Orthopsychiatry, 4,* 193–202.

Allen, F. H. (1940). Otto Rank. *American Journal of Orthopsychiatry, 10,* 186–187.

Alleridge, P. (1979). Hospitals, madhouses and asylums: Cycles in the care of the insane. *British Journal of Psychiatry, 134,* 321–334.

Allport, F. H., & Allport, G. W. (1921–1922). Personality traits: Their classification and measurement. *Journal of Abnormal and Social Psychology, 16,* 6–40.

Allport, G. W. (1921). Personality and character. *Psychological Bulletin, 18,* 441–455.

Allport, G. W. (1924–1925). The study of the undivided personality. *Journal of Abnormal and Social Psychology, 19,* 132–141.

Allport, G. W. (1928–1929). A test for ascendence-submission. *Journal of Abnormal and Social Psychology, 23,* 118–136.

Allport, G. W. (1929–1930). The study of personality by the intuitive method: An experiment in teaching from *The Locomotive God. Journal of Abnormal and Social Psychology, 24,* 14–27.

Allport, G. W. (1937). *Personality: A psychological interpretation.* New York: Holt.

Allport, G. W. (1940). The psychologist's frame of reference. *Psychological Bulletin, 37,* 1–28.

Allport, G. W. (1955). *Becoming: Basic considerations for a psychology of personality.* New Haven: Yale University Press.

Allport, G. W., & Vernon, P. E. (1931). *A study of values.* Boston: Houghton Mifflin.

American Board of Examiners in Professional Psychology. (1959). *American Psychologist, 14,* 827–829.

American Psychiatric Association. (1987). *Diagnostic and statistical manual of mental disorders* (3rd ed.). Washington, DC: Author.

American Psychological Association. (1981). Ethical principles of psychologists. *American Psychologist, 36,* 633–638.

American Psychological Association Clinical Section. (1935). Guide to psychological clinics in the United States. *Psychological Clinic, 23,* 9–140.

American Psychological Association Committee on Ethical Standards for Psychology. (1951). Ethical standards in clinical and consulting relationships. *American Psychologist, 6,* 57–64.

American Psychological Association & American Association of Applied Psychology Committees on Graduate and Professional Training (1945). Subcommittee report on graduate training in clinical psychology. *Journal of Consulting Psychology, 9,* 243–266.

American Psychological Association Committee on Legislation. (1967). A model for state legislation affecting the practice of psychology. *American Psychologist, 22,* 1095–1103.

American Psychological Association Committee on Test Standards. (1952). *American Psychologist, 7,* 461–475.

American Psychological Association Committee on Training in Clinical Psychology. (1947). Recommended graduate training program in clinical psychology. *American Psychologist, 2,* 539–558.

Anastasi, A. (1958). Heredity, environment, and the question "how?". *Psychological Review, 65,* 197–208.

Anastasi, A. (1967). Psychology, psychologists, and psychological testing. *American Psychologist, 22,* 297–306.

Anastasi, A. (1982). *Psychological testing* (5th ed.). New York: Macmillan.

Anderson, J. E. (1939). The limitation of infant and preschool tests in the measurement of intelligence. *Journal of Psychology, 8,* 351–379.

Anderson, J. E. (1948). Personality organization in children. *American Psychologist, 3,* 409–416.

Andreasen, N. C. (1988). Brain imaging: Applications in psychiatry. *Science, 239,* 1381–1388.

Angell, J. R. (1907). The province of functional psychology. *Psychological Review, 14,* 61–91.

Angyal, A. (1941). *Foundations for a science of personality.* New York: Commonwealth Fund.

Ansbacher, H. L. (1950). Testing, management, and reactions of foreign workers in Germany during World War II. *American Psychologist, 5,* 38–49.

Ansbacher, H. L., & Ansbacher, R. R. (1956). *The individual psychology of Alfred Adler.* New York: Basic Books.

Appel, K. E. (1930–1931). Drawings of children as aids to personality studies. *American Journal of Orthopsychiatry, 1,* 129–144.

Ardila, R. (1982). Psychology in Latin America today. *Annual Review of Psychology, 33,* 103–122.

Arieti, S. (1955). *Interpretation of schizophrenia.* New York: Bruner.

Aron, A., & Aron, E. N. (1986). *Love and the expansion of self.* New York: Hemisphere.

Aserinsky, E., & Kleitman, N. (1953). Regularly occurring periods of eye motility, and concomitant phenomena, during sleep. *Science, 118,* 273–274.

Atkinson, J. W. (1960). Personality dynamics. *Annual Review of Psychology, 11,* 255–290.

August, H. E. (1935). Newer attitudes toward mental subnormalities. *American Journal of Orthopsychiatry, 5,* 49–56.

Averasturi, L. G. (1980). Psychology and health care in Cuba. *American Psychologist, 35,* 1090–1095.

Axelrode, J. (1940). Some indications for supportive therapy. *American Journal of Orthopsychiatry, 10,* 264–271.

Ayllon, T., & Azrin, N. H. (1968). *The token economy.* New York: Appleton-Century-Crofts.

Ayres, L. P. (1911–1912). The Binet-Simon measuring scale for intelligence: Some criticisms and suggestions. *Psychology Clinic, 5,* 187–196.

Bandura, A. (1971). *Psychological modeling.* Chicago: Aldine.

Bandura, A. (1974). Behavior theory and the models of man. *American Psychologist, 29,* 859–869.

Bandura, A. (1977). *Social learning theory.* Englewood Cliffs, NJ: Prentice-Hall.

Barber, T. X. (1956). Physiological effects of "hypnosis." *Psychological Bulletin, 53,* 210–226.

Barber, T. X. (1965). Experimental analyses of "hypnotic" behavior: A review of recent empirical findings. *Journal of Abnormal Psychology, 70,* 132–154.

Barber, T. X. (1982). Hypnosuggestive procedures in the treatment of clinical pain: Implications for theories of hypnosis and suggestive therapy. In T. Miller, C. J. Green, & R. B. Meagher, Jr. (Eds.), *Handbook of clinical health psychology.* New York: Plenum.

Barcus, R. A. (1982). Clinical psychology and mental health in South Korea. *The Clinical Psychologist, 35*(Spring), 16–19.

Bard, M. (1966). Clinical psychology in Scandinavia. In L. E. Abt & B. F. Riess (Eds.), *Progress in clinical psychology* (Vol. 7). New York: Grune & Stratton.

Barron, F. (1953). An ego-strength scale which predicts response to psychotherapy. *Journal of Consulting Psychology, 17,* 327–333.

Bartlett, F. C. (1932). *Remembering: A study in experimental and social psychology.* Cambridge: Cambridge University Press.

Bartlett, F. C. (1947). Visitor to America. *American Psychologist, 2,* 372–374.

Batchelor, W. (1984). AIDS: A public health and psychological emergency. *American Psychologist, 39,* 1279–1284.

Bateson, G., et al. (1956). Toward a theory of schizophrenia. *Behavioral Science, 1,* 251–264.

Bayley, N. (1955). On the growth of intelligence. *American Psychologist, 10,* 805–818.

Bayley, N. (1969). *Manual for the Bayley Scales of Infant Development.* New York: Psychological Corporation.

Beaglehole, E. (1938). A note on cultural compensation. *Journal of Abnormal and Social Psychology, 33,* 121–123.

Beck, A. T. (1972). *Depression: Causes and treatment.* Philadelphia: University of Pennsylvania Press.

Beck, A. T. (1976). *Cognitive therapy and the emotional disorders.* New York: International Universities Press.

Beck, S. J. (1930). The Rorschach test and personality diagnosis: I. The feebleminded. *American Journal of Psychiatry, 10,* 19–52.

Beck, S. J. (1933). The Rorschach method and the organization of personality. *American Journal of Orthopsychiatry, 3,* 361–375.

Beck, S. J. (1935). Problems of further research in the Rorschach test. *American Journal of Orthopsychiatry, 5,* 100–115.

Beck, S. J. (1936–1937). Psychological processes in Rorschach findings. *Journal of Abnormal and Social Psychology, 31,* 482–488.

Beck, S. J. (1937). *Introduction to the Rorschach method: Monograph No. 1.* New York: American Orthopsychiatric Association.

Beck, S. J. (1944). *Rorschach's test: Vol. I. Basic processes.* New York: Grune & Stratton.

Beck, S. J. (1945). *Rorschach's test: Vol. II. A variety of personality pictures.* New York: Grune & Stratton.

Beck, S. J. (1948). Rorschach's test in this anniversary year. In L. G. Lowrey & V. Sloane (Eds.), *Orthopsychiatry 1923–1948: Retrospect and prospect.* New York: American Orthopsychiatric Association.

Beck, S. J. (1963). Personal communication to author.

Bednar, R. L., Burlingame, G. M., & Masters, K. S. (1988). Systems of family treatment: Substance or semantics? *Annual Review of Psychology, 39,* 401–434.

Beers, C. W. (1908). *A mind that found itself.* New York: Longmans, Green.

Bellak, L. (1948). *Dementia praecox.* New York: Grune & Stratton.

Bellak, L. (1964). *Handbook of community psychiatry and community mental health.* New York: Grune & Stratton.

Benassi, V., & Lanson, R. (1972). A survey of the teaching of behavior modification in colleges and universities. *American Psychologist, 27,* 1063–1069.

Bender, L. (1938). *A visual motor gestalt test and its clinical use.* New York: American Orthopsychiatric Association.

Bender, L. (1947). Childhood schizophrenia: A clinical study of one hundred schizophrenic children. *American Journal of Orthopsychiatry, 17,* 40–56.

Bender, L. (1956). *Psychopathology of children with organic brain disorders.* Springfield, IL: Charles C Thomas.

Benedict, R. (1934). *Patterns of culture.* Boston: Houghton Mifflin.

Bentley, M. (1926). The major categories of psychology. *Psychological Review, 33,* 71–105.

Benton, A. L. (1950). The experimental validation of the Rorschach test. *British Journal of Medical Psychology, 23,* 45–58.

Bergin, A. E. (1966). Some implications of psychotherapy research for therapeutic practice. *Journal of Abnormal Psychology, 71,* 235–246.

Bergin, A. E., Garfield, S. L., & Thompson, A. S. (1967). The Chicago conference on clinical training and clinical psychology at Teacher's College. *American Psychologist, 22,* 307–316.

Berliner, B. (1941). Short psychoanalytic therapy: Its possibilities and limitations. *Bulletin of the Menninger Clinic, 5,* 204–213.

Berman, L. (1921). *The glands regulating the personality.* New York: Macmillan.

Bernreuter, R. G. (1933–1934). The measurement of self-sufficiency. *Journal of Abnormal and Social Psychology, 28,* 291–300.

Bersoff, D. N. (1973). Silk purses into sow's ears: The decline of psychological testing and a suggestion for its redemption. *American Psychologist, 28,* 892–899.

Beschner, G. M., & Friedman, A. S. (1979). *Youth drug abuse.* Lexington, MA: Lexington Books.

Bettelheim, B. (1947). The dynamism of anti-semitism in gentile and Jew. *Journal of Abnormal and Social Psychology, 42,* 153–168.

Bettelheim, B. (1950). *Love is not enough.* Glencoe, IL: Free Press.

Bettelheim, B. (1967). *The empty fortress.* New York: Free Press.

Bettelheim, B., & Sylvester, R. (1948). A therapeutic milieu. *American Journal of Orthopsychiatry, 18,* 191–206.

Beutler, L. E. (1979). Toward specific psychological therapies for specific conditions. *Journal of Consulting and Clinical Psychology, 47,* 882–897.

Bickman, L. (Ed.). (1987). Resolutions approved by the National Conference on Graduate Education in Psychology. *American Psychologist, 42,* 1070–1084.

Billingslea, F. Y. (1963). The Bender-Gestalt: A review and a perspective. *Psychological Bulletin, 60,* 233–251.

Binder, H. (1937). The "light-dark" interpretations in Rorschach's experiment. *Rorschach Research Exchange, 2,* 37–42.

Binet, A., & Henri, V. (1896). La psychologie indiviuelle. *L'annee Psychologique, 2,* 411–465.

Binet, A., & Simon, T. (1962). Upon the necessity of establishing a scientific diagnosis of inferior states of intellignece: The development of the Binet-Simon Scale. In F. Rosenblith & W. Allinsmith (Eds.), *The causes of behavior: Readings in child development and educational psychology.* Boston: Allyn & Bacon.

Bingham, W. V. D. (1952). Autobiography. In E. G. Boring et al. (Eds.), *A history of psychology in autobiography* (Vol. 4). Worcester, MA: Clark University Press.

Black, J. D. (1949). Survey of employment in psychology and the place of personnel without the Ph.D. *American Psychologist, 4,* 38–42.

Blake, R. R., & Mouton, J. S. (1959). Personality. *Annual Review of Psychology, 10,* 203–232.

Blanchard, P. (1935). Psychogenic factors in some cases of reading disability. *American Journal of Orthopsychiatry, 5,* 361–374.

Blanck, G., & Blanck, R. (1974). *Ego psychology: Theory and practice.* New York: Columbia University Press.

Blanck, G., & Blanck, R. (1979). *Ego psychology II.* New York: Columbia University Press.

Blank, L., Gottsegen, G. B., & Gottsegen, M. G. (1971). *Confrontation.* New York: Macmillan.

Bleuler, E. (1950). *Dementia praecox or the group of schizophrenias.* New York: International Universities Press.

Block, N. J., & Dworkin, G. (Eds.). (1976). *The IQ controversy: Critical readings.* New York: Pantheon.

Blum, G. S. (1949). A study of the psychoanalytic theory of psychosexual development. *Genetic Psychology Monographs, 39*, 3–99.

Bordin, E. S. (1950). Counseling methods: Therapy. *Annual Review of Psychology, 1*, 267–276.

Borehoutsos, J. C., & Roe, K. V. (1984). Mental health services and the emerging role of psychology in Greece. *American Psychologist, 39*, 57–61.

Boring, E. G. (1929). The psychology of controversy. *Psychological Review, 36*, 97–121.

Boring, E. G. (1950). *A history of experimental psychology.* New York: Appleton-Century-Crofts.

Boring, E. G. (1952). Autobiography. In E. G. Boring et al. (Eds.), *A history of psychology in autobiography* (Vol. 4). Worcester, MA: Clark University Press.

Bourg, E. F., Bent, R. J., McHolland, J., & Stricker, G. (1989). Standards and evaluation in the education and training of professional psychologists: The National Council of Schools of Professional Psychology Mission Bay conference. *American Psychologist, 44*, 66–72.

Bowlby, J. (1988). Developmental psychiatry comes of age. *American Journal of Psychiatry, 145*, 1–10.

Brackbill, G. A. (1956). Studies of brain dysfunction in schizophrenia. *Psychological Bulletin, 53*, 210–226.

Bradley, C. (1941). *Schizophrenia in childhood.* New York: Macmillan.

Brain, W. R., & Walton, J. N. (1969). *Brain diseases of the nervous system.* London: Oxford University Press.

Brennan, M., & Gill, M. M. (1944). *Hypnotherapy.* New York: Josiah Macy, Jr. Foundation.

Brickman, L. (Ed.) (1987). Resolutions approved by the National Conference on Graduate Education in Psychology, *American Psychologist, 42*, 1070–1084.

Bridges, J. W., & Coler, L. E. (1917). The relation of intelligence to social status. *Psychological Review, 23*, 303–331.

Brigham, C. C. (1923). *A study of American intelligence.* Princeton: Princeton University Press.

Brigham, C. C. (1930). Intelligence tests of immigrant groups. *Psychological Review, 37*, 158–165.

Britt, S. H., & Morgan, J. D. (1946). Military psychologists in World War II. *American Psychologist, 1*, 423–437.

Bronner, A. F. (1916). Attitude as it affects performance of tests. *Psychological Review, 23*, 303–331.

Brotemarkle, R. (1947). Clinical psychology, 1896–1946. *Journal of Consulting Psychology, 11*, 1–4.

Brown, J. F. (1929). The methods of Kurt Lewin in the psychology of action and affection. *Psychologial Review, 36*, 200–221.

Bruner, J. S., & Goodman, C. C. (1947). Value and need as organizing factors in perception. *Journal of Abnormal and Social Psychology, 42*, 33–44.

Bry, A. (1975). *est.* New York: Harper & Row.

Bryngelson, B. (1935–1936). A method of stuttering. *Journal of Abnormal and Social Psychology, 28*, 291–300.

Buchsbaum, M. S., & Haier, R. J. (1983). Psychopathology: Biological approaches. *Annual Review of Psychology, 34*, 401–430.

Buck, J. N. (1948). The H-T-P technique: A qualitative and quantitative scoring manual. *Journal of Clinical Psychology,* (Monograph Supplement No. 5).

Buckle, D. F., & David, H. P. (1967). Psychologists in European health services. *The Clinical Psychologist, 21*(1), 11–16.

Buie, J. (1990). President signs Medicare bill. *The APA Monitor, 21*(1), 17.

Burns, E. M. (1947). *Western civilizations: Their history and their culture.* New York: Norton.

Buros, O. K. (1941). *The 1940 mental measurements yearbook.* Highland Park, NJ: Mental Measurements Yearbook.

Buros, O. K. (1953). *The fourth mental measurements yearbook.* Highland Park, NJ: Gryphon Press.

Buros, O. K. (1970). *Personality tests and reviews.* Highland Park, NJ: Gryphon Press.

Burrows, G. D., & Deunerstein, L. (1981). Depression and suicide in middle age. In J. G. Howells (Ed.), *Modern perspectives in the psychiatry of middle age.* New York: Bruner/Mazel.

Burrows, T. (1939). The economic factor in disorders of behavior. *American Journal of Orthopsychiatry, 9*, 102–108.

Burt, C. (1925). *The young delinquent.* New York: Appleton.

Burt, C. (1940). *The factors of the mind.* London: London University Press.

Burt, C. (1952). Autobiography. In E. G. Boring et al. (Eds.), *A history of psychology in autobiography* (Vol. 4). Worcester, MA: Clark University Press.

Burt, C. (1958). The inheritence of mental ability. *American Psychologist, 13,* 1–15.

Buss, A. H., & Durkee, A. (1958). Conditioning of hostile verbalizations in situation resembling a clinical interview. *Journal of Consulting Psychology, 22,* 415–418.

Buss, A. H., & Gerjuoy, I. R. (1958). Verbal conditioning and anxiety. *Journal of Abnormal and Social Psychology, 57,* 249–250.

Buss, A. H., & Lang, P. J. (1965). Psychological deficit in schizophrenia. *Journal of Abnormal Psychology, 70,* 2–24, 77–106.

Byrn, D. (1936–1937). The problem of human types: Comments and experiment. *Character and Personality, 5,* 48–60.

Byrne, D. (1971). *The attraction paradigm.* New York: Academic Press.

Cacioppo, J. T., & Tassinary, L. G. (1990). Inferring psychological significance from physiological signals. *American Psychologist, 45,* 16–28.

Calder-Marshall, A. (1962). Ellis, H. *Collier's Encyclopedia* (Vol. 9). New York: Crowell-Collier.

California Schoool of Professional Psychology. (1972). *Catalog of courses for the 1972-73 session.*

Calkins, M. W. (1906). A reconciliation between structural and functional psychology. *Psychological Review, 13,* 76.

Calkins, M. W. (1930). Autobiography. In C. Murchison (Ed.), A history of psychology in autobiography (Vol. 1). Worcester, MA: Clark University Press.

Calkins, M. W., & Gamble, E. A. M. (1930). The self-psychology of the psychoanalysts. *Psychological Review, 37,* 277–304.

Cameron, N., & Magaret, A. (1957). *Behavior pathology.* Boston: Houghton Mifflin.

Campbell, K. J. (1932–1933). The relation of the types of physique to the types of mental diseases. *Journal of Abnormal and Social Psychology, 27,* 147–151.

Cannon, W. B. (1929). *Bodily changes in pain, hunger, fear, and rage.* New York: Appleton.

Cantril, H. (1949). Psychologists working for peace. *American Psychologist, 4,* 69–73.

Carey, B. (1989, January 11). Jump-starting our sexual underachievers. *Chicago Tribune,* Sec. 5, pp. 1, 5.

Carmichael, L. (1927). A further study of the development of behavior in vertebrates experimentally removed from the influence of external stimulation. *Psychological Review, 34,* 34–47.

Carrigan, P. M. (1960). Extraversion-introversion as a dimension of personality: A reappraisal. *Psychological Bulletin, 57,* 329–360.

Carson, R. C., Garfield, S. L., Strupp, H. H., Adams, D. E., & Katkin, E. S. (1982). Whatever happened to clinical psychology: The academic view [Symposium]. *The Clinical Psychologist, 36*(1), 4–11.

Casey, R. J., & Berman, J. S. (1985). The outcome of psychotherapy with children. *Psychological Bulletin, 98,* 388–400.

Cates, J. (1970). Psychology's manpower: Report on the 1968 National Register of Scientific and Technical Personnel. *American Psychologist, 25,* 254–263.

Cattell, J. M. (1890). Mental tests and measurements. *Mind, 15,* 373–381.

Cattell, J. M. (1896). Address of the president before the American Psychological Association, 1895. *Psychological Review, 3,* 134–148.

Cattell, J. M. (1937). Retrospect: Psychology as a profession. *Journal of Consulting Psychology, 1,* 1–3.

Cattell, J. M. (1946). Retrospect: Psychology as a profession. *Journal of Consulting Psychology, 10,* 289–291.

Cattell, J. M., & Farrand, L. (1896). Physical and mental measurements of the students of Columbia Unviersity. *Psychological Review, 3,* 618–648.

Cattell, P. (1940). *The measurement of intelligence of infants and young children.* New York: Psychological Corporation.

Cattell, R. B. (1939). The status of applied psychology in England. *Journal of Consulting Psychology, 3,* 76–79.

Cattell, R. B. (1968, March). Are IQ tests intelligent? *Psychology Today,* 56–62.

Challman, R. C. (1951). Clinical methods: Psychodiagnostics. *Annual Review of Psychology, 2,* 239–258.

Chapman, L. J., & Chapman, J. P. (1967). Genesis of popular but erroneous psychodiagnostic observations. *Journal of Abnormal Psychology, 72,* 193–204.

Chapman, L. J., & Chapman, J. P. (1969). Illusory correlation as an obstacle to the use of valid psychodiagnostic signs. *Journal of Abnormal Psychology, 74,* 271–280.

Chauncey, H. (1959). Some notes on education and psychology in the Soviet Union. *American Psychologist, 14,* 307–312.

Chidester, L. (1934). Therapeutic results with mentally retarded children. *American Journal of Orthopsychiatry, 4,* 464–472.

Ching, C. C. (1980). Psychology in the People's Republic of China. *American Psychologist, 35,* 1084–1089.

Claparède, E. (1930). Autobiography. In C. Murchison (Ed.), *A history of psychology in autobiography* (Vol. 1). Worcester, MA: Clark University Press.

Cleary, T. A., Humphreys, L. G., Kendrick, S. A., & Wesman, A. (1975). Educational uses of tests with disadvantaged students. *American Psychologist, 30,* 15–41.

Cofer, C. N. (1959). Motivation. *Annual Review of Psychology, 10,* 173–202.

Coleman, R. E. (1971). Clinical psychology in Canada. *The Clinical Psychologist, 25*(1), 4–5.

Columbia-Greystone Associates. (1949). *Selective partial ablation of the frontal cortex.* New York: Hoeber.

Committee of the National Research Council. (1945). *Psychology for the returning serviceman.* New York: Infantry Journal; Penguin Books.

Committee on Nomenclature and Statistics of the American Psychiatric Association. (1952). *Diagnostic and statistical manual.* Washington, DC: American Psychiatric Association.

Committee on Nomenclature and Statistics of the American Psychiatric Association. (1968). *Diagnostic and statistical manual of mental disorders (DSM-II).* Washington, DC: American Psychiatric Association.

Committee on Scientific and Professional Aims of Psychology. (1967). The scientific and professional aims of psychology. *American Psychologist, 22,* 49–76.

Cordes, C. (1986). Intelligence. *The APA Monitor, 17*(1), 7–9.

Corsini, R. J. (1957). *Methods of group psychotherapy.* New York: McGraw-Hill.

Cortes, J. B., & Gatti, F. M. (1965). Physique and self-description of temperament. *Journal of Consulting Psychology, 29,* 432–439.

Cotton, H. A. (1921). *The defective delinquent and insane.* Princeton: Princeton University Press.

Cotton, H. A. (1922). The etiology and treatment of the so-called functional psychoses. *American Journal of Psychiatry, 2,* 157–210.

Cowen, E. L., Gardner, E. A., & Zax, M. (1967). *Emergent approaches to mental health problems.* New York: Appleton-Century-Crofts.

Crane, L. (1931–1932). The limitations of psychometrics in clinical practice. *Journal of Abnormal and Social Psychology, 26,* 199–202.

Crane, L. (1925–1926). A plea for the training of psychologists. *Journal of Abnormal and Social Psychology, 20,* 228–233.

Cronbach, L. J. (1956). Assessment of individual differences. *Annual Review of Psychology, 7,* 173–196.

Cronbach, L. J., & Meehl, P. E. (1955). Construct validity in psychological tests. *Psychological Bulletin, 52,* 281–302.

Crutchfield, R. S. (1955). Conformity and character. *American Psychologist, 10,* 191–198.

Cummings, N. A. (1984). The future of clinical psychology in the United States. *The Clinical Psychologist, 37*(1), 19–20.

Dahlstrom, W. G. (1970). Personality. *Annual Review of Psychology, 21,* 1–48.

Daily, J. M. (1953). Verbal conditioning without awareness. Unpublished doctoral dissertation, Iowa State University.

Darrah, L. (1940). Should we differentiate between schizophrenia and dementia praecox? *Journal of Nervous and Mental Disease, 91*, 323-328.

Dashiell, J. F. (1939). Some rapprochments in contemporary psychology. *Psychological Bulletin, 36*, 1-24.

David, H. P. (1959). Clinical psychology abroad. *American Psychologist, 14*, 601-605.

Davids, A. (1975). Therapeutic approaches to children in residential treatment: Changes from the mid-1950s to the mid-1970s. *American Psychologist, 30*, 809-814.

Davies, A. E. (1926-1927). An interpretation of mental symptoms of dementia praecox. *Journal of Abnormal and Social Psychology, 21*, 284-295.

Davis, P. A. (1940). Development of electroencephalography: Retrospect and outlook. *American Journal of Orthopsychiatry, 10*, 710-718.

Day, R. H., & Taft, R. (1988). Psychology in Australia. *Annual Review of Psychology, 39*, 375-400.

DeAngelis, T. (1989). Suit opens doors to analysis training. *The APA Monitor, 20*(6), 16.

Dejerine, J., & Garkler, E. (1913). *Psychoneurosis and psychotherapy.* Philadelphia: Lippincott.

DeLaCruz, F. F. (1985). Fragile X syndrome. *American Journal of Mental Deficiency, 90*, 119-123.

Dement, W. (1960). The effects of dream deprivation. *Science, 131*, 1705-1707.

Dement, W., & Kleitman, N. (1957). The relation of eye movements during sleep to dream activity: An objective method for the study of dreaming. *Journal of Experimental Psychology, 53*, 339-346.

Dennis, W., & Boring, E. G. (1952). The founding of the APA. *American Psychologist, 7*, 95-97.

Denton, L. (1989). Fowler aims for bettter finances, staff morale. *The APA Monitor, 20*(8), 3.

DePue, R. A. (1979). *The psychophysiology of the depressive disorders.* New York: Academic Press.

Deri, S. (1949). *Introduction to the Szondi Test: Theory and practice.* New York: Grune & Stratton.

Deutsch, A. (1937). *The mentally ill in America.* Garden City, NY: Doubleday.

Deutsch, C. P. (1958). After legislation—what price psychology? *American Psychologist, 13*, 645-652.

Devereux, G. A. (1939). A sociological theory of schizophrenia. *Psychoanalytic Review, 26*, 315-342.

DeVos, G. A., Murakami, E., & Murase, T. (1964). Recent research, psychodiagnosis, and therapy in Japan. In L. E. Abt & B. F. Riess (Eds.), *Progress in clincial psychology* (Vol. 4). New York: Grune & Stratton.

Dodd, S. C. (1928). The theory of factors. *Psychological Review, 35*, 211-234, 261-279.

Dodge, R. (1913). Mental work: A study in psychodynamics. *Psychological Review, 20*, 1-42.

Doll, E. A. (1935). A genetic scale of social maturity. *American Journal of Orthopsychiatry, 5*, 180-190.

Doll, E. A. (1940). The nature of mental deficiency. *Psychological Review, 47*, 395-415.

Doll, E. A. (1941). The essentials of an inclusive concept of mental deficiency. *American Journal of Mental Deficiency, 46*, 214-219.

Dollard, J., Doob, L. W., Miller, N. E., Mowrer, O. H., & Sears, R. R. (1939). *Frustration and aggression.* New Haven: Yale University Press.

Dollard, J., & Miller, N. E. (1950). *Personality and psychotherapy.* New York: McGraw-Hill.

Dollard, J., & Mowrer, O. H. (1947). A method of measuring tension in written documents. *Journal of Abnormal and Social Psychology, 42*, 3-32.

Dorfman, D. D. (1978, September 29). The Cyril Burt question: New findings. *Science, 201*, pp. 1177-1186.

Dörken, H. (1980). Psychology abroad. *The Clinical Psychologist, 33*(4), 14.

Dreger, R. M., & Miller, K. S. (1960). Comparative psychological studies of Negroes and whites in the U.S. *Psychological Bulletin, 57*, 361-402.

Dubois, P. (1908). *The psychic treatment of mental disorders.* New York: Funk & Wagnalls.

Dunaif, S., & Hoch, P. H. (1955). Pseudopsychopathic schizophrenia. In P. H. Hoch & J. Zubin (Eds.), *Psychiatry and the law.* New York: Grune & Stratton.

Dunbar, H. F. (1938). *Emotions and bodily changes.* New York: Columbia University Press.

Dunlap, K. (1923). The foundations of social psychology. *Psychological Review, 30*, 81-102.

Dunlap, K. (1932). *Habits: Their making and unmaking.* New York: Liveright.

Dunlap, K. (1932). Autobiography. In C. Murchison (Ed.), *A history of psychology in autobiography* (Vol. 2). Worcester, MA: Clark University Press.

Durant, W. (1927). *The story of philosophy.* Garden City: Garden City Publishing.

Durant, W. (1950). *The story of civilization. Vol. 4. The age of faith.* New York: Simon & Schuster.

Durant, W., & Durant, A. (1961). *The story of civilization. Vol. 7. The age of reason begins.* New York: Simon & Schuster.

Durant, W., & Durant, A. (1963). *The story of civilization. Vol. 8. The age of Louis XIV.* New York: Simon & Schuster.

Durant, W., & Durant, A. (1967). *The story of civilization. Vol. X. Rousseau and revolution.* New York: Simon & Schuster.

Durca, M. A. (1927–1928). The province and scope of mental hygiene. *Journal of Abnormal and Social Psychology, 22,* 182–193.

Duval, A. M., & Hoffman, J. L. (1941). Dementia praecox in military life as compared with dementia praecox in civil life. *War Medicine, Chicago, 1,* 854–862.

Edwards, A. L. (1954). *Edwards Personal Preference Schedule.* New York: Psychological Corporation.

Edwards, A. S. (1928). Intelligence as the capacity for variability and versatility of response. *Psychological Review, 35,* 198–210.

Eggen, J. B. (1926–1927). Is instinct an entity? *Journal of Abnormal and Social Psychology, 21,* 38–51.

Ellenberger, H. F. (1954). The life and work of Hermann Rorschach (1884–1922). *Bulletin of Menninger Clinic, 18,* 173–209.

Ellenberger, H. F. (1974). Psychiatry from ancient to modern times. In S. Arieti (Ed.), *American handbook of psychiatry* (Vol. 1). New York: Basic Books.

Ellis, A. (1946). The validity of personality questionnaires. *Psychological Bulletin, 43,* 385–440.

Ellis, A. (1958). Rational psychotherapy. *Journal of General Psychology, 59,* 35–49.

Ellison, G. D. (1977). Animal models of psychopathology: The low-norepinephrine and low-serotonin rat. *American Psychologist, 32,* 1036–1045.

English, H. B., & English, A. C. (1958). *A comprehensive dictionary of psychological and psychoanalytic terms.* New York: Longmans, Green.

English, H. B., & Killian, C. D. (1939). The constancy of the IQ at different age levels. *Journal of Consulting Psychology, 3,* 30–32.

Epstein, S. (1979). Explorations in personality today and tomorrow: A tribute to Henry A. Murray. *American Psychologist, 34,* 649–653.

Erikson, E. H. (1950). *Childhood and society.* New York: Norton.

Erikson, E. H. (1959). Identity and the life cycle. *Psychological Issues, V 1*(1).

Erickson, M. H., Rossi, E. L., & Rossi, S. I. (1976). *Hypnotic realities.* New York: Irvington.

Estes, S. G. (1947). Book review of *Psychoanalytic therapy. Journal of Abnormal and Social Psychology, 42,* 137–142.

Ethical standards of psychologists. (1959). *American Psychologist, 14,* 279–282.

Exner, J. E. (1974). *The Rorschach: A comprehensive system.* New York: Wiley.

Eysenck, H. J. (1949). Training in clinical psychology: An English point of view. *American Psychologist, 4,* 173–176.

Eysenck, H. J. (1952a). The effects of psychotherapy: An evaluation. *Journal of Consulting Psychology, 16,* 319–324.

Eysenck, H. J. (1952b). *The scientific study of personality.* New York: Macmillan.

Eysenck, H. J. (1961). The effects of psychotherapy. In H. J. Eysenck (Ed.), *Handbook of abnormal psychology.* New York: Basic Books.

Fagan, T. K. (1986). School psychology's dilemma: Reappraising solutions and directing attention to the future. *American Psychologist, 41,* 851–861.

Fancher, R. E. (1979). *Pioneers of psychology.* New York: Norton.

Fancher, R. E. (1987). Henry Goddard and the Kallikak family photographs: "Conscious skullduggery" or "Whig history"? *American Psychologist, 42,* 585–590.

Fantham, H. B. (1933–1934). Charles Dickens: A biological study of his personality. *Character and Personality, 2,* 222–230.

Farber, M. L. (1938). A critique and an investigation of Kretschmer's theory. *Journal of Abnormal and Social Psychology, 33,* 398–404.

Fenichel, O. (1945). *The psychoanalytic theory of neurosis.* New York: Norton.

Fernald, G. G. (1920–1921). Character vs. intelligence in personality studies. *Journal of Abnormal Psychology, 15,* 1–10.

Fernberger, S. W. (1928). Statistical analyses of the members and associates of the American Psychological Association, Inc. in 1928. *Psychological Review, 35,* 447–465.

Fernberger, S. W. (1931). History of the psychological clinic. In R. A. Brotemarkle (Ed.), *Clinical psychology: Studies in honor of Lightner Witmer.* Philadelphia: University of Pennsylvania Press.

Fernberger, S. W. (1932). The American Psychological Association: A historical summary, 1892–1930. *Psychological Bulletin, 29,* 1–89.

Fernberger, S. W. (1933). Shepherd Ivory Franz: 1874–1933. *Psychological Bulletin, 30,* 741–742.

Fernberger, S. W. (1938). The scientific interests and scientific publications of the members of the American Psychological Association. *Psychological Bulletin, 35,* 261–281.

Fernberger, S. W. (1940). On election to membership in the APA. *Psychological Bulletin, 37,* 312–318.

Ferrari, G. C. (1932). Autobiography. In C. Murchison (Ed.), *A history of psychology in autobiography.* (Vol. 2). Worcester, MA: Clark University Press.

Ferster, C. B. (1973). A functional analysis of depression. *American Psychologist, 28,* 857–870.

Festinger, L. (1957). *A theory of cognitive dissonance.* Stanford, CA: Stanford University Press.

Feuerstein, M., & Schwartz, G. E. (1977). Training in clinical psychophysiology: Present trends and future goals. *American Psychologist, 32,* 560–567.

Fichter, M. M., & Wittchen, H-W. (1980). Clinical psychology and psychotherapy: A survey of the present state of professionalization in 23 countries. *American Psychologist, 35,* 16–25.

Finch, F. H., & Odoroff, M. E. (1941). Employment trends in applied psychology. *Journal of Consulting Psychology, 5,* 275–278.

Fink, M. (1984). Meduna and the origins of convulsive therapy. *American Journal of Psychiatry, 141,* 1034–1041.

Fischer, R. P., & Hinshaw, R. P. (1946). The growth of student interest in psychology. *American Psychologist, 1,* 116–118.

Fitts, P. M. (1946). German applied psychology during World War II. *American Psychologist, 1,* 151–161.

Fitzgerald, L. F., & Osipow, S. H. (1986). An occupational analysis of counseling psychology: How special is the specialty? *American Psychologist, 41,* 535–544.

Ford, D. H., & Urban, H. B. (1963). *Systems of psychotherapy.* New York: Wiley.

Fordham, F. (1953). *An introduction to Jung's psychology.* London: Penguin.

Forel, A. (1907). *Collected papers.* Baltimore: Phipps Psychiatric Clinic.

Foster, A., Benton, A. L., & Rabin, A. I. (1952). The internship in clinical psychology: Three alternative plans. *American Psychologist, 7,* 7–13.

Fowler, R. D. (1985). Report of the Treasurer. 1984: Starting to come out of the woods. *American Psychologist, 40,* 613–616.

Fox, R. E., Kovacs, A. L., & Graham, S. R. (1985). Proposals for a revolution in the preparation and regulation of professional psychologists. *American Psychologist, 40,* 1042–1050.

Frank, J. D. (1973). *Persuasion and healing: A comparative study of psychotherapy.* Baltimore: Johns Hopkins Press.

Frank, L. K. (1939). Projective methods for the study of personality. *Journal of Psychology, 8,* 389–413.

Frank, L. K. (1948). *Projective methods.* Springfield, IL: Charles C Thomas.

Frankl, V. (1960). *The doctor and the soul.* New York: Knopf.

Frankl, V. (1962). *Man's search for meaning.* Boston: Beacon Press.

Franz, S. I. (1912). The present status of psychology in medical education and practice. *Journal of the American Medical Association, 58,* 909–911.

Franz, S. I. (1912). Experimental psychopathology. *Psychological Bulletin, 9,* 145–154.

Franz, S. I. (1917). Psychology and psychiatry. *Psychological Bulletin, 14,* 226–227.

Franz, S. I. (1921). Cerebral-mental relations. *Psychological Review, 28*, 81–95.

Franz, S. I. (1922). Psychology and psychiatry. *Psychological Review, 29*, 241–249.

Franz, S. I. (1923). *Nervous and mental re-education.* New York: Macmillan.

Franz, S. I. (1932). Autobiography. In C. Murchison (Ed.), *A history of psychology in autobiography.* (Vol. 2). Worcester, MA: Clark University Press.

Fraser, G. M. (1988). *The Hollywood history of the world.* New York: William Morrow.

Freeman, F. N. (1920). Mental tests. *Psychological Bulletin, 17*, 353–362.

Freeman, F. S. (1950). *Theory and practice of psychological testing.* New York: Holt.

Freeman, W., & Watts, J. W. (1941). The frontal lobes in their relationship to the ego and the future. *North Carolina Medical Journal, 2*, 288–290.

Freeman, W., & Watts, J. W. (1942). *Psychosurgery.* Springfield, IL: Charles C Thomas.

Frenkel-Brunswik, E., & Sanford, R. N. (1945). Some personality correlates of antisemitism. *Journal of Psychology, 20*, 271–291.

Freud, A. (1928). *Technic of child analysis.* New York: Nervous & Mental Disease Publishing Company.

Freud, A. (1937). *The ego and the mechanisms of defence.* London: Hogarth.

Freud, A. (1965). *Normality and pathology in childhood.* New York: International Universities Press.

Freud, A. (1971). *The psychoanalytical treatment of children.* New York: Schocken Books.

Freud, S. (1910). The origin and develoment of psychoanalysis. *American Journal of Psychology, 21*, 181–218.

Freud, S. (1927a). *The ego and the id.* London: Hogarth.

Freud, S. (1927b). *The problem of lay analyses.* New York: Brentano's.

Freud, S. (1936). *Inhibitions, symptoms, and anxiety.* London: Hogarth.

Freud, S. (1938). *The basic writings of Sigmund Freud.* A. A. Brill (Ed.) New York: Modern Library.

Freud, S. (1942). *Beyond the pleasure principle.* London: Hogarth.

Freud, S. (1959a). Turnings in the ways of psychoanalytic therapy. In *Collected papers* (Vol. 2). New York: Basic Books. (orig. pub. 1919)

Freud, S. (1959b). Analysis of a phobia in a five-year-old boy. In *Collected papers* (Vol. 3). New York: Basic Books. (orig. pub. 1909)

Freud, S. (1959c). Analysis terminable and interminable. In *Collected papers* (Vol. 5). New York: Basic Books. (orig. pub. 1937)

Freud, S. (1959d). On the history of the psychoanalytic movement. In *Collected papers* (Vol. 1). New York: Basic Books. (orig. pub. 1914)

Freud, S. (1959e). On narcissism: An introduction. In *Collected papers* (Vol. 4). New York: Basic Books. (orig. pub. 1914)

Freud, S. (1959f). The psychogenesis of a case of homosexuality in a woman. In *Collected papers* (Vol. 2). New York: Basic Books. (orig. pub. 1920)

Freud, S. (1959g). Psychoanalytic notes upon an autobiographical account of a case of paranoia. In *Collected papers* (Vol. 3). New York: Basic Books. (orig. pub. 1911)

Freyd, M. (1924). Introverts and extroverts. *Psychological Review, 31*, 74–87.

Friedlander, I. W., & Sarbin, T. R. (1938). The depth of hypnosis. *Journal of Abnormal and Social Psychology, 33*, 453–475.

Friedman, H. S., & Booth-Kewley, S. B. (1987). The "disease-prone personality": A meta-analytic view of the construct. *American Psychologist, 42*, 539–555.

Friedman, M., & Rosenman, R. H. (1974). *Type A behavior and your heart.* New York: Harper & Row.

Fromm, E. (1950). *Escape from freedom.* New York: Rinehart.

Fromm, E. (1955). *The sane society.* New York: Rinehart.

Fromm-Reichmann, F. (1950). *Principles of intensive psychotherapy.* Chicago: University of Chicago Press.

Frostig, M., & Horne, D. (1964). *The Frostig program for the development of visual perception.* Chicago: Follett.

Fulkerson, S. C., & Barry, J. R. (1961). Methodology and research on the prognostic use of psychological tests. *Psychological Bulletin, 58*, 177–204.

Fuller, G. B., & Laird, J. T. (1963). The Minnesota Percepto-Diagnostic Test. *Journal of Clinical Psychology,* Monograph Supplement No. 16.

Galton, F. (1909). *Memories of my life.* New York: E. P. Dutton.

Garfield, S. L. (1981). Psychotherapy: A 40-year appraisal. *American Psychologist, 36,* 174–183.

Garfield, S. L., & Bergin, A. E. (1978). *Handbook of psychotherapy and behavior change: An empirical analysis.* New York: Wiley.

Garmezy, N. (1978). *DSM-III:* Never mind the psychologists; Is it good for the children? *The Clinical Psychologist, 31*(3, 4), 1, 4–6.

Garner, A. M. (1958). Abnormalities of behavior. *Annual Review of Psychology, 9,* 391–418.

Garrett, H. E. (1947). A developmental theory of intelligence. *American Psychologist, 2,* 372–374.

Garth, T. R. (1925). A review of racial psychology. *Psychological Bulletin, 22,* 343–364.

Garth, T. R. (1930). A review of race psychology. *Psychological Bulletin, 27,* 329–356.

Gay, P. (1988). *Freud: A life for our time.* New York: Norton.

Geiser, D. S. (1989). Psychosocial influences in human immunity. *Clinical Psychology Review, 9,* 689–715.

Gemelli, A. (1952). Autobiography. In E. G. Boring et al. (Eds.), *A history of psychology in autobiography* (Vol. 4). Worchester, MA: Clark University Press.

Gesell, A. (1925). *The mental growth of the preschool child.* New York: Macmillan.

Gesell, A. (1929). *Infancy and human growth.* New York: Macmillan.

Gesell, A. (1952). Autobiography. In E. G. Boring et al. (Eds.), *A history of psychology in autobiography* (Vol. 4). Worcester, MA: Clark University Press.

Gesell, A., & Thompson, H. (1938). *The psychology of early growth.* New York: Macmillan.

Geyer, G. A. (1985). Our disintegrating world: The menace of global anarchy. *Britannica Book of the Year,* 11–25.

Gill, M. (1959). The present state of psychoanalytic theory. *Journal of Abnormal and Social Psychology, 58,* 1–8.

Gitelson, M. (1938). Section on "play therapy." *American Journal of Orthopsychiatry, 8,* 499–524.

Glasser, W. (1965). *Reality therapy.* New York: Harper & Row.

Glueck, S., & Glueck, E. (1950). *Unraveling juvenile delinquency.* New York: Commonwealth Fund.

Goddard, H. H. (1912). *The Kallikak family.* New York: Macmillan.

Goddard, H. H. (1914). *Feeblemindedness: Its causes and consequences.* New York: Macmillan.

Goddard, H. H. (1928). *School training of gifted children.* Yonkers, NY: World.

Goldberg, P. A. (1965). A review of sentence completion methods in personality assessment. In B. I. Murstein (Ed.), *Handbook of projective techniques.* London: Basic Books.

Golden, W. L., Dowd, E. T., & Friedberg, F. (1987). *Hypnotherapy: A modern approach.* New York: Pergamon.

Goldstein, K. (1939). *The organism.* New York: American Book Company.

Goldstein, K. (1959a). Functional disturbances in brain damage. In S. Arieti (Ed.), *American handbook of psychiatry* (Vol. 1). New York: Basic Books.

Goldstein, K. (1959b). Concerning the concreteness in schizophrenia. *Journal of Abnormal and Social Psychology, 59,* 146–148.

Goldstein, K. (1967). Kurt Goldstein. In E. G. Boring & G. L. Lindzey (Eds.), *A history of psychology in autobiography.* (Vol. 5). New York: Appleton-Century-Crofts.

Goleman, D. (1989, August 15). Brain's design emerges as a key to emotions. *The New York Times,* p. 15.

Gollin, E. S., & Bradford, N. (1958). "Faulty" communication and the spiral aftereffect. *Journal of Abnormal and Social Psychology, 57,* 122–123.

Goodenough, F. L. (1926). *Measurement of intelligence by drawings.* Yonkers, NY: World.

Goodstein, L. D., & Ross, S. (1966). Accreditation of graduate programs in psychology: An analysis. *American Psychologist, 21,* 218–223.

Gould, D. W. (1981). Mental health. *Britannica Book of the Year,* pp. 420–421.

Gould, D. W. (1982). Mental health. *Britannica Book of the Year,* pp. 418–419.

Gould, D. W. (1983). Mental health. *Britannica Book of the Year,* pp. 413–414.

Gould, S. J. (1981). *The mismeasure of man.* New York: Norton.

Graff, M., & Clair, T. N. (1973). Requirements for certification of school psychologists: A survey of recent trends. *American Psychologist, 28,* 704–705.

Gray, J. S. (1935). An objective theory of emotion. *Psychological Review, 42,* 108–116.

Greenspoon, J., & Gersten, C. D. (1967). A new look at psychological testing: Psychological testing from the standpoint of a behaviorist. *American Psychologist, 22,* 848–853.

Grinker, R. R., & Spiegel, J. P. (1945). *Men under stress.* Philadelphia: Blakiston.

Groth-Marnet, G., & Shumaker, J. (1989). Computer-based psychological testing: Issues and guidelines. *American Journal of Orthopsychiatry, 59,* 257–263.

Group for the Advancement of Psychiatry Committee on the Family (1989). The challenge of relational diagnoses: Applying the biopsychosocial model in *DSM-IV. American Journal of Psychiatry, 146,* 1492–1494.

Guertin, W. H., Frank, G. H., & Rabin, A. I. (1956). Research with the Wechsler-Bellevue Intelligence Scale, 1950–1955. *Psychological Bulletin, 53,* 235–257.

Guertin, W. H., Rabin, A. I., Frank, G. H., & Ladd, C. E. (1962). Research with the Wechsler intelligence scales for adults, 1955–1960. *Psychological Bulletin, 59,* 1–26.

Guilford, J. P. (1934). Introversion-extroversion. *Psychological Bulletin, 31,* 331–354.

Guilford, J. P. (1940). Human abilities. *Psychological Review, 47,* 367–393.

Guilford, J. P. (1948). Some lessons from aviation psychology. *American Psychologist, 3,* 3–11.

Guilford, J. P. (1950). Creativity. *American Psychologist, 5,* 444–454.

Guilford, J. P. (1959). Three faces of intellect. *American Psychologist, 14,* 469–479.

Guilford, J. P. (1966). Intelligence: 1965 model. *American Psychologist, 21,* 20–26.

Guilford, J. P., & Guilford, R. B. (1933–1934). An analysis of the factors in a typical test of introversion-extroversion. *Journal of Abnormal and Social Psychology, 28,* 377–399.

Guthrie, E. R. (1927). Measuring introversion and extroversion. *Journal of Abnormal and Social Psychology, 22,* 82–88.

Guthrie, E. R. (1933). On the nature of psychological explanations. *Psychological Review, 40,* 124–137.

Hacker, A. (1980). Survey of the '70s. *Britannica Book of the Year,* 129–143.

Hall, C. (1933–1934). A comparative psychologist's approach to problems in abnormal psychology. *Journal of Abnormal and Social Psychology, 28,* 1–5.

Hall, C. S., & Lindzey, G. (1957). *Theories of personality.* New York: Wiley.

Hall, C. S., & Lindzey, G. (1970). *Theories of personality* (rev. ed.). New York: Wiley.

Hall, G. S. (1894). Laboratory of the McLean Hospital. *American Journal of Insanity, 51,* 358–364.

Hall, G. S. (1923). *Life and confessions of a psychologist.* New York: Appleton.

Hall, M. E. (1949). Current employment requirements for school psychologists. *American Psychologist, 4,* 519.

Hall, M. H. (1967, September). An interview with B. F. Skinner. *Psychology Today, 1,* 20–23, 68–71.

Hall, M. H. (1968, February). A conversation with Viktor Frankl of Vienna. *Psychology Today, 2,* 57–63.

Hallowell, D. K. (1927). Mental tests for preschool children. *Psychological Clinic, 16,* 235–276.

Hannah, B. (1976). *Jung: His life and work.* New York: G. P. Putnam's Sons.

Hardaway, R. A. (1990). Subliminally activated symbiotic fantasies: Facts and artifacts. *Psychological Bulletin, 107,* 177–195.

Harlow, H. F. (1958). The nature of love. *American Psychologist, 13,* 673–685.

Harlow, H. F. (1962). The heterosexual affectional system in monkeys. *American Psychologist, 16* 1–9.

Harmon, L. R. (1961). Production of psychology doctorates in the United States. *American Psychologist, 16,* 717.

Harris, A. J., & Shakow, D. (1937). The clinical significance of numerical measures of scatter on the Stanford-Binet. *Psychological Bulletin, 34,* 134–150.

Harris, B. (1979). Whatever happened to little Albert? *American Psychologist, 34,* 151–160.

Harris, T. A. (1967). *I'm OK—you're OK: A practical guide to transactional analysis.* New York: Harper.

Harrower-Erickson, R., & Steiner, M. E. (1943). Modifications of the Rorschach method for use as a group test. *Journal of Genetic Psychology, 62,* 119–133.

Harthshorne, H., & May, M. A. (1928). *Studies in deceit.* New York: Macmillan.

Hartley, D., Roback, H. B., & Abramowitz, S. I. (1976). Deterioration effects in encounter groups. *American Psychologist, 31,* 247–255.

Hartmann, H. (1958). *Ego psychology and the problem of adaptation.* New York: International University Press.

Hartmann, H., Kris, E., & Loewenstein, R. M. (1946). Comments on the formation of psychic structure. *Psychoanalytic Study of the Child, 2,* 11–38.

Hathaway, S. R. (1951). Clinical methods: psychotherapy. *Annual Review of Psychology, 2,* 259–280.

Hathaway, S. R., & McKinley, J. C. (1940). A multiphasic personality schedule (Minnesota): I. Construction of the schedule. II. A differential study of hypochondriasis. *Journal of Psychology, 10,* 249–268.

Hathaway, S. R., & McKinley, J. C. (1943). *The Minnesota Multiphasic Personality Inventory.* New York: Psychological Corporation.

Hathaway, S. R., & Meehl, P. E. (1951). *An atlas for the clinical use of the MMPI.* Minneapolis: University of Minnesota Press.

Healy, W. (1914). A pictorial completion test. *Psychological Review, 21,* 189–203.

Healy, W. A. (1915). *The individual delinquent.* Boston: Little, Brown.

Healy, W., & Bronner, A. F. (1926). *Delinquents and criminals, their making and unmaking: Studies in two American cities.* New York: Macmillan.

Healy, W., & Bronner, A. F. (1948). The child guidance clinic: Birth and growth of an idea. In L. G. Lowrey & V. Sloane (Eds.), *Orthopsychiatry 1923–1948: Retrospect and prospect.* New York: American Orthopsychiatric Association.

Hebb, D. O. (1958a). The motivating effects of exteroceptive stimulation. *American Psychologist, 13,* 109–113.

Hebb, D. O. (1958b). Alice in Wonderland, or psychology among the behaviorial sciences. In H. F. Harlow & C. N. Woolsey (Eds.), *Biological and biochemical bases of behavior.* Madison: University of Wisconsin Press.

Heidbreder, E. F. (1927–1928). The normal inferiority complex. *Journal of Abnormal and Social Psychology, 22,* 243–258.

Heiser, K. F. (1950). Survey of departments giving instruction in clinical psychology. *American Psychologist, 5,* 610–619.

Henry, J. (1941). Rorschach technique in primitive cultures. *American Journal of Orthopsychiatry, 11,* 230–234.

Herron, W. G. (1962). The process-reactive classification of schizophrenia. *Psychological Bulletin, 59,* 329–343.

Hertz, M. R. (1935). The Rorschach Ink-Blot Test: Historical summary. *Psychological Bulletin, 32,* 33–66.

Hertz, M. R. (1943). Modification of the Rorschach Ink Blot Test for large scale application. *American Journal of Orthopsychiatry, 13,* 191–211.

Hertz, M. R., & Rubenstein, B. B. (1939). A comparison of three "blind" Rorschach analyses. *American Journal of Orthopsychiatry, 9,* 295–314.

Hess, E. H., Seltzer, A. L., & Shlien, J. M. (1965). Pupil response of heterosexual and homosexual males to pictures of men and women: A pilot study. *Journal of Abnormal Psychology, 70,* 165–168.

Hess, W. R. (1954). *Das Zwischenhirn: Syndrome, Lokalisationen, Funktionen.* Basel: Schwabe.

Hilgard, E. R. (1945). Psychologic preferences for divisions under the proposed APA by-laws. *Psychological Bulletin, 42,* 20–26.

Hilgard, E. R. (1949). Human motives and the concept of self. *American Psychologist, 4,* 374–384.

Hilgard, E. R. (1978). Hypnosis and pain. In R. A. Sternbach (Ed.), *The psychology of pain.* New York: Raven Press.

Hilgard, E. R. (1980). Consciousness in contemporary psychology. *Annual Review of Psychology, 31,* 1–26.

Hilgard, E. R. (1987). *Psychology in America.* New York: Harcourt Brace Jovanovich.

Hilgard, J. R., & LeBaron, S. (1984). *Hypnotherapy of pain in children with cancer.* Los Angeles: William Kaufmann.

Hirsch, J. (1967). Behavior-genetics, or "experimental," analysis: The challenge of science versus the lure of technology. *American Psychologist, 22,* 118–130.

Hobbs, N. (1966). Helping disturbed children: Psychological and ecological strategies. *American Psychologist, 21,* 1105–1115.

Hoch, E. L., Ross, A. O., & Winder, C. L. (1966). Conference on the professional preparation of clinical psychologists: A summary. *American Psychologist, 21,* 42–51.

Hoch, P. H., & Polatin, P. (1949). Pseudoneurotic forms of schizophrenia. *Psychiatric Quarterly, 23,* 248.

Hodges, W. L. (1960). State certification of school psychologists. *American Psychologist, 15,* 198–200.

Hoffman, L. (1981). *Foundations of family therapy.* New York: Basic Books.

Hollingworth, L. S. (1926). *Gifted children: Their nature and nurture.* New York: Macmillan.

Hollingworth, L. S. (1942). *Children above 180 IQ.* Yonkers, NY: World.

Holmes, D. S. (1984). Meditation and somatic arousal reduction: A view of the experimental evidence. *American Psychologist, 39,* 1–10.

Holt, R. R. (1970). Yet another look at clinical and statistical prediction: Or, is clinical psychology worthwhile? *American Psychologist 25,* 337–349.

Holtzman, W. H., Thorpe, J. S., Swartz, J. D., & Herron, E. W. (1961). *Inkblot perception and personality.* Austin: University of Texas Press.

Horn, P. D. (1973). Psychology. *Britannica Book of the Year,* pp. 566–567.

Horney, K. (1937). *The neurotic personality of our time.* New York: Norton.

Horney, K. (1942). *Self analysis.* New York: Norton.

Horney, K. (1950). *Neurosis and human growth.* New York: Norton.

Horton, L. H. (1920–1921). Old and new in mental tests. *Journal of Abnormal Psychology, 15,* 57–64.

Hothersall, D. (1990). *History of Psychology. Second edition.* New York: McGraw-Hill.

Howard, A., et al. (1986). The changing face of American psychology: A report from the Committee on Employment and Human Resources. *American Psychologist, 41,* 1311–1327.

Howard, K. I., Kopta, S. M., Krause, M. S., & Orlinsky, E. E. (1986). The dose-effect relationship in psychotherapy. *American Psychologist, 41,* 159–164.

Hug-Hellmuth, H., von (1921). Zur Technik der Kinderanalyse. *Internationale Zeitschrift für Psychoanalyse, 7.*

Hull, C. L. (1928). *Aptitude testing.* Yonkers, NY: World.

Hull, C. L. (1929–1930). Quantitative methods in investigating waking suggestion. *Journal of Abnormal and Social Psychology, 24,* 153–169.

Hull, C. L. (1937). Mind, mechanism, and adaptive behavior. *Psychological Review, 49,* 1–32.

Hull, C. L. (1952). Autobiography. In E. G. Boring et al. (Eds.), *A history of psychology in autobiography* (Vol. 4). Worcester, MA: Clark University Press.

Hunt, J. M. (1936). Psychological experiments with disordered persons. *Psychological Bulletin, 33,* 1–58.

Hunt, J. M., & Cofer, C. N. (1944). Psychological deficit. In J. M. Hunt (Ed.), *Personality and the behavior disorders.* New York: Ronald.

Hunter, W. S. (1932). The psychological study of behavior. *Psychological Review, 39,* 1–24.

Hunter, W. S. (1946). Psychology in the war. *American Psychologist, 1,* 479–492.

Hutt, M. L., & Milton, E. O. (1947). An analysis of duties performed by clinical psychologists in the Army. *American Psychologist, 2,* 52–56.

Hutt, R. B. W. (1923). The school psychologist. *Psychological Clinic, 15,* 48–51.

Isaacs, S. (1961). Obituary: Melanie Klein 1882–1960. *Journal of Child Psychology and Psychiatry, 2,* 1–4.

Itard, J. M. G. (1962). *The Wild Boy of Aveyron.* New York: Appleton-Century-Crofts.

Jablonsky, A. (1971). Status report on compensatory education. *IRCD Bulletin, 7,* (1, 2).

Jackson, D. N., & Paunonen, S. V. (1980). Personality structure and assessment. *Annual Review of Psychology, 31,* 503–551.

Jackson, G. D. (1975). On the report of the Ad Hoc Committee on Educational Uses of Tests with Disadvantaged Students: Another psychological view from the Association of Black Psychologists. *American Psychologist, 30,* 88–93.

Jahoda, M. (1958). *Current concepts of positive mental health.* New York: Basic Books.

James, W. (1890). *Principles of psychology.* New York: Holt.

James, W. (1895). The knowing of things together. *Psychological Review, 2,* 105–124.

James, W. (1897). *The will to believe and other essays in popular psychology.* New York: Longmans, Green.

James, W. (1902). *Varieties of religious experience.* New York: Longmans, Green.

James, W. (1907). *Pragmatism.* New York: Longmans, Green.

Janet, P. (1914–1915). Psychoanalysis. *Journal of Abnormal Psychology, 9,* 1–35, 153–187.

Janov, A. (1972). *The primal revolution.* New York: Touchstone.

Jarvik, L. F., Klodin, V., & Matsyama, S. S. (1973). Human aggression and the extra Y chromosome. *American Psychologist, 28,* 674–682.

Jastrow, J. (1901). Some currents and undercurrents in psychology. *Psychological Review, 8,* 1–26.

Jastrow, J. (1930). Autobiography. In C. Murchison (Ed.), *A history of psychology in autobiography* (Vol. 1). Worcester, MA: Clark University Press.

Jelliffe, S. E. (1913–1914). Some notes on "transference." *Journal of Abnormal Psychology, 8,* 302–309.

Jensen, A. R. (1958). Personality. *Annual Review of Psychology, 9,* 295–322.

Jensen, A. R. (1969). How much can we boost IQ and scholastic achievement? *Harvard Educational Review, 39,* 1–123.

Jensen, A. R. (1978). Sir Cyril Burt in perspective. *American Psychologist, 33,* 499–503.

Jersild, A. T. (1951). Self-understanding in childhood and adolescence. *American Psychologist, 6,* 122–126.

Johnson, D. L. (1989). Schizophrenia as a brain disease: Implications for psychologists and families. *American Psychologist, 44,* 553–555.

Johnson, L. B. (1971). *The vantage point.* New York: Holt, Rinehart & Winston.

Johnson, R. C., et al. (1985). Galton's data a century later. *American Psychologist, 40,* 875–892.

Joint report on relations between psychology and psychiatry. (1960). *American Psychologist 15,* 198–200.

Jolliffe, N. (1940). The influence of alcohol on the adequacy of the B vitamins in the American diet. *Quarterly Journal of Alcohol, 1,* 83.

Jones, E. (1911–1912). Book review of *Die Psychoanalyse Freuds: Verteidigung und kritische Bemerkungen,* by E. Bleuler. *Journal of Abnormal Psychology, 6,* 465–470.

Jones, E. (1928–1929). The development of the concept of the super-ego. *Journal of Abnormal and Social Psychology, 23,* 276–285.

Jones, E. (1953). *The life and work of Sigmund Freud* (Vol. 1). New York: Basic Books.

Jones, E. (1955). *The life and work of Sigmund Freud* (Vol. 2). New York: Basic Books.

Jones, E. (1957). *The life and work of Sigmund Freud* (Vol. 3). New York: Basic Books.

Jones, K., Smith, D., Ulleland, C., & Streissguth, A. (1973). Patterns of malformation in offspring of chronic alcoholic mothers. *Lancet, 1,* 1267–1271.

Jones, M. C. (1924). A laboratory study of fear: The case of Peter. *Pediatric Seminary, 31,* 308–315.

Jones, N. F. (1975). Continuing education: A new challenge for psychology. *American Psychologist, 29,* 441–449.

Judd, C. H. (1910). Evolution and consciousness. *Psychological Review, 17,* 7–97.

Jung, C. G. (1916). *Psychology of the unconscious.* New York: Moffat, Yard.

Jung, C. G. (1920). A contribution to the study of psychological types. In *Collected papers on analytical psychology.* London: Bailiere, Tindall, & Cox.

Jung, C. G. (1925). Psychological types or the psychology of individuation. *Psychological Bulletin, 33,* 1–58.

Jung, C. G. (1933). *Modern man in search of a soul.* New York: Harcourt, Brace.

Jung, C. G. (1936). The psychology of dementia praecox. *Nervous Mental Disease Monograph Series,* No. 3.

Jung, C. G. (1963). *Memories, dreams, reflections.* New York: Pantheon.

Kaczkowski, H. (1967). Psychology in Poland. *American Psychologist, 22,* 79–80.

Kagan, J. (1967). On the need for relativism. *American Psychologist, 22,* 131–142.

Kagan, J., Reznick, J. S., & Snidman, N. (1988). Biological bases of childhood shyness. *Science, 240,* 167–171.

Kahn, E. (1985). Heinz Kohut and Carl Rogers: A timely comparison. *American Psychologist, 40,* 893–904.

Kallmann, F. J. (1938). *The genetics of schizophrenia: A study of heredity and reproduction in the families of 1,087 schizophrenic families.* New York: Augustin.

Kallman, F. J. (1959). The genetics of mental illness. In S. Arieti (Ed.), *American handbook of psychiatry* (Vol. 1). New York: Basic Books.

Kamin, L. J. (1974). *The science and politics of IQ.* Potomac, MD: Erlbaum.

Kanner, L. (1943). Autistic disturbances of affective contact. *Nervous Child, 2,* 217–250.

Kanner, L. (1951). The conception of wholes and parts in early infantile autism. *American Journal of Psychiatry, 108,* 23–26.

Kanner, L., & Eisenberg, L. (1955). Chapter 13. In P. H. Hoch & J. Zubin (Eds.), *Psychopathology of childhood.* New York: Grune & Stratton.

Kantor, R. E., Wallner, J., & Winder, C. L. (1953). Process and reactive schizophrenia. *Journal of Consulting Psychology, 17,* 157–162.

Kardiner, A. (1939). *The individual and his society.* New York: Columbia Univeristy Press.

Katz, E. (1941). The constancy of the Stanford-Binet IQ from three to five years. *Journal of Psychology, 12,* 159–181.

Kazdin, A. E. (1988). *Child psychotherapy.* Elmsford, NY: Pergamon.

Kelley, T. L. (1923). *Interpretation of educational measurement.* Yonkers, NY: World.

Kelley, T. L. (1930). The inheritence of mental traits. In C. Murchison (Ed.), *Psychologies of 1930.* Worcester, MA: Clark University Press.

Kelly, E. L. (1954). Theory and techniques of assessment. *Annual Review of Psychology, 5,* 281–310.

Kelly, E. L. (1955). Consistency of the adult personality. *American Psychologist, 10,* 659–681.

Kelly, E. L., & Fiske, D. W. (1950). The prediction of success in the VA training progam in clinical psychology. *American Psychologist, 5,* 395–406.

Kelly, E. L., Miles, C. C., & Terman, L. M. (1935–1936). Ability to influence one's score on a typical pencil-and-paper test of personality. *Character and Personality, 4,* 206–215.

Kelly, G. A. (1955). *The psychology of personal constructs.* New York: Norton.

Kendler, T. S. (1950). Contributions of the psychologist to constitutional law. *American Psychologist, 5,* 505–510.

Keniston, K. (1968). *Young radicals: Notes on committed youth.* New York: Harcourt, Brace & World.

Kent, G. H. (1942). Emergency battery of one minute tests. *Journal of Psychology, 13,* 141–164.

Kent, G. H., & Rosanoff, A. J. (1910). A study of association in insanity. *American Journal of Insanity, 67,* 37–96, 317–390.

Kiernan, J. G. (1909). Limitations of the Emmanuel Movement. *American Journal of Medicine, 16,* 1088–1090.

Kihlstrom, J. F. (1987). The cognitive unconscious. *Science, 237,* 1445–1452.

Kimble, G. A. (1984). Psychology's two cultures. *American Psychologist, 39,* 833–839.

King, P. (1989, October). The chemistry of doubt. *Psychology Today,* pp. 58, 60.

Kirk, S. A., McCarthy, J. J., & Kirk, W. D. (1968). *Examiner's manual Illinois Test of Psycholinguistic Abilities.* Urbana: University of Illinois Press.

Klein, M. (1932). *The psycho-analysis of children.* New York: Norton.

Kleinmuntz, B. (1967). Sign and seer: Another example. *Journal of Abnormal Psychology, 72,* 163–165.

Klineberg, O. (1935). *Negro intelligence and selective migration.* New York: Columbia University Press.

Klopfer, B. (1938). The shading responses. *Rorschach Research Exchange, 2,* 76–79.

Klopfer, B., & Kelley, D. M. (1937). The technique of the Rorschach performance. *Rorschach Research Exchange, 2,* 1–14.

Klopfer, B., & Kelley, D. M. (1942). *The Rorschach technique*. Yonkers, NY: World.

Knight, M. (1950). *William James*. London: Penguin.

Kohut, H. (1971). *The analysis of the self*. New York: International Universities Press.

Kohut, H. (1977). *The restoration of the self*. New York: International Universities Press.

Kopeloff, N., & Cheney, C. O. (1922). Studies in focal infection: Its presence and elimination in the functional psychoses. *American Journal of Psychiatry, 2*, 139–156.

Kora, T., & Sato, K. (1958). Morita therapy: A psychotherapy in the way of Zen. *Psychologia, 1*, 219–225.

Korchin, S. J., & Schuldberg, D. (1981). The future of clinical assessment. *American Psychologist, 36*, 1147–1158.

Korman, M. (1974). National conference on levels and patterns of professional training in psychology: The major themes. *American Psychologist, 29*, 441–449.

Korzybski, A. H. (1941). *Science and sanity*. Lancaster, PA: Science Press.

Kossakowski, A. (1980). Psychology in the German Democratic Republic. *American Psychologist, 36*, 276–289.

Kraepelin, E. (1919). *Dementia praecox and paraphrenia*. Edinburgh: E. & S. Livingston.

Kraskin, L. H. (1940). Psychotherapy for optometrists. *American Journal of Optometry, 127*, 492–413.

Krasner, L., & Houts, A. C. (1984). A study of the "value' system of behavioral scientists. *American Psychologist, 39*, 840–850.

Kretschmer, E. (1925). *Physique and character*. New York: Harcourt, Brace.

Kringlen, E. (1966). Schizophrenia in twins. *Psychiatry, 29*, 172–184.

Krugman, M. (1945). Recent developments in clinical psychology. *Journal of Consulting Psychology, 9*, 342–353.

Kunkel, F. (1932–1933). Sex and society. *Journal of Abnormal and Social Psychology, 27*, 1–28.

Ladd, G. T. (1894). President's address before the New York meeting of the American Psychological Association. *Psychological Review, 1*, 1–21.

Laing, R. D., & Esterson, A. (1964). *Sanity, madness, and the family. Vol. 1. Families of schizophrenics*. London: Tavistock.

Lamiell, J. T. (1981). Toward an idiothetic psychology of personality. *American Psychologist, 36*, 276–289.

Landesman, S., & Butterfield, E. C. (1987). Normalization and deinstitutionalization of mentally retarded individuals. *American Psychologist, 42*, 809–816.

Landi, A. (1989, April). When having everything isn't enough. *Psychology Today*, pp. 27–30.

Landis, C. (1930). Psychology and the psychogalvanic reflex. *Psychological Review, 37*, 381–398.

Lane, H. (1976). *The wild boy of Aveyron*. Cambridge, MA: Harvard University Press.

Lanyon, R. I., & Goodstein, L. D. (1971). *Personality assessment*. New York: Wiley.

Lashley, K. S. (1938). The thalamus and emotion. *Psychological Review, 45*, 42–61.

Lawson, G., et al. (1940). Section meeting, 1939. Old age and aging. *American Journal of Orthopsychiatry, 10*, 27–87.

Lazell, E. W. (1921). The group treatment of dementia praecox. *Psychoanalytical Review, 8*, 168–179.

Lecky, P. (1945). *Self consistency*. New York: Island Press.

LeCompte, W. A. (1980). Some recent trends in Turkish psychology. *American Psychologist, 36*, 276–289.

Lehman, H. C., & Witty, P. A. (1926). Playing school: A compensatory mechanism. *Psychological Review, 33*, 480–485.

Lehner, G. F. J. (1955). Psychological training facilities in Austria and West Germany. *American Psychologist, 10*, 79–82.

Leonard, J. R. (1965). Hypnotic age regression: A test of the functional ablation hypothesis. *Journal of Abnormal Psychology, 70*, 266–269.

Lerner, B. (1967). Dream function reconsidered. *Journal of Abnormal Psychology, 72*, 85–100.

Levine, M. (1981). *The history and politics of community mental health*. New York: Oxford University Press.

Levy, D. M. (1939). Release therapy. *American Journal of Orthopsychiatry, 9*, 713–736.

Levy, J. (1938). Relationship therapy. *American Journal of Orthopsychiatry, 8,* 64–69.

Lewin, K. (1935). *A dynamic theory of personality.* New York: McGraw-Hill.

Lewin, K. (1951). *Field theory in social science.* New York: Harper.

Lewis, N. D. C. (1974). American psychiatry from its beginning to World War II. In S. Arieti (Ed.), *American handbook of psychiatry* (Vol. 1). New York: Basic Books.

Lewontin, R. C., Rose, S., & Kamin, L. J. (1984). *Not in our genes.* New York: Pantheon.

Lidz, T. (1958). Schizophrenia and the family. *Psychiatry, 21,* 21–27.

Lidz, T., et al. (1958). The intrafamilial environment of the schizophrenic patient: 4. The transmission of irrationality. *Neurological Psychiatric Archive, 79,* 305–316.

Lidz, T. (1963). *The family and human adaptation.* New York: International Universities Press.

Lindner, R. M. (1946). Hypnoanalysis. In P. L. Harriman (Ed.), *Encyclopedia of psychology.* New York: Citadel.

Linton, R. (1938). Culture, society, and the individual. *Journal of Abnormal and Social Psychology, 33,* 425–436.

Littell, W. M. (1960). The WISC: Review of a decade of research. *Psychological Bulletin, 57,* 132–156.

Liverant, S. (1960). Intelligence: A concept in need of re-examination. *Journal of Consulting Psychology, 24,* 101–110.

Lockman, R. F., & Thorne, F. M. (1966). Manpower and training in clinical psychology. *Progress in Clinical Psychology, 7.*

Loehlin, J. C. (1989). Partitioning environmental and genetic contributions to behavorial development. *American Psychologist, 44,* 1285–1292.

Loehlin, J. C., Lindzey, G., & Spuhler, J. N. (1975). *Race differences in intelligence.* San Francisco: Freeman.

Loevinger, J. (1959). Theory and technique of assessment. *Annual Review of Psychology, 10,* 287–316.

Lomov, B. F. (1982). Soviet psychology: Its historical origins and contemporary status. *American Psychologist, 37,* 580–586.

London, I. D. (1953). Therapy in Soviet psychiatric hospitals. *American Psychologist, 10,* 287–316.

Lorr, M. (1965). Client perceptions of therapists: A study of the therapeutic relation. *Journal of Consulting Psychology, 29,* 146–149.

Louttit, C. M. (1939). The nature of clinical psychology. *Psychological Bulletin, 36,* 361–389.

Lowenfeld, M. (1954). *The Lowenfeld Mosaic Test.* New York: Psychological Corporation.

Lowrey, L. G. (1948). The birth of orthopsychiatry. In L. G. Lowrey & V. Sloane (Eds.), *Orthopsychiatry 1923–1948: Retrospect and prospect.* New York: American Orthopsychiatric Association.

Lubin, B., Larsen, R. M., & Matarazzo, J. D. (1984). Patterns of psychological test usage in the United States, 1935–1982. *American Psychologist, 39,*·451–454.

Lubin, B., Larsen, R. M., Matarazzo, J. D., & Seever, M. (1985). Psychological test usage patterns in five professional settings. *American Psychologist, 40,* 857–861.

Luborsky, L., et al. (1965). Looking, recalling, and GSR as a function of defense. *Journal of Abnormal Psychology, 70,* 270–280.

Luborsky, L., & Strupp, H. H. (1962). Research problems in psychotherapy: A three year follow-up. In H. H. Strupp & L. Luborsky (Eds.), *Research in psychotherapy.* Washington, DC: American Psychological Association.

Lurie, L. A., Schlan, L., & Freiberg, M. (1932). A critical analysis of the progress of fifty-five feeble-minded children over a period of eight years. *American Journal of Orthopsychiatry, 2,* 58–69.

Lutz, J. (1937). Uber die Schizophrenie im Kindesalter. *Schwiezer Archive Neurologie und Psychiatrie, 39,* 335–372; *40,* 141–163.

Machover, K. (1948). *Personality projections in the drawing of the human figure.* Springfield, IL: Charles C Thomas.

Machover, K. (1980). Reflections of a pioneer. *The Clinical Psychologist, 34*(1), 5–7.

MacKinnon, D. W. (1953). Fact and fancy in personality research. *American Psychologist, 8,* 138–146.

MacLeod, R. B. (1938). William Stern (1871–1938). *Psychological Review, 45,* 347–353.

Maher, B. A., & Maher, W. B. (1979). Psychopathology. In E. Hearst (Ed.), *The first century of experimental psychology.* Hillsdale, NJ: Erlbaum.

Maher, B. A., & Maher, W. B. (1985a). Psychopathology: I. From ancient times to the eighteenth century. In G. A. Kimble & K. Schlesinger (Eds.), *Topics in the history of psychology* (Vol. 2). Hillsdale, NJ: LEA.

Maher, B. A., & Maher, W. B. (1985b). Psychopathology: II. From the eighteenth century to modern times. In G. A. Kimble & K. Schlesinger (Eds.), *Topics in the history of psychology* (Vol. 2). Hillsdale, NJ: LEA.

Mahler, M. S. (1958). Autism and symbiosis: Two extreme disturbances of identity. *International Psychoanalytical Journal.*

Mahler, M. S. (1968). *On human symbiosis and the vicissitudes of individuation.* New York: International Universities Press.

Mahler, M. S., Pine, F., & Bergmann, A. (1975). *The psychological birth of the human infant.* New York: Basic Books.

Maier, H. W. (1965). *Three theories of child development.* New York: Harper.

Maller, J. B. (1934). Forty years of psychology. *Psychological Bulletin, 31,* 533–559.

Mandler, G. (1984). *Mind and body: Psychology of emotion and stress.* New York: Norton.

Magaret, A. (1952). Clinical methods: Psychodiagnostics. *Annual Review of Psychology, 3,* 283–320.

Mariner, A. S. (1967). A critical look at professional education in the mental health field. *American Psychologist, 22,* 271–281.

Masling, J. (1960). The influence of situational and interpersonal variables in projective testing. *Psychological Bulletin, 57,* 65–85.

Maslow, A. H. (1943). A theory of human motivation. *Psychological Review, 50,* 370–396.

Maslow, A. H. (1948). Some theoretical consequences of basic need-gratification. *Journal of Personality, 16,* 402–416.

Masserman, J. H. (1955). *The practice of dynamic psychiatry.* Philadelphia: W. B. Saunders.

Masson, J. M. (1984). *The assault on truth: Freud's suppression of the seduction theory.* New York: Farrar Straus Giroux.

Masterpasqua, F. (1989). A competence paradigm for psychological practice. *American Psychologist, 44,* 1366–1371.

Masterson, J. F. (1972). *Treatment of the borderline adolescent: A developmental approach.* New York: Wiley.

Matarazzo, J. D. (1981). David Wechsler. *American Psychologist, 36,* 1542–1543.

Maupir, E. W. (1962). Zen Buddhism: A psychological review. *Journal of Consulting Psychology, 26,* 362–378.

May, R., Angel, E., & Ellenberger, H. F. (Eds.) (1958). *Existence.* New York: Basic Books.

McCary, J. L. (1956). The psychologist as expert witness in court. *American Psychologist, 11,* 8–13.

McClelland, D. C. (1961). *The achieving society.* New York: Free Press.

McClelland, D. C., & Atkinson, J. W. (1948). The projective expression of needs: I. The effect of different intensities of the hunger drive on perception. *Journal of Psychology, 25,* 205–222.

McConnell, J. V., et al. (1958). Subliminal perception: An overview. *American Psychologist, 13,* 229–242.

McDougall, W. (1908). *Introduction to social psychology.* London: Methuen.

McDougall, W. (1921–1922). The use and abuse of instinct in social psychology. *Journal of Abnormal and Social Psychology, 16,* 285–333.

McDougall, W. (1923). *An introduction to social psychology.* Boston: John W. Luce.

McDougall, W. (1925–1926). A great advance of the Freudian psychology. *Journal of Abnormal and Social Psychology, 30,* 43–47.

McDougall, W. (1928). Men or robots? In C. Murchison (Ed.), *Psychologies of 1925.* Worcester, MA: Clark University Press.

McDougall W. (1930). Autobiography. In C. Murchison (Ed.), *A history of psychology in autobiography* (Vol. 1). Worcester, MA: Clark University Press.

McDougall, W. (1936–1937). Dynamics of the gestalt psychology (Part 3). *Character and Personality, 5,* 61–82.

McFadden, J. H. (1932). The will-o'-the-wisp "intelligence." *Psychological Review, 39,* 225-234.

McGinnies, E. (1960). Psychology in Japan. *American Psychologist, 15,* 556-562.

McKeachie, W. J. (1976). Psychology in America's bicentennial year. *American Psychologist, 31,* 819-833.

McKinney, F. (1960). Psychology in Turkey. *American Psychologist, 15,* 717-721.

McLean, H. V. (1946). Psychodynamic factors in social relations. *Annals of American Academy of Politial Science, 244,* 159-166.

McNemar, Q. (1940). A critical evaluation of the University of Iowa studies of environmental influences upon the IQ. *Psychological Bulletin, 37,* 63-92.

McNett, I. (1982, January). Psy.D. fills demand for practitioners. *APA Monitor, 13,* 10-11.

McPherson, F. M. (1986). The professional psychologist in Europe. *American Psychologist, 41,* 302-305.

McReynolds, P. (1987). Lightner Witmer: Little-known founder of clinical psychology. *American Psychologist, 42,* 849-858.

Mead, M. (1934-1935). The use of primitive material in the study of personality. *Character and Personality, 3,* 3-16.

Mead, M. (1935). *Sex and temperament.* New York: Morrow.

Meehl, P. E. (1960). The cognitive activity of the clinician. *American Psychologist, 15,* 19-27.

Melikian, L. (1964). Clinical psychology in the Arab Middle East. *Progress in Clinical Psychology, 6.*

Menninger, K. (1942). *Love against hate.* New York: Harcourt, Brace.

Menninger, W. C. (1950). The relationship of clinical psychology and psychiatry. *American Psychologist, 5,* 3-15.

Mensh, I. N. (1960). An historical footnote. *American Psychologist, 15,* 221-222.

Merrill, M. A. (1951). Oscillation of progress in clinical psychology. *Journal of Consulting Psychology, 15,* 281-289.

Meyer, A. (1908). The role of the mental factors in psychiatry. *American Journal of Insanity, 65,* 39-56.

Meyer, A. (1919). August Hoch, M.D. *Archives of Neurology and Psychiatry, 2,* 573-576.

Meyer, A. (1924-1925). G. Stanley Hall, Ph.D., LL.D. *American Journal of Psychiatry, 81,* 151-153.

Meyer, A., Jelliffe, S. E., & Hoch, A. (1911). *Dementia praecox: A monograph.* Boston: Gorham Press.

Meyer, M. (1933). That whale among the fishes: The theory of emotions. *Psychological Review, 40,* 292-300.

Miles, W. R. (1943). Red goggles for producing dark adaptation. *Federation Proceedings, 2,* 109-115.

Miller, G. A. (1953). What is information measurement? *American Psychologist, 8,* 3-11.

Miller, J. G. (1946). Clinical psychology in the Veterans Administration. *American Psychologist, 1,* 181-189.

Miller, J. G. (1955). Toward a general theory for the behavioral sciences. *American Psychologist, 10,* 513-531.

Miller, N. E. (1958). Central stimulation and other new approaches to motivation and reward. *American Psychologist, 13,* 100-108.

Mirsky, A. F., & Duncan, C. C. (1986). Etiology and expression of schizophrenia: Neurological and psychosocial factors. *Annual Review of Psychology, 37,* 291-319.

Mitchell, D. (1931). Private practice. In R. A. Brotemarkle (Ed.), *Clinical psychology: Studies in honor of Lightner Witmer.* Philadelphia: University of Pennsylvania Press.

Mitchell, K. M. (1974). Effective therapist interpersonal skills: The search goes on. In A. I. Rabin (Ed.), *Clinical psychology: Issues of the seventies.* East Lansing: Michigan State University Press.

Money, J. (1987). Sin, sickness, or status? Homosexual gender identity and psychoneuroendocrinology. *American Psychologist, 42,* 384-399.

Monroe, R. (1941). Inspection technique: A modification of the Rorschach method of personality diagnosis for large scale application. *Rorschach Research Exchange, 5,* 166-190.

Montagu, A. (1968, October). Chromosomes and crime. *Psychology Today, 2,* 43-49.

Moore, E. H. (1935). A note on the recall of the pleasant vs. the unpleasant. *Psychological Review, 42,* 214-215.

Moore, H., & Steele, I. (1934-1935). Personality tests. *Journal of Abnormal and Social Psychology, 29,* 45-52.

Moreno, J. L. (1932). *Application of the group method to classification.* New York: National Committee on Prisons and Prison Labor.

Moreno, J. L. (1952). *Who shall survive?* New York: Beacon House.

Morgan, C. D., & Murray, H. A. (1935). A method for investigating fantasies: The Thematic Apperception Test. *Archives of Neurology and Psychiatry, 34,* 289-306.

Morrow, A. J. (1969). American Board of Professional Psychology: 1968 annual report. *American Psychologist, 24,* 151-154.

Moss, C. S. (1967). Visitation to mental health progarms in Eastern Europe. *American Psychologist, 22,* 452-456.

Mowrer, O. H. (1939). A stimulus-response analysis of anxiety and its role as a reinforcing agent. *Psychological Review, 46,* 553-565.

Mowrer, O. H. (1950). *Learning theory and personality dynamics.* New York: Ronald.

Mowrer, O. H. (1954). The psychologist looks at language. *American Psychologist, 9,* 660-694.

Mowrer, O. H. (1960). "Sin," the lesser of two evils. *American Psychologist, 15,* 301-304.

Mowrer, O. H., & Mowrer, W. M. (1938). Enuresis: A method for its study and treatment. *American Journal of Orthopsychiatry, 8,* 436-459.

Münsterberg, H. (1909). *Psychotherapy.* New York: Moffat, Yard.

Münsterberg, H. (1913). *Psychology and industrial efficiency.* Boston: Houghton Mifflin.

Murphy, G. (1945). The freeing of intelligence. *Psychological Bulletin, 42,* 1-19.

Murphy, G. (1950). *Historical introduction to modern psychology.* New York: Harcourt, Brace.

Murray, H. A. (1937). Visceral manifestations of personality. *Journal of Abnormal and Social Psychology, 32,* 161-184.

Murray, H. A., et al. (1938). *Explorations in personality.* New York: Oxford.

Myrdal, G., et al. (1944). *An American dilemma.* New York: Harper.

Naccarati, S., & Garrett, H. E. (1924). The relation of morphology to temperament. *Journal of Abnormal and Social Psychology, 19,* 254-263.

Nathan, R. G., Lubin, B., Matarazzo, J. D., & Persely, G. W. (1979). Psychologists in schools of medicine: 1955, 1964, & 1977. *American Psychologist, 34,* 622-627.

National Science Foundation (1974). *US scientists and engineers, 1974.* Surveys of Science Resources Series (NSF 76-329).

Nelson, P. (1989). Accreditation grows, but values remain same. *APA Monitor, 20*(9), 29.

Nemir, R. (1980, November). Lessons on sunset. *APA Monitor, 11,* 33-34.

Newell, H. W. (1941). Play therapy in child psychiatry. *American Journal of Orthopsychiatry, 11,* 245-251.

New York Psychiatrical Society (1917). Activities of clinical psychologists. *Psychological Bulletin, 14,* 224-225.

Norcross, J. C., Prochaska, J. O., & Gallagher, K. M. (1989). Clinical psychologists in the 1980s: 2. Theory, research, and practice. *The Clinical Psychologist, 42,* 45-53.

Norsworthy, N. (1906). The psychology of mentally defective children. *Archives of Psychology,* No. 1.

Nunez, R. (1976, Fall). The profession of clinical psychology in Mexico. *The Clinical Psychologist, 30,* 2-3, 27.

Nunn, P. T. (1920). *Education: Its data and first principles.* London: Arnold.

Oberndorf, C. P. (1953a). Autobiography of Josef Breuer (1842-1925). *International Journal of Psychoanalysis, 34,* 64-67.

Oberndorf, C. P. (1953b). Dr. Karen Horney. *International Journal of Psychoanalysis, 34,* 154-155.

O'Donnell, J. M. (1979). The clinical psychology of Lightner Witmer: A case study of institutional innovation and intellectual change. *Journal of the History of the Behavioral Sciences, 15,* 3-17.

Ogden, R. M. (1911). The unconscious bias of laboratories. *Psychological Bulletin, 8,* 330-331.

Orlansky, H. (1949). Infant care and personality. *Psychological Bulletin, 46,* 1-48.

Orlinsky, D. E. (1989). Researchers' images of psychotherapy: Their origins and influence on research. *Clinical Psychology Review, 9,* 413-441.

Orne, M. T. (1959). The nature of hypnosis: Artifact and essence. *Journal of Abnormal and Social Psychology, 58,* 277–299.

Osgood, C. E. (1953). *Method and theory in experimental psychology.* New York: Oxford University Press.

OSS Staff (1948). *Assessment of men.* New York: Rinehart.

Otis, A. S. (1923). *Otis Classification Test.* Yonkers, NY: World.

Otis, A. S. (1941). *Otis Classification Test: Revised forms R, S, T.* Yonkers, NY: World Book.

Page, H. E. (1967). On planning psychology facilities. *American Psychologist, 22,* 421–422.

Park, D. G. (1931). Freudian influence on academic psychology. *Psychological Review, 38,* 73–85.

Parloff, M. B., London, P., & Wolfe, B. (1986). Individual psychotherapy and behavior change. *Annual Review of Psychology, 37,* 321–349.

Parloff, M. B., Waskow, I. E., & Wolfe, B. (1978). Research on therapist variables in relation to process and outcome. In S. L. Garfield & A. E. Bergin (Eds.), *Handbook of psychotherapy and behavior change.* New York: Wiley.

Parsons, C. J. (1917). Children's interpretation of ink-blots: A study of some characteristics of children's imagination. *British Journal of Psychology, 9,* 74–92.

Patterson, C. H. (1989). Eclecticism in psychotherapy: Is integration possible? *Psychotherapy, 26,* 157–161.

Penrose, L. S. (1935). Two cases of phenylpyruvic amentia. *Lancet, 228,* 23–24.

Perloff, R. (1972). Enhancing psychology by assessing its manpower. *American Psychologist, 27,* 335–361.

Perls, F. S. (1969a). *Ego, hunger and aggression.* New York: Vintage.

Perls, F. S. (1969b). *Gestalt therapy verbatim.* New York: Bantam.

Pervin, L. A. (1960). Existentialism, psychology, and psychotherapy. *American Psychologist, 15,* 305–309.

Pervin, L. A. (1985). Personality: Current controversies, issues, and directions. *Annual Review of Psychology, 36,* 83–114.

Peterson, D. R. (1971). Status of the Doctor of Psychology program, 1970. *Professional Psychology, 2,* 271–275.

Peterson, J. (1925). *Early conceptions and tests of intelligence.* Yonkers, NY: World.

Phares, E. J. (1976). *Locus of control in personality.* Morristown, NJ: General Learning Press.

Phillips, J. S., & Bierman, K. L. (1981). Clinical psychology: Individual methods. *Annual Review of Psychology, 33,* 405–438.

Piaget, J. (1926). *The language and thought of the child.* New York: Humanities Press.

Piaget, J. (1952). Autobiography. In E. G. Boring et al. (Eds.), *A history of psychology in autobiography* (Vol. 4). Worcester, MA: Clark University Press.

Piaget, J. (1958). Biography. In M. D. Candee (Ed.), *Current biography yearbook, 1958.* New York: H. W. Wilson.

Piaget, J. (1972). *The principles of genetic epistemology.* New York: Basic Books.

Pines, M. (1962). Training housewives as psychotherapists. *Harper's, 224,* 37–42.

Pintner, R., & Paterson, D. G. (1917). *A scale of performance tests.* New York: World.

Piotrowski, C., & Keller, J. W. (1984). Psychodiagnostic testing in APA-approved clinical psychology programs. *Professional Psychology: Research and Practice, 15,* 450–456.

Piotrowski, C., & Keller, J. W. (1989). Psychological testing in outpatient mental health facilities: A national study. *Professional Psychology: Research and Practice, 20,* 423–425.

Piotrowski, C., & Lubin, B. (1989). Prescription privileges: A view from health psychologists. *The Clinical Psychologist, 42,* 83–84.

Poffenberger, A. T. (1936). Psychology and life. *Psychological Review, 48,* 9–31.

Poffenberger, A. T. (1939). Specific psychological therapies. *American Journal of Orthopsychiatry, 9,* 755–760.

Porter, F. (1915–1916). Difficulties in the interpretation of mental tests—types and examples. *Psychological Clinic, 9,* 140–158, 167–180.

Potter, H. W. (1933). Schizophrenia in children. *American Journal of Psychiatry, 12,* 1253–1270.

Pratt, J. H. (1906). The home sanitarium treatment of consumption. *Johns Hopkins Hospital Bulletin, 17,* 140–144.

Pratt, J. H. (1945). The group method in the treatment of psychosomatic disorders. *Sociometry, 8,* 323–331.

Premack, D. (1972). The education of Sarah. In *Readings in Psychology Today* (2nd ed.). Del Mar, CA: CRM Books.

Pressey, S. L. (1921). A group scale for investigating the emotions. *Journal of Abnormal and Social Psychology, 16,* 55–64.

Price, A. C., & Deabler, H. L. (1955). Diagnosis of organicity by means of spiral aftereffect. *Journal of Consulting Psychology, 19,* 299–302.

Prince, M. (1906–1907). Hysteria from the point of view of dissociate personality. *Journal of Abnormal Psychology, 1,* 170–187.

Prince, M. (1908–1909). The unconscious. *Journal of Abnormal Psychology, 3,* 261–297.

Prince, M. (1909–1910). The psychological principles and field of psychotherapy. *Journal of Abnormal Psychology, 4,* 72–98.

Prince, M. (1925–1926). $5,000 award. *Journal of Abnormal and Social Psychology, 20,* 1–6.

Prince, M. (1928). The problem of personality: How many selves have we? In C. Murchison (Ed.), *Psychologies of 1925.* Worcester, MA: Clark University Press.

Protho, E. T., & Melikan, L. H. (1955). Psychology in the Arab Near East. *Psychological Bulletin, 52,* 303–310.

Puig-Antich, J., & Gittelman, R. (1980). Depression in childhood and adolescence. In E. S. Paykel (Ed.), *Handbook of affective disorders.* London: Churchill Livingston.

Purdy, D. M. (1936–1937). The biological psychology of Kurt Goldstein. *Character and Personality, 5,* 321–330.

Putnam, J. J. (1909–1910). Personal impressions of Sigmund Freud and his work, with special reference to his recent lectures at Clark University. *Journal of Abnormal Psychology, 4,* 293–310, 372–379.

Rabin, A. I. (1945). The use of the Wechsler-Bellevue Scale with normal and abnormal persons. *Psychological Bulletin, 42,* 410–422.

Rabin, A. I. (1958). Behavior research in collective settlements in Israel: Infants and children under conditions of intermittent mothering in the kibbutz. *American Journal of Orthopsychiatry, 28,* 577–286.

Rabin, A. I., & Geurtin, W. H. (1951). Research with the Wechsler-Bellevue test, 1945–1950. *Psychological Bulletin, 48,* 211–248.

Rabin, A. I., & Hurley, J. R. (1964). Projective techniques. *Progress in Clinical Psychology, 6.*

Rachman, S. (1959). The treatment of anxiety and phobic reactions by systematic desensitization psychotherapy. *Journal of Abnormal and Social Psychology, 58,* 259–263.

Raimy, V. C. (1948). Self-reference in counseling interviews. *Journal of Consulting Psychology, 12,* 153–163.

Raimy, V. C. (1950). *Training in clinical psychology.* Englewood Cliffs, NJ: Prentice-Hall.

Raimy, V. C. (1952). Clinical methods: Psychotherapy. *Annual Review of Psychology, 3,* 321–350.

Ramul, K. (1960). The problem of measurement in the psychology of the eighteenth century. *American Psychologist, 15,* 256–265.

Ramul, K. (1981). The problem of measurement in psychology. In C. E. Walker (Ed.), *Clinical practice of psychology.* New York: Pergamon.

Rank, O. (1950). *Will therapy and truth and reality.* New York: Knopf.

Rapaport, D. (1953). Personality and psychotherapy: An analysis in terms of learning, thinking, and culture. *American Journal of Orthopsychiatry, 23,* 204–208.

Rapoport, J. L. (1988). *The boy who couldn't stop washing.* New York: Dutton.

Redl, F., & Wineman, D. (1951). *Children who hate.* Glencoe, IL: Free Press.

Reisman, J. M. (1971). *Toward the integration of psychotherapy.* New York: Wiley-Interscience.

Reisman, J. M. (1974). Implications of humanism and behaviorism for training in treatment. In A. I. Rabin (Ed.), *Issues in clinical psychology in the seventies.* East Lansing: Michigan State University Press.

Reisman, J. M. (1975). Trends in training and treatment. *Professional Psychology, 6,* 187–192.

Reisman, J. M. (1981). History and current trends in clinical psychology. In C. E. Walker (Ed.), *Clinical practice of psychology.* New York: Pergamon.

Reisman, J. M. (1986). Psychotherapy as a professional relationship. *Professional Psychology: Research and Practice, 17,* 565–569.

Reisman, J. M. (1988). Professional psychology in the Hungarian People's Republic. *Professional Psychology: Research and Practice, 19,* 483–485.

Report of Committee of Clinical Section of American Psychological Association (1935). *Psychological Clinic, 23,* 1–140.

Report of Committee on Clinical Training of Psychologists (1940). *American Journal of Orthopsychiatry, 10,* 166–171.

Rhine, J. B. (1936–1937). Some selected experiments in extra-sensory perception. *Journal of Abnormal and Social Psychology, 31,* 216–228.

Ribble, M. A. (1941). Disorganizing factors of infant personality. *American Journal of Psychiatry, 98,* 459–463.

Rich, G. J. (1928–1929). A biochemical approach to the study of personality. *Journal of Abnormal and Social Psychology, 23,* 158–175.

Riggs, A. F. (1929). *Intelligent living.* New York: Doubleday.

Rivers, W. H. R. (1923). *Conflict and dreams.* New York: Harcourt, Brace.

Robinson, D. N. (1970). *Heredity and achievement.* New York: Oxford University Press.

Robinson, M. F. (1946). What price lobotomy? *Journal of Abnormal and Social Psychology, 41,* 421–436.

Rogers, C. R. (1931). *Measuring personality adjustment in children nine to thirteen years of age.* New York: Teachers College.

Rogers, C. R. (1937). Three surveys of treatment measures used with children. *American Journal of Orthopsychiatry, 7,* 48–57.

Rogers, C. R. (1939). Needed emphases in the training of clinical psychologists. *Journal of Consulting Psychology, 3,* 141–143.

Rogers, C. R. (1940). The process of therapy. *Journal of Consulting Psychology, 4,* 161–164.

Rogers, C. R. (1942). *Counseling and psychotherapy.* New York: Houghton Mifflin.

Rogers, C. R. (1946). Significant aspects of client-centered therapy. *American Psychologist, 1,* 415–422.

Rogers, C. R. (1947). Some observations on the organization of personality. *American Psychologist, 2,* 358–368.

Rogers, C. R. (1951). *Client-centered therapy.* Boston: Houghton Mifflin.

Rogers, C. R. (1957). The necessary and sufficient conditions of therapeutic personality change. *Journal of Consulting Psychology, 21,* 95–103.

Rogers, C. R. (1958). A process conception of psychotherapy. *American Psychologist, 13,* 142–149.

Rogers, C. R. (1959). A theory of therapy, personality, and interpersonal relationships, as developed in the client-centered framework. In S. Koch (Ed.), *Psychology: A study of a science* (Vol. 3). New York: McGraw-Hill.

Rogers, C. R. (1961). *On becoming a person.* Boston: Houghton Mifflin.

Rogers, C. R. (1967). *The therapeutic relationship and its impact: A study of psychotherapy with schizophrenics.* Madison: University of Wisconsin Press.

Rogers, C. R. (1980). *A way of being.* Boston: Houghton Mifflin.

Rogers, C. R., & Dymond, R. F. (1955). *Psychotherapy and personality change.* Chicago: University of Chicago Press.

Rome, H. P., et al. (1966). Psychiatry viewed from the outside: The challenge of the next ten years. *American Journal of Psychiatry, 123,* 519–530.

Rorer, L. G., & Widiger, T. A. (1983). Personality structure and assessment. *Annual Review of Psychology, 34,* 431–463.

Rorschach, H. (1921). *Psychodiagnostik.* Bern: Huber.

Rorschach, H., & Oberholzer, E. (1924). The application of the interpretation of form to psychoanalysis. *Journal of Nervous and Mental Disorders, 60,* 225–248, 359–379.

Rosanoff, A. J. (1920). A theory of personality based mainly on psychiatric experience. *Psychological Bulletin, 17,* 281–299.

Rosanoff, I. R., & Rosanoff, A. J. (1913). A study of association in children. *Psychological Review, 20,* 43–89.

Rosen, J. N. (1947). The treatment of schizophrenic psychoses by direct analytic therapy. *Psychiatric Quarterly, 21,* 3–38.

Rosenthal, R. (1967). Self-fulfilling prophecy. In *Readings in Psychology Today.* Del Mar, CA: CRM Books.

Rosenthal, R., & Jacobson, L. (1968). *Pygmalion in the classroom: Teacher expectation and pupil's intellectual development.* New York: Holt, Rinehart & Winston.

Rosenwald, A. K., & Gould, D. W. (1975). Mental health overview. *Britannica Book of the Year,* pp. 348–353.

Rosenzweig, M. R. (1984). US and world psychology. *American Psychologist, 39,* 877–884.

Rosenzweig, S. (1938). A basis for the improvement of personality tests with special reference to the M-F battery. *Journal of Abnormal and Social Psychology, 33,* 476–488.

Rosenzweig, S. (1948). Projective techniques: The progress in the application of psychodynamics. In L. G. Lowrey & V. Sloane (Eds.), *Orthopsychiatry 1923–1948: Retrospect and prospect.* New York: American Orthopsychiatric Association.

Rosenzweig, S. (1985). Freud and experimental psychology: The emergence of idiodynamics. In S. Koch & D. E. Leary (Eds.), *A century of psychology as science.* New York: McGraw-Hill.

Rosenzweig, S., Mowrer, O. K., Haslerud, G. M., Curtis, Q. F., & Barker, R. G. (1938–1939). Frustration as an experimental problem. *Character and Personality, 7,* 126–160.

Ross, A. O., & Pelham, W. E. (1981). Child psychopathology. *Annual Review of Psychology, 32,* 243–278.

Rotter, J. B. (1953). Clinical methods: Psychodiagnostics. *Annual Review of Psychology, 4,* 295–316.

Rotter, J. B. (1966). Generalized expectancies for internal versus external control of reinforcement. *Psychological Monographs, 80*(1, Whole No. 609).

Rotter, J. B. (1975). Some problems and misconceptions related to the construct of internal versus external control of reinforcement. *Journal of Consulting and Clinical Psychology, 43,* 56–67.

Rousseau, J. J. (1911). *Émile; or, education.* New York: Dutton.

Rubenstein, E. R., & Parloff, M. B. (1959). *Research in psychotherapy.* Washington, DC: American Psychological Association.

Rutter, M., & Schopler, E. (1987). Autism and pervasive developmental disorders. *Journal of Autism and Developmental Disorders, 17,* 159–186.

Safir, F. M. (1950). Certification versus licensing legislation. *American Psychologist, 7,* 105–106.

Salter, A. (1949). *Conditioned reflex therapy.* New York: Creative Age.

Sanford, F. (1958). Psychology and the mental health movement. *American Psychologist, 13,* 80–85.

Sann, P. (1967). *Fads, follies, and delusions of the American people.* New York: Bonanza Books.

Santos, J. F., & VandenBos, G. R. (1982). *Psychology and the older adult: Challenges for training in the 1980s.* Washington, DC: American Psychological Association.

Sanua, V. D. (1966). Clinical psychology in France. *Progress in Clinical Psychology, 7.*

Sapir, E. (1932–1933). Cultural anthropology and psychiatry. *Journal of Abnormal and Social Psychology, 27,* 229–242.

Sarason, S. B. (1949). *Psychological problems in mental deficiency.* New York: Harper.

Sarason, S. B. (1954). *The clinical interaction, with special reference to the Rorschach.* New York: Harper.

Sarason, S. B. (1976). Community psychology, networks, and Mr. Everyman. *American Psychologist, 31,* 317–328.

Saslow, G. (1962). Final summary. In H. Strupp & L. Luborsky (Eds.), *Research in psychotherapy.* Washington, DC: American Psychological Association.

Saudek, R. (1929). *Experiments with handwriting.* New York: Morrow.

Saudek, R. (1933–1934). Can different writers produce identical handwritings? *Character and Personality, 2,* 231–245.

Saxe, L., Dougherty, D., & Cross, T. (1985). The validity of polygraph testing: Scientific analysis and public controversy. *American Psychologist, 40,* 355–366.

Schafer, R. (1954). *Psychoanalytic interpretation in Rorschach testing.* New York: Grune & Stratton.

Schafer, R., & Murphy, G. (1943). The role of autism in a visual figure-ground relationship. *Journal of Experimental Psychology, 32,* 335–343.

Schilder, P. (1934–1935). The somato-psyche in psychiatry and social psychology. *Journal of Abnormal and Social Psychology, 29,* 314–327.

Schilder, P. (1938). *Psychotherapy.* New York: Norton.

Schlenker, B. R. (1985). *The self and social life.* New York: McGraw-Hill.

Schneidman, E. S. (1947). The Make-A-Picture-Story (MAPS) projective personality test: A preliminary report. *Journal of Consulting Psychology, 11,* 315–325.

Schwabb, S. I. (1919–1920). The mechanism of the war neuroses. *Journal of Abnormal Psychology, 14,* 1–8.

Schwartz, L. (1932). Social-situation pictures in the psychiatric interview. *American Journal of Orthopsychiatry, 2,* 124–133.

Schwing, G. (1940). *Ein Weg zur Seele des Geisteskranken.* Zurich: Rascher.

Scott, W. D. (1908–1909). An interpretation of the psychoanalytic method in psychotherapy with a report of a case so treated. *Journal of Abnormal Psychology, 3,* 371–377.

Scott, W. D. (1920). Changes in some of our conceptions and practices of personnel. *Psychological Review, 27,* 81–94.

Seashore, C. (1930). Autobiography. In C. Murchison (Ed.), *A history of psychology in autobiography* (Vol. 1). Worcester, MA: Clark University Press.

Sechehaye, M. A. (1951). *Symbolic realization.* New York: International Universities Press.

Sechrest, L. B. (1985a). President's message. *The Clinical Psychologist, 38*(1), 1, 3.

Sechrest, L. B. (1985b). President's message. Shall we, then, all hang separately? *The Clinical Psychologist, 38*(4), 73, 75.

Seligman, M. E. (1975). *Helplessness.* San Francisco: Freeman.

Selye, H. (1956). *The stress of life.* New York: McGraw-Hill.

Shaffer, G. W., & Lazarus, R. S. (1952). *Fundamental concepts in clinical psychology.* New York: McGraw-Hill.

Shaffer, J. B., & Galinsky, M. D. (1974). *Models of group therapy and sensitivity training.* Englewood Cliffs, NJ: Prentice-Hall.

Shaffer, L. F. (1953). Of whose reality I cannot doubt. *American Psychologist, 8,* 608–623.

Shakow, D. (1939). The functions of the psychologist in the state hospital. *Journal of Consulting Psychology, 3,* 20–23.

Shakow, D. (1945). One hundred years of American psychiatry: A special review. *Psychological Bulletin, 42,* 423–432.

Shakow, D. (1948). Clinical psychology: An evaluation. In L. G. Lowrey & V. Sloane (Eds.), *Orthopsychiatry 1923–1948: Retrospect and prospect.* New York: American Orthopsychiatric Association.

Shakow, D. (1965). Seventeen years later: Clinical psychology in the light of the 1947 Committee on Training in Clinical Psychology report. *American Psychologist, 20,* 353–362.

Shakow, D., & Rosenzweig, S. (1939–1940). The use of the tautaphone ("verbal summator") as an auditory apperceptive test for the study of personality. *Character and Personality, 8,* 216–226.

Sharp, S. E. (1899). Individual psychology: A study in psychological method. *American Journal of Psychology, 10,* 329–391.

Shaver, P., & Hazan, C. (1988). Being lonely, falling in love: Perspectives from attachment theory. In M. Hojat & R. Crandall (Eds.), *Loneliness: Theory, research, and applications.* Newbury Park, CA: Sage.

Sheldon, W. H. (1940). *The varieties of human physique: An introduction to constitutional psychology.* New York: Harper.

Sheldon, W. H. (1942). *The varieties of temperament: A psychology of constitutional differences.* New York: Harper.

Sheldon, W. H. (1944). Constitutional factors in personality. In J. M. Hunt (Ed.), *Personality and the behavior disorders.* New York: Ronald.

Sheldon, W. H. (1949). *Varieties of delinquent youth: An introduction to constitutional psychiatry.* New York: Harper.

Sherif, M. (1935). A study in some social factors in perception. *Archives of Psychology*, No. 187.

Shipley, W., & Kent, F. (1940). The insulin-shock and metrazol treatments of schizophrenia with emphasis on psychological aspects. *Psychological Bulletin, 37,* 259-284.

Shoben, E. J., Jr. (1956). Counseling. *Annual Review of Psychology, 7,* 147-172.

Shuey, H. (1933). A new interpretation of the Rorschach Test. *Psychological Review, 40,* 213-215.

Sidis, B. (1911-1912). Fear, anxiety, and psychopathic maladies. *Journal of Abnormal Psychology, 6,* 107-125.

Siegel, N., & Bernreuter, R. G. (1951). Foreign language requirements for reading current psychological literature. *American Psychologist, 6,* 179.

Silverman, L. H. (1976). Psychoanalytic theory: The reports of my death are greatly exaggerated. *American Psychologist, 31,* 621-637.

Silverman, L. H., & Weinberger, J. (1985). Mommy and I are one: Implications for psychotherapy. *American Psychologist, 40,* 1296-1308.

Simmel, E. (1946). Otto Fenichel. *International Journal of Psychoanalysis, 27,* 67-71.

Singer, J. L., & Kolligian, J., Jr. (1987). Personality: Developments in the study of private experience. *Annual Review of Psychology, 38,* 533-574.

Skinner, B. F. (1936). The verbal summator and a method for the study of latent speech. *Journal of Psychology, 2,* 71-107.

Skinner, B. F. (1958). Reinforcement today. *American Psychologist, 13,* 94-99.

Skinner, B. F. (1967). Autobiography. In E. Boring and G. Lindzey (Eds.), *History of psychology in autobiography* (Vol. 5). New York: Appleton-Century-Crofts.

Skinner, B. F. (1971). *Beyond freedom and dignity.* New York: Knopf.

Skinner, B. F. (1974). *About behaviorism.* New York: Knopf.

Skodak, M. (1936). Children in foster homes: A study of mental development. *University of Iowa Studies on Child Welfare, 16*(1).

Skraggs, E. B. (1934). The limitations of scientific psychology as an applied or practical science. *Psychological Review, 41,* 572-576.

Slavson, S. R. (1940). Group therapy. *Mental Hygiene, 24,* 36-49.

Slavson, S. R. (1943). *An introduction to group therapy.* New York: Commonwealth Fund.

Slavson, S. R. (1951). *The practice of group therapy.* New York: International Universities Press.

Smith, M. B. (1959). Research strategies toward a conception of positive mental health. *American Psychologist, 14,* 673-681.

Smith, M. B. (1973). Is psychology relevant to new priorities? *American Psychologist, 32,* 752-777.

Smith, M. L., & Glass, G. V. (1977). Meta-analysis of psychotherapy outcome studies. *American Psychologist, 32,* 752-777.

Smith, M. L., Glass, G. V., & Miller, T. I. (1980). *The benefits of psychotherapy.* Baltimore: Johns Hopkins University Press.

Snyder, C. R. (1989). Illusions about the self: Taking stock of the new "right stuff." *Journal of Social and Clinical Psychology, 8,* 113.

Snyder, W. V. (1947). The present status of psychotherapeutic counseling. *Psychological Bulletin, 44,* 297-386.

Solomon, M. (1916-1917). Book review of *Psychology of the unconscious* by C. G. Jung. *Journal of Abnormal Psychology, 11,* 277-279.

Spaulding, E. R. (1921-1922). The role of personality development in the reconstruction of the delinquent. *Journal of Abnormal and Social Psychology, 16,* 97-114.

Spearman, C. (1904). General intelligence objectively determined and measured. *American Journal of Psychology, 15,* 201-292.

Spearman, C. (1922). A friendly challenge to Professor Thorndike. *Psychological Review, 29,* 406-407.

Spearman, C. (1927). *The abilities of men.* New York: Macmillan.

Spearman, C. (1930). Autobiography. In C. Murchison (Ed.), *A history of psychology in autobiography* (Vol. 1). Worcester, MA: Clark University Press.

Spearman, C. (1939). Thurstone's work re-worked. *Journal of Educational Psychology, 30,* 1–16.

Speer, G. S. (1950). A survey of psychologists in Illinois. *American Psychologist, 5,* 424–426.

Spence, J. T., Carson, R. C., & Thibaut, J. W. (1976). *Behavioral approaches to therapy.* Morristown, NJ: General Learning Press.

Spielberger, C. D. (1989). Report of the Treasurer, 1988. Turning the deficit around: Better days ahead. *American Psychologist, 44,* 987–992.

Spielberger, C. D., Sarason, I. G., & Milgram, N. A. (1982). *Stress and anxiety.* (Vol. 8). Washington, DC: Hemisphere.

Spitz, R. A. (1946). Hospitalism: A follow-up report. *Psychoanalytic Study of the Child, 2,* 113–117.

Spitzer, R. L., Williams, J. B., Kass, F., & Davids, M. (1989). National field trial of the DSM-III-R diagnostic criteria for self-defeating personality disorder. *American Journal of Psychiatry, 146,* 1561–1567.

Spitzer, R. L., Williams, J. B., & Skodal, A. E. (1980). DSM-III: The major achievements and an overview. *American Journal of Psychiatry, 137,* 51–164.

Spranger, E. (1928). *Types of men.* Halle (Saale): Niemeyer.

Sprinthall, R. C., & Sprinthall, N. A. (1974). *Educational psychology: A developmental approach.* Reading, MA: Addison-Wesley.

Spruill, J. (1987). Stanford-Binet Intelligence Scale, fourth edition. In D. J. Keyser & R. C. Sweetland (Eds.), *Test critiques* (Vol. 4). Kansas City, MO: Test Corporation of America.

Staff. (1912). Alfred Binet [obituary]. *American Journal of Psychology, 23,* 140–141.

Staff, Psychological Research Project (Pilot). (1946). Psychological research on pilot training in the AAF. *American Psychologist, 1,* 7–16.

Stampfl, T. G., & Levis, D. J. (1967). Essentials of implosive therapy. *Journal of Abnormal Psychology, 72,* 496–503.

Stapp, J., Fulcher, R., & Wicherski, M. (1984). The employment of 1981 and 1982 doctoral recipients in psychology. *American Psychologist, 39,* 1408–1423.

Stapp, J., Tucker, A. M., & VandenBos, G. R. (1985). Census of psychological personnel, 1983. *American Psychologist, 40,* 1317–1351.

Starr, H. E. (1933). Promethian constellations. *Psychological Clinic, 22,* 1–20.

Stein, G. M., & Sauta, J. L. (1975). The academic job hunt: Is it more frustrating than it has to be? *American Psychologist, 30,* 861–863.

Stephenson, W. (1935–1936). Correlating persons instead of tests. *Character and Personality, 4,* 17–24.

Stern, A. W. (1956). The nature of *g* and the concept of intelligence. *Acta Psychologia, 12,* 282–289.

Stern, W. (1914). *The psychological methods of testing intelligence.* Baltimore: Warwick & York.

Stern, W. (1925). The theory of the constancy of intelligence. *Psychological Clinic, 16,* 110–118.

Stern, W. (1930). Autobiography. In C. Murchison (Ed.), *A history of psychology in autobiography* (Vol. 1). Worcester, MA: Clark University Press.

Stern, W. (1935–1936). On the nature and structure of character. *Character and Personality, 4,* 270–289.

Stern, W. (1937–1938). Cloud pictures: A new method for testing imagination. *Character and Personality, 6,* 132–146.

Stevens, S. S. (1935). The operational definition of psychological concepts. *Psychological Review, 42,* 517–527.

Stevenson, G. S. (1948). Child guidance and the National Committee for Mental Hygiene. In L. G. Lowrey & V. Sloane (Eds.), *Orthopsychiatry 1923–1948: Retrospect and prospect.* New York: American Orthopsychiatric Association.

Stoddard, D. G. (1943). *The meaning of intelligence.* New York: Macmillan.

Stogdill, R. M. (1934). Neurosis as learned behavior. *Psychological Review, 41,* 497–507.

Stolz, S. B., Wienckowski, L. A., & Brown, B. S. (1975). Behavior modification: A perspective on critical issues. *American Psychologist, 30,* 1027–1048.

Stone, A. A. (1981). Recent developments in law and psychiatry. In S. Arieti & H. K. Brodie (Eds.), *American handbook of psychiatry* (Vol. 7). New York: Basic Books.

Stone, H. K., & Dellis, N. F. (1960). An exploratory investigation into the levels hypothesis. *Journal of Projective Techniques, 24,* 333–340.

Stratton, G. M. (1909). Toward the correction of some rival methods in psychlogy. *Psychological Review, 16,* 67–83.

Strauss, A. A., & Lehtinen, L. E. (1947). *Psychopathology and education of the brain injured child.* New York: Grune & Stratton.

Strickland, B. R. (1988). Clinical psychology comes of age. *American Psychologist, 43,* 104–107.

Strong, E. K., Jr. (1958). Satisfactions and interests. *American Psychologist, 13,* 449–456.

Strupp, H. H. (1976). Clinical psychology, irrationalism, and the erosion of excellence. *American Psychologist, 31,* 561–571.

Sullivan, H. S. (1947). *Conceptions of modern psychiatry.* Washington: William Alanson White Psychiatric Foundation.

Sullivan, H. S. (1953). *The interpersonal theory of psychiatry.* New York: Norton.

Sullivan, H. S. (1954). *The psychiatric interview.* New York: Norton.

Sulloway, F. J. (1979). *Freud: Biologist of the mind.* New York: Basic Books.

Summerfield, A. (1958). Clinical psychology in Great Britain. *American Psychologist, 13,* 171–176.

Sundberg, N. D. (1954). A note concerning the history of testing. *American Psychologist, 9,* 150–151.

Sundberg, N. D. (1961). The practice of psychological testing in clinical services in the U.S. *American Psychologist, 16,* 79–83.

Sweetland, R. C., & Keyser, D. J. (1983). *Tests.* Kansas City, MO: Test Corporation of America.

Sweetland, R. C., & Keyser, D. J. (1986). *Tests* (2nd ed.). Kansas City, MO: Test Corporation of America.

Sylvester, R. H. (1913–1914). Clinical psychology adversely criticized. *Psychological Clinic, 7,* 182–188.

Symonds, P. M. (1931). *Diagnosing personality and conduct.* New York: Century.

Symonds, P. M. (1947). The sentence completion test as a projective technique. *Journal of Abnormal and Social Psychology, 42,* 320–329.

Szasz, T. S. (1960). The myth of mental illness. *American Psychologist, 15,* 113–118.

Szondi, L. (1947). *Szondi Test: Experimentelle Triebdiagnostik.* Bern: Hans Huber.

Taft, J. (1958). *Otto Rank.* New York: Julian.

Tanner, A. (1915). Adler's theory of *Mindeswertigkeit. Pedagogical Seminary, 22,* 204–217.

Tanney, F. (1983). Hospital privileges for psychologists. *American Psychologist, 38,* 1232–1237.

Taylor, J. (1953). A personality scale of manifest anxiety. *Journal of Abnormal and Social Psychology, 48,* 285–290.

Taylor, W. S. (1921–1922). A hypnoanalytic study in two cases of war neuroses. *Journal of Abnormal and Social Psychology, 16,* 344–355.

Tendler, A. D. (1933). A reorientation in psychotherapy. *Psychological Clinic, 21,* 253–259.

Terman, L. M. (1911–1912). The Binet-Simon Scale for measuring intelligence. *Psychological Clinic, 5,* 199–206.

Terman, L. M. (1916). *The measurement of intelligence.* Boston: Houghton Mifflin.

Terman, L. M. (1921). Symposium: Intelligence and its measurement. *Journal of Educational Psychology, 12,* 123–147, 196–216.

Terman, L. M. (1922). A new approach to the study of genius. *Psychological Review, 29,* 310–318.

Terman, L. M. (1924). The mental test as a psychological method. *Psychological Review, 31,* 93–117.

Terman, L. M. (1932). Autobiography. In C. Murchison (Ed.), *A history of psychology in autobiography* (Vol. 2). Worcester, MA: Clark University Press.

Terman, L. M., et al. (1925). *Genetic studies of genius: Vol. 1. Mental and physical traits of a thousand gifted children.* Stanford, CA: Stanford University Press.

Terman, L. M., & Merrill, M. A. (1937). *Measuring intelligence.* Boston: Houghton Mifflin.

Terman, L. M., & Merrill, M. A. (1960). *Stanford-Binet Intelligence Scale.* Boston: Houghton Mifflin.

Terman, L. M., & Oden, M. H. (1947). *The gifted child grows up: Twenty-five years' follow-up of a superior group.* Stanford, CA: Stanford University Press.

Thelen, M. H., & Ewing, D. R. (1970). Roles, functions, and training in clinical psychology: A survey of academic clinicians. *American Psychologist, 25,* 550–554.

Thomson, G. H. (1916). A hierarchy without a general factor. *British Journal of Psychology, 8,* 271–281.

Thomson, G. H. (1919). The proof or disproof of the existence of general ability. *British Journal of Psychology, 9,* 321–336.

Thomson, G. H. (1952). Autobiography. In E. G. Boring et al. (Eds.), *A history of psychology in autobiography* (Vol. 4). Worcester, MA: Clark University Press.

Thorndike, E. L. (1906). *The elements of psychology.* New York: A. G. Seiler.

Thorndike, E. L. (1913). Ideo-motor action. *Psychological Review, 20,* 91–106.

Thorndike, E. L. (1920a). A constant error in psychological rating. *Journal of Applied Psychology, 4,* 25–29.

Thorndike, E. L. (1920b). Intelligence and its uses. *Harper's, 140,* 227–235.

Thorndike, E. L. (1921). On the organization of intellect. *Psychological Review, 28,* 141–151.

Thorndike, E. L. (1936). Autobiography. In C. Murchison, (Ed.), *A history of psychology in autobiography.* (Vol. 3). Worcester, MA: Clark University Press.

Thorndike, E. L., Bregnan, E. O., Cobb, M. V., & Woodyard, E. (1927). *The measurement of intelligence.* New York: Columbia University Press.

Thorndike, R. I. (1940). "Constancy" of the IQ. *Psychological Bulletin, 37,* 167–186.

Thorndike, R. L., Hagen, E., & Sattler, J. (1986). *Stanford-Binet Intelligence Scale, fourth edition.* Chicago: Riverside.

Thorne, F. C. (1948). Principles of directive counseling and psychotherapy. *American Psychologist, 3,* 160–165.

Thurstone, L. L. (1926). The mental age concept. *Psychological Review, 33,* 268–271.

Thurstone, L. L. (1928). The absolute zero in intelligence measurement. *Psychological Review, 35,* 175–197.

Thurstone, L. L. (1931). Multiple factor analysis. *Psychological Review, 38,* 406–427.

Thurstone, L. L. (1934). The vectors of mind. *Psychological Review, 41,* 1–32.

Thurstone, L. L. (1938). *Primary mental abilities.* Chicago: University of Chicago Press.

Thurstone, L. L. (1948). Psychological implications of factor analysis. *American Psychologist, 3,* 402–408.

Thurstone, L. L. (1952). Autobiography. In E. G. Boring et al. (Eds.), *A history of psychology in autobiography* (Vol. 4). Worcester, MA: Clark University Press.

Thurstone, L. L., Leuba, J. H. Lashley, K. S., & Jastrow, J. (1924). Contributions of Freudianism to psychology. *Psychological Review, 31,* 175–218.

Thurstone, L. L., & Thurstone, T. G. (1930). A neurotic inventory. *Journal of Social Psychology, 1,* 3–30.

Tien, H. C. (1960). Organic Integrity Test (OIT). *Archives of General Psychiatry, 3,* 43–52.

Tiffany, F. (1892). *Life of Dorothea Lynde Dix.* Boston: Houghton, Mifflin.

Tolman, E. C. (1922–1923). Can instincts be given up in psychology? *Journal of Abnormal and Social Psychology, 17,* 139–152.

Town, C. H., et al. (1933). Report on the survey of training and duties of clinical psychologists. *Psychological Exchange, 2,* 109–114.

Truax, C. B., & Carkhuff, R. R. (1967). *Toward effective counseling and psychotherapy: Training and practice.* Chicago: Aldine.

Tryon, R. C. (1932). Multiple factors vs. two factors as determiners of ability. So-called group factors as determiners of abilities. *Psychological Review, 39,* 324–351, 403–439.

Tryon, R. C. (1963). Psychology in flux: The academic-professional bipolarity. *American Psychologist, 18,* 134–143.

Tulchin S. H. (1930). The psychologist. *American Journal of Orthopsychiatry, 1,* 39–47.

Turkington, C. (1982, March). Hypnotic memory is not always accurate. *APA Monitor, 13,* 46–47.

Turkington, C. (1986). Professional practice: The fight for survival in a changing world. *APA Monitor, 17*(1), 4–5.

Twitmyer, E. B. (1931). The correction of speech defects. In R. A. Brotemarkle (Ed.), *Clinical psychology: Studies in honor of Lightner Witmer.* Philadelphia: University of Pennsylvania Press.

Tyler, L. E. (1973). Design for a hopeful psychology. *American Psychologist, 28,* 1021–1027.

Ullmann, L. P., & Krasner, L. (1965). *Case studies in behavior modification.* New York: Holt.

Unamuno, M. (1954). *The tragic sense of life.* New York: Dover.

Varnon, E. J. (1935). The development of Alfred Binet's psychology. *Psychological Monographs, 46*(Whole No. 207).

Varnon, E. J. (1936). Alfred Binet's concept of intelligence. *Psychological Review, 43,* 32–58.

Vassiliou, V., & Vassiliou, G. (1966). Clinical psychology in Greece. *Progress in Clinical Psychology, 7.*

Vaughan, W. F. (1926). The psychology of compensation. *Psychological Review, 33,* 467–479.

Vaughan, W. F. (1926–1927). The psychology of Alfred Adler. *Journal of Abnormal and Social Psychology, 21,* 358.

Vernon, P. E. (1933). The biosocial nature of the personality trait. *Psychological Review, 40,* 533–548.

Vernon, P. E. (1941). Psychological effects of air-raids. *Journal of Abnormal and Social Psychology, 36,* 457–476.

Vernon, P. E., & Allport, G. W. (1931–1932). A test for personal values. *Journal of Abnormal and Social Psychology, 26,* 231–248.

Viteles, M. S. (1924). Vocational guidance and job analysis. *Psychological Clinic, 15,* 157–182.

Vitiello, M. V., Carlin, A. S., Becker, J., Barris, B. P., & Dutton, J. (1989). The effect of subliminal oedipal and competitive stimulation on dart throwing: Another miss. *Journal of Abnormal Psychology, 98,* 54–56.

Voelker, P. F. (1921). Vocational guidance and job analysis. *Teachers College Contributions to Education,* No. 112.

Vokey, J. R., & Read, J. D. (1985). Subliminal messages: Between the devil and the media. *American Psychologist, 40,* 1231–1239.

Volkmar, F. R., Bregman, J., Cohen, D. J., & Cicchetti, D. V. (1988). DSM-III and DSM-III-R diagnoses of autism. *American Journal of Psychiatry, 145,* 1404–1408.

Vorhaus, P. G. (1960). Bruno Klopfer: A biographical sketch. *Journal of Projective Techniques, 24,* 232–237.

Walker, C. E., Bonner, B. L., & Kaufman, K. L. (1988). *The physically and sexually abused child: Evaluation and treatment.* New York: Pergamon.

Wallace, I., Wallace, A., Wallechinsky, D., & Wallace, S. (1981). *The intimate sex lives of famous people.* New York: Delacorte Press.

Wallerstein, R. S. (1989). The Psychotherapy Research Project of the Menninger Foundation: An overview. *Journal of Consulting and Clinical Psychology, 57,* 195–205.

Wallin, J. E. W. (1913–1914). Re-averments respecting psycho-clinical norms and scales of development. *Psychological Clinic, 7,* 89–96.

Wallin, J. E. W. (1914). *The mental health of the school child.* New Haven: Yale University Press.

Wallin, J. E. W. (1917–1918). The phenomenon of scattering in the Binet-Simon Scale. *Psychological Clinic, 11,* 179–195.

Wallin, J. E. W. (1922–1923). A study of the industrial record of children assigned to public school classes for mental defectives, and legislation in the interest of defectives. *Journal of Abnormal and Social Psychology, 17,* 120–131.

Wallin, J. E. W. (1929). The nature of *G,* as seen by the clinical psychologist. *Psychological Clinic, 18,* 196–198.

Wallin, J. E. W. (1929–1930). Shall we continue to train clinical psychologists for second string jobs? *Psychological Clinic, 18,* 242–245.

Wallin, J. E. W. (1961). A note on the origin of the APA Clinical Section. *American Psychologist, 16,* 256–258.

Walsh, J. J. (1913). *Psychotherapy.* New York: Appleton.

Warren, H. C. (1914). The mental and the physical. *Psychological Review, 21,* 79–100.

Watson, H., & Levine, M. (1989). Psychotherapy and mandated reporting of child abuse. *American Journal of Orthopsychiatry, 59*, 246–256.

Watson, J. B. (1913). Psychology as the behaviorist views it. *Psychological Review, 20*, 158–179.

Watson, J. B. (1916). The place of the conditioned-reflex in psychology. *Psychological Review, 23*, 158–179.

Watson, J. B. (1924). *Behaviorism.* New York: Norton.

Watson, J. B. (1928). What the nursery has to say about instincts. Experimental studies on the growth of the emotions. Recent experiments on how we lose and change our emotional equipment. In C. Murchison (Ed.), *Psychologies of 1925.* Worcester, MA: Clark University Press.

Watson, J. B. (1936). Autobiography. In C. Murchison (Ed.), *A history of psychology in autobiography* (Vol. 3). Worcester, MA: Clark University Press.

Watson, J. B., & Raynor, R. (1920). Conditioned emotional reactions. *Journal of Experimental Psychology, 3*, 1–14.

Watson, R. I. (1951). *The clinical method in psychology.* New York: Harper.

Watson, R. I. (1953). A brief history of clinical psychology. *Psychological Bulletin, 50*, 321–346.

Watson, R. I. (1956). Lightner Witmer, 1867–1956. *American Journal of Psychology, 69*, 680–682.

Watson, R. I. (1963). *The great psychologists from Aristotle to Freud.* Philadelphia: J. B. Lippincott.

Webb, E. (1915). Character and intelligence. *British Journal of Psychological Monographs*, Supplement 3.

Wechsler, D. (1939). *The measurement of adult intelligence.* Baltimore: Williams & Wilkins.

Wechsler, D. (1949). *WISC manual.* New York: Psychological Corporation.

Wechsler, D. (1950). Cognitive, conative, and non-intellective intelligence. *American Psychologist, 5*, 78–83.

Wechsler, D. (1955). *Manual for the WAIS.* New York: Psychological Corporation.

Wechsler, D. (1958). *The measurement and appraisal of adult intelligence* (4th ed.). Baltimore: Williams & Wilkins.

Wechsler, D. (1967). *Manual for the Wechsler Preschool and Prelimary Scale of Intelligence.* New York: Psychological Corporation.

Weiner, D. B. (1979). The apprenticeship of Philippe Pinel: A new document, "Observations of Citizen Pussin on the Insane." *American Journal of Psychiatry, 136*, 1128–1134.

Weisz, J. R., Weiss, B., Alicke, M. D., & Klotz, M. L. (1987). Effectiveness of psychotherapy with children and adolescents: A meta-analysis for clinicians. *Journal of Consulting and Clinical Psychology, 55*, 542–549.

Wellman, B. L. (1932–1933). The effect of preschool attendance upon the IQ. *Journal of Experimental Education, 1*, 48–69.

Wellman, B. L. (1938). Our changing concept of intelligence. *Journal of Consulting Psychology, 2*, 97–107.

Wellman, B. L. (1954). IQ changes of preschool and nonpreschool groups during the preschool years: A summary of the literature. *Journal of Psychology, 20*, 347–368.

Wells, F. L. (1914). The systematic observation of the personality in its relation to the hygiene of mind. *Psychological Review, 21*, 295–333.

Wells, F. L. (1924). Attesting psychologists for public servce. *Psychological Review, 31*, 328–335.

Wells, F. L. (1927). *Mental tests in clinical practice.* Yonkers, NY: World.

Wentworth, M. M. (1923–1924). Two hundred cases of dementia praecox tested by the Stanford Revision. *Journal of Abnormal and Social Psychology, 13*, 378–384.

Werner, H. (1940). *Comparative psychology of mental development.* New York: Harper.

West, P. R., & Lips, O. J. (1986). Veterans Administration psychology: A professional challenge for the 1980s. *American Psychologist, 41*, 996–1000.

West, R. (1936–1937). Is stuttering abnormal? *Journal of Abnormal and Social Psychology, 31*, 76–86.

Weston, D. (1989). Are "primitive" object relations really preoedipal? *American Journal of Orthopsychiatry, 59*, 331–345.

Wetheimer, M., Barclay, A. G., Cook, S. W., Kiesler, C. A., Koch, S., Riegel, F. K., Rorer, L. G., Senders, V. L., Smith, M. B., & Sperling, S. E. (1978). Psychology and the future. *American Psychologist, 33*, 631–710.

White, R. W. (1941). A preface to the theory of hypnotism. *Journal of Abnormal and Social Psychology, 36,* 476–505.

White, R. W. (1959). Abnormalities of behavior. *Annual Review of Psychology, 10,* 265–286.

White, W. A. (1917–1918). The Adlerian concept of the neuroses. *Journal of Abnormal Psychology, 12,* 168–173.

Wildman, R. W., & Wildman, R. W., II. (1965). The uncertain present and future of clinical psychology. *The Clinical Psychologist, 24*(4), 19–22.

Windle, C. (1952). Psychological tests in psychopathological prognosis. *Psychological Bulletin, 49,* 451–482.

Winkler, J. K., & Bromberg, W. (1939). *Mind explorers.* New York: Reynal & Hitchcock.

Winter, J. E. (1936). The postulates of psychology. *Psychological Review, 48,* 130–148.

Wissler, C. (1901). Correlation of mental and physical tests. *Psychological Monographs,* No. 16.

Witkin, H. A. (1965). Psychological differentiation and forms of pathology. *Journal of Abnormal Psychology, 70,* 317–336.

Witmer, L. (1907). Clinical psychology. *Psychological Clinic, 1,* 1–9.

Witmer, L. (1908–1909a). Retrospect and prospect: An editorial. *Psychological Clinic, 2,* 1–4.

Witmer, L. (1908–1909b). The treatment and cure of a case of mental and moral deficiency. *Psychological Clinic, 2,* 153–179.

Witmer, L. (1909–1910). The restoration of children of the slums. *Psychological Clinic, 3,* 266–280.

Witmer, L. (1915). On the relation of intelligence to efficiency. *Psychological Clinic, 9,* 61–86.

Witmer, L. (1922). Intelligence—a definition. *Psychological Clinic, 14,* 65–67.

Witmer, L. (1925). Psychological diagnosis and the psychonomic orientation of analytic science. *Psychological Clinic, 16,* 1–18.

Witmer, L. (1930). Psychonomic personeering. *Psychological Clinic, 19,* 73.

Wittman, P. (1933–1934). The Babcock Deterioration Index Test in state hospital practice. *Journal of Abnormal and Social Psychology, 28,* 70–83.

Witty, P. A., & Lehman, H. C. (1927). Drive: A neglected trait in the study of the gifted. *Psychological Review, 34,* 364–376.

Witty, P. A., & Lehman, H. C. (1933). The instinct hypothesis vs. the maturation hypothesis. *Psychological Review, 40,* 33–59.

Witty, P. S., & Theman, V. (1934). The psychoeducational clinic. *Journal of Applied Psychology, 18,* 369–392.

Wolberg, L. R. (1945). *Hypnoanalysis.* New York: Grune & Stratton.

Wolf, T. H. (1973). *Alfred Binet.* Chicago, University of Chicago Press.

Wolff, W. (1948). *Diagrams of the unconscious.* New York: Grune & Stratton.

Wolfle, D. (1946). The reorganized American Psychological Association. *American Psychologist, 1,* 3–6.

Wolfle, D. (1947). Testing is big business. *American Psychologist, 2,* 26.

Wolpe, J. (1958). *Psychotherapy by reciprocal inhibition.* Stanford, CA: Stanford University Press.

Wolpe, J., & Lazarus, A. A. (1966). *Behavior therapy techniques.* Elmsford, NY: Pergamon.

Woodworth, R. S. (1917). *Personal Data Sheet.* Chicago: C. H. Stoelting.

Woodworth, R. S. (1917–1918). Some criticisms of the Freudian psychology. *Journal of Abnormal Psychology, 12,* 174–194.

Woodworth, R. S. (1918). *Dynamic psychology.* New York: Columbia University Press.

Woodworth, R. S. (1928). Dynamic psychology. In C. Murchison (Ed.), *Psychologies of 1925.* Worcester, MA: Clark University Press.

Woodworth, R. S. (1930). Dynamic psychology. In C. Murchison (Ed.), *Psychologies of 1930.* Worcester MA: Clark University Press.

Woodworth, R. S. (1932). Autobiography. In C. Murchison (Ed.), *A history of psychology in autobiography* (Vol. 1). Worcester, MA: Clark University Press.

Woodworth, R. S. (1937). The future of clinical psychology. *Journal of Consulting Psychology, 1,* 4–5.

Woodworth, R. S. (1948). *Contemporary schools of psychology.* New York: Ronald.

Wright, L. (1988). The Type A behavior pattern and coronary heart disease: Quest for the active ingredients and the elusive mechanism. *American Psychologist, 43,* 2–14.

Wright, M. E. (1957). Abnormalities of behavior. *Annual Review of Psychology, 10,* 265–286.

Wyatt, H. G. (1926). Intelligence in man and ape. *Psychological Review, 33,* 375–384.

Wyatt, H. G. (1927). The recent anti-instinctive attitude in social psychology. *Psychological Review, 34,* 126–132.

Yarrow, L. J. (1961). Maternal deprivation: Toward an empirical and conceptual re-evaluation. *Psychological Bulletin, 58,* 459–490.

Yerkes, R. M. (1919). Report of the Psychology Committee of the National Research Council. *Psychological Review, 26,* 83–149.

Yerkes, R. M. (1933). Concerning the anthropocentrism of psychology. *Psychological Review, 40,* 209–212.

Yerkes, R. M., Bridges, J. W., & Hardwick, R. S. (1915). *A point scale for measuring mental ability.* Baltimore: Warwick & York.

Yoakum, C. S., & Yerkes, R. M. (1920). *Army mental tests.* New York: Holt.

Young, K. (1924). The history of mental testing. *Pedagogical Seminary, 31,* 1–48.

Young, M. L., & Odbert, H. S. (1960). Government support of psychological research. *American Psychologist, 15,* 661–664.

Young, P. C. (1926). Hypnotism. *Psychological Bulletin, 23,* 504–523.

Young, P. C. (1927–1928). The nature of hypnosis: As indicated by the presence or absence of post-hypnotic amnesia and rapport. *Journal of Abnormal and Social Psychology, 22,* 372–382.

Zaidi, S. M. H. (1959). Pakistan psychology. *American Psychologist, 14,* 532–536.

Zax, M., & Klein, A. (1960). Measurement of personality and behavior changes following psychotherapy. *Psychological Bulletin, 57,* 435–448.

Zilboorg, G. (1939). Overestimation of psychopathology. *American Journal of Orthopsychiatry, 9,* 86–94.

Zilboorg, G., & Henry, G. W. (1941). *A history of medical psychology.* New York: Norton.

Zimet, C. N. (1981). The clinical psychologist in the 1980's: Entitled or untitled. *The Clinical Psychologist, 35*(1), 12–14.

Zimmerman, F. T., & Burgemeister, B. B. (1951). Permanency of glutamic acid treatment. *Neurological Psychiatric Archive, 65,* 291–298.

Zubin, J., & Spring, B. (1977). Vulnerability—a new view of schizophrenia. *Journal of Abnormal Psychology, 86,* 103–126.

INDEX